J. Ranade Workstation Series

LOCKHART • *OSF DCE: Guide to Developing Distributed Applications,* 0-07-911481-4

WIGGINS • *The Internet for Everyone: A Guide for Users and Providers,* 0-07-067019-8

CHAKRAVARTY • *Power RISC System/6000: Concepts, Facilities, and Architecture,* 0-07-011047-6

SANCHEZ, CANTON • *High Resolution Video Graphics,* 0-07-911646-9

DEROEST • *AIX for RS/6000: System and Administration Guide,* 0-07-036439-7

LAMB • *MicroFocus Workbench and Toolset Developer's Guide,* 0-07-036123-3

JOHNSTON • *OS/2 Connectivity & Networking: A Guide to Communication Managers/2,* 0-07-032696-7

SANCHEZ, CANTON • *PC Programmer's Handbook, Second Edition,* 0-07-054948-6

WALKER, SCHWALLER • *CPI-C Programming in C: An Application Developer's Guide to APPC,* 0-07-911733-3

SANCHEZ, CANTON • *Graphics Programming Solutions,* 0-07-911464-4

CHAKRAVARTY, CANNON • *PowerPC: Concepts, Architecture, and Design,* 0-07-011192-8

LEININGER • *UNIX Developer's Tool Kit,* 0-07-911646-9

HENRY, GRAHAM • *Solaris 2.X System Administrator's Guide,* 0-07-029368-6

RANADE, ZAMIR • *C++ Primer for C Programmers, Second Edition,* 0-07-051487-9

PETERSON • *DCE: A Guide to Developing Portable Applications,* 0-07-911801-1

LEININGER • *Solaris Developer's Tool Kit,* 0-07-911851-8

JOHNSTON • *OS/2 Productivity Tool Kit,* 0-07-912029-6

LEININGER • *AIX/6000 Developer's Tool Kit,* 0-07-911992-1

GRAHAM • *Solaris 2.X: Internals and Architecture,* 0-07-911876-3

BAMBARA, ALLEN • *PowerBuilder: A Guide for Developing Client/Server Applications,* 0-07-005413-4

SANCHEZ, CANTON • *Solutions Handbook for PC Programmers, Second Edition,* 0-07-912249-3

LEININGER • *HP-UX Developer's Tool Kit,* 0-07-912174-8

ROBERTSON, KOOP • *Integrating Windows and Netware,* 0-07-912126-8

CERVONE • *AIX/6000 System Guide,* 0-07-024129-5

CHAPMAN • *OS/2 Power User's Reference: From OS/2 2.0 through Warp,* 0-07-912218-3

KELLY • *AIX/6000 Internals and Architecture,* 0-07-034061-7

MULLER • *The Webmaster's Guide to HTML,* 0-07-912273-6

LEININGER • *HP-UX Developer's Tool Kit,* 0-07-912175-6

GOPAUL • *OS/2 Programmer's Desk Reference,* 0-07-023748-4

To order or receive additional information on these or any other McGraw-Hill titles, in the United States please call 1-800-822-8158. In other countries, contact your local McGraw-Hill representative.

KEY = WM16XXA

PowerBuilde

Object-Oriented Design and Developm

William Green

Millard Brown III

McGraw-Hill

New York   San Francisco   Washington, D.C.   Auckland   Bogotá
Caracas   Lisbon   London   Madrid   Mexico City   Milan
Montreal   New Delhi   San Juan   Singapore
Sydney   Tokyo   Toronto

Library of Congress Cataloging-in-Publication Data

Green, William (William T.)
    Powerbuilder 5 : object-oriented design and development / William
Green, Millard Brown III.
        p.   cm.—(J. Ranade workstation series)
    Includes index.
    ISBN 0–07–024469–3
    1. Application software—Development. 2. PowerBuilder. 3. Object
-oriented methods (Computer science) I. Brown, Millard.
II. Title. III. Series
QA76.76.A65G73   1997
005.2—dc20   96–27612
                                      CIP

McGraw-Hill

*A Division of The **McGraw·Hill** Companies*

1 2 3 4 5 6 7 8 9 0 DOC/DOC 9 0 1 0 9 8 7 6

P/N 024550-9
PART OF
ISBN 0-07-024469-3

*The sponsoring editor for this book was John Wyzalek and the production
supervisor was Suzanne Rapcavage. It was set in Century Schoolbook by
Graphic World Inc.*

Printed and bound by R. R. Donnelley & Sons Company.

This book is printed on recycled, acid-free paper containing
a minimum of 50% recycled, de-inked fiber.

McGraw-Hill books are available at special quantity discounts to use as pre-
miums and sales promotions, or for use in corporate training programs.
For more information, please write to the Director of Special Sales, McGraw-Hill,
11 West 19th Street, New York, NY 10011. Or contact your local bookstore.

Millard and I would like to take this opportunity to raise awareness of the people who suffered losses during the bomb attack in Oklahoma City in April 1995. We would like readers of this book to remember these folks, and especially the children who could have been the future PowerBuilders of the world.

About the Authors

William Green is Vice President of client-server technology with RCG Information Technology, a consulting company. He was a contributing author for the books *Secrets of the PowerBuilder Masters* and *PowerBuilder 4.0 Developer's Guide.* Mr. Green writes a regular column for *PowerBuilder Advisor* magazine, and also contributes to *The PowerBuilder Developer's Journal.*

Millard Brown is the founder and co-owner of Gateway Systems, a consulting company that specializes in the business use of personal computers. He writes a regular column for *PowerBuilder Advisor* magazine, and also contributes to *The PowerBuilder Developer's Journal.*

Contents

Preface

What Is Covered in the Book?

This book is about PowerBuilder development. It begins by discussing the issues facing management when deciding to use the tool. It then goes on to discuss how to build an enterprise-wide foundation for reusability. It next discusses techniques to promote and achieve reusability following the object-oriented paradigm. The book is intended to cover advanced topics and techniques rather than reprint the user manual. We cover the design, development and deployment of class libraries and applications from an enterprise perspective, although commercial developers could use the information as well, tailoring the deployment part for themselves.

We are trying to cover the entire development cycle using OO techniques sensibly. It is easy to get caught up in too much theory and not enough practicality, and we are not trying to create a theoretical book. Everything contained in this book is the result of our experiences in designing, developing, and deploying class libraries and applications for clients. I have researched and reviewed several IS managers, as well as Powersoft, to investigate aspects of operations I am not familiar with. (For example, I do not make corporate decisions for Fortune 500 clients. I do advise these clients on approaches and techniques, however.)

As a supporter of the OO paradigm and a more than avid supporter of the PowerBuilder family of products, I was disappointed by the lack of advanced discussions on how to correctly apply these techniques for PowerBuilder development; this book attempts to address this void.

Who Is the Intended Audience?

Managers, lead architects, and project managers are the focus of Part I.

The book is targeted at two groups of people. First, the book is targeted at anyone in a managerial position who is interested in promoting reusability in his or her organization. Millard and I both feel that getting everyone to agree that reusability, and the associated costs, are worth the investment made is critical. Part I of the book deals with every issue we have come up against in the struggle to accelerate the paradigm shift.

> *Senior developers, lead architects, and designers are the focus of Parts II, III, IV, and V, although inexperienced developers can gain a lot of insight and direction as well.*

The second group targeted is advanced designers and developers. This is not a how-to-use PowerBuilder book. It is intended to promote the successful design of PowerBuilder applications from the enterprise level down. The theory being reiterated by this book is that successful development of PowerBuilder applications depends heavily on successful design, commitment to productive use of available tools, and successful deployment of the application once the development cycle has been completed.

Our goal with this book is to definitively describe the entire process of client-server design, development, and deployment using PowerBuilder, and to promote reusability of every aspect of the tasks that lay ahead for us all.

How the Book Is Structured

The book is divided into five distinct parts, separated by design to be distinguishable and useful by themselves.

Part I: PowerBuilder for Managers

> *Target: senior managers, project managers, and lead developers*

The first part deals with management's commitment to reusable objects. It explores why this approach is more beneficial than others, why the commitment to the approach must be made at the managerial level, and how the commitment can be transferred and encouraged throughout the organization. It discusses reusability as a goal and details topics such as why a class library should be used, why reusable objects are cost-justifiable, and what is currently available in the marketplace to help promote the development cycle.

Part II: Developing a Class Library

> *Target: senior managers, project managers, lead developers, library architects, and developers*

This part discusses issues pertaining to class library analysis, design development and deployment, and more, guiding the reusable class designer through the decision processes required to create a library of reusable objects that will benefit their organization for several years to come. We discuss techniques we have developed, often through trial and error, to provide a comprehensive set of tools to aid in this process.

We go through the entire process of developing a class library, detailing concepts and techniques wherever they are relevant.

Part III: Application Development

Target: project managers and application developers

This part covers the development cycle of an application. We focus on determining requirements from a business process workflow, defining the logical and physical classes and objects that will make up the application, mapping the defined objects to preexisting class library objects available (if any), building and integrating the application, and finally, addressing documenting, testing, and deployment issues related to the development effort. The focus is on the whole process, modeling the application to the business domain, basing physical objects on preexisting classes, and producing tight, integrated objects that can be reused themselves.

Part IV: Documentation Development

Target: all

This part describes the need for, and how to get, living documentation. There is a noticeable lack of effective documentation tools on the market, and this part shows the developer how to develop documentation that makes sense, is reusable throughout the development cycle, and becomes the end-product documentation. We also describe the readily available yet undocumented features of the ORCA library, Powersoft's open Application Programming Interface (API) to the underlying structure of our object libraries.

Part V: Implementation and Beyond

Target: senior managers, project managers, and lead developers

The final part deals with issues that arise in deploying PowerBuilder libraries and applications. A sample implementation plan is created throughout the part until an implementation plan is built that allows the development group to make sure nothing slips through the cracks. Though not foolproof, the plan will eliminate many common headaches that arise in the client-server world simply because of the environment.

Object-Oriented Concepts and Technologies as Implemented in PowerBuilder

Many people will argue that PowerBuilder is not a true object-oriented (OO) language. They are correct. PowerBuilder is an object-oriented development tool. It allows developers to use object-oriented techniques to develop reusable objects and code. But what is object-oriented technology and how does this benefit us, the developers? More importantly, how does it benefit the user?

First, let's dispense with one myth. Object-oriented technology does not make a developer's job easier. It makes developers more productive and successful, if used correctly. The key to it all is in the words *object-oriented.*

How object-oriented languages and tools are used is determined by whether certain aspects of object-oriented technology are supported and how they are managed. SmallTalk and SmallTalk-based tools, for example, *enforce* object-oriented techniques. C++ and other tools and languages *allow* object-oriented techniques to be used, but do not require it. In the purists' eyes, if your development efforts are not object-oriented from start to finish, you aren't developing OO systems. I agree, although I add that the language or tool is not what determines the level of object orientation. It is the developer. And, it is the developer who must learn that OO systems do not just happen. They are created. From the depths of the design chamber to the frantic final keystroke, OO systems must be carefully designed and planned *before* development teams bring the objects to life.

As PowerBuilder developers, we have learned that object-oriented development means that we develop systems using objects that contain methods and attributes. Well, this part is at least easy. Why? Because everything developed in PowerBuilder *is* an object. Thus, by definition, we are all object-oriented developers. How much we orient ourselves to object development is the key to success.

There are some terms that are useful to get to know, however. These are each discussed below, and I have attempted to give both a real-world and a PowerBuilder example of the following terms:

- Inheritance
- Encapsulation
- Polymorphism
- Function overloading
- Classes
- Methods and attributes
- Objects
- Instances
- Events, functions, and variables
- Overriding and extending
- Global, shared, instance, and local variables
- Private, protected, and public
- Messages, triggers, and posts
- Object typing and pointers

Inheritance

Inheritance is the cornerstone of object orientation.

If you asked 10 people what they thought was the most important aspect of object-oriented technology, 9 out of 10 would say reusability. Inheritance is the cornerstone of reusability. The difference between inheritance and copying is that a copy is a self-standing entity that is not altered automatically if the original is altered.

Think about a form letter. Once it is printed, it is indeed a copy. If you change the original, the printed copy does not automatically change. If you photocopy the printed copy, you are extending the *branching* of the copied data. The more copies you make, the harder it is to go back and change the person's name on the original and roll that change out to all copies of the document. Figure PR.1 demonstrates copying. If this were source code, you would end up with many *code trees* and be unable to maintain changes to every branch of the tree.

With inheritance, the content of the original is not copied. It is linked in, or *referenced*. Now, when the original changes, the change is also visible in the linked copy, although nothing actually changes in the copy. Through this mechanism, you are able to retain the original data in only one place and any change is reflected in the descendants. Figure PR.2 shows the effect reduced when the parent object is retained as part of the object. Changes made to the parent are automatically reflected in the child.

The potential savings that can be realized are obvious. Inheritance is the foundation on which reusable code is based. PowerBuilder supports the inheritance model easily and intuitively, but the developer must take the time to plan and design for reuse. It will pay big dividends down the road.

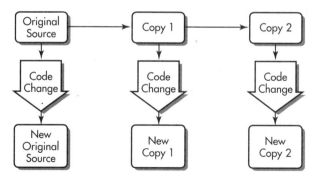

Any changes made to an object must be manually applied to copies or object originals. Chance of error is high.

Figure PR.1 Source branching: copied objects.

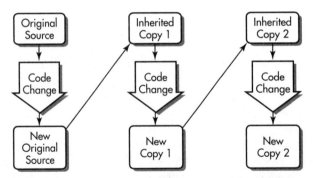

Changes made to objects at any level are automatically inherited into the derived copies. Chance of error is low.

Figure PR.2 With inheritance, source branching is eliminated.

Encapsulation

> *Encapsulation is the process of hiding the implementation of an object's functions and data from objects external to it.*

In object-oriented terms this means that objects must use a common set of entry points to communicate with another object. This eliminates the need to modify every program or object that uses the object in question every time a minor change is made to the object's internals. Only when an access method changes should there be any effect outside the object.

This concept is very powerful. Once an object is established with common entry points (or public methods), the effect of change to this object is virtually nil. Compare this to every time a program module or subroutine was modified in a more procedural mainframe environment. No change could be taken lightly. The object-oriented environment lends itself well to building an insulated code structure that can withstand changes and make excessive maintenance costs a thing of the past. Figure PR.3 shows how a well-written object interface can both protect the object and the developer.

Indeed, the environment itself supports the paradigm to the extent that if you make a change to an object, you need not even recompile (or rebuild) your applications that use the object. I would stress, however, that this is limited solely to changes that do not affect entry points.

Polymorphism

> *Polymorphism is the means by which a common interface is presented, but actual execution varies based on the required input or output data.*

Polymorphism, from the Greek words meaning *changing form,* is one of the most powerful techniques available to OO development. It allows you to define a method whose implementation is hidden from the developer, but whose in-

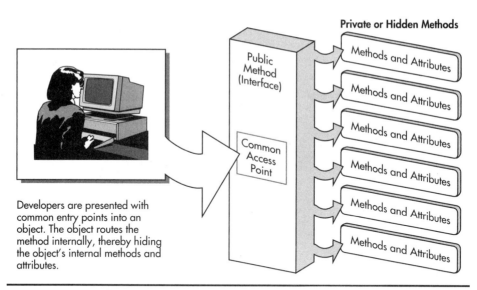

Private or Hidden Methods

Public Method (Interface)

Common Access Point

Methods and Attributes

Methods and Attributes

Methods and Attributes

Methods and Attributes

Methods and Attributes

Methods and Attributes

Developers are presented with common entry points into an object. The object routes the method internally, thereby hiding the object's internal methods and attributes.

Figure PR.3 Encapsulated objects present well-defined entry points to developers while hiding the functionality of the object, allowing for easy change.

terface is common. In other words, it allows you to develop functionality based on the same name and concept, but implement the functionality differently depending on the object.

An example would be to devise a method called Print. Although *print,* on a general level, always means the same thing (print the contents of the object), each object might implement printing in a different way. All the developer needs to know, however, is that he or she needs to call the Print method on the object. The object's code will take care of the rest. Figure PR.4 shows how the Print method in different objects presents a like interface where a developer calls the same method and achieves different results.

Function overloading

Another means of achieving polymorphism is via function overloading. This is a technique whereby the same function name is implemented multiple times within an object hierarchy, and the data being passed as the argument to the function or the result returned from the object is different. When the function is called, a specific version of the function that matches the argument list provided is executed. An example of this in PowerBuilder is the TriggerEvent function shown in Figure PR.5.

As can be seen, when the developer calls the TriggerEvent function, you can supply the parameters required to satisfy any of the possible combinations provided, and the correct function will execute.

This is a powerful feature of an object-oriented language, but it was limited in its implementation in PowerBuilder 4.0 to overloading by inheritance. A

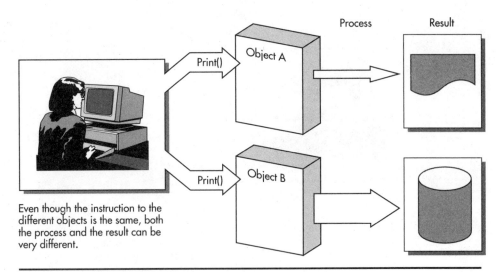

Even though the instruction to the different objects is the same, both the process and the result can be very different.

Figure PR.4 Calling the Print method on one object creates a report, whereas the same method on another object prints the data to a file.

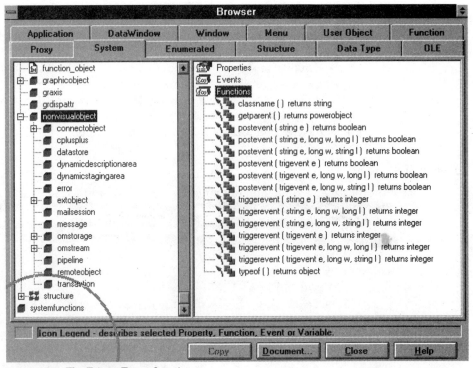

Figure PR.5 The TriggerEvent function.

function within an object could be overloaded by declaring an identical function in a descendant with a different argument list. PowerBuilder 5.0 allows you to directly overload functions as described previously. PowerBuilder also allows you to overload functions directly if the functions are external. Figure PR.6 shows an overloaded external function declaration. Note that the parameters can then be used as any combination of string or integer types.

PowerBuilder 5.0 supports true function overloading, so object functions may be overloaded within the same object. Figure PR.7 shows an example of function overloading.

Classes

> *A class is a definition of the collective capabilities and attributes of the objects derived from the class.*

Typically, a class is made up of methods and attributes. The attributes are data, sometimes static, usually variable. The methods are the insulation layer, protecting the attributes from outside agents. A class is the *definition* of the collection of methods and attributes. Figure PR.8 demonstrates this definition of a class.

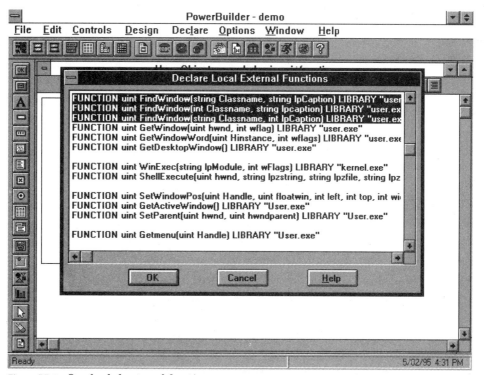

Figure PR.6 Overloaded external functions.

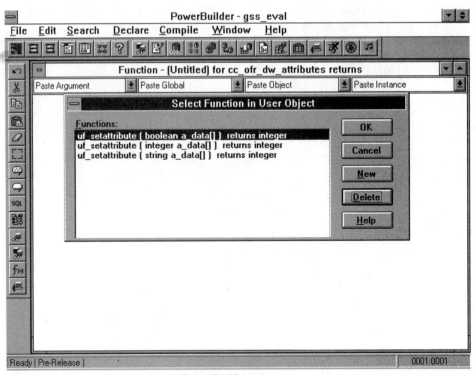

Figure PR.7   Function overloading in PowerBuilder 5.0.

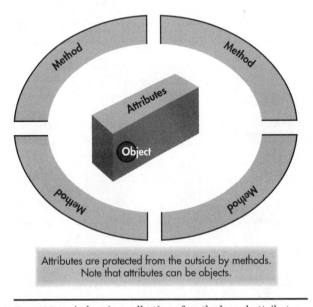

Attributes are protected from the outside by methods.
Note that attributes can be objects.

Figure PR.8   A class is a collection of methods and attributes.

Methods and Attributes

Methods protect attributes from agents outside of the class. Attributes are the variable data stores for the class.

A method is defined as a means to accomplish a task. The method requires that it be activated via a defined mechanism (message, function call) and the method will implement one or more functions to achieve the desired result. Functions are specific tasks that accomplish specific goals within the object. Attributes are the variables defined within the object as well as the various characteristics of the object itself (such as size and name). Figure PR.9 shows both interobject communication between methods and method-to-attribute communication internally.

Objects

An object is a physical representation of a class and is functionally independent of other objects. It encapsulates functionality and data within itself, can be adapted and extended, and can be reused without code modification.

According to Dr. David Taylor, renowned author on object-oriented technology, an object is "a software packet containing a collection of related data (in the form of variables) and methods (procedures) for operating on that data." This

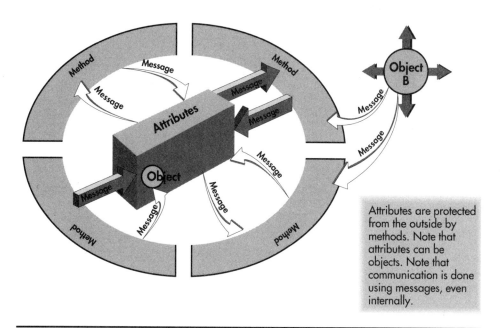

Attributes are protected from the outside by methods. Note that attributes can be objects. Note that communication is done using messages, even internally.

Figure PR.9   Methods and attributes. Methods protect attributes from external objects.

is virtually identical to the definition of a class. The difference is that an object is a physical implementation of a class.

Objects are the foundation for the development of OO systems. To relate this back to the real world of application development, an object would have a specific purpose within your system, would contain all of the functions necessary to accomplish that purpose, and would have attributes or variables that would store the data necessary to accomplish its goal. The object could then be used from within your application and, if designed and implemented in a true object-oriented fashion, by any other application that requires that type of functionality.

Classes are definitions. Objects are implementations.

For example, if you create a class nvo_ancestor in PowerBuilder, you have actually defined the class. When you create a nonvisual object and save it as nvo_ancestor, you are implementing the class, creating a physical object that you will save in a library. In Figure PR.10, nonvisualobject is the class and nvo_ancestor also appears as a class.

By virtue of the fact that nvo_ancestor is actually implemented in a Power-Builder library (Figure PR.11), we say that nvo_ancestor is an object rather than a class.

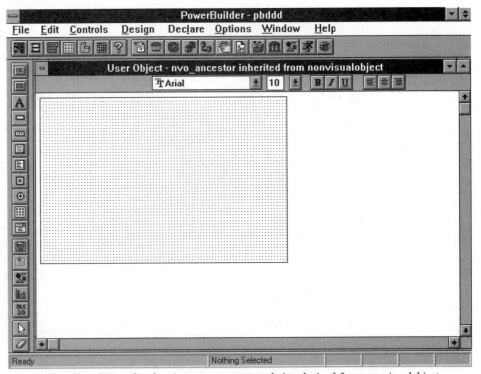

Figure PR.10 Class hierarchy showing nvo_ancestor as being derived from nonvisualobject.

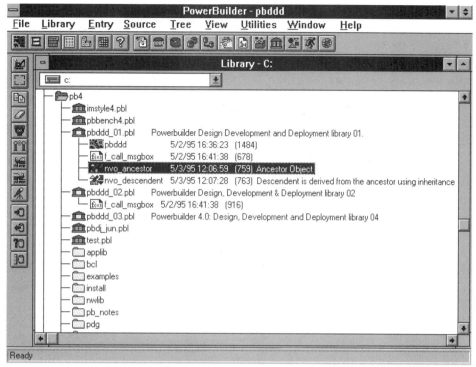

Figure PR.11 Class nvo_ancestor implemented as object nvo_ancestor.

Descendant objects are said to be derived from a class.

When you derive a descendant from the nvo_ancestor and save it as nvo_descendant, you can refer to the nvo_descendant object as being descended from the nvo_ancestor class. The distinguishing factor is that you are referring to the definition of the object's ancestor. A descendant object is derived from the parent object's definition. Figure PR.12 shows that nvo_descendant is *derived* (inherited) from nvo_ancestor.

Instances

> *Instances are physical realization of objects.*

An instance is a physical realization of an object. The creation of an instance of an object in memory is called *instantiation*. Many instances of the same object or object class may be instantiated. All instances share the same foundation of methods and attributes; that is, all instances of the class receive a copy of the attributes of the class. Once the object is instantiated, the values of the variables can be altered without affecting other instances of the class. The exception to this rule is shared variables. Shared variables create only one copy

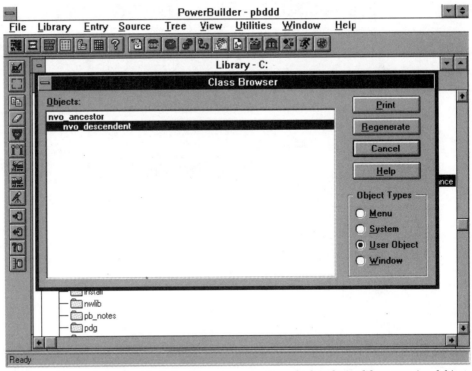

Figure PR.12 nvo_descendant is derived from nvo_ancestor, which is derived from nonvisualobject.

of the variable for the entire class. In Figure PR.13, we have instantiated three copies of the nvo_descendant class. All three instances contain the attribute ii_id, but can contain differing values within the attribute.

Events, functions, and variables

Events, functions, and variables make up the methods and attributes of an object.

Each object built in the PowerBuilder environment contains a combination of functions, events and variables. Events are reactions to messages directed at the object. The object may respond to a system message or a message sent by another object. PowerBuilder provides great flexibility in allowing the definition of custom user events linked to respond to system or object messages. Functions are called directly, passing parameters to be acted on and responded to. Variables are the data that the events and functions act on. Although variables are generally declared as predefined data types, variables can be objects themselves. This adds to the power and flexibility of the tool as fully functional objects can be imbedded within objects, their functionality initiated by the encompassing object. Figure PR.14 shows this scenario.

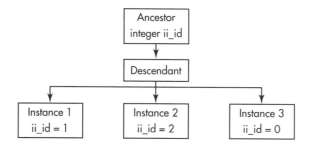

Note that the descendant and each instance of the descendant automatically receives the ii_id attriubute declared in the ancestor, but that each instance of the descendant can maintain the value of the attribute independently.

Figure PR.13 Multiple instances of nvo_descendant. Note that all three classes contain a variable called ii_id, which is declared in the ancestor object. Each object contains its own copy of this attribute.

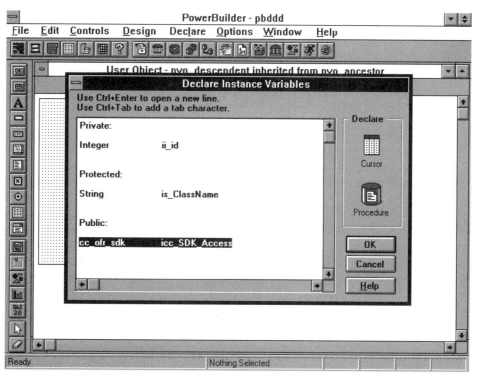

Figure PR.14 Data within an object can be an object.

Overriding and extending

One of the features and capabilities of the object-oriented paradigm is the ability to extend or override functions or events. The capability to extend inherited functionality is powerful. Code written in an inheritable object can be used in another object by simply inheriting from the object. Any code required specifically for the inherited object can be added to the object easily. If the functionality is not required in the object, it can also be overridden. Figure PR.15 demonstrates the possibilities of this feature.

Global, shared, instance, and local variables

Global variables are not recommended as a good practice in OO systems as they violate the rules of encapsulation. They also make objects within an application dependent on the variable and therefore nonportable to other applications. Even though it is tempting to make a variable accessible to all objects within an application, any object that references the variable will require the variable to be declared wherever else it might be used. This applies to global external functions as well.

Shared variables are variables that are shared among all instances of a class. That is to say that only one copy of the variable is created for all of the instances of the class, rather than each instance getting its own copy of the variable. This has both power and limitations and should be used carefully.

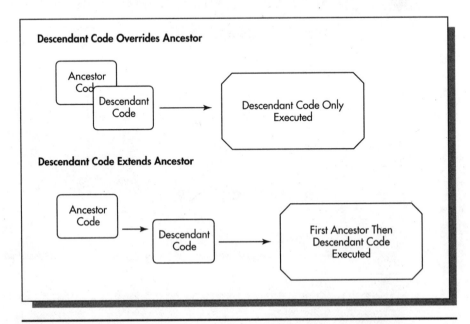

Figure PR.15   Extending and overriding (adding or removing features of an object).

Instance variables are the variables created for each instance of the object. Each object contains its own copy of the variable. Instance variables can be declared as private, protected, or public.

Local variables are declared within events and functions and are limited to the scope of the event or function.

Private, protected, and public

Private functions and variables are the code and data that operate solely within the object. No other objects, including descendant objects, have access to private functions and variables.

Protected functions and variables are code and data that are private to the object and the object's descendants. Objects not descended from the object do not have access to the functions and variables.

Public functions and variables are the common means of interobject communication. Public functions are accessible by the object, its descendants, and any other object. Public variables are directly accessible by any object and should be used sparingly and carefully, as they violate the rules of encapsulation. They are sometimes necessary, however, and should not be totally discarded.

Messages, triggers, and posts

Objects communicate using messages. Messages can be either triggered (synchronous) or posted (asynchronous).

Messages.   Messages are the means by which objects communicate with each other. A call to an object's methods is actually one object sending a message to another object to invoke a method on the object. This is done by building a message by combining the object name and the function name and separating them by a defined notation. A message is either inserted into the message queue or added to the end of the queue.

Trigger and post.   In PowerBuilder, events are either triggered or posted. Functions are always triggered. Triggered events and functions are messages that require the application to wait until the message is processed; in other words, triggered events and function calls are synchronous. Posted events are messages that are added to the system's message queue to be processed in turn. These events are called asynchronous.

There is a limit to the number of messages you can post to the message queue, so posting should not be a recursive implementation. Also, certain synchronous functions, such as message boxes, can actually drop the remaining message queue elements and create problematic situations (mainly because message boxes are modal, and the message queue is periodically cleared of unprocessed messages). Finally, if you are expecting your object to have to wait for a message in the message queue, use of the Yield() function allows waiting messages to be processed.

Pointers and object typing

Pointers are references to physical objects without the overhead of the actual object. Typing is the means by which the power and flexibility of a pointer are restricted or enhanced.

Casting a pointer is a term often used in C and C++ development, and is becoming more common in PowerBuilder development as well. A pointer is a reference variable through which objects can communicate with each other. A pointer is also much smaller than the object it references, and thus has much less overhead. When you, as the developer, call a function where one of the arguments is an object, and the argument is defined as being by reference, the function actually receives a pointer back to the original object, and the function then has access to the attributes and functions associated with the object type.

This brings up the point of object typing. When you develop an object and encapsulate methods, functions, and attributes to that object, you are in fact creating an object type. When referencing the object as a variable declared as being of the *type* object name, you are declaring a *hard typed pointer*. I also refer to it as an intelligent pointer because it can reference the variables and functions of the type specified and higher.

For example, if you create a user object called cb_ofr_base, you can type this object as either commandbutton, or as cb_ofr_base within variables. If you type it as commandbutton, you have access to all methods and attributes of the commandbutton class, but none of those defined in the cb_ofr_base object. Hard typing of the cb_ofr_base object allows you to reference the contents of the object.

Function arguments and return values

An object that is passed to a function by value receives a copy of the object, rather than a pointer to the original object. This limits what you can really do with the object internally, but may also be a desired behavior, as you may not want any change to be made permanently to your original copy.

Some of the internal PowerBuilder objects, such as Transaction and Message, are always passed by reference, regardless of argument type settings. Be aware of this, as it forces certain behaviors on you. For example, if you create a variable of type Transaction (My_Transaction) and assign the values of the SQLCA transaction to this object (My_Transaction = SQLCA), what you are in fact doing is establishing a pointer to SQLCA. Any changes made to My_Transaction will also change SQLCA and vice versa. To create a copy of SQLCA, you need to create your transaction object and then assign each of the SQLCA attributes to your transaction object individually, as follows:

```
Transaction My_Transaction
My_Transaction = Create Transaction
My_Transaction.Userid = SQLCA.Userid
```

Now My_Transaction contains data that, when modified, will not affect the original SQLCA values. This is commonly referred to as a *deep copy* and is a requirement for establishing objects within dynamic arrays in PowerBuilder 5.0.

Summary

These are the terms most often used to define object orientation used in PowerBuilder. Understanding these terms will begin to paint the picture of the power of this tool, and hopefully will also highlight the danger of misuse. This book is dedicated to highlighting power and flexibility of PowerBuilder, as well as warning of the danger of diving in unprepared.

Foreword

This is no ordinary PowerBuilder book you are holding.

There are plenty of PowerBuilder how-to books on the market. They show you how to use the various PowerBuilder painters as well as how to build windows and other common objects. However, none of them show you how to put together a full life-cycle PowerBuilder application. This book does. I have known one of the principal authors for over a year and heard about the innovative and leading-edge development techniques described in this book as they were being developed. I am very pleased to see that the authors put their ideas, experiences, successes, and failures down on paper for the world to see. I'm sure you'll find this book a great learning tool—I surely did.

This is an object-oriented design and project management technique book. It just happens to use PowerBuilder as its core. This book shows that object-oriented programming for the corporate client-server developer is here—and working—in PowerBuilder. If you are finishing your twentieth PowerBuilder project or just beginning your first, you will learn a good deal from this book.

You will find that the authors concentrate on two areas: class library design and GUI client-server project management. These are two of the most critical topics in PowerBuilder development (and almost all new development) today. I am pleased that there is a heavy emphasis on object-orientation theory and code!

A brief glance through this book shows that PowerBuilder *is* an object-oriented language. The Green-Brown Methodology shows that you can do object-oriented PowerBuilder programming. More and more PowerBuilder shops around the world are moving toward object orientation. Moreover, it will be the way to program in PowerBuilder within a year. Why? Because Powersoft is committed to making it even more object-oriented. The fact that Powersoft is moving toward a richer, more robust OO model is a clear sign that its customer base—namely corporate IS development shops—should also begin to move toward OO.

PowerBuilder and other visual client-server development tools have forced software developers to change the way they construct software. The tried-and-true ways of developing software have to be modified. Today's development has different requirements from the old ways: new standards, object models, dynamic models, functional models, class libraries, application partitioning, object-oriented testing—the list goes on and on. If you are trying to figure out just how to manage such a development project, this book is for you.

If you wish to survive as a programmer, analyst, designer, architect, project lead, or project manager through the 1990s, you must learn the concepts this book teaches: object-oriented design and today's project management techniques.

Thank you, Bill and Millard. Thanks for sharing your experience with the rest of us. This book will raise the debate among development techniques and methodologies in the PowerBuilder community to a higher level.

Steve Benfield
Executive Editor, PowerBuilder Developer's Journal
President, CCS Consulting

Acknowledgments

There are many people to thank for their contributions, both philosophical and physical, in making this book possible. Both of us would like to take a moment to acknowledge those who contributed both in spirit and in deed to the completion of this book. There are many others whom we would like thank, but we would need to write another book to thank all of you who helped. There are some who require more thanks than others, those who gave more than we could have ever asked for, with little return. To these people, we would like to extend more personal thanks.

First and foremost, I want to thank Coleman Sisson. Coleman Sisson was a vice-president at Powersoft and he and I started conversing on CompuServe before Powersoft even had its own forum. Coleman was instrumental in getting me to believe in the quality and power of this development tool we have all grown to love/hate. By showing the willingness to listen to a lowly programmer who was determined to prove that the product was not good enough, Coleman convinced me that Powersoft was going to make the effort to listen to its clients and make this a product that would take the client-server world by storm. It is easy to look back now and admire his foresight. I'm just glad he was convincing enough to keep me going in this direction. Thank you, Coleman, for your guidance, trust, and friendship.

To my daughters, Lauren and Alicia, for their endless love and patience in waiting for Dad to stop working long enough to play with them.

To my partner in crime, Millard Brown III, who taught me to laugh in the face of death, that OO purism is an oxymoron, and that Elvis will return someday.

To the late Dan Allen, my friend and mentor, who was instrumental in my getting to work on personal computers. Dan was an inspiration to me, and taught me that to become an expert in any field requires a thirst for knowledge and a passion for teaching.

To my father, Vincent, who taught me to love what I do with passion, and to stand up and be counted, and my mother, Ruth, who taught me to dare to dream.

And last, but most importantly, to my wife, Terri, for the love and support that makes this kind of effort worth it. Thank you for the many hours that passed where you probably got more attention from Federal Express than from me, and decided not to send me and the book by overnight express to destinations unknown.

Bill Green

To Millard F. Brown, Jr., for teaching me everything I know about conquering technology and communicating with others.

Sinclair Brown, for putting up with my long hours and reminding me of my commitment to quality.

John Louchheim, for general great counsel and introducing me to Power-Builder.

Millard F. Brown III

Additionally we would both like to thank several other people for their contributions, both direct and indirect, to making this the best book on Power-Builder we could. These people include Ed Gaudet, SQA Inc.; Alex Whitney, Powersoft Corp.; the members of TeamPowersoft for guidance, support, and their seemingly unlimited sources of technical expertise, and special thanks to Jon Credit, Steve Benfield, and Andy Tauber for their advice and support. To the hard-working crew at Graphic World, especially Marcia Craig and the amazing art department, our undying gratitude. Thank you all for the great job. Finally, out thanks to Jay Ranade of McGraw-Hill for believing in us and the book; and to our editor, John Wyzalek, who left no stone unturned to help us accomplish our dream.

PowerBuilder for Managers

Introduction

There are many things that go into building successful applications. When an enterprise makes a commitment to a technology, they are basically banking on the success of the technology, hence the reluctance to put all their eggs into one basket. Some companies attempt to remain on the cutting edge of technology, occasionally getting burned, but doing everything they can to remain ahead of their competition.

Client-server technology promised huge rewards in reduced costs, labor requirements, and increased productivity. I believe this was originally overstated when the theory of savings was tabulated. On paper it does seem that the technology will reduce the historically high maintenance costs. What we have come to learn is that there are savings to be had. But these savings are not as large as once thought, and the environment requires at least as much planning and interdepartmental communication as before.

Specialized support personnel focusing on smaller sections of the environment are typical.

The mainframe environment typically had a technical support staff and operations staff who supported and ran the mainframe, usually in a single location. Now the client-server juggernaut is spreading these people out to distant sites within the enterprise, requiring different teams of specialists to monitor and support these distributed operations. The number of systems and technical support personnel required in a diverse and widespread enterprise usually grows rather than shrinks.

Still, the cost of this environment is lower than that of the typical mainframe environment. With the powerful tools available on a multitude of platforms, development costs are expected to fall rapidly. Again, it is a mistake to assume that this will happen. It can be achieved, but the planning and commitment required are beyond that which most people are used to. Thus, companies entered the distributed client-server era looking for the pot of gold at the end of the rainbow.

Object-oriented technology is introduced to the business sector. RAD becomes the new buzzword.

Then, as if life were not complicated enough, someone introduced object-oriented technology to the business environment. Even though object-oriented technology has been around since the early 1960s, it was not until the 1980s that the idea began to permeate the business environment. Initially developed to support scientific simulations, the technology showed promise as a business technology tool. The possibilities, again, seemed endless.

Visions of an enterprise built on this reusable foundation stirred the hearts of the dreamers, the idea generators. Rapid application development (RAD) replaces the steady yet plodding procedural mainframe design and development techniques. Once again, the hard facts of reality have brought us crashing back. The very idea of a centralized building block foundation is ripped apart by the notion of the distributed environment. We have separated the people and equipment that build and house our applications, but expect to take advantage of the reusable aspect of the technology.

The tools we use develop faster than the technology they support.

This is a quandary that has industry experts changing their opinions regularly. Although I do not consider myself an industry expert, I have seen several companies go through the throes of technology implementation. Some companies have not only survived, but flourished. Others have floundered, some even giving up on the technology and reverting back to their centralized procedural "safe" environment. A few companies have held back, waiting for the technology to stabilize.

This is not going to happen any time soon! Technology is increasing and improving at an exponential rate. It is quite a simple formula. A technology is born and begins to grow. At first it grows slowly, steadily. Then tools are born to help use the technology. The technology is like a photographer's wide-angle lens, however, trying to keep everyone moving forward. The tool vendors—small, lean, and competitive—exploit the technology and the market, building better, faster tools, quickly outstripping the technology they are there to support. Their focus is much narrower, the competition fiercer.

Soon, the technology has to speed up to try to keep pace, and now the technology is trying to satisfy the tool vendors rather the maintaining its original objectives. This is a reality, and will not change. The more focused tool vendors will always advance technically much more quickly than the environment can. Sometimes an improvement of magnitude occurs in the technology, gaining ground on the technology tools, and we witness almost a rebirth of the technology.

Three-tiered architecture is a major advancement in client-server technology.

Today, three-tiered architecture is seen as this type of advance in the client-server arena. But again, we are witnessing the tools gathering momentum and rushing headlong to catch up. Three-tiered architecture is not the savior, however. It is an advancement in the technology; perhaps we could even call it a breakthrough. But it also adds a new level of complexity with new tools to analyze and new methods to adopt. One thing remains constant: the need for careful planning and design.

Enter the Internet.

It seems that the next leap will be the use of the Internet. Globally interconnected applications are available to any target user. Incredible possibilities—perhaps! I believe the next 18 months will either prove or destroy the Internet as an application delivery vehicle. (No predictions—I am eager to start developing for the Internet, but filled with trepidation at the thought of how much traffic this development will generate. Today's physical limitations will become either the back-breaker of the Internet or the cause of the next technological breakthrough).

Hardware is also a technology.

Into this mix, we throw hardware technology. For years, hardware technology could not keep up with the advances in software engineering. Now we are witnessing new and faster chip sets being developed almost every year. Hard drives that cost thousands of dollars just a few short years ago now cost a few hundred dollars, and are being bought more and more by home PC users. Mobile computers are bringing the technologies into every facet of business, large and small. The "it's obsolete when development is completed" syndrome is shifting from software to hardware.

Technology: boon or bane?

We have three different technologies rushing madly into the future, and we are left hanging on by our fingertips, adjusting and accelerating to try to keep pace. Well, this is when I tell the senior managers of large enterprises, "Slow down! By trying to keep up, you are getting left behind. Remain leading-edge, not bleeding-edge.

Build a foundation and build on that foundation.

Build a foundation for the technology you choose. Design an architecture that you believe in, and then decide whether the technology is there to satisfy your objectives. Do not let the technology dictate to you. When your foundation is set, gather and train your employees to support the technology no matter how the personnel are dispersed physically. Then build on your foundation, and if your planning and design are done well, you will see a momentum gathering that will quickly allow your company to achieve significant cost savings. Your employees are your most important asset, and you need their commitment to the architecture. This is the tactic common to the successful companies I have had the pleasure to associate with.

Today's environment dictates full-throttle ideals and burn-out schedules. Driving too fast may give you a rush, but you may not get to the other side alive.

Part Objectives

The objectives of this part of the book are to explain the building blocks we feel are necessary in order for your enterprise to use this technology successfully. The techniques are targeted at managers, rather than developers, including project managers, lead analysts, and architects. Everyone in the organization must know what the architecture is and how to use it.

Although I have not experienced all walks of this technology, nor do I intend to, I have decided on a path. That path is object-oriented technology and the tools used to promote reusable aspects of system development. PowerBuilder is one of the key tools that promote this model and even after being considered an expert in this field, I find that I am constantly learning and discovering ways to improve the level of reusability that can be achieved.

I want to share with you the foundation building blocks that I have seen and been a part of in order to prepare you for successful enterprise development. I cannot make an organization successful, but I can share the tools I have seen, used, and developed to help guide you to success. Some of the building blocks I want to emphasize are as follows:

- Obtaining management commitment
- Developing useful guidelines and best practices
- Developing a strategy for reuse
- Developing and using a class library
- Developing reusable business object libraries
- Using effective pilot projects
- Building on the foundation
- Using the tools and components available

By the end of this part, you will have a grasp of what it takes to prepare your organization for successful client-server development with PowerBuilder. You will also have a sense of what others around you are doing, or need to do, to continue to build on the success.

My methodology is not vastly different from others. I am not against RAD, reiterative prototyping, or any other development discipline. Rather, I want to emphasize the pieces of the puzzle that have been omitted from many plans, strategies, and discussions: the need for planning and design *followed by* development, testing, documentation, and deployment.

My methodology is based on the building block approach. Figure p1.1 shows the enterprise development pyramid as we have developed it to this day. Each piece is an integral piece of the final picture, although any given piece can be modified or enhanced. It can comprise its own architecture, and it is fully replaceable.

As you can see, the base of the pyramid is management commitment. Standards and strategies are the guide mechanisms that control the flow and direction of the development efforts. You will also notice the triple-layered development section made up of the class library or application framework library layer, the business or reusable objects library layer, and the applica-tion layer. These three layers should be integrated and yet separate to allow swapping in and out of features and objects. Good design and testing techniques help guide these processes, ending with good documentation and carefully thought-out implementation plans. All of these elements

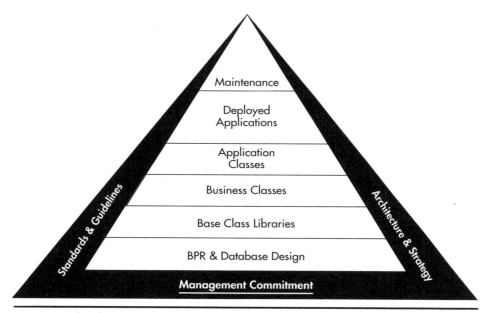

Figure P1.1 The enterprise development pyramid, showing how each layer of the pyramid builds on the layer beneath it.

add up to successful client-server development, and especially development using PowerBuilder.

Summary

I want to assure you that successful client-server development is not only possible, but ensurable. You have to measure your success and adjust your planning where necessary to continue to be successful. Remember that the technology is young but is maturing constantly. Give the technology, yourself, and your staff the tools to make the technology work for you. Above all, make a commitment to the technology and make it work for you, not the other way around.

1

Management Commitment

Introduction

The decision to dedicate time, money, and effort to new technology must be supported by a solid commitment from senior management. As with any major decision in a company, getting the commitment to ensure that achievable goals are set and plans are developed and followed is not easy. This is especially true when managers are facing increasing pressure to provide higher quality service to their clients at lower cost.

This chapter deals with how to obtain that management commitment. Your mission is to promote the idea that reusability begets profitability, but it takes time and effort to plan and design for reusability. Reusability does not happen by accident, or as a by-product. Reusability must happen by design. Remember the very essence of the reason companies decide to use a tool such as PowerBuilder in the first place: Increased productivity through the power of reusability leads to decreased costs.

When you have completed this chapter, you will be able to convince management that implementation must be built on a strong foundation of design and concepts. You will understand the strategy of reusability as it applies to the business environment, not just the programming world.

Informed Decision Making

The management of a company is charged with making decisions that maximize the company's overall profitability. These decisions are not made in a vacuum. An effective argument in favor of a strategy must be based on benefits that outweigh costs. The key to effectively pursuing any agenda is the targeted organization of appropriate information. That is, you need to separate the relevant from the irrelevant and prepare it in such a way that management concerns are addressed clearly and efficiently. This is called structuring information for decision.

Information that is structured for decision has most (if not all) of the following attributes:

- Summary comes first.
- Focus is on benefits versus costs.
- Alternatives are presented unambiguously, with attention to the differences that will drive the decision-making process.
- Undesirable consequences and side effects are addressed as part of the summary as well as the detailed exposition.

Do you see a trend emerging? The idea is to communicate with management. The more you stack the deck with information that they can use, structured in a way that answers their questions, the better your communication will be.

Reusability Is a Goal, Not a Method

It is important for management of companies to realize that reusability must be planned. The planning does not begin and end with application development. It begins with determining the enterprise architecture and continues through every process used in the organization. Reusability is a goal, not a means to achieve a goal. Every aspect of the enterprise development effort must strive for reusability and flexibility. The strategy begins with the architecture, where a foundation for reuse is built. This foundation must be communicated throughout the echelons to ensure that every person involved is aware of the goal. Design, planning, and communication are all necessary when a tool such as PowerBuilder is selected as the development environment.

Why PowerBuilder?

You may need to begin by convincing management of the viability of PowerBuilder as a tool. What are the benefits that the company gains through the use of PowerBuilder?

Benefit: Training time and costs decrease.

PowerBuilder is described as a fourth-generation language (4GL). This is distinct from a third-generation language (3GL) such as C. Unlike a 3GL, PowerBuilder allows a high degree of visual development within the graphical user interface. Instead of meticulously coding each piece of the presentation layer, the developer "paints" the objects within the PowerBuilder development environment. Many of the elements of interacting with the user and the graphical environment are handled automatically by PowerBuilder. Visual objects created with PowerBuilder conform to the expected user interface standards with little or no coding needed. The business impact of this ease of use is that the amount of training a developer needs is greatly reduced. Of course, some training is still required if the developer is to make optimum use of all of the features provided by PowerBuilder.

Benefit: Business needs can be answered readily.

PowerBuilder has an enormous amount of power and flexibility. Depending on the business need, a developer can choose from a vast array of implementation styles. Class and component libraries can provide a component-assembly style of programming to answer simple information-handling needs. The object-oriented nature of PowerBuilder also allows the developer to accommodate increasingly complex needs, simply by extending and overriding attributes and behaviors inherited from basic PowerBuilder objects or external class libraries. This means that the company can expect to be able to answer a large variety of business needs using a single tool. In addition, PowerBuilder 5.0 provides the capability to build business solutions using distributed objects, allowing you to create middle-tier objects that run on different platforms and can be used by any number of client PowerBuilder applications.

Benefit: Company strength means a firm foundation.

Powersoft is exceptionally strong as a company. Their product is an accepted standard for graphical client/server development. The company's strength means that PowerBuilder should exist as a standard for some time to come, and that support will be readily available.

Benefit: PowerBuilder's popularity means better availability of personnel.

It is easy to find people who know PowerBuilder programming and can build or maintain your applications. It is also easy to find people with a desire to learn PowerBuilder to enhance their own career opportunities. This means that you can expect to find available and eager PowerBuilder developers.

Why Should We Reuse?

Your strategy must be one of pursuing object-oriented development techniques to maximize reusability of code and objects and to increase developer output. You must convince your management that the seemingly increased cost of planning for reuse and promoting an enterprise-wide reusability strategy will lead to increased developer productivity, better quality, and lower maintenance costs.

Benefit: Increased productivity comes from reusable objects.

From the developer's viewpoint, an important feature of PowerBuilder is the ability to produce reusable objects. What is the impact of this feature on the business decision makers? The first and most important objective of company management is to increase productivity in line with overall company goals. Reusing existing code and objects increases developer productivity. Of course, this still depends on how well your reusable objects are developed. Management will see increased productivity only as a result of a planned strategy involving reusable objects. Increased productivity means better performance for the same cost, or a lower cost for equivalent performance.

Reusability is a difficult goal to achieve. You must fight the "not developed here" syndrome, you must teach your developers that reusability must be their goal in every application, and you must have a dedicated team promoting and teaching reusability throughout the organization. If management support exists for this effort, your projects will benefit enormously from the strategy of reuse.

Benefit: Reuse of objects allows better planning and budgeting.

A strategy that involves reusable objects also pays off in the area of cost estimation and planning. Any object that already exists and is known to satisfy a business need can be included in a development plan with very little uncertainty about its incremental cost. This means that plans based on reuse will produce more accurate time and budget estimates.

Benefit: Reuse of objects leads to reduced cycle time.

Reusable code that is effective reduces project development time dramatically. Every object that is reused provides code that the developer does not have to write. And if you do not have to write the code, the chances of introducing a defect are dramatically reduced. This leads into the next topic: quality.

Benefit: Reuse of objects leads to improved quality.

When an object is first developed, the law of averages says there will be a defect in it somewhere. If the object is never used again, the defect stands a good chance of staying there until the most inopportune moment, when it will surface and create havoc. When the object is reused by several other projects, the chances of early discovery rise exponentially. Early discovery, early correction, and reused code mean fixes are applied in only one area. Furthermore, new reusers of the object get an object that is defect-free. Defects are detected earlier and fixed earlier and reusers get continually improved quality in their applications without effort. This raises the standards of the quality in both systems and applications.

Benefit: Reuse of objects reduces maintenance costs.

Improved quality virtually ensures reduced maintenance. There is an old adage that says, "If it ain't broke, don't fix it." I add to this, "If it is broke, make sure it's someone else's object so you don't have to fix it." Reused code means that maintenance costs that normally invade all applications now occur only in one area. The original object is the object that gets repaired. If you have a team of expert developers taking care of your reusable code, you are ensured of fast and accurate repairs that do not have to be made by your application.

Benefit: Object reuse promotes component-based software engineering.

Reusable code changes our way of thinking of how objects should be designed and built. When you build an object for your application, if you are not thinking reuse, you may build the object to suit only your application. Now, with a strategy based on reuse, you think about building reusable components. This promotes more generic thinking, more adherence to object-oriented design principles, and higher quality. You will produce feature-rich reusable components that save time and dollars.

Benefit: Reuse promotes consistency across applications, reducing training time and costs.

Reusable objects also promote consistency across applications. If an object conforms to your standards, and the object is reused, you are guaranteeing yourself a much higher level of consistency and conformity to standards throughout the enterprise. A consistent look and feel is often underestimated as being simply a means of making a user comfortable across applications. It is much more than this. Consistency reduces maintenance costs as developers are already familiar with objects they might not have written, and user training costs are reduced as users already know to expect certain behavior from certain application features. This benefit should not be underestimated.

The Myths and the Realities

The term object-oriented conjures ivory tower visions, wrapped in exotic notations, swept up in a panoply of ill-defined buzzwords, with the promise of instant productivity and gratification. In view of this, it is important to set management's expectations to more accurately match the realities of the technology and the tools. We must help management be ready in the following ways:

- Prepare for the learning curve
- Understand that the technology makes people more productive if applied in a planned, consistent, and systematic manner
- Understand that the power and diversity of the tool may leave gaps in quality
- Set realistic expectations for productivity gains and cost reduction

Benefits of the technology

Object orientation (OO) is a discipline with many faces. One of the least productive yet most entertaining aspects of the current state of the technology is the ongoing semireligious debate among the proponents of various OO methodologies. However, we can easily identify the real and tangible benefits of object-oriented technology as it is embodied in our tool of choice, PowerBuilder.

Benefit: Shared development compresses development time.

The encapsulation of functionality within discrete objects makes shared development of enterprise-scale projects much easier to manage. If the interfaces are designed rigorously and the specifications adhered to throughout development, each developer can concentrate on the internal implementation of the functionality, without concern that the resulting object will not fit into the whole of the development effort.

Benefit: Prior costs are leveraged by building on proven code.

In addition, the developer can extend and override the functionality of existing objects, leveraging prior development costs by building on proven code. The benefit is greater functionality in less time with a higher success rate.

Benefit: Increased quality leads to decreased cost.

The development of reusable business objects according to a well-defined set of standards increases the quality of the end product. The developers benefit by having an increasing pool of objects to draw from. The end users gain a more consistent presentation and functionality throughout the company's information systems. The reuse of proven objects also decreases the maintenance cost of the components of each application.

Benefit: Visual development environment increases developer productivity and end-user satisfaction.

PowerBuilder provides a comprehensive visual development environment. Developers create a window by "painting" visual elements onto a representation of that window at design time. The feedback to the developers is immediate, and helps them design windows that provide the end user with high information bandwidth. If the need to alter the visual presentation arises, it is easy to accomplish without disturbing the underlying logic.

Why the technology can fail

Object-oriented technology and PowerBuilder join together to provide a rich and powerful toolset for application development. The opportunities are vast, but the technology can fail. There are steps you can take to avoid the pitfalls, and the more you prepare, the more you will increase your chances of success.

Danger: Excessive expectations lead to disappointment.

Do not set expectations, yours or management's, too high. PowerBuilder is a tool, not a miracle. You will certainly realize productivity and quality gains using PowerBuilder in conjunction with the methods and techniques of object orientation, but you will not see an instant improvement. You will find that a certain amount of investment in time, training, planning, and organization is needed to fully reap the benefits of the tool and the technology. You should factor that time and cost into your cost/benefit analysis, and make sure management is never surprised by the need to invest in future productivity. Maintain a realistic outlook.

Danger: Prematurely loading an incomplete foundation can cause it to fail.

Starting too many projects before the foundation is established is a prescription for disaster. If you are to reap the most benefit from the use of object technology, you need a solid foundation of design methodologies, reusability strategies, standards, and competent and informed practitioners. Standards and practices take some time to evolve from academic aphorisms to practical guidelines. Give the new technology a chance to breathe.

Make sure your foundation plan includes a plan for project loading. Start with only a few pilot projects to prove new concepts and methodologies. As your foundation develops, you will be able to comfortably support more development efforts.

Danger: Lack of experienced guidance increases your chance of failure.

Experience counts. Object orientation does not automatically lead to better programming. PowerBuilder is a vast and powerful tool that allows you to reach the same goal by following a number of paths. Your developers will re-

quire time, study, and hands-on experience to fully apply the concepts and realities of object orientation and PowerBuilder.

It is extremely important that you build some experience into your program from the beginning. Knowledgeable mentoring, coupled with experience in the realities of object-oriented development, will help your project
teams to succeed.

Reusability issues

Several issues must be resolved concerning reusability and its foundation in
order for it to be justifiable. Management must be aware of these issues, and
your planning must include and make allowances for them. These issues are
detailed below.

Issue: Time frames for application delivery are often unrealistically short. Reusability helps.

It seems that every time someone says "Here's a tool that will reduce development times," all of our application schedules are cut by 10%, even if it is not a
technology we are using. Reusability is one technology that promises shorter
time frames for application delivery and can deliver. Project schedules are so
aggressive today that it is imperative that this technology be used. Reusing
proven code helps ensure that development efforts can focus on delivering
completed products on time.

Issue: Plans must address and solicit cross-organizational funding.

In any large organization there are two major obstacles that stand in the way
of new technology: politics and logistics. Today's environments are widely distributed, often across international boundaries. Depending on whose idea it is
and which area controls the power of the organization, an idea may be accepted, rejected, or enforced without cooperation. If you can get beyond these
obstacles, you often run into a third obstacle: Who is going to pay for all this?
Getting multiple organizations to share in the funding of a concept whose benefit is still unrealized is a daunting task. Be prepared for this tough issue with
solid evidence of cost benefits and value added by this technique.

Issue: Cross-application dependencies must be addressed as part of the overall enterprise information strategy.

Data, business rules, and processes can and will cross application boundaries in an enterprise information environment. A strategy that actively
promotes reusable objects will certainly help manage the complexity of
this issue. As much as you can, encapsulate business rules, data access, and

standard processing into reusable objects. The benefit to you and your management will be ease of sharing these resources among applications. If it fits your corporate information strategy, these objects can be created as distributed middle-tier ware using PowerBuilder 5.0's distributed object capability.

Issue: "Real programmers don't reuse" syndrome.

You may face a real battle with your more experienced developers. Some of these developers will readily accept the concept of reusability. Others may be more reluctant. After all, the reasoning may go, the really good programmer has no need to reuse objects developed by others of less stature. This prima donna attitude resides within all competent developers. Those who are able to suppress it and use their talents as part of a team with a common goal are a great benefit to your organization and will adapt and promote reusability very quickly. Those who will not or cannot suppress this attitude are a counterproductive influence that can hamper the gains in productivity resulting from reuse. They must be convinced or reassigned. These people might be your most talented developers, and they are often vital to your organization. They will also be the most fervent promoters of your goals if they can be convinced of the benefit of the technology.

These are the developers who will tell you that they can develop the same object, along with their original application objects, in less time than it will take them to learn about the reusable object. This might actually be true the first time, but the benefits of reuse are not rooted in increased productivity alone. Redevelopment is counterproductive in the long run.

Issue: Generic objects may not address specification complexity.

Often, one of the key obstacles in reusable code is that developers may believe that the object does not satisfy their applications' complex requirements. This might be true. Objects usually cannot satisfy all of the complex requirements of differing systems. They are not intended to. They are intended to form a common base from which to build applications, eliminating the need for the developer to redevelop common code and objects. For example: If an application specification indicates that 10,000 lines of code will be generated, a reduction of 1,000 lines of code by reusing prebuilt and pretested objects is a 10 percent savings in development cost. It also reduces testing costs, documentation costs, and maintenance costs. Developers need to be aware of this. Keep looking at the big picture.

Setting expectations

If one potential problem area is unrealistic expectations, what expectations should you have? What goals can you realistically set for savings using object-oriented technology? The savings in cost and time will accrue during initial development, subsequent maintenance, and later development.

Benefit: 21 percent cost savings during initial development.

Our experience indicates that you can realistically expect a 21 percent cost benefit during the initial development of an application. The saving stems from increased productivity because of focused application of object-oriented technology. A class library is an important part of the foundation that facilitates increased productivity. Developers use proven objects to solve development and business needs, and are free to concentrate on the specialized needs served by their particular application.

Benefit: 33 percent cost savings during maintenance.

One persuasive benefit of the consistent application of reuse through object-oriented design is reduced maintenance cost. Each application springs from a common, thoroughly tested set of objects. The chances of building a flaw into your application decrease. If a bug does turn up in the base objects, the fix can be propagated to all applications simply by recompiling.

Benefit: 21 percent reduction in cycle time after first project.

Once the developers throughout the company have started using OO methodologies and your class library, the time to develop each subsequent application drops by about 21 percent. This results primarily from familiarity with the objects and their functionality. Once learned, the base class objects do not need to be relearned.

In fact, you will see a cost/benefit ratio that constantly improves. The consistent use of standards, reusable objects, and rigorous design methodologies will pay increasing dividends with each new project.

Once again, you and your management can expect significant savings in cost and time as your investments in PowerBuilder as a tool and object orientation as a discipline begin to pay off:

- 21 percent cost benefit (development)
- 33 percent cost savings on maintenance
- 21 percent cycle time reduction after the first project
- Increasing ratio of benefit to cost

How to Maximize Productivity

Management commitment will come when you have convinced management that the technology (object orientation) and the tool (PowerBuilder) will maximize productivity and yet contain costs. The key concepts to emphasize are as follows:

- Preparation and planning speed development
- Solid architecture accelerates development of business functionality
- Training helps developers maximize their use of the technology
- Mentoring spreads the experience base

Preparation and planning are essential, and will speed and guide development efforts. The objects you build, the flow of the work, and the sequence of events leading to completion of a project must be planned and integrated into the overall strategy. Remember that reusability requires planning and design, but reusability pays in time, money, and quality.

A solid architecture frees your developers to concentrate on business solutions, while the architecture attends to the underpinnings. You need to develop an architecture based on creating and reusing common objects and integrating new objects into the common base. The benefit is that your developers will be far more productive because they can devote most of their time to solving business information problems.

Training is essential. The tools and methodologies must be understood to be used properly. If understood, the tools and methodologies are powerful. Your developers will benefit because they know the details of the architecture and the intent of the methodologies. You will benefit from greater productivity: more solutions, more accurately, in less time.

We have already said that experience counts. We have pursued a strategy of mentoring with great success. We try to make sure that a highly experienced person is placed on each development team. The result is that all other team members gain from interaction with an expert in object-oriented development in general, with a class library, and with PowerBuilder. Mistakes are fewer, solutions come faster. Again, productivity is up, cost is down.

Summary

This chapter dealt with the many questions senior managers have when choosing a technology. There are clearly benefits and costs associated with the technology, but as can be seen, the benefits outweigh the costs significantly, and the gap continues to increase with each reuse that occurs. Remember that reusability should occur at all levels of the development cycle, not just the physical object development. Reuse is a goal, not a methodology.

2

Developing a Strategy for Reuse

Introduction

When deciding to embark on the journey to the Oz of client-server development, we must establish certain goals and build a foundation to support achieving the goals. Several issues must be resolved at the management level to prepare the enterprise for development using PowerBuilder. It has become evident that companies are spending more time justifying decisions when it comes to this new technology, and the leg work up front does pay dividends down the road.

This chapter deals with the issues an enterprise faces when adopting the technology.

Chapter Objectives

The objectives of this chapter are to define an easy-to-follow strategy to implement reusability as a goal in the enterprise. The strategy must include developing practical means of measuring reusability, setting goals for development of standards, building a high-quality development and support infrastructure, deciding on the reuse mechanism, and implementing the mechanism.

The Reusability Strategy

In determining a reusability strategy, it is important to accomplish the following tasks:

- Obtain senior management support
- Develop a cost/benefit model
- Promote standards

- Build a library team
- Establish a class library
- Build business-oriented objects on top of your class library to support the business infrastructure
- Select a high-visibility, low-risk pilot project
- Develop or purchase high-quality objects
- Implement an object repository
- Perform training
- Perform ongoing support

Let's break each of these components down and discuss how we can go about ensuring success.

Obtain senior management support

As discussed in Chapter 1, it is vital that management be committed to the goal of reuse. I have already broken down the reasons why this is a good approach; now we need to figure out how we can continue to provide management with feedback on progress, benefits being reaped by reuse, and emerging goals to ensure their continued support. One of the most effective means of achieving ongoing support is to provide a meaningful cost/benefit analysis.

The cost/benefit analysis

In order to build a cost/benefit analysis, there are several factors to weigh. What are our goals? What are the real and intangible costs? What are the real and intangible benefits? There are intangible costs and benefits associated with any technology. We do not want to hide these, because for the most part they favor reusability.

Setting realistic goals. We have found through our experience with class libraries that you must set realistic goals. We began with a goal of 10% cost reduction over 1 year for project teams using the library. We soon realized that the savings were much closer to 25%. With more objects and features being added, we expect that this goal can be increased with each application built on this foundation.

By the same token, we began with a cycle time reduction goal of 25%, but scaled this back to 15%. This is because project teams began estimating their project schedules with the class library in mind and because project teams added more functionality to their finished product without adjusting their schedules to reflect this functionality.

Our final goal was to determine how much we saved in maintenance costs. An example of a real case shows that an application with 187 objects took almost 18 worker-months to build. Maintenance costs were running around 1.2 worker-months each month. Almost two full-time staff members supported and enhanced the application. We retrofitted the application to use a class library and immediately reduced the object count to 112. (Most of these objects were datawindows). Application code was cut by almost 40%. Maintenance costs were immediately reduced to less than 1 worker-month per month. Given the shared maintenance costs of the class library (0.1 worker-months per month for each of 10 projects), we realized an effective savings of 33% or more! Obviously, this scale project may not apply to your organization, but Table 2.1 shows how effective this method becomes with each project added to the plate.

As you can see, each project added reduces its own maintenance costs, and the per-project cost of supporting the class library continues to decrease with each application added. Of course, new projects do not gain the immediate reduction in maintenance costs. Or do they? If we now had to develop a new application of roughly the same size, we would expect to deliver 180 objects. We can therefore project that our savings would be in the region of 0.7 worker-months. These numbers were typical of projects we looked at. Using a class library reduces the number of objects and lines of code in an application. Maintenance costs are reduced because the maintenance cost per object is shared among users of the objects, the number of actual application objects is reduced substantially, and a class library typically delivers a higher-quality and more feature-rich set of functions because more people test the objects. The graph in Figure 2.1 shows typical savings increasing to overtake project costs by about the fourth project. This makes it obvious that spending a lot of money on a class library and on internal infrastructure development is not cost-justifiable if you are planing to do only one project, unless you are leveraging the skills of an external vendor who is following the same strategy.

The graph shows that breakeven points vary depending on how much reusability is attained. Reusability is expressed as the percentage of the project's objects that will be derived from your library objects. Twenty-five percent

TABLE 2.1 Incremental Maintenance Benefits[1]

Number of apps	Initial objects	Maintenance costs	After retrofit	Project maintenance cost	Library maintenance cost[1]	Modified total cost
1	180	1.2	112	0.9	1.0	1.9
2	180	1.2	112	0.9	0.5	1.4
3	180	1.2	112	0.9	0.33	1.23
4	180	1.2	112	0.9	0.25	1.15

1. Library Maintenance Costs are shown as one full-time person doing strictly maintenance on the library.

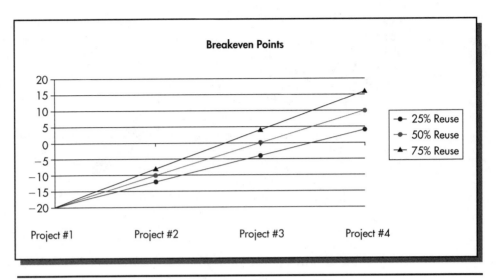

Figure 2.1   Cost-savings breakeven points, depending on reusability.

is a very low estimate for a truly reusable class library; 75% is a difficult goal to reach, but should be where you are aiming. The graph is based on starting project costs at 20% more than normal if a class library is used (to account for training time and the learning curve). Project costs begin to be reduced after two to four projects start using the library. Costs really begin to dip when employees start working on their second project with the library as some of the up-front costs are eliminated.

Intangibles.   You cannot judge how much a team would have spent to develop a version of a class library object because they will not develop to the same level of genericism and feature count, and because the development will also be based on the project need. For example, a project team developing a Sort object (dialog window with sort capabilities) might develop the sort to support only text and decimal columns if that is what their project requirements are. However, a class library object must include date, time, and integer sort capabilities. The same applies to Find and Filter functions. We estimate that project implementation of a class library object is 33% of the development time of the class library object (including research and testing). Project teams that use this object can expect this saving in their development effort and gain the benefit of more robust functionality.

 We also find that we sometimes have objects that are simply not used by project teams. We cannot include these in a post-development cost/benefit analysis. Our cost/benefit analysis now begins to assume the appearance, as shown in Figure 2.2.

 Another intangible is the benefit a project team gets by gaining functionality not included in their project plan. An example of this again is Sort/Filter

Library component	Library Development Effort (MM)	Application Savings on Reuse (MM)	Total Savings
Standard Components			
Application Initialization	0.12	0.040	
Application Version Control	0.25	0.083	
User Login Services	0.25	0.083	
User/Application Security	0.75	0.250	
Standard MDI Framework	0.50	0.167	
Print Functionality	0.25	0.083	
			0.707
Datawindow Value-Added Functionality			
DW Sort	0.12	0.040	
DW Filter	0.12	0.040	
DW Find	0.12	0.040	
			0.120
Core Services			
Application Configuration Control	0.50	0.167	
Error Handling	1.00	0.333	
Interobject Messaging	1.00	0.333	
Object Management	0.75	0.250	
			1.063
Additional Services			
Edit Rules Processing	0.50	0.167	
Database Connection Management	0.50	0.167	
Transaction Management	1.00	0.333	
User Message Processing	0.50	0.167	
Windows SDX Functionality	0.50	0.167	
			1.000
Totals:	8.73		2.910

Figure 2.2 Cost/benefit analysis: project development.

and Find. Some project teams will not even include this functionality (or part thereof) in their project planning. It is not required according to initial specifications. When a requirement does come along, the project team must design, develop, and test the object in the project. By using a class library, the objects are already available and need only be activated. These benefits must be included in the cost/benefit analysis simply because they provide added functionality and features to the finished application.

The final intangible cost we found was one of user training. When users are trained in the use of an application, a certain amount of money is spent. When the user must learn a second application, any behavioral differences are actually harder to learn. Applications built from a common base inherit the same basic behavior and this reduces the amount of relearning that the users have to do.

When we add all of these elements together, you can see that the potential savings look extraordinary. Keep in mind that some of the benefits are intangible and cannot accurately be gauged. Determine what objects will provide benefit to the developers and build a means to demonstrate these ongoing savings to your management.

Promote the use of standards

You must develop, maintain, and promote the use of standards for your enterprise development solution. This not only keeps your developers thinking along similar lines, but also keeps them informed of the direction and commitment of the company. Standards are often seen as a waste of time and effort and you must make sure your standards are not overly restrictive. Give your developers room to breathe while developing a feeling of consistency.

Build an effective development/support infrastructure

In order to effectively build or promote a class library within an organization, you must establish a library team to take on this chore full time. The library team should be a small group of highly skilled employees who understand the value of reusability as a goal and of PowerBuilder as a means to achieve the goal. The best way I have seen this team structure implemented is as shown in Figure 2.3.

The inner circle represents the core group of developers. It is important that this group remain small, staffed by highly skilled developers with as few distractions as possible in a normal enterprise environment. (Because these people are often your best developers, there is always a demand for their skills. Too many distractions from their central tasks will detract from your overall achievement of goals.)

The second (middle) circle represents personnel from each main organizational area in your enterprise, or roughly one person for each two to eight projects that use the library, depending on your internal architecture. These people must be trained in the use of the reusable objects and serve to promote the reusability to development groups. Services such as internal training, internal consulting, and support during development testing and implementation phases are performed by these people. They should represent leadership within the groups they support. They are also responsible for the design, development, and deployment of business-specific object classes required by ap-

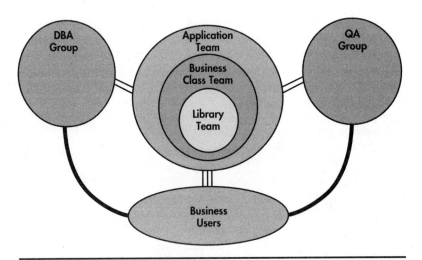

Figure 2.3 Library support infrastructure.

plication teams. Business objects, if designed correctly, will reap even larger benefits than the initial class library, but a solid base is necessary to realize this benefit.

The outer ring represents the application developers. This structure serves to promote feelings of access to support, interest in the development process, and targets for developers to be aiming for. (Developers should aim for the support ring as part of their career development. The support ring should be aiming for the core development team. The core developers should move into more senior positions after gaining experience in the development team.

The support infrastructure therefore serves to promote internal competition, allowing further employee career growth and goal establishment.

Class libraries

Of course, much of what we have said in this chapter is based on your having, acquiring, or building a class library. The class library is one of the most important tools for achieving reusability in the organization. With the benefits we have discussed it becomes easy to see that the class library is almost a prerequisite to successful reuse. How you build or buy your class library is discussed in detail in other chapters in this book.

Business object layer

Building business-oriented objects on top of your class library increases the reusability of your objects a great deal. Not only do business objects model your business, but they are built on a proven set of base objects. These will raise the confidence levels of your application developers and users alike, resulting in systems being developed faster and more efficiently and, most importantly, encapsulating real business solutions that are consistent with actual business processes.

Selecting a pilot project

You must select a pilot project that can prove that the procedures you have built and put in place work for your organization. Choose a high-visibility, low-risk project for this role, but be prepared to follow it very closely with higher-risk projects. You need the high visibility to make sure that more people are aware of what you are trying to accomplish. You need a low-risk project in order not to jeopardize an ongoing time-critical effort using software and procedures that have not been tested. Changes in design and operation are a way of life. We are providing tools to help reduce the number of "violent" changes (changes where developers glare at you with obvious violence when you announce a change in structure or architecture), but you will never eliminate change.

Develop or purchase high-quality objects

All object requirements should be addressed individually, as components. You need to make careful decisions on what you should develop and what you should buy. Look at this from the component level all the way up through the class library level.

Implement an object repository

When gathering objects, you need to develop an object repository, or a central area where all reusable objects will ultimately be stored. This area must be read-accessible to everyone in your organization, and everyone should be encouraged to learn about the area and its contents.

Perform training

Always continue to train your staff. From your leading expert down, your staff needs to learn continuously. Many times, employees or their supervisors are reluctant to take time out from a development effort to do training. Remember that this employee will need the skills eventually; employees who are not afforded the same training opportunities as their peers cannot compete for advancement. You will find that most people have an insatiable need for knowledge. Be careful that this does not turn into an unmanageable nightmare. Your developers need to see your continued commitment to their future, not just the future of the company.

Perform ongoing support

Libraries and development teams need continued support efforts. All stages, from planning through design and development and finally to testing and deployment must be continually supported by the class library team no matter how you choose to structure the team.

Summary

In conclusion, we know that building a strategy for successful reuse helps assure people that the goals are not only quantifiable, but justifiable and measurable. Success is often measured by perception. Hard evidence goes a long way to build the relationship between reusable class developers, application developers, and the business users they support. A shortcoming in any of these areas can jeopardize the overall success of this effort. Most of all, organizational commitment to this type of effort must be complete.

3

Standards and Guidelines

Introduction

Standards have been around forever. I remember my first day of training in the computer sciences, when the words ANSI STANDARD were used. As a junior developer, I hated standards. Standards "restricted my creativity." My second job introduced me to systems maintenance, where I had to maintain both packaged software and in-house developed code. I was astounded at the varieties of coding techniques I saw in those systems. I was also distressed every time I had to go into certain programs whose contents were irreverently called "spaghetti code." I began to appreciate standards, but still felt they applied more to those who were undisciplined.

I performed my first mission-critical on-line systems development a few years later. Again, I was surprised at the many ways the same data could be presented. And accepted! It was at this time that I began to develop a feel for what users felt was simple for them to use. It was also around this time that I heard of CUA standards and SQL standards.

By this time I was a veteran consultant, with 10 years of development and maintenance experience behind me, and I had come to the realization that all those managers I had ridiculed for wanting to limit my creativity were in fact right. Development without standards can cost you about half of your development cycle costs in maintenance.

Then came the true turning point in my career when it comes to standards. I began developing on personal computers, specifically client-server. Suddenly there were many different tools available to do any given thing, none (or very few) with standards of any kind. The technology was simply too young. I realized that the costs of maintenance on systems developed without standards on the client-server platform would be even more costly than they were in the mainframe world. At least the languages used on the mainframe had standards. On the PC, new tools were being born regularly.

I have gone through several iterations of standards development for this platform. The most common problem is the technology momentum. By the time we had established a standard or a guideline, the technology would change in some way. It was a difficult period. Now things seem to be settling down. Technology advances are still frighteningly rapid, but the direction of change appears to be consistent now. Some technology advances can even be prepared for ahead of time.

Standards aid consistency

Standards are the cornerstones of consistency. Not only do they help reduce maintenance costs, but by providing users with an application interface that is consistent, standards reduce training costs. The human mind can grasp only five to seven units of information at any given time. Consistent interfaces allow the users to focus on the business instead of trying to figure out why File–Open means different things in two applications. Standards aid consistency for the developer as well. Knowing how to name an object, approach a problem, comment code, or document new functions reduces the constant stress of decision making.

Standards must be easy to apply and enforceable

Standards are pretty useless if not applied. But how do you make sure that everyone is following standards? The simple answer is, you cannot. It would cost you so much to determine whether standards are being followed or met that it would not be cost-justifiable. The answer is in training. Make learning the standards a part of every employee's training . We teach our employees the "standard" for approaching human resources for benefit information, or how to go about reporting sick days, but we seldom train people on how to design and develop mission-critical applications. Millions of business dollars are being wasted trying to figure out what someone was intending to do or where an object resides. Standards are becoming crucial.

> *OO technology helps not only introduce standards but, in some cases, enforce them.*

Object-oriented technology introduces the first paradigm I have seen that helps enforce standards even before you start. The paradigm allows us to shift the bulk of standards decisions away from the application developer to the class architect. The class architect has to be aware of the company standards, and may even help to create them. If object classes are designed and built to a set of standards, then the developer using those classes is practically forced to follow suit. With the environment being as complicated as it is, developers will gladly adopt useful, practical standards, especially if they are already enforced.

How does this occur? As an example, let's take a simple command button often seen on a window. A command button typically has two important attributes: size and font. (Location is often important, too.) If we establish a size and font we want as standard for our organization and then do not create a class object for developers to use, we will succeed only half of the time in enforcing this standard. If we create a class object using the size and font we have established, and provide this to developers as the inheritance model, the developers know that by inheriting the object they are already complying with corporate standards and they do not have to look up the standard in a 3-inch-thick manual somewhere. Compliance rises to 95%! Automatic collaboration virtually ensures compliance! This also ensures that the end-user will see and recognize consistency. The look and feel of the application become consistent. User training costs go down, development costs go down, and productivity goes up.

Published guidelines

Standards are also useless if they are not readily available. Make sure you publish your standards in a form that can be easily found. Standards should always be published as guidelines. Good developers are typically creative. Eliminating creativity is a side-effect of standardization that can reduce productivity. Developers often strive to prove why a standard should not be followed in a particular case, but if the standard is published as a guideline and is an inheritable attribute of their environment, they will be more likely to comply. Thoughtful guidelines aid in productivity.

Easier maintenance

One of the largest benefits of applying standards is in reducing the complexity level of maintenance. Maintenance costs are typically higher than the development costs over the lifetime of an application. These costs should be a focus element for an organization. Applying a simple naming convention helps maintenance programmers to locate the object or function they are looking for much more easily, thereby making them more productive. Standardized coding techniques help maintenance programmers to find and understand the area of code they will work with, further reducing the effort.

Referring back to the command button example, if the company standard changes and the buttons should now be 2 units larger or smaller, or a different font is required, changing the object class from which application command buttons are derived automatically ensures that all objects derived from the class will reflect the changed model. Instead of requiring maintenance of several thousand buttons to ensure compliance (or as is the case in many environments, simply not changing preexisting code because of the effort required), you can simply rebuild applications to pick up the new standard.

Chapter Objectives

The objectives of this chapter are to discuss the various standards I have seen or helped to develop. Standards must follow one simple rule: A standard must be a guideline to ensure consistent behavior. Presentation guidelines are necessary, but must be flexible to allow applications to provide users with the results they want. The categories of standards I have felt to be necessary are outlined below and discussed in detail in this chapter.

- *GUI or presentation guidelines:* Standards defining presentation, or look and feel, aid in application consistency.
- *Coding guidelines:* Standards defining naming conventions and coding techniques aid productivity and reduce maintenance.
- *Planning guidelines:* Standards applicable to the planning of projects ensure consistency and allow fewer problems to slip through the cracks.
- *Design guidelines:* Standards can be used to ensure consistent design approaches. If designs are consistent, application of internal structures will be consistent and reusability of common objects and code is promoted.
- *Development guidelines:* Standards define how certain elements within an application should be approached (such as the use of stored procedures versus standard datawindow SQL).
- *Testing guidelines:* Testing is critical in the client-server environment. By following a set (and tested) practice, we can ensure higher application quality.
- *Documentation guidelines:* Documentation is crucial to maintenance efforts, as is user training. Consistency of documentation, not only of content but of which documents should be produced, reduces both maintenance and user training costs.
- *Deployment guidelines:* Standard deployment techniques ensure a more successful implementation of the final product. This is one area where more standardization is good. Leaving anything to chance during deployment can result in huge costs being incurred if something goes wrong because it was not checked.

Graphical User Interface (GUI) Development Guidelines

The graphical user interface (GUI) is the portion of the application that the user sees. As we said before, if a user recognizes a feature as having a specified behavior in one application, he or she will expect that feature to behave the same way in a second application. Similarly, if an application window contains three buttons of inconsistent shape, size, or color, the user will be confused as to the relative importance of the differences rather then the functional difference. Larger buttons may be perceived as being more important.

A different font can reduce the importance. Placing buttons on the right side of one window and on the left side or bottom of the next window forces the user to search for them. Of considerable importance is the fact that users typically work with commercial applications as well. If a commercial application presents an item with a specified behavior, your users will expect similar behavior in your application if the same item is presented.

PowerBuilder is a proprietary development tool without any widely accepted GUI standards. Windows development is more recognizable as having some standards. A typical Windows application contains a File menu as the first item on the menu bar. The File menu relates to all functions that require or perform input and output (I/O). (Thus, File–Open usually initiates a dialog to locate and select a specific file to open.) Recently, Microsoft has been promoting several of its products as having consistent menu structures in different applications to allow more conformity of applications using their object linking and embedding (OLE) technology. For examples of this, review any of the applications in the Microsoft Office Suite. Consistency is the key element here. Whichever approach you decide to use, it should be consistent throughout your organization. Such cross-application standards are important to your application development effort. We have included our GUI Guidelines skeleton document,[1] which you can use to continue to develop your own organization's standards. Where applicable, we have noted the source of some published standards we have referenced. Of special note is the reference to behavioral standards, which we find are sometimes more important than presentation standards.

With the growing popularity of products that transcend physical platform barriers, there is an additional concern of applying standards that can be met on multiple platforms. If your organization is one where processing of a GUI front-end is expected to cross platform boundaries, make sure that the GUI guidelines reference the applicable platform whenever possible.

Coding and Naming Guidelines

Ask any developer who has tried to locate an object that is named differently (in structure) from what he or she is used to, and he or she will invariably state that the object was incorrectly named. There is so much freedom when it comes to naming objects in PowerBuilder that this type of inconsistency is almost unavoidable. Decide on an approach before imposing this type of guideline. These standards need to be much more rigid and static than other standards typically are because object inheritance requires the developer to know the physical name of the parent objects.

In addition, applying a standard for coding conventions helps ensure that a maintenance programmer will understand code he or she did not write. Our coding standards include naming conventions, function comments, code indentation specifications, and the use of capitals in names.

---

1. See chap03\gui_guid.doc and chap03\gui_guid.hlp on the CD. The document was produced using WexTech's Doc-2-Help system.

Naming conventions

Figures 3.1 through 3.5 describe the naming conventions we have established, used, and enforced before and have applied to our own code in this book.

Naming Standards

Conventions Used in the Naming Standards

<name>	Required: *name* defines what is required.
{ }	Optional.
{.}	Choice of.
xx_xx	Underbar is a connector and is required.

Figure 3.1 Conventions used in the naming standards.

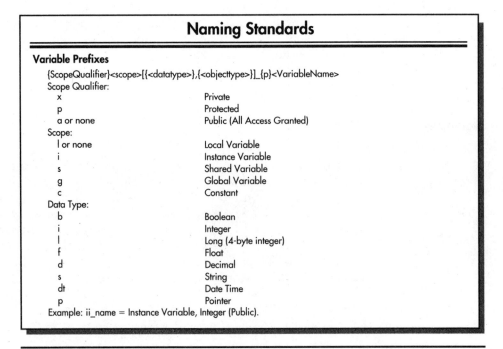

Naming Standards

Variable Prefixes

{ScopeQualifier}<scope>[{<datatype>},{<objecttype>}]_{p}<VariableName>

Scope Qualifier:

x	Private
p	Protected
a or none	Public (All Access Granted)

Scope:

l or none	Local Variable
i	Instance Variable
s	Shared Variable
g	Global Variable
c	Constant

Data Type:

b	Boolean
i	Integer
l	Long (4-byte integer)
f	Float
d	Decimal
s	String
dt	Date Time
p	Pointer

Example: ii_name = Instance Variable, Integer (Public).

Figure 3.2 Variable prefixes.

Naming Standards

Object Types

{ObjectType>{_<ObjectTypeStyle>}_{ObjectClassStyle}<SA>_ObjectName
ObjectTypes include:

s_	Data Structure
f_	Global Function
w_	Window
m_	Menu
d_	Datawindow
dddw_	DropDownDatawindow Object
uo_	Custom UserObject
uo_<style>_	Standard User Object
uo_vbx_	VBX User Object
uo_ex_	External User Object
cc_	Custom Class (nonvisualobject)
cc_<style>_	Standard Class (nonvisualobject)
cpp_	C-Plus-Plus Class (nonvisualobject)

ObjectTypeStyle refers to the standard object style being used (e.g., cb = Command Button).
ObjectClassStyle refers to the class style defined at design time (e.g., i = Interface).
SA = System Acronym (2 or 3 characters).
Example: UO_DW_Datawindow = User Object Datawindow.

Figure 3.3 Object types.

Naming Standards

Function Prefixes

Functions
<Object Qualifier>f_{<FunctionType>}_<SA>_FunctionName

Object Qualifier = 'o' if function is an object function.
FunctionType:

i	Interface Function
p	Protected Function
a	Public Function
x	Private Function

SA = System Acronym.

Examples:
f_a_OFR_Function = Global Function, public access (all), Object Framework function.
f_OFR_Function = Global Function, public access (all), Object Framework function.
of_i_OFR_Function = Interface Function in a User Object or Window.

Figure 3.4 Function prefixes.

Naming Standards

Event Prefixes

Events

{c}ue_{Eventtype_}<defining<SA>>_EventName

CUE	Custom User Event
Defining SA	System Acronym where the event is originally defined

EventType:

i	Interface Event
o	Object Specific User Event
c	Class Specific User Event
r	Reserved Uncoded User Event
None	Normal User Event addition

Examples:

CUE_i_OFR_ExtraClicked = Interface Event.

CUE_r_OFR_Reserved01 = Reserved Event.

UE_OFR_Print = Normal User Event defined in the Object Framework.

Figure 3.5 Event prefixes.

Coding guidelines

Comments. Figure 3.6 shows a standard comment block we have developed. This comment block is applied to all functions in our code. The use of special characters such as "&&" provides us with access points for some automated documentation programs we have developed and help indicate the beginning and end of a comment block. You can adjust the comment block to suit your organization. Use of the standard comment block in all functions aids not only in documentation but also in understanding the function for development.

We also feel that events require standard comment blocks, but that perhaps less information (or different information) is required for events. Figure 3.7 shows our standard event comment block.

Code. Some elements of code are useful standard additions. For example, all objects should contain an initialization routine and a place where object attributes can be set up or modified before object initialization. Another element we found applicable to all objects is an exception handler. Our coding standards therefore include standard elements as well as coding style conventions.

```
*************************************************************************
**
* FUNCTION   :Sample Function Preamble
* PURPOSE    :Function Description goes here
*
* Author     :Bill Green
* Date       :Aug. 15, 1996
*
*
* A R G U M E N T S
* ----------------
* Type       Description
* -------    ----------------------------
* (None)     Sample
*
*
*
* R E T U R N   V A L U E S
* -----------------------
* Type       Description
* -------    ----------------------------
* (None)     Sample Return Value
*
*
* HISTORY
* -------------
* Date       Init      Description of Change
* --------   ----      ------------------------
* 08/15/95   xxx       Initial Coding...
*
*************************************************************************
*/

RETURN
```

Figure 3.6 Standard comment block (function preamble).

You will notice these elements throughout our objects as events INIT, SETUP, and CLOSEQUERY and functions CheckException, Intfc_Load, and Intfc_Unload. We decided to use the word *exception* rather than *error* because the word *error* indicates that something is wrong. An exception is behavior or results differing from expected results or behavior, which is not necessarily invalid. Figure 3.8 details the standard behavior we find necessary in all object classes.

Under coding style conventions we reiterate the requirement to apply correct indentation of iterative or decision processes such as If . . . Then . . . Else . . . End If or Do While . . . Loop.

We added that Powerscript standard notations be indicated in all capital letters; for example, we code If . . . Then . . . Else . . . End If script as IF . . . THEN . . . ELSE . . . END IF. PowerBuilder's own code generation assistant painter generates script with the static script elements capitalized, so we adopted that standard to add to consistency levels.

Along with these, we indicated that code contained within blocks such as IF . . . THEN . . . ELSE . . . END IF would be indented one tab position from

```
********************************************************************************
**
* EVENT        :Sample Event Preamble
* PURPOSE      :Event Description goes here
*
* Author       :Bill Green
* Date         :Aug. 15, 1996
*
*
* A R G U M E N T S
* ----------------
* Longparm:          Describes contents of Longparm if any
* WordParm:          Describes contents of Wordparm if any
* Other:             Describes the use of any other arguments defined for the
event
*
* R E T U R N S
* ----------------
* Type               The type of data returned
* Description        Describes the return value
*
* O V E R R I D E / E X T E N D
* ----------------------------
* Ancestry:          Describes event ancestry
* Override Details:  Describes override characteristics
* Extend Details:    Describes extend characteristics
*
* HISTORY
* -------------
* Date              Init     Description of Change
* --------          ----     ------------------------
* 08/15/95          xxx      Initial Coding...
*
********************************************************************************
*/

RETURN
```

Figure 3.7   Standard comment block (event preamble).

the block identifiers. Figure 3.9 shows the standard block code convention we have adopted.

Finally, we decided *for* using CapWord notation for object and function name references; that is, the first letter of each word is capitalized. For example, a function call to the PowerBuilder SETTRANSOBJECT function appears as SetTransObject. It has no functional purpose other than adding readability to the code. Figure 3.10 documents these conventions. We decided to adopt this standard even though PowerBuilder's built-in Paste functions (paste instance name, paste object name, etc.) automatically convert everything to lowercase. I feel the effort will pay dividends in readability later on. We limited use of the underbar (_) to separate main identifying elements of a word.

You will notice that our guidelines are all small, well-defined elements that are easy to digest and therefore easier to follow. We also propose that these

Figure 3.8 Common functionality standard.

Standard Attributes, Events and, Functions

Attributes:

Scope		Type	Name	Default
Protected	Instance	Integer	ii_Return	Const.OK
Return Value used in function calls				
Protected	Instance	Integer	ii_Severity	Const.Fatal
Severity Code used for exception handling				
Protected	Instance	Boolean	ib_ContinueAction	True
Action Code used to control logic flow				

Methods:

Scope	Type	Prefix	Name	Link
(None)	Event		Constructor	
Description	Launch any object initialization routines			
Specification	• Trigger *cue_setup* event • Post *cue_init* event			
Overrides	None			
Extensions	Should not be extended unless a step is required between the setup and init events.			

Parameters	Description	Reference
(None)		(None)

Scope	Type	Prefix	Name	Link
(None)	Event		Destructor	
Description	Launch any functionality to be executed prior to object shutdown			
Specification	• Trigger *closequery* event/function to determine validity of closing down the object • Determine whether object may be closed or not (*ContinueAction = True*) • Fire *intfc_unload* function to deactive interfaces used if closedown approved			
Overrides	None			
Extensions	Should not be overridden. Can be extended to add additional setup behavior.			

Parameters	Description	Reference
(None)		by Value

Scope	Type	Prefix	Name	Link
(None)	Event		CloseQuery	
Description	Event fired from the Close/Destructor event to perform application			

(continued)

Figure 3.8 *(Continued)*

	processing prior to shutting down the object. Allows checking of data changed without being saved, etc.		
Specification	• None		
Overrides	None		
Extensions	Should not be overridden. Usually extended to change default object behavior.		
Parameters	**Description**		**Reference**
(None)			by Value

Scope	Type	Prefix	Name	Link
(None)	Event	cue_	Setup	
Description	Event fired from the constructor event to setup the object			
Specification	• None			
Overrides	None			
Extensions	Should not be overridden. Usually extended to change default object behavior.			
Parameters	**Description**			**Reference**
(None)				by Value

Scope	Type	Prefix	Name	Link
(None)	Event	cue__	Init	
Description	Event posted from constructor to perform object initialization after the object build is complete			
Specification	• None			
Overrides	None			
Extensions	Should not be overridden. Can be extended to add additional setup behavior.			
Parameters	**Description**			**Reference**
(None)				by Value

Scope	Type	Prefix	Name	Link
Protected	Function	of_p	Intfc_Load	
Description	Function utilized to instantiate declarative interfaces			
Specification	• Scan for declared interfaces • Check if interface loaded • If not loaded, instantiate the interface • Obtain a pointer to the interface • Increment the usage count			
Overrides	None			
Extensions	Can be extended by developer to add additional interface declarations			
Parameters	**Description**			**Reference**

(None)				
ReturnValue		Success or Failure indicator		Constant

Scope	Type	Prefix	Name	Link
Protected	Function	of_p	Intfc_UnLoad	
Description	Function utilized to de_instantiate declarative interfaces			
Specification	• Decrements interface usage counter • If usage count reaches zero, interface can be unloaded completely.			
Overrides	None			
Extensions	Can be extended by developer to add additional interface declarations			
Parameters	Description			Reference
(None)				
ReturnValue	Success or Failure indicator			Constant

Scope	Type	Prefix	Name	Link
Protected	Function	of_p	Raise_Exception	
Description	Function utilized to process exceptions raised by the object/object class			
Specification	• None			
Overrides	None			
Extensions	Can be extended by developer to add to the exception handling capabilities of the class.			
Parameters/Return Value	Description			Reference
(None)				by Value
SeverityCode	Returns Severity code			Return

guidelines are maintained in an easily accessible format, either printed or in Windows on-line help format.

Planning Standards

It is obvious that standards are necessary for development. What is often over-looked is that planning and design are as vitally important as the development effort itself, But how many standards are available for planning and design? Even in the relatively new world of client-server, standards committees abound to develop standards for languages such as SQL. But, I have yet to see a standard for project planning or system documentation.

It seems that RAD has lowered everyone's guard as to how much planning and design are required. We found that it is extremely difficult to standardize

```
IF<condition> THEN                DO WHILE <condition>
        <action>                          <statementblock>
END IF                            LOOP

IF <condition> THEN               DO
        <action1>                         <statementblock>
ELSE                              LOOP UNTIL <condition>
        <action2>
END IF                            DO
                                          <statementblock>
IF <condition1> THEN              LOOP WHILE <condition>
        <action1>
ELSEIF <condition2> THEN          FOR <varname>*<start> TO <end>
        <action2>                         <statementblock>
END IF                            NEXT

IF <condition1> THEN              FOR <varname>*<start> TO <end> STEP <increment>
        <action1>                         <statementblock>
ELSEIF <condition2> THEN          NEXT
        <action2>
ELSE                             CHOOSE CASE <expression>
        <action3>                        CASE <item>
END IF                                           <statementblock>
                                         {CASE ELSE
DO UNTIL <condition>                              <statementblock>}
        <statementblock>         END CHOOSE
LOOP
```

Figure 3.9 Capitalized script.

CapWord Notation Indicates Use of Capitals on Each Word Segment

Instance Integer variable for result code:
ii_ResultCode
ii is lowercase, indicating identification elements only.
Separator (_) splits the scope and type of the variable from the variable name.
ResultCode is a combination of Result and Code.

Alternative

ii_result_code

Another Example

Object Names:
    cc_Base_Interface
    cc_Intfc_SQLConverter
Base and Intfc are group identifiers and are separated from the names
Interface (no caps on *face*) and SQLConverter.

Figure 3.10 CapWord notation.

everything, but by creating some standards to include in all application development projects, we were able to introduce a consistency in estimation, project control, and on-time delivery. An immediate benefit was that tasks sometimes omitted (and we found at least one task omitted in every project we looked at) were now handled. Even a task that took no time at all, but raised consciousness of a possible shortfall, paid off handsomely in project delivery.

The most important aspect of the development cycle, I feel, is that deadlines are established before the full extent of the development effort is known. By breaking up the project into two distinct parts, (planning, analysis, and logical design, then physical design, construction, testing, and deployment), we feel we can much more accurately estimate a project. Based on our methodology, we can establish the equivalent of *function points,* which we can use to estimate and plan the development cycle. The planning and design phase can be estimated and planned according to the known business processes involved. Thus, we can create a working plan that develops almost iteratively, as defined in RAD. I say *almost* iteratively because we try to limit the iterations to keep the project under control. Figures 3.11 and 3.12 show some of the planning tasks we estimated for sample projects. The tasks remain the same for larger projects, the amount of effort required simply adjusts along with the project size. Notice the additional columns added to enter class/object function points to aid in the estimation process.

	Task Name	Work	Detail
1	**Sample Project Plan**	0h	
2	**Planning Tasks**	0h	
3	Model the Business Function	0h	Develop workflow of business functions
4	Develop Requirement Summary	0h	Develop list of requirements based on workflow
5	**Logical Design**	0h	
6	Define Requirements	0h	# of Requirements
7	Define Method Collections	0h	One line for each method collection
8	**Define Methods**	0h	
9	Define Actions	0h	One line for each method
10	Define Attributes	0h	One Line for each Action
11	**Define Test Procedures**	0h	
12	Define Test Plan	0h	One line for each method
13	Define Test Cases	0h	One line for each test procedure
14	Define Messages	0h	As Needed
15	Define Logical Classes	0h	# will vary based on like methods
16	**Physical Design**	0h	
17	Design Physical Classes	0h	May be several physical classes for each Logical Class
18	Define Physical test plans	0h	At least one for each NEW method defined in the class
19	**Object Construction**	0h	

Figure 3.11 Planning, analysis, and design tasks required (sample).

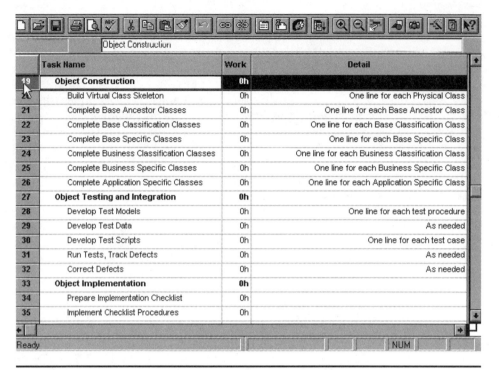

Figure 3.12 Development, testing, and deployment tasks required (sample).

Design Standards

As stated before, design techniques are often not standardized, even within an organization. It is difficult to impose standards on a design, as this is usually the most creative time of the project cycle. Unfortunately, this creativity is also the area that needs the most standardization. We have not tried to impose a design standard in this book, but we have developed a methodology that, if used correctly, will help bring the project to completion on time and under budget. This methodology provides us with a standardized approach to object-oriented design.

The need for a standard in design techniques arises because if development teams are designing differently, the chances of reusability are reduced exponentially with each different style used. If everyone is approaching the design in the same way (specifically, with reuse in mind), the chances of ending up with a more reusable result are much higher.

As a test of this theory, we had two different groups prepare a design of a small system. We then had independent teams develop an application based on the design. We found that the result was two very similar applications, at least in the users' eyes. Both systems satisfied the business problem. When we looked at the objects and classes that were designed and built however, we found that the application designed from the ground up using OO techniques had a reusability index of 80%. That is, 80% of the objects (excluding datawindows) could be reused in other applications with little or no modification. The second application was designed along more traditional lines, where the design closely modeled the available development objects. This application had a reusability index of less than 20%. In terms of large-scale application development, this represented a 40% increase in development cost of a second application using similar objects.

This simple test made us very aware of the results of the design phase. The methodology we have developed, called cooperative business modeling, is shown in Figure 3.13 and is described in detail in Part II of this book.

Using this methodology as a standard design guideline ensures that you address the business problems in such a fashion as to produce highly reusable classes of objects.

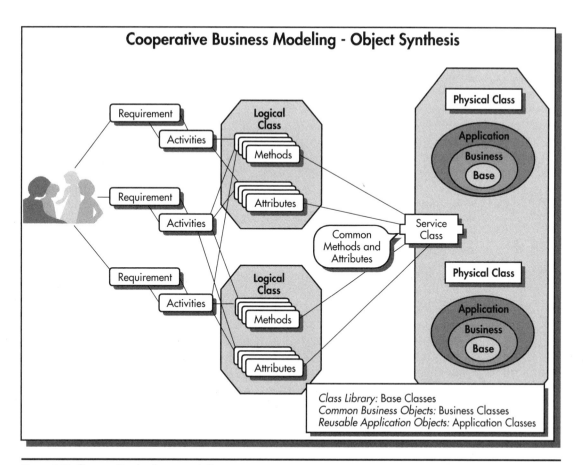

Figure 3.13 Cooperative business modeling.

Diagram notation

One of the most often mentioned guidelines available for OO design is diagram notation. We looked at the notations offered by leading experts in the field of OO design. Although all of these notations contained many valid points, we felt it would be impossible to choose one as the method we recommend. Each style has its own benefits and drawbacks. We found that the methods were actually very similar and therefore recommend that if you choose to adopt an OO standard for diagrammatic notation, you research these methods and use the one that is most applicable to your environment.

We also found, however, that although many people know of these methodologies and guidelines, few followed the techniques for one common reason: practical timely use. With deadlines shrinking, project teams need a methodology that is easy to use and provides a means to achieve the desired result. Our documentation methods are shown later on in this chapter and discussed in detail in other chapters in the book.

Two other elements of our methodology are the navigation workflow and object map. These are application design diagrams we found to be extremely useful to our efforts. Figures 3.14 and 3.15 show examples of these diagrams. Note that we deliberately omitted the use of any notation.

The navigation workflow documents the system as the user will see it and use it. It is useful in determining where links between windows occur and how different objects are linked together. It is not intended to be a detailed object workflow or a repeat of a business process workflow, but rather a simple aid to help determine object integration.

The object map is one of the most useful diagrams we have developed. This simple chart of objects shows the object hierarchy (where each object is derived from), and helps greatly in determining which class library objects (if any) should be used for the object. This simple planning step can save weeks of effort if attempted later during the development cycle. It is also extremely useful in documenting the system for later maintenance and enhancement, as it tells the maintenance programmer instantly which classes are involved.

Development Guidelines

Development guidelines are another very useful collection of guidelines that are established over time. This collection is, and should remain, a living document, growing in content over time with useful tips on development techniques that reduce the learning curve for newer developers and help to bring more experienced developers who are new to your organization up to speed quickly. Guidelines that should be included in such a document are how to code access to stored procedures, useful Windows SDK functions (not included in your class library), and steps to follow to migrate applications through development tool or class library upgrades. This document is most useful in the Windows on-line help format, which can be easily researched and printed topic by topic. A printed copy of the entire document should also be easily attain-

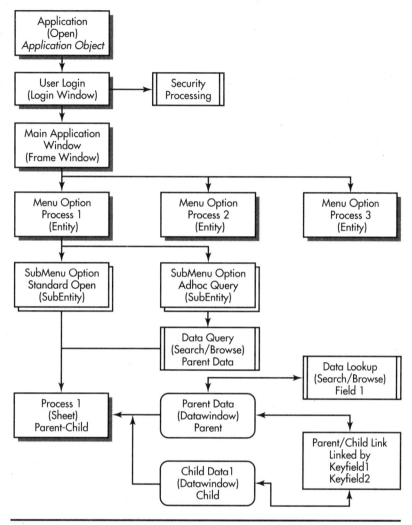

Figure 3.14 The navigation workflow.

able. A sample of such a document is included on our attached CD.[2] The document includes only a few items so that you can use it as a beginning for your own organization.

The final benefit of such a document is that it enables developers to prevent mistakes, rather than discovering the mistake later on and suffering the cost of correcting a known problem or technique. Powersoft originated this idea with the tips help file distributed with version 3.0a and has extended with their InfoBase CD.

_____

2. See chap03\dev_guid.doc and chap03\dev_guid.hlp.

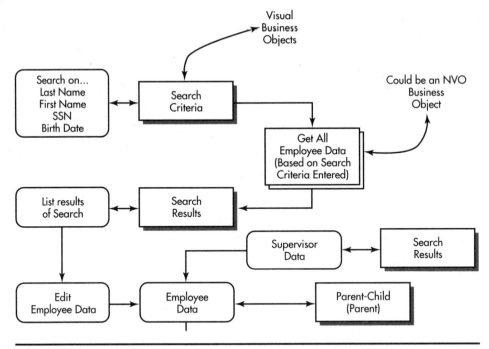

Figure 3.15 The object map.

Testing Standards

Software testing usually accounts for more than 30% of application development costs. Yet most people are under the impression that software is not fully tested. The cause of this contradiction is twofold. First, software testing of client-server applications, and of event-driven languages in particular, is extremely difficult. The permutations of events and functions being fired are almost unquantifiable. Second, testing is often done without following a clear methodology. We all strive for fully-tested, bug-free software, but as is clearly evident, there is not a software program available today, commercial or proprietary, that is error-free. However, there are some things that can be done with tools available today to help reduce the level of defects.

The need for this methodology is clear. The methodology we recommend, teach, and follow is the methodology developed by SQA, the leading provider of automated testing tools for Windows. With their permission and assistance, much of the documentation of testing practices in this book is derived from the work they have put into their guide to automated testing, SQA Process.[3] I highly recommend that your organization obtain this document, whether you plan to use an SQA product or not.

---

3. See chap03\sqa_data.doc and the SQA Demo on the CD for additional information.

In the world of client-server, processing is often distributed across large, decentralized networks, and when you add the client software to this mix, with its rich user interface, nonsequential processing, and architectural complexity, it becomes easy to see why testing practices have suffered. Object-oriented technology does provide some relief in that classes of objects designed for reusability provide a high-quality base for application development. However, it does not alleviate the testing burden completely.

To apply good testing practices, it is important that a major portion of the testing be done using automated tools. We realize that a portion of the testing cycle has to be done manually, but most testing can be done with the tools available today. Automated testing tools are also worth their weight in gold when it comes to regression testing. A good testing tool must allow for solid regression testing. Figure 3.16 shows the testing life cycle required to promote more effective testing of software.

As can be seen, planning, design, and execution of testing occur in conjunction with the relative development cycle. This promotes location of defects much earlier in the development cycle.

Documentation Standards

Documentation is generally left "at the bottom of the food chain." Documentation, other than user documentation, is seldom performed. There is just no time in project schedules to allow developers to create sensible documentation. The emphasis here is on *sensible*. Mounds upon mounds of technical jargon are almost as useless as no documentation at all. Most of all, in the RAD environment we live in today, it is vital that documentation be *living* documentation. If documentation is out of date by the time someone reads it, it is not very useful. We found an astonishing lack of high-quality tools

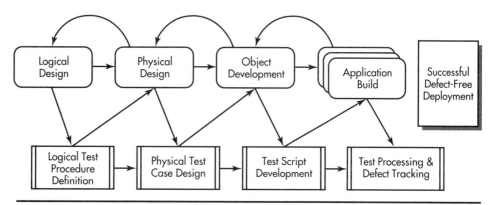

Figure 3.16 Software testing cycle.

capable of producing and maintaining living documentation. In fact, at the time of writing, we knew of only two such tools. One of these is CyberDoc, described in much more detail later in this book.

We provide simple yet effective means to document the development life cycle, including testing. Figure 3.17 describes the documents we expect to produce at the various stages of development and how they contribute to the final documentation of the system.

These forms are described in detail in Part II and Part III of this book. They are summarized in Part IV, and are also included as samples on the attached CD.

Deployment Guidelines

Deployment guidelines consist of checklists to ensure that all facets of implementation are covered. We are aware of the changing face of client-server and realize that these checklists will be modified and updated continually in an attempt to cover every aspect of application deployment. We have also separated the deployment guidelines for application delivery and class library delivery because they are different. One set of guidelines is targeted

Design Documentation

Business Model/Navigation Workflow
Requirement Definition
Method Definition
  Attribute Definitions
  Test Procedure Definitions
   Test Case Definitions
Logical Class Definitions
Physical Class Definitions
Object/Class/Method Map

Cross Reference Documents

Requirement Summary
Method Summary
Attribute Summary
Test Procedure Summary
Test Case Cross Reference
Logical Class Cross Reference
Physical Class Cross Reference

Implemented Software Documents

Technical

Technical Reference
  Based on Design Documentation
User Guide
Knowledge Base
Object/Function Reference
Quick Reference

Nontechnical

User Guide
Technical Support Issues
Quick Reference: Keyboard
Quick Reference: Navigation Map

Figure 3.17 Sample documentation forms.

for an end-user application, in which typically more components are distributed than with a class library, which is targeted at the developer. Tables 3.1 and 3.2 show the checklists we have produced. Each of these is discussed in more detail in their relevant chapters.

TABLE 3.1 Class Library Implementation Checklist

Network preparation	Scheduled	Completed
Identify development locations		
Identify servers		
Create library directories		
Establish user group rights		
Installation preparation		
Documentation distribution		
Library installation routine		
Replication plan		
User training		
Prepare user training		
Communications		
Set up user training		
Perform user training		
Library considerations		
Library bug reports		
Library change requests		
Library version control		
Production source control		
Library build	**Scheduled**	**Completed**
Freeze source code		
Update version information		
Copy to secure location		
Regenerate libraries		
Optimize libraries		
Build library PBR files		
Build dynamic libraries		

©Copyright 1995, Unpublished, Castle Software Engineering, William T. Green and Millard F. Brown III. Document may be used without restriction.

TABLE 3.1 Class Library Implementation Checklist *(Continued)*

Software check			
OS software	Minimum	Excluded	Verified
DOS			
Windows			

Software	Verified

TABLE 3.2 Application implementation checklist

Environment preparation		
Network preparation	Scheduled	Completed
LAN/WAN testing		
Add-user process		
Communication protocol		
Gateway requirements		
Server configuration test		
Create user groups		
Database preparation		
Database turnover request		
Database load		
Database access requests		
Environment preparation		
Documentation dibstribution		
Application installation routines		
Environment preparation		

TABLE 3.2 Implementation Checklist *(Continued)*

Environment preparation (Continued)		
Network preparation	**Scheduled**	**Completed**
User training		
Prepare user training		
Environment training		
Communications		
Set up user training		
Perform user training		
Application considerations		
Application bug reports		
Application change requests		
Application version control		
Production source control		
Other considerations		
Mainframe turnover procedures		
User equipment		
Additional hardware and software		

Installation preparation		
Installation build	**Scheduled**	**Completed**
Freeze source code		
Copy to secure location		
Update version information		
Optimize libraries		
Build dynamic libraries		
Build application PBR		
Create project file		
Run project make utility		
Archive all .exe, .pbd, and .pbr's		
Installation prep		
Refresh deployment kit .DLLs		
Make sure DDK .DDLs are included		
Include application files		

TABLE 3.2 Implementation Checklist *(Continued)*

Installation preparation *(Continued)*

Installation prep	Scheduled	Completed
Include routines to update users WIN.INI		
If ODBC is used, include routines to update ODBC data sources		
Include setup program instructions		
Test on user machine		
Application installation		
Create application directories		
Create development tool directories		
Update WIN.INI		
Update ODBC data sources		
Create program group and items		
Run application, test key features		

Hardware and software

Resource	Minimum	Verified
CPU		
Local hard disk available		
System memory		
Video resolution and colors		
Screen size		
CD-ROM drive		

OS software	Minimum	Excluded	Verified
DOS			
Windows			

Software		Verified

Summary

In conclusion, the standards and guidelines presented above will help you and your organization to develop your own standards and guidelines. These guidelines are crucial to the success of client-server development, particularly if reusability is your goal.

4

Class Libraries

Introduction

As a class library developer and user, I am, quite frankly, disappointed in the class libraries available. It seems that the drive has been financial gain rather then quality of product—at least until recently.

At the time of writing, I know of at least a dozen commercial-strength class libraries of varying quality, depth, and object-oriented design. Of all of these libraries, I have come to know several of them really well. They all provide benefit to the developer. Of this, there is no question. However, the amount of benefit varies depending on how the library is implemented and the architecture behind it.

Some libraries are more object-oriented than others. Some cover the full spectrum of development, providing comprehensive application frameworks, whereas others are more component-oriented. The key is that they all provide some benefit to the developer. The hard part is determining what constitutes an acceptable level of benefit.

Chapter Objectives

This chapter delves into many areas of a class library. What is a class library? What do class libraries give you (not always good), and what do they not give you (not always bad)? I show you the flaws in some of these libraries to help you to understand what not to do. I also give you the means by which to perform your own evaluation of the products. (Number of objects, for example, is not a good estimate of benefit.) I also discuss the different alternatives available to you in building or buying a class library.

What is a class library?

A class library is a collection of reusable components that, combined or separate, give developers a jump start on their development effort. Class libraries should eliminate some of the more redundant tasks facing developers and, at the same time, provide some comprehensive objects to make the more difficult tasks easier. Class libraries are designed specifically for reuse, and their level of reusability drives how much benefit you can expect.

There are different styles of class libraries today. They can be classified as one of three styles.

- Component-based
- Integrated framework
- Service-based architecture

Component-based libraries provide a collection of mostly independent objects designed and developed to solve a particular business problem. Most of the objects can be used by themselves without the need for integration with other objects in the library.

Framework-style libraries are integrated objects that are almost all reliant on other objects in the library. These objects are precoded to communicate internally with each other and provide a high level of reuse and inheritance.

Service-based libraries contain objects that have their functionality implemented as services. This makes the reusable objects easier to use and allows a high level of flexibility. The integration level falls between that of component-based and framework-style libraries.

The style of the library is not nearly as critical as what the library contains and how well it is designed and coded.

What they give you, what they do not

Most class library vendors boast a "complete set" of objects needed to promote successful development reuse. These statements are often linked with a bunch of marketing hype that will lead you to believe that the tool is the silver bullet for the client-server woes you are, or will be, experiencing. Unfortunately, the client-server werewolf is apparently impervious to the silver bullets of the world. This monster can be tamed only by careful planning and strategic application of solid practices. Don't be fooled by the marketing hype.

Class libraries are basically collections of reusable objects. The objects contained in the library vary greatly from simple, easy-to-use convenience objects to complex, integrated objects designed to solve common business problems. Most libraries contain at least one object from each extreme. The good libraries solve more business needs than the basic list of reusable objects. Libraries should contain basic objects, though. The purpose is to eliminate, to the greatest degree possible, tasks and business problems that occur more than once! Therefore, a good library contains a fair share of the basic elements to reduce the coding effort. A good library also uses these basic objects as a basis for enhanced functionality to add value to the process, as well as deliver complex integration strategies to solve business problems we all face.

The class library should present a common, standardized presentation layer that conforms to generally accepted standards. All of the objects with presentation capabilities must be able to be modified, however, to take on the presentation format chosen by the enterprise. These objects should be easily accessible and clearly defined as the modifiable presentation layer. There is nothing more frustrating than having to make significant adjustments to reusable objects in order to satisfy your own standards, and having trouble locating and modifying the necessary objects. Libraries that provide a user-customizable layer get an extra point from me.

Like the basic objects, libraries should provide a comprehensive set of utility functions to help enhance your applications capabilities. However, they should not be replacements for existing built-in functionality.

Class libraries will not have an immediate impact on your productivity. Your top developers will pick up on the concepts and techniques quickly, but even they will have a learning curve. The average developer will also have to add the learning curve for the library to the continuing learning curve of the tool itself. Add a paradigm shift from procedural to object-oriented concepts to the mix, and you are likely to have developers who are confused as to which objects should be reused and why they should be reused in the first place. Libraries that offer hands-on training workshops get an extra plus from me, as training is vital to getting your organization up to speed. The training should include not only what objects are in the library, but how to use, integrate, and test them. The training materials should also emphasize the concepts and techniques encouraged by the library and how they apply to the developers using the library.

Strategy for development

Once you have decided on the architecture you want to use for your enterprise, you are faced with an entirely different question. How will you acquire the class library you need? First you need to decide whether to buy or build. There are pros and cons for each. Part of this decision is to evaluate the libraries that are available. You then need to prepare yourself and your organization for the thrill-ride of PowerBuilder application development, class library development, and deployment.

Buy versus build.   When trying to decide whether to buy or build, you need to know the benefits and drawbacks of each approach. Weigh the different approaches with a view to the elements that are most critical to your organization, such as cost, development cycle time, and internal requirements. If you decide to buy a product, evaluate the options available and make an informed choice. Spending a little time here could save you a lot of time and effort down the road.

Buying a commercial product:

Key benefits: lowest initial cost, fastest initial implementation.

Key drawbacks: least customized, most reliance on outside vendor.

Buying allows you to implement a predefined set of objects quickly and jump-start your development processes. It is also often cheaper to buy than build. The drawbacks are that no library will ever be customized exactly for your organization. One factor in evaluating the libraries available is therefore to determine how much customization would be needed to meet your enterprise standards and needs.

The second drawback is that your are reliant on a vendor to upgrade and enhance the toolset. This means reapplying customizations with each major release. I think you will find that if designed correctly, customizations will be made through inheritance and will be easier to reapply, if even necessary. This approach is most beneficial if the vendor assumes the responsibility of tailoring the library to your standards without additional cost.

Developing your own library:

Key benefits: most customized, least reliant on outside support.

Key drawbacks: highest cost, longest development cycle.

Building your own library obviously means a longer development cycle. You should be prepared for this. There are also different ways to base your development effort. You can start from scratch, defining requirements for reusable classes (I strongly suggest getting an experienced consultant to assist in this process) and designing and building your classes. You will also need to prepare your development teams for using this library. The second method involves developing a class library as a by-product of a large-scale application development effort. This simply means you are driving your requirements process from existing project development needs. Building your own library means that you will have a customized set of objects that meet your application development needs and standards. However, you are not reliant on an outside vendor for support or enhanced capabilities. It does mean that your library development process will be an ongoing one, affected by internal staff turnover and politics. Finally, it is usually considerably more expensive than buying an off-the-shelf product.

Developing jointly with experienced vendor:

Key benefits: very customized, compact development cycle, experience obtained from vendor partnership.

Key drawbacks: high cost, long development cycle, reliant on vendor expertise.

The third alternative combines the two previous approaches: hiring an external vendor to come in with their existing library as a base, and through a joint effort, tailoring the product for your enterprise at significantly reduced cost. The vendor gains a much improved class library and you have a class library that meets your needs. It is the best of both worlds. The drawbacks here are minimal, although significant. You have to find a vendor that has a library that is a suitable foundation for this effort, the enhancements you propose must be accepted by the vendor and provide significant improvements to the existing base, and you must end up with co-ownership of the product, that is, fully implied licensing of the product. Maintenance costs should be picked up by the vendor, while internal support and additional business specific development are done by the enterprise. This can be a winning solution if done with an experienced vendor who has qualified personnel and who is willing to pay a good portion of the development costs.

Using the Powersoft Foundation Class Library:

Key benefits: no cost, no development cycle; it is provided with PowerBuilder Enterprise.

Key drawbacks: not customized.

The fourth alternative takes advantage of the Powersoft Foundation Classes (PFC), a library introduced with PowerBuilder 5.0. The Foundation Classes use many of the techniques we espouse throughout this book, including the concept of service providers. PFC adheres to object-oriented concepts, including inheritance, encapsulation, and polymorphism. PFC is also the first library to take advantage of PowerBuilder 5.0's ability to overload functions.

PFC provides service objects, implemented as custom-class user objects. PFC service groups include the following:

- Application services
- Window services
- Datawindow services
- File services

- DBMS services
- Date/time services
- String services
- SQL parsing services

PFC also provides a single layer of extension objects. This allows customization at the application level to be provided in the context of PFC services and objects. It should be noted that PFC is the foundation on which to develop your enterprise class library, not your applications.

The costs and benefits of all four of these alternatives should be weighed to determine which approach is best for your organization.

Evaluating Class Libraries

Class libraries today are much more sophisticated than they were two years ago, when I last performed a major evaluation of those available. At that time the major players were PowerClass and PowerTool. Both libraries were developed with PowerBuilder 2.0, and it showed. Now there are at least a dozen class libraries with varying degrees of sophistication, object-oriented techniques, and quality. I am not going to perform an evaluation in this book. That will be up to you. What I will do is provide you an "evaluation recipe" to aid you in the evaluation of the class library.[1]

Executive summary

Summarize the findings of your evaluation. Highlight the strengths and weaknesses of the library and indicate a per-developer cost based on single-copy, server license, and site licensing options. Summarize the usefulness of the library, training requirements, and availability. Finally, indicate other products or clients that are using the library for development. This should be no longer than a page and should highlight the bottom-line recommendation.

Company analysis

This section should detail what you have found out about the company. To get this information, make sure you consult various sources, including the library vendor (find out what they think of themselves and their position in the marketplace), the tool vendor (find out from Powersoft what their impression of the vendor is), and clients (determine what clients using the software think about the library and the vendor), and finally, solicit responses through additional media (such as CompuServe) to find out how typical users feel about the

---

1. A product called Electronic Evaluation Database by Grey Stallion Software provides a very good unbiased evaluation of several of the class libraries, as well as other product comparisons.

company and the product. Consult experts who have knowledge on the subject materials (such as TeamPowersoft). Your list of topics covered should include the following.

Company and library profile. Profile the company and the library. How long have they been around? Are they a well-known vendor? How well has the company been doing? Are the employees involved in the development effort knowledgeable in the toolset being used and offered?

Company reputation with tool vendor. Find out from Powersoft whether the vendor is a Code Partner, working with Powersoft to provide the best product for the tool. If possible, investigate common client complaints by referring to the Powersoft Infobase and Powersoft Customer Services.

Installed base. Find out how many clients the vendor is installed at and get names of clients whom you can call to get additional feedback. Established vendors are not necessarily better than new tool vendors, but they have a longer track record with clients, which will help you to form a more accurate picture.

Reputation with current clients. Call the client contacts you receive and find out from them about the quality of the product, the service provided by the vendor, and the level of satisfaction from the client base.

Market position. Find out where the company is positioned in terms of market share or market strength. This should be done to help determine whether the vendor will be around over the long haul to support the tool.

Subjective views of other users or evaluators. Ask questions of other users of the libraries. Join a local Powersoft User Group, solicit members on CompuServe and other electronic media, and check articles from major publications.

Object analysis

This section should provide an overview of the objects contained in the library. To get this viewpoint, you should make sure you get an evaluation copy of the software and try out a few of the key features as well as some more obscure features your organization requires. See how hard it is to find information you need and whether that information helps you to quickly solve the problem at hand. The evaluation should include the following items.

Object count and type. Counting the objects in a class library does not give you an indication of the scope, complexity, or completeness of a library, but a library with 50 objects is almost always going to contain more functionality and usefulness than a library with 5 objects. A library with 500 objects is quite likely to have too many for you to review, let alone use. The numbers alone give you a basic idea of the library contents. If you categorize the objects into object types, the numbers will begin to help more.

The number of objects in each object category will help to make your estimation of value more accurate. By assigning values to an object type, you can assess, with some degree of accuracy, an object value.

For example, a library that contains 20 windows of which 19 are dialogs is likely to be of lesser value than a library whose 20 windows consist of 10 dialogs and 10 other styles including master-detail and parent-child. One very real rule is to count the number of objects that make up the bottom layer of the library's inheritance hierarchy.

Usefulness.   Determining object usefulness requires that you have an understanding of the objects' capabilities and your organization's needs. The closer these two elements are, the more useful the object is going to be. Determine a scale with which you can assess a usefulness value to each object.

Completeness.   Determining whether the library is complete is again something you have to judge based on your own needs. One hard factor you can look at is whether the library handles things like transaction management and database connectivity management. Determining a list of requirements for your organization is an important step in measuring the benefit of a commercial library.

Upgradability.   Determine from the vendor, other users, and your own observations whether upgrading either PowerBuilder or the product will cause you any problems. Upgrading is something that will occur on a regular enough basis to be of major concern. If you have to put twice as much effort into upgrading one library as another, the overall cost of the library rises dramatically.

Functionality.   One of the hardest tasks you will have to perform is determining the functionality contained in a library. Again, if you have already determined the type of functionality you need, it will be slightly easier to judge. Once again, get the opinions of others to assist in your assessment.

Reusability.   Determine how reusable the library is. To do this, you will have to look at each object and determine the number of times it will be reused, how much change there might be in each reuse, and finally, how easy it is to reuse any particular object. Look for elements that are not reusable to determine whether the functionality is of the type you would commonly reuse.

Code efficiency.   The library must be performance-aware. Hierarchical layers do not determine code efficiency, but unnecessary layers in a hierarchy can indicate a lack of code efficiency. Code should be encapsulated as much as possible without affecting overall ease of use. Have an expert look at the code to help determine whether it is well-written. Large numbers of user events could be a factor in this element of the evaluation.

Stability.   The tool should have gone through a few development iterations before you buy it. Version 1 of any tool very often indicates a lack of maturity. This is not a determining factor, but it can give you an idea of the product's stability. Try to find out how much technical support has been required by other users of the tool and what types of problems they encountered. Show-stopper bugs are a good indication of lack of product stability.

Cost/benefit analysis.   Determining the value of each object is obviously important. Assessing how much time it would take you to redevelop each object helps to determine an estimated cost for each object. By adding up all of these values you will be able to determine the value of the library.

Installation

Installing the library in your environment should not cause major distribution headaches. The more professional the installation, the more likely a vendor has paid attention to the other details associated with class library development. Installation procedures should be simple to follow and work as easily on network installations as on desktop installations. Because you are going to reuse this library throughout your organization, the ability to network the library is essential.

Retrofitting.   If you already have development efforts underway, you should try to find out how easy it is to retrofit some or all of that development based on your library of choice. You will achieve maximum benefit only if all development efforts are based on the library. Try to get a feel for this from both the vendor and other users. (Experience is a useful evaluation tool.)

Distribution.   You must be able to distribute both the library source code and applications developed using the library freely within your organization. Runtime costs associated with a class library are often indicative of revenue generators rather than toolset promotion; in other words, you should not have to pay a runtime cost to distribute your applications through your organization.

Training requirements

You must figure the cost of training into your budget. As stated before, a class library adds a learning curve on top of the learning curve associated with the language. Training should be readily available at a reasonable cost per student. Hands-on training workshops are very efficient in hurdling the learning curve.

Instructor-based training.   The vendor should offer instructor-based training to help your developers and support staff become familiar with the software. The better tool vendors offer a more advanced training course for your intended support staff to make them familiar with the inner workings of the library.

Computer-based or video-based training.   Self-study training, if offered by the vendor, reduces the overall cost of your training needs but reduces the effectiveness of the training. If these forms of training are offered, get an evaluation of these courses to determine their usefulness to your developers.

Documentation

Critical to a class library's success is the quality of the documentation. Thorough, accurate, and easy-to-use documentation is a must for using a library whether it be purchased or home-grown. Library documentation should include the following:

- Technical reference explaining techniques, conventions, and architecture
- Function reference explaining all functions contained in the library and when and how to use them
- User guide or knowledge base explaining how and when to use various objects

If these documents are also available in an on-line format (such as on-line help or Adobe Acrobat), they will prove to be more useful to the developers. These need not be in separate documents, but the contents of each of these should be available and of high quality.

Libraries should also include some tutorials, sample code, and reference materials.

Finally, look at the code itself. All objects and their methods should be well documented internally. Developers often look inside an object to figure out how it works, determine whether it does what they need, and learn how code development should be done. Self-documenting code is an absolute requirement.

Support

Support for the library must be readily available from the vendor. If you are basing strategic and tactical development efforts on the library, your developers should have quick access to support paths. A comprehensive support agreement should be available from the vendor.

Support plan.   Compare the vendor's support plan with those of other tools you are using. A commercial class library is another tool in your toolset and should offer the same or better support than your other tools.

Support costs.   Support costs should not rise to match the cost of the actual software purchase. You are only buying the software once and support costs should be no more than 10% of the cost of the software. If the support costs include the next major upgrade of the tool, make sure these costs are based on the delivery of the upgrade, not on the promise of an upgrade.

Client references.   I cannot stress enough how important it is to get the opinions of clients using the tool. These client references relate to support as well. Try to talk to the clients yourself rather than accepting letters of recommendation. Maintain an open-ended dialog with these references as part of your information-gathering strategy.

Effectiveness of support.   Having support readily available with a good support contract is one piece of the puzzle. You must also try to find out how effective the support is. Ineffective support is throwing money down the drain.

Costs

Everyone's favorite part: How much does the tool cost? Cost should not be an overriding factor, but in many situations it is. The cost of the tool must be weighed against its benefit. I think you will find that most class libraries provide enough benefit to justify their cost. When determining cost you should obtain cost estimates for the following:

- Per-developer licenses
- Server licenses
- Site licenses

Site licenses should be readily available and should also recognize the global scope of some companies. They should not include portions of software that cannot be licensed in other countries. For example, software that offers encryption routines is functionally richer than software that does not. This functionality becomes useless to a U.S. company that has global organizational needs if the encryption is based on a DES algorithm, which may not be used outside the United States. These types of issues must be addressed.

Conclusion

Add any topics that are important to your organization and get as much information as you can before making a decision. Uninformed decision making often results in poor choices. Making a decision with data to back up your decision makes you more accurate. You can always get information from periodical reviews, current users and evaluators of the tools, and the opinions of the vendor's competition. Getting the negatives is important and is what we most often do, but in this case, you should also focus as strongly, if not more so, on the positives. The benefits of reuse drive your object development strategy and should drive your evaluation strategy as well.

Implementation plan

When you make a recommendation for one of the libraries, you should also outline a plan to purchase, implement, and train employees in the use of the tool.

Where Can You Get More Information?

Look at the trade publications available today and you will often find reviews of tools. Remember that these evaluations are often performed specifically for a review. Get on-line on CompuServe, the Internet, or other electronic communication media and get the opinions of other users, industry experts, and other vendors. Obtaining competitive white papers from various vendors can often tell you more in an hour than you can learn in a week any other way. Other evaluation services such as the Electronic Evaluation Database can also be useful resources.

What Libraries Are Available?

At the time of writing, there are a growing number of commercially available class libraries. Table 4.1 shows these libraries and the contact information that was made available to us. You can also get this information directly from Powersoft.

TABLE 4.1   Vendor List

Vendor	Product	Architecture
Janiff Software	APOL-Advanced PowerBuilder Object Library	Nonvisual based object library
Financial Dynamics	Cornerstone 5.0	PFC-base application framework
PowerCerv	FLOWBuilder	Workflow development tool separate from application
PowerCerv	PADLock	Security application with links to PowerTool
PowerCerv	PowerTool	Template-based application framework
ObjectWorks	ObjectFrame	Framework & object library
BusinessSoft	ObjectSolutions	Framework & object library
Greenbrier & Russell	ObjectStart	Application framework
Outlook Systems	OK-PowerBase	Application framework
Case/Mate	PowerAid	Source code class library
Millenium	PowerBase	Application framework, security, and adhoc report management
ServerLogic	PowerLock	Security
ServerLogic	PowerObjects	Advanced objects library
ServerLogic	PowerClass	Class library
Metasolv Software	PowerFrame	Application framework
N.E.Solutions	PowerLib	Function library
Paradigm Computer	PowerPlate	Application framework
Beard Technology	ProFrame	Foundation classes
Applied Knowledge	Progeny	Component-based class library
QuadriTech	Q-Frame v1.5	Application framework
Advanced Business	RAD-Tool	Object library
Systems Evolution Inc.	SEI Object Class Library 3.0	Application framework
SalesVision	SalesVision Framework	Framework for sales automation business
Castle Software Engineering	ObjectFramework	Service-based class library

Summary

As you can see, simply deciding how to build your reuse base is difficult. It takes a significant effort to gather the information you need to make the most informed decision possible. Base your decision on facts rather than assumptions to make the best decision for your organization, and use all of the tools available to you.

5

Developing Reusable Classes

Introduction

Deciding to develop your own library raises additional issues. Do you develop from the ground up, start from a proven base, or build as a by-product of development? And how do you go on from there?

If you choose to purchase a class library, your development efforts are ready to begin. You may have some customization to perform to suit your organizational needs, but your library development effort, at least the initial one, is complete. If you choose to develop your own library, either on your own or by using a base set of objects, you will follow one of three approaches:

- Build from the ground up
- Build from a base
- Build as a by-product of development

We will take a look at each of these approaches and highlight some of the benefits and pitfalls of each approach.

Chapter Objectives

The objectives of this chapter are to provide you with the information needed to decide how you will develop your reusable classes. Regardless of the approach you take, you need to be aware that designing and developing reusable classes takes considerably more effort than straight development. The result more than justifies this effort, however, as is demonstrated in Figure 5.1.

As you can see, although the cost of developing reusable classes is often two or three times the cost of a straight development effort, but the cost is earned back by the time the objects are reused the fourth or fifth time. The more generic and reusable the object, the quicker you will reach the breakeven point. Your goal should be to achieve 75% reusability for an object. This percentage is determined as the amount of the work that is necessary for a developer to use the reusable object as a percentage of the amount of work it would take a developer to develop the entire object him- or herself.

Comparing the Different Approaches to Building Reusable Classes

Let's take a more in-depth look at the different approaches to building reusable classes. As I stated before, the three approaches have benefits and pitfalls. The following breakdowns will help you to make your own decisions on which approach to use.

Approach: building from the ground up.

If you decide to build your library completely from the ground up, you have a lot of work ahead of you. This approach is covered in depth in this book, but the principles remain the same regardless of the approach. You need to define an architecture for your library. Several are discussed in the chapters describing class library development. Develop a set of design objectives that your class library must attain. Set the objectives at a high but achievable level. Survey the users

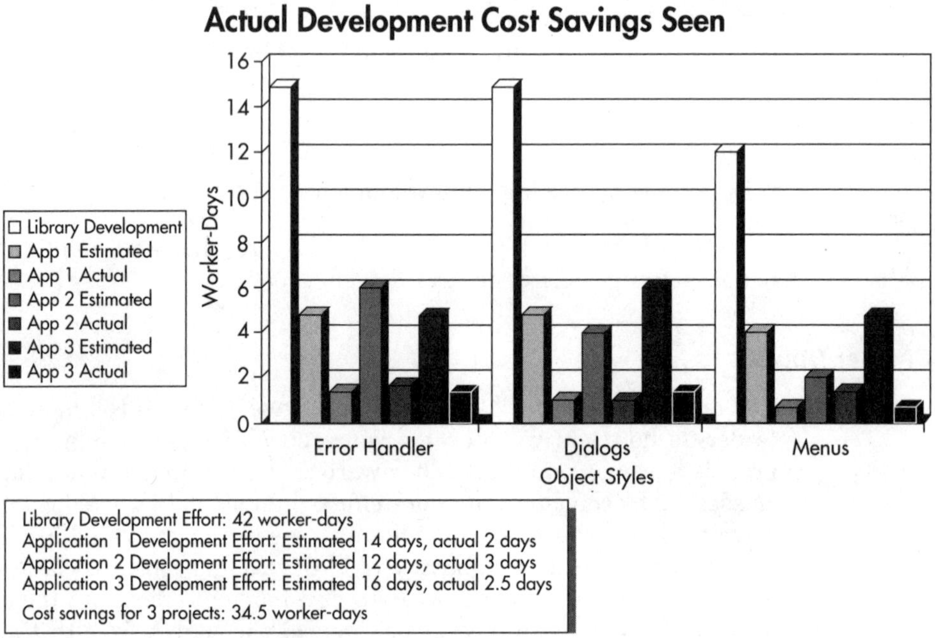
Actual Development Cost Savings Seen
Library Development
App 1 Estimated
App 1 Actual
App 2 Estimated
App 2 Actual
App 3 Estimated
App 3 Actual
Worker-Days
0
2
4
6
8
10
12
14
16
Error Handler
Dialogs
Menus
Object Styles
Library Development Effort: 42 worker-days
Application 1 Development Effort: Estimated 14 days, actual 2 days
Application 2 Development Effort: Estimated 12 days, actual 3 days
Application 3 Development Effort: Estimated 16 days, actual 2.5 days
Cost savings for 3 projects: 34.5 worker-days

Figure 5.1 Cost justification of reusable classes.

and developers in your organization to gather a thorough set of requirements, set the scope for your project, and prepare a plan for the development effort. Remember that planning is still the most important aspect of your development effort. Without a plan, how will you know when you have reached your goal?

The second most important aspect of your class library development effort is the design. The best developers in the world cannot develop a good system if it is based on a poor design. Design carefully and follow object-oriented techniques, but don't let them rule you. The whole purpose of object-oriented techniques is to make you more productive and develop systems that work in the real world. The techniques should be used where they are best suited. Do not avoid them because you do not understand them.

Building from the ground up provides you the most flexibility, but also affords the most room for project scope creeping and political battles among the designers. Be aware of the dangers of using this approach. Set the project scope as early as possible and stick to it.

Approach: building from a base.

If you are building your library from a base, you will gain structure and quality and lose some flexibility. Your architecture is determined by the base objects, as these are the objects that form the architecture. This may seem restrictive, but it does help to prevent the political battles that architectural decisions always seem to spawn. Your project scope is also predetermined in a sense. You will base development on the objects that you already have, with the goal of developing a set of classes that will complement and supplement your base. Objects that benefit your users and developers will already have a base, and can be designed and built much more quickly and efficiently. You are also basing your development effort on proven and reliable code, which aids in developing more robust and higher-quality objects. In other words, you are already gaining the benefits of reusability!

The trade-off between quality and flexibility is one you need to watch very carefully. A faultless object that has a completely single-minded purpose might not get reused as often as a lower-quality but much more flexible object. On the other hand, an object that fits nicely into many situations will often be ignored if it is of such poor quality that reusing it reduces productivity and overall quality.

> *This approach can begin with using the Powersoft Foundation Class Library as your base. This library comes free with the enterprise edition of Power-Builder, and thus reduces the cost of developing some of your base objects.*

Approach: building as a by-product of development.

The final approach to developing reusable classes is to build your classes based on reusable objects developed during a major development effort. The greatest benefit of this approach is that the classes that are developed relate much more closely to real-life development needs. The major drawback is that the development effort itself is often delayed by class development or correction. There cannot be an aggressive deadline on this project.

This approach lends itself to using correct object-oriented design techniques to design the application, and then applying the class library design techniques to design the physical classes. One item to note is that this approach sometimes has the effect of developing classes that are well suited to one application but not to others. If you are in the position to use multiple development efforts on which to base the design of your classes, you are far more likely to design generic reusable classes. This approach is often more appropriately used as a way to build your business class objects rather than a class library or application framework.

Designing Reusable Classes

Once you have a class library, or your base, you need to continue to build reusable objects. Designing reusable objects for PowerBuilder is no simple task. PowerBuilder makes it easy to develop objects quickly, but to make your objects realize the true power of the PowerBuilder development tool, they must be designed with more than the current project's or program's scope in mind. A little thought before coding pays off in the long haul.

Programmers are typically scavengers. Good developers always try to find well-written code to reuse before they write it themselves. This trait can pay big dividends when it comes to PowerBuilder development. But if reuse means copying and modifying, then the code or object is not being reused but recycled. This process means that the original object is of no use once the new object is created. It also means that changes made to either of the objects are usually not made to the other. This is called source code tree branching, which is something the object-oriented thinker has to avoid at all costs.

To demonstrate the difference between designing an object to be used in the current project and designing one to be reused, I am going to design an object from the ground up and show all of the intricacies involved in designing and developing objects to be reused from day one.

Objective: to develop a reusable logon procedure for applications.

This procedure is required by virtually all projects. It should be an object that can be put together relatively quickly and can effectively deliver the functionality desired. It should also be an object that can be reused in virtually every project. It is a great candidate for reuse. So why is it that every Power-Builder developer has written a database login window at least once in his or her career? One reason is that developers feel a need to know how to do something. Although this is good for the developer, it is not good for the company the developer works for. If it takes a developer a single day to design, develop, and test a database login window, even one that is copied from somewhere else, then the company is losing one worker-day every time a developer writes the login procedure. On top of this, the login procedures will vary from developer to developer in functionality and robustness. On top of the development time, you can add the time needed to test the objects, make modifications, and train users to use the sometimes widely different approaches, all for a simple object to log a user on to a database.

The solution we will work through in this chapter requires more than a day to design and develop. The result, however, is a standard procedure that can be implemented into a system easily and seamlessly. There is only one set of source code that needs to be archived, tested, regression-tested with upgrades, and enhanced.

This is not without its drawbacks, however. Truly reusable objects require a much more controlled environment. This means that someone, or a group of people, must maintain, develop, and support these objects. However, the costs of controlling the environment are offset by the savings that can be achieved. A more controlled environment lends itself to additional benefits by virtue of the fact that developers are taught to design in an object-oriented fashion, making them more productive in the long run.

Logical function design

A typical approach to achieve our object would be to develop a window to accept user input for the user's ID and password, a function to retrieve some database settings from an .INI file, and a function to attempt the connection to the database. Simple enough. It seems to fit the OO mold. Functionality is self-contained and the object can be reused and controlled. But to really design the object, we need to go deeper.

First, we can break down the functionality into more distinctive groupings. Our objective states that we need login procedures for systems. We know that we will need to obtain data from an external file that describes the connection. The connection may or may not be to a database. A connection is therefore an object or method that connects our application to a target. We need to retrieve settings that describe the target. We need connection methods for each target (even though they may be the same today, they may not be tomorrow). To plan ahead, we want to be able to maintain multiple connections simultaneously, so we also need a method or object to maintain and manage existing connections. As with any object, we also need some error-processing capabilities.

Already we have expanded the requirements to a level that will allow us to design a comprehensive and robust set of functionality to connect our application to a specified target. For this example, we will narrow the scope a little. (Expanding the scope, in an OO world, is accomplished quite easily, as we will see later in this chapter.) We can narrow the scope because we need to connect only to a Sybase and a Watcom database. We do need to be able to connect to both, and we may require multiple connections for each (for databases on different servers). Table 5.1 shows how we begin to capture our requirements and build object classes.

Already we can begin to see that there is much more to a connection than a login window and a couple of functions. The requirements above would satisfy the objective of any application being able to connect to any target.

TABLE 5.1 Object Requirements

Object	Processes	Methods and Attributes	Description
Settings Processing			Object that can get settings from an external file.
Login Data Manipulation			Object to capture the user-entered data required for the connection.
Connection object			Connects the application to the specified target.
Connection Manager			Maintains connections once established.
Error Handler			Handles all errors from the objects above.

We can now begin the physical design of the objects. In order to do this effectively, we need to understand a little more about the objects. We do this by expanding our logical design to include processes. We are not yet describing methods and attributes, but processes, which can be considered collections of attributes and methods (functions or events) that will interact to perform a single task.

The Settings Processing object can be expanded as follows. We need a process to locate the file where the settings are maintained. Another process that is required is to retrieve particular settings from the file. To think ahead, we can also build processes to support setting various options in the settings file. Although settings are usually stored in an .INI file, this is a MS Windows feature, and we do not want to restrict the object in any way, so we will not rename this object to Ini_File_Processor. We also do not want to restrict the object to just database connection data. It could also process other application settings or preferences.

The Login Data object does not require a great deal of expansion—at least not yet. It is a simple container object that will allow the user to enter his or her user ID and password. It is not a processing object. The connection object will perform the processing itself. Thus, the login data object will not require processes other than a simple communication process to send data to and receive data from the connection object.

The Connection object is more complex. It will take the data captured or retrieved, attempt to connect to the target, process any security requirements, and, once established, provide the necessary information to any portion of the program that needs it. This includes the Transaction object.

Another important part of the project is the Connection Manager. This object needs processes to log and store connection objects, keep track of which connections are established in order to reuse objects wherever possible, and properly dispose of objects once they are not needed.

Finally, we need some error processing. Again, to promote reusability, I classify the error processing as an object. We will see only a portion of the error processing required because error processing can be a complex area. But, we will show the design in such a way that the object will be able to deal with all errors directed toward it. Briefly, the error processor must contain processes to determine error severity, decide how to act on the error, display the error to the user, and react to the user's response. I have also found a need to log errors and send notification messages on demand.

We can now tabulate the objects with their proposed processes, as depicted in Table 5.2. Your own design may vary, but your approach in creating the design should be the same. Expand the logical design to satisfy the objectives of your project, but keep in mind the reusability factor. The more reusable the object, the higher the cost savings.

We are not going to go into the full effort of breaking out logical classes, but I do want to emphasize that there is much more to the design than shown here. I am merely attempting to demonstrate the thought process that is required before you can actually develop an object.

The physical design

At this point, we are ready to begin designing our object classes. As we indicated before, we are going to concentrate on the Connection object itself, but we will make references to the other objects and their methods.

The first step in designing our objects is not an actual design step but a decision on how we intend to implement the object class . (Remember that in object-oriented design, we are designing classes of objects, not the object itself. An object is a physical instantiation of one of these object classes.) Some object classes will be implemented in a physical manner. A window is an example of this, as is our Data Capture object. Other classes are implemented as nonvisual classes. We need to make sure we can distinguish the two. This is relatively simple, as we can distinguish between visual and nonvisual objects quite easily. The second distinguishing factor is not quite as simple. This is a term I call *functional dependency*.

Functional dependency means that we need to determine whether the object can be implemented by itself or whether it will always be dependent on another object for its implementation. This does not depend on the object being visual or nonvisual.

To distinguish the types of object classes, I name them differently. The first is the easiest. It is the reusable object class, the normal type of object that is intended to be implemented as a physical object. The second is the base object class, an object whose primary purpose is to be the basis for the development of derived or descendant objects, although it could, in some circumstances, be used as an object. The third class I call a service provider class, indicating that the object is intended to always operate as part of another object to enhance the capabilities of the object(s).

The reason this is important is twofold. Objects that have user interaction must control the input and make sure it is correct. Service provider objects can assume a higher level of correctness, in that the communication is generally from another object leading to a more controlled environment. Derived classes, on the other hand, need to know at what level of ancestry functionality is required in order to implement the functionality at the right time. The second

TABLE 5.2 Logical Design Expanded

Object	Processes	Methods and attributes	Description
Settings Processor			Object to process settings from an external file.
	Locate Settings file		Determine where the Settings file is located.
	Retrieve settings data		Retrieve the settings data.
	Modify settings data		Update data in the Settings files.
Login Data Manipulation			Object to capture the user-entered data required for the connection.
	Build Data Capture object		Get information supplied and prepare an input object for the user to complete the connection data.
	Send connection data		Send captured data to the Connection object.
Connection object			Connect the application to the specified target.
	Get database connection information		Get all captured data and build the data required to make the connection.
	Object connect		Execute a connect function to the target.
	Register connection		Register successful connections with the Connection Manager
Connection Manager			Maintain connections once established.
	Register connections		Register a connection made.
	Allocate a transaction		Create and allocate a transaction for each separate connection request.

TABLE 5.2 Logical Design Expanded   *(Continued)*

Object	Processes	Methods and attributes	Description
	Dispose of connection		Dispose of connections.
	Suspend connection		Suspend a connection by disconnecting the transaction, albeit logically.
	Activate suspended connection		Reactivate a suspended transaction.
Error Handler			Handle errors generated by the application.
	System Error Handler		Handle system errors.
	Database Error Handler		Handle database errors.
	Application Error Handler		Handle application errors.

reason is that the service provider object class generally contains more Get/Set functions than others.

Our physical design can now go forward, and we can break down the objects to a physical class hierarchy. A key concept is that all objects should be derived from a base object. Although we are always deriving our object classes from PowerBuilder object classes, we do not have access to the PowerBuilder objects themselves to modify their behavior and functionality before we inherit the objects. Our first step is therefore to determine which PowerBuilder object classes we will use and create our base object classes from them. We can determine that most of the connection objects will be nonvisual. We can therefore state that we need to create a base object class for nonvisual objects. To do this, we can define an object class for nonvisual objects. So we can define that all of our nonvisual objects can be derived from this base object, indicating that the object is our base custom nonvisual object. We also need to define the characteristics of the object classes, and we need to determine to what level of a class hierarchy the functionality should go. To do this, we apply three questions to each process expected.

- Does this process apply to all objects of this class?
- Is the functionality required by other object classes?
- Does this functionality need to be broken down further to answer the first two questions?

TABLE 5.3 Object Classes Assigned

Object	Processes	Class type	Description
Base nonvisual class		Nonvisual, base	Base object for all derived nonvisual objects.
	Initialization		Method to set default attributes and behavior for the object class.
	Identification		Method built into the object to identify itself and any method being processed. Useful in registration and debugging options.
	Print		Method to print the contents of the object.
	Error Processing		Method to invoke the Error Processing object
Settings Processor		Nonvisual, service	Object to process settings from an external file.
	Locate Settings file		Determine where the Settings file is located.
	Retrieve settings data		Retrieve the settings data.
	Modify settings data		Update data in the Settings files.
Login Data Manipulation		Visual, reusable	Object to capture the user-entered data required for the connection.
	Build Data Capture object		Get information supplied and prepare an input object for the user to complete the connection data.
	Send connection data		Send captured data to the Connection object.
Connection object		Nonvisual, service	Connect the application to the specified target.
	Get database connection information		Get all captured data and build the data required to make the connection.
	Object connect		Execute a connect function to the target.

TABLE 5.3 Object Classes Assigned   *(Continued)*

Object	Processes	Class type	Description
	Register connection		Register successful connections with the Connection Manager.
Connection Manager		Nonvisual, service	Maintain connections once established.
	Register connections		Register a connection made.
	Allocate a transaction		Create and allocate a transaction for each separate connection request.
	Dispose of connection		Dispose of connections.
	Suspend connection		Suspend a connection by disconnecting the transaction, albeit logically.
	Activate suspended connection		Reactivate a suspended transaction.
Error Handler		Nonvisual, service	Handle errors generated by the application.
	System Error Handler		Handle system errors.
	Database Error Handler		Handle database errors.
	Application Error Handler		Handle application errors.

A base object class is usually not expected to be instantiated as an object. It also dictates, by definition, that only functionality that will be required by all objects derived from this class should be encapsulated within the class. My base object classes are usually defined with some standard behavior that I expect will be required by all objects of the class. These include an Initialization method, an Object Identification method, a Print method, and an Error Processing method. All objects derived from these base object classes will therefore inherit these characteristics. Table 5.3 shows the base object class defined.

Features of the design that I will reuse include the common processes and methods of the base nonvisual class. I can implement these into other classes I design. Standardizing on common functionality also helps makes object classes reusable. One final point about the design so far is the prospect of the Error Handler object. This object falls into the nonvisual interface style of object, but, would cause some severe problems in attempting

Figure 5.2   Physical class definition form.

Physical Class Data

Physical Class ID:	PCD_Form	Version:	1.0
Physical Class Name:	Sample Physical class		
Author:	William Green	Update Date:	July 31, 1995

Object Identification Data

Functional Layer:	Base ancestor	Ancestry:	Nonvisualobject
Object Name:	cc_Base	Library:	Base objects
Object Type:	Custom class	Xref:	

Object Class Description/Purpose

Description
Description of class goes here

Methods and Attributes

Inherited Attributes

Scope		Type	Name	Defined In
Inherited	Instance	Integer		Ancestor ID

Attributes

Scope		Type	Name	Default
Protected	Instance	Integer	Attribute name	Default value

Inherited Methods (Standard Base Object methods are shown)

Name	Override Criteria	Defined In
Constructor	None	
Destructor	None	
CloseQuery	Extend for class	
Setup	Extend for class	
Init	Extend for default overrides	
Service_Load	Extend for class	
Service _Unload	Extend for class	
Raise_Exception	Extend for class	

Methods:

Scope	Type	Prefix	Name	Xref Link
Protected	Function	of_p		
Description:	Description of method			
Specification:	1. Steps in the method			
Overrides:	None			
Extend:	No	None		
Parameters		**Description**		**Reference**
(None)				(None)

to implement it as part of the base object because it would be derived from the base object. This is a feature I call embedded object references. How do you implement an object within an object that is derived from the object? The answer is that you don't. (*Really bad idea* is an alternative name for an embedded object reference.) Even if you think you have figured out a foolproof method to implement this, (and it is done quite often), remember that reusable objects are usually reused by someone who might not be aware of some of the particularly gruesome results of embedded object references.

The final aspect of my physical design is to break down the processes into methods (functions and events) and detail the attributes that will belong to each object. To do this, I use a form that Millard and I and another colleague[1] adapted from the C++ book *Object-Oriented Development* by Charles Brumbaugh. The form is shown in Figure 5.2 as it would be for a class about to be inherited from the base object.

Without going into detail for every object, you can see how this form will help to ensure that you look at all aspects of the object and question how the developer might use the object, and also serves as technical design documentation of your objects.

Our final functional design table (abbreviated form of each object definition form) is shown in Table 5.4.

Where do we go from here?

We have just begun to open up the design process, but even at this point it is obvious that the objects would continue to expand and develop with each iteration we go through. Every object, function, and event requires revisiting, questioning, and careful design. Expanding gradually allows you to maintain your objectives and develop comprehensive reusable objects by design rather than by accident. The final step is to map the object definitions back to exist-

---

1. Acknowledgment to Richard J. Mohr.

Table 5.4 Technical Design Summary Table (in process)

Object	Process	Type/process data	Description
Base nonvisual Class		Nonvisual, base	Base object for all derived nonvisual objects.
	Initialization		Method to set default attributes and behavior for the object class.
		Init event	Initialization event, sets object defaults.
		PostInit event	Event that fires after the Init event to execute any default functions to further prepare the object.
	Identification		Method built into the object to identify itself and any method being processed. Useful in registration and debugging options.
		IdentifyMe function	Function to identify the object to another object requesting the information.
	Print		Method to print the contents of the object.
		Print event	Event containing code to print the contents of the object. If more than one print method exists for the object, additional print functions could be defined.
	Error processing		Method to invoke the Error Processor object.
		Object Error function	Function used to invoke the error processor.
Settings processor		Nonvisual, service	Object to process settings from an external file.
	Locate settings file		Determine where the settings file is located.
		Get Windows INI path.	Function to get the path and name of the Windows INI file. Similar functions could be coded to get the location of other system initialization files.
		Get App INI File path	Function to obtain the path of the Application INI file based on information retrieved from the Windows INI file. Similar functions could be coded for retrieving the path in alternative fashions.

Table 5.4   **Technical Design Summary Table (in process)**   *(Continued)*

Object	Process	Type/process data	Description
		INI File path locator	Special function for when the file specified cannot be found. Invokes a common file open dialog that allows the user to locate the INI file to use.
	Retrieve settings data		Retrieve the settings data.
		Retrieve topic data	Retrieve data from the INI file based on a section and topic provided.
	Modify settings data		Update data in the settings files.
		Set topic data	Set data from the INI file based on a section and topic provided.
	Error processing		Derived from ancestor object.
Login Data Manipulation		Visual, reusable	Object to capture the user-entered data required for the connection.
	Build Data Capture object		Get information supplied and prepare an input object for the user to complete the connection data.
	Send connection data		Send captured data to the Connection object.
Connection object		Nonvisual, service	Connect the application to the specified target.
	Get database connection info		Get all captured data and build the data required to make the connection.
	Object connect		Execute a connect function to the target.
	Register connection		Register successful connections with the Connection Manager
Connection Manager		Nonvisual, service	Maintain connections once established.
	Register connections		Register a connection made.
	Allocate a transaction		Create and allocate a transaction for each separate connection request.
	Dispose of connection		Dispose of connections.

Table 5.4   Technical Design Summary Table (in process)   *(Continued)*

Object	Process	Type/process data	Description
	Suspend connection		Suspend a connection by disconnecting the transaction, albeit logically.
	Reactivate connection		Reactivate a suspended transaction.
Error Handler		Nonvisual, service	Handle errors generated by the application.
	System Error Handler		Handle system errors.
	Database Error Handler		Handle database errors.
	Application Error Handler		Handle application errors.

ing classes in your base class to determine which objects are already defined and need to be expanded.

Summary

This chapter discussed the various approaches to developing reusable objects and briefly discussed the intricacies involved in designing truly reusable classes. This is not a technique for the faint of heart, but is an absolute must for organizations wanting to take advantage of the true power of the object-oriented nature of reusable classes.

Chapter

6

Common Reusable Object Libraries

Introduction

There is another layer of objects that resides between your class libraries and your application. These are called common reusable objects (CRO) and common business classes (CBC), and include both business-specific objects and other reusable objects not specifically included in your class library. These objects are designed to handle specific functionality requirements without requiring integration into either your class library or an application.

Most suitable for this layer are classes that contain reusable business calculations, specific data access functionality, and utility objects such as access to fax services that are not normally needed by applications and not normally provided in your class library. (Another example is HLLAPI services to access your mainframe, which is not required in every application.)

The distinction between these types of classes does not necessarily have to be made, but it does help to categorize and group the functionality into plug-'n'-play libraries that applications can simply include in their search paths and code calls to the defined entry points.

All of your developers must be trained to think reuse all the time. Every object developed will probably be needed elsewhere in the organization. Functionality such as building a new account number or accessing customer address information should be built into reusable business objects, providing a single point of maintenance effort when business requirements change. Figure 6.1 demonstrates where this layer resides in the development pyramid.

Chapter Objectives

The goal of this chapter is to introduce the reusable thinking concepts that you need to pass on to developers. We go through a couple of examples that demonstrate how these objects should be categorized, designed, and built and demon-

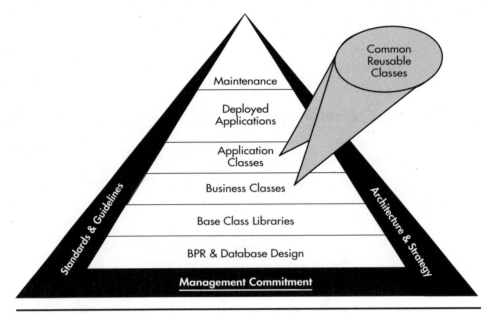

Figure 6.1 Development pyramid: common reusable classes.

strate the savings potential that these types of objects could have in your organization. We specifically want to achieve the following objectives:

- Determine the benefit of these object libraries to your organization
- Demonstrate how to encourage object reuse thinking
- Show how to construct CRO and CBC libraries
- Emphasize the importance of getting the buy-in of project teams
- Reinforce the need to design specifically for reuse

How Do These Objects Benefit Your Organization?

Obviously, there will always be a benefit to your organization if specific business-oriented functionality can be reused. If we take a simple set of functionality such as retrieving customer data based on their account number or name, you can see how many times throughout your organization this functionality is required. Once? Not likely. Up to 10 times? More than likely. More than 10 times? Also very likely. Without reuse of the functionality, we can see that if 15 different projects requiring access to customer data code this functionality themselves, we are more than likely going to have 15 different ways of achieving this end. We are also likely to end up with 15 different sets of code that need to be tested, maintained, and documented. If an account number structure changes, we need to search out all of this code and make modifications, again followed by testing and documenting. This can get expensive after a while, and there is always the danger of missing a piece of code that needs changing. And we all know that that piece of code will come up and fail when the most important client is on-site and asks to see his or her information! Having one object class take care of this required functionality makes sense.

The object is designed based on business need, and provides an easily used interface such as Get_Account_Data or, even more appropriately, Get_Data which, being reused in many business objects, promotes polymorphism. Applications simply include the object wherever needed and call the interface functions. When account number structure changes, or retrieval needs to access an additional set of data, the changes are made to the single object and applications automatically pick up these changes when they next rebuild the system. Quality is ensured because the single object is thoroughly tested and documented.

Based on this scenario, the cost savings of following this approach can easily be diagrammed. Figure 6.2 shows the cost savings you could expect, assuming that the development effort for the reusable object is 5 days, whereas 2 days are required to develop each application separately. It typically takes longer to design and develop more generic objects due to the nature of designing an easy-to-use interface and the completeness of functionality needed.

As can be seen, your costs are recouped roughly between three and four applications reusing the object, coupled with a reusability index of 50%. The reusability index varies from object to object, but typically, well-designed ob-

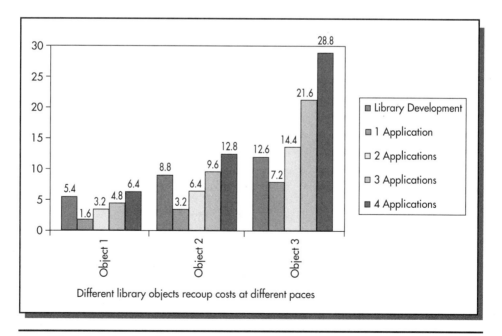

Different library objects recoup costs at different paces

Figure 6.2 Projected cost savings.

jects can achieve a much higher reusability index. (This method of establishing benefit is well worth the time and effort).

___

Benefit: Developers begin to think reuse.

An intangible benefit to this approach is that your developers begin to think reuse. On one side of the scale, your developers will become used to scanning your library first to see whether the object they need is there, and on the other end of the scale, developers begin to design their objects with reusability in mind, promoting further reuse. This benefit cannot be measured in dollars and cents, but developer productivity will continue to rise. As more and more objects are added to your library, you will notice that more object-oriented design techniques are used.

How to Encourage the Paradigm Shift

Making the change from procedural thinking to object-oriented thinking is not easy. Even though object-oriented technology is touted as being a more natural thought process, our training over the past few decades has been geared toward logically progressive procedural thinking. This is a hard habit to break, especially for developers who have been successful with more procedural languages. Convincing your developers can be the hardest task you face. To overcome this you need to make an initial financial sacrifice to achieve long-term savings.

___

Training and education

Training and education are the first steps in promoting the development and the reuse of your business objects. Class libraries are generally accepted as the building blocks for reusable development. Business-oriented object development is not quite as generally accepted, but can actually yield higher savings than the more accepted class library. Developers need to be taught not only how to develop reusable objects, but why they should be developed. There are several course offerings that teach the how. There are none that teach why. You will have to take on this responsibility.

Your organization needs to be prepared to spend the time and money up front in order to achieve the long-term savings the technology can offer. Not only are you investing in the employees' future, you are also easing the transition to the object-oriented paradigm. This will make your developers more productive sooner.

Once you begin this approach, you also need to keep your eyes open for developers who grasp the concepts and the benefits of the approach more quickly than others. These are the people you need in order to build teams that specialize in the development of business class objects. These developers will raise the standards of your development efforts and provide higher-quality solutions all around. Let them swim in the pool of technology available. Make the tools available to them to accomplish their goals and your long-term benefits will astonish you.

Mentoring

Mentoring is another very successful way to help make the paradigm shift. Developers often listen more closely to another developer than to a trainer or manager. The peer relationship fosters a sense of camaraderie that makes what the mentor is saying more believable. After all, this is a person who has had to go through the same thing before. Most consulting companies working with Powersoft offer mentor programs. Use these carefully and you will notice an increase in interdeveloper knowledge transfer and a more rapid adoption of the technology in your employee base.

How to Construct CRO and CBC Libraries

Building CRO and CBC libraries is much like class library development. The design approaches remain consistent: Each object must meet the needs of multiple applications, be as comprehensive as possible, and yet offer an easy-to-use and intuitive interface consistent with your class library. Maintain your architectural decisions and reinforce your enterprise design objectives.

One element that is often overlooked in the development of common reusable classes is the support infrastructure required to perpetuate the objects throughout your organization. If your organization is as distributed as many of the major corporations are today, this can be a daunting task. The team must not only make the paradigm shift, but also be forceful and determined to market the objects internally. The team becomes an internal vendor with many of the same responsibilities a vendor has. The objects must be marketed, improved, and supported by the team. Documentation must be comprehensive, accurate, and easy to get. Creating professional-looking user manuals helps you to achieve general acceptance. The team should be highly visible in the organization and be set up to accept input from all of the developers and business users. Input from these sources is vital to acceptance of the end products.

Build the library like a class library by gathering the requirements, defining logical classes, designing the physical class hierarchy, and mapping the classes back to your class library. Build on the class library from the word go in order to continue to achieve the power and flexibility of the class library. By following the same approach, you will find it much easier to get your developers to accept the objects, especially those who are already using the class library. Remember, the business layer should be an extension of your class library, not a replacement.

Remember that all of the development layers should be replaceable or extendible. The business layer should follow this ideal as well, with the idea that any element or object in the business layer should be replaceable without impact to the application or class library layer. It also allows us to separate the business domain from the application domain and we can easily see that if the business objects ever end up in a multitier environment, we should be able to move them from one domain server to another with little or no impact on the functionality. Figure 6.3 illustrates how we should separate the domains in order to allow this functionality splitting to occur.

Buy-in from Project Teams

Getting development teams to buy into the process is another difficult task developers of business classes face. One aspect that makes this easier than class library acceptance is the fact that the objects model the business, and therefore their benefit is much more obvious and immediate. However you must still take the time and effort to develop cost/benefit models to demonstrate how the objects can save time and effort for the development teams.

Build on successes by showing off applications that use the objects. Demonstrate the savings that the objects offer with clear and accurate models, and build the objects to meet the needs of the development teams. This will build a feeling of confidence in the development teams that you must nurture and encourage.

Most important of all, you need to build confidence in the development teams that the objects are well supported, not only by the object developers, but by senior management. Developers need to know that if they get stuck

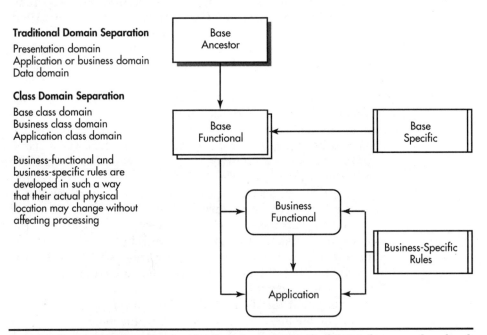

Figure 6.3 Separation of business domain allows business-specific objects to be removed, replaced, or moved to different domain servers easily.

with anything, the answer to their questions is never more than a phone call or e-mail away. Major vendors have found electronic media to be a great source of support for their products; you should understand that this works from within, too. Set up the network in such a way that key people are easily accessible. Make sure that the team also realizes the importance of this aspect of their development effort. It is time-consuming, but it is crucial to the success of the object library.

One final point: Don't oversell the library. It is important that the library be seen as a benefit and productivity enhancement, not as the ultimate solution to all problems.

Designing Specifically for CRO Use

Designing objects specifically for common reusable class reuse is, as stated before, very similar to class library development. The design effort is identical; the major difference is that the scope of each object or group of objects is clearly defined to satisfy a business need. This makes the design task slightly easier, but you have to be prepared to take the extra time necessary to design efficient generic classes to satisfy the business need. Following object-oriented design and development techniques as discussed throughout this book will help to make your objects successful.

Summary

This chapter discussed some of the issues facing the reusable class developer. We did not go into a lot of detail, as this is covered more thoroughly in later chapters. I do want to stress the importance of this layer of the development model. A class library is extremely beneficial, but business classes are much more visible and will be reused much more vigorously. We discussed the benefit of these object libraries to your organization and showed you how to develop cost/benefit models to support the objects in your organization. We also discussed how to encourage object reuse as a paradigm in your organization. Making the paradigm shift is difficult and often time-consuming. Make the effort up front to invest in a reusable future.

We showed you how to construct the object libraries physically and create the support infrastructure necessary to support the effort, both during and after development.

We emphasized the importance of getting project teams to buy into the technology and direction and the importance they play in the entire process. These are your customers, and should be treated as the valuable resources they are.

Finally, we reinforced the necessity for designing specifically for reuse. If every developer built only one object that is reusable in your organization, you would save many developer hours in your organization in a very short time span.

Keep developing on this base and using the methodology—after all, success breeds success.

Chapter

7

The Pilot Project

Introduction

An important part of our methodology for introducing, proving, and improving a class library is the completion of a pilot project. In this chapter we examine the ways you can ensure that the pilot project you select will enhance and promote the acceptance of your class library.

Why a pilot project?

The pilot project provides a proving ground for new methodologies and technology introduced with your class library. You will discover which features are best used by developers and which are less important. The major features will be exercised and proven in the pilot project.

The pilot project helps shake out the class library. The process of building the pilot project using your library will help reveal bugs, errors, and omissions. Your exposure remains at one project, rather than a handful. Any problems that require architectural or behavioral changes to the library will affect only the pilot project.

Finally, the pilot project provides a showcase for your class library's features and functionality. A real-world project, completed with the help of your library, will demonstrate to other developers the value of using your library. The pilot project will show the gains in productivity, consistency, and robustness that your library provides. Consider the pilot project one of the most important tools in your marketing effort.

Elements of the perfect pilot

The suitability of the pilot project is key in this crucial process. It is important to select a project that incorporates an ideal team as well as ideal project characteristics. In this chapter you will learn the elements that constitute the ideal pilot project.

The pilot project team will be the first to use any new methodologies you introduce with your class library. They will need training and support to apply these methodologies properly and to overcome the "not invented here" mentality that often greets new approaches.

You will also see that one of the keys to a successful pilot is providing enhanced support to the team. Your pilot project will have a lot of hurdles to overcome, and your support must be up to the challenge. You will need to react quickly to help with usage questions, techniques, and strategies, as well as the occasional bug fix.

The Selection Process

What are the elements of an ideal pilot project? Simply put, the pilot project should exercise and demonstrate the key features of the class library, provide a visible benefit to the company, have experienced developers on the team, and be realistically planned to allow time and resources for both training and problem solving. Figure 7.1 shows the elements of a perfect pilot project.

The pilot project should provide maximum coverage of the available features of your class library. It is important to demonstrate the features and functionality your library can provide to the developers. The pilot project provides a real-world opportunity to do so. You will find that following our application workflow and object mapping methodology enables you to easily identify the level of coverage any particular project will offer. You will not execute a complete workflow and object mapping during the initial selection process, but you should follow as much of the methodology as you need to identify the suitability of the project.

The pilot project should provide a visible business benefit to the company. Steer clear of projects with a dubious future. Projects that contribute only to the political process in the company can be volatile, to say the least. Your job is to enhance the profitability and efficiency of the company, not to expand someone's turf (unless that someone is your boss). Look for a project that addresses a need in the company that is currently unmet, but provides functionality that is needed in a key business area.

You should pick a project that has less aggressive deadlines than most. The pilot project gives the developer community their first glimpse of the class library in action, and slipped schedules will leave them with a poor first impression of your library. Remember that you will be facing new code and new methodologies. Bugs will happen. Even though you have tested exhaustively, your users will find situations you did not anticipate and did not test for. You will also need to provide mentoring and training in the best way to apply your methodologies and library objects. All of this takes time. The moral of the story is to pick a project with a schedule that will accommodate these and other strains on project deadlines.

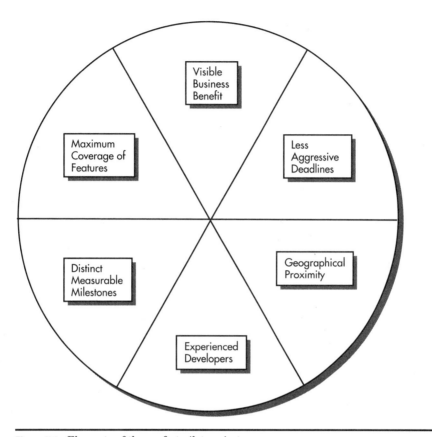

Figure 7.1 Elements of the perfect pilot project.

Strive to find a project with distinct, measurable progress milestones. It is important to measure progress of the project incrementally. This allows you to gauge the areas of your library and methodology that bring increased productivity to your developers. It also gives you the opportunity to intervene with increased support or expertise if the project's schedule slips.

The pilot project team must have enough experienced developers. An experienced developer should have completed at least one development effort using PowerBuilder, and preferably more. That developer should have a complete understanding of object-oriented technology and terminology, as well as a complete understanding of Windows development and standards. Our experience indicates that a project team should have a minimum of one such experienced developer for every two less-experienced developers.

Although it is less important, you should be aware of another consideration when selecting the pilot project: location. If your company has multiple development sites, try to pick a project that is based at the same site where the library development and support team is based. The initial support effort will require a more hands-on approach because the library developers and the application developers will both be treading unfamiliar ground. "Show me" becomes a powerful tool in these circumstances. As the developers and support personnel become more familiar with the types of issues raised, the need for close contact will diminish.

Building on the Methodology

Once you have selected a pilot project that will enhance the acceptance of your class library, it is time to begin using your methodologies to accelerate the development of the pilot project. Your pilot project's initial exposure to your methodologies, architecture, and class library objects must be orchestrated for maximum efficiency and information transfer. Begin using the methodologies rigorously, and resist the temptation to skip steps.

Work closely with the project team to develop the application workflow document. This document will be the basis of the continued development of the project. It also will provide the basis for the object mapping step, in which the class library objects are mapped to the steps and objects in the workflow document.

The next step is to adjust the plans and schedule for the pilot project to reflect what you have learned through the development of the application workflow and the object map. Some of the objects that occupy a large part of the project's schedule will be easily mapped to one of your library's objects, thus reducing their impact on the schedule. You may require some modification to the architecture of the application to better take advantage of the library's features. For this you will need to allow more time. Also be sure to allow time for false starts and rewrites as the developers find their way through the features and architecture of your class library.

Supporting the Pilot Effort

As we have already stated, the support effort for the pilot project is absolutely critical. The success of your library depends in large part on the first impression you make during the pilot project. Remember that many software companies have made their reputation based on the quality and accessibility of their support. You can enhance your library team's reputation greatly by providing top-quality support for all development teams, especially the pilot project.

Quick response is prized as a characteristic of your support infrastructure. You should make your team aware that support requirements take absolute priority over all other considerations. The developers are your customers. The developers are also your advertisements. The word-of-mouth promotion you will get from happy developers will help to ensure the success of your library in the corporate culture. The way to make the developers happy is to respond instantly, deploy massive force, and fix their problems.

Note: The support questions will range from simplistic PowerBuilder questions, through advice for objects and techniques, all the way to true support issues for your class library. Treat each problem as an opportunity. Even if you seem to spend a great deal of time answering simple questions, the stature of the library team will grow as you are increasingly seen as experts. More importantly, you will maintain closer contact with the developers, and you will be alerted to real class library issues in time to provide elegant and timely fixes.

Provide the pilot project developers direct access to support personnel. Use direct phone access, specific e-mail addresses, and automated bug-reporting tools to provide maximum coverage on all communication channels.

For direct phone access, consider a hotline dedicated to the support of your library. Be sure to alert your support team to the necessity to provide complete coverage for the hotline. You should also make known the phone numbers for each member of your support team.

E-mail can provide support through the company's own network, using products such as cc:Mail, Lotus Notes, and MS Mail. You should consider using a dedicated address for library support issues. The library mailbox should be checked at least once a day, preferably more often. In keeping with the idea of quick response, an acknowledgment of a problem report should be sent to the user immediately.

You can also use the various network service providers such as CompuServe and America Online, as well as the Internet for support coverage. Newsgroups, bulk mail, and other large-scale distribution features can make the dissemination of information and patches effective and easy.

Conversely, the library support team needs direct access to project personnel. The library team needs to communicate solutions quickly, not only to the person who reported the issue but to all the members of the pilot project team. The more you can increase contact between your support team and the project team, the higher your chances are of success. Figure 7.2 illustrates the support channels you can provide for your pilot project.

Marketing Success

The pilot project is one of the most important facets of the marketing effort you will use to promote your library. The results and progress of the pilot project will be closely watched throughout the company. This means that your success and the success of the pilot project are inextricably intertwined. Do not make the mistake of underestimating the value and power of the word-of-mouth promotion resulting from a successful pilot project. Also remember that a failed pilot project takes a lot of effort and subsequent success to overcome. Do everything in your power to make the pilot a success.

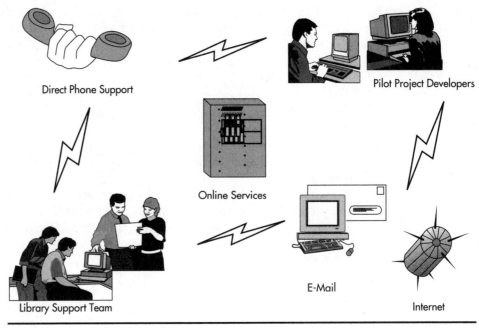

Figure 7.2 Support channels for the pilot project.

Your successes will market your library better than any amount of glossy brochures. Market your successes. Use examples of projects that have achieved their goals using your library. Gather statistics on the reuse of your objects and the savings that have been realized. Make sure the developers in your company are aware of the ways other teams have produced more, with less effort, using your methodologies and objects. Show the savings in maintenance for applications that are based on objects reused from your library.

On the other hand, do not oversell. Take pains to ensure that the claims you make for increased productivity and functionality are borne out by the facts. The pilot project is invaluable for this. You will find out where savings are realized in time, money, or effort, and where functionality was increased over what the developers would have provided without your library. You will also find out where you will need to increase your concentration and support to avoid problems in future projects. Use these data to make realistic statements about the benefits and features of your library.

Summary

Selecting the right pilot project is crucial to the success and acceptance of your class library. In this chapter we have examined the elements that contribute to the success of the pilot project:

- Selecting the right project
- Supporting the pilot project
- Using the methodologies to facilitate the pilot project
- Marketing your successes

Selecting a pilot project involves evaluating the characteristics that help define the ideal pilot project and project team:

- Maximum coverage of available class library features
- Visible business benefit
- Less aggressive project deadlines
- Measurable project milestones
- Experienced developers
- Geographical proximity

We showed you the importance of support for the pilot project and outlined the steps you can take to ensure top-quality support for the users of your library:

- Quick response
- E-mail and network services for communication channels
- Direct access to support personnel
- Direct access to project personnel

Finally, we outlined the ways to increase the marketing potential of your successes, starting with the pilot project.

My mother exhorted me, at the beginning of each school year, to work especially hard during the first few months. The point was to enhance the first impression that the teachers had of my abilities and work habits. It worked! The teachers learned quickly that I was a capable student, and through the remainder of the year, any problems I had were treated as isolated problems rather than a trend. In the same way, you should look at the pilot project as the vehicle through which you will establish your class library as a capable, solid performer. From the outset, if you establish a track record of success, the likelihood of your library's acceptance throughout the company is enhanced. Treat the pilot project as your first line of marketing, and do whatever it takes to ensure its success. You will be rewarded.

8

Building on the Foundation

Introduction

The foundation we have built up to this point is strong and ready for expansion. It is neither an incomplete facade nor a finished edifice. Now you must add, expand, and continue to build.

Use the technology—do not let it use you. This means that you must keep a cool head and maintain mastery over your tools. If you know what your tools can do and how to apply them, you will be their master.

Chapter Objectives

This chapter tells you how to achieve and maintain that dominance. You will learn the technique of knowledge dissemination through mentoring. You will see that designing with the judicious use of a methodology and an established set of guidelines can lead to greater productivity and an ever-expanding working knowledge. You will also learn the value and the process of expanding the object base as your development teams use the methodology to create reusable business objects.

Building on the Foundation

The skills you need to move forward and build on the foundation are based on the conviction that knowledge is paramount. You need to know how to use the tools and the technology, and you need to spread that knowledge around. The success you achieve is tied to three factors:

- Disseminating knowledge
- Learning to design with the methodology
- Expanding the object base

We will examine each of these in greater detail.

Disseminating knowledge

Having a methodology and a base of reusable objects is not enough. You need to have a growing base of knowledgeable people who can apply the tools. You can accomplish this goal through the twin processes of training and mentoring.

Training your developers is an ongoing process, not a one-time effort. Strive to maintain a flow of people through the stages of training. Start by teaching the basic techniques of applying the objects that already exist. Then train your people to rigorously apply your methodology as they create new objects. Finally, you should impart to them the details and purposes behind your architecture and encourage them to improve on what exists.

Once developers have been trained, they should become trainers themselves. Their knowledge is fresh and imbued with a sense of where they have started and how far they have come. They know the questions they had when they started, and they know where the training process needs better clarity or thoroughness. In addition, the act of teaching a discipline requires that the teacher become increasingly familiar with that discipline.

Show teams how to do it right. The process of mentoring allows you to leverage your knowledge base among the entire development community. Place a developer who is well-trained and intimately knowledgeable of the methodology and tools with each development team at the start of their project. This mentor has dual objectives. The first is to increase the team's chance of success by applying the methodology properly. The second, more important objective is to actively promote understanding of the methodology, the architecture of the class library, and the objects themselves. By this simple expedient, more developers gain more knowledge faster. Once their project is completed, they can become mentors to other groups within the company.

Learning to design with the technology

Using a methodology is not a matter to be discussed, agreed on, and then set aside. The temptation is always there to abandon the seeming constraints of the methodology and simply build the project. Do not even think about it! Your methodology is the key to consistency and reusability. Reusability is the key to a repeatable pattern of success and productivity.

The Cooperative Business Modeling (CBM) methodology we have used in this book enhances the prospect of reusability. You use the methodology to constantly build on the base of knowledge and objects you have acquired. By adhering to your established techniques, you will promote the construction of objects that mesh with your base. You will ultimately save time, accumulated over all of the projects in your company. Do not lose that opportunity just to make a "quick kill."

Following the established guidelines will bring a coherence to the objects developed throughout your company. Less time will be spent rewriting. Less time will be spent redesigning objects that did not meet requirements. And, less time will be wasted trying to figure out why something was built a particular way, and how to make it compatible with the rest of the object base.

Remember, you need not build everything yourself. You need to find out what is available in the rest of the company and the industry at large. There are probably objects already developed throughout the company that can easily be retrofitted to conform to your architecture. There are certainly tools available that will enhance your ability to speedily design and develop objects using the methodology.

Expanding the object base

Living objects grow, and so should your library. Every time you complete a development effort, you are left with a collection of objects. Many of these objects serve a valuable business function. Their functionality can be replicated every time a project needs it, or they can be reused. Your goal is to build each object for reuse. Then, make sure that its functionality is documented and available so that it gets reused.

Designing for reuse must come first. Encourage the developers to create everything with an attitude that it will be reused. This means knowing and using the methodology to create objects that encapsulate a coherent set of related functions in a standard, predictable way.

The CBM methodology builds reuse into the objects starting at the design phase. The analysis and design documents lead to physical implementations that are grouped according to functionality. The documents produced throughout the process enhance reusability by rigorously documenting the details of the objects' architecture, implementation, testing, and usage.

As you develop more and more business objects and add them to your object base, you need to be aware of the effect that this ever-expanding collection of objects has on the development environment. Separate the implementation of these objects so that only the objects a project team requires need be inserted into the search path. This keeps unused objects out of the search path, minimizing the performance impact that would result from the need to scan through them.

The CBM methodology encourages and enables you to build and expand on existing objects. You do not rewrite unless you have to. The process of object mapping allows the developer to discover existing objects that address a given requirement. If an existing object has a subset of the required functionality, you can extend the object instead of starting over.

Finally, if you need to rewrite part of an object, ensure backward compatibility. This may sometimes require that you build parallel lines of functionality either within existing objects or with the addition of new objects. Freeze the old functionality and build on the new.

Supporting the Foundation

The foundation will not persist solely through its own momentum. It must be maintained and promoted. You need to actively champion the techniques, standards, and processes you have established. Your goals as you maintain the prominence of your development foundation will be as follows:

- Enforce the use of standards
- Maintain developers' productivity at a high level
- Increase availability of the technology
- Guide people through the process

Enforce the use of standards

Why enforce standards? As an integral part of the methodology, standards for design, coding, and documentation will provide consistency throughout your company's projects. The benefits of consistency are many. Your developers will be able to move freely from one project team to another without meeting yet another learning curve. Successful strategies will propagate while less successful ones die away. End users will benefit, too, as the applications they use perform more consistently, especially when addressing a given business function.

We recommend a preproject review process as a way of evaluating each project's adherence to standards. At this time, you can make sure that the project team has access to the expertise necessary to apply the methodology. You can also verify that the time frame stated for the project is realistic and allows enough time for the team to use the methodology to its fullest. Finally, verify that training is available for the team members in both the methodology and the available base and business class objects.

Maintain developers' productivity at a high level

The payoff for standards and for following the methodology is increased productivity. Any given project will always have stumbling blocks.

Incomplete training.   If a developer does not understand the objects, technology, and methodology, he or she stands a great chance of misapplying any or all of them. Do not wait for misapplication to wreck a project. Monitor the project's progress and consult with the members of the team often enough to gauge the level of their understanding. Make sure that any additional training the developers need is made available immediately.

Object blindness. Object blindness occurs when the team needs functionality that already exists in some form, but they do not see it. Sometimes this happens because much of the functionality exists in a fashion that is not immediately obvious (for instance in an object that must be extended to provide the ultimate qualities the developers need). The goal of the library support team in this case is to intercept these needs before developers reinvent anything. Point out that the object exists and guide them in the effort of extending the behaviors and attributes of the object to meet their own needs. Always keep in mind that the objects that they develop can probably be used in other projects.

Support blockage. Sometimes a project reaches a point where all progress stops because a support issue remains unresolved. This is beyond doubt a reason for that support request to be given the highest priority. You need to devote every resource available to ensure that the support need is answered and the project gets back on track.

Increase availability of the technology

Part of the support effort in favor of the foundation is to ensure that the base of committed users of the technology continues to grow. Your vistas can include the following:

- Expanding to other installations
- Integrating with other reusable libraries
- Providing other development platforms access to your business objects

As your object base grows, and as the methodology evolves to meet your company's needs, your focus should remain on increasing the coverage of your technology within the company.

If your company does application development in other countries, you will eventually need to deal with internationalization issues. Budget time for this endeavor in your support plan. There is no good reason to limit your development foundation's influence to the country where it originated.

Guide people through the process

Be present or easily accessible during all phases of project development. You must actively participate, especially during the initial design portion. This is where the mapping from desired functionality to existing objects is carried out. Your guidance will ensure that the object mapping process is carried out smoothly and accurately, and that the existing object base is used fully.

As the project follows through to conclusion, monitor its progress and help the developers where necessary. Provide support and show them how to apply the methodology. Help them to fit their business objects in the framework you have built for development.

Summary

Throughout this section, we have shown you how to create a development foundation that promotes reusability and enhanced productivity. In this chapter you learned how to build on that foundation. You found out that you must maintain mastery of your tools and environment. We explained the techniques of training and mentoring as they apply to enlarging and enhancing the development foundation. You learned how to create a climate of learning and growth through knowledge dissemination, mastery of the methodology, and expansion of the object base.

We showed you how to support the foundation. You must concentrate on the following areas:

- Enforcing the use of standards
- Maintaining developers' productivity at a high level
- Increasing availability of the technology
- Guiding people through the process

The important thing to remember is that no foundation is static. You must continually improve, expand, and hone the tools and methodologies you use. You need to provide a consistently high level of support, and help the practitioners of your methods to become the teachers.

The development foundation is never complete. Use your skills to direct its growth and you will be rewarded with better, more consistent products and more productive, more fulfilled developers.

9

Third-Party Software

Introduction

The history of software development sometimes resembles the history of the invention of the wheel—over and over and over. The dreaded not-invented-here syndrome combined with a general uncertainty about the quality and utility of the available offerings leaves many developers reimplementing solutions that are already available. Rest assured, there is no shortage of high-quality, useful third-party software to aid the PowerBuilder designer and developer. In this chapter we present a sampling of the types of the available third-party tools and libraries. We touch on some of the specific products in each area, but many equally good ones are not mentioned. This is not in any way an exhaustive list, nor is it meant to be any kind of recommendation. Evaluate a tool carefully before settling on it as a standard part of your development foundation.

Third-Party Software
Computer aided software engineering tools

Computer aided software engineering (CASE) tools enable designers to define their data and process characteristics. The resulting information can then be used to construct databases from schemas defined within the CASE tool. Extended attributes for columns can be defined within the CASE tool and used to populate the PowerBuilder data dictionary tables. In addition, some CASE tools also allow the creation of PowerBuilder objects, such as datawindows, based on the design created within the tool.

A brief listing of some PowerBuilder-compatible CASE tools follows.

System Architect, Popkin Software Systems, Inc. System Architect is a suite of tools including SA Screen Painter, SA Reverse Data Engineer, SA Schema

Generator, SA/PowerBuilder Link, SA OOA&D, SA Project Documentation Facility, and SA/Interface Manager.

The link between System Architect and PowerBuilder allows you to exchange design information back and forth between System Architect and PowerBuilder.

Systems Engineer, LBMS. Systems Engineer provides design, management, and control facilities to support enterprise-wide client/server development. Systems Engineer provides bidirectional integration with PowerBuilder with SE/Open for PowerBuilder. This link provides integrated object storage in the LBMS repository, version control, and configuration management.

What makes Systems Engineer different from the other CASE tools is its ability to import existing PowerBuilder objects and register them as classes to use during your design process. This allows the designer to use predefined classes to design objects, which Systems Engineer can generate into your code library. The drawback is cost. Systems Engineer has a one-time server cost (central repository) of around $45,000, to which you add the individual cost per seat.

In addition, Systems Engineer includes PowerProcess, a client-server methodology geared especially toward PowerBuilder users.

Database design tools

S-Designor, Powersoft Corporation. S-Designor provides an environment for powerful data modeling that enjoys bidirectional integration with PowerBuilder. S-Designor extracts information such as validation rules, edit styles, and format masks from PowerBuilder. These items are saved in S-Designor as extended attributes.

S-Designor allows graphical database modeling, including integrity rules, indexes, and PowerBuilder extended attributes. You can create complete databases, including triggers for over 30 database systems. S-Designor also supports reverse engineering of existing databases.

Version 5.0 of S-Designor shows a distinct trend toward full CASE capability. Powersoft has added a process modeling module, ProcessAnalyst, and an application modeling module for PowerBuilder, AppModeler, to the product. The data modeling module is called DataArchitect, and S-Designor also includes a project and dictionary management module called MetaWorks

ErWin, LogicWorks. ErWin is a popular choice for data modeling. It supports most database languages, reverse engineering, stored procedure and trigger generation, and extended attribute synchronization.

ErWin is easy to use and flexible, and it is able to generate complete databases. ErWin lacks the logical-to-physical capabilities found in some higher-level products such as Bachman, but remains one of the more popular database modeling tools available.

Version control

Version control systems enable you to manage complete releases of an application or library. They allow you to track source code changes and maintain an archive of all of the source code as it relates to each given release.

PVCS, Intersolv, Inc.   PVCS integrates with the PowerBuilder Library Painter and allows complete control over the management of all development objects. PowerBuilder check-in and check-out capabilities are used to manage the storage of source code in archive files.

PVCS provides a full GUI interface that allows the management of objects beyond just PowerBuilder development objects. For instance, you can place under version control the automated testing scripts that you use to test a particular release.

Source Integrity, Mortice Kern Systems, Inc.   Mortice Kern Systems (MKS) provides Source Integrity, a configuration management and version control system. MKS began providing an interface to the PowerBuilder Library Painter with the release of version 4 of PowerBuilder.

Source Integrity provides "sandboxes," which mirror the structure of a project. Sandboxes allow each developer to work on a component of the project and use the sandbox as a private build location.

Source integrity also makes full use of the security functionality provided by Novell Netware.

Object Manager, LBMS.   Object Manager is a subset of the LBMS System Engineer product that has now been separated from the main product so that it can be used standalone as a version control system. Object Manager differs from the PVCS/Source Integrity products as being one of the few products that archives versions into a database instead of a text file.

Object Manager is also the same system used internally by LBMS's System Engineer product to provide version control of the remainder of the LBMS objects such as data models and class models.

Object Cycle, Powersoft.   With version 5.0 of PowerBuilder, Powersoft is also introducing a version control system called Object Cycle. Object Cycle provides full team development support in a network client-server environment. Object Cycle uses an SQLAnywhere database to keep track of object versions. Object Cycle was written using PowerBuilder 5.0.

Class libraries

The list of class libraries available grows almost daily. Since PowerBuilder 2.0, vendors have been striving to provide their customers with a set of reusable classes that help developers to assemble functional application components quickly and efficiently. How the libraries are designed and built is what makes them really different. Below is a brief list of some of the class libraries we have come into contact with. If you are evaluating class libraries, contact several vendors and find out what their underlying strategy is. Pick the tool that best serves your need or, if you decide to build your own, learn from what these vendors offer.

PowerTOOL, PowerCerv. An integrated multiple document interface (MDI) application framework, PowerTOOL is one of the oldest and most mature libraries. Unfortunately, PowerTOOL also contains code and objects to support legacy applications written in older versions of PowerBuilder. However, PowerTOOL does support these important paradigms.

- MDI window ancestor hierarchy
- Datawindow ancestor hierarchy
- Data driven navigation and security methodology
- Intersheet communications
- Install program for PowerBuilder applications
- "Search as you type" object

Enterprise Builder, Icon Solutions, Inc. Enterprise Builder is a comprehensive application framework comprising an integrated suite of objects geared toward supporting parent-child or master-detail behavior. The library's strength (and possibly its weakness) is in its datawindow classes. Both of the authors have had some involvement in the design and development of this library. Some of the features of Enterprise Builder are as follows:

- Offers declarative control of object behavior.
- Complete save-cycle support is available.
- Datawindow hierarchy includes base, search criteria, search result, parent-child and group-assign.
- Window hierarchy includes base, dialog, and parent-child.
- Includes comprehensive error trapping and handling.
- Supports multiple concurrent database connections using "super-transactions."
- Supports publish/subscribe messaging between objects.
- Includes Object and script wizards.

Object Framework, Castle Software Engineering. Object Framework 5.0 is a class library built on PowerBuilder 5.0 technology with the future in mind. Object-oriented techniques are used heavily throughout, making it easy for the user to add on and into the library. The support for real business objects is what distinguishes this class library from others. Automatic execution of business rules and support for all of the datawindow styles currently being used allow for maximum flexibility.

Ease of use is enhanced by reducing the number of visual objects and adding a layer of functional service objects that control each object's capabilities. Developers need not choose which style of datawindow they want from a list of visual presentations; rather, they always choose a datawindow object and then specify what functionality on the object they want to activate. This is the service-based architecture (SBA) that we have used throughout this book. Object Framework Enterprise supports these features:

- Object-oriented approach

- Dynamic interface instantiation

- Automated business rule execution

- Customized single-layer object hierarchy (unique among class libraries)

- Object and object script wizards

Powersoft Foundation Classes. Powersoft ships the Powersoft Foundation Class (PFC) library with PowerBuilder 5.0. This is a collection of objects that you can use to form the basis of a more complete class library or application framework. PFC is based on what Powersoft calls Service Architecture, which corresponds well to the service-based architecture (SBA) we have detailed elsewhere in this book.

Add-on components

Component Pack, Powersoft Corporation. The Component Pack from Powersoft includes two controls from Visual Tools, Inc.: the Formula One spreadsheet, giving you a control with Excel-like capabilities, and a spell checker. Both tools are dynamically linking library (DLL) driven with customized PowerBuilder Userobjects to speed integration with your application.

Translation Assistant, Powersoft Corporation. The Translation Assistant add-on provides support for languages such as French and German. The add-in DLLs make it easier for project teams to develop international applications. Support for additional languages is planned. This allows developers to develop multilingual international applications.

Documentation

DesignDoc, Castle Software Engineering. DesignDoc is a collection of Word for Windows macros and templates that make it easier for developers to capture class design documentation before development. The documentation deliberately avoids choosing a CASE tool notation to allow the users to use whatever

CASE tool they prefer. Hyperlinks allow the designer to link documents together and automate cross-referencing, allowing the successful design of logical and physical classes.

CyberDoc, Gateway Systems, Inc. CyberDoc™ is Gateway Systems' automated documentation helper. CyberDoc was written to address five specific documentation needs of project teams: design and specification, standardized object documentation, organization of auxiliary documents, production of user and technical manuals and automated PBL scanning. First, CyberDoc aids the development of design and specification documents by guiding the designer through a standard sequence of data-gathering steps. Once the data are entered, CyberDoc produces the design documents automatically. CyberDoc uses sorting and searching techniques to help identify commonality among objects, thus helping the designer to avoid redundancy and plan ancestry. Second, CyberDoc helps create the tables and forms that make up a great deal of the typical user or technical manual. The design and development data entered into CyberDoc is massaged and formatted, then used to produce class, object, method and attribute documents. Third, CyberDoc allows the technical writer to organize and classify auxiliary documents for ease of retrieval. Fourth, CyberDoc compiles and prints user and technical manuals using a combination of the standard Cooperative Business Modeling (CBM) forms and the auxiliary documents entered by the technical writers. Finally, CyberDoc scans the PowerBuilder libraries used in an application or class library, and maintains lists of objects, methods, and attributes found.

Automated testing tools

Automated testing tools are one of the most important additions to your toolset that you can make. The bane of the application developer is in quality of testing, not quantity. Automated testing tools give you something that is rarely, if ever, found in human testing: consistency. The ability to run the same tests time after time and be able to identify possible problems quickly is a definite advantage—in my opinion, a necessity. The only shortfall of these tools is that the test scenarios must be designed and developed by hand. The tools cannot, as of yet, interrogate your objects and build test cases for you. These tools are also very dependent on visual presentations. Complicated internal functions must still be tested the old-fashioned way.

Most of the tools operate in the same manner, although ease of use, quality of object testing, and platform independence will vary. The tools allow you to record events and monitor the results of simulated human interaction. The depth of the object monitoring varies from tool to tool, ranging from antiquated recording of mouse movements and events to state-of-the-art object event recorders that can check and measure the state of the various objects in your system. Regardless of the tool you choose, it is important that you do choose one.

QA Partner, Segue. QA Partner from Segue is an automated testing tool with a long history and some unique features that distinguish it from the other tools in its class. Some of these features are as follows:

- Supports more than 25 platforms
- Is object-aware
- Uses object-oriented scripting language
- Includes window declarations to simplify keeping up with changes
- Allows definition of pretest and posttest setups to ensure that data and conditions remain consistent

SQA Suite, SQA, Inc. SQA Suite (formerly known as SQA TeamTest) is a top-quality product whose testing environment is the easiest to get used to and also has built-in test management capabilities. Its object comparator allows for test prediction and records the states of your objects before your code is actually ready to run them.

SQA has the advantage of being able to import your application's PBLs to create the start of your test plan. It becomes a matter of filling in the various test cases required to test each of the objects listed.

SQA is also object-aware. By this we mean that SQA has the unique ability to access all attributes of PowerBuilder objects, including the datawindow. This allows you to capture the object and then specify various object characteristics that indicate success.

Help-authoring software

RoboHelp, Blue Sky Software Corporation. RoboHelp is an add-in for Microsoft Word that allows graphical development of your on-line help. RoboHelp is not a manual-to-help compiler. It is specifically designed for the development of on-line help. The resulting document is simply a container of your on-line help topics, not a user manual.[1]

RoboHelp supports the development of on-line help files for Windows and Windows 95. RoboHelp can also take an existing help file and import it back into a document for review, correction, and recompilation.

ForeHelp, ForeFront, Inc. ForeHelp is a visual help development system that enables the help designer to quickly and easily create Windows help files. Unlike many other help-authoring systems on the market, ForeHelp does not require the use of an external word processor. You construct the help file in Fore-Help's own what-you-see-is-what-you-get (WYSIWYG) word processor, and no longer need to keep track of (or see) arcane rich text format (RTF) codes.

---

1. See Chapter 30 for more detail on developing on-line help.

ForeHelp supports all Windows help file constructs, including banners, pop-ups, hypertext links, and secondary windows. You can import your existing help projects and RTF files into ForeHelp, so you don't need to recreate them. Once you have created your help file, you can test it in ForeHelp's test mode, then compile the final .HLP file.

Doc2Help, WexTech, Inc.   Doc2Help is a Microsoft Word add-in that uses templates and styles for the development of on-line help. Doc2Help is well suited for the development of a user manual that can be compiled into on-line help. Doc2Help supports multiple file documents and can compile large on-line help systems.

Other development tools

An often overlooked but powerful add-on application for PowerBuilder Developers is another language or development tool. Tools such as Borland's Delphi and Powersoft's new Optima++ are ideal additions to your arsenal of PowerBuilder tools.

These tools can augment PowerBuilder by allowing the developer to add OCX and DLLs to PowerBuilder applications quickly and easily. Combining the best of both types of tools, PowerBuilder's powerful data access and visual capabilities and Optima++'s (or Delphi's) ability to generate custom controls can give you the ability to deliver better, more powerful, and more professional applications.

Summary

The software market for PowerBuilder products, add-ons, and other development aids to complete the enterprise development effort continues to grow at an astonishing pace. This chapter only grazes the surface of the products available now, and with PowerBuilder 5's support for OCXs, the marketplace will soon be booming with third-party custom controls that can easily be added to your software arsenal. Make sure you review the tools you want to use carefully. You have made a significant investment in client-server technology. Third-party tools will round off your development environment nicely if chosen well.

Developing a Class Library

Introduction

A class library is the foundation of reusable object development that will enhance the productivity, stability, and maintainability of applications.

In approaching the development of reusable classes, I found that generic design is a far more complex approach to take. The first issue to overcome is that of justification. Justifying spending additional time to design an object to be reusable is at best an inexact science. Having gone through the process several times, we are able to look back and realize that the justification is often understated. The savings achieved through well-designed, reusable classes is staggering. In several cases, we found that objects almost entirely eliminated (and in some cases did eliminate) development costs for those specific objects. The illustration in Figure P2.1 shows some of the savings factors we have seen.

This illustrates how costs for the more generic development effort are usually about three times as high as the cost of developing a similar object for an application. There are two reasons for this. The library effort is much more generic (and therefore more complex), and is usually much more feature-rich. Applications usually develop the functionality needed for their application only. We are also only showing cost savings for three objects. As is evident, the savings will continue to grow with the number of objects used by the application that are provided by the class library.

The reverse can also be true. Occasionally, we found objects that were seldom (if ever) used because they provided no real benefit to the application or were too complex and created more work than their justification level. Dividing these groups is a task that the reusable class developer needs to be aware of and complete.

Some classes we developed in our first library did not reach their full potential because we realized that the design had not gone far enough, and could be modified or enhanced. One of the most difficult decisions, once the justification issue is resolved, is that of the depth of the object-oriented design. Just

- Development of an object for a project takes less time than that for a library.

- Library development effort occurs only once. Project effort is cumulative.

- Library offers standard API and structure. Projects have as many different results as there are projects.

- Maintenance of the object from one project to the next carries no learning curve.

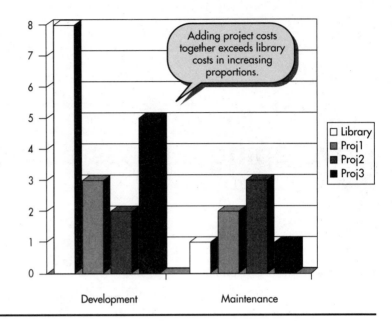

Figure P2.1 Potential cost savings.

how far do you go to design a reusable class without adding so much complexity as to make the class virtually unusable? In this and in subsequent chapters, we try to help you make such decisions more confidently.

The importance of documentation also becomes obvious. Reusable classes without documentation are almost useless, as developers under strict schedules and tight budgets will use their creativity to get the task done if the object is not flexible and usable. This is one of the reasons that we decided to devote an entire section of this book to documentation. This part introduces some of the documentation types we found useful in the development of two different class libraries and several applications with these libraries. Being a user of reusable classes gives a different perspective on how the documentation should guide the developer through using the objects. It should leave them feeling that the task was accomplished in much less time than it would have taken them to write their own object class, and with the realization that they now have a much richer set of features than they would have developed.

Part Objectives

This part discusses these issues, and more, guiding reusable class designers through the decision processes required to create a library of reusable objects that their organizations will benefit from for several years to come. We discuss some of the techniques we have developed, often through trial and error. There is no unimportant facet to reusable class design. From requirements gathering and analysis through design, development, testing, and deployment, a reusable class library must provide high-quality objects that developers will use. Even the most well-designed object is worthless if it is not used.

We go through the entire process of developing a class library, detailing concepts and techniques wherever they are relevant. We do not intend to describe the entire development effort that goes into designing and developing every object, but I do want to make sure that every step is covered. The diagram in Figure P2.2 shows the steps we follow to develop a library. Each block in the diagram relates to a specific chapter in this part of the book.

By the end of the part you will have a clear understanding of why we adopted the approaches we did and how these techniques guided our efforts toward a successful class library design. We will also have established the proven design techniques that can guide you in future efforts.

Methodologies

We introduce or reinforce several methodologies we have developed or enhanced through our experience. The methodologies, though not all new or revelatory, are molded and enhanced to allow the developer of reusable classes to use a more automated approach to the design, development, and deployment of reusable class libraries. We discuss, demonstrate, and reinforce common object-oriented techniques. We also introduce a methodology of our own, which we call object synthesis. This methodology allows us to take requirements

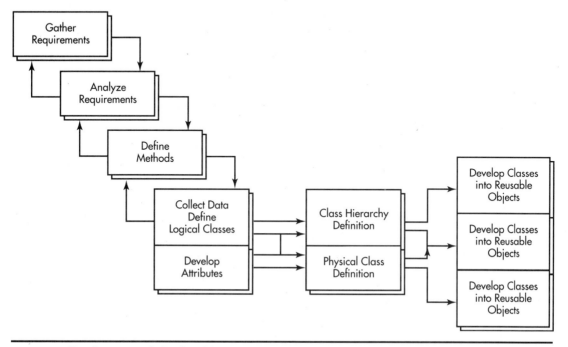

Figure P2.2 Development path for class libraries.

through predefined steps to ultimately end up in physical class definitions. This methodology is molded from proven reusable object design techniques used in real development efforts. Figure P2.3 shows the workflow from start to finish.

Object synthesis involves gathering requirements; analyzing the requirements; grouping requirements; defining logical classes, methods, and attributes; analyzing methods and attributes to define interfaces; and, finally, designing physical classes to represent the definitions. During the whole process, test procedures are being defined to ensure that your reusable classes are of the high quality needed to gain acceptance.

Reusable class library design must follow object-oriented techniques because any change, no matter how small or large, affects multiple projects, each with users depending on the system for daily business processing. This can be a daunting task, forcing harder questions to arise when any change comes on the drawing board. On the other hand, libraries must continue to evolve, to solve more application development issues. Sometimes new products are released to make the tool more efficient and provide more functionality. Class libraries must evolve with the development tool, taking advantage of new fea-

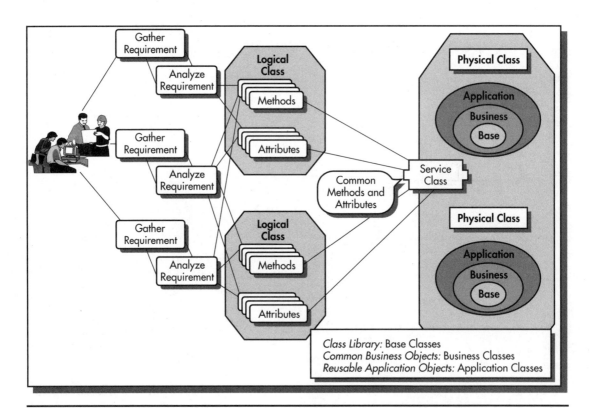

Figure P2.3 Object synthesis (from CBM).

tures, new thinking, and new techniques. The class library developer has to be aware of all of this and more, and there are some techniques he or she can use to minimize the effect of change. This part brings many of these issues to the table and presents you with real-life solutions.

Case Study: Object Framework

To further illustrate the validity and the benefits of the techniques we discuss in this part, we look closely at Object Framework, a commercially available class library we have developed and refined over the past two years. We attempt to describe a wide variety of the objects included and to illustrate each technique or methodology we use. Object Framework is the culmination of our learning so far, and we acknowledge that the learning isn't over yet.

10

Requirements Analysis

Introduction

In the client-server environment today, and especially in the environment of PowerBuilder development, there is a tendency to dive into development, relying on the RAD process to continually build the application until it reaches a point of acceptability. Although this may work, and occasionally meet budget objectives, the approach makes it very difficult to build truly reusable objects. The crux of the problem is that once an object is built, it is often more difficult to make the object generic than to build a more generic object from the ground up. The point that needs to be emphasized is that RAD is not a substitute for planning and design. Rather, it is a means by which to implement the design.

The first part of planning and designing a class library is to assemble the requirements, along with the expected benefit of the requirement, that will drive the process. There has to be a goal that can be established early. When gathering requirements, do not discard any idea, however big or small. All ideas have their place. When you have determined the scope of your development effort, then you can eliminate ideas and requirements through a predetermined process until a comfortable scope is achieved. The requirements discarded from your first development effort should be merely shelved until you are ready to expand on your base. Your class library should satisfy the needs of your developers, not hinder them through over-abundance and complexity.

Chapter Objectives

The goal of this chapter is to describe what a requirement is and to explain the requirement-gathering process. (See Figure 10.1.) We accomplish this by describing the requirements we have gathered over several such efforts. In the course of this chapter we do the following:

- Define a requirement
- Decide on a library approach
- Establish design objectives
- Define the library architecture
- Design and document object-naming conventions
- Describe the requirement-gathering process
- Detail the requirements
- Categorize the requirements
- Weigh the costs and benefits of each requirement
- Define the activities for each requirement

This is a period of creative abandon. Every idea you gather can make a difference to your final product. The ideas not included in the first development cycle can be included when you continue to build the library.

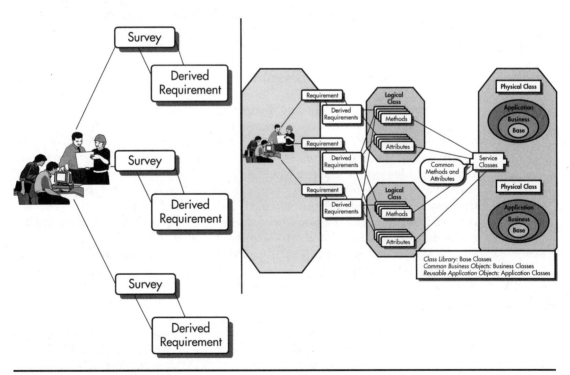

Figure 10.1 Focus on gathering requirements.

Where to Start

There are different types of class libraries available today. Some are true efforts to promote object reuse. Others, unfortunately, contain barely enough to merit the classification of class library, promoting the vendor rather than the benefit they should be providing to the developer.

In order to classify a library, we need to look at the development approach. We have determined four categories of class libraries. The list below describes these categories, the types of objects they include, and the development approach taken to achieve this style.

- *Component class library:* Develop classes of objects that can be used individually or in small groups.

- *Application framework class library:* Develop an integrated framework of object classes that are closely linked together by common features, functionality, and services. Objects rely on the framework for integrated services.

- *Business object library:* Develop reusable classes of objects that relate to the business area (usually based on a base set of objects).

- *Service-based object framework:* Develop a group of objects that rely on services imbedded in the objects to provide the level of functionality desired. The objects provide a common interface to developers and can allow services to be activated or deactivated through declarative attributes.

Although these approaches result in different libraries being built, the design approach must remain the same. Gather the requirements first, define the classes, design, build, and test the objects, and deploy them in applications. The approach that is best for your organization is determined by your organization's needs. We adopted the service-based object framework style because this best represented what we wanted to establish: a suite of object classes that could be used by themselves, or used together as a framework, with services built in that developers could activate declaratively.

Library Design Objectives

All development efforts should have an objective. Developing a class library is no different. Aside from the objective of developing the class library, it is important to have design objectives to ensure that there is a consistency in the design to add benefit to the developer. The list below shows our top 10 design objectives. These objectives are discussed in detail in this chapter and redisplayed in each design chapter in an abbreviated table. We have to emphasize the need to focus on the design objectives to be completely successful.

- The library must satisfy at least 75 percent of object requirements for any given project to be considered useful. This is not to say that no coding effort is required, but rather that objects to be used in a project should be derived from a library object that contains basic code. For obvious reasons, this does not include datawindow objects, but does include datawindow controls.

- The library must be manageable. This is harder to accomplish than the first objective because it is easy to continually extend the scope of a project of this nature. The scope must be clearly defined and both the number and types of objects should be kept to manageable numbers.

- The library must be easy to use, and provide as much off-the-shelf usability as possible. In addition, objects should be kept as simple as possible while providing maximum flexibility and extendibility. Even objects that are extremely well written, provide major functionality, and are flexible will not be accepted or used to their full potential if they contain too many user events and functions. This only makes it difficult for the developer to locate the functionality he or she requires.

- The library must be an extension of the environment, not a replacement or a hindrance.

- The library must reduce the time it takes to develop a full-featured Power-Builder application.

- The library must improve the consistency and reliability of PowerBuilder applications.

- The library must implement the defined requirements for the application framework within the confines of the PowerBuilder development environment to improve the portability to other supported PowerBuilder platforms.

- Objects developed as part of the class library must be accessible to existing PowerBuilder applications or applications developed outside of the proposed application framework.

- The implementation of the application framework must be independent of the database server.

- Strive to design objects that are independent of the implementation of other objects. If an object must rely on the behavior of another object, use the target object's interface to access these behaviors. This single design principle provides the most flexibility and reduces the impact of changes made to either object.

All of these objectives make the task of designing a truly reusable class library a daunting one. The result, however, will more than justify the effort if the objects are well designed and thoroughly tested.

With these objectives in place, we adopted the methodology of definable services, established at runtime through declarative attributes. To accomplish this, we needed to figure out a way to implement the services in such a way as to not impose any restrictions on the use of the services or make the services difficult to use or understand. We also had to figure out a way to allow objects to communicate with each other without knowing anything about each other.

Basic Methodology

The first step in beginning the design of a class library is to define clearly how the library will be built, not what should go in it. You absolutely must agree on a library architecture. All access to features and functionality in a library must be consistent. Inconsistencies will drive your developers nuts and will make your library unusable, or at least not user friendly, thereby failing one or more of our design objectives. Therefore, decide on the library architecture before beginning anything else.

Next, decide on naming conventions that follow your corporate standards or help to set your corporate standards. Do not create naming conventions for the sake of creating naming conventions. Keep them simple and usable while clearly showing the object, function or attribute's purpose and scope. Keep your names short and to the point, but do not abbreviate to the point where names become little more than a group of indistinguishable letters.

Only after completing the groundwork can you begin to gather requirements from your developers and users to build your requirements list. There is often confusion as to what a requirement actually is.

Once your requirements are gathered, categorize them and establish the cost, benefit, and business purpose of each one. This will assist in defining the scope for your development effort and, if your requirement-gathering process is thorough, will leave you with a substantial future requirements list.

Deciding on a Library Architecture

Our library is based on user-definable services presenting common access methods to the developer. The goal is to use the power of polymorphism as much as possible, reducing the number of different functions a developer needs to learn while providing an easily expandable collection of objects that use a common methodology.

By using a service, we are able to change the processing or presentation at the back end of the functionality. This level of flexibility is not easy to achieve. We need the ability to easily and dynamically modify the object that will be used at the back end.

Note that the architecture allows the flexibility of using an application's own objects as the back end. The flexibility level of this type of library is huge. One other key point to mention is that the library imposes *no* presentation style on the developer. *Any* object that has a graphical representation allows the developer to modify the presentation aspects of the object. The developer, in many cases, also controls the services. Services can be enhanced, extended, or, in some cases, overridden and replaced without the library even being concerned. This type of architecture is called a service-based architecture.

Service-based architecture

PowerBuilder has matured to the point at which the developers of a few years ago, eagerly diving in to produce applications as quickly as their budgets would allow, are looking back and asking that ages-old question, "How could I have done this better?" I'm one of those developers, and the answer to the question, for me, is in the architecture. We tried the traditional inheritance model and achieved a great deal of reuse, often at the expense of ease of use. As the technology and our knowledge grew, we continued to add new features, extending the inheritance model to its limits. Now it is time to adapt. We need to use the technology for what it can provide. For this we need a new architecture, and with this architecture comes the requirement for a new methodology.

The window inheritance model.   In the beginning, we decided that the window was the key component to our applications. Everything was shown in a window (remember the days of no NVO?), and we built our inheritance model around the window. We then derived new classes of windows to satisfy particular needs. Some classes included datawindows, others related multiple datawindows, and others knew how to communicate to a menu. The result was a very rigid inheritance model with new branches extending to satisfy the multitude of business needs. Figure 10.2 shows how this model might have looked.

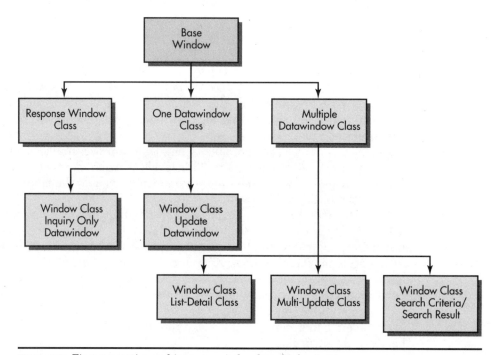

Figure 10.2   First-generation architecture: window-based inheritance.

The datawindow inheritance model.   We quickly discovered the limitations of the window inheritance model. Whenever you needed a datawindow to behave differently, either you had to do a lot of overriding or extending, or you built a new branch. We learned that the datawindow played a more vital part in our applications and built the second generation of inheritance models based on the datawindow (inherited as a user object) as the key object, with windows acting more like a container object class. This second generation of inheritance models was still based on the traditional inheritance model, but the window hierarchy grew a little more flat. Figure 10.3 shows what a typical datawindow inheritance model might look like.

Introducing service-based architecture.   We found out that the datawindow inheritance model placed too much emphasis on the datawindow object and this portion of the inheritance model outgrew our other objects rapidly. It also became more difficult to add new functionality because the location of the function within the hierarchy now became more critical. We also discovered that changing the level of functionality we wanted required significant effort, even if we could actually choose which level of the inheritance tree we wanted to use in the first place. We needed more separation of functionality from our basic objects. We wanted more encapsulation, improved ease of use, better performance, less maintenance, and greater flexibility.

Enter service-based architecture (SBA). SBA is derived from our cooperative business modeling (CBM) design methodology, which places the emphasis of the processing within a service object. The service object should be compact, combining functionality that relates specifically to its purpose. It is more encapsulated and is easier to maintain. The architecture grew out of a need to separate functionality (separation is similar to encapsulation) and provide

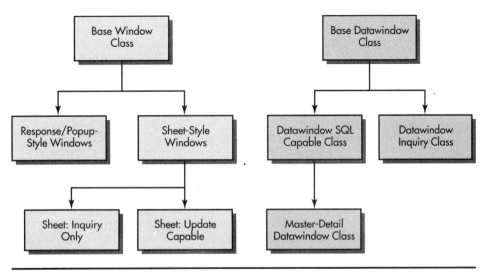

Figure 10.3 Second-generation architecture: datawindow inheritance strategy.

more capability and flexibility to developers while retaining the common access point to the objects' functionality. This basic premise for the architecture is shown in Figure 10.4.

Enhancing ease of use, flexibility, maintainability, and encapsulation. The service-based architecture model gives the developer much fewer and, in many cases, a single choice in deciding which object to use. For example, instead of the traditional choice of master-detail style, query style, or single-update style of datawindow class, the developer chooses the datawindow class and then chooses which services the datawindow class should support. This results in improved ease of use, better performance (services not required are simply not carried as overhead), and more flexibility. You can choose to use another service by "turning the service on." Figure 10.5 depicts the service-based inheritance model.

Note that the usable object is part of the flat inheritance model whereas services are part of a traditional model. We still rely on the traditional model to promote reuse within the service hierarchy, but the developer does not have to be aware of this. As can also be seen, this model allows PowerBuilder to gain the benefits of multiple inheritance without the complexity.

Implementation options. We also learned that the service itself may need to be implemented in different ways, sometimes dynamically changing the typical implementation. We discovered that services could be instantiated in the ways shown in Figure 10.6.

The service scope determines how long the service will be active, which also determines when it should be removed from memory. The instantiation style indicates whether the service is loaded as part of the container's construction event or is driven by runtime requirements. When the object that uses the services is loaded, the services themselves are loaded by definition only. This

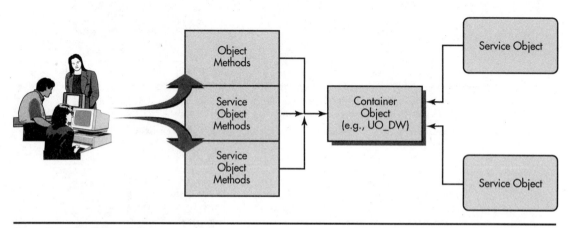

Figure 10.4 The SBA premise.

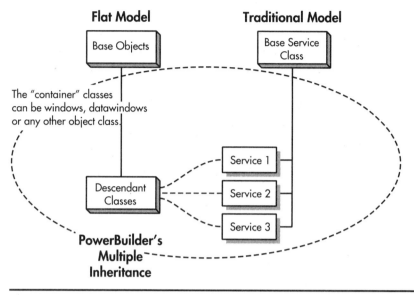

Figure 10.5 The next generation: Service-Based Architecture.

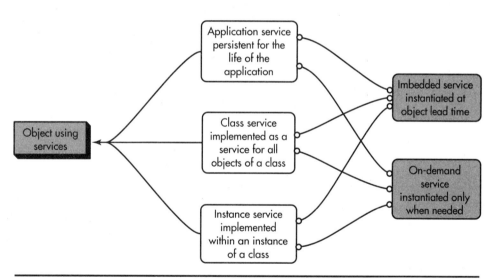

Figure 10.6 Service implementation styles.

makes the object load faster than before because load processing is shifted from a time when delays are noticed to a time when delays are not noticed. Service classes are typically nonvisual in nature, which results in faster load times than visual objects. This architecture can therefore improve performance.

Deciding on implementation.   Now our model is nearing completion. Developers using the classes developed in this fashion have an easier job of object selection. Reusable class developers, on the other hand, are still faced with the choice of which level of object a service should be implemented in. The answer to this is demonstrated in Figure 10.7.

The flexibility of the service classes is such that they can actually be implemented in any layer of the hierarchy, even within other service classes, although more care must be exercised when implementing services within services.

To summarize, we have learned the following:

- *SBA is more powerful:* Service-based architecture is PowerBuilder's multiple inheritance, albeit simulated instead of applied.

- *SBA performs better:* Smaller physical objects are loaded. Services can be loaded when needed, improving overall performance.

- *SBA is more encapsulated:* Processing is encapsulated at the service level; objects are smaller, with less code to maintain.

- *SBA is easier to use:* Objects follow a flatter hierarchy model, enhancing ease of use while services are selected using declarative attributes.

- *SBA is more maintainable and promotes reuse:* Services follow a traditional inheritance model promoting reuse and maintainability.

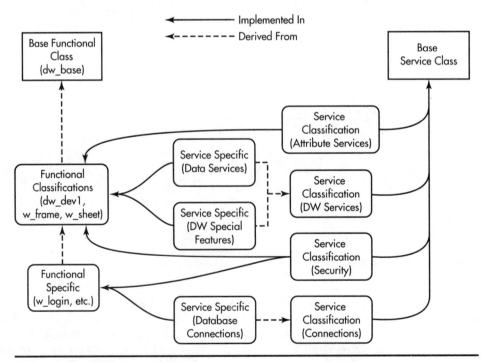

Figure 10.7 The CBM common hierarchy.

- *SBA is more flexible:* Objects need not necessarily be instantiated. Developers can control them by using declarative attributes. Developers can change object capabilities by changing an attribute, not the object's ancestry.[1]

Agreeing on Naming Conventions

The naming conventions of objects might seem trivial, but it is actually crucial to reducing maintenance costs. Having to figure out what an object is before finding out *where* it is, wastes time. When an object or object function describes the object or function clearly and is short enough to reduce the amount of coding, you have succeeded.

Many companies and people have shared their naming conventions with the rest of us. Some of these people were early pioneers and developed a solid groundwork for the rest of us to build on. For this, they deserve our gratitude.

We have (of course!) developed our own standard that we believe is a short enough list to be learned easily, because a concept applies, not just terminology.[2]

Gathering Requirements from Developers and Users

REQUIREMENT: A requirement is a high-level description of an action or condition that must be satisfied to accommodate the needs of the project.

In deciding what our requirements were, we were faced with two questions. How much data do we need to collect about the requirements, and how do we establish the requirements that will provide the most benefit? We found out that the second question was much harder to answer than the first.

For the first step, we realized that the best way to gather the requirements was a poll of developers' object wish lists. This provided us with a list of objects that developers felt would benefit them the most in their development efforts. Developing a survey that asks the right questions eliminates many arguments later in the process. One thing we found that was extremely useful was surveying developers who had just completed a development effort. Their perspectives reflected the current state of the environment and their frustrations (if any) were still fresh enough to provide useful information.

We have developed a survey form that can be used to poll developers and users for their opinion on requirements. It is a very simple form requesting information on the requirement, its expected benefit, who receives the most benefit, and what prompted the requirement. Finally we ask for a priority rating in order to help determine the importance of the requirement to the originator. The form is shown in Figure 10.8.

---

1. Naming conventions are described in Chapter 3.

2. We have included a technical paper and PowerPoint presentation on the latest advancements to SBA on the CD.

Survey Data

Survey ID:				
Survey Name:		Update Date:	April 23, 1996	
Contact:	William Green	Author:	William Green	

Topic

Topic Description

Cost/Benefit Data

Benefit	CBA Value:	1.00
Describe the benefit of this survey item	CBA Rating	Medium

Survey Details

Survey Details

Figure 10.8 Requirement survey form.

The second poll is an end-user poll. All system development ends up on users' desktops. Users are the people who drive business requirements and their requirements are as important as developers' requirements. Many of these requirements, especially when presented as a generic requirements list rather than a specific business need, often came from features and functionality the users were used to having in the commercial applications they worked with.

For companies that are just getting started on the client-server journey with PowerBuilder, this could obviously be restrictive. Polling developers using other development tools will help, but it is not the final answer.

Like developers, users not familiar with the platform may feel restricted in this process. Remind them that they will still bring with them the features and functionality they found useful on whichever platform they have been using. It cannot be emphasized enough that this step should be taken to ensure that developer needs are not the only ones represented. Keep the user community aware of the standard look and feel that using a class library will help provide. This will make them feel more comfortable with new systems more quickly, thereby reducing training costs in the long run.

Remember that viewpoints will differ and that none are invalid. Getting agreement about opposing views on a single requirement may take time, but it will be worth the effort.

Build the Project Requirements List

Combining these lists forms the project requirements list. This list is then narrowed down to a manageable scope through a second voting process in which developers, users, and library architects rank and prioritize the benefits of the requirements, and a cutoff point is established so that a functional library can be developed in a reasonable time frame.

The list in Figure 10.9 shows the results of this information-gathering process, which were obtained from several sources. You may find that it represents many of your own requirements, and may offer some that would not ordinarily be raised in a given environment.

Our field experience has afforded us the opportunity to do a little Monday-morning quarterbacking, reassessing some of the requirements and reevaluating some of the benefits, so our lists are based not only on requirements, but on retrospective thought and new or improved techniques. Figure 10.9 shows our project summary document. We will revisit some of these requirements in much greater detail over the next few chapters of the book.

Cost/Benefit Study of Requirements

A full-blown CBA takes a lot of time and resources that often will cost more than the development effort. We have reduced this to a simple model in which we ask ourselves, the developers, and the users to estimate what portion of a $100 budget they would spend to develop the objects that would satisfy each requirement. We ask them to try to get as close to the $100 as possible, but they may go under or over $100 as the need arises.

What you will invariably find is that when the total exceeds $100, there are actually too many requirements that employees feel are important to include in this project scope. If the total does not reach $100, the general feeling is that there may be key elements in the requirements but there are not enough requirements for this effort to be worthwhile. You will have to make the call when determining what should be included in your project scope, and what should not.

Figure 10.10 shows a partial table of our requirements cost/benefit sheet showing averages we accumulated.

Project Scope Definition

Now that the cost/benefit sheet is completed, we go back to the developers and users and discuss established priorities. This should no longer be a difficult task. With the benefits established and the importance poll results indicating

Project Data

Project ID:	OFR_PROJ		
Project Name:	Project Objectives Collection - Object Framework		
Contact:	William Green	Update Date:	May 16, 1996
		Author:	William Green

Project Description

Description
The objective of this project is to build a collection of reusable classes that will satisfy the following goals: 1. Satisfy more than 80% of infrastructure requirements   2. Provide solid reusable classes to develop business classes   3. Provide cross-platform support   4. Be language-independent, although designed specifically with PowerBuilder in mind

Specific Objectives

Objective	Xref	Status
1. Control multiple instances of the application	OFRO0001	
2. Verify and control system resources	OFRO0002	
3. Maintain application and user preferences	OFRO0003	
4. Provide user feedback	OFRO0004	
5. Establish and maintain the application environment	OFRO0005	
6. Identify and report version information	OFRO0006	
7. Validate user authorization	OFRO0007	
8. Manage application connections	OFRO0008	
9. Support and manage data access	OFRO0009	
10. Handle errors	OFRO0010	
11. Apply application security constraints	OFRO0011	
12. Interface with operating system services	OFRO0012	
13. Manage print settings	OFRO0013	
14. Support the MS Windows clipboard services	OFRO0014	
15. Trace execution and debug environment/objects	OFRO0015	
16. Support interobject communication	OFRO0016	
17. Manage the MDI environment	OFRO0017	
18. Manage dialog windows	OFRO0018	
19. Manipulate and display calendar data	OFRO0019	
20. Support custom visual presentations	OFRO0020	
21. Provide and manage ad-hoc reports	OFRO0021	
22. Implement reusable business/edit classes	OFRO0022	
23. Support remote system administration	OFRO0023	
24. Support netware library access	OFRO0024	
25. Support Lotus note library access	OFRO0025	

Figure 10.9 Project summary form.

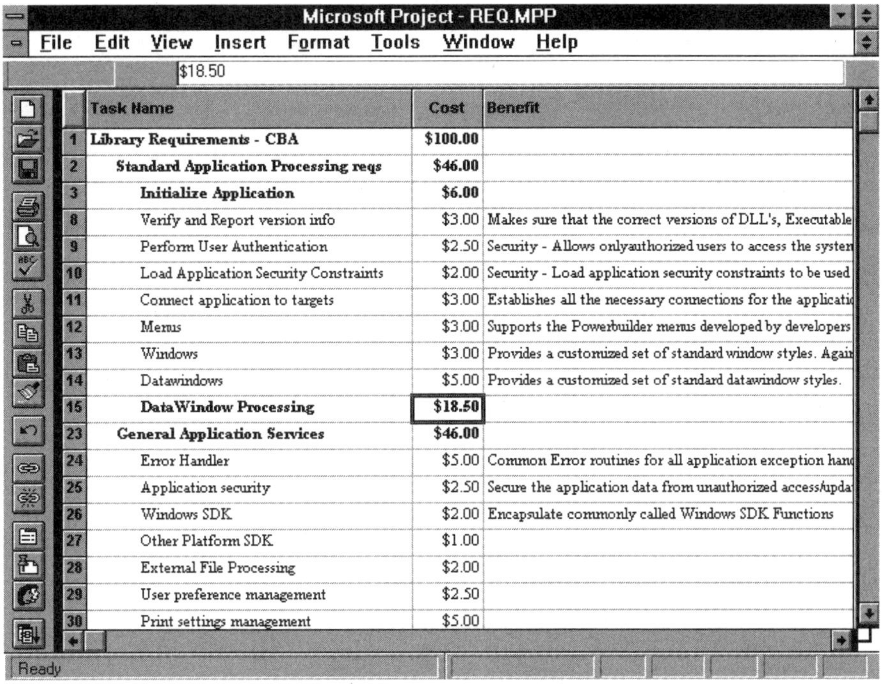

Figure 10.10 Assigning priorities using the $100 approach.

what everyone felt was vital, your priority list should be very close to complete. This is more of a chance to allow anyone to restate a priority that they might feel is too high or too low on the list.

Finally, we need to establish a cutoff point for what we want to accomplish during this development effort. This should be based on the average of what everyone thought the requirement was worth versus the benefit the requirement brings. Keep in mind that the value of the requirement can change very quickly as new needs arise. It is important to use the average of the employees surveyed. We established a cost/benefit rating for our requirements, ranging from high to low. Figure 10.11 is a snapshot of our requirements cost/benefit rating showing the priority ratings we assigned.

Finally, we go through an analysis to determine which requirements are important to us and the users and provide the greatest benefit. This is accomplished by balancing the expected benefit with the current priority rating.

This final list determines the project scope, to which we add a project scope definition statement that describes verbally what we intend to accomplish with this implementation.

Determine Requirement Activities

In breaking the project requirements into activities, remember that the activity must be able to" do something to satisfy the requirement. For example,

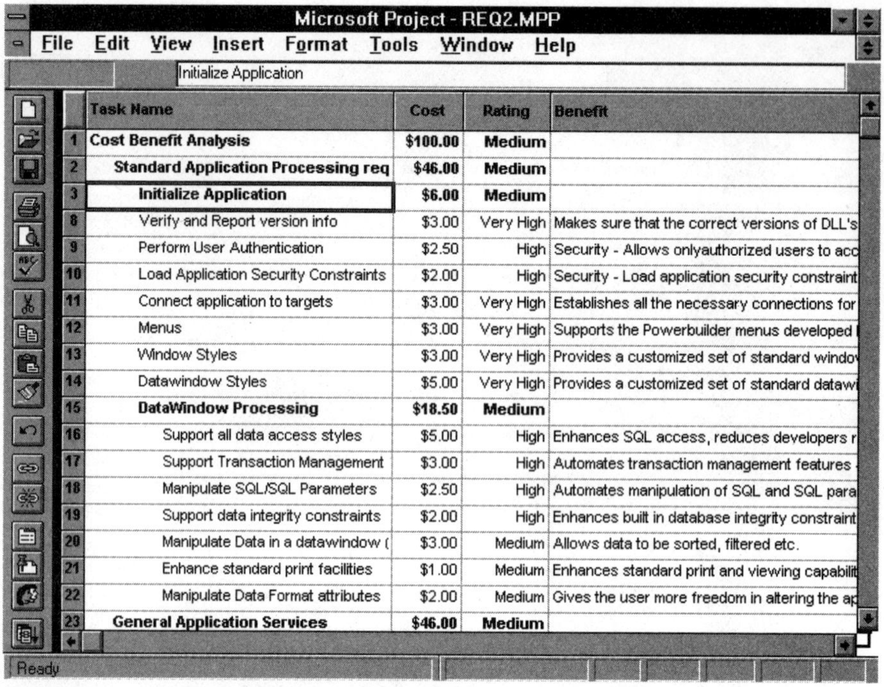

Figure 10.11 Cost/benefit rating.

under the requirement "Manage application connections," there are nine defined activities, as shown in Table 10.1.

Each activity describes what must be done to satisfy all or part of the requirement. For example, connections must be able to capture user information in order for a connection to happen. Notice that there is nothing that defines what a connection is; we have maintained a level of abstraction. This allows us to define generic behavior for connections, thus avoiding the pitfall of defining implementation before the design is complete. Through a reiterative process, we can gather all of the activities necessary to meet the project scope.

Summary

Obviously, a library containing objects to satisfy all of these requirements would take several years to develop, and would be too cumbersome to provide the right level of functionality. We need to take this list of requirements into the next phase of the design and continue to expand on them and build them into, ultimately, powerful classes of objects that will make developers much more productive.

To recap this chapter, we have gathered a bunch of requirements from user surveys and categorized them. Categorizing does little more than apply a

TABLE 10.1 General Connection Services

Activities	Xref ID
Obtain connection data from an external source	
Capture user information	
Check user authorization	
Create a persistent connection	
Maintain a collection of current connections	
Connect to target connection	
Disconnect from target connection	
Provide a connection to application classes	
Maintain connection-specific data for application use	

group name to a set of features, but identification of a requirement is important, regarding both what it is and where the author of the requirement expects it to provide the most benefit.

We also detailed how to solicit the data you need from different people. Remember that not everyone speaks PowerBuilder jargon, or even Windows for that matter, so a requirement may be described by someone who has no knowledge of the capabilities of the tool and is describing a feature he or she is used to using or defining a requirement that was always a wish but was never implemented on the current platform.

We discussed the need to establish design principles early, to agree on an architecture you will use, and to establish naming conventions if none exist.

If you do not have a user base or developer base to solicit, collect all your own ideas, contact other PowerBuilder developers through user groups or electronic mail media, or use some of ours.

Logical Class Definition (Class Library)

Introduction

This chapter focuses on logical class definition. Figure 11.1 shows the focus area.

Using the object synthesis methodology, we begin to analyze the activities for each of the requirements we have defined. Each activity is broken down into methods and attributes that ultimately satisfy the requirement. These methods and attributes also have a test plan associated with them that drives the development of a thorough set of test procedures, resulting in a solid reusable class library that will achieve the benefits expected from a class library. But what are methods and attributes?

Attributes are the data elements of a class or object. Methods are the means by which attributes are affected. Think of methods as the shields that protect attributes from objects outside the realm of the encapsulating object, just as a cell wall in the human body protects the contents of the cell. It is also, like the human blood cells, the vehicle for communication between objects or cells. A message is passed to the method, which in turn directs the message to affect, manipulate, or be manipulated by attributes of the object. Figure 11.2 depicts this mechanism.

In PowerBuilder terms, to access the contents of a datawindow we are required to use a datawindow function to retrieve the contents of a row/column. (GetItem would be a method, whereas GetItemNumber and GetItemString are functions, or physical implementations of the method).

This chapter defines the methods and attributes that are required to satisfy a particular activity. Once the methods and attributes are defined, we go back and group methods and attributes into logical classes. A logical class is a collection of methods and attributes that are logically connected. You will see that there are methods and attributes that are shared across logical classes. These methods and attributes automatically define a service class, a key element of

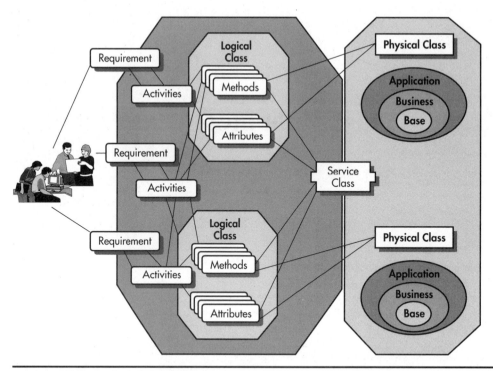

Figure 11.1 Focus on logical class definition.

our class library structure. This is a class that needs to be implemented in more than one object.

Figure 11.3 shows the process flow we use to expand the activities from method definitions through attribute definitions, and finally to class definitions.

Still, the first step is to establish the scope of the project we are about to undertake. We do this by analyzing the requirements we have gathered and developing a cost/benefit analysis (CBA). Once we do this, we will have determined our project scope and we can begin to define the methods and attributes required.

Remember that at this point we are still not defining implementation. We have not yet decided on a class hierarchy or library names; rather, we are establishing the groundwork for the physical design.

Chapter Objectives

The goals of this chapter are to take the requirements to the next level: logical class definition (or requirements analysis). Here we want to make sure we accomplish the following:

A Class is a definition of Methods and Attributes.
Communication is done using messages.

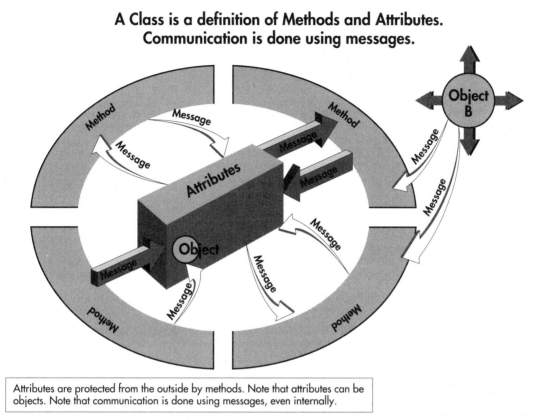

Attributes are protected from the outside by methods. Note that attributes can be objects. Note that communication is done using messages, even internally.

Figure 11.2 Definition of a class.

- Reemphasize design objectives
- Derive methods and attributes for each activity
- Create method test plans and attribute definitions
- Collect methods and attributes to define logical classes

Design Objectives

As previously stated, we want to reemphasize the design requirements in every design phase. Table 11.1 shows the design objectives again.

Defining Logical Classes

Now that we know what requirements define the scope of the project, we can begin the task of defining classes. Unlike an application, where a class can relate to a physical task, a class library tries to provide generic behavior. This

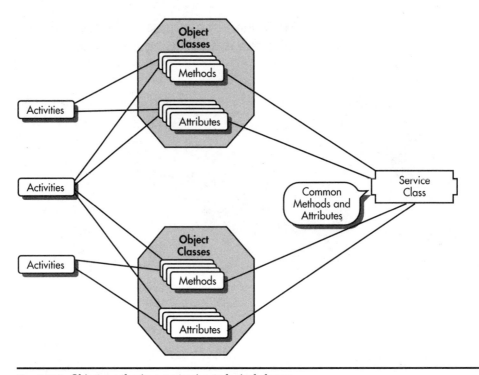

Figure 11.3 Object synthesis: progression to logical classes.

makes the task of logical class definition a little more difficult, but the rules of expanding requirements into classes are very much the same. Expand the requirement into activities, and then into methods and attributes. Once this is accomplished, not a trivial task to be sure, the methods and attributes go through a phase of aggregation. A logical class is made up of methods and attributes that will accomplish a task. This does not mean that a logical class will satisfy a requirement. A requirement may be fulfilled by multiple classes, one or more of which may be a service class (more on service classes a little later in this chapter).

One of the elements to watch during this phase of the design is the object-oriented design depth. In a class library, requirements must be expanded to the lowest level of functionality possible (the what) without defining implementation (the how). The design depth, therefore, is usually at the deepest level possible without defining implementation.

Once the requirements have been expanded into methods and attributes, we go through a process of collecting methods and attributes into logical classes. While this process is going on, we will also be categorizing the type of class. Typing the class is not crucial to the design but helps to portray how the class will be physically designed later on. We have defined the following types of classes:

- *Object class:* a normal class that will ultimately end up being the container class object for developers.

- *Service class:* a class whose methods span multiple requirements. This class will become an integral part of the library.

- *Service collection class:* a class defined as not being part of a requirement. It provides a service to multiple classes and objects, but is not implemented as an interface. In other words, it is a class defined to collect information about services for easy access by objects and interfaces. Classes defined as managers fall into this category.

- *Data interface class:* a class defined as a data repository for information that must be available across multiple classes. An example would be user preference data or application description data.

You will become very familiar with these classes as we begin to build on our design, and the categorizations will become much more obvious when the classes become objects.

TABLE 11.1 Design Objectives

The library must satisfy at least 75% of object requirements for a given project.
The library must be manageable and easy to use and provide as much off-the-shelf usability as possible.
The objects should be kept as simple as possible while providing maximum flexibility and extendibility.
The library must be an extension of the environment, not a replacement or a hindrance.
The library must reduce the time it takes to develop a full-featured PowerBuilder application.
The library must improve the consistency and reliability of PowerBuilder applications.
The library must implement the defined requirements for the application framework within the confines of the PowerBuilder development environment to improve portability to other supported PowerBuilder platforms.
The objects developed as part of the class library must be accessible to existing PowerBuilder applications or applications developed outside of the proposed application framework.
The implementation of the application framework must be independent of the database server.
Each object in the library should be independent of the application framework and of the implementations of other objects.

Expanding Activities

The first step in this phase is to expand requirements into activities that satisfy all or part of a requirement.

When expanding the activity, remember the following: Expand the activity into *logical* methods and attributes. You will have to concentrate on avoiding the natural inclination to design the implementation of an anticipated object. If a method or an attribute appears more than once, mark it as a possible interface class. If an activity spawns another activity, remember to apply the same measures as before to determine importance.

In expanding the activities, we take each one and determine the methods that will satisfy the activity statement. For example, the "retrieve application preferences" activity needs a method to obtain data from an INI file. The method is not "Use the GetProfileString function to get the preference value." This is the how rather than the what. We will expand methods into functions and events during physical design.

Remember that we have not yet begun to define classes. Referring to activities may seem like referring to classes and objects, but we are trying to establish ways to satisfy the activity. How this will be implemented is not yet determined. Keep the language as simple as possible. Referring to methods and attributes as if functions and physical data types are involved would be inviting implementation design to take place.

One key element to help in this effort is to try to forget the language you will use. Language guides implementation. Design should be implementation-independent.

Activity-to-method synthesis

There are really only three rules to follow in expanding activities to methods and attributes.

- Define the *what* not the *how*.
- There must be at least one method for each activity.
- Methods act on attributes, so there should be at least one attribute targeted by each method. This reference may be implied rather than physical.

The first step in method synthesis is to expand the activity into method definitions. Method definitions are high-level descriptions of what the method must do (they define the goal of the method). At this point, we do not determine specifically what the method must do or what the attributes it affects look like. To demonstrate this capability we will look at a few of the activities defined in Chapter 10 and break these out as examples.

**The first requirement: control multiple instances
of the application**

This requirement is based on a need to avoid running the same application more than once. The requirement is quite simple and we defined three activities associated with this requirement:

- Establish whether verification is required.

- Check whether multiple instances exist.

- Take action based on the existence of another instance.

These activities are shown on the requirement form, and along with them we associate a cost/benefit rating and an overall requirement test plan. These are simply to help in prioritizing the work and to provide a check-off to determine when we are done. Figure 11.4 shows the completed requirement definition.

Note the first activity is to check whether this entire activity is even necessary. In some environments, or for a particular application, multiple instances of the application may be allowed without question! So we need an attribute that will tell us whether we need to perform this check. Second, the application needs a method to get and set the attribute. Get and Set are very common methods, and encapsulate the access to an attribute within a method. Remember that the method protects the attributes. Notice that we are not defining implementation. We have described *what* needs to be done for the activity, not *how* to achieve it. I will reiterate this point many times during this chapter as it is a crucial aspect of defining the methods and attributes. Figure 11.5 shows the method definitions expanded into actual method actions and attributes.

Before we go much further into details, let's take a quick tour of the types of methods we typically will define. Knowing this helps to determine actions later on in physical class definition.

Attribute methods act on the attribute.

Attribute methods.   Note that each activity definition explodes down to one or more specific methods, often including Get or Set methods. Remember the diagram showing how methods protect the attributes of a class? You can easily see how the attributes are accessed by methods. The methods that get or set attributes are called attribute methods.

Action methods perform processing using one or more attributes.

Action methods.   Some methods do not take action directly on an attribute. Instead, they perform a particular function and then might use an attribute

Requirement Data

Requirement ID:	OFRR0001		
Requirement Name:	Control multiple instances of the application		
Version:	1.0	Update Date:	April 29, 1996
Survey Xref:	OFRS0169	Author:	William Green

Requirement Definition

Description
Determine whether multiple instances of the application exist and if so, perform some predetermined processing.

Cost/Benefit Data

Benefit	CBA Value:	1.00
Prevents the running of multiple instances of the application if desired by the developer/user.	CBA Rating:	Medium

Activities

Description	Xref
Establish whether verification required	OFRM0101
Check whether multiple instances exist	OFRM0102
Take action based on existence	OFRM0103

Requirement Test Definition

Test Definition
Tests should indicate whether the application is already running and take appropriate action.

Figure 11.4 Requirement definition: control multiple instances of the application.

method to set an attribute. These are called action methods; they define a specific action that is not directly related to the getting and setting of attributes (Get Application Exists and Take Specified Action). These methods perform processing that will exist potentially outside of the activity. Note that we still do not define *how* to perform Get Application Exists. This will come in the physical design.

Activity Data

Activity ID:	OFRM0101		
Activity Name:	Validate multiple instance check required		
Version:	1.0	Update Date:	April 19, 1996
Type:		Author:	William Green

Activity Definition

Description
Validates whether there is a requirement to check for multiple instance syndrome.

Methods and Attributes

Method	Attribute	Expected Result	Test Plan
Get an attribute indicating whether check is required	Multiple Instance Indicator	Gets the Multiple Instance Indicator, which determines whether we need to test for multiple instances	Test what happens if attribute is never set Test with valid attribute
Set an attribute indicating whether check is required (reciprocal method)	Multiple Instance Indicator	Sets the Multiple Instance Indicator	Test what happens if attribute is never set Test with valid attribute

Figure 11.5 Method definition: multiple instance check required.

Reciprocal methods are defined to maintain object harmony.

Reciprocal methods. Quite often we will define a method required for an activity where there is an obvious need for another method that counteracts the defined method. Often these take the form of Gets or Sets. These are methods defined as reciprocal methods. Based on the laws of nature (which we are modeling in object-oriented technology, aren't we?), every action has an equal but opposite reaction. In OO-speak, this translates to "every Get Attribute method requires a Set Attribute method. Likewise, every Set method requires a corresponding Get method." If this activity needs to Get an attribute's value, we know there will be a need to Set the attribute's value. We define this method now because we know it will be required later. Reciprocal methods are usually attribute methods that do not strictly belong to this activity.

Attribute definitions. In Figure 11.5 we saw the actions that must take place to accommodate the activity definition. These are the actual methods we are defining for the activity. Note that each method has a test plan associated with it. Also note that the methods have an attribute associated with them. This is the means by which we link attributes and test plans to the methods, even at this early stage. Let's dig into an attribute or two to see how these are defined.

Attribute definitions: classifying the attribute

Breaking out the definition of the attributes means we take each attribute and attempt to classify it. We are not defining the data type, but the different values and types of values an attribute might have. Figure 11.6 shows the attribute definition for the attribute Multiple Instances Allowed.

Here we can see that the attribute has characteristics and allowed values. The characteristics here show that the attribute might well be held in a data repository with other application and user preferences, but to make that assumption now would be to define implementation, which we want to avoid.

Going back to our activities, let's look at the next activity definition. We can see a few different methods associated, which are shown in Figure 11.7. Here we can see another two methods defined. Check whether another instance of the application exists and then set an indicator that indicates whether another instance exists.

Attribute Data

Attribute ID:	OFRA0001			
Name:	Multiple Instances Indicator			
Version:	1.0		Update Date:	August 11, 1995
			Author:	William Green

Attribute Definition

Description
Indicator that stores a value indicating whether multiple instances of an application are allowed.

Characteristics

ID	Location	Allowed Values
	Preferences Data Repository	True, False

Figure 11.6 Attribute definition: Multiple Instances Indicator.

Activity Data

Activity ID:	OFRM0102		
Activity Name:	Check whether multiple instances exist		
Version:	1.0	Update Date:	April 96
		Author:	William Green

Activity Definition

Description
Check whether another instance of this application exists. Set an attribute to indicate that an instance exists.

Methods and Attributes

Method	Acts Upon	Expected Result	Test Plan
Check for application instance	Application Handle	Returns an indication of whether the application is already running	Test with another instance of the application running Test with no other instance of the application running
Set an attribute indicating whether multiple instances exist	Multiple Instances Exist	Attribute is set to a true or false value	If another instance is running, value should be true If not, value should be false

Figure 11.7 Activity definition: check whether multiple instances of application exist.

It is only when we get to the third method that we begin to see some more complex methods. Take a look at Figure 11.8 to see the methods required.

Now we can see a few different methods being shown. The first is a normal Attribute method, getting the Action to Be Taken indicator. When we look at the attribute definition, however, we can see something a little different about this attribute definition. A link is defined to a reusable attribute list.

A reusable attribute list is a list of values that are predefined and can be used in several places. For example, a list of possible button combinations on a message box might be a valid reusable attribute list because there is no reason why we should redefine these attributes over and over again. So, we simply indicate that the attribute is taken from a list of valid combinations.

Method Data

Method ID:	OFRM0003			
Method Name:	Take action based on existence of another instance of the application			
Version:	1.0		Update Date:	April 29, 1996
			Author:	William Green

Method Definition

Description
When another instance of the application exists, some action must be taken. This method defines the action based on defined attribute settings.

Actions and Attributes

Action Method	Acts Upon	Expected Result	Test Plan
Get action attribute	Multiple Instance Action	Gets the action to take if another instance of the application is found	Test that attribute style returns the action required
[Warn User]	Application Message: Application already running	Displays a warning message to the user	Verify message is correct and that correct button options are set
Take action based on indicator	Application Flow	Continue, halt and activate original instance or halt processing	Check that correct logic flow ensues

Figure 11.8 Method definition: take action based on existence of application.

Reusable attribute lists might be classified as enumerated data types in languages that support such typing. Figure 11.9 shows a typical reusable list definition.

Another new element shown in this activity is an application message. We immediately create an application message definition, which serves two purposes. First, it allows us to keep track of messages we might need in the classes; second, it defines the options we expect to see on the message display. Figure 11.10 depicts our message definition form.

Note how the message definition not only spells out the text of the message (allowing for optional text portions) but also defines what buttons might appear as user-selectable options. Finally, note how the return values from the message are set (in this case) as constants. We have an additional cross-

List Data

List ID:	OFRLS001		
List Name:	Multiple Instance Action Indicator list		
Version:	1.0	Update Date:	August 11, 1995
		Author:	William Green

List Definition

Description
List of valid actions: Combine values to determine actions allowed Example: 15 = Show Message, Allow Continue, Activate Original, and Halt

Values and Definitions

Link	Value	Definition
	1	Show Application Message (Continue, Activate, Halt)
	2	Allow Continue
	4	Allow Activate Original
	8	Allow Halt

Figure 11.9 Reusable attribute list.

reference form where we store all defined constants. This is simply a list of the name of the constant, a category, and a value.

Finally, we want to visit the column of the activity definition form that highlights the test plans. We showed that there was a method test plan associated with each method. This is one of the key aspects of our methodology. The test plans are defined long before a class is even developed or designed. Once we define the test plan for the method, it travels with the method wherever it gets used, resulting in comprehensive and successful test plans. One of the test plans we defined was a two-part procedure: Test the method with another instance of the application running, and test without another instance of the application running. We document this test procedure in a form such as the one shown in Figure 11.11.

The method test procedure defines test cases that will determine the success of the method. This test procedure highlights two test cases. If we take a look at one of these, you will see something like the definition shown in Figure 11.12.

Here you can see outlined the steps that a developer would need to know to build this test procedure. The procedure is already named, even though

Message Data

Message ID:	OFRX0001
Message Name:	User Message: Application already running
Version:	1.0

		Update Date:	April 29, 1996
		Author:	William Green

Message Definition

Definition
Displays a message to the user indicating that another instance of the application is running. Buttons shown depend on the Multiple Instance Action indicator.

Message Text

Description
Another instance of the application is running. Continue? [To continue, press Yes]. [To revert to original instance, press No], [To quit processing, press Cancel]

[..] indicates an optional portion of the text.

Message Attributes

Button	Default	Button Action	Return Value
Yes	Yes	Indicates to continue with the process	Constant Yes
No	No	Stop current processing and revert to original application	Constant No
Cancel	No	Stop current application launch	Constant Cancel

Figure 11.10 Application message definition.

we do not have a clue what the class or object will be. This is one of our goals: spending time up front to cover the details we normally try frantically to catch up on later when time is much more precious.

Other activities. Some activities are the result of knowledge of the environment rather than a more tangible self-standing activity. Menus, windows, and datawindows are examples of these. They are activities that refer to collective implementations of other activities.

Test Procedure Data

Test Procedure ID:	OFRT0004			
Test Procedure Name:	Test the check for existence of application			
Version:	1.0		Update Date:	April 96
			Author:	William Green

Test Procedure Definition

Description
Test with another instance of the application running
Test with no other instance of the application running

Test Procedure Objectives and Expected Results

Test Case ID	Test Objective	Expected Result
OFRC_001	Return true from test if another instance of the application exists	Constant Exists
OFRC_002	Return false from test if another instance of the application does not exist	Constant DoesNotExist

Figure 11.11 Method test plan: test for existence of application.

The activities for menus, for example, are actually derived from other activities. An example of this is the ability to copy data to and from the clipboard. The method for the activity is Copy Data to Clipboard. A menu option would support the clipboard methods. A datawindow may also support the clipboard methods by invoking the clipboard methods on the menu. The reason menus, windows, and datawindows are included is to force thought, at least on methods that are specific to the objects. A menu must support synchronization of menu attributes, windows must manage their appearance and location, and datawindows have several required processing methods.

Using the methodology described above, we can continue to break out each activity into method definitions, methods, and attributes.

When we have completed the method definitions, we need to define classes. A class is a logical collection of methods and attributes used to form the basis of objects. What this means is that through a process of collecting methods and attributes from the method definitions we have done, we can begin to define classes.

Test Case Data

Test Case ID:	OFRC_001		
Test Case Name:	Duplicate Application Instance: Perform Check for True		
Version:	1.0	Update Date:	April 30, 1996
Test Plan Xref:	OFRT0004	Author:	William Green

Test Case Definition

Description
Return true from test if another instance of the application exists

Test Case Steps:

Step	Step Data	Expected Result
1	Test procedure initialization: Make sure environment is clear	Application should not be in the environment.
2	Launch application	Application should start up. Method should return FALSE.
3	Launch application again	Application should begin to initialize. Method should return TRUE.
4	Test procedure cleanup	TBD

Figure 11.12 Test case definition: duplicate application instance.

The process of collecting the methods and attributes that make up a class requires that we first take the methods defined for all activities and create one single list. We sort the list by method name and attribute, which allows us to go through the list and make our method and attribute names a little more consistent. Figure 11.13 shows a portion of our list of methods (based on what we have done so far).

What we then need to do is go through the list and assign a logical class, which is done simply by grouping and identifying like methods that can then be assigned to classes as they develop. We do this by adding a column to the methods cross reference as shown in Figure 11.14. Now we sort the table again, this time by logical class name and then by method and attribute. This gives us a nice list of the classes we expect to need. As you can see, there are four logical classes so far: Application Flow Control, Application Initialization, Attribute Management (various flavors), and User Feedback. This may seem like a lot of work, but as your definitions grow, so will your understanding of why this is necessary.

Method	Attribute	Expected Result	Test Plan
Check for application instance	Application Handle	Returns an indication of whether the application is already running	Test with another instance of the application running Test with no other instance of the application running
Display Application Message	Application Message: Application already running	Displays a warning message to the user	Verify that message is correct and that correct button options are set
Get action attribute	Multiple Instance Action	Gets the action to take if another instance of the application is found	Test that attribute style returns the action required
Get an attribute indicating whether check is required	Multiple Instance Indicator	Gets the Multiple Instance Indicator, which determines whether we need to test for multiple instances	Test what happens if attribute is never set Test with valid attribute
Set an attribute indicating whether check is required	Multiple Instance Indicator	Sets the Multiple Instance Indicator	Test what happens if attribute is never set Test with valid attribute
Set an attribute indicating whether multiple instances exist	Multiple Instances Exist	Attribute is set to a true or false value	If another instance is running, value should be true If not, value should be false
Take action based on indicator	Application Flow	Continue, halt, and activate original instance or halt processing	Check that correct logic flow ensues

Figure 11.13   Cross-reference: methods without logical class identification.

Summary

In this chapter we reemphasized the design objectives. We then took the requirements list generated, performed a cost/benefit analysis for each activity, and produced a final list of requirements that defined our project scope. We then took the requirements and expanded them into method definitions. For each method definition, we determined the methods and attributes. For the attributes, we defined tangible values wherever possible. These were all documented in the method definition document.

Finally, we collected methods and attributes into logical classes by class type and produced a class definition. We documented these in our class definition document. These two documents, combined with the reusable attributes list,

Method	Attribute	Expected Result	Test Plan	Logical Class
Take action based on Multiple Instance Action indicator	Multiple Instance Action	Continue, halt, and activate original instance or halt processing	Test all combinations of Multiple Instance Action	Application Process Flow
Check for application instance	Application Handle	Returns an indication of whether the application is already running	Test with another instance of the application running Test with no other instance of the application running	Application Service Instance Check
Set an attribute indicating whether multiple instances exist	Multiple Instances Exist	Attribute is set to a true or false value	If another instance is running, value should be true If not, value should be false	Application Service Instance Check
Get Multiple Instance Action Attribute	Multiple Instance Action	Gets the action to take if another instance of the application is found	Test that attribute style returns the action required	Application Service Instance Check
Get an Attribute indicating whether check is required	Multiple Instance Indicator	Gets the Multiple Instance Indicator, which determines whether we need to test for multiple instances.	Test what happens if attribute is never set Test with valid attribute	Application Service Instance Check
Set an attribute indicating whether check is required	Multiple Instance Indicator	Sets the Multiple Instance Indicator	Test what happens if attribute is never set Test with valid attribute	Application Service Instance Check
Display Application Message	Application Message: Application already running	Displays a warning message to the user	Verify message is correct and that correct button options are set	User Feedback Application Message

Figure 11.14 Cross-reference: methods with logical class identification.

form our requirements analysis document. We have now successfully completed our logical design.

What should be apparent is that this process is not an easy one, or one that should be approached with trepidation. The steps are complex, yet flow into each other. It is not easy to design a class correctly, but using this methodology will help you to do so.

Physical Class Design

Introduction

Welcome to Physical Class Design 101. At last we can begin to create a picture of what our objects will look like. If the previous steps have been done well, this step will flow smoothly, although there will probably be some heated debates in your design group as to how and where objects and object classes fit together. This process will be a fruitful one, though, as there is a more definite goal: clearly defined object classes ready for construction. This is a much more tangible (and therefore satisfying) result.

For this reason, it is also easy to get carried away in this phase. Make sure your team remains focused on your project scope. Some new ideas will arise during this phase, a few of which you may include in your end product. Others should be added to the future expansion list. Do not allow the project scope to escape you now.

Designing physical classes brings up many of the issues PowerBuilder application designers face every day. How many times have you looked at an object that you, or someone else, developed, and said, "We should have done this differently," or "An ancestor class would have been really useful," or "we made this much too complex." My very first project involved developing reusable objects along with an application. I could easily do both today in less than half the time it took me then. Looking back on my early days with PowerBuilder, I realized that what I had missed were some definitive guidelines on developing reusable classes, guidelines that would help to define and design the objects correctly the first time. The "dive in and develop" methodology that is often used simply does not work. The first reusable classes I built, even though I spent considerable time on the design of the objects, would barely be considered object-oriented. Remember that there is no substitute for experience. Having an experienced developer on your team during this phase will help you avoid some pitfalls early on.

Spend some time in this phase revisiting designs from different angles. Remember that application developers will use these objects. Keep your design objectives in mind for every object, and do not be afraid to set up a class in design and modify the class later. Until construction begins, you have free reign over your creative abilities. You will need less time during the construction phase if this phase is done well.

For the same reason, this is the most crucial step in the process. Mistakes made during design, if carried over into development, can prove extremely costly. Catch the mistakes now, and cost is minimal. Revisiting a design after development is not feasible in an object-oriented environment. A single change to an object's entry point can affect many users. The goal is to define the entry points clearly and correctly. The back-end code, or other objects used beyond the developer's interface, can be modified without fear because the entry points are visible only to your reusable classes. This is another feature of object-oriented development. Objects should be easily modifiable without impact.

If complete sets of functionality are omitted, the impact is less severe. We show how to prepare your object for future modification using virtual methods. Virtual methods, as opposed to their definition in a language such as C++, are entry points to an object where the back-end code or interobject links are not defined. Having the entry point available means that applications using the library can code to these entry points knowing that when the functionality is completed, their application will not require modification to gain access to the functionality. Do not be afraid to incorporate entry points into your objects if the entry point is clearly defined and is not expected to change.

These, and many other techniques, are discussed in this chapter. We also completely design several object classes to fully demonstrate how these techniques help to build accuracy and confidence.

Chapter Objectives

In this chapter, we need to keep our design objectives in mind. Along with these design objectives, we have identified the following goals:

- Maintain our design objectives
- Adhere to our design principles
- Use our design methodology
- Design the needed class hierarchy
- Define the functions, events, and attributes for each class
- Define performance metrics
- Build an object test plan

As we go through the steps of designing the physical objects and their ancestral hierarchy, we need to keep one very important goal in mind: the KISS principle (Keep it simple, Sir!).

Maintaining Our Design Objectives

The design objectives were defined in Chapter 11. We need to continually re-mind ourselves about these objectives. Although there is a great deal of self-satisfaction in designing and building a class library, remember that you have two levels of users—developers and end-users—who are relying on high-quality functionality and easy-to-use features. To continue to ensure that we stay on track to meet our design objectives, I again include the De-sign Objectives Checklist (Table 12.1).

Adhering to Design Principles

Everyone should have principles. But what good is having principles if you do not adhere to them?

The methodology we used to design our library adheres to some basic design principles:

- Avoid the use of global variables.
- Use nonvisual objects (NVOs) for nongraphical processing.

TABLE 12.1 Design Objectives

The library must satisfy at least 75% of object requirements for a given project.
The library must be manageable and easy to use and provide as much off-the-shelf usabil-ity as possible.
The objects should be kept as simple as possible while providing maximum flexibility and extendibility.
The library must be an extension of the environment, not a replacement or a hindrance.
The library must reduce the time it takes to develop a full-featured PowerBuilder appli-cation.
The library must improve the consistency and reliability of PowerBuilder applications.
The library must implement the defined requirements for the application framework within the confines of the PowerBuilder development environment to improve portability to other supported PowerBuilder platforms.
The objects developed as part of the class library must be accessible to existing Power-Builder applications or applications developed outside of the proposed application framework.
The implementation of the application framework must be independent of the database server.
Each object in the library should be independent of the application framework and of the implementations of other objects.

- Build a solid, identifiable class hierarchy with common methods.
- Identify object styles, types, and scopes.
- Use declarative services.
- Use pointers to declared objects.
- Develop and use constants.
- Design application templates.
- Use and extend the PowerBuilder environment as much as possible.

Following these principles will help you avoid many of the traps that await the unwary designer during the construction phase. I have seen many objects redesigned during the construction phase as the library architect realizes that the design will not meet the design objectives. You may have different design principles, but your ultimate goal is still the same. You must make sure you at least address the issues of using constants, templates, and pointers, avoiding globals, using NVOs, and extending the environment as much as possible. The result will be a faster, more reusable, easier-to-use class library.

Avoiding globals

Beware the global variable. It waits patiently to be used, appearing friendly, but is ready to stab reusability in the back.

Using global variables violates the most basic principle of object orientation. Making a variable available to every object appears to be useful, and at times even necessary, but every object that references a global variable, or a global external function, requires the globally declared object to be carried with it and redeclared if reused in another application. This can be quite a problem. For example, a global external function is declared to call a Windows SDK function. For this example we will use GetSystemMetrics(). This is a simple function that returns a variable of type long containing information about your environment. We create an object that calls this SDK function when needed. The object turns out to be useful because of its encapsulated functionality. If we want to reuse the object, we have to declare the external function in every application that needs it. If we declare the function as a local external function in the object, simply reusing the object ensures that the declared function is accessible.

Using global variables also violates the principle of encapsulation. Encapsulation dictates that the attributes and methods of an object should be "hidden" from all other objects other than the required public access methods defined by the developer. A global variable is accessible to all objects and can be modified unexpectedly. Again, the problem this creates is demonstrable using an example.

A global variable is declared to hold a user ID for an application. This variable is then expected to contain this information for the duration of the application. When some of the objects in the application are reused by another application, the global variable must be declared for that application, too. The developer of the second application requires a user ID field to use for an e-mail connection, notices the global variable, and assumes that it is usable. Now you no longer have a guaranteed value in the variable, and application errors can result.

Avoiding the use of global variables is not easy. There are times when a globally available variable (or object) would make life simple. We need to focus on object encapsulation to ensure that we do not need any global variables. We have found that every global variable we thought was necessary was really needed only for specific objects or object classes, and thus could be instantiated within the object or object class. Some developers use their MDI frame as a holding pen for "globally accessible" variables. Although this is infinitely better than a global variable, it still is not the complete solution. A method has to be defined to access the frame window by hard typing, which, in turn, makes the frame less reusable. If the variables are contained in the base class of a frame, and all applications inherit their frame window from this class, the problem is alleviated a little more. However, this assumes that all the "globally accessible" variables are defined in the base class. Again, developers are restricted.

The only solution that makes sure that the developer continues to have free reign of the environment is to define the variables at the class level of the objects that require access to the variables. The use of services and object brokers helps alleviate this symptom. A service is a collection of methods that provide functionality to an object or group of objects. An object broker is a specialized object whose sole responsibility is to be aware of the objects around it and to be able to direct messages between objects that are (and should be) totally unaware of each other.

Does this rule apply to global functions?   Yes and no. A global function is different in that it encapsulates functionality and is itself an object, an attribute desired in object-oriented applications. The global function is also accessible to all objects in the application. The only problems with using a global function are the lack of the ability to inherit and extend the function if a variation or extension of the function is required, and the fact that the loading and unloading of function objects is not in the developer's control. You can code around these issues by calling a global function from within another global function and declaring and creating global functions dynamically into reserved memory areas. Generally speaking, you would be better off grouping functionality into NVOs, which can be inherited, extended, or overridden more easily. This does not mean you should never use a global function, but you should take the time to justify the need for the function to be declared as global. If functional boundaries are clearly defined, global functions are seldom justifiable.

According to developers at Powersoft, global functions are not loaded piece-meal into memory depending on script length, a myth I subscribed to until looking into it for this book. A function is an object in PowerBuilder and, as such, is loaded entirely into memory when needed. The difference between a function object and an NVO is that you are responsible for creating and destroying the NVO. PowerBuilder automatically unloads the global function from memory after an elapsed period. This implies that a global function may be loaded and reloaded (a potentially slow task) each time the function gets used, whereas an NVO would be loaded and unloaded when needed as determined by the developer. This level of control may or may not be what you desire. We prefer to use the power of the nonvisual object.

Using NVOs for nongraphical processing

The nonvisual object, or custom class object as it is now known, is one of the most powerful features in PowerBuilder. This object comes closest in defining a true class, although it cannot contain graphical qualities. Even though the object is now called a custom class, if we look at the object class hierarchy, the nonvisual object class is still evident. Descended directly from a PowerObject, the building block of all PowerBuilder objects, it carries with it very little overhead, making it one of the quicker loading and executing objects available.

The nonvisual object is also available as a standard class or a C++ class in PowerBuilder 4 and 5. These forms of NVOs enhance the power of the development tool even more, enabling developer access to objects that were only wished for before. PowerBuilder 5.0 also allows nonvisual objects to be compiled as OLE 2.0 Inbound Automation Servers, a topic we address later in the book. Figure 12.1 shows the nonvisual class hierarchy.

One of the key elements we used throughout our library is the custom class. We used nonvisual objects heavily as services, object brokers, service managers, and data structures. There are multiple reasons for this, the main one being that the nonvisual object, being higher up in the object class hierarchy, carries very little overhead. The object can be created and destroyed as needed and can encapsulate attributes, functions, and events. This object can also be used to encapsulate business logic, making it even more powerful.

The standard classes offered in PowerBuilder 5 include the datastore or nonvisual datawindow. We immediately created a class of datastore objects for our own use. Many of our general datawindow services were built into this object, with a few others that are specific to our needs for this object. We also built custom class objects for the other standard custom classes available. This will be revisited in various parts of the book as the need arises.

One thing PowerBuilder allows you to do is to modify an object that will be used as a PowerBuilder global object, such as the error, message, or transaction objects. We felt that this might be beneficial and powerful, but it again detracts from the reusability of the application. Every application that uses the

Figure 12.1 The nonvisual class hierarchy.

object will have to change the global objects specified, and also exposes a danger for future upgrades to the environment.

If you choose to use these objects and change your environment, I suggest you do it with careful consideration of the implications of such a change.

The C++ Class Builder, optionally available in the PowerBuilder Enterprise edition, is a real door opening. Now an object can be created that is hot-wired into a C++ DLL, which is a great speed improvement. However, this feature is limited to new C++ DLLs. It would have been used far more in the object framework were it available to attach to an existing DLL and build the hot-wired PowerBuilder object. We opted not to introduce C++ objects into our library, mainly due to the cross-platform issues we were trying to avoid. In addition, the compiled nature of PowerBuilder 5.0 detracts from the performance gains once touted by the C++ Class Builder.

Using the C++ Class Builder can add speed of execution to your application, but decreases its portability. If multiplatform convergence is an issue for you, the C++ Class Builder should be approached with caution.

For the most part, we stuck to the custom class, the old nonvisual object that has become so familiar to us. An important PowerBuilder 4 enhancement to this object was making PostEvent available as a function. The other functions available on the nonvisual class are shown in Figure 12.2.

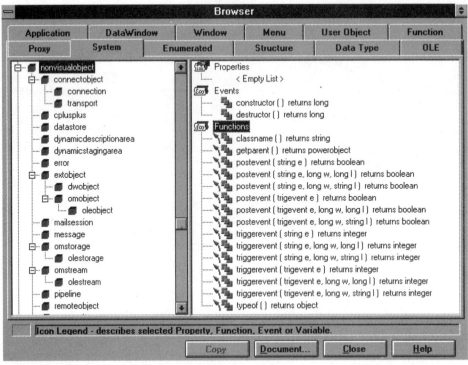

Figure 12.2   The nonvisual object (custom class) functions.

Services or service modules

One of the methods of keeping your object hierarchies as flat as possible, while providing the maximum amount of functionality possible, is to use a service object. These are typically nonvisual classes that are instantiated within an object class, depending on the need. For example, a datawindow that requires SQL processing might instantiate a SQL service that can build and manipulate SQL. The service would not be instantiated if the datawindow did not need the SQL processing capabilities. This reduces overhead and enhances ease of use because developers do not have to look at code they are not using.

Determining when to instantiate the service is influenced by several factors:

- *Persistence required:* How long should the service be made available and when should it be created?

- *Commonality of functionality:* If services will be common to different object classes, then the service should be made more global in nature and also be more persistent. If the service relates more specifically to the active object, it might be required on each instance of the object class.

- *Performance:* If object performance is critical, it would be wise to have the services instantiated before the object is instantiated.

To this end, we can identify three different styles of services:

- *Static services,* which are always required by the object or class of objects. Services that manage the object's attributes are typical of this style.

- *Declarative services,* which are instantiated depending on developer/user set choices. Services that distinguish different behavior typically fall into this category, such as SQL processing on a datawindow object.

- *On-demand services,* which are a permanent part of the object, but are instantiated only when needed and then destroyed after use. Error handling is typical of this style.

Even with these styles, there are different implementation methods available for the services, as follows (these are discussed in more detail later in this chapter):

- *Application (global) services:* services available to the entire application
- *Class services:* services available to a class of objects
- *Object services:* services available to a specific object
- *Service managers:* services to manage the services defined

Application services: global service modules. We have already discussed the need to avoid the use of global variables. But, there are some occasions when you really need a service available globally. One example of this is an object manager that tracks which window, menu, and objects are currently in control. The way to create the service as a global service without using a global variable is as follows:

1. Create the object that will encapsulate the processing needs. Save this object using a normal naming convention such as cc_ofr_object_manager.
2. Create an inherited level of this service using the name you will use in your application, such as ObjMgr.
3. Instantiate the service in your application open event; thus, ObjMgr=CREATE ObjMgr.

ObjMgr is now a globally accessible service in your application. NOTE: Be sure to destroy the service in your Application Close event as follows:

```
IF isValid(ObjMgr) THEN DESTROY ObjMgr
```

The drawback of this approach is that the object is not easily visible in the debugger. To you as a class library developer this may not seem to be much of a hindrance, but to someone using your library, it could be a severe handicap.

Class services: implementing shared variable services. Class services are services that are required by all members of a class. For example, we have a
datawindow user object class that we use instead of the standard datawindow
object. This user object class has built-in functionality to manage its attributes
and handle retrieves, inserts, and deletes. Most of the services for this object
class pertain specifically to the instance of the class, such as attribute management. Other services are more general in nature, such as error handling,
and do not vary from instance to instance. For this type of service, we determined that the best performance boost we could attain would be to have the
service instantiated a single time for all instances of the class. This means
that the service is not made available until needed, but once created, remains
available until all instances of the datawindow class are closed. To do this, we
created a new type of service called the shared service module. This relies on
one of the less-used features of PowerBuilder, the shared variable.

The shared variable is a seldom-used variable that is available to an entire
class of objects: The variable is defined once for a class of objects. When the
shared variable's data changes, its changed attribute is visible to all instances
of the class. One minor problem arises, though. Shared variables are automatically scoped as private variables. They are private to the object class and
are therefore useful only to that class and instances of the class. In the world
of defining classes intended to be inherited, the usefulness of this variable dis-
sipates. Only the ancestor class can affect the variable, and the variable is not
exposed to the class's descendants.

It seemed a shame to waste an obviously valuable tool, so we figured out
that the variable could still be used if a public method of access was provided
to the variable. The solution? Define an access method for the shared variable
that defines a more public pointer to the variable. Again, the usefulness
seemed limited. Pointers can be established only to objects. Data types such as
strings and integers are still limited to the defined class. This is okay. We need
the strategy to work only for objects, specifically our shared service objects.
Still, we found a few more obstacles along the way. Defining the access methods in the ancestor was not enough. When inherited, the methods now pointed
to the descendant class. The pointer definition had to be done in the ancestor
class, and had to point to the ancestor class when instantiated in a descendant
class. This meant we had to make sure the instantiation calls to the service object had to use hard typing; that is, the reference had to use the object's physical name rather than the keyword *This*.

Using NVOs as services means physically creating the object. This means
we need to keep control of the object and make sure it was created only once
per class. Figure 12.3 shows what we are trying to achieve.

> *Goal: Instantiate the service object as part of the ancestor object in such a
> way that only one copy of the service is instantiated and is available to all
> objects of the class and its descendants.*

The Constructor event of our base object triggers the object's Setup event,
which is used to establish default attributes. This is followed by firing the Init

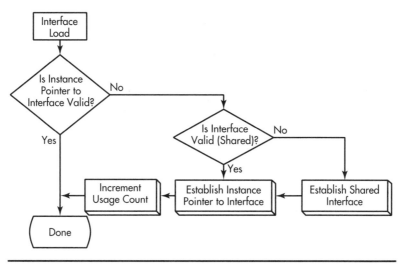

Figure 12.3 Establishing a shared service interface.

event, which then performs initialization functions using the attributes. The Setup event is where we allow the developer to establish the attributes of the object that will control which services are instantiated. Figure 12.4 shows the Setup event script from our datawindow user object.

This script shows how we instantiate our datawindow attribute manager service as an "always-required instance service." By this we mean that the service is always required, and is therefore instantiated as soon as possible, whereas "instance service" indicates that the service is required for each instance of the datawindow object. The next two functions are our attribute default settings. These specialized functions take an array of constants as input and call a function on the datawindow attribute manager, which sets the attributes accordingly. This technique allows us to define a set of three functions to handle all of our attributes instead of a pair of wrapper functions for each attribute. The constants (such as Const.dw_StatusBar) have specific array index values so the array processing is direct and fast. Adding an attribute to the object is a matter of adding a constant with a new array value. (The array could also be replaced by a datastore object in PowerBuilder 5.0).

Our final function is one that establishes the SQL access style for the object. Our SQL Processor object is instantiated if we indicate that SQL will be used. This also results in the SetTransObject() being fired.

In Figure 12.5 we see the call being made to the function that will instantiate the service objects required. In this example, we are calling a function to instantiate our datawindow column attribute service module. If we have selected automatic column attribute management, then this service will look at the datawindow and extract information pertaining to the columns. This can then be used later on for other processing needs such as sorting. If manual column manipulation is selected, we provide another function where the developer can provide column information to be used.

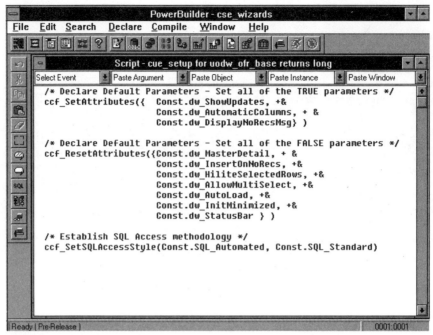

Figure 12.4 Ancestor object Setup event.

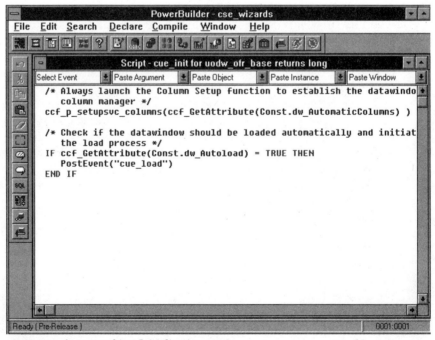

Figure 12.5 Ancestor object Initialization event.

We also determine at this point whether data are automatically loaded into the datawindow (via an attribute setting) and initiate the datawindow object's Load event.

If we look at how the service is instantiated, we can see that this service is an on-demand service; that is, it is instantiated if required, and each object instantiates its own copy of the service. Datawindow column information is specific to the object. Figure 12.6 shows how this service is loaded.

Sometimes, however, we would like to instantiate the service at the class level. This would be done for services that contain no object specific data, but rather a predetermined set of functionality that is required by all objects of the class (in our example, the datawindow class). For example, error handling is required by all datawindow objects, and the standard error handling does not vary from object to object. For this purpose, we instantiate a special form of the service. First, we declare a variable for the service. The variable is declared as a shared variable. This makes the service persistent for the class. Because the shared variable is automatically private, however, we need to establish a pointer to the service for each instance of the object class. For this, we declare an instance variable of the same type (but not the same name) as the shared variable. We will get a pointer to the shared variable and assign this to the instance variable, thus establishing a public pointer to a shared interface (or service) module. To demonstrate this, Figure 12.7 shows the service setup function ccf_p_SetupSVC_Error().

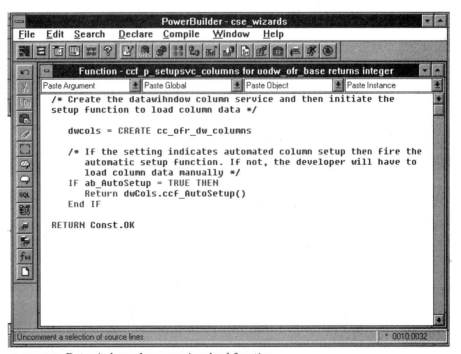

Figure 12.6 Datawindow column services load function.

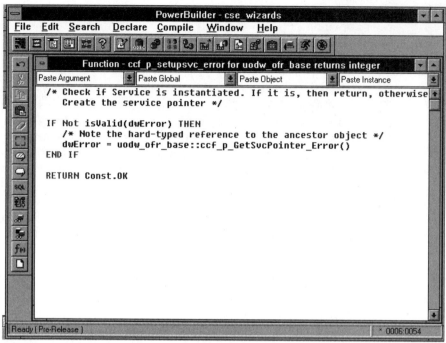

Figure 12.7 Error services load function.

As you can see, the function checks whether the service exists. If it does not, it calls another function to get the service pointer. Note that the function call *requires* that the actual ancestor object be hard-typed to allow access to the shared variable. The ccf_p_GetSvcPointer_Error() function does the rest, as shown in Figure 12.8. This code physically creates the service object only once for the entire class of objects. Each subsequent instance of the container class instantiates a pointer to the service module and increments the usage count in the service module. This controls how long the service module is active.

Once this pointer is established, you have access to all of the service's functionality without every object carrying the overhead, and without creating a global variable. The service is created only once for the class and all of its descendants. Of course, there may be an occasion when the same service is used on a different class (for example, the constants will be used in every class), and services such as these should be global, but again, the overhead is minimal enough that we do not mind establishing the service in a class-by-class manner.

Accessing functionality on the service itself is a simple matter of checking whether the service is valid and executing a function on the service. For example, a call to the error services would look like this:

```
/* Call Error Handler function
IF isValid(dwError) THEN dwError.ccf_p_LogError(ii_ErrorSource, ii_ErrorNumber)
```

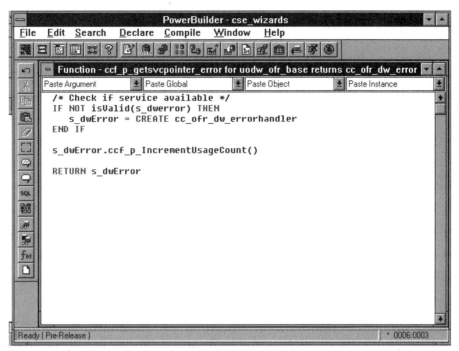

Figure 12.8 Get Pointer function for error services.

The overhead carried by the isValid statement is far outweighed by the flexibility gained by being able to precode statements into your code that execute when the service they seek is available. Depending on the need, the code could call the setup function if the service is expected to be there. (In our case here, we would call the ccf_p_SetupSVC_Error() described earlier).

Of course, when your object gets destroyed you need to make sure that the services it has loaded get unloaded.

The Unload function is interesting in that it really does not "unload" the service, at least not in the case of error services. What it does is call the Decrement Usage Count function on the service, which returns a value indicating how many *other* objects have pointers to the service. When this count reaches zero, the service itself can be unloaded. The object services are all unloaded using the Destroy function. Figure 12.9 shows the Service Unload function.

As is evident, the error service object is instantiated only once for the ancestor object class and all descendants of the ancestor. Through the instantiation of an instance variable pointer (you will notice that the object is neither created nor destroyed; it is treated as a pointer), we have access to the functionality of the service object while carrying the overhead of the object only once. This technique is used often in the object framework class library, allowing services to be declared as needed.

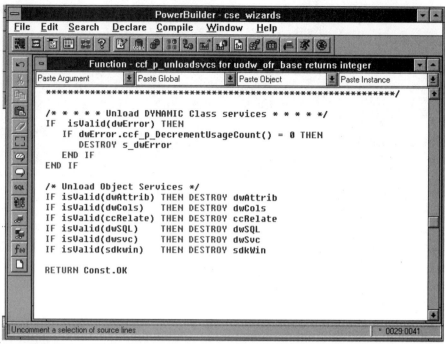

Figure 12.9 Service Unload function.

The method shown is similar to that used by DLLs. When a DLL is loaded, it is physically loaded into memory. When another application or object needs the DLL, Windows knows that the DLL is loaded and increments a Usage Counter. When this count reaches zero again, Windows knows to unload the DLL. Our technique does the same thing. The service object is created the first time, and a usage counter controls when the object is destroyed.

Now we have a means to create a service object once for each object class that needs it, and it is available automatically to all members and descendants of the class. If not instantiated, the overhead associated with the service is not carried in the object. If it is instantiated, it is created only once for all objects of the class, and overhead is still kept to a minimum. This can be used for all services that do not deviate for members of the class.

One question that comes to mind when looking at this approach is, if the service is so similar to a DLL, why don't we use a DLL? One reason is portability to other platforms. A second issue is of a little more concern. DLLs allow the sharing of methods very nicely. However, they also share the attributes, and allow multiple applications access to the same variable. This not only violates the rules of encapsulation, but could be downright dangerous. DLLs that are simple collections of methods (no attributes shared) could be used if deemed useful. This same principle applies to the service object. Establish the service as shared only if the methods and attributes can be truly shared among members of the class. If not, the service can be instantiated as an instance variable instead of as a shared variable and all other code and reference code remains the same. For example, an SQL access service class would be instantiated within a datawindow, but as an instance service because the SQL being used belongs to the datawindow only. Other general datawindow functionality can most assuredly be built into a shared variable service (Cut, Copy, Paste, etc.).

Use the technique carefully with some planning and you will find that your objects will remain small, fast, and extremely powerful.

Object services: instantiation on-demand.   One of the most powerful techniques available to developers of PowerBuilder applications is the ability to instantiate objects on demand. You can encapsulate services in an object such as an NVO, and have the services instantiated only when necessary. Error handling services fall into this category. Why carry the overhead of error handling services until you encounter an error? Instantiated services can be destroyed after use or, using an approach similar to the class services, can remain in memory for use by other members of the class.

Another feature of on-demand services is that you can define the service in your object and have instantiation take place based on declarative attributes. A master-detail relationship between datawindows can be encapsulated into a relationship service object, which is instantiated if the developer elects to indicate that the service is required. Figure 12.10 shows a service being instantiated on demand.

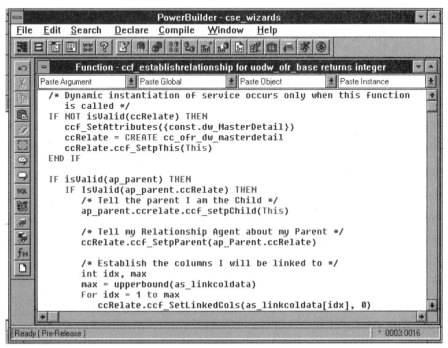

Figure 12.10   Instantiate service on demand.

Service managers: collection objects.   One problem with having services instantiated all over the place is in managing them. Some of our services have built-in management capabilities whereby they are capable of managing dependent service objects. One such service is a relationship object. The relationship object is capable of maintaining a relationship with its immediate parent and its immediate children. It can maintain all of the knowledge required about its children and has the capability to inform its parent of any change in status. Relationship objects also provide the means of communication between the objects they are housed in. For example, when RowFocus changes on a parent or master datawindow object, it no longer has to communicate to other datawindows. It communicates to its relationship object, which in turn looks at its dependent object collection and notifies these dependents that a specific action must take place. The object also maintains knowledge about whether any of the dependent objects have unsaved changes and acts accordingly.

Using NVOs instead of structures

The data structure is a powerful data typing object capable of collecting many variables into a single structure. Structures can be passed as parameters to functions or between objects. The only problem is that you cannot define internal processing or initial values within a data structure. It is also a meaningful task to release the memory allocated to a structure dynamically.

Imagine a data structure that is self-initializing. If you declare an NVO for use as a data structure, you have the capabilities of the data structure, but you also have the ability to define internal processing. Furthermore, the NVO can be passed by reference or returned as a pointer, reducing overhead. The only negative side effect is that the NVO must be created and destroyed, but this is also a positive point. To remove the object from memory and free up the memory, destroy it. To use it again, create it.

Creating an effective class hierarchy

When designing the objects for your library, it is crucial that you establish and build an effective class hierarchy.

- The hierarchy must be as flat as possible (reduces complexity).
- The hierarchy must be as useful as possible (self-documenting, feature-rich).

Succeeding in these two goals is not simple task. To accomplish this, we found that a layered approach works best. We found the following layers of objects to be most typical:

- Base or ancestor class
- Classification classes
- Functional classes

TABLE 12.2 Class Hierarchy Layer Criteria

Layer	Criteria
Ancestor	Needed by all objects descended from this class.
Classification	Divides classes into specific classifications of classes. Although these classes might be used as is, it is more typical that this class serves as the functional split zone. An example is an NVO that defines datawindow services. Descended from an nvo_base object, it still serves no particular purpose other than to define the ancestor for all datawindow service classes, and separates these from other services such as window service classes.
Functional	Needed by this object. Very little overlap to other classes of the same ancestry.

The layers might incorporate a hierarchy within the layer depending on the object class requirements, but should be kept as flat as possible (up to the application layer). The important thing is to determine in which layer functionality and attributes should go. We found that the criteria shown in Table 12.2 are best suited to this approach.

By following this layered approach, it becomes easier to determine how the classes must be built and where functionality must be placed. You will notice this approach used for all the objects in our object framework. Sometimes, the classification layer is not required. When the hierarchy does not have to go below one layer before being used in the application, we can easily omit the classification layer. Although I do not recommend this (it is far more difficult to add a layer between two layers than to use a layer with no added code), you may choose to use this approach to reduce the number of objects. For example, we created a class hierarchy for command buttons (yes, we advocate the creation of user objects for all of the standard PowerBuilder controls), which did not need to go beyond the base level before being provided to the application. However, we still created the classification layer for future use. Just because there is no need for functionality now does not mean there never will be. The final benefit of this approach is that all objects follow the same hierarchy. This makes maintaining and finding an object much easier.

Remember that we said there may be a mini-hierarchy within a layer. For example, we could create what we feel is a typical use of the datawindow class (master-detail relationship) and create a customized class of the user object datawindows, with this interrelationship in place. We could have, but we did not. Instead, we created this capability within a service that could be instantiated in any of the datawindows to automatically form this relationship. The service is an object that provides a known linkage point between objects. An object never actually has to know about another object; its linkage service provides that capability. Think of it as a message relay object. Figure 12.11 depicts this strategy.

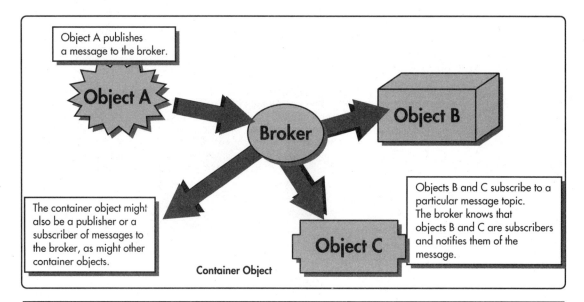

Figure 12.11   The linkage object is categorized as an object broker.

Once we have established the class hierarchy, we can begin to place methods and attributes into the hierarchy. Again, knowing we have the three layers (or that we will have three layers) helps us to determine where functionality goes.

Using declarative services

> ### *A declarative service provides a common access point to functionality.*

One of the key aspects of our design is the use of services that are created only when needed. This allows us to reuse common code between objects of the same or different hierarchies and to provide the developer with a common means of accessing functionality. Based on the layered approach, all services would be derived from the custom class base (cc_ofr_base), then the custom class services base (cc_ofr_Service_base). Notice the mini-hierarchy within the base layer here. We do this because different types of custom classes can be created. We do not have this additional layer for the standard class objects because they are not derived from a common base (uodw_ofr_base and uocb_ofr_base are both standard user object classes, but we do not have a uostd_ofr_base because the standard classes must choose an ancestor path following a standard PowerBuilder class). Figure 12.12 shows the various standard classes available in PowerBuilder 5.0.

Declarative services reduce overhead. By virtue of the fact that the service can be created only once for the entire class hierarchy (Shared Service class),

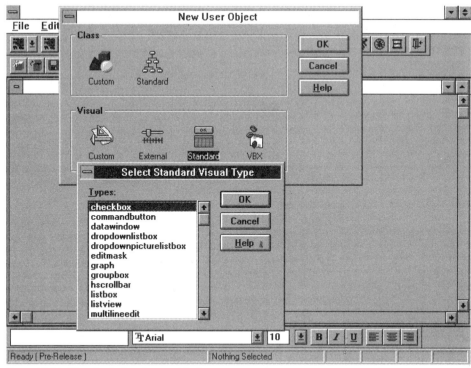

Figure 12.12 Standard visual user objects.

and each object in the hierarchy establishes only a pointer to the service, the overhead is minimal in each object. In addition, declarative services provide the flexibility of being able to add or remove a service dynamically by activating or deactivating a specific service whenever needed.

Finally, declarative services allow us to encapsulate processing. If a service performs a specific function and is used in many places, we can modify the service object and have the modification reflected in all objects using the service. One item to note here: Services must have clearly defined entry points, which should not be subject to change. Entry point changes require modification to objects that use that entry point specifically. This is not too bad when you figure that services are precoded in inheritable objects, but developers often write code to access service functions, too. Do not change the argument list for the object's setup routines, for example.

Using pointers in PowerBuilder

POINTER: A pointer is a persistent link between two objects.

Using pointers is a means of getting access to an object without carrying the overhead of the object. A pointer also allows you to modify the access privileges of a class (establishing a public pointer to a private variable, for example).

Why should you use a pointer? As we said, pointers carry less overhead than passing around the actual object, so only one copy of the object resides in memory at any given point.

How do you establish a pointer? There are generally two ways to establish a pointer. One is proactive, the other reactive. A proactive pointer is created when an object is passed to a function by reference. The function gets a pointer back to the original object. Any changes made using the pointer change the original object. A reactive pointer is what we use for our service classes. The simple process of returning an object from a function automatically passes a pointer to the object. This allows us to use a custom class, for example, without issuing a Create or Destroy. The original object must be instantiated before you establish a pointer. Figure 12.13 shows the difference between these types of pointers.

Naming convention for pointers. To identify when pointers are used, we use a data type of "p." Thus, instead of the typical "ii" (instance variable, integer data type), we use "ip" (instance pointer). Because pointers are related to specific objects, we have determined that specifying the scope of the pointer is not always necessary. Thus, a pointer to the debugger can be called pDebug rather

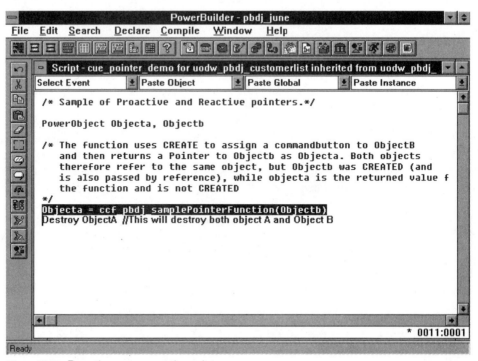

Figure 12.13 Proactive versus reactive pointers.

than the more typical ip_Debug. However, we still prefer to establish the scope of the pointer, so our naming conventions dictate the use of ip_Debug rather than pDebug.

Example of using a pointer: the debug object.   When using a pointer to access objects, your code should ensure that the object exists. Adding isValid() to your code carries very little overhead and prevents the common Null Object Reference error from becoming a prominent piece of your architecture. Accessing a debug function for example, is shown as follows:

```
IF isValid(ip_Debug) THEN ip_Debug.Function(args).
```

This simple precaution prevents errors, especially in the declarative service environment we advocate. If an object pointed to is expected to be present, then the ELSE leg of the IF statement can contain exception handling code or, in the case of on-demand services, can actually create the service before attempting to execute the code.

Developing and using constants

You might have noticed the common reference to constants in the debugger example shown before (c.OK, c.ToMicrohelp etc.). Constants are variables with predefined constant values.

Constants allow you to reference values using a common name. For example, a message box with OK and Cancel buttons will return 0 for OK and 1 for Cancel. When the same message box is used with Yes, No, and Cancel buttons, Yes = 0, No = 1 and Cancel = 2. Your program needs to determine the context of the return value before determining what the value means. In our replacement message box (a simple dialog window that simulates a message box), we return constants relating to the button; c.OK always means OK was pressed, c.Cancel always means Cancel, etc. The developer does not have to remember that OK = 0 (when OK and Cancel are options), or figure out that Cancel = 1 when OK and Cancel are options and Cancel = 2 when Yes, No, and Cancel are used.

Another benefit is that of readability of code. IF button_returned = 1 tells you very little. IF Button_Returned = c.Cancel tells you that the Cancel button was pressed.

How can you define constants in PowerBuilder?   PowerBuilder 5 allows the definition of constants by adding the keyword *Constant* as a scope identifier. The constant becomes persistent depending on the declaration. In other words, the constants provide a means of "privatizing" the contents of a variable, much like you can hide the attributes and methods of any other object by making them private. To those who are familiar with constants, this is PowerBuilder's implementation of the sorely missed programming technique.

Another technique we use is to declare all of our constants in one object specially defined as a constants container object. The object is a nonvisual object where our constants are declared as instance variables. Figure 12.14 shows some of our declared constants.

To use the constants throughout the application, we need a method to define the constants as global. We have a technique that allows us to do this without defining a global variable.

The object is instantiated within the application as self-referencing. By this we mean that the object is created as a type of itself. This allows us to create the object without ever declaring a variable for the object. To do this, we follow these simple steps.

1. Create a nonvisual object; ours is called cc_ofr_base_constants.

2. Derive a developer-customizable level of this object by inheriting the object. Save this object using the name you will use in your application. Our constants' object-customizable layer is called CONST.

3. In your application object's open event, create the object as self-referencing; that is, Const = CREATE Const.

You can now reference the Const object as if it were declared as a global variable in your application, without actually declaring any variable for the object.

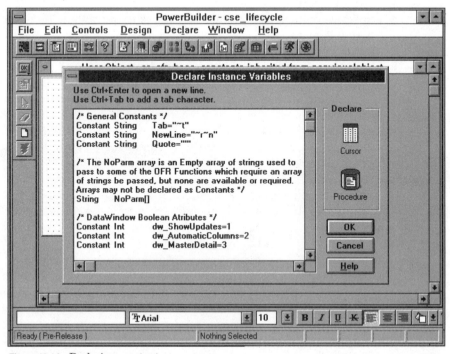

Figure 12.14   Declaring constants.

Remember that this method of declaration might make certain objects in your application nonreusable as standalone objects. If your object is intended for use as an OLE object/server or as a distributable object, it must be fully encapsulated and not reference objects not in its path. If this is the case, use the class-wide service instantiation methods described earlier.

Developing and using dynamically inherited objects (customization levels)

A dynamically inherited object (DIO) is one that is inherited from a library object by the library team and library code refers to the object already. This works as though the developer inherited the object, built the code, and when he or she uses the object, the library dynamically changes its inheritance path to include the developer's object. These are sometimes called template objects, but they are not true templates as they are not meant to be inherited from. Basically, the inheritance is done for you and the object is a customizable layer object that is already referenced from the base class library.

How is this useful?   This technique becomes useful when you want the library to instantiate the developer's version of the object at runtime and refer to that version in the library code. For example, our Datawindow Attribute service object is very useful to *us*. If a developer wanted to add an attribute or function, he or she would need to derive his or her own object and replace code in objects where he or she wanted to use the services.

Instead, the base class developers, create the application customization layer and call the object cc_ofr_dio_dw_Attributes. The *ofr* refers to the object framework. The *dio* refers to the dynamically inherited object layer or customization level. DIO objects can reside in the same library as their ancestor object, copied out to the developer library only when the need arises to override it, or they can all be placed in a special DIO library to facilitate ease of finding the objects. We prefer the former because it allows us to exclude certain processing features altogether.

The developer can now modify the DIO object (application layer), and it is this object that is instantiated in the library object code. This is shown graphically in Figure 12.15.

Different types of DIOs.   There are also different types of DIOs. One type is the normal inherited object such as the constants object described previously, usually a service object. These are the objects that manage the way your framework works, and DIOs provide a means to extend or modify that behavior.

A second type is in using a datawindow to hold predefined data that the developer can modify. This datawindow is already imbedded in a user object

Figure 12.15 Dynamically inherited objects (customization levels).

datawindow accessed by the library. We call these data-retained-on-save datawindows. We include these in the developer library and these include such items as predefined dropdown lists. The datawindow cannot be inherited, but it can be predefined and prereferenced.

Another type of DIO is an object that is particularly useful, but not necessarily dynamically referenced by the class library. Instead, it is ready to be used to help reduce development time. An example of this type of DIO is a pre-built Message Box dialog window. The library refers to this object but an application level is provided that the developer can modify for presentation or behavior.

Extending the environment

One of the features of object-oriented technology is the ability to extend the functionality of an object or function. One of our design objectives is to extend the natural environment. Putting these two elements together allows us to extend the functionality of the environment. For example, the various flavors of TriggerEvent satisfy most needs. One method is missing: the ability to pass an object as a parameter with a TriggerEvent. We can extend the environment by adding another TriggerEvent function to our base objects. By modifying the parameter set to include an object reference, we can extend the environment

```
/*******************************************************************************
 * FUNCTION : triggerevent
 * PURPOSE : Special Overload layer to add PowerObject as a
            Parameter
 *
 *   Author : Bill Green
 *     Date : Sept. 11, 1995
 *
 *
 * A R G U M E N T S
 * ----------------------------
 *
 * Type           Description
 * ----           --------------------------------------
 * String         EventName
 * Integer        WordParm
 * PowerObject  Object
 *
 * R E T U R N   V A L U E S
 * --------------------------------------
 *
 * Type      Description
 * ----      ---------------------------------
 * Integer        1 = success, -1 = failed
 *
 *
 * History
 * --------
 * Date       Init  Description of change
 * ------     ----  --------------------------------
 * 09/11/95  xxx  Initial Coding...
 *
 *
 *
 *******************************************************************************/
 /* Move the powerobject argument to the message object */
 message.powerobjectparm = objectparm

 /* Call the Standard triggerevent function so that the object being passed
            can be utilized */
 RETURN Super::TriggerEvent(eventname, wordparm, -1)
```

Figure 12.16 Overloading PowerBuilder functions.

using function overloading. Figure 12.16 shows the TriggerEvent function coded in our custom class base object.

By doing this, we are extending the environment and adding a useful feature to the natural TriggerEvent function. Note that PostEvent is not a good candidate for this feature because the message object is used and its contents are not persistent. If we look at the function hierarchy of the object, you can see what looks like a regular PowerBuilder function added to the classes' capabilities. The function hierarchy of our custom class is shown in Figure 12.17.

Another means of extending the environment is the use of the global PowerBuilder objects. Objects such as Message and Transaction, for example, can be

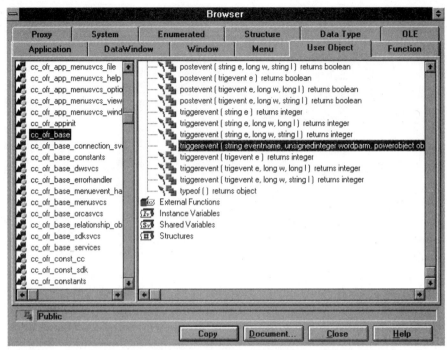

Figure 12.17 Overloaded Triggerevent on the object browser.

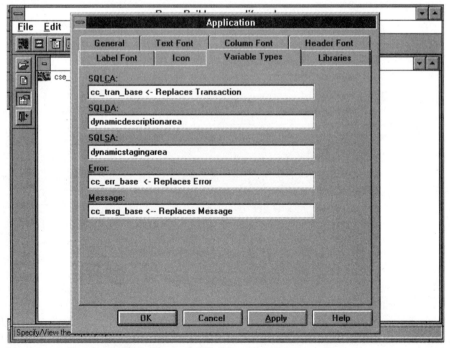

Figure 12.18 Standard global objects modified for an application.

replaced with standard classes derived from the original objects. The capabilities of the object are then extended and the reference to object modified in the global object painter. An example of the global object painter with modified natural objects is shown in Figure 12.18. Remember that this technique reduces the portability of your code in that the objects must be included with any application that uses your library. This must be weighed against the power that can be added to your applications by using extensions of these global objects.

Library structure development

The final piece of our design theory is the development of library structures. It is important to do this before beginning development so there are natural libraries defined where objects belong. Moving objects around and creating new libraries or removing old libraries leads to confusion. There are also a few techniques that can improve the efficiency of your compile and runtime performance. One of these is to place the base layer objects in one library and place this at the end of your search path. As most, if not all, objects are inherited from these objects, it is important that the search engine find these objects as quickly as possible, at least initially, so techniques such as preloading can help to preload the ancestor object class definitions. Preloading can be accomplished by simply declaring a variable (instance) of the object type. Instantiation is not necessary, as the declaration requires that the reference be resolved, and the ancestor's definition will be loaded into memory. You might not be able to measure the effect of this technique, but it does provide a benefit.

These results and knowledge of how objects are loaded into memory help us to build a library structure that has meaning beyond being the location where our objects will be stored.

One other fact we discovered (and this applies to class libraries more than to application libraries) is the possibility of building libraries that can be totally excluded from the search path of the application if the functionality is not desired. For example, our collection of debugger objects is housed in a OFR_DEBG.PBL, which can be excluded from the search path. OFR's Object Manager checks the search path to determine what feature sets are included and adjusts the service objects included dynamically. (We do require a certain subset of libraries, which the Object Manager also checks). You will notice that OFR has an apparent abundance of libraries, some of which are required and some of which can be excluded. A sample library list is shown in Figure 12.19.

As you can see from some of the comments shown in Figure 12.19, some of the libraries are listed as optional such as the Debug library and Custom Frame library. If you follow this approach, you must ensure that objects in required libraries do not reference objects in optional libraries.

Library facts.   Once you have decided on a library structure, you need to keep a few things in mind. The following facts relate to all PowerBuilder development, not just class libraries.

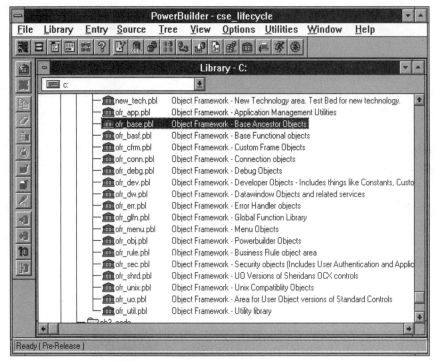

Figure 12.19   Sample application library list.

Moving and deleting objects.   Moving and deleting objects are common occurrences during the development cycle. Remember to optimize your libraries regularly to keep the libraries clean.

Optimizing libraries.   Optimizing rebuilds the library, eliminating dead space left by objects deleted or moved. Optimizing helps keep your libraries as compact as possible and ensures that object reference pointers have less chance of getting lost.

TIP: Novell Network Users

On a Novell Network, you might encounter the occasional "Save failed. Possible I-O error." This is most often caused by developers accessing objects in the same libraries. The cause of the problem lies in the way libraries are handled between PowerBuilder and Novell. Novell has file attributes similar to a DOS file system. One of these attributes is the file share attribute. This attribute allows files to be shared between developers or applications. When a PowerBuilder library is first created, and when it is optimized (which creates a new library anyway), this attribute is automatically set to "not shared." You need to reset this attribute to avoid the sharing errors. To do this, follow these simple steps.

1. At a DOS prompt, go to your source directory.
2. Type FLAG *.PBL

   This displays a list of your libraries and their Novell file attributes.

3. Type FLAG *.pbl +s

   This turns the shared attribute on for all of your libraries and virtually eliminates the sharing violations.

Size limits. Library size has often been bandied about. Back in the days of PowerBuilder 2.0, size limits were established as real limits: less than 600 KB in size, no more than 50 objects. From PowerBuilder 3.0 onward, however, these limits have been reduced to guidelines. They have never been eliminated, but a few tests we ran showed no visible limitations with version 3.0, 4.0, or 5.0. We have built a library containing over 160 objects, resulting in a library some 2.8 MB in size. It is a little slow (actually, 10 to 12 seconds on my 486DX4 75Mhz NEC) when opening, and finding the object you want is a little tedious, but it does not seem to affect the development environment or the execution environment. What it does do is eliminate the possibility of duplicate objects.

Common sense tells us that this is not an optimal condition, though. It is counterproductive to the developer. A 10- to 12-second delay every time you open your library can add up to a lot of wasted time. We recommend trying to limit the number of libraries you use, but keep them at sensible levels.

Having 40 libraries with 10 objects each is also not a wise decision, especially if using PowerBuilder Dynamic Libraries (PBDs). Objects are loaded from PBDs when needed. This means a physical file I/O for each object you need. The PBD needs to be opened only once, but physical reads are not cheap, especially across a network. Finding the right balance is important and you may need to experiment a little in your environment to determine the most effective solution. We found that running on a token ring network at 16 MB/second was okay in most situations. Another network running a 4 MB/second ring was painfully slow loading PBDs across the network. The best solution is to have an automated software distribution solution that automatically updates the user's machine locally with the latest versions of EXEs and PBDs. You achieve optimal speed, although you sacrifice a little in terms of execution safety; that is, it becomes a little harder to guarantee that the user is using the correct set of executable code.

Physical Class Definition

After all the theory, it is time to put the methodology to the test and begin defining our physical classes. During this phase, we will design the physical class structure based on classes we have defined logically. Looking at our class definitions (you can pick any one to start with, but I prefer starting at the beginning), we can begin putting similar object definitions together. At this point we need to decide where in an object hierarchy each method and attribute goes. We also need to decide whether a method will be serviced by a function, an event, or a combination of functions and events. There does not have to be a correlation between a method and a function or event. A method is a definition of the functionality required. Another thing we do is determine the scope and access privileges of each attribute and method. While breaking the methods and attributes out into their respective positions in the class hierarchy and expanding the methods into functions and events, we also need to continue to build on our test plan. Finally, we need to make sure we maintain accurate and informative documentation on each object defined.

Function or event decision process

Before we begin designing our physical classes, we need to establish certain criteria. One of these is the decision process in deciding whether a method should be created as a function or an event. There are three elements that affect this decision: performance, extendibility and access privilege.

Performance. In Chapter 18 we delve into the performance aspects of using functions and events, but in short, functions outperform events easily. Build as many of your methods as possible into functions and keep the number of user events to a minimum. This might seem like it will detract from the ease of use, but you have to remember that the final product must satisfy a user. Developers can be taught how to extend and overload functions. Users cannot be taught to accept bad performance.

Extendability. If the method is one that is intended to be extended by the developer and is not performance-dependent, an event may be used. Events are generally easier to extend or override than functions. They also make it easier for developers to see what the ancestor is doing.

Access privilege. If a method is determined to be a public method, that is, accessible to all classes, then it may be an event. If any form of protection is required, the method should be a function. Remember that only functions can have access privileges defined.

All functions should start out protected, and those that are private to the class should then be declared as private. Functions that are for public use can then be defined as public. Events, by default, are always public.

Scope and access privileges of attributes

Attributes should also start out as protected. Attributes that are required solely for the internal use of the object should be made private. Attributes that must be accessible to descendants of the object should be classified as protected. Attributes that simply define characteristics of the object can be made public, as it is often less efficient to code a Get and Set function that simply changes a value of an attribute or retrieves that value. If changing the value of the attribute results in additional processing, then the attribute should be defined as protected (at the minimum) to avoid accidental change to the value.

Attributes should also default to being instance variables. The only exception is the declaration of services that are declared as shared variables. Shared variables are, by default, private to the class. Attributes required solely by a method, and not required to be persistent for the life of the object, should be declared as local.

Building the object hierarchy

The first element we need in designing our physical classes is to determine what layers of inheritance are going to be used. We have already established that we will use the SBA architecture, so we know that our inheritance layers will follow the CBM hierarchy as shown in Figure 12.20.

Note that the left-hand side of the hierarchy is flatter than the service class side. This is our goal, to flatten the inheritance hierarchy of object classes. You will also notice that there are in reality three layers of inheritance. (Layers are different from levels because you may have multiple levels of inheritance within a layer. We'll see an example of this later in this chapter.)

These layers are defined as follows:

BASE ANCESTOR CLASS: Contains basically only the methods and attributes required to "manage" the class. Basic services for the entire class can be implemented here. Class-wide services are also implemented here.

CLASSIFICATION CLASSES: These are classes that define a classification of functionality, such as datawindow classes. Although you might have a dw_base class, in reality the dw_base class would be more apt if it were a uo_base class because datawindows are classified as user objects. Another example is a classification of a type of service; for example, attribute management, error handling, or constants are service classifications. These might be further specialized into functional classes.

FUNCTIONAL CLASSES: These are either the classes that implement declarative type services, or the service objects that implement functionality, such as database error handling. (Note that datawindow error handling is not a specialization. Datawindows can implement various error handler services to handle developer requirements.)

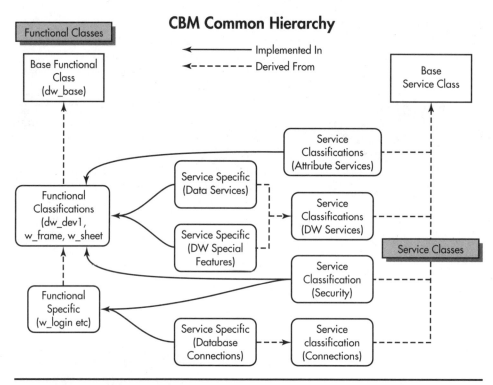

Figure 12.20 The CBM standard inheritance hierarchy.

Now all we have to do (although it is not quite as simple as it sounds) is to place methods of our logical classes into one of these layers. For example, if we look at the logical class cross-reference we defined in Chapter 11 (see Figure 12.21), we can begin to put together the physical classes we will need.

To follow this in a step-by-step fashion, we first need to make use of a form called the physical class hierarchy (PCH). Our first logical class (and method) shown is Application Service Instance Check. This class is pretty specialized, so we slot this class and its method into the hierarchy. Figure 12.22 shows this first step.

Before we go any further, we know that a class cannot just "hang out"; we need some ancestry (we gotta know our roots, right?). We can therefore determine that this class needs an ancestor and what better than a classification class for all application services? Figure 12.23 shows this class inserted into the hierarchy.

Again, we can determine that application services are a classification of a type of service. As there are bound to be others (service-based architecture would be more of a service-based tent if there were only one service), we can determine quite safely that there will be a base service class. We add this to

Method	Attribute	Expected Result	Test Plan	Logical Class
Check for application instance	Application Handle	Returns an indication of whether the application is already running	Test with another instance of the application running Test with no other instance of the application running	Application Service Instance Check
Get Multiple Instance Action attribute	Multiple Instance Action	Gets the action to take if another instance of the application is found	Test that attribute style returns the action required	Application Service Instance Check
Set an attribute indicating whether check is required	Multiple Instance Indicator	Sets the Multiple Instance Indicator	Test what happens if attribute is never set Test with valid attribute	Application Service Instance Check
Set an attribute indicating whether multiple instances exist	Multiple Instances Exist	Attribute is set to a true or false value	If another instance is running, value should be true If not, value should be false	Application Service Instance Check
Get an attribute indicating whether check is required	Multiple Instance Indicator	Gets the Multiple Instance Indicator, which determines whether we need to test for multiple instances	Test what happens if attribute is never set Test with valid attribute	AutoVerification
Take action based on Multiple Instance Action indicator	Multiple Instance Action	Continue, halt, and activate original instance or halt processing	Test all combinations of Multiple Instance Action	Process Flow
Display Application Message	Application Message: Application already running	Displays a warning message to the user	Verify message is correct and that correct button options are set	User Feedback Application Message

Figure 12.21   Cross-reference: method/logical classes.

the PCH and we now have our first complete class hierarchy. (No, don't start coding yet!) Figure 12.24 shows this in place.

This process continues for all of the logical classes until they are all slotted into the hierarchy and have parentage defined. For this brief example, we ultimately end up with the hierarchy shown in Figure 12.25. The next step is to design a physical class for the classes listed in the hierarchy. (Isn't it amazing how many classes seem to be needed for something any experienced programmer knows is a simple "IF Handle(This) : 0 THEN . . . Exists?) The goal is truly reusable classes, and this type of breakout pays big dividends when code gets more complicated. The same code may be used, but instead, it is imbedded in a physical class, which can now be extended for other use.

Base Ancestor Classes

Type	Name	Methods	Ancestor	PCD Xref
		•		

Classification Classes

Type	Name	Methods	Ancestor	PCD Xref
		•		

Specialized Classes

Type	Name	Methods	Ancestor	PCD Xref
Service	Application Instance Check	• Check for application instance	SvcApp	AppCheck

Figure 12.22 Physical class hierachy: application instance check.

Base Ancestor Classes

Type	Name	Methods	Ancestor	PCD Xref
		•		

Classification Classes

Type	Name	Methods	Ancestor	PCD Xref
Service	Application Services	• Generic Application Service Behavior	SvcBase	SvcApp

Specialized Classes

Type	Name	Methods	Ancestor	PCD Xref
Service	Application Instance Check	• Check for application instance	SvcApp	AppCheck

Figure 12.23 Physical class hierarchy: application services defined.

For the class definition, we use a form called physical class definition, which looks like that shown in Figure 12.26. The form is separated into distinct sections. The first is the physical class data. Here we simply describe the class identification attributes such as the name (descriptive, not symbolic), the version, author, and date.

The next section is the identification section for the ultimate object, where we describe the hierarchical layer, the predicted ancestry, a "real" class name,

Base Ancestor Classes

Type	Name	Methods	Ancestor	PCD Xref
Service	Base Services	Generic Behavior for All Service Classes	None	SvcBase

Classification Classes

Type	Name	Methods	Ancestor	PCD Xref
Service	Application Services	Generic Application Service Behavior	SvcBase	SvcApp

Specialized Classes

Type	Name	Methods	Ancestor	PCD Xref
Service	Application Instance Check	Check for an instance of an application • Check for application instance	SvcApp	AppCheck

Figure 12.24   Physical class hierarchy: base services defined.

what library the object will most likely reside in (remember that this is still the design phase and things can change), a description of the class, and, finally, how we predict the class typically will be used. This may seem excessive, but when you figure that you can pull something like the typical usage element from every class, you have an immediate index to likely functionality, something a developer will love you for.

The third section deals with class specifications. This area is then subdivided into four subsections:

- *Implementable services:* These are services that will probably be implemented within this class, a key aspect for an SBA architecture. Note the key elements of SBA: scope, type, and implementation. These will drive how the services are used.

- *Attributes:* This is simply a list of the attributes we expect to see in the object. Again based on SBA, we choose to implement most static attributes in an attribute service, reducing the overall number.

- *Methods:* This is the key element of the class definition. First we define the method itself, identifying scope, implementation type, and a name and prefix. Then we define the arguments and return values associated with the method. Finally, we describe the physical elements of the method, including what exceptions can arise and what tests would ensure quality. (Note that a lot of the test case information comes directly from the original method test plan.)

Again, the information might seem excessive, but to truly succeed in reusable class development it is important to focus on the details of the de-

Base Ancestor Classes

Type	Name	Methods	Ancestor	PCD Xref
Service	Base Services	• Initialize Class • Process Exceptions • Load Services • Unload Services	None	SvcBase
Service	Process Flow Control	• Interrogate Style • Initiate User Feedback • Return Flow Control	None	pFlow
Service	Attribute Services	Attribute Managment Service (See PCD for attributes defined) • GetAttribute • SetAttribute • ResetAttribute	SvcBase	SvcAttr

Classification Classes

Type	Name	Methods	Ancestor	PCD Xref
Service	Application Services	• Generic Application Service Behavior	SvcBase	SvcApp
Service	User Feedback	• Generic User Feedback Service Behavior	SvcBase	SvcFbck

Specialized Classes

Type	Name	Methods	Ancestor	PCD Xref
Service	Application Instance Check	• Check for application instance • Get Multiple Instance Action attribute • Set an attribute indicating whether check is required • Set an attribute indicating whether multiple instances exist	SvcApp	AppCheck
Service	Application Messages	• Display Application Message	SvcFbck	AppMsg

Figure 12.25 Physical class hierachy: other classes defined.

sign and have documentation for developers to build the classes or develop from the classes.

Now we start to fill one of these in. (There will be a slight twist later, but we will wait for that.) We begin with the Base Service class. The physical class definition tends to get pretty long at times, so we break this one up into digestible parts.

Class data. Figure 12.27 shows the physical class data for the Base Service class. Note that the object identification section indicates the hierarchy layer being used.

Physical Class Data

Physical Class ID:		**Version:**	1.0
Physical Class Name:			
Author:	William Green	**Update Date:**	May 1, 1996

Object Identification Data

Functional Layer:	Base Ancestor	**Ancestry:**	NonVisualObject
Object Name:		**Library:**	
Class Description:			
Typical Usage:			

Class Specifications

Implementable Services

Scope	Type	Name	Implementation

Attributes

Scope	Type	Name	Default

*Note: When default indicates a Class ID (eg PCD_xxxx), variable is defined in that class.

Methods

General Specifications			
Scope	**Type**	**Prefix**	**Name**
Public	Event	*cue_*	Method Name
Arguments/Return Values/Extension			**Scope**
Extend:	No	None	
Argument:	None		
Return:	None		Reference
Description		**Exceptions**	**Test Xref**
Description of method			
• Specification		Exception_id	Test Procedure

Figure 12.26 Physical class definition.

Physical Class Data

Physical Class ID:	SvcBase		Version:	1.0
Physical Class Name:	Base Services Class			
Author:	William Green		Update Date:	May 1, 1996

Object Identification Data

Functional Layer:	Base	Ancestor	Ancestry:	None (Nonvisual Class)
Object Name:	cc_SvcBase		Library:	Base Ancestors
Class Description:	Base object for all service classes			
Typical Usage:	Used primarily as an ancestor to other service classes			

Figure 12.27 Physical class definition: base services class.

In Figure 12.28, we show the first two subsections from the Specifications section.

Here we can see how the base service class attributes are defined, as well as an imbedded service, the result code processor. This is a small service we designed to handle return codes better. The service contains attributes for the return code, as well as some others for information when the return code is bad. It also dynamically links to error handlers.

Class Specifications

Implementable Services

Scope	Type	Name	Implementation
Class	SvcResult	Result Code Processing Services	Static

Attributes

Scope	Type	Name	Default
Private	Instance	SvcResult	i_pResult Pointer to result code processor	Constant OK
Protected	Instance	Integer	ii_UsageCount Maintains a count of how many objects are utilizing this service. When this reaches zero, service may be unloaded	0
*Note: When default indicates a Class ID (eg PCD_xxxx), variable is defined in that class.				

Figure 12.28 Physical class definition: base services class.

For our final look at this class, we look at the methods defined. Figure 12.29 shows the methods defined for the class. Note the exception specifications at the end.

When we define the next layer in this hierarchy, we need to take some information from the parent class with us. The parent class becomes a template for its descendant. In Figure 12.30 we show the PCD for our Application Services class. Note the addition of three more groups of data.

- *Implemented services:* services implemented in an ancestor class

- *Inherited attributes:* attributes from the ancestor class, even the private attributes

- *Inherited methods:* methods already defined for this class

Nothing else is added for this class because nothing else has been added. Yet.

If we look further down into the hierarchy, we find the first class we defined, the Application Instance Check specialized class. This class has some behavior defined and this is shown in Figure 12.31.Note that in the inherited methods section we have added to the Initialize method the instantiation of attribute services and a *potential* service OS API services. A potential class is one that comes out of vision rather than requirement. We can easily see that a check for an application instance need not necessarily be for the current PowerBuilder application. Instead, we might want to be able to check whether Excel or some other application is running. This Application Instance Check service could well be used for this purpose also.

We also show the potential service in the implementable services and in the attributes sections. We then added three methods that were required: Get Attribute, Set Attribute, and Check Instance. Our goals for the class are defined in the hierarchy as follows:

- *Check for application instance:* satisfied by Instance Check

- *Get Multiple Instance Action* attribute: satisfied by Get Attribute

- *Set an attribute indicating whether check is required:* satisfied by SetAttribute

- *Set an attribute indicating whether multiple instances exist:* method determined to be a derivable value and therefore omitted from the actual class

Congratulations! You have defined a complete class hierarchy for the Application Instance Check logical class. It has been a long haul, but you are ready to start coding. How? Well, using CBM, you can begin coding as soon as you complete a PCD. The amount of detail requires so much extra thinking that your design turns out to be more complete. Entry points (public methods) are clearly defined, and using the SBA techniques allows us to predict when and how services will be used. The SBA technique of service and attribute man-

(Text continued on p. 202)

Figure 12.29   Physical class definition: base services class.

Methods

General Specifications			
Scope	**Type**	**Prefix**	**Name**
(None)	Event	*None*	Constructor

Arguments/Return Values			Reference
Extend: No	None		
Argument: None			
Return: None			

Description	Exceptions	Test Xref
Launch any object initialization routines		
• Execute Setup method	None	Ensure that Setup method fires
• Execute Initialize method	None	Ensure that Initialize method fires

General Specifications			
Scope	**Type**	**Prefix**	**Name**
(None)	Event	*None*	Destructor

Arguments/Return Values			Reference
Extend: No	None		
Argument: None			
Return: None			

Description	Exceptions	Test Xref
Performs all cleanup processing		
• Execute Service Unload method	None	Ensure that all services are unloaded

General Specifications			
Scope	**Type**	**Prefix**	**Name**
Public	Event	*cue_*	Setup

Arguments/Return Values			Reference
Extend: Yes	Developer can extend this event and add specific setup instructions		
Argument: None			
Return: Integer	Constant OK		Reference

Description	Exceptions	Test Xref
Setup method provides an area for developers to specify the behavior that the object will implement		
•	None	

General Specifications			
Scope	**Type**	**Prefix**	**Name**
Public	Event	*cue_*	Initialize

Arguments/Return Values		Reference
Extend: Yes	Developer can add behavior to the default behaviors defined	

Argument:	None			
Return:	Integer	Constant OK		Reference
Description			**Exceptions**	**Test Xref**
Initializes the object and implements required behavior				
•			None	

General Specifications				
Scope	**Type**	**Prefix**	**Name**	
Protected	Function	*uf_*	SvcLoad	
Arguments/Return Values				**Reference**
Extend:	No	Not necessary - Will function for any service type		
Argument:	Any	Service Object class		Value
Return:	svcBase	Instantiated service of type SvcBase		Reference
Description			**Exceptions**	**Test Xref**
Instantiate a Service				
• Check if Service instantiated			None	Test with service instantiated Test with service not instantiated
• Instantiate service into service array			svcLoad_001	Check that array is incremented correctly and service object successfully created
• Return pointer to instantiated service			None	Check that pointer is valid upon return

General Specifications				
Scope	**Type**	**Prefix**	**Name**	
Protected	Function	*uf_*	SvcUnload	
Arguments/Return Values				**Reference**
Extend:	No	Not required - All instantiated services will be unloaded		
Argument:	None	N/A		Reference
Return:	ResultCode	Result OK		Const.OK
Description			**Exceptions**	**Test Xref**
Performs all cleanup processing				
• Decrementally destroy all services in service array			SvcUnload_001	Test with null array Test with valid array

General Specifications				
Scope	**Type**	**Prefix**	**Name**	
Protected	Function	*uf_*	Try	
Arguments/Return Values				**Reference**
Extend:	No	None		
Argument:	Function	A function to be executed		

(Continued)

Figure 12.29   *(Continued)*

Return:	Integer	Constant OK		Reference
Description		**Exceptions**	**Test Xref**	
The Try method is an automatic exception handling method designed to allow developers to safely execute instructions with a guaranteed exception process			Check what happens when a null Result Code object is passed	
• Check Result Code		None	Result code should contain a success or failure code	
• Check Exception Code			If Result code is success, then Exception code should be null. If not, Exception code should contain a value which translates to a specific exception condition and invoke the exception handler	

General Specifications				
Scope	**Type**	**Prefix**	**Name**	
Public	Function	*uf_*	IncrementUsageCount	
Arguments/Return Values/Extension				**Scope**
Extend:	No	None		
Argument:	None			
Return:	ResultCode	Returns usage count with OK result		Reference
Description		**Exceptions**	**Test Xref**	
Increments the service object usage count				
• Increment UsageCount attribute		None	Ensure that count increases by 1	

General Specifications				
Scope	**Type**	**Prefix**	**Name**	
Public	Function	*uf_*	DecrementUsageCount	
Arguments/Return Values/Extension				**Scope**
Extend:	No	None		
Argument:	None			
Return:	ResultCode	Returns usage count with OK result		Reference
Description		**Exceptions**	**Test Xref**	
Decrements the service object usage count				
• Decrement UsageCount attribute		None	Ensure that count decreases by 1	

Exception Handling Specifications

Exception Code	Method	Description	Reference
SvcLoad_001	SvcLoad	A service failed to load correctly	SvcErr01
SvcUnload_001	SvcUnload	A service failed to unload	SvcErr02

Figure 12.30 Physical class definition: application services (classification).

Physical Class Data

Physical Class ID:	SvcApp		Version:	1.0
Physical Class Name:	Application Services (Classification)			
Author:	William Green		Update Date:	May 2, 1996

Object Identification Data

Functional Layer:	Service	Classification	Ancestry:	SvcBase
Object Name:	cc_SvcClass_App		Library:	Base Ancestors
Class Description:	Generic service class for all application services			
Typical Usage:	Used primarily for inheritance of specific services			

Implemented Services

Scope	Type	Name	Implemented
Class	SvcResult	Result Code Processing Services	SvcBase

Inherited Attributes

Scope		Type	Name	Default
Protected	Instance	SvcResult	i_pResult	Constant OK
Private	Instance	SvcBase	i_pServices[...]	Null
Protected	Instance	Integer	ii_UsageCount	0

Inherited Methods

Scope	Type	Prefix	Name
(None)	Event	*None*	Constructor
(None)	Event	*None*	Destructor
Public	Event	*cue_*	Setup
Public	Event	*cue_*	Initialize
Protected	Function	*uf_*	SvcLoad
Protected	Function	*uf_*	SvcUnload
Protected	Function	*uf_*	Try
Public	Function	*uf_*	IncrementUsageCount
Public	Function	*uf_*	DecrementUsageCount

Inherited Exception Handling

Exception Code	Method	Description	Reference
SvcLoad_001	SvcLoad	A service failed to load correctly	SvcErr01
SvcUnload_001	SvcUnload	A service failed to unload	SvcErr02

(Continued)

Figure 12.30   *(Continued)*

Class Specifications

Implementable Services

Scope	Type	Name	Implementation

Attributes

Scope		Type	Name	Default

*Note: When default indicates a Class ID (eg PCD_xxxx), variable is defined in that class.

Methods

General Specifications			
Scope	Type	Prefix	Name
(None)	Event	*None*	

Arguments/Return Values			Reference
Extend: No		None	
Argument: None			
Return: None			

Description	Exceptions	Test Xref
•		

Exception Handling Specifications

Exception Code	Method	Description	Reference

agement affords us the luxury of knowing that adding more later is really quite simple. In Chapter 13, we develop these three classes, and use them briefly, and we also see how the addition of another class in the overall schema affects this.

One other technique we use is to simply gather all exception codes and predicted constant value into a single repository, allowing rapid access to all of the messages, attributes, and constants our library will need.

Figure 12.31 Physical class definition: application service instance check.

Physical Class Data

Physical Class ID:	AppCheck		Version:	1.0
Physical Class Name:	Application Service: Instance Check			
Author:	William Green		Update Date:	May 13, 1996

Object Identification Data:

Functional Layer:	Service	Specialized	Ancestry:	SvcApp
Object Name:	cc_svc_AppCheck		Library:	Application Services
Class Description:	Application service to check for instances of a specified application			
Typical Usage:	Implemented as an application load check for the current application or as a service to look for an instance of a specified application			

Implemented Services

Scope	Type	Name	Implemented
Class	SvcResult	Result Code Processing services	SvcBase

Inherited Attributes

Scope		Type	Name	Default
Private	Instance	SvcResult	i_pResult	Constant OK
Private	Instance	SvcBase	i_pServices[...]	Null
Protected	Instance	Integer	ii_UsageCount	0

Inherited Methods

Scope	Type	Prefix	Name
(None)	Event	*None*	Constructor
(None)	Event	*None*	Destructor
Public	Event	*cue_*	Setup
Public	Event	*cue_*	Initialize • *OS Api Services??*
Protected	Function	*uf_*	SvcLoad
Protected	Function	*uf_*	SvcUnload
Protected	Function	*uf_*	Try
Public	Function	*uf_*	IncrementUsageCount
Public	Function	*uf_*	DecrementUsageCount

Inherited Exception Handling

Exception Code	Method	Description	Reference
SvcLoad_001	SvcLoad	A service failed to load correctly	SvcErr01
SvcUnload_001	SvcUnload	A service failed to unload	SvcErr02

(Continued)

Figure 12.31 *(Continued)*

Class Specifications

Implementable Services

Scope	Type	Name	Implementation
Protected	*OSApi*	*OS Api Services*	*Dynamic*

Attributes

Scope		Type		Name	Default
Protected	*Instance*	*OSApi*	*I_*	*OSAPI*	*Null*
Protected	Instance	Boolean	ib_	Verification Required	True
Protected	Instance	Integer	ii_	MultipleInstanceAction	0

Methods

General Specifications			
Scope	**Type**	**Prefix**	**Name**
Public	Function	*uf_*	CheckInstance

Arguments/Return Values/Extension			Scope
Extend:	Overloaded	Can check an Application Handle or another application class name	
Argument:	Overloaded	Handle/String	
Return:	ResultCode	rcBoolean	Reference

Description	Exceptions	Test Xref	
Checks if the handle (or classname) being passed already exists and reports	ChkInst_001	Test with no target passed Test with valid target passed Test with invalid target passed	
• If Application Handle is valid then application instance already exists		• Make sure application handle can be used here	
• *If ClassName can be found using an OS API call, then application instance exists*		*Test with FindWindow, GetModule, and other API functions to determine the best one.*	

General Specifications			
Scope	**Type**	**Prefix**	**Name**
Protected	Function	*uf_*	GetAttr_VerificationRequired

Arguments/Return Values/Extension			Scope
Extend:	No	None	
Argument:	None		
Return:	boolean	ib_VerificationRequired	

Description	Exceptions	Test Xref	
Gets the attribute which indicates whether verification is actually required for the multiple instance check			

General Specifications				
Scope	**Type**	**Prefix**	**Name**	
Protected	Function	*uf_*	GetAttr_MultipleInstanceAction	
Arguments/Return Values/Extension				**Scope**
Extend:	No		None	
Argument:	None			
Return:	Integer		ii_MultipleInstanceAction	
Description		**Exceptions**	**Test Xref**	
Gets the attribute which dictates what kind of action will be taken if multiple instances of specified application are found		ChkInst_002	Test all action code combinations: Warn User; Continue Processing, Quit Processing, Swap to Active Instance, etc.	

Exception Handling Specifications

Exception Code	Method	Description	Reference
ChkInst_001	CheckInstance	Instance cannot be checked because no instance handle was passed	AppChk03
CHKInst_002	GetAttr	Attribute Invalid - Illegal combination	AppChk04

Virtual events

One final technique used in our class library is the use of virtual events. A virtual event is one that is referenced in an object, but is never actually defined in the object. This serves the purposes of reducing the overhead of declared user events with no code and providing extendable support for a set of functionality. One common use for this is Post-Insert, Delete, Update, and Retrieve events. A class library typically does not do much in a Post event. Developers quite often want to extend the functionality of the object using the Post events. When a Post event is required, the developer simply declares the event and writes the code. The event is automatically called. Figure 12.32 shows the virtual event in action. Note that even the name of the event can be changed by the developer.

Test procedures

Test planning should continue. We have established method tests to ensure that each method defined is tested during our test phase. Now we can relate each method test to its location in the object hierarchy and group the tests by object definition. By doing this we find it is quite easy to build a test plan that covers most of the testing we will need to do. Testing procedures are discussed in more detail later in this book.

```
/* Trigger the Virtual Event cue_RetrieveSetup, which does not exist in the
base class, but can be added by the developer. The actual event name can
also be changed by the developer because ve_retrievesetup is actually a
STRING instance variable that can be set, reset etc.... If the virtual
events are held in a special event service object, the string reference
could be replaced by a function call */
TriggerEvent(ve_retrievesetup)

/* This is part of a Relationship - Obtain any joined values */
IF is Valid(ccRelate) THEN ccRelate.ccf_GetKeyData()

/* IF the SQL Processor is being utilized, call the retrieve
         Function on the SQL processor */
IF is Valid(dwSQL) THEN
          dwSQL.ccf_Retrieve(ccRelate)
/* If not, the developer can extend this event to perform the retrieve
          any way they want */
END IF
```

Figure 12.32   A virtual event being called. Note that the virtual event is called ve_retrievesetup in this example only to highlight the call.

Object class documentation

While the design effort continues, it is important to make sure that the documentation being produced remains up-to-date and accurate. The documentation we will produce from the physical design phase is an object definition document. Based on this document, we should be able to turn the development effort over to our developers and be confident that the final result will match the design.

Summary

This chapter dug deeper into the object synthesis submethodology of the CBM methodology. We described several factors that we feel are guiding principles when it comes to designing and developing class libraries, particularly in the physical design of object classes. We discussed the process of taking a logical class and breaking it out into the physical class structures we felt would make up the physical characterization of the logical design. We also discussed some of our philosophies of library design: how they differed from other libraries and why. This is not a better mousetrap. It is a technological advance in mousetraps. The ability to distinguish between what is needed and how easy it should be to use is, we believe, tantamount to why we developed our methodology in the first place. Adhering to our design principles is crucial and requires significant discipline. But the rewards far outweigh the effort required.

Object Construction

Introduction

In this chapter we put all of the design effort to the test. We build the object classes based on our design and begin to note where design and implementation can differ. By building the objects in the fashion described, you ensure that the objects match their definition and design, thereby meeting the objectives we established.

Chapter Objectives

The goals of this chapter are quite simple: to build the library we have spent so much time designing. This is when you find out how close you really were. There will be objects that you will alter the design of, but this does not mean your design failed. Good developers rely on instinct, just as good athletes do. Sometimes your instincts point you in a different direction.

The purpose of the exercise is to see just how much the design plays a part in your construction. If you have done the design portion well, the construction effort should be relatively simple. However, there are some techniques that will make life easier.

Remember that the goal of OO technology is to do everything only once. But, we have to be aware of the consequences of making anything overly complicated.

This phase is also where we begin to put our test cases and documentation together in preparation for the testing and implementation efforts. This is a class library, so your users will be highly critical of your efforts. They will ask why you did things a certain way, suggest how it could be done differently (not always better, but differently), and most of all, learn from what you have done. When you build foundation classes of any kind, you are becoming a teacher. Keep this in mind when you "don't feel like putting in the comments," or you decide to "get to that documentation a little later." The sooner you apply the basics, the sooner employees will start looking at what you are preparing. What we want to do is to develop the following:

- Sound object administration techniques
- Solid construction principles
- Tips and techniques for development
- Samples and examples that serve to teach and to test
- Solid test cases and procedures
- Usable, living documentation

Object Administration

One of the key elements in development is administering the objects you and your team develop. Keeping track of objects, functions, and sample code is an arduous task at best, bordering on frightening at worst, and when your project team numbers more than one, you have an administrative headache that the tools of today do very little to alleviate.

It seems that the more advanced we get, the more tools we throw into the mix, and none of the tools solves all of the problems they were designed to solve. If I have to hear (or say, for that matter), "in the next release . . ." once more, I think I will pass the hundred-excuse limit. The fact of the matter is that no one has the unlimited time and resources needed to create the perfect tool, and even if someone did, we would eventually get a tool that would have been perfect 5 years earlier.

Think about it. Those of us who "got our feet wet" with PowerBuilder 1.0 can remember the feeling that there was something good coming. If PowerBuilder as it is today had surfaced 4 years ago, we would have been even more impressed. But, within days we would have found a few things we would like to work differently, or, in pushing the envelope as so many of us are doing these days, we would have found the limits of the tool for a specific task.

This does not mean we should lose heart and not bother doing anything (then I would be out of a job, and would have to resort to *real* work); instead, we should try to plan ahead. When you find out as much as you can about the tools you plan to work with, you can get a pretty good idea of where the vendor is heading.

Object administration is no different. Two years ago, the *only* tool you had for version control of PowerBuilder objects was a very DOS-oriented PVCS. Today, there are no fewer than five vendors, including the makers of PVCS, that provide some sophisticated software to help manage your objects. None are perfect, but some are better than others. Even Powersoft has leapt into the fray to provide a tool (ObjectCycle) that will adequately support its products. Microsoft did the same thing when it purchased SourceSafe some time ago.

We are not here to extol the virtues of the different vendors, but to discuss what we need to do to effectively administer the objects we are developing. We will mention capabilities of different vendors with the different tools we have worked with, but we have not worked with every tool. (If anyone out there has, I have a job for you on the second edition of this book!)

I have, however, had the opportunity to work with several vendors in this area. I still use some manual administration even with the best of the tools. If I could combine all of the tools, I think we might have a tool that will solve more than 80 percent of our requirements.

The object repository

Your PowerBuilder libraries are your repository for your objects. This is a given. What you really need is a cross-reference library of object definitions that relate directly to your actual objects, your test plans, and your documentation, all of which is updated simultaneously whenever you change any of them. Microsoft calls this linking and embedding. The problem is that linking and embedding is a technique, not a tool.

LBMS's Object Manager comes close in this regard in that PowerBuilder object definitions can be "imported" into the LBMS repository and actually used as inheritable class definitions that can be exported back into PowerBuilder objects. This exchange is not quite dynamic, however. Object Manager will also version-control your objects. Their philosophy on version control is reactive. Your objects can be changed multiple times and a version stamp put on the object only when you choose to. Changes made on either side of the fence require manual interaction to keep the other updated. This is not the perfect solution.

PVCS, MKS, and ENDEVOR are the more traditional version control tools. They vary in philosophy and some interact better with PowerBuilder than others, but they are all based on the "archive the exported object" technology. ENDEVOR archives the objects into a database repository, but MKS and PVCS both use the text file on the network approach.

MKS's approach to text file archiving is based on their UNIX experience, where they are the leading provider of version control software, but this environment is different.

How many times have you wondered about the possibility of multi-level check-out, object function versioning, or controllable make-file delivery? Part of each of these requirements is available to one extent or another in all of the tools, but no single tool manages to create the whole environment.

The most popular version control tool is PVCS. This tool interacts quite nicely with the PowerBuilder environment and does not require that you work with the PVCS infrastructure once established. (Although setting up the environment to work with PVCS is somewhat like getting the seven dwarfs to guard Michael Jordan. It can be done, but it is not easy.)

The point is that you need object administration. Picking the right tool to do this invariably amounts to a combination of manual and automated effort on your part. How much you automate and how much remains manual is the determining factor. Your environment might dictate some of the rules for you.[1] Your administration techniques should cover these main points.

- Control who is working on which object
- Control who is working on which version of an object
- Maintain the relationship between design, construction, and documentation

If you succeed in these tasks, you will be able to manage your objects more effectively without the myriad of problems often found in this type of effort.

Object Construction

In building our objects, we need to determine a few factors. How do we go about building these objects, knowing that they must be glued together at some point with little or no effect on the desired result?

The answer is quite simple. Build the objects based on your hierarchy and create test objects to effectively cover the associated test plans. If you are working on this effort by yourself, this will be easy to do. But we generally find a team of developers working on this effort, and you are not building an application—you are building pieces of a large and sophisticated puzzle. If the piece is not built correctly, it will not fit.

As you are aware, the governing body of all the objects we create is the base ancestor layer. You have to build this layer before any of the other layers can even be approached. And yet you do not have to build the object completely in order to start on the next layer. Welcome to virtual development.

Virtual development, like anything virtual, is something that is not really there. The method definitions are built without a concern for the actual functionality in order to provide a base for other object construction to begin. As the methods are fleshed out, the descendant objects gather their own strength and functionality.

Quite simply, it describes the development of the ectodermal layer of your library. All of your objects are designed, so you can go in and build the object hierarchy from the ground up without concern for content. The entire hierarchy can be built in your "development sandbox," where everyone has access to the pool of objects. As object methods are completed, and the object reaches a level of completion that can be effectively tested, the object can be moved into its final deployment area. This allows much easier control over who is working on what because the check-in/check-out facilities can be used. Objects that are completed are moved out of the sandbox so that oth-

---

1. Chapter 9 discusses the various tools in more detail.

ers can easily be seen to be completed, and the remaining objects provide an easy method of identifying what remains to be done.

For example, the base custom class object we have designed contains several defined methods. To create a virtual object, we need only define the entry points, that is, the functions, events, and attributes that are required. The next few figures walk you through the steps as we go about virtualizing the first of our objects.

Create the object

First of all, we create our basic object. The object is descended from a nonvisual object, so we create a new custom class.

Figure 13.1 shows the Create New Custom Class dialog.

Add attributes

Once we save this blank object as our Base Services class (cc_SvcBase; I prefer to use cc_ to identify custom classes instead of the more customary nvo_ or n_), we can begin to define the attributes, the methods, and the services. First, we look at the attributes required (see Figure 13.2). Figure 13.3 shows these variables defined in the Instance Variable dialog.

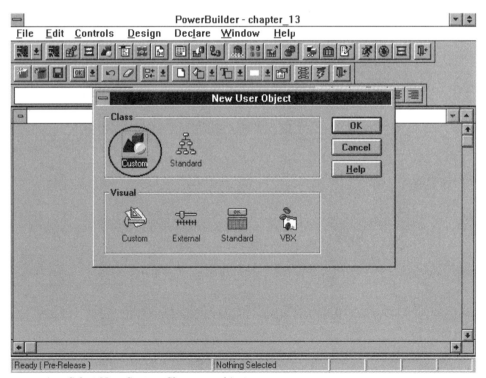

Figure 13.1 Select New Custom Class user object.

Figure 13.2 Declared attributes.

Scope		Type	Name	Default
Protected	Instance	Result	i_pResult Pointer to result code processor.	Constant OK
Protected	Instance	Integer	ii_UsageCount Maintains a count of how many objects are using the service. When this reaches zero, service may be unloaded.	0

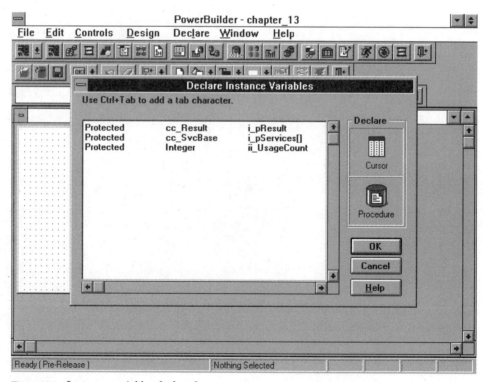

Figure 13.3 Instance variables declared.

Define methods (functions)

Our next step is to define all of the functions we have identified, including their arguments and return values. Figure 13.4 shows the definitions of our functions and Figure 13.5 shows them defined.

Define methods (new custom user events)

Finally we define the custom user events needed, which in this case are the Setup and Initialize events, as shown in Figure 13.6.

At this point, we have a skeleton object that forms the basis for all of our service classes. Even though no code has actually been written, we can begin to develop the next layer of the hierarchy. So, Developer 1 (Bill) moves on to create the next class in the hierarchy, the Application Services classification class. Note that Developer 2 (Millard) will begin fleshing out the details of the base class, so the next few steps actually are occurring at the same time. (By the way, Developer 3, you, are continuing to flesh out the design of our classes, adding new ones, and adding to existing ones, so there is still plenty for all of us to do, but it is going to start moving faster.)

Filling in the blanks

Now you can begin to put together the internal functionality. Slowly and carefully, you can flesh out the methods you have designed. We will adopt a "conversational" approach to explaining the development process. This is a different style of explaining things, but it should indicate how many employees can work on objects once they are virtualized.

Developer 1: Create new Application Services class.

Creates a new class based on the Base Services class. Figure 13.7 shows the Base Services class being inherited.

Developer 2: Constructor event of Base Services class.

While Developer 1 is creating a new class based on the base class, Developer 2 is fleshing out the details of the base class. First of all, code is added to implement the details of the Constructor event (call the Setup and Initialize routines). This code is simply:

```
This.Triggerevent("cue_setup")
This.Triggerevent("cue_init")
```

Developer 2 adds this code and saves the object.

Developer 1: Create Application services, Instance Check class.

Developer 1, in the meantime, closes the Application Services module (as there is nothing to add at this time), marks the class as created, and moves on to the

(Text continued on p. 217)

Figure 13.4 Methods defined as functions.

Functions:			
Scope	**Type**	**Prefix**	**Name**
Protected	Function	*of_*	SvcLoad

Arguments/Return Values/Extension			Reference
Extend:	No	Not necessary; will function for any service type	
Argument:	Any	Service Object class	Value
Return:	svcBase	Instantiated service of type SvcBase	Reference

Scope	**Type**	**Prefix**	**Name**
Protected	Function	*of_*	SvcLoad

Arguments/Return Values/Extension			Reference
Extend:	No	Not required; all instantiated services will be unloaded	
Argument:	None	N/A	Reference
Return:	ResultCode	Result OK	Const. OK

Scope	**Type**	**Prefix**	**Name**
Protected	Function	*of_*	Try

Arguments/Return Values			Reference

Extend:	No	None	
Argument:	Function	A function to be executed	
Return:	Integer	Constant OK	Reference

Scope	Type	Prefix	Name
Public	Function	*of_*	IncrementUsageCount

Arguments/Return Values/Extension			Scope
Extend:	No	None	
Argument:	None		
Return:	ResultCode	Returns usage count with OK result	Reference

Scope	Type	Prefix	Name
Public	Function	*of_*	DecrementUsageCount

Arguments/Return Values/Extension			Scope
Extend:	No	None	
Argument:	None		
Return:	ResultCode	Returns usage count with OK result	Reference

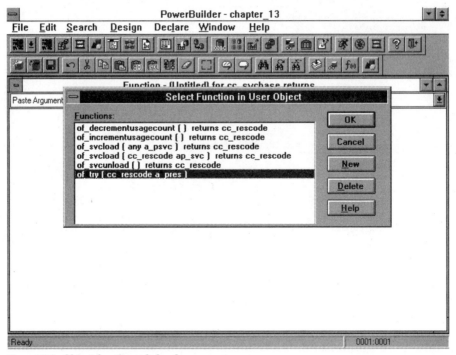

Figure 13.5 Object functions defined.

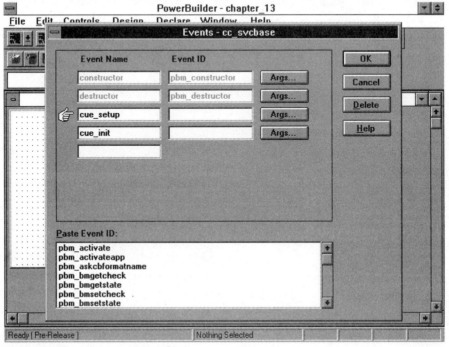

Figure 13.6 Custom user events added.

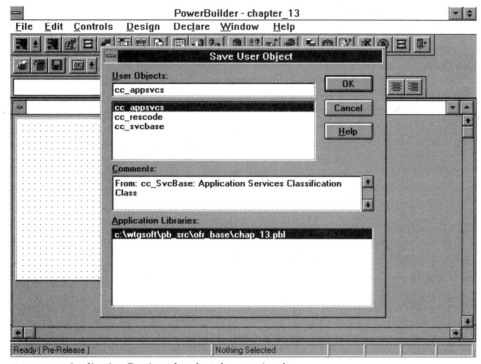

Figure 13.7   Application Services class based on service class.

next class, the Application Services Instance Check class. This class is quickly created by inheriting from the Application Services class.

Developer 2: Code SvcLoad function on Base Services.

Developer 2 moves on to code the functions within the Base Services class, beginning with the of_svcload(). The SvcLoad() uses the new power of the overloaded function in PowerBuilder 5.0 to allow different services to be instantiated using the same function name: of_SvcLoad(). As the argument defines the type of service (passed by reference), the created service is immediately loaded into the instance variable service pointer for the service. The code for this function is shown in Figure 13.8.

Another alternative to this approach is to use a Services Manager that controls which objects are instantiated and where, and provides service class pointers to those who ask. Although this method is more encapsulated and more flexible, it is also a performance hit as the manager must scan for the service each time it is instantiated. We opted for the simpler approach of Overloading when needed.

Figure 13.8 The of_SvcLoad() function for the result code processor.

Developer 1: Application Services Instance Check.

As Developer 2 saves this latest change, Developer 1 is beginning to fill out the code needed for the Application Services Instance Check service. First, add any new attributes, in this case ib_VerificationRequired and ii_MultipleInstanceAction; one is a boolean and the other is an integer.

Next we note that there is an extended event shown. Figure 13.9 shows the inherited methods specifications.

You can see that there are operating system application programming interface (OS API) services declared for the Instance Check class. Why? Because at some point we might want to check for an instance of a different class, which will require a call to the operating system's API.

The OS API services are declared here as a possible service. It is not required for this class, at this particular point in time, but may be needed for something we can foresee in the future. For now, we will leave this out. To continue, we can see three new methods required for this class. Two of these are pretty simple, the third a little more complex. The first two are simple Get Attribute operations, which return the value of an attribute. The attributes are a boolean for Verification Required and an integer comprising the combination of possible actions, or a "style" variable.

A style variable is one that offers several possible values in powers of two (1, 2, 4, 8, 16, etc.). This offers the ability to create unique combinations (which

Figure 13.9 Inherited methods with possible extensions noted.

Scope	Type	Prefix	Name
(None)	Event	*None*	Constructor
(None)	Event	*None*	Destructor
Public	Event	*cue_*	Setup
Public	Event	*cue_*	Initialize OS Api Services??
Protected	Function	*of_*	SvcLoad
Protected	Function	*of_*	SvcUnload
Protected	Function	*of_*	Try
Public	Function	*of_*	IncrementUsageCount
Public	Function	*of_*	DecrementUsageCount

could be considered a bit-wise operation, that is, a combination where the binary representation has the effect of on–off switches, where 1 = 0001, 2 = 0010, 3 = 0011, etc.), allowing you to offer choices such as "warn the user," "continue with current load," "swap to original instance," or "abort current load." Sometimes combinations are invalid (and must therefore be checked), such as "continue with current load" and "abort current load." However, you can continue current load and swap to original instance, even though it probably does not make too much sense to do so.

Getting back to the code, Developer 1 can ignore the possible service implementation for now, and can code the two Get functions shown in the Methods spec of the class specifications, as shown in Figures 13.10 and 13.11.

Developer 2: Service Unload function.

Developer 2 is busy coding the Service Unload function (shown in Figure 13.12).

Figure 13.10   Get Verification Required method.

General Specifications			
Scope	**Type**	**Prefix**	**Name**
Protected	Function	*of_*	Get_VerificationRequired

Arguments/Return Values/Extension			Scope
Extend:	No	None	
Argument:	None		
Return:	boolean	ib_VerificationRequired	

Description	Exceptions	Test Xref
Gets the attribute that indicates whether verification is actually required for the multiple instance check		

This service is invoked to remove all services instantiated. Here we again adopted the simple approach to physically checking for and destroying each service we know about, while providing the developer the means to add on to this process. The service manager would already know which services were instantiated, and would destroy all of them in turn.

The difference in the code comes in deactivating class-wide services. These services use the Usage Count attribute to determine whether they are being used by any other object before allowing the physical destroy to occur. The code for all the service object destroys still looks the same.

```
If isValid(SVCName) THEN
   IF SvcName.DecrementUsageCount() = 0 THEN
     DESTROY SvcName
   END IF
END IF
```

So far we have only one service defined, and that is for the Result Code processor, so our code for SvcUnload() looks like this:

```
If isValid(i_pResult) THEN
   IF i_pResult.of_DecrementUsageCount() = 0 THEN
    Destroy i_pResult
   End If
End If
```

Note that because the Result Code processor is descended from the base services class, it automatically inherits the Usage Count manipulation methods already described.

Developer 1: Code Instance Check function.

Developer 1 now begins to code the Instance Check function itself. Based on the specifications shown, in Figure 13.13, we know to allow the method to look for any application, even though we will be coding only for the current PowerBuilder application at this time.

We can also see, however, that the way we will allow extension of this class is through overloading. Developer #1 can declare the object function

General Specifications			
Scope	**Type**	**Prefix**	**Name**
Protected	Function	*of_*	Get_MultipleInstanceAction

Arguments/Return Values/Extension				**Scope**
Extend:	No	None		
Argument:	None			
Return:	Integer	ii_MultipleInstanceAction		

Description		Exceptions	Test Xref
Gets the attribute that dictactes what kind of action will be taken if multiple instances of specified application are found		ChkInst_002	Test all action code combinations; Warn User, Continue Processing, Quit Processing, Swap to Active Instance, etc.

Figure 13.11 Get Multiple Instance action.

Figure 13.12 The Service Unload function.

General Specifications			
Scope	**Type**	**Prefix**	**Name**
Protected	Function	*of_*	SvcUnload

Arguments/Return Values/Extension			Reference
Extend:	No	Not required; all instantiated services will be unloaded	
Argument:	None	N/A	Reference
Return:	ResultCode	Result OK	Const.OK

Description	Exceptions	Test Xref
Performs all cleanup processing		
Decrementally destroy all services in service array	SVCUnload_001	Test with null array Test with valid array

required with an unsigned integer (UINT) argument for requests pertaining to a handle, and a String argument for additional other checks. The Instance Check code itself is still relatively simple, especially because the handle to the currently active application instance is being passed to the function anyway. We just need to check whether the Handle function tells us there is another instance of the application elsewhere.

There is another reason we are not jumping onto the API bandwagon here. We want to be as platform-independent as possible, and some API functions do not translate. Most functions translate over to UNIX very well, using library name substitution (such as LIBUSER.OS instead of User.exe, or User32.exe), so we would be okay if we chose an API function from the user library. If we chose an API function not in the three generic libraries (User, Kernel, and GDI), we might start finding some that do not exist elsewhere, and thus jeopardize our goal.

The code for our function at this point looks like this:

```
If isValid(a_hAPP) THEN
  /* Handle passed is invalid - Raise an exception */
  OF_SetReturn(Exception, chkinst_001)
  RETURN i_Presult
END IF
IF Handle(a_hApp, True) : 0 THEN
  /* Another instance exists. Return this information */
  of_SetReturn(OK, TRUE)
ELSE
  of_SetReturn(OK, False)
End If
RETURN i_PResult
```

Note that the first segment of the code results in an exception being raised, and that the exception is identified as chkinst_001, the same ID we assigned in the physical class design document.

General Specifications			
Scope	**Type**	**Prefix**	**Name**
Public	Function	*of_*	CheckInstance
Arguments/Return Values/Extension			**Scope**
Extend:	Overloaded	Can check an Application Handle or another application classname	
Argument:	Overloaded	Handle/String	
Return:	ResultCode	rcBoolean	Reference
Description		**Exceptions**	**Test Xref**
Checks if the handle (or class-name) being passed already exists and reports		ChkInst_001	Test with no target passed Test with valid target passed Test with Invalid target passed
If Application Handle is			Make Sure application

Figure 13.13 The Check Instance method.

Developer 2: Increment and Decrement Usage Count attribute

Meanwhile, Developer 2 has begun coding the usage count methods, as described in Figure 13.14.

These functions are relatively simple in that they simply increment or decrement the usage count variable and return the current value:

```
il_UsageCount ++
RETURN il_UsageCount
```

and

```
il_UsageCount − −
Return il_UsageCount
```

The object is once again saved.

Note that we did not code the OF_TRY() or the OF_SETRETURN() mainly because our physical class design was incomplete at this point, showing only a portion of the design effort. To complete the effort sufficiently, we had Developer 3 build the Return Code processor object, which is a standard nonvisual object inherited from the standard nonvisual object class and saved as cc_Rescode. To this object we added a variable called iRes of type ANY and two functions: OF_SetReturn() and OF_Exception(). OF_SetReturn takes as its parameter a data type of ANY, allowing you to return any kind of data to your user in the Return Code object, while at the same time setting a positive return code. OF_Exception works the same way except that the return code is negative and the parameter is usually a long value identifying the exception code.

The OF_Try() is intended to take the return code, along with associated results, and determine whether this is an exception condition for this object at this time. It is a further level of abstraction, allowing an easy way to check for errors almost automatically.

At this point, these objects are saved and stored snugly in their beds, dreaming of roaring performance and sharing encapsulated variables, or whatever objects dream about. We, Developers 1 and 2, have begun to build a hierarchy that will ultimately result in a truly solid class library.

If you were to try these classes out right now, you would find that they work very well. Try the following. Create a new application and in the open event add the following code:

```
/* Testing first service object */
cc_appsvcs_instance cc_appchk
cc_rescode acRes
boolean lb_checkres
cc_appchk = CREATE cc_AppSvcs_Instance
acRes = cc_AppChk.of_CheckInstance(This)
Messagebox("Application Instance Check", String(acRes.iRes))
Destroy cc_AppChk
```

This will display a message box containing False the first time and True the next time.

Figure 13.14   Increment and Decrement Usage Count attribute.

General Specifications				
Scope	**Type**	**Prefix**	**Name**	
Public	Function	*of_*	IncrementUsageCount	
Arguments/Return Values/Extension				**Scope**
Extend:	No	None		
Argument:	None			
Return:	ResultCode	Returns usage count with OK result		Reference

Description		Exceptions	Test Xref	
Increments the service object's usage count				
Increment UsageCount attribute		None	Ensure that count increases by 1	

General Specifications				
Scope	**Type**	**Prefix**	**Name**	
Public	Function	*of_*	DecrementUsageCount	
Arguments/Return Values/Extension				**Scope**
Extend:	No	None		
Argument:	None			

(Continued)

Figure 13.14 *(Continued)*

Return:	ResultCode	Returns usage count with OK result		Reference
Description		**Exceptions**	**Test Xref**	
Decrements the service object's usage count				
Decrement UsageCount attribute		None	Ensure that count decreases by 1	

Tips and Techniques

During our travels we have found several interesting and innovative ideas, from solving a specific problem to using what is already available; the following techniques will allow you to get more out of your environment.

General development techniques

Building environmental controls. Managing your environment is no easy feat. There are so many things that can go wrong, it is almost impossible to plan for all of the conditions you might encounter. One of the most unstable and inconsistent of these is the environment surrounding your application, the Windows environment. Every object you develop adds to the burden the Windows resources must handle. If you have more than 4 MB of RAM and a permanent swap file, chances are you will not have memory problems before you encounter graphical device interface (GDI) and user resource problems. These must be monitored carefully, as they are consumed extremely rapidly. Consider that a program such as Excel can swallow up 20 percent of your GDI resources in a single gulp. If you paint a window with several controls on it, you will consume these valuable and precious resources quickly, too.

Try to keep as few individual controls as possible in a single window. This reduces the load on the environment, promotes better graphical performance, and makes maintenance easier. A datawindow is a great tool for collections of controls. External datawindows can be built with checkboxes, radio buttons, list boxes, and many other characteristics to simulate a collection of controls. And it uses fewer resources. (You also have the flexibility of loading the default attributes of the datawindow with a single instruction.)

You can also use a Windows API function to check the resources available before or during the opening of a window. The function call is quite simple. Declare an external function as follows:

```
FUNCTION uint GetSystemMetrics(int wflag) LIBRARY 'user'
```

You can then call GetSystemMetrics(parm) where parm contains 0, 1, or 2. You will get the lowest of your available resources from 0, 1 will return the user resources and 2 will return the GDI resources. All of these are returned as a percentage. If your resources reach a limit (which you can establish), for example 30 percent, you can abort the open with a message to the user indicating that system resources are low and suggest closing a few application windows (you can easily check to see how many are open), or closing down other applications that are open. (Checking for these is more difficult, but can be done using additional API calls). This provides you with a modicum of control over your environment and prevents nasty "Out of memory" or "Resources too low" messages.

Scripting techniques.   There are several techniques you can use to make your scripts faster and more efficient. The first of these is simply to keep each individual function or event as short and to the point as possible. Below are a few other techniques we have picked up.

Array processing.   Have you ever tried to load an array with a list of items? Building a loop to increment the index value and setting each element in the array can be not only time consuming but painful. Here is a technique to load the entire array with one statement, no indexing required.

```
String MyArrayOfStrings[]
MyArrayOfStrings = {Value1, Value2, Value3, Value4}
```

This loads the values into the first four elements of the array. You will notice that we have used this technique quite successfully in the Object Framework class library.

Another tip is to try to use fixed-size arrays as much as possible. Fixed-size arrays reserve memory in advance and thus perform much better at load time. Remember to try to free up the array as soon as possible to free up the memory it is using. This can be done quickly with a null array of the same type:

```
String ArrayOfNulls[]
SetNull(ArrayOfNulls)
MyArrayOfStrings = ArrayOfNulls
```

One final technique is to use the Destroy function on the array if it is an array of structures or objects. For example:

```
s_Structure MyArrayOfStructures[]
...Some processing that loads and uses the array
FOR idx = UpperBound(Myarrayofstructures) to 1 STEP -1
  DESTROY MyArrayOfStructures[idx]
Next
```

Avoiding long executing statements.   One of the things shown above is a no-no: the use of a function to set a range. The one used above is not as bad as the other way around. For example:

```
For idx = 1 to UpperBound(MyArrayOfStructures)
```

Using UpperBound in this type of statement means that the function is executed for each iteration of the loop. Instead, assign UpperBound to a holding variable and use the holding variable to test the range:

```
int max
max = UpperBound(MyArrayOfStructures)
for idx = 1 to max
```

Knowing what the current window and control are.   It is almost always necessary to know what the current active window and control are. It is also relatively simple to keep track of these elements. Assigning a pointer to a globally accessible variable from a window or Controls Activate/GetFocus event will ensure that you always have the pointer to the currently active object. In using sheets, the function GetActiveSheet() will tell you which sheet is currently active. (It will not tell you whether a child or popup window is currently active.)

> *Remember that response windows activate events do not fire. You must manually set the active object pointers in these cases.*

Events to watch out for.   Some events do not react kindly to developers and can introduce severe complications if used incorrectly. The list below shows a few of these.

- *RetrieveRow:* Executes script for each row of data returned. Use carefully, if at all, as it will significantly slow your retrieval times.
- *Other:* Executed for every message the object is capable of receiving. Do not execute any code that results in the generating of a message.
- *Activate / GetFocus:* Executed whenever an object receives the focus. Do not execute code that forces the object to lose focus, such as a message box.

Application object

The Application object is the one object that is accessed by many developers throughout the development cycle. This makes any form of change tricky. Here are some tips in using the Application object.

- *Version control:* Do not version-control your application object. If you do, every time you check this object out, you will actually be creating a new application.
- *Using functions:* Call functions from your application object as much as possible. This reduces the amount of changes that are required in this object.
- *The idle event:* The idle event should be used to deactivate the application if not in use for a period of time. I open up a dialog box for the user to reenter their user ID and password and then minimize the application. When the user reactivates the application, he or she must enter a user ID and password, connections can be reestablished if necessary, and the user taken back

to the point where he or she left off. You may choose other processing, but use this event to safeguard your application.

- *The SystemError event:* The SystemError event traps all system errors automatically. The function SignalError() also triggers this event. Use this built-in capability to process errors of a single-cycle nature (that is, show an error, expect a response). For multiple-error processing, use a separate routine.

Frame windows

Frame windows are the top-level windows in MDI applications and come in two forms, standard and custom. Standard frames are frames that use only the standard PowerBuilder status bar and toolbars. Custom frames make use of user-defined objects for status bars and toolbars. Frames contain an area called MDI_1, the MDI client area. This area is what your sheet windows will use during application processing.

Resizing the client area. The client area must be manually resized if a custom frame is used. The code required to do this is shown in Figure 13.15.

Note that we are calling a couple of external functions here. The first, ccf_p_GetToolbarWindow() locates the toolbars (if any) and stores the handles

```
/**************************************************************************
*
* METHOD   : Resize Event
* PURPOSE  : Resize the MDI Client area to cater for toolbars
*
*  Author  : Bill Green
*   Date   : 5/17/96
*
* History
* --------
* Date    Init   Description of Change
* ------  ----   ----------------------------------
*
**************************************************************************
*/
/* Check if Custom Frame is being used */
IF NOT ib_usecustomframe THEN RETURN

     int NumToolbarsAtBottom=0
     int ii_width, ii_height, ii_x, ii_y
     s_sdk_rect       1_tb_dimensions[2]
     UINT                     tb_hWnd[2]

     ii_width   =     WorkSpaceWidth(This)
     ii_height  =     WorkSpaceHeight(This)
     ii_x       =     WorkSpaceX(This)
     ii_y       =     WorkSpaceY(This)
```

Figure 13.15 Resizing the frames client area.

```
        num_tbars = sdkwin.ccf_p_GetToolbarWindow(Handle(this), tb_hWnd )

        num_tbars = sdkwin.ccf_p_GetToolbarWindow(Handle(this), tb_hWnd)

        /* If we don't have toolbars, standard resizing is done    */
        If num_tbars < 1 THEN
            IF Isvalid(iw_StatusBar) THEN
                MDI_1. Resize(ii_Width, ii_Height - iw_StatusBar.Height)
                iw_StatusBar.TriggerEvent("cue_resize")
            END IF
            RETURN
        END IF

/* Get the Toolbar sizes */
sdkwin.ccf_p_GetWindowRect(tb_hWnd, 1_tb_Dimensions)

/* Check position of Frame toolbar */
Choose Case This.ToolbarAlignment
    Case AlignmentAtBottom!
        NumToolbarsAtBottom ++
End Choose
/* Get a pointer to the Active Sheet */
Window aSheet
aSheet = This.GetActiveSheet()

/* Check position of sheet toolbar */
IF IsValid(aSheet) Then
    IF aSheet.ToolbarVisible THEN
        Choose Case aSheet.ToolbarAlignment
            Case AlignAtBottom
                NumToolbarsAtBottom ++
        End Choose
    END If
END IF

/* Note: Adjusting width by fixed factor of 5 to cater for borders
    May be replaced with SDK function if desired
*/
IF 1_tb_Dimensions[1].width < (ii_width - 50) THEN
    ii_width = ii_width - 1_tb_Dimensions[1].width + 5
END IF
IF1_tb_Dimensions[2].width < (ii_width - 50) THEN
    ii_width = ii_width - 1_tb_Dimensions[2].width + 5
END IF

/* Check if any toolbars are at the bottom of the screen because this affects
    the location of the Status Bar Window */
IF NumToolbarsAtBottom = 1 THEN
    IF 1_tb_Dimensions[1].height < 200 THEN
        ii_height = ii_height - 1_tb_Dimensions[1].height
    ELSE
        ii_height = ii_height - 1_tb_Dimensions[2].height
    END IF
END IF

If NumToolbarsAtBottom = 2 THEN
        ii_height = ii_height - 1_tb_Dimensions[1].height
        ii_height = ii_height - 1_tb_Dimensions[1].height
END IF

/* Resize the Statusbar */
IF Isvalid(iw_StatusBar) THEN
    MDI_1.Resize (ii_width, ii_height - StatusBar.height)
```

to these toolbars, as shown in Figure 13.16. The second executes a function to determine the size of the toolbars, and this is used in the resize event to resize the custom frame MDI client area. Figure 13.17 shows the code required to obtain the size and position of the toolbars.

You will notice, however, that if you use a custom frame with standard toolbars, you will need to fire the resize event manually when the toolbars are moved. Trapping the toolbar movement messages is done in the ToolbarMoved event (pbm_tbnMoved). Remember to post the event to make sure the movement messages are completely processed before you attempt resize processing.

Using the frame as a global storage area.   Many developers use the frame window to store attributes and methods that they wish to have globally accessible. This is one way to avoid using global variables, but does mean that you need to establish a general pointer back to your frame window. You should not have developers referencing the frame window using hard typing (such as w_myFrame or w_yourFrame). Instead, your frame window should "register"

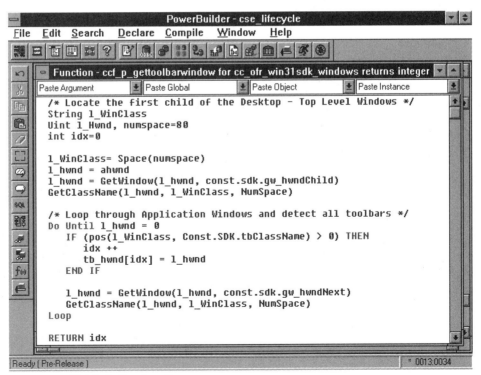

Figure 13.16   Obtain toolbar handles.

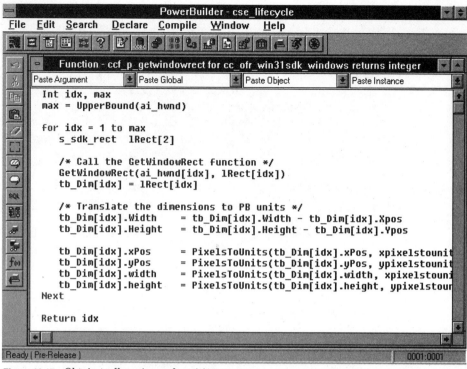

Figure 13.17 Obtain toolbar size and position.

itself to provide a pointer to its functionality. We store the pointer to the frame in our Global Object Manager, and can then reference the frame using ObjMgr.theFrame. This avoids referencing the frame by name.

Menus

Menus are the least exciting of the PowerBuilder objects. There is often much functionality that needs to be put into menus that cannot be because the events available are not customizable. Menus are also almost all pure graphical processing, which use multiple sets of arrays to locate items. This makes them quite slow in comparison to most other objects. They are also the most difficult object to extend and enhance. (Inserting menu items, for example, is tricky and not very fast). Use your menus carefully.

The Menu Service object. We have developed a Menu Service object where all code is processed, separating menu processing from the menu completely. This gives us much more flexibility in building the menu processing hierarchy. Our menus all contain a single line of code.

```
Mf_Event(<eventclass>,<eventname>)
```

Eventclass is a constant identifying the menu item category such as File or Edit, and the MenuName is typically the Menu Items ClassName().

Our Menu Service objects are broken up by a top-level menu item, separating processing even more, and contain custom user events for each menu item to be processed. The hierarchy for this is shown in Figure 13.18.

We need to establish only the services that are being used; the menus should contain the absolute minimum code, resulting in improved load performance. We can also use the service objects to determine whether a particular item in the menu is available by doing a simple IsValid(), followed by the object being able to set the menu attributes associated with it.

Using system information.   There are different ways to show system resources. Here are a few ideas we have used.

One method is to use a custom status bar that continually updates system resource information and displays this textually in the custom status bar. This is similar to what PowerBuilder shows.

A second method is to have a dialog window that can be opened from the menu that displays resources graphically. A window that does this is included in the example application with PowerBuilder and also with the application library in PowerBuilder 3 and PowerBuilder 4. This checks system resources and displays a graph showing the available resources.

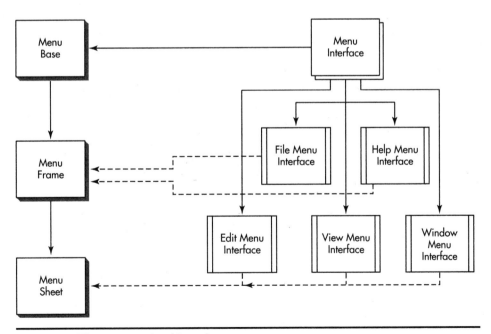

Figure 13.18 The menu services hierarchy.

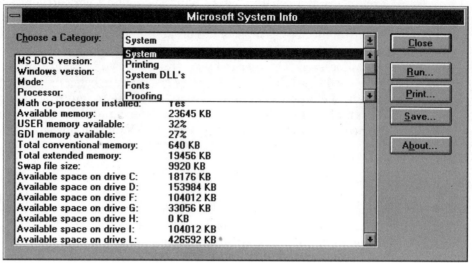

Figure 13.19 MS System Info box.

If you use Microsoft Office, there is a program that shows detailed system information that you can call from your application. The MSInfo.Exe module can easily be called, and has a display as shown in Figure 13.19.

About boxes. There are two methods to display an about box for your application. The first is obviously to code your own. The second involves a system call to display the standard about box as used by Windows applications. (See the Program Manager about box.) This function is shown in Figure 13.20 and the resulting about box is shown in Figure 13.21.

The System Menu box. At the top left corner of every window is the System Menu box. This contains the normal attributes of Restore, Move, Resize, Minimize, Maximize, Close, and Switch To, which are all handled for you by Windows. You can add to this menu with a simple function call and have a window from your application (or processing, for that matter) fired from the menu. The function used to do this is shown in Figure 13.22.

Sheet windows Sheet windows are the mainstay of the MDI application. They contain the processing scripts required by the application. Here are a few tips and techniques regarding sheet windows.

Long-running activate events. Try not to place too much code in the window's activate event. The activate event occurs when you open the sheet and when you switch between sheets. The activate event already has a processing overhead because it has to switch your menus from sheet to sheet, a possibly expensive process. Adding to this will visibly slow down the switching process. A

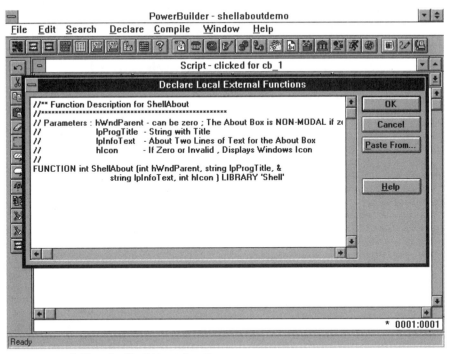

Figure 13.20   Calling the ShellAbout function.

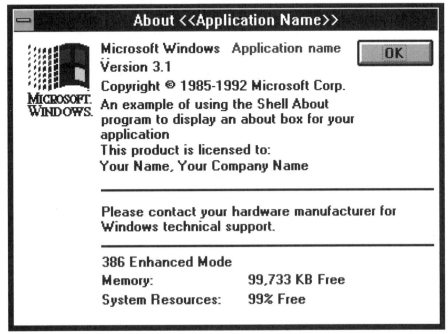

Figure 13.21   The ShellAbout display.

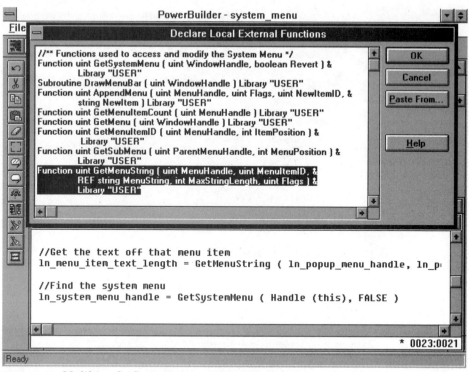

Figure 13.22   Modifying the System menu.

side effect of this is that in debug mode, you cannot step out of the activate event. Why? Because the activate event is the window's GetFocus event and is fired whenever the window receives focus. The debugger forces the window to LoseFocus and it then Gets the focus as soon as the event script is complete, in which case it fires the activate event again. Make sure you put your stops *after* the activate event.

Long-running scripts during the open cycle.   Long-running scripts during the open cycle of the window give an artificial appearance of slow load performance. Remember that the building of the objects contained in your window is in process at this time and will already be starting graphical processes; the user may see portions of objects drawing and redrawing themselves. You would be much better off *posting* an event to perform processing so that the window loads quickly, and the first step of your processing can display feedback to the user as to what it is doing (for example, retrieving data). A progress bar or updatable messages prove useful for this.

Registering and keeping track of sheets.   In PowerBuilder 3, there was no way to keep track of sheets or access them. PowerBuilder 4 has two functions geared specifically to sheets: GetActiveSheet() and GetNextSheet(). This is often still not enough. Using a Window Registry object that each sheet window registers itself in is a useful method of maintaining control over the sheets in your application. If done correctly, the registry can also maintain an accurate view of the hierarchy in which your sheets were opened, providing thread-management capability.

CloseQuery and Show.   Two other events in the window are often misunderstood: the CloseQuery event and the show event. The Show event is fired *after* the activate, and immediately before you see the results on the screen. If you want to affect the appearance of a window (position, size, etc.), this is the event in which to do so. You will therefore avoid the flickering often seen with applications changing appearance in the Open event.

The CloseQuery event fires from the Close event automatically, and allows you to control whether the window closes. Checking for such things as data that have changed without being saved should be done here. If you wish to prevent the window from closing, set the MESSAGE.RETURNVALUE = 1. Windows that must remain open at all times can be controlled here.

Remember that if you use this form of processing to prevent the window from being closed, you need to make sure you provide at least one method whereby it can be closed, or you will never be able to close your application. Note: In Powerbuilders 5, use RETURN(1) instead of MESSAGE RETURNVALUE.

Response and popup windows

Response and popup windows are dialog windows that provide information to the user. The response window is modal. That is, the user must respond to the window before being able to do anything else in the application. A popup window is nonmodal, so it can display information without preventing the user from doing something else in the application. Response windows have a nasty habit of clearing the message queue. Because message loops are not infinite, and the queues are cleared periodically, your messages awaiting processing (from posted events, for example) might be cleared because the response window will wait until the user does something. Therefore, these windows should be used with care and planning.

Popup windows are useful for imparting information to the user on an ongoing basis (such as a progress bar) without preventing the user from continuing. One use for this is business rule error messaging, because you might receive multiple error messages, which can be displayed in a scrolling list.

Positioning the windows.   Do not rely on your design mode positioning for your dialog windows. Changes in video drivers or screen resolution can make this positioning inadequate. A call to the windows GetSystemMetrics() function will tell you what your screen resolution is, and you can adjust your window position according to the user's environment. This adds some polish to your application. The GetEnvironment() function returns this information for you as well, and

Figure 13.23   Window Positioning function.

```
/*********************************************************************
 *
 * FUNCTION : of_Set_WindowPosition
 * PURPOSE : Sets the position of the window based on screen metrics
             rather than rely on set metrics
 *
 *  Author : Bill Green
 *
 * ARGUMENTS
 * --------
 * Type      Description
 * ----------------------------------
 * uint      hWnd - Handle of the window to be positioned
 * Int       Window Position Desired - Constant value representing quadrant
                  such as Top Left, or Centered, or Bottom Right
 * Int       XOffset - Number of units to offset the x-position by (LEFT)
 * Int       YOffset - Number of units to offset the y-position by (Top)
 *
 * RETURN VALUES
 * -------------------------
 *
 * Type      Description
 * ----      -------------------------
 * Int              Const.OK, Const.Failed
 *
 *
 * History
 * --------
 * Date      Init Description of Change
 * --------  ---- -------------------------
 * 09/32/95 BTG   Initial Coding...
 *
 *********************************************************************/
/* Local Variables Used */
int winwidth, winheight, leftpos, toppos
int ScreenWidth, ScreenHeight, Res

/* If the window type is a child window, call the childwindow pos
          function instead*/
IF              hWnd.WindowType = Child! THEN
          Of_SetChildWindowPos(hwnd, ipos, xoffset, yoffset)
          return 1
END IF

/* Continue for normal window positioning*/
if (Screen Width = 0) OR (ScreenHeight = 0) then
          /* If screen metrics have not yet been obtained, get them
             using the GetSystemMetrics() sdk function */

          ScreenWidth = GetSystem Metrics(0)
          ScreenHeight = Get System Metrics(1)
end if

/* Convert the width and height of the actual window to Pixels */
winwidth = UnitsToPixels(hWnd.width,xunitstopixels!)
winheight = UnitsToPixels(hWnd.height,yunitstopixels!)
winheight = winheight

/* Check which position is required and calculate the actual coordinates */
```

```
  Choose Case iPos
  Case Const.topleft
     leftpos = 0 + xoffset
     toppos = 0 + yoffset
  Case Const.topcenter
     leftpos ((ScreenWidth − winwidth) / 2) + xoffset
     toppos = 0 + yoffset
  Case Const.topright
     leftpos (ScreenWidth − winwidth) + xoffset
     toppos = 0 + yoffset
  Case Const.centerleft
     leftpos = 0 + xoffset
     toppos = ((ScreenHeight − winheight) / 2) + yoffset
  Case Const.centered
     leftpos ((ScreenWidth − winwidth) / 2) + xoffset
     toppos = ((ScreenHeight − winheight) / 2) + yoffset
  Case Const.centerright
     leftpos (ScreenWidth − winwidth) + xoffset
     toppos = ((Screen Height-winheight)/2 + yoffset
  Case Const.bottomleft
     leftpos = 0 + xoffset
     toppos = (ScreenHeight − winheight)) + yoffset
  Case Const.bottomcenter
     leftpos ((ScreenWidth − winwidth) / 2) + xoffset
     toppos = (ScreenHeight − winheight) + yoffset
  Case Const.bottomright
     leftpos (ScreenWidth − winwidth) + xoffset
     toppos (ScreenHeight − winwidth) + yoffset
  End Choose

//** Set the windows position
uint lparam
Setnull(lparam)

/* Set the window position */
res = SetWindowPos (handle(hWnd),0, &
+         leftpos, toppos, winwidth, winheight, lparam)
```

you can use the results of this call to position your window. The code to perform this kind of processing is shown in Figure 13.23.

For the more simple need to position windows to the center of the screen based on the system metrics, use the GetEnvironment function as shown in Figure 13.24.

Datawindows. Datawindows are the most often used, and most powerful, objects in the PowerBuilder repertoire. This object is used on almost every window in applications to display and manipulate data. The object is extremely powerful, and is well-documented. Here are a few tech-niques we have picked up on that enhance its processing capabilities even more.

Describe, Modify, and Create. The Describe, Modify, and Create functions are tools used to manipulate, create, and describe your datawindows. The only problem is the use of the syntax. Well, there is a simple solution. The

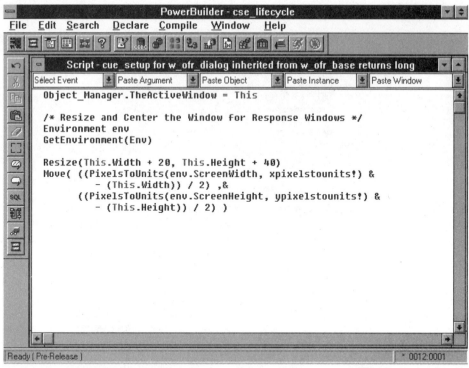

```
Object_Manager.TheActiveWindow = This

/* Resize and Center the Window for Response Windows */
Environment env
GetEnvironment(Env)

Resize(This.Width + 20, This.Height + 40)
Move( ((PixelsToUnits(env.ScreenWidth, xpixelstounits!) &
        - (This.Width)) / 2) ,&
      ((PixelsToUnits(env.ScreenHeight, ypixelstounits!) &
        - (This.Height)) / 2) )
```

Figure 13.24   Window Positioning function.

dwSyn050.exe program that is shipped with PowerBuilder Enterprise allows you to visually select the attributes and various describe and modify syntaxes as necessary. This allows you to create the statements you need without the normal fear of syntax overload. Use this program to generate error-free syntax for using these powerful features. Figure 13.25 shows the DWSyntax program in action, displaying the attributes for a modification of the Table.Select clause.

ImportString().   How often have you heard employees say SetItem() is too slow? Well, the truth of the matter is that it is too slow. Unfortunately, there are no alternatives for setting individual data elements into a datawindow, other than keyed data. But when a new row must be inserted with default values, remember the following function. ImportString() will take a comma- or tab-delimited string of data that matches your columns and insert this data into your datawindow in one step. Multiple columns of data are inserted in about the same amount of time as a single SetItem. This capability is also useful wherever you use datawindows to capture manual data, as in an error dialog window.

Data Retained on Save datawindows.   Datawindows have another useful capability: To act as a data store for static data. Imagine creating the elements of a dropdown datawindow manually, saving these and then using the data in a dropdown without accessing your database or using the much slower and more cumbersome SetValue or DropDown listbox. New data can be added and the data can be filtered, sorted, and manipulated in any fashion with the final outcome being exactly what you started with.

Using this feature is simple. In any datawindow, select the Rows and then Data menu items. This will present you with a grid where data can be entered. Once you enter the data, you can save these data along with your datawindow and when the datawindow is loaded, the data are automatically loaded with it. The data can then be sorted, filtered, and otherwise used, giving you data access with a database.

Interobject messaging

A feature that is used throughout any PowerBuilder application is interobject messaging. This is also the crux of object-oriented programming: objects communicating to each other through the use of messages. PowerBuilder provides a specialized message object to use in passing data between objects: the Message object. However, it is not the ultimate solution. You often need to enhance the capabilities of the message object through the use of other objects such as a message manager.

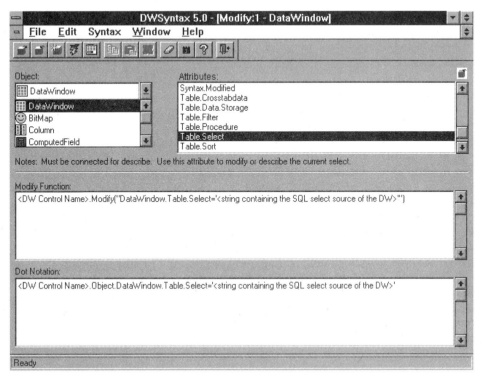

Figure 13.25 The DWSyntax generator for Create, Modify, and Describe.

The message manager, simply put, is an object that maintains a list of objects that can communicate with each other. (Windows does this for all of its communications with and between tasks.) The best use of this type of feature is a Publish and Subscribe methodology.

An object need not know about any other object being used in the system. It knows what messages it can publish and which messages it should subscribe to and process. Thus, when it needs to communicate with another object, it publishes a message. The message manager is the target of all messages. The message manager receives the message and determines who among its list of subscribing objects should receive this message and then publishes the message to all of the recipient objects. Each object that wants to accept and subscribe to a message notifies the message manager at instantiation that it is a subscriber of a particular message and the message manager registers the object for the messages it wants to receive. It then automatically notifies the object when that particular message is published.

Interapplication messaging

An extension of the messaging capability is interapplication messaging. There are two forms: communication within a single environment and communication to an application on another workstation via a network. The first of these is easy to accomplish, the second more difficult, requiring a knowledge of Windows sockets and UNIX processes.

To communicate between applications on the same workstation, you need a communication vehicle. Windows is this vehicle. All you need to do is register a special Windows message class, send a message, and code the recipient application to receive and process the message.

Registering the message class.   To register a special Windows message class, you need a simple function call to the Windows operating system. The function call needed is shown in Figure 13.26. This process returns an unsigned integer that references the message class you created. Each application that wants to publish or subscribe to the message class must register. Using the same string value returns the same message number for use.

Sending a message.   To send a message to all of the subscribers you need the Windows SendMessage function. (The PowerBuilder Send() function will also work.) The arguments for this function are as follows:

- hWnd of the recipient window/object
- Message number to be published
- Long parameter value
- Word parameter value

The Long and Word parms contain the data you wish to communicate. The recipient object must know what to do with the parameters. The message

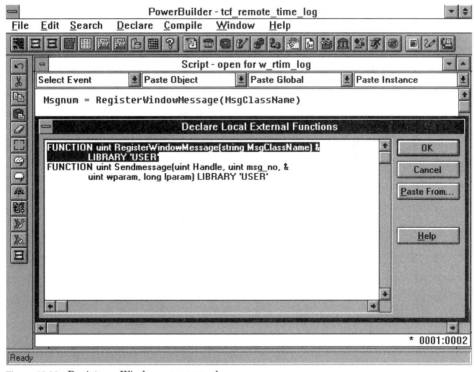

Figure 13.26   Register a Windows message class.

number is the number that was returned from the register function. The hWnd is the handle of the window you are publishing the message to. To send this message to applications of which your application has no knowledge, you need to publish a general target message. To do this you use a special handle called the Broadcast handle. This value is 65535 and will broadcast the message to all top-level windows. (Your frame is your top-level window in an MDI application. The active window is the top-level window in a non-MDI application.)

Receiving a message.   The receiving window needs processing capabilities to process the message. This means it must register the message class so it can receive the message and provide code to process the message. The register function is the same as before, whereas the receiving end requires that you place code in the *other* event to trap the message, check for the message number, and then initiate the processing for the message. An example of this processing is shown in Figure 13.27.

A typical use.   One useful idea for this type of processing is a remote logging facility that can log application messages or debugging information, or audit data. The benefit is that no overhead is added to the application. The draw-

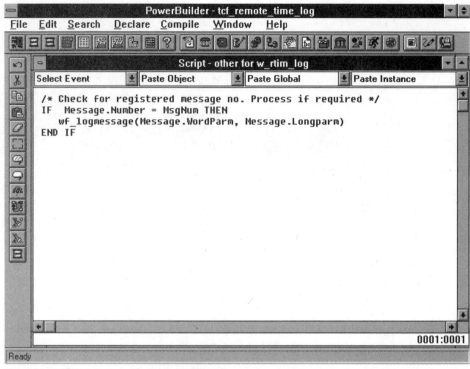

Figure 13.27   Process an application registered message.

back is that the receiving application must know quite a bit about how to process the message with its parameters.

PowerBuilder controls

I recommend creating user object versions of PowerBuilder controls. You can greatly add to the flexibility and versatility of certain objects. The example we will show is the command button.

The command button user object.   In our command button user object we code four events. The first is in the constructor, where we capture and store the handle of the parent window/object. This is done using the Parent() function and assigning the result to a variable of type window. (Exercise care in placing buttons on a user object. The user object must obtain the handle to the parent window and then pass this on to the command button.) The second item we place code in is the Mousedown or Rbuttondown event (or whichever event you wish to use to publish help on). This event then extracts the tag value of the object and displays this in your Microhelp to inform the user of the button's functionality.

The third event is the clicked event. This event needs to trigger (or post) an event back on the parent window (to which you have the handle).

All that remains is to decide which event should be triggered. To do this, we use the code shown in Figure 13.28.

What this code does is use the button's text (you could use the tag value or ClassName() for this as well), from which any accelerator character (&) is extracted and your event prefix added (Cue_). This means that this single button can be placed on any window, with the name changed to represent what you want to execute on the window, and no coding is involved. An OK button, for example, would translate to triggering the *cue_ok* event on whichever window it was placed. No code required!

Side benefit

Another benefit of this approach is, of course, standards. If all of your buttons are derived from this object class, then all of your buttons will be the same size, use the same font, and perform processing in identical fashion. No maintenance required, either!

PowerBuilder samples and example code.   One of the products delivered free with the PowerBuilder product (all levels) is the examples and samples of PowerBuilder code. Although they may not all necessarily be examples of good object-oriented programming, they can definitely reduce the amount of time it

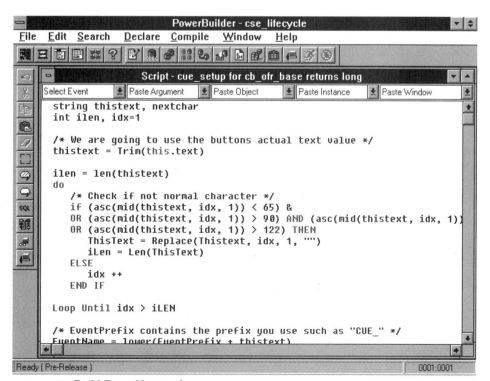

Figure 13.28   Build Event Name code.

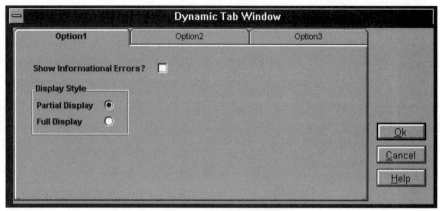

Figure 13.29   Dynamic tabbed folder display (Powerscript version).

takes to learn how to perform a certain function or create a specific object. For example, in PowerBuilder 4.0 an example program by Steve Benfield[2] showed how to create tabbed dialogs. While everyone was rushing around trying to find the right tab object to purchase, one was already right there. In fact, I used this object to develop my own tabbed dialogs that, with a few functions, became a very simple and dynamic tabbed dialog window, as shown in Figure 13.29.

Of course, PowerBuilder 5.0 comes with a built-in tab folder object. This meant I had to change the way the tab object was used, but the functions I had built were still usable; my dynamic tabbed dialog window now uses the Power-Builder 5.0 tab object, but still uses the dynamic tab instantiation functions I built using Steve's tab builder code.

The point is that there is a lot of code already done for you. You just need to take the time to look at it, learn what it does, and use the code or the concept for yourself. There is much to be learned, and some of the information is wait-ing right under your nose!

Summary

This chapter dealt with the tasks we face in developing class library objects. We discussed the need for and some options for object administration, the need for solid construction principles such as virtual class development, how to use samples and examples to test our objects, and the need for testing and docu-mentation.

---

2. Steve Benfield is an acknowledged expert on PowerBuilder and a fellow member of Team PowerSoft.

14

Object Testing and Documentation

Introduction

Testing is a crucial stage of development. Historically, project teams spend 30 to 40 percent of the total development effort on testing. It may not seem that way, but when you add up the time spent on test development, bug tracking, and bug fixing/testing, it adds up.

Usually this is because development is moving forward at breakneck speed and very little time is allowed for testing, or rather test development, during the development effort. Even less effort is expended during the design phase.

In our methodology, we highly recommend that you design, develop, and use test procedures from the start of the development effort. Every action method relating to a method definition must have an associated method test plan. Each method test plan remains with the method, regardless of which class, or how many classes, the method is implemented in. During the physical design phase, the method test plans are further expanded into the test cases or scenarios that are needed to satisfy the test plan.

This provides you with the necessary tools to develop and implement thorough testing of all methods used, with confidence in the result. Logical grouping of test cases results in a test plan of solid and thorough regression test suites that will always completely test the product.

This may seem expensive and time-consuming, but is less time-consuming than waiting until after the development effort is complete to try to develop sufficient and complete tests. By using the design phase to design the test cases to match the methods, you are assuring yourself of having a test plan that matches, therefore ensuring good coverage.

Add to this a test plan that matches the business requirements, and you can guarantee that you will reduce your risk of defects.

Another aspect of development that is often overlooked is documentation. Documentation of a class library is critical to its success. The documentation should tell developers as little or as much as they want to know about the object. Include design documents as part of the package. These give the developers some insight as to how and why objects work the way they do. A user guide, technical reference, and function reference are the key elements. A quick reference guide explaining what is available and where to look up more information ensures that the documentation does not go to waste. These four documents are crucial. If desired, a knowledge base document containing answers to frequently asked questions (FAQ) and tips and techniques (TAT) are other useful but not crucial documents. This may sound like a lot, but if the design is done carefully and the classes, objects, and functions documented properly up front, the penalty at the end is minimal.

I do not want to trivialize documentation, as this is done daily at most organizations, and I also do not want to state that without good documentation, your code will not work; rather, without good documentation, your product will not be used as effectively, you will answer more support calls, and developers will have a little less faith in the product. Spend the time scheduled for documentation on documentation, and start early.

Chapter Objectives

The goals of this chapter are to introduce the techniques we have developed and used to prepare for and execute solid and thorough object testing, and to prepare and produce complete documentation that grows with the product. The elements we cover in depth in this chapter include the following:

- Using the requirement test plan
- Using the method test plans
- Preparing test cases
- Building a regression test suite
- Using samples and demos for testing
- Using automated testing tools
- Test management
- Putting together technical documentation

Object Testing
The testing hierarchy defined

When putting together a test plan for your library, it is important that you understand all of the elements that go into producing an effective testing strategy. There is much more to developing tests than recording repeatable scripts. A good deal of planning and forethought can go a long way to raise the level of quality delivered by any development effort. The development of the test plan follows the same path as the development of the remainder of your system, be it library or application. Figure 14.1 shows a timeline that represents the most effective strategy in developing an effective test plan.

As you can see, test development begins in the design phase. Each phase of the design process produces a part of the test plan. This allows the testing criteria to mirror the design, raising the confidence level when determining whether a system is fully tested.

Just as the design phases build on each other, so do the testing design phases. We have developed a hierarchy of test development that shows the various elements of the overall test plan from requirement test plan through to test development. Your quality assurance can be measured by the test plan you develop. More is not better, but completeness certainly is! Figure 14.2 shows our testing hierarchy.

Note that not all levels require specific test cases to be defined. The requirement test definition is one that ensures that the requirement has been satisfied. This can sometimes be a simple visual check. Each of the levels of the hierarchy is further explained in this chapter.

Building the requirement test plan

Each requirement that a development effort is based on must have an associated test plan. This test plan will not be a technical one, but will focus on satisfying a business function rather than an object's specific methods. The test

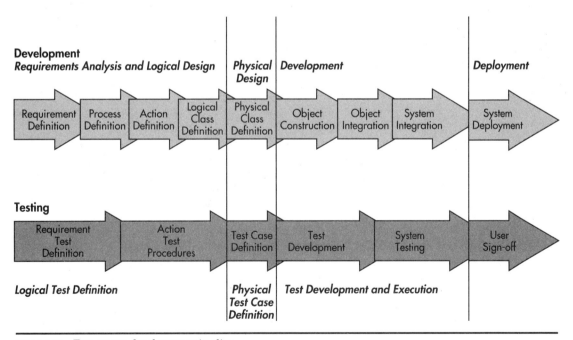

Figure 14.1 Test versus development timeline.

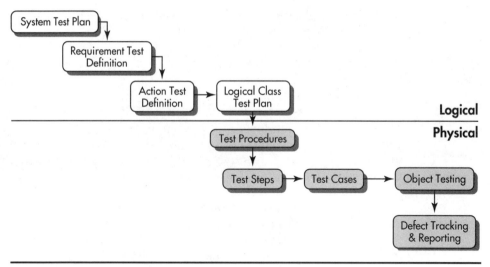

Figure 14.2   The testing hierarchy.

is usually implemented as a visual test, relying on knowledgeable users to detect any defects in the process. The tests focus not only on results but on workflow as well. These tests are usually carried out after each requirement's methods have been developed. The test plan should include tests by method and also a test by object to ensure complete coverage. This might seem like a lot of work, but it is work that must be done in order to ensure good-quality objects.

An example of a requirement test plan (with the associated requirement) is shown in Figure 14.3.

Test procedures

A test plan is made up of test procedures. In our example shown in Figure 14.3 we can see that the requirement is made up of three processes:

- Verify whether the requirement is warranted
- Check for multiple instances of the application
- Take appropriate action based on the results of the check.

The first of these is very simple. An attribute is checked to determine whether the process should take place. The second process defines the actual test required. If we look at this process definition, we can see that there are several actions defined. Figure 14.4 shows an extract from the process definition.

The test plans are designed to test all facets of the implemented functionality. In some cases, however, the definition of the test is as simple as defining the possible values that will be set or returned from an attribute check, as in the second action shown in Figure 14.4.

Requirement Data

Requirement ID:	OFRR0001		
Requirement Name:	Interrogate and Intepret Multiple Application Instances		
Version:	1.0	Update Date:	March 25, 1996
Survey Xref:	OFRS0169	Author:	William Green

Requirement Definition

Description
Determine whether multiple instances of the application exist and, if so, perform some predetermined processing

Cost/Benefit Data

Benefit		CBA Value:	1.00
Provides a mechanism to control user resources		CBA Rating:	Medium

Processing Required

Process	Process ID
Establish whether verification required	OFRM0001
Check whether multiple instances exist	OFRM0002
Take action based on existence	OFRM0003

Requirement Test Definition

Test Definition
Test both with and without another instance of the application running and verify that correct feedback is invoked and the appropriate defined action takes place

Figure 14.3 Requirement Definition: interrogate and interpret multiple application instances.

Action	Acts Upon	Expected Result	Test Plan
Application Instance Check	Application Handle	Returns an indication of whether the application is already running	Test with another instance of the application running Test with no other instance of the application running
SetAttribute	Multiple Instance Exist	Sets a variable indicating whether multiple instances exist	Possible Values: True/False

Figure 14.4 Check whether another instance of the application exists.

In most cases, however, the test procedures defined outline the testing necessary to verify the success of the action. It is important to note that an action may have a positive or negative result. This does not define a test failure, but instead defines the expected results of the action, each of which must be tested. As shown in Figure 14.4, the first action has two possible test procedures: a test with another instance of the application running, and one without another instance of the application running. This describes the two possible scenarios the action will operate under. These scenarios describe the test procedures. These are shown in Figure 14.5.

If we look at one of the test procedures we have defined, we can see the individual test cases required to satisfy the method actions. In expanding the test procedures into test cases, we need to establish the steps required to fully test the object. Figure 14.6 shows the test case for the first test plan.

What we see here is that the test case describes the steps and actions necessary to complete the test. Step 1 is to set up the environment for the test case.

Note that the first step in test case definitions always describes the setup process for the test case. This serves two purposes. The first is to show where to begin recording the test case, and the second is to provide a logical progression of test recording so that a test suite can be built that follows a logical path.

Step 2, in this case, is to start up the application. Step 3 is to start the application a second time. The result of this portion of the test is that the test for existing application should return True. This test should then be logged (preferably with an automated testing tool). This method of preparation leaves nothing to chance. Test case 2 would obviously follow similar steps but omits the final step, and the final result should be False.

Preparing test cases

It is a good idea to start preparing test cases early. Use the tools available to prepare solid test cases for the product you are developing, and reduce the quickly rising defect rate that is becoming the status quo. For the test case we have just defined, we require that an application be ready to run as an executable file. As described, our first step is to prepare the environment. In this case, this requires that we verify visually that the application is not already running. Other test procedures might require other preparatory steps.

Step 2 requires that we launch the application. Step 3 requires that we launch the application again. Now we can record a specific test case. On one hand, we have to verify that the test picks up the multiple instances. This we mark as a positive or expected return. On the other hand, if the result is negative, our code has failed and we need to report a defect.

In this particular case, it might be difficult to trap the return from the test because it lacks the visual component that a testing tool requires in order to capture a test state. What I do in this case is define a condition in the testing tool that I can set programmatically. Different tools provide different mecha-

Test Plan Data

Test Plan ID:	OFRT0004		
Test Plan Name:	Test the Check for Existence of Application		
Version:	1.0	Update Date:	March 25, 1996
		Author:	William Green

Test Plan Definition

Description
Check to ensure that the test to determine whether another instance of this application exists returns a correct value

Test Plan Objectives and Expected Results

Test Case ID	Test Objective	Expected Result
OFRC_001	Return True from test if another instance of the application exists	Const.Exists
OFRC_002	Return False from test if another instance of the application does not exist	Const.DoesNotExist

Figure 14.5 Method Test Plan: test check for existence of application.

Test Case Data:

Test Case ID:	OFRC_001		
Test Case Name:	Duplicate Application Instance: Perform Check for True		
Version:	1.0	Update Date:	May 17, 1996
Test Plan Xref:	OFRT0004	Author:	William Green

Test Case Definition:

Description
Return True from test whether another instance of the application exists

Test Steps:

Step	Step Data	Expected Result	Test Case Recording
1	Test initiation point: application is not running		
2	Launch application	Application should start up	Application Main Window Exists
3	Launch application again	Second instance of application should initiate; test for multiple instances should return true	Record result of Multiple Instance Check

Figure 14.6   Test Case Definition: duplicate application instance; perform check for True.

nisms to do this. My tool of choice, SQA, allows me to do this quite easily. I attach an additional line of code in my object that checks an environment variable that tells it we are running a regression test. The code checks for this and initiates the Log Test Result function, which invokes a mechanism that the testing tool can record. Every time this test procedure runs, this test will verify that the Check for Existing Applications method works correctly.

Using automated testing tools

There are several automated testing tools available today that should enhance the level of quality of your development effort. Use the tools effectively and you can reduce the risk and cost of defects. Using an automated testing tool allows you to record each test case individually, and then combine test cases to form solid test procedures for each method action. Combining all of the test plans applicable to an object class results in a thorough compilation of test procedures that can be reused to build a solid test foundation.

Using a tool such as SQA, WinRunner, or QA Partner, allows differing degrees of test recording, test script editing, and unattended automated testing. It may be debated which tool is better, but there is no doubt that the level of testing that can be achieved with these tools far surpasses manual methods.

Your test procedures should be built individually, and then combined to form tests that can be run unattended (or at a minimum, automated). The results will be a measurable contribution to the success of your development effort.

Using samples and demos for testing

Excellent tools that should be used for testing and for the building of test cases are samples and demo programs. By developing a sample application using the class library, you are emulating, to an extent, the actual developer environment. Remember that the developers who use the product will often use the available functionality differently than will the person who developed the library. Library objects are developed with a specific goal in mind and are designed with a specific use in mind. This is sometimes not the way the object will really be used. Developing an application with the objects gives the library developer a different perspective on how the object can be used.

All sample and demo programs should also be used to build the user guide, which instructs the developer on how the objects should be used.

Using bug reports to build additional tests

Another useful method of testing is to build tests that highlight specific error conditions found. If a bug is reported and code is developed to demonstrate the bug as well as prove that a code fix works, it should be included in every test suite. This ensures that old bugs do not come back, as often happens. Capture these test cases with the bug report number or identifier as the key so that you can quickly establish that a test case relates to a specific method or to a specific reported bug.

Building a regression test suite

A regression test suite is a collection of test cases that are used to test changes made to the library. Changes should not affect existing code, so the regression test suite should be run after any change to the code or the environment. This includes elements such as development tool upgrades, operating system updates, database changes and code changes. Using an automated testing tool often allows unattended regression testing, which can reduce this type of effort by 80 percent or more. For the most part, all that needs to change in the regression test suite is to add any new test cases developed, and to modify some expected results if code is expected to operate differently because of the change.

Test Management

Test management is a very important aspect of system testing. Test management includes setting up the test environment, preparing the test suite, managing defect reporting, scheduling any enhancements that are required, and keeping track of defects reported by users. The automated tools available provide means of tracking and reporting test cases run and defects produced.

The test environment

The test environment should emulate a production environment as closely as possible. All network settings, databases, and other elements normally found in the production environment should be established on a machine separate from the development machine if at all possible. The development tool should be installed on this machine just as it would be in the developer environment, but you should also allow the access to the development tool to be turned off at any point so that runtime issues can also be addressed.

The test environment should not be subject to a great deal of change. Rather, it should be a stable environment for consistent testing.

Preparing the test suite for execution

Once all of the test cases have been built and established to perform the correct test, you need to collect them all into a test suite. This might involve some manual effort or, with some tools, you can build a totally automated test suite. The test suite should be run completely with each major test cycle, but test procedures should be separated in such a manner that smaller portions of the system can be tested individually if necessary. If the tool you are using supports unattended testing (this means that the tool has built-in recovery procedures to handle any unexpected errors that occur and should be able to reset the program to a point where testing can continue, rather than fail the test and all others following), you should be able to run a comprehensive test suite overnight rather than using several precious days of effort.

Tracking and reporting defects, scheduling, and tracking changes

All testing tools, automated or manual, must effectively report and track defects. Each defect that is noted during a test run must be logged, a scheduled correction date assigned, and the defect reporter notified of this schedule. Use an automated system to log and track defects as they go through the correction cycle. Once all known defects are traced, logged, and corrected, you can deliver a high-quality product to your users.

Other Testing Considerations

Coverage testing

One key element of testing is to ensure that you perform coverage test analysis. This means that you should establish what portion of your overall code will be covered by testing. With the complexities of the GUI development, distributed client-server development, and multiplatform considerations, it is important that your testing cover the key aspects of the library. It might prove impossible to test every single line of code, but by using the method test planning we recommend, it becomes more comforting to know that much of the code you build will be thoroughly tested.

Coverage testing can also be accomplished using software, but as of yet, there is no tool that provides test coverage analysis of PowerBuilder programs. These tools are considered white box tools rather than black box tools. The difference between the two is that a black box tool does not have to know the insides of your code. Tests are based on your input and results are tested, not lines of code. White box tools are code-aware; that is, they are intelligent enough to be able to read and analyze your actual code and prepare test coverage analysis to determine whether every function in your application or library has been tested.

Stress testing

Stress testing is usually associated with application development rather than library development, but you, as the library developer, should be aware of this and realize that applications will stress-test the code built on the library, so you still have a responsibility to the application developers to ensure that library code will perform well under stress. Some changes may be generated by the application team for this purpose and these changes should be incorporated and tested in the library code as much as possible.

Object Documentation

Design documentation

The design documentation for any system developed using the CBM methodology is automatically done. The output from each step results in a form of document. (We are working on an automated system to support CBM.) When you combine these documents, you will have not only a thorough design for your system, but also a very effective design document. The important thing at this point is to ensure that the design document stays current. Using the same methodology to design new objects will automatically update the overall design document. Changes made in physical processing to accommodate bug fixes or minor enhancements usually affect only the physical class definition document. Without being automated, it is up to the system architects to ensure that the design document stays current with the actual classes.

Enforcing this strategy requires significant discipline, but also ensures that changes go through a design process, resulting in much more effective code enhancement.

Technical documentation

A class library of any kind is intended for use by developers. Developers are the users in this case, and the documentation must be slightly different from normal application documentation. The documentation we feel is important to developers includes the following:

- User guide
- Technical reference
- Function reference
- Quick reference

There are other useful documents, such as a knowledge base, which can be added as time passes, but these four are critical to the acceptance of your product, be it commercial or proprietary.

User guide.   The user guide is very important, especially to new users. This document should detail how to build any object based on a class library object. The user guide should include the following:

- An overview
- Support details
- How to install the library
- What key objects and architectures are used
- Where to get more information

The overview.   The overview of the document should detail what the library is all about, why it came about, how it benefits the user, and where the library and information about the library can be obtained.

Support details.   Support details should include where and how the users of the library can obtain the technical support they need. Details of the support services offered should also be included. Another detail often overlooked is a procedure to report bugs and enhancement requests and the chain of events that will occur when this procedure is invoked.

Installation procedures and requirements.   Here you should detail how to install the library and list the minimum hardware and software needed to use the library. If several components can be installed, each component should be described as well as the effect of not installing the component.

Key objects and architecture. Detail the key objects offered in the library. Describe the architecture behind the library objects and how they are intended to make the developer's task easier. Reference the other technical guides offered for additional information.

Where to get more information. A key element of the overview is where to obtain additional information about the library and its contents. Describe the various manuals that are offered and state whether they are available in electronic format.

Technical reference. The technical reference should be the ultimate how-to guide for all of the objects in the library. The technical reference should include details on how objects should be used together. For example, if a dialog window is developed with an object in it, the technical reference should detail not only the use of the window, but also the nature of the object within the window. The technical reference should be developed in such a manner that it can be compiled into an on-line help file. The value of on-line help cannot be overstated.

Function reference. The function reference should be a complete guide to all of the functions available in the library and which objects they reside in or are used from, and should describe in detail the calling conventions (parameters, return values), override capabilities (can the function be overridden or extended by the developer?), and details of any related functions or objects.

Quick reference The quick reference guide is a very brief outline of the objects and functions available in the library, often taken from the table of contents of the technical and function references. A brief (one-line) description of the function or object should be included as well as details of where the object or function is described in more detail. This should be able to be printed and handed out to all developers with the library and will get more use than most other manuals.

Summary

This chapter was intended to shed light on the procedures that must be followed in order to establish good testing design practices, which in turn will help produce solid and reliable code. Every aspect of testing is important and should be approached with as much care and concern as the development effort itself. In a library development effort, it becomes even more important. Developers will build more and more mission-critical applications using your code as a foundation, and the foundation must be rock-solid.

The QA process is a vital one and should not be left until after the development cycle is complete; rather, it begins very early on in the design, as does the documentation effort. Start early and avoid the desperate dash for the finish line; you will produce a more polished application. Effort put into testing and documentation is rewarded very quickly.

15

Productivity Aids

Introduction

Productivity! It is the measure of what we do and how well we do it. It is the mantra of the middle manager. It is the pot of gold at the end of the rainbow. However you look at it, productivity (along with quality and stability, of course) is the goal of the class library designers and builders. However, once you have constructed and deployed your class library, there is still more you can do to help the developers.

Chapter Objectives

This chapter introduces the concepts and techniques you can use to build productivity aids (also known as wizards) in PowerBuilder. We discuss our definition of productivity aids and show you how to apply the power of Power-Builder to create simple, effective tools to increase developers' productivity.

What are productivity aids?

Productivity aids or wizards guide the user through the steps necessary to complete a task. In the specific case of a PowerBuilder class library, wizards are used to create objects based on the class library objects. Through a simple question-and-answer process, the wizard gathers the information necessary to produce the code that implements the object.

Why build productivity aids?

Wizards can be used to simplify the construction of complex objects. The wizards use a simple Previous/Next/Finished interface to guide the user through the steps necessary to completely specify an object. The creator of the wizard controls both the static and the user-definable aspects of the object in question. The makeup of an arbitrarily complex object is broken into manageable chunks, wrapped in a simple and understandable interface. This enables a larger body of developers to make use of the features of your class library.

Furthermore, the use of wizards helps to ensure adherence to best-practice guidelines. Because the wizard process guides the user through a sequence of questions, then creates the code to implement the object, the code can be created to make best use of the technology embodied in your class library. The code created through this process follows the intent of the creator of the wizard, and implements the object in the most efficient manner.

Wizards also help teach the use of your objects. Through repeated use of the wizards, the developers come to know the requirements and options associated with any of your objects. The order and grouping of the data elements that the user must specify help him or her to understand the relationships involved. Developers are soon able to implement objects based on class library objects without the help of the wizards.

The wizard process

The wizard process consists of three steps:

1. Gather the information.
2. Format the substitution values.
3. Execute the substitution engine to create the final object.

The first step, gathering the information, varies according to the complexity of the object the wizard is creating. For a very simple object, a single screen may be all that is needed to gather the user input. For more complex objects, numerous screens may be required. In addition, the answers given on one screen may influence how subsequent screens are presented. You need to provide a mechanism that allows the user to move back and forth at will between screens, such as Previous and Next buttons.

The second step, formatting the substitution values, reflects the fact that a wizard is simply a sophisticated substitution engine. For any object, a certain amount of the code remains static. The remainder of the code is the variable part. The variable part of the code is generated by the wizard according to the input gathered in Step 1 of the wizard process. The substitution values must be formatted in such a way as to allow them to be inserted into the substitution template in an unlimited number of places and in any order.

The final step, executing the substitution engine to create the final object, is where the magic of the wizard process manifests itself. The synergy between the substitution values, the substitution engine, and the template allows for unlimited flexibility in the generation of the final object. However, to adequately support this level of flexibility, the substitution keys and the template must be created very carefully.

Simple Wizards

A simple wizard uses only one or a few screens to gather information and creates only a single type of fundamental object. The requirements for flexibility are not as stringent as they are in the case of more complex wizards. That means that the underlying information-gathering engine and the substitution engine can be created easily for each separate object.

One example of a simple wizard is a preamble wizard. This wizard creates the standard preamble for a function or event and places it on the clipboard for easy pasting into your code. Figure 15.1 shows the first information-gathering screen from Castle Software Engineering's preamble wizard. This screen allows input of the name of the function or event, the author, and the function description. Subsequent screens lead the user through the description of arguments and return types. Then, when the user presses Done, the properly formatted preamble comments are placed on the clipboard, from which they may be pasted into the function script.

Extendible Wizards

An extendible wizard uses a database to define the objects that can be created, and the steps necessary to create these objects. The information-gathering

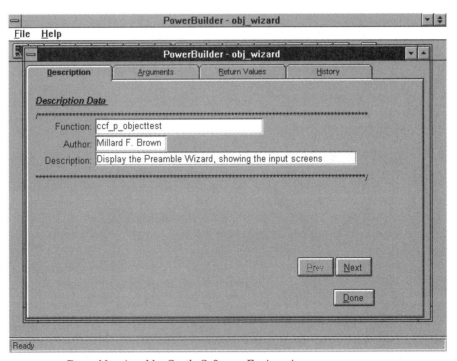

Figure 15.1 Preamble wizard by Castle Software Engineering.

process must be flexible and generic to allow for the many and varied pieces of user input that must be accepted. The benefit of this architecture is that objects of arbitrary complexity can be generated simply by defining the input-gathering objects for each step.

Figure 15.2 shows a typical information-gathering screen of an extendible object wizard.

The design of an extendible wizard involves several elements:

- *The wizard database:* The database contains the definitions of the objects that the wizard can generate and the steps that must be taken to define each object.

- *The wizard process windows:* These windows, each based on a common ancestor, contain the code and datawindows that guide the object-generation process.

- *The wizard user objects:* This collection of user objects, again with common ancestry, provides the intelligence for the data-gathering phase of object generation.

- *The wizard script templates:* This is the basic script that defines each object, with substitution arguments where the user input will be added.

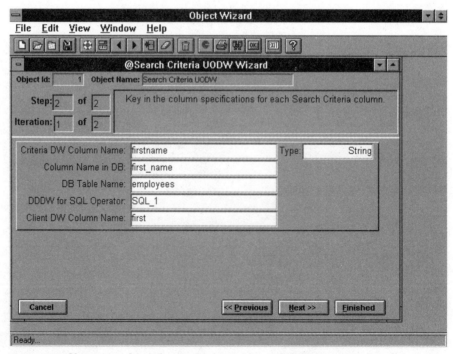

Figure 15.2   Object wizard search criteria object column definition screen.

The wizard database

The simplest example of a wizard database consists of two tables:

- The wizard objects table
- The wizard steps table

Figure 15.3 shows the wizard tables.

The wizard objects table defines each object that the wizard is able to generate. The rows of the wizard objects table contain the following:

- *Object ID:* a unique identifying key for each object
- *Object name:* a descriptive name that is displayed on the wizard window during the object-generation process
- *Object description:* a string that provides a detailed description of the object to be generated

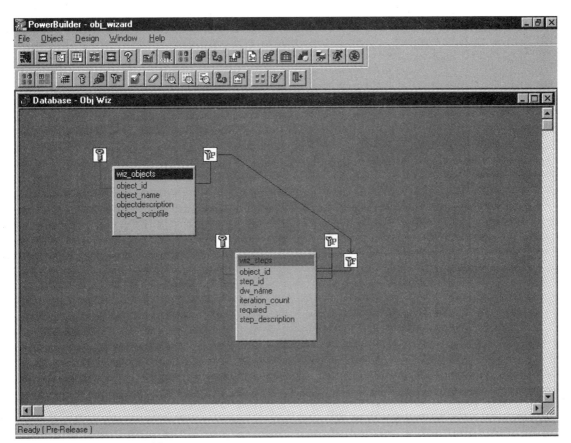

Figure 15.3 Object wizard tables.

- *Script template file:* the full path to the file containing the script template for the object

The wizard steps table defines the steps that the information-gathering process works through to accumulate user input to generate each object. The table is keyed on the object ID and step number. The rows of the wizard steps table contain the following:

- *Object ID:* a foreign key linking the steps table to the objects table
- *Step ID:* a sequential ID that is unique when combined with the object ID
- *Wizard user object dw name:* the object that is used to gather the input from the user for this step
- *Iteration count:* a number that specifies the number of times this step will be performed
- *Required:* indicates whether this step may be skipped by the user
- *Step description:* a detailed description of the purpose of the step, displayed on the wizard process window during the data collection for each step

The wizard process window

Figure 15.4 is a schematic of the wizard process window. Figure 15.5 depicts the wizard process. First, the user selects the object to be generated. The record defining that object is then retrieved from the wizard objects table. The object record is retrieved into a hidden datawindow, dw_objects. Note that you could use a datastore instead of the various hidden datawindows, which would save graphic resources. We used datawindows for this example to make the internal structure more obvious to the reader.

Next, the steps defined for that object are retrieved into another hidden datawindow, dw_generate_steps, sorted by step number. The name of the wizard user object is read from the first step record, and the object is opened on the window. You will note that each step record also contains a value for the number of iterations. This allows a given step to be repeated as many times as necessary. The iteration count may also be overridden by entering code into the cue_i_getCount event.

When the user presses the Previous, Next, or Finished buttons, the data that have been entered into the datawindow are saved in another hidden datawindow, dw_storage. This allows the user to move freely among the steps, using the Next and Previous buttons. The next step or iteration is then executed.

Once the user has entered all of the data necessary to define the object, he or she presses the Finished button to trigger the construction of the object. The Finished button begins the object build process to construct the importable source code for the target object. First, the build process steps through the user's responses and constructs the substitution key-value records.

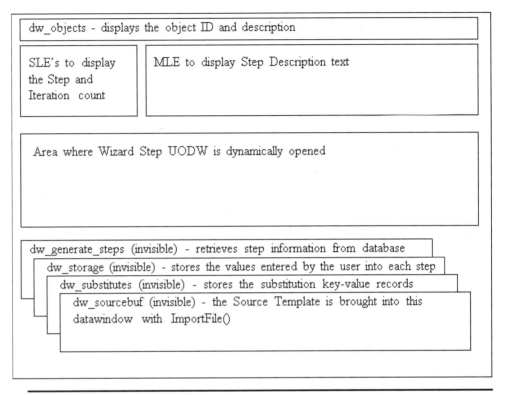

Figure 15.4 The wizard process window.

Once the key-value records are created, the process of substituting the replaceable parameters in the script template begins. The source template is imported into the source datawindow, dw_source. Then, the substitution engine is executed for each source line. The substitution engine examines the source line for each substitution key. If the key is found, the substitution is repeated for that source line as many times as is necessary to exhaust all references in the source line as well as all occurrences of that key in the key-value table. Finally, the stock substitutions, which are standard, built-in substitutions, are performed on the source line. An example of a stock substitution is $CRLF$, which is the substitution key for the Carriage ReturnLine Feed pair. Once all substitutions are performed, the source line is written to the output file.

The object build process is depicted graphically in the bottom half of Figure 15.5.

The object build process creates an output file that can be imported using the import facility of the Library Painter. Alternatively, you could use Open Repository Case API (ORCA) to construct a DLL that would programmatically import the source code into the target object, eliminating all manual steps.

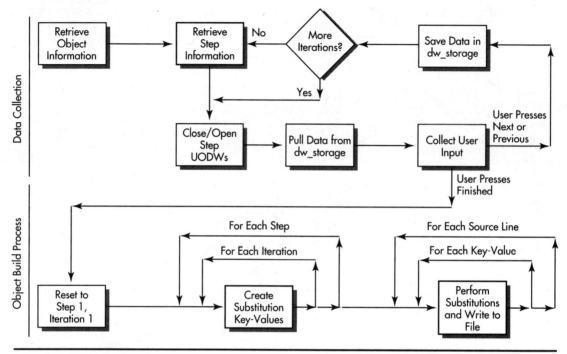

Figure 15.5 The wizard process.

However, without some fancy footwork, the string you can import using ORCA is limited to 60 K.

The wizard user object

The user is led through the wizard step by step, filling in the responses that eventually are used to construct the final object. Each step uses a datawindow user object to gather the user input. Let's examine the wizard user object in greater detail.

The wizard user objects inherit from a common ancestor, uodw_wiz_base. There are several custom user events defined on the base wizard user object:

- cue_i_execute_step: This event iterates through each successive data-gathering step.

- cue_i_execute_iteration: This event iterates through multiple occurrences of a single step.

- cue_i_defaults: Initially empty, this event allows the wizard developer to establish any default values for the user object.

- cue_i_getCount: This event allows the iteration count of the next step to be overridden based on data gathered in the current user object.

- `cue_i_buildstring`: This event constructs the substitution record that will be used for constructing the object.

In addition, the uodw_wiz_base user object inherits the standard User Object DataWindow (UODW) events from the base UODW object, including the Init and Setup events, as well as Next and Previous.

A user object function, ccf_build(), triggers the cue_i_buildstring event. The substitution key-value record is placed in the instance variable is_buildstring, then returned from the ccf_build() function.

The wizard script template

The wizard script template is a text file with a copy of the script for the target object. Within the template, the variable information that the user supplies when the wizard is executed is replaced by substitution keys. The keys should be constructed such that the key string does not occur accidentally within ordinary exported script. Our keys are constructed by enclosing the key string between dollar signs. However, you must be careful not to use the key string $PBExport-Header$ or other strings that begin with $PB because those strings are generated by PowerBuilder and can occur in any exported file. Listing 15.1 shows a typical script template. Except for $PBExportHeader$, all of the strings enclosed in dollar signs are substitution keys that will be replaced by user-entered values in the final stages of the wizard process.

LISTING 15.1 Object wizard script template.

```
$PBExportHeader$$object_name$.sru
forward
global type $object_name$ from uodw_search_criteria
end type
end forward

global type $object_name$ from uodw_search_criteria
int Width=1212
int Height=465
end type
global $object_name$ $object_name$
on cue_i_ofr_setup;call uodw_search_criteria::cue_i_ofr_setup;
// Enter Setup Script Here
//$ofr_setup$
end on
on cue_i_ofr_init;call uodw_search_criteria::cue_i_ofr_init;
// Enter Init Script Here
//$ofr_init$
end on
```

The next task is to add objects to the wizard so that the users can generate them.

Adding an Object to an Extendible Wizard

Once the superstructure is in place for the extendible wizard, it is a fairly simple matter to add a new object. The steps are shown in Figure 15.6.

Create an object record and script template

Your first task is to create and insert a record into the wizard objects table. You will need to specify the values for each field in the record: Object ID, Object Name, Description, and ScriptFile.

Next, you will create a script template. You derive a wizard script template from an object of the type that you ultimately want to generate. That is, if you are creating a wizard for a Search Criteria user object, first create an instance of that object. Populate all of the events that you will eventually generate code for with representative code. Be sure that any objects, instance variables, and event scripts are placed into the object. Then export the script to an .SR? file.

Using the exported file, determine the areas in which the user will supply information that replaces code in the exported source code. Make note of the code that you will have to supply from the object build process, then delete the representative code from the script, replacing it with a substitution key. Figure 15.7 illustrates how a section of script is replaced by a key string. Note that you can use the same substitution key anywhere in the script. In fact, it is necessary to do so for every instance where you want the same substitution performed. Save the resulting file with a .TXT ex-

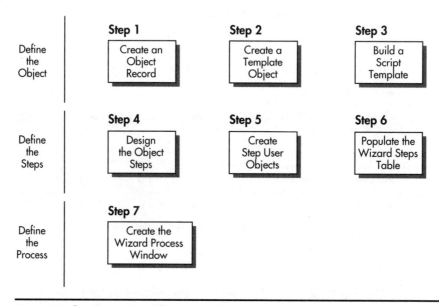

Figure 15.6 Creating a wizard for a new object.

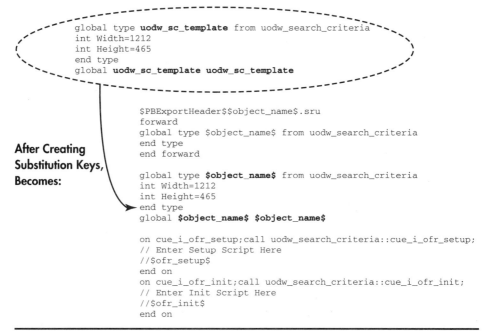

```
        global type uodw_sc_template from uodw_search_criteria
        int Width=1212
        int Height=465
        end type
        global uodw_sc_template uodw_sc_template
```

**After Creating
Substitution Keys,
Becomes:**

```
                        $PBExportHeader$$object_name$.sru
                        forward
                        global type $object_name$ from uodw_search_criteria
                        end type
                        end forward

                        global type $object_name$ from uodw_search_criteria
                        int Width=1212
                        int Height=465
                        end type
                        global $object_name$ $object_name$

                        on cue_i_ofr_setup;call uodw_search_criteria::cue_i_ofr_setup;
                        // Enter Setup Script Here
                        //$ofr_setup$
                        end on
                        on cue_i_ofr_init;call uodw_search_criteria::cue_i_ofr_init;
                        // Enter Init Script Here
                        //$ofr_init$
                        end on
```

Figure 15.7   Replacing source code with a substitution key.

tension so that you can use the ImportFile() function to load it into the dw_source datawindow.

Design the object steps

Now you need to lay out the steps that the user will cycle through to specify the object. Each step should gather a logically related group of information that will be translated to one or more key-value records during the object build process. For this example, we will create a wizard that will generate a Search Criteria object. A Search Criteria object is an object that allows the user to specify a set of criteria that the program will attempt to match and display in a Search Results object. The Search Criteria object contains the intelligence to collect and validate the user input, as well as to format the final SQL statement that will retrieve the desired result set. To completely specify a Search Criteria object, we need to collect the following from the user:

- The name of the object to be generated
- Various declarative options
- The number of columns that may be included in the generated SQL

- Information that defines the link between criteria columns, database columns, and result set columns.

  This example is based on a business object that encapsulates the functionality necessary to gather and manipulate search criteria. It is an example only, and is based on the experience accumulated over a number of development efforts. The purpose of including it here is to show, by example, how the wizard process gathers and substitutes the necessary user-supplied data to create the object.

The majority of the functionality in the Search Criteria object will be inherited from a business object, uodw_search_criteria. The developer would ordinarily inherit from the base object, then supply the declarative information to set up the options and link the columns.

Figure 15.8 shows the sequence of steps that will be used to generate our example Search Criteria object.

Create a user object for each step

Once you have designed the steps, you will create a user object to collect the data for each step. First, construct an external source datawindow with fields on it for each parameter that the user will supply for that step. Then create a user object datawindow, inheriting from the base wizard user object. You can add any validation as necessary to ensure that users enter accurate data. Add code for the events in the user object as follows:

- cue_i_defaults: Supply any default values to the datawindow.
- cue_i_buildstring: Extract the values from the datawindow and construct one or more substitution key-value records.

Supplying the defaults: cue_i_defaults.   Listing 15.2 shows a typical script for the cue_i_defaults event. This script sets up any values that you want to al-

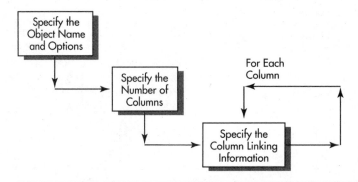

Figure 15.8   The steps for specifying a search criteria object.

ready exist in the datawindow when the user receives control. Note the use of the ImportString() function to boost performance of this script.

LISTING 15.2   The cue_i_defaults event script.

```
Reset()
ImportString("False~tTrue~t2~t")
```

Building the substitution values: cue_i_buildstring. The script for the cue_i_buildstring event is shown in Listing 15.3. This listing shows how the substitution key-value records are constructed based on the data that the user entered. Each key-value record is generated as a string containing a tab-separated pair. The value that will be substituted into the script is a combination of code wrapper and data extracted from the wizard datawindow. The key-value data created by this script consist of one pair made up of ofr_setup and several lines of script. The script lines are delimited using the $CRLF$ stock substitution. The complete key-value string is recorded in the storage datawindow, dw_storage, using the ImportString() PowerScript function.

TIP

You can add multiple key-value pairs to one string by separating the successive key-value pairs by a Carriage Return–Line Feed pair, ~r~n. In the same vein, do not allow literal ~r~n pairs in the string, or you will force a new record during the ImportString() function. Instead, use the $CRLF$ stock substitution.

LISTING 15.3   The cue_i_buildstring event.

```
is_buildString = "ofr_setup~t"+&
  "istr_Columns["+String(ii_current_Iteration)+&
  "].dwColumnType = "+ GetItemString(1,"dwcolumnType") +"$CRLF$"+&
  "istr_Columns["+String(ii_current_Iteration)+&
  "].dwColumnName = ~""+ GetItemString(1,"dwcolumnName") +"~"$CRLF$"+&
  "istr_Columns["+String(ii_current_Iteration)+&
  "].dbTableName = ~""+ GetItemString(1,"dbTableName") +"~"$CRLF$"+&
  "istr_Columns["+String(ii_current_Iteration)+&
  "].dbColumnName = ~""+ GetItemString(1,"dbcolumnName") +"~"$CRLF$"+&
  "istr_Columns["+String(ii_current_Iteration)+&
  "].dwSQLOperatorName = ~""+ &
  GetItemString(1,"dwSQLOperatorName") +"~"$CRLF$"+&
  "istr_Columns["+String(ii_current_Iteration)+&
  "].ResultdwColumnName = ~""+ &
  GetItemString(1,"ResultdwcolumnName") +"~"$CRLF$$CRLF$"
```

Create the wizard process window

Establish a wizard process window for the new object. You will inherit this window from the base wizard process window. Note that the bulk of the code is housed in the base window, but the inheritance model allows for greater flexibility as the wizard is extended. The specialized code in the wizard process window will establish the object ID and the name of the output file.

Add the steps to the wizard steps table

Insert a record into the wizard steps table for each step you have defined. You will need to specify the step ID, the name of the wizard user object for that step, the user object name, the iteration count, the required flag, and the description of the step. If the step is to occur multiple times, enter the iteration count as the number of times that you want that step to execute. Otherwise, set the iteration count to 1.

> *You can override the iteration count for the next step by coding the cue_i_getcount event to set the ii_iterationcount value on the parent window.*

Test the functionality of the wizard

Now that you have completed the steps necessary to define your wizard, it is time to try it out. Select the new object from the object list, then proceed through the steps you have defined. Make sure you exercise the limits of your input collection datawindows:

- Test the validations
- Leave out required fields
- Change the values that control subsequent iteration counts
- Use the Previous and Next buttons to move between steps, checking that previously entered data are displayed for each step.

Once you have cycled through the steps, press the Finished button and make sure that object generation proceeds smoothly. Then use a text editor to examine the final script file. If all looks well, use the Entry | Import command of the Library Painter to import the file. If the import completes without error, try to open the object. Then examine the instance variables, style settings, functions, and scripts that have been generated by the wizard. Once you are satisfied that the wizard is functioning, turn it over to a potential user for further testing. The test with the actual user will probably unearth a few bugs and situations that you never considered. Once you have met any challenges raised by the user testing, you can release your wizard to the rest of the developers.

Summary

The construction of productivity aids or wizards allows more developers to use your base class objects. Because the wizard process controls the generation of the code, you will be able to ensure that objects built using the wizard use your base class functionality optimally. You will also find that developers will gain knowledge about the requirements for using your objects through the use of wizards. Thus, wizards are tools for enhancing developer productivity, code efficiency, and developer training.

In this chapter, we showed you the characteristics of both simple wizards and the more complex extendible wizards. You found out how to design an extendible wizard application that will generate objects of arbitrary complexity based on entries in a database. Finally, we showed an example of how to create the database entries and PowerBuilder objects needed to define a new object to be included in an extendible wizard.

The techniques demonstrated in this chapter need not be restricted to building PowerBuilder objects, either. You can apply these techniques any place where you can use a template containing key-value substitution fields.

A well-crafted wizard application improves developer productivity and enhances the image of the library team. It is also a blast to build one. Have fun.

Support Infrastructure Development

Introduction

Your job is not over once the library is deployed. Next thing you know, someone out there is going to start using it, and that leads to support calls. For a class library to succeed, the level of support must be high. The way we handle the support requirements of our library's users has a direct impact on the reputation and the longevity of the class library.

The developers are your customers. Maintaining the ongoing relationship with them depends on a consistently high level of support.

Chapter Objectives

In this chapter, we examine the goals your support organization needs to pursue. You will see the components that make up an ideal support system. Finally, we help you with tips and techniques for ensuring that the quality of your support remains high.

Goals of the Support Infrastructure

The support team should strive to strengthen the corporate commitment to the library. They do this primarily by enabling the current and potential users of the library to address their business issues more productively through the use of the library. The support team keeps the library running smoothly and according to specifications. They also provide expert help, answering technical questions and resolving bug reports.

The support organization also is responsible for providing startup training to new users of the library. In the cases where the formal training function has been assigned to the support team, they will need to produce, schedule, and administer the formal training courses.

An important goal of the support team is to ensure that no reported bug goes unanswered. Any bug report should be acknowledged immediately. The steps taken to resolve the bug should be tracked and recorded. The support organization should never allow a problem to slip through the cracks. The ill will that results from an overlooked bug report can be very damaging to the library's reputation in the company.

Components of the Ideal Support Infrastructure

Ideal support is readily accessible to the users. They should be able to make bug reports at any time, without interrupting their work. This requires that you set up multiple lines of communication to the support team, each one accessible by the developers.

Ideal support is adequately staffed. If the support team is stretched too thin, they will lose ground and be overwhelmed by the developers' demands. Problems will take too long to be resolved, or they will be forgotten entirely. If this occurs the library loses credibility and, subsequently, users. If you take this to its logical conclusion, you can see that there will eventually be no need for support staff.

Depending on the complexity and maturity of the library, one support person can cover three to six current development efforts, plus six to ten existing projects. In addition, you will need a support team leader and one person to handle the administrative tasks.

Ideal support gives quick, meaningful feedback to the user. The user should always be assured that the problem or question he or she has reported has been noted and will be acted upon. You also need to give some idea of the turnaround time users can expect on their problems. Finally, once a solution is found and the problem report is closed, the user must be notified and informed of the procedure for applying the fix.

Ideal support provides methods for assigning priority to a reported problem. Users often perceive their problem as having a high priority even if it does not. You need solid criteria that define the various priority levels so you can assign priority and explain the reasons to the users. You should report the priority you have assigned to the problem to the user, and ensure that their assessment of priority matches yours.

Ideal support has automatic escalation of unclosed problems. Whether you use a manual mechanism or an automated one, a problem should not be allowed to sit around very long without being resolved. Either assign more people to the problem, or give the problem to one of your top performers.

Ideal support always has a person-of-last-resort that a dissatisfied user can report a long-standing problem to. This is usually the manager of the team, but you can also set up a special position to handle these types of problems.

Ideal support has mechanisms for ensuring that the developers are using the correct versions of all library components. It is frustrating for developers and support personnel to chase a problem around for hours, only to discover that components of the user's version of the library must be updated. Tools can be created to check time stamps and file sizes. You can also embed version information in the library objects and build a mechanism to query each object for its version.

The Nature of Support

No matter how you choose to provide access to your support services, you need to provide some mechanism to accomplish the following:

- Bug reporting and resolution
- Answers to technical and usage questions
- Training
- Distribution of bug fixes

Figure 16.1 shows the services provided by the support organization. Let's examine some ways to address each of these items.

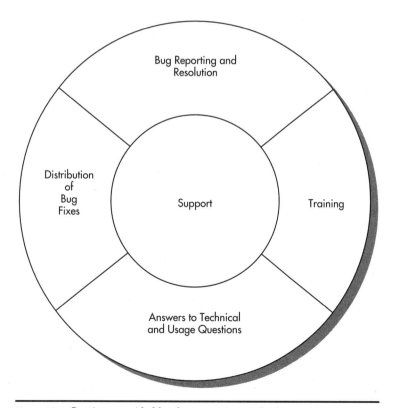

Figure 16.1 Services provided by the support organization.

Bug reporting

You need to allow bug reporting access to all users of your library. There are a number of ways to accomplish this. First, you can make sure that each user has a phone support number that they can call at any time. This number can simply be the desk phone of your lead support person. You should consider installing a hotline for support. This is a phone line that is not assigned to any one support person, but is guaranteed always to have coverage. You can use mechanisms such as automatic forwarding to make sure that any call to the hotline eventually is routed to a support person.

This is as good a time as any to mention a personal pet peeve: voice mail! Voice mail has its places, but support is not one of them. Yes, you should have voice mail as the final recourse if a call is not answered by a person. However, that situation should never be allowed to arise. Voice mail is not closed; that is, the caller leaves a message, but has no idea whether it ever will reach human ears. This is not adequate for a high-quality support organization. As I have already mentioned, feedback is an essential part of good support service. Staff your support organization adequately, so that you will never shuffle a caller off to voice mail. Track absences and vacations, and make sure that everyone in your support group is aware that coverage is a top priority.

You can also use groupware, such as Lotus Notes, to facilitate bug reporting. It is a simple matter to set up a database into which developers can enter problem reports. Then the support staff can scan the database for new entries, make assignments, issue replies, and close any problems reports that have been solved. The benefit to this approach is that the users get direct, immediate entry of their problem reports. The downside is that the user-entered problem logs receive no immediate feedback from the support staff. In this sense, it is not much better than voice mail.

Answers to technical and usage questions

Users often have questions about how to apply your class library to their business problem. This is certainly not a bug, but it must be handled with the same speed and accuracy. You should have specific people assigned to handle these technical issues. Their communication skills and patience must be especially keen for this duty. What is obvious to a person who is intimately familiar with the inner workings of the library may seem hopelessly opaque to a green developer. The support person in this case must be at least as much trainer as technician.

The same mechanisms that you use to provide user access, feedback, and priority assessment for bug reports will come in handy for these technical questions. If a question cannot be answered immediately, let the user know the priority assigned to his or her question and the expected turnaround time. Once the question has been answered, record the answer and close the issue. Over time, the accumulated questions and answers can be used to create a knowledge base that will further assist both the support staff and the developers.

Support can be administered using home-grown sets of tools developed in PowerBuilder, as well as spreadsheets such as Excel, or even word processors. In addition, you can use commercial help-desk systems to track bugs and other support issues. But, whatever method you choose must allow each problem report to be tracked from its inception through closure.

Training

Typically, training falls under the umbrella of support. The support team is charged with creating the training courses, as well as scheduling and conducting them.

The task of creating a training course for the class library can be outsourced to external training organizations. Likewise, the courses can be presented by professional trainers. However, the task of ensuring that the potential users of your library have ready access to training falls on the support team.

In brief, the tasks that make up the training effort are as follows:

Creating training

- *Assessing need:* You will need to determine the number of users who require training.

- *Scheduling:* Schedule enough classes to satisfy the demand, and spread them over a period of time so that all developers can take advantage of them.

- *Manage the environment:* Make sure that all required materials and hardware are on hand, installed, running, and properly configured before the classes begin.

- *Run the classes:* Take charge of conducting the class, whether you draw on internal resources or outsource the instruction.

- *Follow up:* Continually strive to improve the content and quality of the classes. Survey the students and incorporate what you learn from them into future classes.

Distribution of bug fixes

The task of distributing fixes to reported (or unreported) problems also falls on the support team. Not only must the fixes be distributed, but they must be free of additional bugs or side effects. If the fixes require changes to developers' code, the necessary changes must be documented and distributed along with the fixes.

Typically, you will use the same channels to distribute bug fixes as you would use for the normal library releases. We have used a technique called automatic correction facility (ACF) to distribute bug fixes. This technique entails adding one more PBL, the ACF PBL, to the search path. The ACF PBL is initially empty, and as changes to objects become available, they are added to that PBL. This allows the class library PBLs to remain at the level that corresponds to the most recent release, but allows the developers access to fixed objects before the next point release occurs. It also simplifies distribution because you need to distribute only the ACF library.

Assigning Priority

Every support request must be assigned a priority. Even if you do not explicitly do so, a de facto priority is established for every support request. You cannot afford to run a support organization based on assessments like "It'll only take a minute to do this one" or "This isn't important. I'll drop it and it won't be a problem anymore." Your reputation will suffer and your users will suffer.

An important maxim of time management is "Do not let the urgent overshadow the important." This is an important distinction, and one that is often hard to draw. Take this example: A little-used feature is reported to you as not working exactly as documented. In fact, there is a particular report that cannot be generated until the bug is fixed. The developers are on a tight schedule, and they can't begin user acceptance testing until the report is complete and operational. No one else has tried to use the flawed feature, and a quick survey of the developers throughout the company reveals that no one else is likely to in the near future. Urgent? Yes, to the single development team that is using the feature. Important? Probably not. The problem needs attention, but if there are problems that affect greater areas of functionality and affect more developers, they are more important, and should be addressed first. Now, let's make things a bit more complicated. It turns out that the report in question is being developed for the president of the company, and is crucial to completing the financial planning for the next five years. Important? Most assuredly.

This points out that there are many components involved in the assessment of priority. You need to consider the following:

- The number of developers affected
- The effect of the problem on the usability of your library (severity)
- The time frames of the affected projects
- The relative importance of the affected projects
- The likelihood that an acceptable workaround exists
- The prominence in the company of the project's sponsors
- The prominence in the company of the person reporting the problem
- Whether the project is for internal or external use

Figure 16.2 is an example of a priority assessment worksheet that we have used with a great deal of success. The example shows the value column filled in to the highest possible value for illustration purposes. The importance and urgency columns each have a weight and a score. The weight assigns the relative effect of each factor on the overall score. The score for each factor is simply the weight multiplied by the number entered in the value column. The sum of all of the values in each column is a number less than or equal to 100. To use the worksheet, simply enter the appropriate value according to the legend shown under "Enter in Value Column." The reported problems should then be addressed in order of importance, where 100 is most important, and then according to urgency. Of course, do not let any tool override common sense. If a problem needs fixing, fix it, no matter what the spreadsheet says.

Developing the Infrastructure

What do you need to do to develop the infrastructure? First, you must make sure that you have commitment and funding from the upper management of the company. The support organization generates no revenue, so you must be ready to defend and justify its existence at any time.

	Enter in Value column	Value	Importance Weight	Importance Score (Weight × Value)	Urgency Weight	Urgency Score (Weight × Value)
Number of developers affected	1 for less than $\frac{1}{3}$ 2 for between $\frac{1}{3}$ and $\frac{2}{3}$ 3 for greater than $\frac{2}{3}$	3	6	18	3	9
Effect on library usability (severity)	0 for no effect 1 if usage is impaired 2 if library is unusable	2	9	18	4	8
Timing of affected projects	1 if within 6 weeks, 2 if within 2 weeks, 3 if within 3 days	3	2	6	9	27
Relative importance of affected projects	1 if not very important 2 if moderately important 3 if very important	3	4	12	2	6
Likelihood of workaround solution	1 if very likely, 2 if somewhat likely, 3 if highly unlikely	3	2	6	9	27
Prominence of project's sponsors	1 if not very important, 2 if moderately important, 3 if very important	3	6	18	4	12
Prominence of person reporting problem	1 if not very important, 2 if moderately important, 3 if very important	3	4	12	3	9
Project for internal or external use	1 if internal use, 2 if external use	2	5	10	1	2
			Importance	100	Urgency	100

Figure 16.2 Priority assessment worksheet.

Next, establish the elements that your support organization needs. Always strive to reach the (admittedly unreachable) ideal support team. The elements that you will address are as follows:

- Staffing
- Accessibility
- Administration tools

Staffing

The essential observation regarding support staffing is the more, the merrier. This applies only within reason, of course. The dynamics of a corporation help to ensure that your support staff is never too large. You will always be fighting pressure to release members of your support staff to other efforts. Remember that response time and coverage are the key ingredients of a successful support effort, and both will suffer if you are understaffed. If your support is seen as inadequate, the reputation, and therefore the degree of usage, of your library will decline.

Cover the phone lines with technically adept, but not necessarily your most knowledgeable people. They need to be able to understand the description of a problem and evaluate its complexity and priority. They also need to know enough to offer suggestions to solve some problems, but to avoid speculation, guesses, and rash promises. The same people who are assigned to the phone can share their time to scan and dispatch e-mail and entries in groupware databases.

The thornier technical issues should be handled by the best and most technically knowledgeable people you have. These people are the key to minimizing your response time and maximizing your impact.

The people you assign to maintain contact with the development teams need good skills in a variety of areas. They must be adept with people and able to handle varying personalities and styles with aplomb. They must have excellent technical skills because they will be in contact with the customer, and must resolve issues quickly and correctly. They must be flexible, able to adapt to varying schedules and changes in priority and requirements.

Finally, your team must have a leader. The leader needs to know the technical details of the library, as well as the different skills and capabilities of the support staff. The leader coordinates the responsibilities and activities of all the members and makes sure that adequate coverage is always maintained. The leader also assigns or assumes responsibility as the last-resort resource for handling problems that he or she feels have not been adequately addressed.

Accessibility

Establish the lines of communication. The first and most important connection between the developers and the library support team is the telephone. As I have mentioned, make sure that the phones are covered at all times. As part of the process of initiating a project, distribute the support phone numbers to the development team members. If you have established a hotline, make sure to specifically identify the hotline to your users. Assign one member of your support team as the person with responsibility for checking and administering voice mail left for the support team. You can increase the coverage dramatically by assigning beeper numbers to several of your support staff, ensuring total coverage even during off hours.

Next establish the various asynchronous contact points: e-mail and groupware. The support team should have at least one e-mail address set up for bug reports and questions. You will need to create procedures that ensure that all support e-mail addresses are checked frequently for messages. Groupware databases also fall into this category. You will need to design the databases, ensure that access is afforded to all of your current and potential users, and set up a rotation to scan the database regularly.

Internet mailing lists and newsgroups are an important addition to your support lines. Users throughout the company can subscribe to your mailing list or newsgroup. They will then receive everything that is posted to the lists. You can use this avenue to distribute notices of bug reports and fixes, as well as usage notes, tips, and techniques.

The nature of some problems requires personal assistance. Assign some of your people to maintain personal contact with the various development teams that are using your library. They should establish regular rounds so that they make contact with each development team about once a week. Problems and questions that the developers have, but did not think were severe enough to warrant a support call, can be discussed and resolved during these visits.

Administration tools

The support team needs tools and procedures to manage support requests and bug reports.

The easiest and most crucial tool for support administration is a bug reporting and tracking system. A simple spreadsheet will serve for the initial effort, but more detail and greater control will be necessary in the long run. The system you use must track the following:

- *Reported problems:* a unique problem ID for each problem
- *Short description:* a one-line description of the problem
- *Library version:* the version of the class library in use when the problem occurred
- *Date:* the date the problem was reported
- *Reported by:* the name, location, and phone number of the person reporting the problem
- *Priority:* the ratings for both importance and urgency
- *Application:* the application where the problem surfaced

- *Application version:* the version of the application
- *Long description:* all detailed information that will help pinpoint and reproduce the problem
- *Assigned to:* the name and phone number of the person assigned to resolve the problem
- *Escalation history:* dates when the problem was escalated, and the adjusted priority ratings
- *Reason:* explanation of how and why the problem occurred
- *Resolution:* the resolution of the problem (this should be explained in detail, so that if a similar problem occurs again, the solution is readily available)

This is a lot of data to house in one small spreadsheet. It will be impossible to see all of it in one screen, and that will reduce its usefulness. A well-designed database that allows you to track these items will smooth the task of administering the support effort.

An important corollary to the bug reporting system is a system for reporting progress back to the user. As we have already mentioned, the user should receive immediate acknowledgment of a reported problem. The user who reported the problem should also receive notice when it is closed or escalated. If you have built a tracking system, it is a simple matter to add e-mail notification to the program.

Another tool that promotes the support organization's reputation while easing its burden is a living, growing knowledge base. Each support request has the potential to generate an entry in the knowledge base. Developers will contact the support team for help in applying the library objects in novel and useful ways. The techniques you develop for using the library's objects should be entered into the knowledge base for all developers to reference. You should also maintain a frequently asked questions (FAQ) list in the knowledge base. This allows the developers to research and solve some of their questions without requiring any direct support.

Remember that you can also purchase commercially available help-desk systems to track problem reports. The system must track all necessary data about problem reports and support requests. Be sure provision is made to notify users of changes in the status of their reports. You should get a system that allows as much customization of bug reporting formats, user notification, problem escalation, and administrative reporting as possible.

Handling a Support Request

Finally, let's examine the workflow that occurs as your team fields a support request. Figure 16.3 depicts the typical workflow.

First, the user submits the request. Receipt of the request should be immediately acknowledged to the user. The mechanism for this varies depending on the method used to submit the problem report. If the report is made by phone,

Actions   ## Notifications

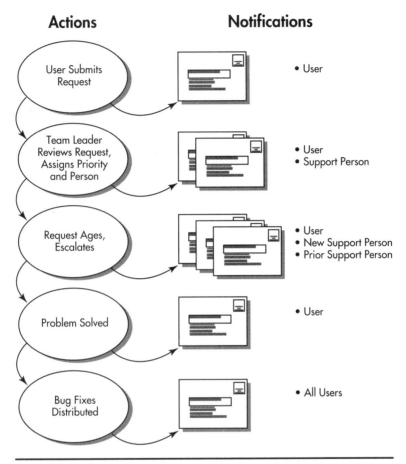

Figure 16.3 Workflow of support requests.

the person taking the request should repeat the problem number to the submitter. If the request is made through an asynchronous channel, such as e-mail, the person responsible for scanning the problem log must generate an acknowledgment through the same channel. Be sure to include an estimate of expected turnaround time for the problem.

Next, the support team leader reviews the support request. The purpose at this stage is to evaluate the importance and urgency of the request and to assign a support person to handle the request. The responsibility for reviewing the request can be delegated to one or more members of the team besides the leader. When a priority and support person have been assigned, the submitter should receive another notification, usually via e-mail, informing him or her of the assignments.

If the problem ages beyond a predetermined period without being closed, it should be escalated. This means that its priority should be increased and, if necessary, the problem should be reassigned to someone on the team with greater knowledge or experience. When a problem is escalated, the user should be notified, as well as both the new and prior support people.

Once the problem is resolved and the fix is tested, the problem should be closed. At this point, the user should be notified that the problem has been closed. Include the explanation of the reason the problem occurred and the way it was solved. Also include the date that the bug fix will be distributed. You should also issue a notification to the team member who administers the knowledge base so the problem and its resolution can be added.

Finally, when the bug fix is distributed to the users, issue a notification to the users that a bug fix is available. You should state the nature of the bugs corrected by the fix, any coding changes required, and any behavioral changes brought about by the fix.

Summary

The support infrastructure is a crucial element in the ongoing success of your class library. In this chapter we examined the reasons you need to provide support and the ways to build an infrastructure that facilitates support. We looked at what you need to provide to ensure ideal support. You have seen that ideal support provides the following:

- Ready accessibility to the user
- Adequate staffing to handle developer demands
- Quick, meaningful feedback to the users
- Reasonable, accurate assignment of priority
- Escalation of unclosed problems
- Last-resort contact for unsatisfied users

We looked at the nature of support requests and the ways that you need to handle the different functions of the support team. The responsibilities of the support team include bug reporting and resolution, providing answers to technical and usage questions, training, and the distribution of bug fixes.

Finally, we showed some techniques that you can use to effectively manage your support effort. You found out how to build a simple spreadsheet that simplifies the task of setting the priority of a support request while increasing your accuracy. We also showed you the data you need to track for each support request submitted.

The pilot project sets the initial expectations for your class library. After the first impressions, the support you provide will cement your reputation and relationship with the developers if you strive for quality and coverage. Go forth and support!

17

Library Maintenance

Introduction

Maintenance, housekeeping, chores—the nature of support is that it produces change. The nature of change is that it ensures a need for cleanup or maintenance.

Maintenance is what we try to leave until we have nothing better to do. That's the wrong time. Maintenance, like all chores, is best done on an ongoing basis. Your goal is prevention, not firefighting.

You need not steel yourself against drudgery, though. The techniques we outline in this chapter will help you accomplish the maintenance your library needs with confidence and ease. We show you the things you need to do, and the order in which to do them. We also provide a checklist to ensure that no step is bypassed.

Maintenance includes the installation of bug fixes and upgrades. It also includes the procedures you need to follow to ensure that the libraries are clean, synchronized, and optimized and have all of their pointers lined up properly.

What happens if you do not do maintenance? Nothing good: GPFs, PBSTUB errors, linkage errors, unresolved references, and more. Program bugs remain unresolved and upgrades do not happen. Admittedly, this is an extreme view. But at the very least, your users will encounter problems not of their own making if the libraries are not maintained properly.

Chapter Objectives

In this chapter, we show you how to maintain your libraries so that you can avoid many of these problems. We show you the steps and the correct order to follow when you make changes to the libraries. You will learn methodologies that make the maintenance job smoother and less prone to error. We also show you some of the symptoms your objects will exhibit when they need maintenance.

Methodologies Introduced

In this chapter, we introduce you to the automatic correction facility (ACF). This is a simple technique that allows you to maintain the libraries at their latest point release while allowing developers access to in-stream fixes.

We show you how to use the methodology of staged maintenance to decrease the likelihood of unexpected errors and side effects affecting your users.

The Automatic Correction Facility

The ACF is a technique we use to allow easy distribution of in-stream fixes to users. *Automatic correction facility* is a long name for a standard Power-Builder library (PBL) that is used to distribute these fixes. The PBL is initially empty, and as fixes are created and certified, they are added to the ACF PBL. Then, the single PBL is sent through your distribution network to each development team. The ACF PBL is always present in every development team's search path, as the first PBL of the class library. That way, any fixes you distribute immediately become available to the developers.

When a new release of the libraries is prepared, you simply use the objects in the ACF PBL to update the corresponding objects in your library PBLs. The ACF PBL is emptied and then distributed along with the rest of the library PBLs.

Staged Maintenance

We use staged maintenance areas to phase in bug fixes and minor upgrades. This is a three-step process. The object that needs repair is copied into a PBL designated as the FIX PBL. If you are using version control, you will check the object out into the FIX PBL. But be aware, you will not check it back in until the next minor release of the library is distributed. The FIX PBL is where the object is modified to bring about the fix.

Once the objects have been modified and tested by the support team developers, they are released to a limited number of development teams (usually one) for further testing and verification. This stage is the equivalent to the beta test stage. You accomplish this by copying the objects into the TST PBL. The TST PBL is sent only to the single development team responsible for shaking out the new or modified objects.

If the testing uncovers the need for additional changes to an object, they should be made to the copy in the FIX PBL, then copied to the TST PBL and sent to the developers once again.

The final stage for the corrected objects is the ACF stage. The objects must be tested and fully certified before you proceed with this step. The objects are copied into the ACF PBL, which is then distributed to all of the developers. You will notice that the changes are always made to the objects in the FIX PBL and copied through the TST PBL into the ACF PBL. This ensures that the objects in the ACF PBL are always identical to their companions in the FIX PBL.

When the next release is prepared, you need to copy the objects in the ACF PBL back into the class library PBLs. If you are using version control, simply check the objects back in from the FIX library. As we have already shown, the objects in ACF are the same as the objects in FIX.

Maintaining Separate Versions

In many cases, it is not practical for applications that are already in production to constantly upgrade to the latest release. There are a few different solutions to this problem. One potential solution is to enforce upgrading by adopting a no-support-for-previous-versions policy. Every time a new release is issued, the old code base is deleted from the production servers. This will not win your class library team a lot of friends.

Not as simple to implement, but far more effective, is a policy of maintaining each major release, frozen at its final incarnation. This increases your maintenance chores, as well as the storage your class library requires on the production servers, but it is a practical way of addressing the need. Older applications will have a stable platform and new ones will have access to new features and corrections.

It is important to observe the key word *frozen*. There is a danger that as the applications using the older versions run their course, problems will surface. Often, it will seem expedient to simply repair the problem in the older code stream. The problems with this approach are many. First, you are creating parallel code streams, each with its own maintenance history. Each code stream requires that its own separate documentation be maintained and changed as the library evolves.

In addition, you run the risk of affecting other users of the same older version. Unless you have completely changed the architecture of the library objects, you will probably need to propagate any changes throughout all existing versions. This increases the exposure of all of your company's development teams to side effects created by the changes. You also run the risk of an inadvertent error in each version you modify.

The only way to keep this scenario clean is to insist that all prior versions remain static. If an insurmountable problem affects an application that uses an older library version, users must upgrade to the latest version to receive the benefits of a bug fix. This seems harsh. But remember, changing one application to conform to the latest version of the library is much less problematic than any changes to an existing, stable class library.

Using Regression Testing

Each change you make to the library brings with it the danger of side effects. You need to take steps to detect and correct any errors that occur because you have modified objects in the library.

In many cases, manual testing is not thorough enough to ensure that the class library functions as intended. People make assumptions, forget things, and overlook symptoms.

The solution is to develop a complete suite for regression testing. The term *regression testing* refers to the characteristic of regressing to the very beginning and testing every method of every object completely whenever a change is made. Sounds appealing, doesn't it?

Several options exist that allow you to automate the regression testing process. These tools consist of applications that work together to help you define, manage, and execute automated testing.

Typically, you will define a test plan that encompasses the entirety of the regression test. Then, for each scenario you want to test, you will define a test procedure to put your library objects through their paces. Within the test procedures, you can specify test cases along the way. Each test case allows you to compare the state of your objects at that point to the expected state of that object. The automated tool records the success or failure of each test case for later analysis.

One tool that follows this model is SQA Team Test. This is a comprehensive set of programs that fully automates the testing process. One component, SQA Robot, allows you to record the steps of your test procedures and stop anywhere along the way to investigate test cases. The abilities of SQA Robot to compare objects are very thorough, and allow you to examine the most minute detail of every object. It can even peer into datawindows, comparing contents row by row.

You need to construct an application to exercise the class library. We do not recommend using demonstration or sample applications for this duty. The purposes of these applications are vastly different from those of a testing application. Demonstration programs showcase features of your library, whereas a properly written testing application exercises the methods of each library object in a systematic way. The demonstration programs should sparkle and be full of life, whereas the testing application will seem stilted, boring, and much too mired in detail.

The costs for both the testing tools and the extra development effort of the testing applications will be high. They may be so high that you are tempted to forgo them. That is a mistake. The second time you run a regression test, you will recover your cost. Unless you want to become a testing robot yourself, invest the time and money in a good tool and a companion application.

Cleaning Up

Every time you make a change to a PowerBuilder object, PowerBuilder must reestablish the path of inheritance and the pointers to and within the object. Sometimes this works well without any intervention from you. Sometimes it does not. "Sometimes" is not good enough odds for a company standard class library. Cleaning up after a change is vital to the health of your library and the satisfaction of your users.

By *cleaning up* I mean regenerating the PowerBuilder objects and optimizing the libraries. PowerBuilder provides the tools to do this. In this section we show you how to use these tools to keep your class library working properly.

You also need to go through the cleanup exercise whenever you upgrade one or more of PowerBuilder's DLLs. Each new release seems to introduce a difference in the way PBLs are managed by the environment. The differences can cause misleading error messages, failed compiles, and other frustrating problems.

How do you tell if your libraries need maintenance? We examine that next.

Symptoms

Changing class library objects or the development environment (PowerBuilder DLLs) without regenerating and optimizing the class library PBLs can cause a number of mysterious problems. The problems you encounter may include the following:

- Unresolved external references
- Erratic operation
- Error in function call
- PBSTUB errors and GPFs
- Programs that mysteriously halt during operation
- Linkage errors when creating an executable file

These problems are often announced by a panic-stricken developer saying, "I haven't changed a thing, and I can't even open my objects! Everything worked yesterday!" A secret to solving these sorts of problems is to recognize that if nothing has changed, nothing will operate the least bit differently. You need to look for the change. Do not challenge the developer, but probe. Make sure his or her conditions and source PBLs really are the same as they were when "everything worked." When you are satisfied that (within the bounds of common sense) the developer's conditions have not changed, begin looking elsewhere for the change. Check the PowerBuilder DLLs that the developer is using. If these have changed, it is imperative that you regenerate and optimize the libraries using the new DLLs. On the other hand, if you have installed a bug fix or enhancement in your class library, you need to regenerate and optimize, then the developer must follow suit. Failure to keep up with this process will bring on one or more of the symptoms I mentioned earlier.

Let's examine each of these symptoms briefly.

Unresolved external reference.   This error message shows up during creation of an EXE, or during execution in development mode. This has several genuine causes, in addition to corrupted libraries:

- Library search path is missing one or more PBLs: Always verify that the library search path contains all of the PBLs necessary to establish addressability to every object.

- Objects or resources missing: The developer may have deleted an object that is referenced somewhere within the application. Refer to Figure 17.1. You can see that the error message (this one from development mode) pinpoints the object, event, and line where the error occurred. This makes it a simple matter to verify whether the reported error is accurate. If it is not, you probably have library trouble.

Erratic operation.   By *erratic operation* I mean that the application behaves differently each time it is run. Sometimes it connects to the database, sometimes it does not. Sometimes an event fires correctly, sometimes it does not. This is an almost sure sign that the libraries have gotten confused.

Error in function call.   When you are saving an object, compiling, or running an application, PowerBuilder may report an error in function call. If this error occurs in code that previously compiled error-free, it is a sure sign that your libraries need some tender loving care.

I have also seen this error produced when the PowerBuilder DLLs are mismatched. That is, the PB???050.DLL files that implement PowerBuilder functionality are from different versions, or builds, of PowerBuilder.

Of course, there are genuine causes for this problem, too. Mistyped external function declarations will generate this problem at runtime. Carefully check your declarations against the documentation for the function. Verify that all arguments are correctly specified and in the right order. Also make sure that the return value is typed correctly.

An example of a mistyped function declaration occurred in the transition from PowerBuilder version 3 to version 4. The following two SDK functions,

Figure 17.1   Unresolved external reference caused by missing PBL.

if used in PowerBuilder 4.0, must be modified from the original Microsoft SDK Definition and from the way they were originally defined in the 3.0 environment.

```
//Powerbuilder 3.0 Definitions
FUNCTION INT GetModuleUsage(long hWnd) LIBRARY "KRNL386.EXE"
FUNCTION UINT GetFreeSystemResources(long SysType) LIBRARY "USER.EXE"

//Powerbuilder 4.0 Definitions
FUNCTION UINT GetModuleUsage(uint hWnd) LIBRARY "KRNL386.EXE"
FUNCTION INT GetFreeSystemResources(int SysType) LIBRARY "USER.EXE"
```

PBSTUB errors and general protection faults. General protection fault (GPF) is Windows's way of saying that it has fallen and it can't get up. PowerBuilder will fail with a GPF showing the module name (such as PBSYB050.DLL) and the address of the failure. This information can help you to track down previously reported GPF errors. If you call Powersoft to report a GPF, be sure to write down everything in the error display.

Memory corruption is the only cause of GPFs. In essence, Windows, with the help of the protected mode operation of the CPU, is telling you that the module in question attempted to access memory that it did not own. The list of ways that memory can be corrupted is practically endless. This usually happens because a pointer gets scrambled or a piece of code tries to write four bytes into a memory area two bytes long. A program may create an object but never destroy it, or the program may destroy something it never created. GPFs can also occur if a program fails to release items that it pushed onto the stack, or if it releases something that it never really put there. Because the stack is the place where return addresses are stored, the program loses its direction quickly. Eventually, a GPF occurs.

A maddening property of GPFs is that they do not always occur immediately following the piece of code that corrupts the memory. The bad pointer can sit there quietly like a time bomb, waiting for an unsuspecting op-code. This is why you often hear tales of intermittent GPFs that occur only some of the times the user is working with an object. The GPF is caused in some other portion of the code, but it does not surface until the object in question is accessed.

Libraries that need to be regenerated create GPFs. The regeneration process lets PowerBuilder tidy up its inter- and intraobject pointers. If you have made changes to ancestor objects, or if you have started using a newer set of DLLs, you should regenerate to restore the PBLÕs internal pointers. Remember, pointer corruption is a chief cause of GPFs. PowerBuilder has a lot to keep track of, especially when you are using complex inheritance hierarchies. If you change the libraries without cleaning up after yourself, you run the risk of GPFs.

You need to recognize that many GPFs are caused by the application code. Questionable programming practices, misuse of arrays, improperly called external functions and mismatched create/destroys all lead to GPFs.

PowerBuilder also contributes to some GPFs. Check the application code, and check the Powersoft InfoBase before you spend half of a lifetime pursuing a problem that is not even caused by the class library objects.

Programs that mysteriously halt during operation. Sometimes, a developer reports that one or more programs are halting without any notice or any error message. Sometimes the machine hangs and must be rebooted. Sometimes, the program simply disappears. Sometimes nothing has focus, and nothing can be given focus, but the program is still running. Except for the case of an infinite loop in the program, these symptoms point almost exclusively to regeneration problems. You can use the debugger to rule out the case of an infinite loop. Then go ahead and regenerate both the class library objects and the application objects.

Maintenance techniques and solutions

There are only a few steps you need to follow to adequately maintain the PBLs that house your class library. You need to follow them rigorously and in the correct order, though. The steps are as follows:

- Regenerate objects
- Optimize PBLs
- Create PowerBuilder dynamic libraries (PBDs)

You must be sure to observe the inheritance structure when you regenerate the objects. Regenerate ancestors first, followed by the descendants.

Now let's look at a bit more detail about the maintenance steps.

Regenerating objects. The single most important maintenance procedure is the regeneration of the PBLs. The class library PBLs must be regenerated whenever you release a change. It is important that you regenerate them in the proper sequence. Ancestor objects must be regenerated before their descendants. If you are using the Library Painter to regenerate, you can accomplish this by regenerating all objects as many times as you have layers of inheritance. Another way to accomplish this is to use the Object Browser to regenerate. The Object Browser regenerates starting at the highest ancestor you select and then propagates the regeneration process to the furthest descendant.

You can also regenerate your objects from the Library Painter. Open up all of the libraries by double-clicking on each library. One by one, regenerate each PBL. Select every object in the PBL. You can accomplish this by selecting the first object, then holding down the shift key and selecting the last object in the PBL. Press the regenerate icon (the little generator) on your PainterBar to regenerate the contents of the PBL.

A better method is to regenerate your objects using the object browser. Select the browser button on the PowerBuilder toolbar. You will see a dialog displaying the tab folder open to the Application tab. If you choose the Window tab, you will see a display similar to the one shown in Figure 17.2. In the example shown, the base window, w_exam_ancestor is highlighted. If you then press the Regenerate button, the entire descendent tree starting with w_exam_ancestor will be regenerated in the proper order. Of course, you can use this capability on other types of objects as well.

Optimizing PBLs.   After you have regenerated all of your class library's objects using either of the two methods described, you should optimize the PBLs. For each PBL, follow this procedure in the Library Painter:

1. Click once on the PBL to select it.
2. Choose Library | Optimize from the Library Painter menu.
3. Press "OK" to complete the operation.

You do not need to follow any particular order when you optimize your PBLs. The optimize procedure simply reorganizes the internal structure of

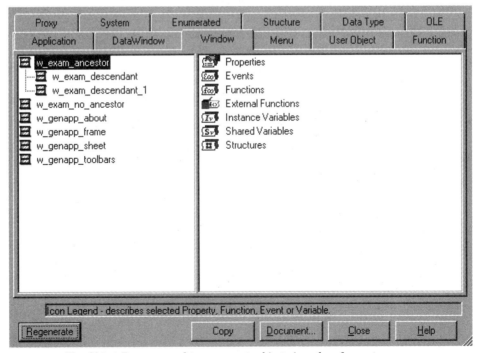

Figure 17.2 The Object Browser used to regenerate objects in order of ancestry.

the PBL, removing unused code. Nothing during optimization affects any dependencies.

TIP: Novell Users

After optimizing libraries, go into a DOS window and use the Novell FLAGS option to reset the shared attributes on the library. By default, new files created on a Novell network are not marked as sharable. Optimizing libraries is accomplished by creating a new library and copying the old source code. Resetting the shared flag prevents a common problem in a multideveloper environment: a "Save Failed—Probable File I-O Error" message when attempting to save an object.

Steps:

1. Go to a DOS prompt.
2. Change to your source directory.
3. Type **FLAGS *.PBL.** This will display a list of your libraries and their file attributes. These are not the same attributes as DOS attributes.
4. Type **FLAGS *.PBL +s.** This will set the shared attribute for each library.

Creating dynamic libraries.   Now that you have optimized the PBLs, you need to create dynamic libraries (PBDs). Once again, the order that you use to create PBDs does not matter. No dependencies are involved. PBDs are essentially PBLs with the source code stripped out.

Using the Library Painter, follow these steps to create PBDs:

1. Click once on the PBL to select it.

2. Choose Utilities | Build Dynamic Library from the Library Painter menu.

3. Press OK to complete the operation. If the library already exists, you will see a dialog requesting confirmation to replace the existing PBD. Choose Yes.

The maintenance application

You can make your life considerably easier by establishing a simple, limited-function maintenance application that uses your class library PBLs in its search path. Set up the path in the same order that you recommend to application developers. Then go through the steps outlined in the previous section, using the maintenance application as your basis.

The Project Painter.   PowerBuilder 4 introduced the Project Painter. Power-Builder 5 has increased our dependency on the Project Painter by eliminating the ability to create an application from the Application Painter. Now all applications must be created using the Project Painter. When you use the Project Painter, you can automate the above steps. (Chapter 33 has a detailed discussion of the Project Painter.)

The Project Painter requires a lot of memory to complete the build of a complex project. An architecture that makes heavy use of inheritance and contains a lot of objects will strain even a 16 MB machine. I strongly urge you to get 20 or even 32 MB of memory and a fast computer if you intend to use the Project Painter to maintain a large class library. The same applies to applications based on the class library.

Panic Time

There will come a time when you have followed all of the proper steps, regenerating and optimizing to the point of frustration, and still, you have some objects that will not behave or will not compile. It's time for emergency measures.

Sometimes you will find that you cannot open (or save) a particular object in a particular PBL without generating a GPF. This may spring from a number of causes:

- The PBL's internal structure is damaged.
- The object is damaged, or contains a reference to an object that is damaged.
- The object is descended from an object that is damaged.

In any case, it is tough to fix the problem when you cannot even open or save the object. Here are two techniques that can get you out of this kind of tight situation.

The PBL shuffle

The first technique is called the PBL shuffle. For this trick, you will need to create a new PBL. Then, one by one, copy each object from the affected PBL to the new PBL. Once you have copied every object into the new PBL, rename the old one with a different name, and rename the new one to the name used by the broken PBL.

Now, regenerate everything in every PBL. Once again, be sure to observe ancestry, and regenerate in the correct order.

Now it is time to see whether it helped. Try to open the broken object. If it opens, try to save it (Use File | Save from the menu). If it all works, congratulations! If not, move on to the next section.

International banking

Not really. But this emergency fix does require a lot of exporting and importing. First, create a new PBL. Put it into your search path. Then, for each object in the broken PBL do the following:

1. Export the object. Click once on the object name to select it. Then select Entry | Export from the Library Painter menu. PowerBuilder will suggest

a name. Be careful with the name. PowerBuilder simply takes the first 8 characters of the object name and uses that for the file name. Keep the ".SR?" extension, but change the name to something unique and meaningful. Then press OK.

2. Import the object into the new PBL. If you encounter a compilation error, you will get a detailed error message that will help pinpoint the problem. If it imports without error, you can move on to the next object.

TIP

If you get a compile error when importing, exit PowerBuilder and start over again before you attempt to import any other objects. I have seen entire PBLs trashed because PowerBuilder got confused after an import error. I do not know the mechanism behind this, but a little caution beats days or weeks of lost work.

If you cannot get an object to import, check the code using the editor of your choice. You may spot some dropped code or other syntax problems in the exported code. Failing that, check the code for object references and ancestors. Then attempt to open any referenced objects or ancestors.

Do not be alarmed if you see code you do not recognize in the exported script. The exported script is a superset of the Powerscript code you write. There are additional syntactical constructs as well as events that you, as a developer, cannot normally reach.

Summary

The maintenance of your class library's source PBLs and PBDs is critical. You need to maintain synchrony among the development and runtime resources that the developers rely on when they use your library. In this chapter, you saw how to use staged maintenance and the automatic correction facility to minimize disruption from unexpected errors and side effects when you change your library's objects. You learned the importance of freezing each delivered release of your library to parallel code streams.

We described the need for regression testing to help you certify each successive release of your library. Then we described the typical steps that you would use to construct a regression test suite using automated testing tools.

You learned the importance of cleaning up after any changes to your objects. We showed you the steps you need to take: regeneration and optimization. We described the symptoms, such as GPFs, that may indicate that you need to regenerate and optimize.

Finally, you learned the steps you can take to recover seemingly unrecoverable objects or PBLs.

With the techniques and methodologies you have learned, you will know when and how to maintain your class library PBLs. Remember, if something is happening but there is no logical reason for it, try regenerating and optimizing.

18

Library Performance Metrics

Introduction

If there is one common complaint heard about the use of PowerBuilder and class libraries, it has to be performance. Many times I have heard people use performance as a reason not to use a class library. The biggest culprit? Inheritance. When you begin to use multiple levels of inheritance, the system gets slower and slower.

Unfortunately, the reports are justified. But I do not believe that it is the fault of the tool. Rather, I think many hierarchies are not built with performance in mind. The truth of the matter is that inheritance can actually be a performance booster if used correctly.

But how do you determine whether your library performs well? One way is to keep the hierarchy as flat as possible. A more effective way is to make sure the class hierarchy is built in an efficient manner. There are techniques you can use to help performance rather than hurt it. There are also means by which you can measure the performance of each object and method you develop to find out where your performance issues arise. This chapter highlights some of the techniques we have developed over the years to measure and to help improve performance.

PowerBuilder 5.0 allows you to compile your code into DLLs and machine code executables. This means that code-intensive operations can run up to 50 times faster than in PowerBuilder 4.0. Does this solve all of our performance issues? Most definitely not. Even if we were writing straight C code, efficiency and performance depend on the developer and the architect. A badly written program in any language does not perform as well as a well-written and well-designed program.

Chapter Objectives

The goals of this chapter are to provide some insight as to where potential performance issues arise, how to measure them, and, most importantly, how to circumvent them. We delve into the myths and realities of performance, describe techniques to measure performance at each level of your hierarchy, and outline the tools and techniques we use to get the most out of the environment. Specifically, we cover the following:

The Perception of Performance

- Inheritance: myths and realities
- Architecture and objects: the role they play
- Functions and events: the debate continues
- Using the library search path
- The environment and its effect on performance
- Compile scenarios
- Performance tricks and tips
- Benchmarking and tuning

The Perception of Performance

When measuring performance, one key aspect is often overlooked: the perception of performance. There is always an area in a system that we feel can, and should, perform better. What we often overlook is what the user perceives to be lackluster performance. There are some things we can do to improve the appearance of performance.

Users recognize performance problems in areas where they are forced to wait for the computer to do something. This often occurs when they are retrieving data or building large, complex screens. Generally, users want the system to perform at their speed, not the CPU's. Their speed is defined by the function they are attempting to complete and their understanding of how long each process should take. If the process takes 5 seconds to accomplish manually, the computer system should do it in less time, regardless of the level of complexity required.

This is often difficult to accomplish. A key element in avoiding this is to avoid long blank pauses. When the user stares at an hourglass waiting for something to happen, the entire system is labeled as slow. When a long process is taking place, keep the user informed with some form of feedback that distracts him or her for at least a portion of the time.

I recently did a presentation on performance using this technique. The audience was mostly technical people who were already using PowerBuilder and knew its strengths and weaknesses. The demonstration involved opening a window and retrieving 120 records from a database. Three scenarios were established.

- **Scenario 1:** Window opened and data retrieved during the open cycle. The process took about 1.1 seconds on average on my Pentium 90. I opened the window and initiated a retrieve, a normal development style. (I had already loaded the window and datawindow and retrieved the data once to ensure that all memory caching would have taken place.)

- **Scenario 2:** Window opened and retrieve posted so that window open completed before the retrieval taking place. In this case, the average was around 0.9 seconds. This difference is not really noticeable to the human eye, but most of the audience agreed that it seemed faster. The difference was more due to the fact that the window opened and displayed fully before the data came back. There was some feedback during the processing cycle, resulting in less dead time.

- **Scenario 3:** Window opened and retrieve posted, as in Scenario 2, but the RetrieveStart event popped up a small dialog window that told the user that a retrieve was about to take place. When the retrieve ended, the popup was closed. Based on the processing load, one would assume that this would almost certainly take longer. It did, averaging around 1.4 seconds—significantly longer than the other two methods.

One startling fact appeared. Almost every single person in the room chose Scenario 3 as the fastest! When I opened up a small time log imbedded in the main window and displayed the average times, there was a buzz in the room. Their perception had been altered. Because the Popup window contained the words *Please Wait,* followed by a brief message explaining the cause for the delay, everyone had been distracted for at least half of the processing time. This is time not measured. Therefore, the third method appeared to run significantly faster than the other two.

Another presentation using the same example on a slower machine emphasized the result. The third method appears to run significantly faster than the others. Keep your users informed! When information is provided, they know the reason for the delay and they are not staring at a blank screen and hourglass, moving the mouse to watch the mouse trails they have turned on for amusement. Reading the message requires time and this time is not accounted for in measuring the performance of the object in question. The object is perceived to perform better than it actually does.

To this end, we established a few guidelines to aid in performance perception:

- *Slow is slow only if it makes you wait.* Only when you wait for a process to do something can it appear to be slow.

- *Keep your user informed.* Even slower processes become more endurable if the reason for the wait is known.

- *Use the available tools to provide as much feedback as possible, and use the right tool in the right place.* In our example, populating Microhelp had far less effect. Many people ignored the Microhelp unless they were looking for something. The popup dialog was much more effective. We also inserted a beep to indicate that the process was done, drawing immediate attention to the fact that it was complete.

- *Longer than 3 seconds is a long time for a user.* Keep updating your feedback (if possible) at least every 3 seconds.

I hope this helps to shed a little light on what your users might perceive to be performance, as opposed to what you know is happening in the system. Keep you user in mind when developing. Performance can be affected in more ways than one.

Inheritance: Myths and Realities

When discussions of performance arise, the first topic brought up is the effect of inheritance on performance. A deep hierarchy does not perform like a flat hierarchy or no hierarchy at all. This is true. Accessing, loading, and building a six-layer hierarchy is less efficient than loading a single-layer hierarchy. However, this type of discussion about the inheritance tree is not as accurate as one might think. Let's first take a look at how PowerBuilder loads objects.

When an object is first referenced, PowerBuilder loads the object's definition into memory. This is the portion that remains in memory. An instance of the definition is then built based on the definition. If the object is inherited, the ancestor's definition has to be loaded first, then the current object's definition, and finally these two combine to build an instance of the object, and so on. The search process for the object's definition can take considerable time if the hierarchy gets deep and distributed among various libraries. Table 18.1 com-

TABLE 18.1 Loading Objects into Memory

Single-Layer Hierarchy	Multiple-Layer Hierarchy
Search for object definition	Search for object definition
Load object defintion	Discover inheritance criteria
Create instance of object	Search for ancestor definition
	Discover inheritance criteria
	Search for ancestor definition
	Discover inheritance criteria
	Search for ancestor definition
	Load object definition
	Create instance of object

pares the load process of a typical object with a four-layer inheritance tree with that of a single layer.

It becomes immediately obvious that the multiple-layered object takes longer to load. This flat comparison does not do justice to reality, however. Typically, an object is not loaded only one time in the life of an application. (If it is, you should take steps to make sure that the object's hierarchy is as flat as possible; Frame windows, for example, fall into this category.)

Case study: Invoice Data object and Company Data object

Let's take a little deeper look into what happens in a more typical case of objects that are used several times in an application and also at the level of functionality that is involved. Take the case of an object that can process Invoice details. A typical hierarchy might look like this:

- Ancestor object
- Business layer
- Application layer

Each of these layers contains functionality. The base level ancestor performs some initialization and could control some general processing, the business layer might implement some rules about the processing capabilities, and the application layer drives the actual processing for the Company Data object. Each layer contains a certain amount of functionality, and requires a certain amount of memory. For the purpose of this discussion, we make assumptions about size, as shown in Table 18.2.

If we developed the Company object without a hierarchy, it would probably *not* add up to 70 K. After all, the various layers would contain functionality for other object classes as well. It would probably add up to about 60 K, or less if all the functionality imbedded in the hierarchy pertaining to Invoice data was to be implemented. This is a key distinction between the two approaches. Class hierarchies generally implement higher levels of functionality than non-hierarchical approaches. If we looked at this hierarchy, we could see something like Figure 18.1.

TABLE 18.2 Object Hierarchy Size: Company Object

Object Layer	Size
Base layer	30 K
Business layer	20 K
Application layer	20 K
Total	70 K

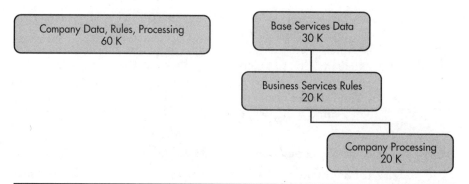

Figure 18.1 Flat model versus traditional inheritance model.

Based on our knowledge of how PowerBuilder objects are loaded, we can see the object load paths following the path described in Figure 18.2.

The difference begins when the second instance is loaded. Now, with both definitions in memory, the two approaches' load times are much more similar. The definitions for both objects are already in memory, so search time is eliminated. Load times are much more similar. Figure 18.3 demonstrates the load steps.

Now we look at a second object. For example, let's define Invoice as another object class. A similar effect is described in the single versus layered approach, with one difference. The layered approach inherits from the same tree as the Company object, resulting in the hierarchy shown in Figure 18.4.

As you can see, the ancestry for the object uses the same Base Ancestor and Base Functional classes. In the flat model, when invoice information is required, the 60 K Invoice object is searched for and loaded into memory. The search process for the Invoice object in the layered approach is more efficient than the first Invoice object loaded because the Base Ancestor and Base Functional layers are already in memory. The search time is comparable, and in fact you might find that the layered Invoice object loads faster than the flat model. The differences in load times between the first load of an instance and the second are far smaller. The layered approach pays a stiffer penalty once, but then continues to be more and more efficient than the single layered approach. This can be demonstrated as shown in Figure 18.5.

As objects continue to be loaded, the total execution time of the flat model approach would soon exceed the time consumed by the layered approach, and ultimately, you would suffer a performance degradation, even if it is not truly noticeable.

One reason for the myth of slow layered approaches is that the single-layer approach does not deviate much at all from object to object, whereas the layered approach can reduce load times by as much as half, or sometimes more, leading the user to believe that there is a performance problem with the object, at least once. It is also not always the same object loaded first, so the user sees the Invoice object take a while longer one day, and the

- ▸ Locate object
- ▸ Load definition
- ▸ Instantiate object
  - • 60 K Loaded
  - • 2–4 seconds

- ▸ Locate object
- ▸ Load definition
- ▸ Locate ancestor
- ▸ Load definition
- ▸ Locate ancestor
- ▸ Load definition
- ▸ Instantiate object
  - • 70 K
  - • 4–6 seconds

Figure 18.2 Load of the first instance: flat model outperforms traditional model.

- ▸ Definition already loaded
- ▸ Instantiate object
  - • Another 60 K
  - • Approximately 1–2 seconds

- ▸ Definitions are loaded
- ▸ Instantiate object
  - • Another 70 K
  - • Approximately 1–2 seconds

Load of the second instance is pretty close to being equal.

Figure 18.3 Loading of second instance is much more efficient. In some cases, the inherited model may outperform the flat model.

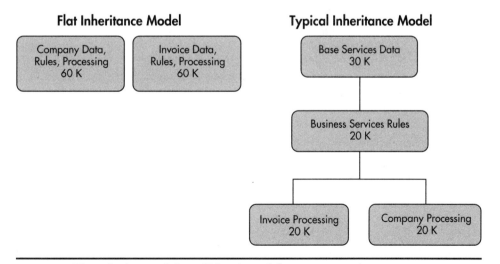

Figure 18.4 Hierarchy is extended to add Invoice and Company processing.

- ▸ Locate object
- ▸ Load definition
- ▸ 2–4 seconds

- ▸ Locate object
- ▸ Load definition
- ▸ Determine ancestry
- ▸ Ancestor definitions already loaded
- ▸ 2–4 seconds, sometimes faster than flat model

Figure 18.5 Second object's load times are reversed in performance. Inherited model outperforms the flat model.

company object run slower the next because of processing flow. Again, this is perception rather than actual performance and can be avoided by preloading ancestor objects, either by using them sooner in the application or by physically preloading the object in question. You can preload an object's definition by simply declaring a variable of the object class in an earlier loading object. This avoids complaints that "The first time is really slow. After that, it's acceptable."

Objects and Architecture: The Roles They Play

Another factor affecting performance is the architecture you choose to implement and the object classes you decide to use. Be aware of the built-in hierarchy of an object class, and also of how much resources each object uses up. (Resource allocation requirements *can* affect performance.)

A nonvisual object loads far faster than a visual object because there is very little overhead required, resource requirements are minimal, and the class is actually closer to the root PowerObject class. This is one reason that many class library vendors have moved to placing services in NVOs. However, simply creating services is not a service-based architecture (SBA), it is moving code from one object to another. SBA attempts to reduce the number of developer usable object class choices as well.

Functions and Events: The Debate Continues

Global versus object functions

There is an ongoing debate over the effectiveness and efficiency of global and object functions. A common myth is that the global function is loaded into memory and discarded after every so many lines of code. This is not true. The global function is an object like any other and once loaded, remains in memory until some time after it is not being used anymore, at which point it is unloaded. This period of time that elapses before the object is no longer resident is unknown. Global functions are generally not used often enough to remain in memory permanently, so there is a potential load penalty involved each time you access them. Object functions, in contrast, remain in memory until the object is unloaded, in which case the developer has much more control over the situation. Besides, when you unload an object, you generally do not need the object's functions anymore.

Object functions do a few things that global functions do not. They encapsulate common groups of functionality, thereby making functions generally needed at the same time accessible. They are inheritable and extendible, providing more flexibility, and they support instance variables, which are then available to all of the functions contained in the object. For this reason, I recommend that functions be grouped together as much as possible and built into objects such as custom classes. Global functions should still be used when functionality must truly be global and the function is not related to other functions.

PowerBuilder 5.0 supports function overloading within objects. This allows you to define the functions with varying parameter clauses to promote further reuse and polymorphism.

Functions versus events

In the bitter battle to decide on the use of functions versus events, there is basically no contest. Functions outperform events (in access time) by about 5 to 1. The reason for this is in binding. Binding is the process by which a piece of script obtains an address to the function or event being called. Functions are tightly bound, whereas events are loosely bound. Tightly bound means that the script accessing the function obtains an address to the function at compile time (or when you save the script). Events are not addressed at compile time, but rather at runtime, when the event's address is first sought out before the script passes control to it. Events are therefore little more than dynamic functions.

Events also have to respond to the Windows message queue. This means that a handler is actually responsible for activating the event. This handler must first seek the address to the event, and then execute the event based on the request's position in the event queue. Processing events is therefore a longer route than processing functions.

This being said, when should we use functions? The answer is quite simple. We should use functions under the following conditions:

- The exact name of the function and arguments is known
- Maximum performance is required
- Functionality must be private or protected

We should therefore use events under the following conditions:

- The exact name of event is not known
- Performance is not a factor
- Function must execute only after other more important functions take place (posted events)
- Method access must always fall into the public realm

One last consideration. Events are easier for developers to extend or override than are functions. If ease of use is most important to you, strongly consider using events. Use of arguments and return values should not play a part in your decision because either method can be used successfully.

Using the Library Search Path

The library search path plays a role in performance as well, although its effect is felt more in large applications with many PBLs than in small applications or applications that use a small number of PBLs. For example, suppose we create an object hierarchy four layers deep (Base Ancestor, Base Functional, Business Layer, and Application Layer). Typically, the application layer comes first in the search path simply because it is the penultimate effect on the remaining classes. This is often the downfall.

Rearranging the libraries to place most-often-used objects at the front of the search path will affect load performance. This might not be much, perhaps even imperceptible to your user, but the increase in performance has the overall effect of making the application run more efficiently. Remember how objects are loaded?

First the object definition is loaded (once it is located). Then PowerBuilder checks the inheritance characteristics of the object, seeks the ancestor, and loads that definition. This continues until the highest-level ancestor is loaded. Once loaded, of course, the ancestor objects remain in memory until the last descendant is unloaded. We can therefore derive that we should do the following:

- Place most-often-used ancestors at the bottom of the search path and try to preload them. Once loaded into memory, the physical object class is not likely to be required very often. This includes static services (those always loaded with objects).
- Implement instantiable services (on-demand) higher in the search path because they are loaded and removed from memory quite often.

The Environment and Its Effect on Performance

One of the elements that has the most significant impact on the performance of your application is also one that is probably least understood: your workstation's environment. The possibility that every user on your system is using a different hardware configuration is actually quite high. Finding the right balance is difficult, as today's configurations call for networks and other drivers to be loaded that use up the most scarce resource, memory below the 1 MB line.

Windows 3.1 and earlier versions still rely on memory below the 1 MB line. Have you ever gotten an "insufficient memory" message when it appears as though Windows has lost its memory because you have 32 MB of RAM and a 50 MB permanent swap file? The cause for this is the memory you have available between the 640 KB line and the 1 MB line of memory, most of which is quickly used up by network cards and other "loaded high" software. Every application, or task, has to register with Windows. A Task database is created for each task started, gobbling up 60 bytes and more of this scarce below-the-line memory. This is a throwback to the days of the DOS extenders and earlier versions of Windows that required program addresses to be located in nondiscardable memory. (Why this never went away when protected mode Windows, or 386 enhanced, came about is a secret buried in the "Boy, that was stupid" vault at Microsoft.) If this was all that used up this memory, though, we would still be okay. (By the way, remember that every DLL loaded is a *task* to Windows.) But we have another problem.

When programs seek nondiscardable memory (this is memory that will not be swapped out, and therefore is always accessible and addressable), they use up the resources that are generally reserved for your task databases. Sometimes this type of memory allocation is required; at other times, it is not. These are called badly behaved programs.

So, there are external forces at large that affect the environment without your even knowing. But there are some things we can do to combat them. One is to create a small module that checks existing resources and determines whether your windows should try to open. The SDK function call to do this is the GetFreeSystemResources() function. This is declared as follows:

```
FUNCTION uint GetFreeSystemResources(int wFlag) LIBRARY 'kernel'
```

By establishing a default minimum resource level in each window of your application, and calling this function using a flag setting of 0 (0 returns the lowest resource level of your user, GDI, and system resources), you can determine whether the open should continue.

Another method of controlling your environment is to use the interface implementation methods referred to in earlier chapters. This allows you to place executable code into memory once instead of once for each object that uses it.

Finally, get your systems and network employees to work on a standard desktop configuration that works within your environment to help ensure that the users you are developing for have a configuration that supports your application. Try not to run too many external applications (such as Word, Excel, and other PowerBuilder applications), as these all use up resources.

Hardware

Of course, the answer to almost every question is more power. Today's machines are bigger, faster, and cheaper than before. Getting users to set up with the right hardware can have a remarkably favorable effect on their perception of your system. Hardware is never the ultimate solution, however, because improved software is just around the corner that will use up more of the hardware's capabilities than ever before.

Operating systems

The operating system you choose also affects performance. A 32-bit compiled application runs faster under Windows NT than under Windows 3.1. A 16-bit application does not perform faster under NT, and in fact may actually be a little slower. Windows 95 is a 32-bit operating system with similar performance credentials to a Windows NT workstation, except that NT handles resources more efficiently. I have found that a Windows NT workstation is the best platform for me to develop and run PowerBuilder applications. Your choice may be different, and sometimes you may not have a choice. Just remember to take your OS into consideration when designing your system.

Compile Scenarios

One of the aspects many programmers complain about is the length of time it takes to perform a compile of their application. My first recommendation is this: Make sure you have 16 MB of RAM or more. PowerBuilder loads and checks many referenced objects at compile time, as well as loading many of the DLLs you will use into memory. When you reach the limit of your physical memory, swapping begins. This extends your compile time exponentially.

Secondly, compile your applications with a little thought about where the PBLs are located. Placing the largest PBL first in line at compile time will also reduce your compile times. This is because when a PBL is loaded, PowerBuilder reserves that memory space. If the next PBL is larger, the memory space is first freed, another section of contiguous free memory is sought, and the PBL loaded. If you load the largest PBL first, the memory is never discarded and other memory is not required.

Third, make sure you have a swap file allocated and make it permanent. This reduces the time Windows takes to swap memory.

Another seemingly insignificant compile enhancer is your Smartdrive option. Smartdrive is often installed for you when Windows 3.1 is installed. Smartdrive handles disk cache, which affects swapping. Disable Smartdrive when compiling, especially larger applications. Leaving Smartdrive running can cause the "infinite compile" syndrome.

Finally, optimize your libraries before you compile. This gets rid of any dead space, which is not included in your executable but nonetheless affects how much contiguous free memory is required.

Benchmarking and Tuning

Once we have the more easily controlled elements satisfied, you need to analyze the library objects to determine where performance setbacks occur. To do this, I use a small application I created along with very small pieces of code added to various objects. The application is a remote log facility that traps Windows messages targeted for it and registers the time and resources available at that time. The main piece of code for this application is shown in Figures 18.6 through 18.9. Because the application is separate from your application, no additional overhead is added to your application.

The functions executed can then perform whatever processing is required. Your application does not wait for this to happen. It continues processing.

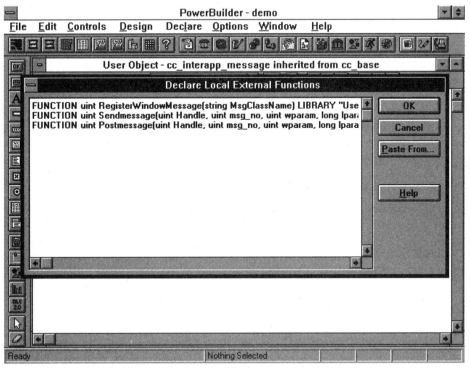

Figure 18.6 Function declarations for interapplication messaging.

```
/*****************************************************************************
 * FUNCTION : ccf_register
 * PURPOSE  : Register a unique message number with Windows
 *  Author  : Bill Green
 *   Date   : Aug. 11, 1995
 *
 *
 * A R G U M E N T S
 * --------------
 *
 * Type       Description
 * ----       ------------------------------------
 * String     Message Name
 *
 * R E T U R N    V A L U E S
 * -------------------------
 *
 * Type       Description
 * ----       ------------------------------------
 * uint       Message Number to be used for communications
 *
 * History
 * --------
 * Date       Init    Description of change
 * ------     ----    -------------------------------
 * 09/11/95   xxx     Initial Coding...
 *****************************************************************************

RETURN RegisterWindowMessage (messagetype)
```

Figure 18.7   Registering a message class.

In your application, you need to use an object called the interobject message manager. This object is instantiated as globally available to your application when activated, and you place strategic calls to the object in your code.

How it works

Basically, both your application and the log facility application register a special Windows message class. When one application sends or posts a message to the message queue containing this unique message ID, the Windows message handler processes the message and notifies the recipient applications.

Your application is coded to first check whether the message manager is available before executing the function call, so there is no overhead other than a very fast isValid() function call if the object is not active. This code looks like this:

```
IF isValid(InterAppObject) THEN InterAppObject.SendMessage(hWndRecipient, Ms-
gnum, longparm, wordparm)
```

The hWndRecipient is the handle of the window that is to receive this message, and can be defaulted to hwnd_broadcast (or 65536). The MsgNum is a

```
/********************************************************************
* FUNCTION : ccf_register
*  PURPOSE : Register a unique message number with Windows
*   Author : Bill Green
*    Date  : Aug. 11, 1995
*
*
* A R G U M E N T S
* --------------
*
* Type       Description
* ----       -----------------------------------
* uint       Recipient Window hWnd (hWnd_Broadcast = All Top Level Windows
*    uint         Message Number
* uint       WordParm
*    Long        LongParm
*
* R E T U R N    V A L U E S
* -------------------------
*
* Type       Description
* ----       ---------------------------------
* (int)      Successfully sent
*
*
*
* History
* --------
* Date      Init   Description of change
* ------    ----   --------------------------------
* 08/11/95  xxx    Initial Coding...
********************************************************************
// If the hwnd received = zero, translate to Broadcast
If WindowID = 0 THEN WindowID = hwnd_BroadCast

// Send the message number to the Windows message queue
RETURN SendMessage (WindowID, MessageID, wparam, lparam)
```

Figure 18.8 Sending a message to the message class.

value returned to you when you register the message with Windows, and the longparm and wordparm contain the values you can use for processing the message. (I use longparm to send an identification of function to the log program, and the wordparm can be used to hold other data such as time).

This little log facility can then be used to trap the start and end times for any object or script and give you real feedback on performance.

How to test

This section describes how to test the library to analyze areas of performance that can be improved or require improvement. The tests will be run using various machine, network, and environment setups.

Use an automated scripting tool to record and run test.   We use the capabilities of SQA Test Suite to record and run our tests. This ensures that we apply con-

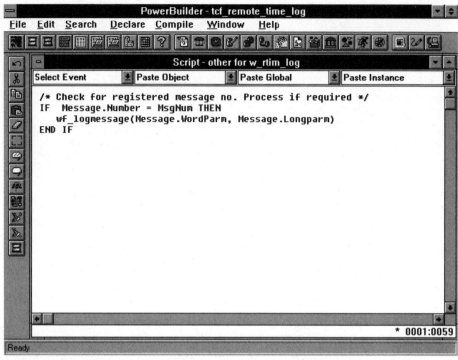

Figure 18.9 Trapping the message and extracting the code depending on it.

sistent parameters and criteria for all tests. We run each situation script a total of 20 times and calculate the average times for each test.

Use the remote log facility to record times.   We have developed a module that can record data, including time and resources, that runs remotely from the application. The application communicates with the log facility by means of Windows messages, thereby having a minimal effect on the performance of the library.

Use a debug version of the library.   We developed a special edition of the library framework that contains the imbedded calls to the Remote Log facility. As specified, the accesses to the log functions are simple Windows message posts to a special Windows message class, reducing the impact on the system.

Analysis.   We recommend that you perform your analysis on various hardware and software configurations. Even if the configuration will not be used in a production environment, it can serve to provide additional information.

PowerBuilder DLLs networked, application EXE/PBDs networked.   PowerBuilder DLLs and application EXE/PBDs all running from the network should give the slowest performance of any version of your library.

PowerBuilder DLLs networked, application EXE/PBDs local. PowerBuilder DLLs running from the network and application EXE/PBDs running locally should result in acceptable performance.

PowerBuilder DLLs local, application EXE/PBDs networked. PowerBuilder DLLs running local, application EXE/PBDs running off the network will boost performance, especially when the combined size of the application's files is less than 8 MB.

PowerBuilder DLLs local, application EXE/PBDs local. PowerBuilder DLLs and application EXE/PBDs all running local is not an optimal condition for running distributed client-server applications, but provides feedback on what performance levels can be attained.

Development versus runtime executable. Running the tests with both development and production environments will help us to analyze how much time is being used by PowerBuilder itself, as most load time taken by PowerBuilder is eliminated in the development environment.

PowerBuilder DLLs preloaded. Preload the PowerBuilder DLLs using a small "shell" application (or in fact, the Remote Log facility, which serves quite nicely as a PowerBuilder DLL loader).

Hardware configurations. If possible, run the various test scenarios on different client platforms to determine how much of an impact upgrading equipment would have on future use. For example:

- 486/33: 16 MB RAM
- 486/75: 16 MB RAM
- Pentium P90: 16 MB RAM

Analyze for different database accesses. In order to complete save cycle testing, we include tests of using Watcom (ODBC) and Sybase (our choices) in the test cycle. We compare normal datawindow SQL access with stored procedure access.

What Should You Test?

Application load time

At application startup, plan to analyze the time it takes to load PowerBuilder and then to load the application.

PowerBuilder load time. PowerBuilder load time is described as the amount of time it takes to load the PowerBuilder runtime DLLs. We are aware that PowerBuilder 4.0 loads much more of the runtime environment up front than does PowerBuilder 3.0, one of the ways PowerBuilder is addressing some of the runtime performance issues. Expect the PowerBuilder load time to be significantly longer than that of PowerBuilder 3.0. PowerBuilder 5.0 loads faster under Windows NT, but slightly slower under Windows 3.1

Library or framework load time.   Analyze the amount of time it takes to load each element or service of the class library application framework. The results will reveal any areas of suspect performance.

Application initialization.   Measure other areas of application initialization such as splash windows, resource checking, and version checking.

Application login

At the login window, we measure the time it takes to connect to various databases and investigate means to improve the connect time required. Various parameter settings are measured in an attempt to determine the optimal settings for each database.

Frame window and menu load

We measure the load time required to load our Frame window and Frame menu and investigate different techniques now available to improve the performance of the initial Frame menu loads.

Often-used dialogs

In this section, we perform analysis of the dialog windows most often used in the library and determine how we can improve the performance of any dialog determined to be nonperformance compliant, that is, performance that does not meet the standards we establish as our goals. For example:

- User preferences
- Window Toolbar dialog
- Help About
- System info
- Sort/Filter/Find dialogs
- Error dialogs
- User message box dialogs

Other key objects

Finally, run tests on all of the other objects most often used, such as parent-child (master-detail) and data retrieval.

Test Results and Analysis

In analyzing the results of the tests, we need to make sure we cover the following points:

- Collect all test results for analysis.

- Analyze test results and determine where effort is required for correction or enhancement, or no change is needed.

- Create the technical specification for changes required.

- Develop recommendations for developers to improve performance through the use of better techniques

- Make all required changes to library code or make recommendations to the vendor for changes that affect the architecture. This effort is very dependent on the results of the analysis, and may either be extended or shortened based on our findings.

Summary

This concludes the performance metrics section. As you can see, there is a lot that can be done to improve performance, and we hope we have dispelled some myths about PowerBuilder and performance. Do not lose hope. Remember that the software will continue to improve, as will your hardware. If your users are critical of performance, convince them to get equipment and configurations that will not affect your application detrimentally. But also remember that getting faster hardware is no excuse to not analyze your libraries' performance.

Retooling Existing Projects

Introduction

What is a retrofit? It is when you change an existing project to make use of your base class objects. The pitfalls are many, but so are the benefits.

Chapter Objectives

In this chapter you will find out how to plan and implement a retrofitting project. You will learn how to estimate the effort required, and how to justify the effort to management.

We show you how to gauge the benefits of applying a retrofit and how to judge whether a retrofit makes sense for any given project.

Methodologies Introduced

This chapter introduces you to the technique of adding an ancestor to an object. You will be able to leverage the functionality of your base class objects using this technique. We will also show how you can, where it is appropriate, change the ancestor of an object. These two techniques will enable you to apply the benefits of your class library without rewriting entire objects.

Class library developers take heed! This chapter is a detailed look at what you and your application developers face if you change the way applications interface with the architecture of your library. Try to get the design and performance right the first time. Observe good object-oriented practice: change the underlying objects if you must, but maintain the interfaces. We speak from experience.

Justifying the Retrofit

Why should working projects be retooled? This question will surely come up. When it does, it pays to be prepared with the answers. The obvious answer, "to use a class library," glosses over important issues of economic effectiveness and incentive when the applications are working without it.

A retrofit costs money and time, sometimes a surprising amount of each. Those who foot the bill have a need and a right to know why the expenditure is worth it.

The first, and perhaps most compelling, reason is that ease of maintenance is enhanced. The features provided by your class library will no longer need to be supported by the maintenance team for that application. Maintenance of these features is, of course, the responsibility of the library team. In addition, when an enhancement to the base functionality is introduced, that enhancement is readily available to the application.

Changing the application to use your class library also helps it to remain consistent with the other applications in the company. Consistency is a benefit for end users, trainers, managers, and developers. It increases the mobility and flexibility of the users, and enables them to apply their skills across different applications. It decreases training time, because of the commonality among applications. Managers and developers benefit because enhancements and maintenance are more easily estimated and implemented.

Retrofitting provides access to the new features of your class library. This may actually reduce the need for anticipated enhancements because the features are already there in the class library.

However, it is important to realize that not all retrofit efforts are justifiable. The size, scope, expected life span, and likelihood of enhancement of each candidate application must all be within a range that makes the effort worthwhile.

When does a retrofit make sense?

A retrofit is indicated when user demands for enhancements point to a measurable benefit from incorporating base class objects. If there is a decent fit between the desired features and the functionality that the class library provides, then you can usually justify a retrofit.

Sometimes, an opportunity simply presents itself. When a production program must be upgraded to match a newer release of PowerBuilder, this can be a perfect time to use the class library to smooth the transition. The base class objects, already in tune with the new PowerBuilder version, bring functionality without increased coding effort.

Throughout the life of an application, it will be fixed and enhanced many times. Sometimes the changes are made in a hurry, without much attention to reusability or consistency. When maintenance demands on an existing application have compromised its reliability or usability, it is a clear candidate for a retrofit.

Some signs that an application will not benefit from a retrofit are as follows:

- The application is near the end of its production life. Under these circumstances, the application will be phased out or replaced. The effort involved in planning, executing, and testing a retrofit probably is not warranted.

- The application is stable. No enhancements are planned, and it is essentially bug-free. There is no benefit to be derived from retrofitting this application to use your class library objects. On the contrary, if you retrofit, you expose the users to changes in the operation of the application, and you expose the developers to another round of testing and user acceptance.

- The application is small. If the application is half a dozen datawindows and one or two windows, it does not make sense to invest in a retrofit. It is better to leave well enough alone and allow the application to serve its users in relative peace.

Estimating a Retrofit

A retrofit project, like any other project, consists of identifiable tasks. Some tasks depend on the completion of other tasks, whereas others are independent or iterative. The tasks involved in a retrofit effort are as follows:

- *Review existing system:* Allow time in your estimates for adequate review of each object as well as the features, workflow, and functionality of the entire application. A simple time factor for conversion, multiplied by the number of objects, gives you a ballpark estimate that you can use as your basis for more refined estimates.

- *Identify dependencies and relationships:* The complexity of the application has a bearing on the time you must allot for this task. The more complex, and the more relationships within the application, the more time is spent on the task of isolating and identifying these relationships and dependencies.

- *Implement framework:* This task does not involve a great deal of time, and prior experience with nonretrofit projects is a good indicator.

- *Convert application windows:* The time that you must allocate for this task varies with the complexity and variety of the windows.

- *Convert application datawindows:* This task involves using the user object datawindow classes that you have developed to add functionality without extra coding. This task takes only a modest amount of time for each affected datawindow, but you need to make sure that you allocate a finite interval for each datawindow.

- *Convert other functionality:* If you can identify other areas where existing functionality is duplicated by the class library, the class library functionality should be used. Allocate time to identify and convert any such areas.

- *Integrate new objects:* Allot time to integrate new objects that replace existing objects with updated functionality or presentation.

- *System testing:* Finally, be sure that you allow time for system testing. The target is completely specified—it already exists! This makes the definition of success easier, but can complicate testing. Even if your retrofitted application is correct with respect to specifications, it needs to be compared with the existing application as well.

You must allow enough time in your estimates for each of these tasks. Obviously, the larger the application you are converting, the more time you must allow for each task. Not so obvious is the fact that as system size and complexity grow, the time needed to perform a retrofit does not grow linearly, but geometrically. The interactions among the objects to be converted must be taken into account when you create the factors used in your estimates.

Finally, remember that estimates must be flexible. Nothing ruins a retrofit project faster than a slavish adherence to an estimate made even before the planning phase has begun. Refine the estimates as the project progresses. You will learn more about the inner workings of the target application than you thought possible. As you learn, your knowledge will affect the precision of your estimates. Early estimates will change. Accommodate the changes, or be prepared to surprise your manager later. Believe me, surprises should be saved for birthday parties.

> *In some cases, you will not be able to complete each defined task linearly, without regard to other tasks. That is okay. The tasks still need to be completed, and estimated. During development, you can postpone completion of windows or other objects until the objects they depend on have been converted.*

Implementing a Retrofit: The Tasks

You can implement the retrofit relatively painlessly by following a plan that encompasses the tasks we have outlined. A project planning tool comes in handy for maintaining the plan for your retrofit. Figure 19.1 shows an excerpt from a retrofit plan, RETRO.MPP, that we built using Microsoft Project. This file is included on the CD for your review.

This project plan contains several macros that automatically estimate the effort required at each step of the retrofit. The formulas have been refined over time to reflect what we have learned over the course of several retrofit projects. Your estimates will indeed vary, though. The structure, architecture, and complexity of your class library and your application will have a significant impact on any retrofitting estimates.

Review existing system

The first task you need to address is a review of the system as it currently exists. Your goal at this point is to discover the real nature of the application.

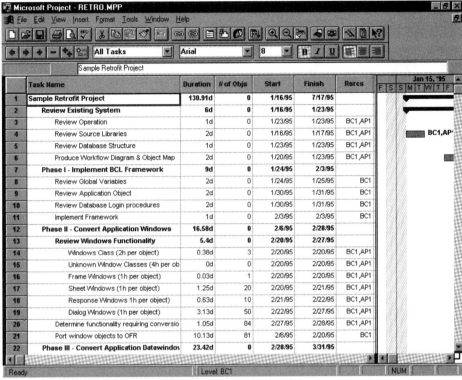

Figure 19.1 A Microsoft Project plan for a retrofit.

Has it evolved beyond its original specifications? Does it contain any long-standing bugs that the users have learned to treat as features? Does it have any hidden functionality that the users count on? Obviously, this stage can be completed more easily with the added involvement of some experienced users.

Review the way the libraries are organized. Also examine the types of objects and their size.

Allow time for an examination of the database structure. This will aid you in following the internals of the application.

You also need to do a count of every object, by type, in the application. As previously mentioned, this step aids in estimating. It also helps you to divide the work among your developers.

Estimate the complexity of the application's objects. You can refine your estimates at this point, giving more time to the conversion of more complex objects and less to the simpler ones. In many cases, the greatest benefits of retrofitting stem from the more complex objects. The retrofit reduces the internal complexity and improves performance and maintainability. Plan to spend the most time on the complex objects to get the most return for your retrofit effort.

Identify dependencies

Examine the application workflow. (If you do not have an application workflow document, now is the time to prepare one.) You can identify the one-to-one, one-to-many, and search criteria/results relationships present in the application by reviewing the workflow document. You can use the object mapping technique we presented earlier to map the objects and dependencies onto your class library objects. Use this knowledge to determine which objects you need to convert in order to use your class library.

As you find dependencies and object relationships, be sure to reevaluate your plan. You need to take into account any new knowledge you have gained during this step.

Implement framework

Next, you need to create the application framework using the standard construction techniques for your class library. Do not deviate from your standard practices here. The goal is to rebuild the application in the image of the applications that have been, and will be, created with your library. If you maintain consistency, future developers will thank you.

Convert application windows

The next step is to convert the application's windows to use your library's functionality. Use the object map created previously to guide you in this phase. Move code out of individual objects on the windows into the window's script wherever possible.

During this step, you need to modify the ancestry of the application's windows. We discuss this in greater detail later in the chapter, but the essence of the method is as follows:

1. Make a backup of the PBL.
2. Verify that you have made a backup of the PBL.
3. Export the window's code.
4. Change (or add) the name of the ancestor.
5. Extend the control array.
6. Detect and remove custom event collisions.
7. Remove or relocate functionality to take advantage of the new ancestor's capabilities.
8. Import the modified window.

Convert application datawindows

As much as is practical, convert the application's datawindows to user objects based on your class library. Use the object map to determine which object best suits a given datawindow's usage. Then add any common code directly to the user objects.

If any datawindow is used in more than one window, you can add the code that is specific to each window once you have placed the object onto the window.

Convert other functionality

At this point, take the opportunity to bring the application's other functionality into compliance with your class library and the standards you have promoted. You can bring much of your class library's might to bear by inheriting the functionality from one of your basic nonvisual objects and using the resulting object as a starting point for objects that encapsulate the specific methods needed for your application.

Examine and analyze these objects thoroughly. You will probably discover common business objects that you can reuse throughout the company. This is an excellent opportunity to show the benefits of designing for reuse.

Integrate new objects

Your converted objects must be reintegrated into the system at this point in the project. Each object should be thoroughly unit-tested before you integrate it into the application. If you are using an automated testing tool, be sure to construct test scripts and test cases at this time.

System testing

The last phase of a retrofit project is the system test. The entire system must be tested to verify that it duplicated the features and functionality of the original system. One of the best ways to ensure that the new system works the way that the old one did is to use a parallel test. Construct, either manually or using a regression testing tool, a set of scripts that you can execute on both systems. Make sure that the scripts produce the expected results on the original system. Then run the scripts against the converted application. The results you obtain along the way and at the end of the scripts should be identical. Be especially careful to note the condition of the database at points during the script's execution. Any differences in the way the database is handled are sure to cause trouble once the system is implemented.

Implementing a retrofit: tips, techniques, and traps

The most important advice I can give you is Do not upgrade! That is, do not enhance the application as you are retrofitting it to use your class library. The temptation is always there to improve on the application's functionality or add a long-awaited enhancement. This is a bad idea. The scope of the project will creep upward with each enhancement, and your target will be constantly moving. Your best chance of success comes when you aim at a well-defined, stationary target. The target already exists: your original application. Strive to replicate as closely as possible the operation of the prior application. Schedule enhancements as a second phase of the project, to begin once the retrofit is proven to be successful.

Also, although it may seem obvious, do not work on the original! Make a copy. Keep the original source code safe and frozen. Do not allow the original to be changed or enhanced while the retrofit is taking place. Of course, if an enhancement is absolutely necessary, either to fix a bug or to satisfy an important need, it should be allowed. But keep the original intact. Remember, that is your target. Any enhancements to the original should be well-documented when they are done, and incorporated as a separate, second project after the retrofit is done. This is the only way to keep your retrofit project safe from scope creep.

You should retrofit only where there is a benefit, and leave well enough alone where there is no benefit. This can best be summed up with an old adage: Never try to teach a pig to sing. It wastes your time and annoys the pig.

Leverage your work. Find areas of common functionality in the application and encapsulate them into common reusable business objects. If functionality in the application is duplicated by your class library objects, use the class library wherever possible.

Find the custom events in currently existing objects. Then isolate and remove conflicts. You can use the Search item on the Library Painter's Entry menu to find the word *event* in the objects you are upgrading. Then you can go into that object's painter and change the definition of the custom events so that they do not collide with any of the standard events supplied by your base objects. This comes in very handy if you decide to add one of your class library objects as an ancestor at a later time.

Sometimes it is easier to export and edit the object's source code directly. Use a text editor (such as the one included with PowerBuilder) to modify the exported code. Then reimport.

TIP

To add the DOS file editor to your PowerBar, first right-click on the PowerBar. Choose "Customize" from the popup menu. Then find the Edit icon in the palette. (It looks like a dog-eared page with a pencil hovering over it.) Drag the icon to the current toolbar in the dialog and let go. I placed my edit button immediately to the left of the Help icon.

Adding an ancestor

The procedure outlined here can damage objects or entire PBLs. Make backups of all of your application's files before you try this. If you get a compiler error or GPF when importing a script file, we strongly recommend that you exit from PowerBuilder and restart before continuing. Make backups!

In some cases you need to add an ancestor to a window that is not inherited. This allows you to take advantage of base class functionality while still retaining the work already done on that window. The first step in changing a window's ancestor is to export the source code. In the Library Painter, select the window you want to export. Then choose Entry | Export from the menu. PowerBuilder will offer a suggestion for the file name. Because this is simply an eight-character name, you should not accept the suggestion. Provide your own descriptive name. Listing 19.1 shows the exported code from a minimal example of a window with no ancestry.

LISTING 19.1 **w_exam _no_ancestor** (Notice that this Window has *Window* as an ancestor.)

```
$PBExportHeader$w_exam_no_ancestor.srw
forward
global type w_exam_no_ancestor from Window
end type
type cb_1 from commandbutton within w_exam_no_ancestor
end type
end forward

global type w_exam_no_ancestor from Window
int X=833
int Y=357
int Width=1998
int Height=1213
boolean TitleBar=true
string Title="Untitled"
boolean ControlMenu=true
boolean MinBox=true
boolean MaxBox=true
boolean Resizable=true
event cue_my_event pbm_custom01
cb_1 cb_1
end type
global w_exam_no_ancestor w_exam_no_ancestor
on w_exam_no_ancestor.create
this.cb_1=create cb_1
this.Control[]={ this.cb_1}
end on

on w_exam_no_ancestor.destroy
destroy(this.cb_1)
end on

type cb_1 from commandbutton within w_exam_no_ancestor
int X=1527
int Y=269
int Width=380
int Height=109
int TabOrder=1
string Text="no ancestor"
int TextSize=-10
int Weight=400
string FaceName="Arial"
FontFamily FontFamily=Swiss!
FontPitch FontPitch=Variable!
end type
```

There are several items to note about this exported source. First, you will see that even a window with no ancestor is actually inherited from *window*. The window has a single custom user event declared, cue_my_event. The event ID of cue_my_event is pbm_custom01. Also, this window has a single control cb_1 on it. You can see that the control (a command button) is inserted into the window's control array in the window's Create event.

You will need to ensure that none of the custom user events (pbm_custom) in the target source have duplicate event IDs in the ancestor window. To do this, you also need to examine the ancestor window to determine its custom user events. You can do this either with the window painter or by exporting the source. Listing 19.2 shows the exported source of our (also minimal) ancestor window.

LISTING 19.2   The Example Ancestor Window: Exported Source.

```
$PBExportHeader$w_exam_ancestor.srw
$PBExportComments$Ancestor window for inheritance example
forward
global type w_exam_ancestor from Window
end type
type cb_1 from commandbutton within w_exam_ancestor
end type
type dw_1 from datawindow within w_exam_ancestor
end type
end forward

global type w_exam_ancestor from Window
int X=833
int Y=357
int Width=1998
int Height=1213
boolean TitleBar=true
string Title="Untitled"
long BackColor=12632256
boolean ControlMenu=true
boolean MinBox=true
boolean MaxBox=true
boolean Resizable=true
event cue_ancestor_event pbm_custom01
cb_1 cb_1
dw_1 dw_1
end type
global w_exam_ancestor w_exam_ancestor

on w_exam_ancestor.create
this.cb_1=create cb_1
this.dw_1=create dw_1
this.Control[]={ this.cb_1,&
this.dw_1}
end on

on w_exam_ancestor.destroy
destroy(this.cb_1)
destroy(this.dw_1)
end on

type cb_1 from commandbutton within w_exam_ancestor
int X=1596
int Y=81
int Width=247
```

```
int Height=109
int TabOrder=10
string Text="Button"
int TextSize=-10
int Weight=400
string FaceName="Arial"
FontFamily FontFamily=Swiss!
FontPitch FontPitch=Variable!
end type

type dw_1 from datawindow within w_exam_ancestor
int X=119
int Y=689
int Width=1687
int Height=361
int TabOrder=20
string DataObject="d_example_1"
boolean LiveScroll=true
end type
```

If you examine the code in Listing 19.2 you will see that the ancestor window also has a custom event, cue_ancestor_event, with an event ID of pbm_custom01. You need to change the event ID for cue_my_event. You can do this either in the window painter or in the exported source. If you are changing the source, simply replace pbm_custom01 with an event ID that does not occur in the intended ancestor. You will find the event declarations in the global type declaration block immediately following the forward declarations block.

For this example, use your editor to change all occurrences of w_exam_no_ancestor to w_exam_descendant_1. This lets you import the source back into your PBL without overwriting w_exam_no_ancestor. In a typical retrofit, of course, you would not change the window name.

You also need to prevent collisions between control names. Notice that both Listing 19.1 (the target window's source code) and Listing 19.2 (the intended ancestor's code) contain a reference to a control called cb_1. You need to change all references to cb_1 in the target to refer to another name. For this example, we will use cb_descendant as the name.

TIP

If you have developed your class library using some reasonable naming standards, you will not encounter this problem very often. The standard names used in your base class objects will not often collide with PowerBuilder's default names. You still need to check, though.

You still have a small control headache to contend with. Remember the Create event? The control array is populated with cb_1 (now called cb_descendant). If you examine the code you will see that whatever was in the control array is simply replaced by the controls on this window. This is exactly the way it should be done on a window with no ancestors. But because we are adding an ancestor, we need another way to set up the control array. Refer to Listing 19.3 for an example of the correct code to use in the target window's Create event. You need to make this change directly in the exported source. The Create event is not accessible through the Window painter.

LISTING 19.3   New Code for the Window Create Event.

```
on w_exam_descendant_1.create
int iCurrent
call w_exam_ancestor::create
this.cb_descendant=create cb_descendant
iCurrent=UpperBound(this.Control)
this.Control[iCurrent+1]=cb_descendant
end on
```

Take note, also, of the call to w_exam_ancestor::create before this window's code executes. You need to add a call to the ancestor's event in each event that occurs in the descendant. Listing 19.4 shows another example of this, in the destroy event. The ancestor's destroy event is called, then the descendant's code executes, destroying the cb_descendant command button.

LISTING 19.4   The Destroy Event for the New Descendant Window.

```
on w_exam_descendant_1.destroy
call w_exam_ancestor::destroy
destroy(this.cb_descendant)
end on
```

Finally, you need to change the ancestor from "window" to "w_exam_ancestor." Use your text editor to search for occurrences of "from Window" and replace them with "from w_exam_ancestor."

Save the source code file. Then exit from the editor, close all PowerBuilder painters except for the Library Painter, and import the source file into one of the application's PBLs. If you get an error, exit PowerBuilder and restart before continuing. If all goes well, you should see your new object appear in the PBL directory listing.

If the import finishes without an error, try to open the new window in the Window painter. Examine the control list. Check out the script editor. You should see the window's ancestor listed on the title bar. Check the user events. You should now have access to the ancestor window's events as well.

Congratulations. You have just performed open-heart surgery on a PowerBuilder window.

Changing an ancestor

If the window already has an ancestor, the process is simpler. You still need to examine the two objects for event and control collisions, but the code required to implement calls to the ancestor events is already in place.

However, if the old ancestor has events, controls, or variables that do not exist on the new ancestor, you need to add these to the new ancestor, or change the descendant so that it does not refer to them. After you have resolved collisions, change the ancestor name using your editor. Search for the name of the ancestor window (do not use *from,* as we did in the previous example) and replace it with the new ancestor. Reimport the source and you are done.

Best practices I: relocate the scripts

You will want to move scripts from the objects and controls on each window that you retrofit. The goal is to bring the coding practices more into line with your established standards and guidelines.

Move code away from command buttons. Your code should exist in NVOs or in the window itself. You can use the window as a container for various objects that initiate actions on the window. An important benefit of this technique is that different objects on the window can fire the same functionality on the window.

Move code out of menus. Menus are such poor performers and grow so fast that you should remove as much code as possible. The ultimate menu script simply triggers an event on a central menu service manager.

Best practices II: banish globals

Examine the existing code for the use of global variables and functions. In many cases, you can narrow the scope of these items by combining them into discrete objects: functions into object methods, variables into object attributes.

In other cases, you can eliminate globals by using messaging methods to pass information from one object to another. However, be aware that huge, unwieldy structures are difficult to maintain and can be prone to bugs. Use a nonvisual object instead, and pass a pointer to the object. Then use a method on that object to go after relevant data.

Summary

A retrofit project is not to be taken lightly. It can consume a lot of time, resources, and money. In this chapter you learned how to determine whether a retrofit is justified. You learned how to plan and carry out a retrofit. Finally we showed you some important techniques you can use to ensure the success of your retrofit project.

Part

Application Development

Introduction

In today's world there are two types of development efforts using client-server technology: successful and unsuccessful. Methodologies are bandied about like an old-fashioned medicine peddler sells sugared water as the elixir of life. RAD, JAD, and waterfall, and reiterative prototyping and are touted as being the savior of the day. They are not. The methodologies are getting better, but they are still a long way from being the silver bullet.

Nothing has come about yet to replace careful planning and design. The more traditional, stoic, step-by-step methodologies still work. All you need to do is modify them to suit the technology. The traditional life-cycle cannot be ignored to get the system out the door faster.

The promise of productivity through client-server has changed the planning and design of systems the most. For the most part, what is most noticeable is the reduction in time spent planning and designing. The number of six-week projects is growing. So is the number of failed projects, or "close enough" projects. I have also been fortunate to see the other end of the scale. A little more time, a little more effort, and the result is a really good system that the users recognize as a technological advance. Taking the right approach, balancing planning and designing with integrated efforts by both the development team and the user, is tantamount to success. Skip a step and you will almost certainly doom yourself to failure in one way or another.

Part Objectives

The goals of this part of the book are to discuss some of the approaches available today and highlight the benefits and deficiencies of each. We also show the methodology we have adopted, and how we use the methodology to improve productivity continuously, not just for a single project.

Application Development Methodologies

There has been a significant change in life-cycle methodology over the past few years. I remember when structured programming and structured analysis and design techniques became popular, and were touted as the next breakthrough in technology. Now, they appear antiquated because the new buzzwords emphasize speed and flexibility. If you look at the differing methodologies, however, you will notice that they are not that different! In fact, the major difference between them is that today's methodologies are trying to envelop *change* as part of the project life-cycle. In my opinion, this is the single largest contributor to the advance in technology. Change is being recognized for what it is: inevitable.

The styles that have emerged over the years include many of the same tasks. You still have to plan, analyze, design, and develop a system. The major difference now is the ability to shorten each of these phases into bite-sized chunks that are more manageable. Now we want users to see what they are getting much sooner in the life-cycle in order to produce a more complete and accurate representation of their needs. Gone are the days of the "development gods" telling the user what they really want. Now we want the user more involved than ever, and object-oriented technology allows this to happen more easily than any prior technology. In my opinion, this is the single greatest technological advance of the computer era.

Not too long ago, we faced what I call the deity syndrome. This happened when users told the IS department what they needed, in general business terms. The IS department, after reviewing what it could accomplish and what it could not, went back to the users and told them what they were going to receive. The users then nodded happily, because they really did not understand a word the IS manager was saying, but expected the programming gods to take over and magically produce the completed product that would solve all of their problems. IS then went away for a year and returned with the product "the users asked for." The users looked at this and frowned deeply because the product resembled the inner workings of a Swiss watch, did not do half the things they expected, glossed over the major business functionality (which had changed in the past year, by the way), but had some great bells and whistles that would make them "more productive." The next eighteen months were spent modifying this system to achieve a more than 60 percent satisfaction of business requirements. The relationship between users and IS was, to say the least, tenuous.

There are other contributing factors to the problems of systems analysis and design, some of which are contributed by the user, some by the IS department. One of these is the law of user requirements: "Give me what I need, not what I ask for." The law has been somewhat modified in the modern era. It now reads, "Give me what I need today, not what I asked for yesterday."

The need to develop systems more rapidly, more accurately, and according to actual business requirements is what makes object-oriented technology as popular as it is. The OO model is able to assimilate the actual business model much more closely than any other technology. User interaction is required much more, and much sooner than ever before in the continuing drive to gain a business advantage. User and IS departments have become development partners, with users who are much more familiar with the environment than before. Let's face it, the odds that users will have PCs in their homes running Excel and Word are much higher than the odds that they will have mainframes, or access to mainframe applications, in their homes.

This in itself drives one problem we face. A user who has purchased a copy of Quicken, for example, is curious about why IS cannot develop a product for his or her business need with the same quality of performance, documentation, and looks. In addition, Quicken costs less than $100, whereas the new business function is going to cost $100,000. It does not take long to explain why. Take the time. It is well spent.

This technological advance is not the end of the road, however. It is merely the beginning of the journey. We discuss the evolution of the development life-cycle, and then describe how to take full advantage of the technology offered today.

The waterfall approach

The waterfall approach was common in the 1970s. The structured approach with specific start and end points for each phase determined a rigid schedule with very little opportunity for change. Added to that is the fact that the development language of choice was COBOL, itself going through some radical change and advance, and development efforts were major undertakings. Changes to requirements led IS to grumble about users who could not make up their minds; users attributed resistance to change to the failure of IS to see that the business was changing. Changes in the business world were the one consistent element. The waterfall development approach was good because it provided a direction, but in retrospect, it can also be seen to be unidirectional with no escape.

Figure P3.1 illustrates the waterfall approach. It is clear that each phase was meant to end at a specific point (often with dramatic "user sign-off" theatricals to enforce the "no changes after this point" philosophy of the day).

The spiral methodology

The next "breakthrough" was the spiral methodology. This was the first methodology that allowed change to occur before the final product was shipped. The problem with the spiral methodology is that significant development takes place before changes enter into the picture. The other problem is that the spiral has no real defined start and end point. You can continue to spiral until your user retires. (This is an excellent method of ensuring that you

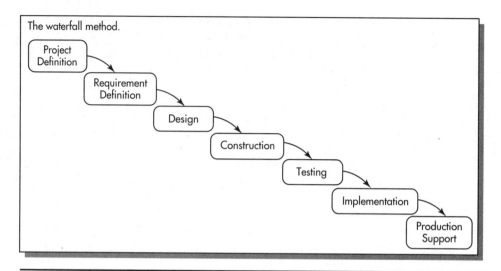

The waterfall method.

- Project Definition
- Requirement Definition
- Design
- Construction
- Testing
- Implementation
- Production Support

Figure P3.1   The waterfall method.

meet users' needs!) The spiral methodology's strength is the fact that it does allow change to take place before the final product is delivered. The spiral methodology is illustrated in Figure P3.2.

Reiterative prototyping (RIP): more than one look at what will not satisfy the original requirement

Reiterative prototyping (RIP) was the next methodology to become extremely popular. Why? It allows for more change and requires more user involvement. These are the two key ingredients for delivering successful projects. However, RIP has its own set of problems.

Prototypes are typically created very quickly, with the user watching, and modified and tweaked until everyone is satisfied that it does what is needed.

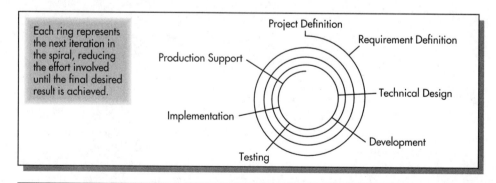

Each ring represents the next iteration in the spiral, reducing the effort involved until the final desired result is achieved.

- Project Definition
- Requirement Definition
- Technical Design
- Development
- Testing
- Implementation
- Production Support

Figure P3.2   The spiral method.

Prototyping is a good design technique, but not a good development technique. It is very difficult to decide when enough prototyping has been done and the objects used are typically built from the ground up with no regard for reusable code elsewhere (there is no time to review other people's objects), which results in "throwaway code." I have seen many prototypes developed and then thrown away when completed because "now the real development starts." This makes prototyping a very expensive design tool. If the prototype becomes the end-product, then the code is very likely to be application-specific and nonreusable, defeating one of the goals of the technology. Figure P3.3 illustrates a typical RIP workflow.

Someone once described RIP as another way to say, "we'll take a stab at it and when we're done, you tell us how close we are." Although more successful and more adaptable to change, it is still not the final solution.

"Not so" rapid application development (RAD)

RAD is the buzzword of the 1990s. It implies ultrafast development that satisfies users' requirements. Unfortunately for RAD, a good idea has gone south

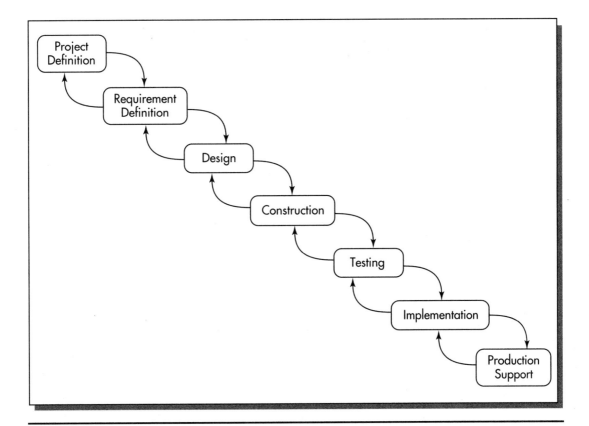

Figure P3.3   Reiterative prototyping.

with bad implementation. It appears that RAD is interpreted to mean, "Skip the planning and design. Just code it. We'll design it while we are coding." This was not the intention of RAD (or its latest cousin, joint application development, or JAD). The side effects of improper use of RAD techniques were driven home to me a few months ago when I heard a developer talking to a user. The user was complaining that he had no specification to which he could compare what the developer was producing. The developer replied, "I know we have no spec, but it's right there on the screen!" The interaction with the user was about the only good thing that resulted. Because so many people have misused the technique, RAD has received very little good press, and has ultimately succumbed to the old adage, "It promised, but it did not deliver." Through no fault of the technique, the developer community has used it as a crutch for lack of planning and design.

Cooperative Business Modeling

Our methodology, which we believe takes the strengths of each technique, is called Cooperative Business Modeling. Based on our development foundation, we understand that it is still necessary to plan and design. In fact, it is more important than before. What is done during the planning and design phase of this technique is radically different from other methods. Figure P3.4 shows our development cycle as a multithreaded development architecture.

Phase I : model the business function, develop a plan.   In Phase I, we gather the user requirements. It has often been said that users have only a vague notion of their requirements. Nothing could be further from the truth. What is much more accurate is that developers have only a vague notion of the business. We do not spend much of our time learning about the user's business function. It is our job to develop the concrete requirements, and to do that we need to ask the users to give us what they do know: a model of their business function. We

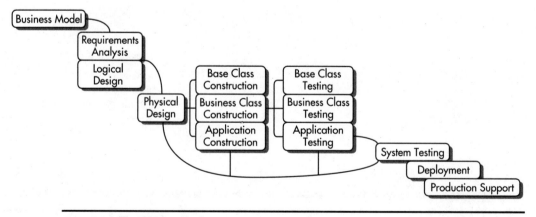

Figure P3.4   The CBM method.

cannot start development until we have this business model. At this point, we can also begin to make an accurate assessment of the estimated development effort. You cannot be completely accurate until the logical design phase is complete, but the estimation process becomes more predictable.

This phase is also where other preparatory tasks take place, such as environment preparation, database preparation, and tool selection.

The final element of the requirement analysis is to develop a prototype of the business model. This does not include well-defined classes and methods, but rather a visual overview of what the final system will look like to the user. Keep in mind that 80 percent of the prototype is typically throwaway code.

If you are using a well-defined base class library during the prototype phase, much less of the prototype will be throwaway code.

Phase II : requirement analysis and logical class definition.   In the second phase, it becomes our job to turn the business model into specific requirements, and then mold these requirements into logical class definitions. User involvement is still high because we need to understand the business model. The definition of requirements and logical classes is limited to defining the "what." All terms used should be confined to simple, clear definitions. This process in itself is re-iterative, albeit confined to this phase. This phase is also the point at which the development estimate can be cast much more accurately than before. By assigning a development effort at each class and method level, you can make the estimation pretty specific, although the multithreaded development nature also means that you need to be careful in the estimate for actual delivery of an object.

Overall delivery time should match up competitively with those resulting from the RIP and RAD/JAD methodologies, but is a little longer due to the single-threaded nature of the analysis effort. The good news is that with each base or business class developed, actual development effort decreases. Revise the project plan to indicate inclusion of reusable classes (base or business) during the object mapping process in Phase III.

Phase III: physical design.   At this point, the straight line development shifts over to a multithreaded, reiterative approach. Based on our logical design, we can begin to accumulate the class definitions and build physical classes. As we design each physical class required, we have to do two things:

- Separate the methods into the architectural layers defined (base, business, or application). Some call these domains. I prefer to keep the simple layered definition, because I can see, and have seen, how classes in the different layers might fit into different domains depending on the driving need. We call this method separation.

- We also need to map the classes back to our base and business class repositories to determine whether the class exists and whether the methods and attributes required exist on the classes. We call this process object mapping.

- With the classes and methods that do not map back to base or business classes, we follow our standard class design methodology and design the objects and classes remaining that will be needed by the application.

As each object or class is designed or mapped, we can begin construction. We should also revise our development estimate. By knowing whether we need to build the class from scratch, enhance an existing class with a new method, or integrate an existing class into our application, we can adjust the development effort required and retask the class.

If we are following the design methodology, we do not have to wait until all of the objects and classes are designed. We can begin to develop sooner this way, begin test development sooner, and have more to show the user with each reiterative build. You will notice that all of the various phases following this begin to mold together. Each development thread follows a reiterative path, allowing modification to enter at any point, but each object or class is handled as a development thread of its own. Even if a class under construction is affected by a class being designed, the modification requirements are noted and dealt with when appropriate. Change management and user interaction are high at all levels and at all times, but the environment is controlled and manageable. Change is handled in small chunks, so it does not send the developer into a panic and it affords the user the satisfaction of seeing the application being constructed to meet the business need.

Phase IV: object development.   Our final phase is actual object development. This phase could be reiterative, but if the planning and design is done correctly, need not be. This phase can be split up into four distinct but overlapping sections:

- Part I: object construction
- Part II: test case development
- Part III: object and system documentation
- Part IV: object testing

During object construction, test plan development, and documentation building, the developers and users interact to define and develop the objects that meet the class designs. If each object is classified as a development thread with reiterative tasks to review the methods, attributes, and overall integration, it becomes very difficult to fail. In addition, each object is individually tested according to the test plan for the object class, ensuring that we are continuing to build on a solid foundation. As the application grows, the number of test cases built grows with it. Use of an automated testing tool becomes even more important than before because, at the end, when all objects are developed, you should have a test bed that will test your system integration as well.

Phase V: documentation and deployment.   All that remains is to run some system tests (including a full run of all test cases developed), pull all the documentation together into user and technical manuals, and then deploy the application. You will probably notice that the following has occurred. Your application layer makes up approximately 35 percent of the development effort, the business layer is responsible for an additional 35 percent, and your base layer accounts for the remaining 30 percent. If your enterprise is structured to deal with this architecture, you have reduced the maintenance costs for the application by 65 percent *before the application is used for the first time!* Now we can begin to see how this technology should be able to continuously reduce the development effort while delivering applications that more closely resemble the user's business and are more adaptable to change.

Summary

In conclusion, I have to warn you that this methodology is not a silver bullet. You must use it correctly to reap its benefits, and your enterprise infrastructure must be prepared to deal with the many complexities the technology reveals. Object administration becomes a crucial role in the organization as more and more common objects are developed. Your base and business layers should continue to evolve and improve, allowing the application developer to do exactly that: develop the application.

Builders of houses do not make the bricks they use. They get them from the people who are experts at making bricks. Your developers and users should develop business solutions, not the objects that make up your development foundation. Solve the users' business problem.

20

Application Planning and Management

Introduction

With so many things that can go wrong, it is a constant wonder to me that we even try to achieve our goals in application development. I am not sure whether it is resilience, a need for constant challenge, or plain stupidity that drives us onward.

With all of the obstacles we face every day, lack of application development planning is the main ingredient for failure. The only other thing that causes as many projects to fail is mismanagement of the development effort. This chapter is devoted to emphasizing the importance of application planning and management.

Chapter Objectives

The goals of this chapter are to lay out the steps we feel are necessary to include in your project planning and management. Although we cannot possibly provide an absolute blueprint for every development effort, we feel that these steps must be executed to ensure a higher degree of success.

In this chapter, we take a look at tasks we feel are vital to the success of your project:

- Development preparation
- Environment preparation
- Team development
- Infrastructure development
- Training
- Tool selection

- Data preparation
- Project plan preparation
- Project management

Preparing for Development

Preparing for the development effort is vital. There are so many things that must be done before you can get started, it is easy to gloss over or omit a task. Every preparation task omitted before development starts must be done at some time during the development effort. This adds time to the project, usually more time than was first anticipated, because the effect has a tendency to ripple, affecting other tasks that might have been dependent. When we go on a long car journey, we usually have our car serviced beforehand, refuel regularly during the trip, and pay close attention to road signs. Development should be approached in an even more thorough manner. After all, this journey is far longer than one we would ordinarily make in a car.

The roadmap

Some of the elements of preparation include preparing the environment, building a development team, establishing communication channels to the user group, analyzing and purchasing the necessary tools, team training, and data preparation. The driving factor, or the fuel for the project, is the business requirements. Analyze the business requirements first, or as soon as possible, before beginning other preparation.

Lay out the tasks that must be done before you start coding. Checklists are extremely useful in ensuring that steps are not missed.

You also need to schedule users' involvement. They are involved in the day-to-day operation of the business. Taking time away from that means they are not doing what they need to do, so you should consider their time precious. Use as much of their time as possible without affecting the day-to-day business.

Try not to determine a project estimate before the preparation is done. You will not have the business requirements nailed down, nor do you know what members your team will have or what business classes are available to you and your team. Your estimate will be based on the few known factors, with too many variables that can affect the decision process. Only with a good business model and knowledge of what tasks are complete and which are not, can you make an accurate assessment of the effort required.

Lastly, plan ahead. Know what is coming before it arrives. This is a powerful technique of project management. Knowing at all times where the development effort lies in the proposed schedule, how much is remaining, and whether you are on track is the mark of a good project manager.

Business modeling

Business modeling, often called business process reengineering or business requirement analysis, usually takes place well before the development effort begins. This is both good and bad. It is good in that the business function is laid out well before the development effort begins, but it is bad in that the business has likely changed since the process took place.

As long as the business analyst can focus on the high-level requirements of the business and stay away from implementation, you should be able to easily incorporate changes to the business function. Your first step is to review the business analysis and ensure that it is as close to the actual business environment as possible.

You should also make sure that the result of the business requirement analysis is something that tells the IS staff how the business operates. Remember that functions involving human interaction are influenced by three types of employees: those who cannot follow the function guidelines, those who follow the function guidelines, and those who are innovative and change the function guidelines. Make sure you talk to the employees actually doing the job to ensure that what the business process is expected to be is what is really taking place.

The end of the Business Requirements Analysis will not only outline the business processes required, but will also provide you with a Navigation Workflow. This is a diagram that shows the interactions between the Entitities and Processes within the Business Function. Entities are concrete "things" such as Users, Data, etc., while processes define actions that will take place. The Navigation Workflow is discussed in more detail in the remainder of this part of the book.

I like to think that as a project manager, I always know what my employees are doing. In truth, all I know is what they *should* be doing, and I trust them to provide me with the expected result. Most of the time, as long as they are delivering what I expect, I do not question their methods. In order to automate any process, you need to find out which methods are being used and select the method that will be most successful.

If a process is automated, you might be meeting the business need in a manner users have rejected as inefficient, thereby giving users an automated way to do something they do not want to do. Be aware of this and talk to as many of the users as possible about their specific business functions.

Environment preparation

Preparing the environment may seem like a waste of time. After all, everyone knows you have to have a copy of the development tool in order to start development. Unfortunately, I have seen enough projects begin without the necessary tools to know that this is something you have to be aware of. Start by making a list of the types of tools you will need during a normal development effort (a database design tool, a development tool, a testing tool, etc.). This helps you to plan the project's budget, an element the user will watch even more closely than your project schedule.

Making sure a database design is in place that supports the business functions you are trying to model is also critical. A changing data model implies one of two things: Either the database design is changing to meet the needs of the business, or it is changing to meet the needs of the project. The second of these situations is very dangerous. The database should reflect the business needs. The database design should be done with development in mind. Having your database highly normalized might seem like the right thing to do. It usually is, but my experience is that highly normalized data do not exactly model the business, which cannot be normalized, and do not make data access simple or efficient. The emphasis here should be on modeling the actual business, allowing for changing business requirements and typical development implementation. The design should make data access easier, not impossible without 14 cartesian joins and multiunion subselects.

The business requirements will change during the life of a development effort. This is a given. Be ready for it, and make sure your database is ready for it, too.

Team development

Once the business requirements are laid out, you should be able to plan the structure your project team will require. Your development team should be comprised of employees who can fill various roles, or should have access to employees who fit the role required.

We all know that we cannot put six or seven employees on every development effort. We should, but it is not feasible. In some cases, we might have only one or two employees on the project team. Remember that these employees must be more than developers. The roles they must take on in order to successfully complete a development effort are as follows:

- Project manager
- Business analyst
- Database administrator and designer
- Project developer
- Development mentor
- Quality assurance specialist
- Technical writer

I am aware that few projects can afford to hire a different person for each of these functions, and many projects will involve people outside the project team to perform these functions (such as a DBA group or a QA group). The important factor to note is that these functions are required for the project to be successful. How you build the project team to perform these functions varies.

Infrastructure development

Along with team development comes infrastructure development. This involves establishing the internal lines of communication in the project team and determining how users will be trained, how mentorship will be provided to the development group, and what communication channels the development team will use to contact other groups. A typical infrastructure chart is shown in Figure 20.1.

This is one of the most successful models I have seen. Separate teams are developed to handle the responsibilities of each area. The class library team handles development, maintenance, and support of the base classes. The business class group is closer to the application developers, and provides mentorship and knowledge about the base classes and the business classes. The application team uses both groups to promote the highest level of reuse possible. All of the groups have clearly defined links to the database administration group, the quality assurance group, and, most importantly, the business users group. Note that the business users also have access to the DBA and QA groups. It is imperative that the business users be involved in all aspects of system development as much as possible.

The lines of communication must be clearly defined so that everyone knows where to go to get something done. There is no confusion, and the project team is able to relax and get the job done without the normal "who do we speak to

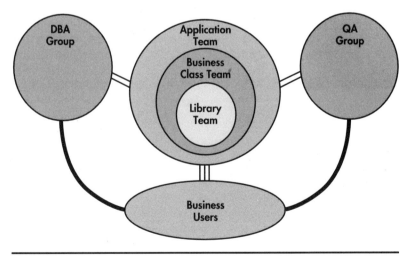

Figure 20.1 A typical team infrastructure.

in order to get this done, and when will they get it done?" I believe that this is crucial to the success of the project team.

Review, analyze, and select tools

This is another important aspect of project planning. No matter how well you plan, manage, and execute, if you are using the wrong tools, or are unsure of which tool to use (or, as is often the case, change the tool midstream) you can add days or even weeks to your project plan. Evaluate the options carefully before you get started, so you know which tools your project team will use and, more importantly, your project team will know which tools to use.

Tools that should be looked at include all of the categories listed below. Your own list may be different, as each project's requirements dictate a different toolset.

- Development tool (we will assume PowerBuilder for this, even though it is understood that this may not be the only tool you need for development)
- Project management
- Database design and administration
- Base class library
- Business class library
- Quality assurance (testing, defect tracking, etc.)
- Software version control
- Project documentation

Evaluate your choices carefully. Your organization may have standards in place for tool selection, making this process simpler, but you still need to ensure that the tools required by your project team are readily available. You can prepare your team for the effort by letting them know which tools they will be using and when they will be using them.

Training

Training is another important aspect of development. In many cases, some of your project team will not have worked with one of the tools in your toolset. If this is the case, I strongly suggest evaluating and obtaining training for team members in the desired tools. Of particular importance is training in the development tools and the base and business class libraries. An accepted method of continuous training is providing a mentor, an expert who is able to disseminate the knowledge he or she has gained using the tools.

The mentor may be part of the development team (in fact I recommend this), but may also be part of a group of people who spend time with various project teams in order to help raise the overall knowledge level of the organization.

Data preparation

With much of the preparation either complete or under way, you can begin to focus on building the external elements of the system. If the database has not yet been designed, this should begin as soon as possible. The development effort itself should not begin until data are available for testing. Development of the database includes the following elements:

- Database design (logical and physical)
- Data preparation (development data)
- Data preparation (test data)
- Data preparation (production data)
- Identification of data access methods (stored procedures, triggers, etc.)

Although the data are often not prepared before the development effort gets under way, the plan to complete data preparation must ensure that the necessary data are ready before the developers begin to test. Changes to data, or incomplete data, can have a severe effect on development, slowing development and frustrating the developers and users. The three sets of data shown have specific purposes.

Development data.

Development data are the data required to help developers ensure that the objects they are building will have the correct results. The data need not reflect production data if this is not possible, but must be in place before the developers need them. Most client-server systems rely heavily on the data and a specific database design during the development effort. Although I have seen some development take place without data being in place, what you are developing requires the data to be available in specific format and quantity. Without it, developers are merely guessing, with perhaps a 50 percent chance of being correct—not good odds for development.

Test data.

The test environment is very crucial to development. Test data should be indicative of the production environment. In fact, the closer your test data matches your production data and environment, the more confident you will be when your system is tested. Test data procedures should also be the means by which data loads, batch processes, and all other elements that will affect the production environment should be tested. Test data should be monitored and updated regularly. Of particular importance is the ability to back up the test environment and restore it at will. This allows regression testing to take place during the development effort and ensures that changes to the system do not affect other areas of the project already developed and tested.

Production data.

Production data preparation includes the setting up of all procedures that affect the data that will end up being the production environment. This includes such elements as bringing data down from a legacy system, preparing the DDL for database creation, and establishing stored procedures or triggers.

The production environment should be established and all necessary procedures tested well ahead of time, because system testing should take place against the production data environment (which means that backup procedures should also be planned, developed, and put in place).

Preparing the Development Project Plan

Added to all these tasks is the preparation of the development effort itself. These days, this is no ordinary task. With reiterative development steps and changing requirements, establishing a start-to-finish development plan is much more daunting. Project planning tools available today cannot deal with the real-world demands placed on the already overburdened project managers (it comes with the job). Our project planning is based on our methodology. You may adopt a different methodology, but the plan is still needed, should be as accurate as possible, and should be managed carefully.

Project planning based on the CBM methodology

Our plan, based on the CBM methodology, is broken down into phases. These phases, we believe, are necessary for any project. The tasks, and how they are planned and used, are what varies.

Everything from the planning and preparation tasks through business function modeling, logical class definition, object mapping, physical class design, and object construction, testing, and implementation must be mapped out and followed. The project plan is your checklist of the project's progress—how will you know you are done without knowing what you need to accomplish?

This is where I believe we have failed with the technology. We have some of the most powerful tools ever available, yet we choose to ignore the foundation, the one element of development that has not changed over the years. The element that has changed with the technology, the methodologies, and the tools is the adaptability to change. The CBM methodology embraces change, breaks the project tasks into easily managed elements, and allows the reiterative type of object building that is the power of the technology.

CBM allows you to build your objects in a reiterative fashion. By this I do not mean the typical practice of reiterative development in which the system is developed and shown to the user, who requests changes, and the whole system is then modified for the next build.

This methodology allows each object class to be built almost as a standalone subproject. Users get to see the project in much smaller pieces, changes are easily identified and incorporated, and the user watches the system grow. As each class is designed, you can begin to build it. Based on the CBM methodology, the physical class design dictates which portion of the class falls into the domain of the base class (or framework), the business class (business functions and business rules), and the application classes. Objects falling outside the realm of the application should not be developed by the application team. We highly recommend the separation of domain infrastructure shown earlier in this chapter. This allows the developers in the various domain areas to concentrate on the aspects of the development process they specialize in. Of course, this implies that more careful scheduling of tasks is required. This is true. It also implies that, because more personnel across different teams are involved, project costs rise. This part is not true.

If you look at how the development teams are involved, you will notice differing percentages of effort required. Once a base set of objects is established (usually by an external process), the involvement of the base class team steadily decreases as the base set of classes becomes more and more complete. The business classes will begin to follow the same pattern, although business classes may be developed by the application development team in your organization due to the various levels of available personnel. Slowly, but steadily, the classes required for development efforts are reduced. Classes become more reusable, and more reused.

Obviously, the project plan cannot foresee how much of the application will be developed externally from the development team. It should not. Only through consistent planning can the benefit of reusable classes be measured and recorded. Once the physical class design is complete and object classes are assigned to the various groups involved, the project manager can assess the development effort saved.

Tasking a CBM project

When tasking a project using the CBM methodology, there is much more overlap and reiterative tasking at much lower levels than before. As soon as a physical class is designed, the task's required hours are a known factor. We use an estimation method for physical classes that reflects the methods and attributes involved. For example, if a physical class contains ten methods and five attributes, we can extrapolate the estimated work effort to hours suitable to accomplish the task.

Our working formula is the sum of (Method + Attributes affected × Method complexity) + 20 percent of the total. The additional 20 percent is built in to embrace change via the reiterative process. We are continually updating this formula as additional history is accumulated with our methodology.

Once we complete the estimate to develop the object class, we can determine that portions of the class will be developed as part of the two higher-level domains: base and business classes. This effort is tasked out of the project, reducing the overall cost of the project. As the base and business class domains grow, the cost of the base and business class development is simply absorbed because the classes and methods already exist. As your developers become more and more familiar with the existing classes and the methodology, the cost of project development continues to decrease. Of course, there is a limit to how much of the development costs can be eliminated. There will always be some application-specific development.

To illustrate a typical development plan using the CBM methods, we have included a sample project plan (using Microsoft Project) on the CD.[1]

Project Management

It is crucial that the project be effectively managed. Even though every project manager works differently, goals should be the same: Get the project completed on time and within the budget constraints, deliver a product that matches the users' requirements, and keep the developers challenged and continually learning. I am not about to preach the virtues of differing management styles. Good managers get the job done and meet their other objectives as well. They also vary their management style depending on the people working for them. What I do want to emphasize is the importance of managing the project carefully.

Using an efficient project planning tool (again, I am not about to delve into the virtues of the various project management tools; they are as good as the people who use them) allows you to plan, monitor, and adjust your project plan according to the requirements and progress being made.

Summary

It is obvious that planning and management of a project are crucial to its success. We discussed several key issues, including environment preparation, data preparation, team structure development, team training, tool selection, project plan development, and project management. I hope we have stressed the importance of planning and management strongly enough.

Finally, we discussed how using the CBM methodology can help you prepare your development effort for success.

---

1. See Chap20\sample.mpp.

21

Application Logical Design (Requirements Analysis)

Introduction

In this chapter we delve into the use of our methodology and apply it to a real-life scenario. This is when the true test of any methodology comes into play. If the end-product is successful after following the methodology, the methodology is successful. Again, the emphasis is on applying the methodology. Writing code and saying you followed a methodology is not a true measurement of the value of the methodology.

Of course, if it takes three times as long to follow the methodology, you still do not have a good compromise (although users will choose right over fast any day). Better, cheaper, and faster will not go away. We need to figure out a way to accomplish these goals.

What we have to relearn is to take a little more time planning and designing in order to reduce the development, testing, and maintenance effort. Remember that maintenance costs, in many cases, equal the total development cost over a 3-year period. Testing applies both to development and maintenance efforts and therefore consumes additional costs continually. Only planning and design cease once development is completed. Unless a class (or a collection of classes) is totally redesigned, most changes to the system are done without the requirement analysis and design phases usually associated with a development effort. More is the pity however, because changes to a system, unless a bug fix is required in a known area, should first be applied at the requirement level and gently cascade through the various design steps until a clear definition of the change required can be outlined and its effect clearly seen.

We reiterate this later in Chapter 26, although we specifically leave out a portion of the system development effort to demonstrate how easily change is adopted into the system using our methodology.

Chapter Objectives

The goals for this chapter are very similar to those outlined in the logical design section of class library development. We need to establish design objectives for the system, model the business, expand the requirements into methods and attributes, and begin building the test plan with the method test plan.

As we go through our case study, a base class library administration system, we highlight each of these key elements and show the results.

The Case Study: Base Class Library Administration

The case study we are going to examine is that of designing an application for administering a base class library throughout an organization. (See Figure 21.1.)

We chose this case study because it is something needed in most organizations that develop with PowerBuilder. Therefore, the result is a product that can also be useful. This avoids the usual problem of having to find something everyone can relate to.

Business statement

The business need here is training, mentoring, and other technical assistance for project teams wanting to use the base class library in their project development. We also want to follow up with the project team as they progress and record any bugs, enhancement requests, and additional business class needs they might have because the development of business classes must be, at a minimum, a joint effort between the development team and the library administration team. Finally, we need to keep track of when the development effort will conclude and enter system testing and implementation so that we can schedule additional support personnel to be available at these crucial times.

The business model

As we develop the business model, I want to stress that we are not using any particular methodology because this varies (often greatly) from organization to

Developers and Users

Describes Workflow

Business Requirements

Developer/Library Team Interaction

Library Team

Figure 21.1 Class library administration module.

organization. For the purposes of this demonstration, we use a simple business model and some assumptions are outlined along the way. We do not support taking any shortcuts, but we want to focus on the key aspects of system design in the limited space available here. There are several good books out on business modeling and business process reengineering, and the methodologies, for the most part, are sound.

Our case study, described in more detail later in this chapter, has a workflow that is very distinct. We receive a request from the "new user" to initiate their project. This process is followed by a series of operations that take us through assisting the project in their design phase, helping define any new classes they will need going forward, developing the new classes and monitoring their progress. Based on the requirements analysis we can begin to develop the navigation workflow, which we will use later on to map back to classes. Figure 21.2 shows a typical workflow diagram. Note that there are no indications as to what kind of class or object will be used, therefore notation is limited. We chose to use normal flowchart symbols that can be

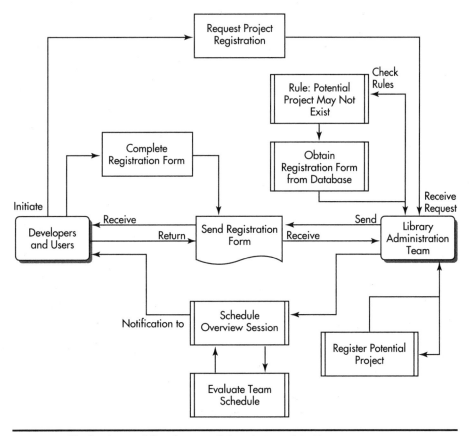

Figure 21.2 Navigation workflow for potential projects registration.

easily drawn and described. We chose to use the shadowed box to indicate an Entity, a regular rectangle to indicate a manual process, a report symbol for any kind of form/document, and a subroutine box (rectangle with extra vertical lines) to indicate an automated process. This same workflow diagram will be used to define the objects that will comprise each element within the workflow. Basically we can see that there are four automated processes.

- Rule Check: Potential Projects must not already exist.
- Obtain a Registration form from our database.
- Prepare a schedule of Administration team involvement with project.
- Check and update the Administration teams schedule data: This process is actually a subprocess of the Prepare Schedule process.

On with the show. The first step is project initiation. Figure 21.3 shows the actions taken by each of the involved parties. The development team issues a request for information about the class library, to use in evaluating which tool they will use for their development effort. The library team receives the request, obtains a registration form, and sends this registration form to the development team. The development team is also added to a potential users list, which is monitored and updated to make sure we do not miss anyone.

The development team is given an overview of the class library, an explanation of how the library team works with them to deliver the final product, and also given other reasons why the library should be used in the development process. (Of course, some organizations may not allow the flexibility of making the choice, but we prefer to allow the developers to make up their own minds.) The development team then evaluates their position and de-

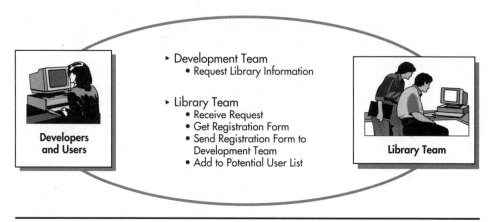

Figure 21.3 Project initiation.

Figure 21.4   Project team registration.

cides whether to use the library. If they decide to proceed, the team is registered as a project team. Figure 21.4 depicts the project team registration process. Even if using the library is a standard that must be followed, you should still provide the development team with plenty of information. It will raise their confidence when they realize you are going to place yourself at their disposal to help make sure their project succeeds and reaps the benefits of the reuse strategy.

The development team now proceeds with logical design. It is important that they prepare the logical design in a manner that allows them to identify methods and classes that are already developed and available in the enterprise repository, either as base classes or business classes. The library team's involvement at this point is to schedule and deliver training to help the development team get up to speed on the methodology and the object classes residing in the repository. The learning curve associated with this approach can appear frightening, but is quite easily handled. The development team, if they have not used this approach or the base and business classes before, may be intimidated or raise any of the other barriers typically associated with reusability strategies.[1] Figure 21.5 outlines the tasks associated with the logical design portion of our workflow.

Now the library team's involvement begins in earnest. The development team must now begin the task of object mapping and become familiar with what is already available to them and what still needs to be done. The library team must assist in this preparation by installing the base and business class libraries on the development servers, applying some QuickStart training in the use of any pro-

---

1. See Part I for detailed explanations of the barriers that arise and how to overcome them.

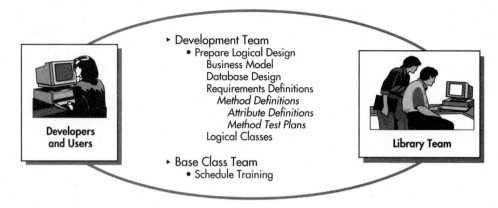

Figure 21.5 Logical design steps.

ductivity tools available such as object wizards, instructing the team in the where-abouts and use of available documentation, and, as in our case, building the application's working shell from the base classes. Figure 21.6 depicts these steps.

In the next step, the library team takes on a primary role in analyzing the physical design of the system. Methods and classes are mapped back to existing objects, classes, and methods, and a development schedule of new required classes comes to light. Additions and enhancements to existing classes are also detailed and scheduled. In preparing the schedule, the development team should be made aware of the scheduled development of additional base or business classes, if they are not going to be the ones developing them, because some of their application development might depend on these classes and methods. In the case of conflicting schedules, we have found the use of virtual methods to be useful. This is the process of defining and creating the new (or enhancements to) classes with the entry points (methods), built even if the

Figure 21.6 Development preparation.

residual functionality is not. (This is sometimes called stubbing.) This allows the development team to continue their efforts and build classes or objects based on the virtual classes and methods. When the base (or business) classes are fleshed out, the development team will not have to change the code, but rather simply test the functionality to determine completeness and accuracy. Figure 21.7 shows the object class analysis step.

Once object development begins, the two teams begin a physical separation previously not evident. The development efforts continue along their different schedules, but with regular status checks. In addition, the development team must now be introduced to the means to request additional development support, bug reporting, and enhancement request reporting. (Yes, we know we will not always hit every object class or method, so enhancements are usually part of the package. Our design is adaptable, however, and change should be quite easily incorporated). Figure 21.8 shows the various elements of the development phase.

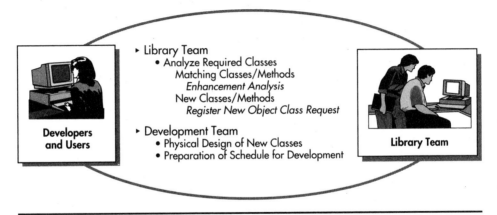

Figure 21.7 Object class analysis.

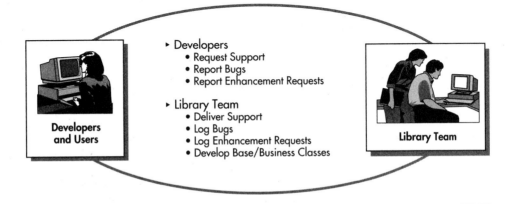

Figure 21.8 Object development.

Figures 21.9, 21.10, and 21.11 are informative requirements detailing the steps needed to handle bug reports, enhancement requests, and new or updated object class requests. These communications are processed quite similarly and can be grouped together.

The library team also has to be able to handle additional requests for support, mentoring, and training. Figure 21.12 depicts the elements associated with this task.

Only two requirements remain, both pertaining to tracking. The library team needs to keep track of which project team is where during the project life-cycle in order to maintain a schedule that provides the most help when and where it is needed the most. Figure 21.13 shows that the development team is asked to inform the library team when each new development stage is entered.

Developers and Users

▸ Development Team
  • Report Bug
▸ Library Team
  • Log Bug in Defect Tracking Database
  • Weekly Defect Status Report to All Users
  • Auto-Schedule Maintenance Based on Priority
  • Update Schedule when Actual Work Begins
  • Update Log when Problem Resolved

Library Team

Figure 21.9   Bug report processing.

Developers and Users

▸ Development Team
  • Report Enhancement Request
▸ Library Team
  • Log Request in Enhancement Database
  • Weekly Enhancement Status Report to All Users
  • Auto-Schedule Maintenance Based on Priority
  • Update Schedule when Actual Work Begins
  • Update Log when Enhancement is Complete

Library Team

Figure 21.10   Enhancement request processing.

▸ Development Team
  • Report New Object Class Request
▸ Library Team
  • Log Request in New Development Database
  • Weekly Status Report to All Users
  • Auto-Schedule Development Based on Priority
  • Update Schedule when Actual Work Begins
  • Update Log when Development is Complete

Developers and Users

Library Team

Figure 21.11   New and updated object class requests.

▸ Development Team
  • Issue Requests for Support/Mentorship
▸ Library Team
  • Log Request
  • Schedule Required Time Based on Priority and Availability
  • Report Scheduled Time to Requestor

Developers and Users

Library Team

Figure 21.12   Support request processing.

▸ Development Team
  • Report Stage Changes
▸ Library Team
  • Track Development Effort
      Requirements Analysis
      Training
      Logical Design
      Physical Design
      Construction
      UAT
      Deployment

Developers and Users

Library Team

Figure 21.13   Project life-cycle tracking.

Figure 21.14   Object and class reuse tracking.

Figure 21.14 shows the other tracking function required. The library team needs to keep track of the following:

- Use of existing classes
- New and enhanced base classes requested
- New and enhanced business classes
- Application classes that might be future candidates for reuse

When the project is about to be deployed, the library team should make a last review of the application class usage and make any necessary adjustments to the registered classes list.

The steps for testing and deployment also require scheduling and tracking, and are triggered by project life-cycle changes.

We have completed our business model. We deliberately went this route because each of the illustrations is included on the CD as a PowerPoint presentation for your own use and adaptation. This route is an integral part of our class library support philosophy.

Now we can begin to gather and expand the requirements into their subelements before beginning the physical design of the system.

Requirement Analysis

In defining our requirements, we find that we can continue to use the same forms and techniques we used in the development of our class library in Part II of this book. The format works for base classes, business classes and application classes.

Let's begin documenting the requirements based on our business model. As you can see in Figure 21.15, the first step is to list all of the requirements involved in the business model.

Project Data

Project ID:	LIB_R000
Project Name:	Library Administration Module
Contact:	William Green

Update Date:	July 7, 1995
Author:	William T. Green

Project Description

Description
The purpose of the system is to allow easy access to: Development Team Schedules (to assist in Support Planning) Support Scheduling Object/Class Repository Maintenance Object/Class Reuse Analysis

Requirements Generated

Requirement	Req_ID	Test_Id
Receive Library Information Request (Manual)	None	LIB_T005
Log Request for Information	LIB_R001	LIB_T006
Send Registration Form	LIB_R002	
Schedule Evaluation Session	LIB_R003	
Deliver Evaluation Session (Manual)	None	
Register Development Team	LIB_R004	
Schedule Training, Planning Assistance	LIB_R005	
Install Library	LIB_R006	
Build Application Shell	LIB_R007	
Analyze Required Classes	LIB_R008	
Register, Schedule, and Report on Support Requests	LIB_R009	
Register, Schedule, and Report on Bug Reports	LIB_R010	
Register, Schedule, and Report on Enhancement Requests	LIB_R011	
Register, Schedule, and Report on New Class requests	LIB_R012	
Develop Classes/Objects: Register Classes, Methods	LIB_R013	
Track Project Lifecycle	LIB_R015	
Track Object Reuse	LIB_R016	
Build an SQL Statement Based on Supplied Criteria	LIB_DR01	
Interpret SQL Execution Return Code and Convert DBMS-Specific Message	LIB_DR02	
Generate Stored Procedure Code from Selected SQL Statement	LIB_DR03	

Figure 21.15 Requirement Summary: library administration module.

Note that not all of the steps outlined end up being requirements. Some processes are, and will remain, manual. Of key importance to us is knowing the status of the project team and maintaining the schedule of the base (and business) classes to accommodate them.

As we continue to expand the requirements, we are also defining the requirements for database access. For example, the requirement "Log Request for Information," outlines three activities, as shown in Figure 21.16.

The first of the three activities is to check whether the project team is already on file as a potential customer. The actions necessary to accomplish this are shown in Figure 21.17.

Requirement Data

Requirement ID:	LIB_R001		
Requirement Name:	Log Request for Information		
Version:	1.0	Update Date:	July 23, 1995
Survey Xref:		Author:	William Green

Requirement Definition

Description
When a request comes in for additional information, log the request to the Potential Projects log.

Cost/Benefit Data

Benefit	CBA Value:	1.00
Keeps track of the potential new users and makes sure our scheduler knows about the upcoming overview session required. Allows library team to keep track of project teams who are considering using the library. This information can be used later in justifying additional development funding.	CBA Rating	Medium

Activities

Activity	Linked ID
Check whether project team already on file	LIB_M001
Prepare log data	LIB_M002
Create new log entry	LIB_M003

Figure 21.16   Requirement Definition: log request for information.

Activity Data

Activity ID:	LIB_M001		
Activity Name:	Check whether project team already registered		
Version:	1.0	Update Date:	July 22, 1995
		Author:	William Green

Activity Definition

Description
Read the Potential Projects log file to determine whether project team is already registered. If it is, return an exception to the calling module.

Methods and Attributes

Action Method	Attribute	Attr_ID	Expected Result	Test_Id
Build Potential Projects SQL Statement	User Data/ SQL Statement	LIB_A001	Loads the expected key values in the SQL Access Structure	LIB_T001
Execute SQL Call	Potential Users Data/SQL Statement	LIB_D001	Executes an SQL Select statement	LIB_T002
Interrogate Return Value	SQL Return Value	LIB_A001	Checks the SQL Return Value and determines whether an error occurred	LIB_T003
[Display Error Message]	SQL Return Code/ Error Message Handler	LIB_A002	Displays an error message if the return value indicated failure	LIB_T004

Figure 21.17   Activity Definition: check whether project team is already registered.

Here you can see there are four actions associated with the method. The first is to build the key to be used for the search against the database. This action uses a data structure called SQL Access Structure. (We are not concerned yet as to whether this structure will be a structure object as is known in PowerBuilder, or a different type of object. We try not to get into implementation at this point.) The attribute definition for the SQL Access Structure is shown in Figure 21.18.

Attribute Data

Attribute ID:	LIB_A001		
Name:	SQL Access Attributes		
Version:	1.0	Update Date:	July 22, 1995
		Author:	William Green

Attribute Definition

Description
SQL Statements contains all of the elements needed to build an SQL statement for either SQL or Stored Procedure access to data. Functionality includes building of where clauses, validating SQL, and generating a stored proc from SQL statement. Also included here should be any capabilities required to convert SQL syntaxes for various DBMSs

Characteristics

Xref/Type	Location/Characteristics	Allowed Values
LIB_DR01*	SQL Statement - Sub Attributes are:	
	• Select Statement	Valid Select statement
	• From statement	Valid From statement
	• Where statement	Valid Where statement
	• Order By statement	Valid Order By statement
	• Group By statement	Valid Group By statement
	• Union statement	Valid Union statement
	• Sub-Select statement	Valid Sub-Select
	• SQL Return Value interpreter	Return Value 0 indicates successful execution of the SQL. Values from different databases are mapped to a common error number for error reporting consistency.
	• Stored Proc converter	The object should have a feature to capture the SQL being used and generate a stored procedure (including parameters) that can be used later on.

*Note: LIB_DRxx indicates a derived requirement.

Figure 21.18 Attribute Definition: SQL access attributes.

As you can see, the SQL Access Structure contains all of the elements needed to build an SQL statement for either SQL or Stored Procedure access to data. Functionality includes building where clauses, validating SQL, and generating a stored proc from SQL statements.[2] Another key feature is the return value interpreter. This characteristic allows the object to convert the DBMS-specific error code into a more general error code established by the organization. If built correctly, the object can "learn" the error codes as it goes, as well as be manually incremented.

Returning to the method definition, we can see that there is a method test plan associated with the method. This is depicted in Figure 21.19.

---

2. Although this is not shown on the attribute definition at this point, it is something we note early to indicate that this would be a nice feature of the object.

Test Plan Data

Test Plan ID:	LIB_T001		
Test Plan Name:	Build Key for Potential Projects Access		
Version:	1.0	Update Date:	July 22, 1995
		Author:	William Green

Test Plan Definition

Description
The key data required for accessing the potential projects file must be built by successive calls to the SQL Access Object. Tests should include sending no data, sending partial data, and sending full key information for both existing and new project records.

Test Plan Objectives and Expected Results

Msg Link	Test Objective	Expected Result
LIB_X001	Test for no data sent	Error value should be returned by the SQL Access object indicating no key data received.
LIB_X001	Test for insufficient data sent	Error value should be returned by the SQL Access object indicating no key data received.
(None)	Test for valid data sent: Nonexistent record	Return Value should be OK.

Figure 21.19 Method Test Plan: build key for potential projects access.

Here we outline the elements of the specific action of the methods we wish to test. Try to be as specific as possible without outlining physical code. We are still designing the what, not the how. Notice here too that we begin to define some messages that are linked to specific test cases. Using this outline, we can begin to put together a list of the messages that will be needed by the application. An example of the message definition is shown in Figure 21.20.

Notice that the message attributes include specifying the buttons that will appear on the message display window and specifying what the effect of

Message Data

Message ID:	LIB_X001		
Message Name:	SQL Error: Insufficient data received to build key		
Version:	1.0		
		Update Date:	July 7, 1995
		Author:	William T. Green

Message Definition

Description
Message is returned when SQL Access object finds insufficient data to build its prescribed SQL statement.

Message

Description
Insufficient data received in order to build proper SQL statement; contact technical support

Note: [ ] indicates optional portion of message. { } indicates replaceable parameter.

Message Attributes

Button	Default	Button Action	Test Plan ID
STD	Yes		
	No		

Note: Buttons indicate what is shown on the mesage box window. STD indicates that the standard error handler is used and buttons are not specified.

Figure 21.20   Application Message Definition: insufficient data for SQL object.

each button should be. Additional test cases can be added to these to ensure that the correct action occurs *after* the message is acknowledged.

Method, attribute, test plan, and message definition summary

This method of creating the definitions for methods, attributes, test plans, and messages continues until all of the requirements have been expanded. This process follows the pattern described above and illustrated in Figure 21.21.

The workflow is shown as a project plan, but the task hours are not set realistically. They have been expanded to show the workflow better.

Logical Class Definition

Now that all of these steps are complete, we can build logical classes from our definitions. To do this, we follow the same methodology described in earlier chapters: object synthesis.

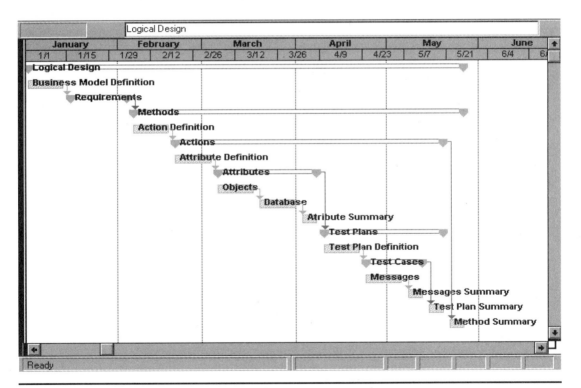

Figure 21.21   CBM definition workflow.

What we do here is collect activities and method actions together in logical groups to form logical classes. The attributes, tests, and messages associated with each method action tag along for the ride. This process is quite simple, requiring only that we copy a method action from the activity definition into the logical class it belongs in.

Note that we are not defining where in the class hierarchy the action will go; rather, we are simply *categorizing* the actions. This helps ensure that the functionalities that belong together go together. Our final product from this effort is a logical class definition that we will use to design physical classes or objects. The form we use for this is shown in Figure 21.22 and includes the logical class definition for the SQL Access Class.

> *Note that we have not defined any presentation elements for the application. The presentation is the easiest element to design, put together, test, and modify. As long as the processing elements are correctly put together, the presentation characteristics should be entirely at the user's and designer's discretion.*

Note that all of the action methods come straight from the first activity we defined, an activity to check whether the project team was already on file. As you can see, this exercise is much more time-consuming than the standard "we need an object to do this" approach. The end result, however, is a much cleaner method of defining what should and should not be included at various levels in the class hierarchy. Also note that the LCD is in turn capable of generating attribute and method requirements.

Database Definition

Organizations vary regarding when and how they implement database design, some forming huge designs of intercommunicating databases for the entire organization, whereas others build on a key subset of data and continue to expand the database. Most organizations would not have a database designed for this particular business need as it does not drive the business. Rather, it is needed to enhance and encourage the reuse of objects during development. We concluded that the database design in this case is the result of the business model, not the driving factor behind it, as is more often the case.

The data elements we need will be highlighted during method and attribute definition. We will then feed these requirements into a database design tool such as ERwin, System Architect, or S-Designor to produce our database design.

After all the definitions are complete, we can scan through the attribute definitions, extract the data elements marked as Persistent or Database, and use these elements to build our database. For our case study application, we used

Figure 21.22   Logical Class Definition: SQL access class.

Logical Class Data

Logical Class ID:	LIB_L001		Version:	1.0
Logical Class Name:	SQL Access Class			
Predicted Ancestry:	NonVisualObject		Update Date:	July 25, 1995
Keywords:	SQL, Select, SQLCode		Author:	William Green

Logical Class Description

Description
SQL Access Class capable of building, executing, and converting SQL and SQL error return values.

Action/Class Hierarchy Characteristics

Action Method		Attribute	Attr ID	Expected Result	Test ID
Build Potential Projects SQL statement		SQL Access Structure	LIB_A001	Loads the expected key values in the SQL Access Structure	LIB_T001

Hierarchy	Level	Method Details			Xref ID
Base	Ancestor	Build key virtual method • A virtual method on the base ancestor class is required by all descendants of the SQL Access Class.			
Base	Functional	Build key method for general SQL capabilities • Generic build capabilities to build an SQL select statement, including dynamic parameter parsing. Generic SQL must be ANSI 92 compliant.			
Base	Specific	Build key method encapsulating SQL dialects from various DBMSs • Convert generic SQL syntax to DBMS-specific SQL syntax.			
Business	Functional	Build key method encapsulating building of Potential Project key data • Build key structure for the Potential Projects access. • Key elements: project team name (ID is not known). • SQL should be a Like clause.			
Business	Rule	None			
Application		None			

(Continued)

Figure 21.22 *(Continued)*

Action Method		Attribute	XrefAttr	Expected Result	XrefTest
Execute SQL Call		Potential Users data/SQL Statement	LIB_D001	Executes an SQL Select statement	LIB_T002
Hierarchy	**Level**	**Method Details**			**Xref**
Base	Ancestor	Virtual method			
Base	Functional	Execute either Embedded SQL or Stored Procedure or Datawindow Select			
Base	Specific	None			
Business	Functional	None			
Business	Rule	None			
Application		None			

Action Method		Attribute	Attr ID	Expected Result	Test ID
Interrogate Return Value		SQL Return Code/Error Message Handler	LIB_A002	Displays an error message if the return value indicated failure.	LIB_T003
Hierarchy	**Level**	**Method Details**			**Xref**
Base	Ancestor	Virtual Method			
Base	Functional	Determine whether code returned is an error			
Base	Specific	Convert DBMS-specific code to generalized code			
Business	Functional	None			
Business	Rule	None			
Application		None			

S-Designor to create our data model. Other tools, such as ERwin and System Architect, are also up to the task.

We also used our data element definition form (targeted from the method definition form) before building the model. We found that this helped us greatly in determining the entities and rules that needed to apply to the various data elements. This form is shown in Figure 21.23. You can use this form to directly populate many items in most data dictionary implementations.

Data Definition

Data Defn ID:	DD_Sample			
Data Defn Name:	Sample Definition Form			
Version:	1.0		**Update Date:**	August 8, 1995
			Author:	William T. Green

Figure 21.23 Data Definition Form.

Figure 21.23 *(Continued)*

Definition

Description
Description of data definition

Data Elements

Element	Description	Entitiy
Elements	Description of the element	Entity the element belongs to

Data Rules

Rule ID	Rule Description	Related Data Item
Rule ID	Description of the rule	Data item (element or entity) that rule pertains to

Summary

We have now completed the logical design portion of the development effort. We have successfully put together a comprehensive list of requirements, expanded the requirements into activities, and then collected the methods and associated actions, attributes, and test plans for each. Where applicable, we associated messages that will be used throughout the application. If you are using a centralized messaging utility, this list of messages is useful. If not, it becomes almost crucial.

Finally, we went through the methods defined and arranged them in logical groupings, which then became our logical class definitions. Now we are ready to move on to physical class design and object and method mapping.

22

Physical Design

Introduction

When we start putting together the physical design of the objects needed for the project, we are actually building a blueprint of how we are going to build on our foundation of base classes and business classes. By keeping in mind that we are helping to build the enterprise architecture and not just one business solution, we emphasize the importance of every application that guides, molds, or directs the organization's business.

Many times application development has been likened to building a house. I used to share that opinion; however, I have changed my opinion somewhat. I have found that application development is more like building a shopping mall, a business campus, or perhaps a complete community. Pieces may be developed sooner or separately from others, but all of them must be aware of the pieces that fit into the puzzle around them. If the whole thing is well-designed, the completed effort will yield the fruits of such an endeavor. If any one piece takes off in a different direction, the whole effort is put in jeopardy.

A community of beautiful homes can be marred by a house that is too extravagant or one left incomplete for too long. All of the pieces fit, and they are all important. Obviously, some are more important than others, but none are more important than the whole.

I could wax philosophical all I want, but the truth of the matter is, "thar's an object in them thar classes, jest awaitin' to be designed." So let's get to it!

Chapter Objectives

The goals of this chapter are to guide you through the steps you need to take the logical design to the next level. We first take the logical classes and begin the task of method separation, which is defining the functional layer where a method logically belongs (base, business, or application). In many cases we have to go even deeper than that and separate the logical location within the functional layer, such as an ancestor class or functional class within the base class layer.

Once we complete this exercise, we begin to scan existing methods defined to determine which methods have been already built into objects and object classes. These methods are then checked to determine whether complete functionality is in place or whether they should be enhanced. This process is called object and method mapping.

The methods that remain undeveloped are then put together in a schedule of hierarchical dependency. By this we mean that we schedule development of objects in a logical, progressive manner as much as possible. We cannot develop an application object that needs to be derived from a base class object that does not exist. (There is a means to accomplish this, which we discuss in this chapter.)

As soon as possible, we can expand the methods into their physical implementation details and hand the specification to a developer. The construction specification should include all the documentation associated with all the methods assigned to the object, including the method test plans.

These test plans are then combined to form an object test plan. The test plans are later expanded to test cases that will thoroughly test each object and its methods.

By sticking to the development of the documentation as an ongoing element of the design, we can be assured of virtually complete object documentation before development is actually completed, or even begun!

Physical Design

Physical design is actually the easy part of the effort. Each method is interrogated and slotted into a functional layer, mapped to existing methods to determine remaining development effort, and finally designed into physical implementation details. After that, we take the navigation workflow developed as part of the requirements analysis and map the physical classes defined back to the elements of the workflow.

The difficult part is in making sure you do not jump ahead too quickly. Spend the extra time required to complete this exercise carefully, and not only will your development costs decrease, but you will be amazed at how well each applications' methods fit into the giant enterprise business collection of methods, rules, and attributes.

The physical design comprises five basic steps:

- Define the class hierarchy.
- Map methods back to existing methods.
- Define any new methods or classes that must be built.

- Accumulate the test plans associated with the class and define actual test cases that satisfy the test plan.
- Map objects to navigation workflow.

Class hierarchy definition

In defining the class hierarchy, much as we did in defining the class library hierarchy, we interrogate each activity or method action and determine where in the functional hierarchy such an element belongs. The determining factors are genericism, business-specific characteristics, and application characteristics. If the method applies generally for all applications (or most), the method probably belongs in a base class. I say *probably* because there are always exceptions to the rule.

Business functionality is divided into two parts: business functions and business rules. Business functions are those that are generalized across the organization whenever the functionality defined is required, whereas a rule is defined as a process whereby the validity of data or functionality is determined *as it pertains to the business.*

Application classes are the easiest. These include any methods that pertain strictly to application execution. To help you visualize this concept, Figure 22.1 depicts graphically the common class hierarchy design I use.

As shown in the illustration, the actual hierarchy is three or four layers deep. The SQL class is actually (at this point in the design) only three layers deep (base ancestor, base functional, and business functional).

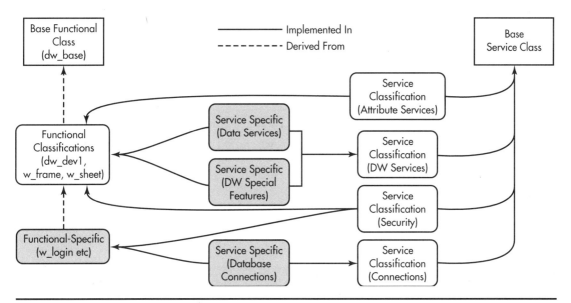

Figure 22.1 The CBM common hierarchy.

Figure 22.2   Logical class definition: SQL Access class.

Logical Class Data

Logical Class ID:	LIB_L001		Version:	1.0
Logical Class Name:	SQL Access class			
Predicted Ancestry:	NonVisualObject		Update Date:	July 25, 1995
Keywords:	SQL, Select, SQLCode		Author:	William Green

Logical Class Description

Description
SQL Access class capable of building, executing, and converting SQL and SQL error return values.

Action/Class Hierarchy Characteristics

Action Method	Attribute	Attr ID	Expected Result	Test ID
Build Potential Projects SQL statement	SQL Access structure	LIB_A001	Loads the expected key values in the SQL Access structure	LIB_T001

Hierarchy	Level	Method Details	Xref ID
Base	Ancestor	Build key virtual method. • A virtual method on the base ancestor class is required by all descendants of the SQL access class.	
Base	Functional	Build key method for general SQL capabilities. • Generic build capabilities to build an SQL select statement, including dynamic parameter parsing. Generic SQL must be ANSI 92 compliant.	
Base	Specific	Build key method encapsulating SQL dialects from various DBMSs. • Convert generic SQL syntax to DBMS-specific SQL syntax.	
Business	Functional	Build key method encapsulating building of Potential Project key data. • Build key structure for the Potential Projects access. • Key elements: project team name (ID is not known). • SQL should be a Like clause.	
Business	Rule	None.	
Application		None.	

Action Method	Attribute	XrefAttr	Expected Result	XrefTest
Execute SQL call	Potential Users data/ SQL statement	LIB_D001	Executes an SQL Select statement	LIB_T002

Hierarchy	Level	Method Details		Xref
Base	Ancestor	Virtual method.		
Base	Functional	Execute either Embedded SQL or Stored Procedure or Datawindow Select.		
Base	Specific	None.		
Business	Functional	None.		
Business	Rule	None.		
Application		None.		

Action Method	Attribute	Attr ID	Expected Result	Test ID
Interrogate Return Value	SQL Return Code/ Error Message Handler	LIB_A002	Displays an error message if the return value indicated failure	LIB_T003

Hierarchy	Level	Method Details		Xref
Base	Ancestor	Virtual method.		
Base	Functional	Determine whether code returned is an error.		
Base	Specific	Convert DBMS-specific code to generalized code.		
Business	Functional	None.		
Business	Rule	None.		
Application		None.		

Let's take a closer look at the class hierarchy mapping of a few of the logical classes defined in Chapter 21. The first is the SQL Access object, whose logical class definition (LCD) is shown in Figure 22.2.

We can see that we have defined the methods that make up this class, and the methods are broken out into the functional layers of our class hierarchy. Remember that the class hierarchy does not always mean that every class will have a six-level hierarchy. In fact, it is more common to see a three- or four-level hierarchy instead: a base ancestor class containing minimal defined functionality, a base functional class that contains most of the generic code required, in some cases a business class, and then an application class. In our example, deliberately chosen because it can fit into all six levels, our base ancestor class contains virtualized methods only. Virtualized methods contain basic construction elements and some routing capabilities, and also serves as the base where most global services and data repository objects are constructed.

The base functional class contains the elements necessary to build SQL statements based on incoming parameters. Our base-specific class contains

DBMS-specific code, SQL conversions, and error code translators. This layer is not a derived layer; rather, it is an imbedded layer, meaning that these are classes separate from the SQL Access object, but whose methods must be imbedded in the SQL Access classes. Our business classes, both function and rule, are derived from the base functional classes. The functional side contains specific data access setups such as checking for duplicate project team information, the code necessary to build and insert a new record, and update capabilities. The business rules contain specific data that control the access and updating of the data. For example, not allowing duplicates could be a business rule. Another rule could be that a project team cannot exist on both the potential projects log and on the active projects log. We would then implement this rule in the business class layer for both potential projects and active projects.

Our LCD (Figure 22.2) does not show any business rules. For the rules, we need to go back to the data definition form, which includes the rules regarding our data (the most common form of business rule because they are most tangible), and extract the rules that pertain to the Check for Duplicate Potential Projects method. Indeed, the whole requirement can be seen to be a rule. In a sense it is, but in reality only the actual rule implementation can be slotted into the "Check Return Code" action method. We can also see that a second action method (Project Already Exists is the first) can be added to check that the project team is not in our active projects log. Thus, we can see that the logical class definition should be revised to show our business rules from our data definitions.

> *Notice how much interaction there can be between the development teams, the DBA team, and the QA team. The business user, in the case of this example, is the development team (us), so presumably the communications channels there are pretty good.*

Figure 22.3 shows our LCD with business rules in place for the SQL Access for Potential Projects class.

Once we go through this exercise for our other LCDs defined, we end up with a thorough picture of our required environment. Now we need to establish what physical objects we will generate in order to build our system. We begin this with object and method mapping.

Object and method mapping

At this point we have a pretty good idea of what objects we need to create. Again, looking at the LCD for the SQL Access class for the potential projects access loop, we can begin to more clearly map out the objects, events, functions, and attributes we need. Now we introduce our final form, shown in Figure 22.4.

The physical class definition is the form that is handed to developers to begin coding. The reiterative portion of the effort now changes slightly in that it be-

Figure 22.3 Logical class definition: SQL Access class with business rules.

Logical Class Data

Logical Class ID:	LIB_L002		Version:	1.0
Logical Class Name:	SQL Access class			
Predicted Ancestry:	NonVisualObject		Update Date:	July 7, 1995
Keywords:	SQL, Select, SQLCode		Author:	William T. Green

Logical Class Description

Description
SQL Access class capable of building, executing, and converting SQL and SQL error return values.

Action/Class Hierarchy Characteristics

Action Method		Attribute	Attr ID	Expected Result	Test ID
Build Potential Projects SQL statement		SQL Access structure	LIB_A001	Loads the expected key values in the SQL Access Structure	LIB_T001

Hierarchy	Level	Method Details			Xref ID
Base	Ancestor	• None.			PCD_0001
Base	Functional	Build SQL method for general SQL capabilities. • Generic build capabilities to build an SQL select statement, including dynamic parameter parsing. Generic SQL must be ANSI 92 compliant. • Call the Translate SQL method on the base-specific class to translate the SQL. • Call the Execute SQL method on the business functional class to complete the SQL statement build depending on SQL data source and to execute the SQL statement.			PCD_0002
Base	Specific	Build SQL method encapsulating SQL dialects from various DBMSs. • Convert generic SQL syntax to DBMS-specific SQL syntax.			PCD_0003
Business	Functional	Build key method encapsulating building of potential project key data. • Build key structure for the potential projects access. • Key elements: project team name or project team identifier.			PCD_0004

(Continued)

Figure 22.3 *(Continued)*

		• SQL should be a Like clause because key identifier might not be fully known at this time and project name might vary.		
Business	Rule	Potential project should not exist on Active Projects log.		PCD_R001
Application		None.		

Action Method		Attribute	XrefAttr	Expected Result	XrefTest
Execute SQL call		Potential Users data/ SQL statement	LIB_D001	Executes an SQL Select statement	LIB_T002
Hierarchy	**Level**	**Method Details**			**Xref**
Base	Ancestor	None.			
Base	Functional	Execute either Embedded SQL or Stored Procedure or Datawindow Select. • Ability to change SQL used to standard Retrieve + Arguments (any). • Ability to change SQL used to Stored Proc Retrieve + Arguments.			
Base	Specific	None.			
Business	Functional	None.			
Business	Rule	None.			
Application		None.			

Action Method		Attribute	Attr ID	Expected Result	Test ID
Interrogate Return Value		SQL Return Code/ Error Message Handler	LIB_A002	Displays an error message if the return value indicated failure	LIB_T003
Hierarchy	**Level**	**Method Details**			**Xref**
Base	Ancestor	Virtual method.			
Base	Functional	Determine whether code returned is an error.			
Base	Specific	Convert DBMS-specific code to generalized code.			LIB_XSQL
Business	Functional	Success: Record Not Found on Potential Projects and Record Not Found on Active Projects log. Fail: Record Found on Potential Projects log. Fail: Record Found on Active Projects log. Fail: Other SQL Error.			
Business	Rule	None.			
Application		None.			

Physical Class Data

Physical Class ID:	Sample		Version:	1.0
Physical Class Name:	Sample			
Author:	William Green		Update Date:	July 7, 1995

Object Identification Data

Functional Layer	Base	Ancestor	Ancestry:	
Object Name:			Library:	

Object Class Description/Purpose

Description

Methods and Attributes

Attributes

Scope	Type	Name	Default

Note: When default indicates a Class ID (e.g., PCD_xxxx), variable is defined in that class.

Methods

Scope	Type	Prefix	Name	Link
(None)	Event		*Constructor*	
Description	Launch any object initialization routines.			
Specification	• N/A			
Overrides	Should not be overridden			
Extend	No	None		

Figure 22.4   Physical class definition.

comes a multithreaded effort instead. A developer can be handed an object definition and begin coding unless an object higher in the hierarchy is not yet created.

It becomes obvious that classes must be developed in the correct sequence, and even more importantly, should not be developed if they already exist. This is where object and method mapping comes into play. Of course, this methodology assumes you have something to map back to. If not, the mapping process will be very short this time around. (Notice that this is an additional way for you to build a base class from the ground up that meets your applications' requirements. Your base class team will certainly be overworked for quite a while, though).

Before we can begin object mapping, we must complete the physical class definitions. The process is quite simply to extract the pieces from the logical class definitions that pertain to the object class, and move them. For example, we have three action methods shown in our LCD example. Each of these is broken up into the layer of functionality that the method belongs in. This stage leaves us with the final design task of building up the object classes we want wrapped around these methods.

The first object class we define is the base ancestor class. This is the class that defines the basic behavior associated with all objects descended from it. This class is derived from a nonvisual object, creating our base custom class object. This object should, and will, contain very little functionality. Its purpose is to allow us to define behavior that controls descendant classes. This class is the base class for many other custom classes, and therefore cannot be specific for any class. You may have noticed that the standard physical class definition contains some predefined methods and attributes. These are object initialization methods and attributes we feel are required by every class. These methods include the following:

- Object initialization
- Exception handling
- Service instantiation and deinstantiation
- Object shutdown processing

Our definition form contains these four elements (eight methods) as part of the template for class definition. This helps us avoid omitting these very important aspects of object development from the start. In addition, we add the attributes shown as defaults, ii_return, ii_severity, and ib_ContinueAction (this is our version of the PowerBuilder SetActionCode, but we wish to separate the two to avoid confusion). These attributes are used as a return value from calls to other methods, an exception code severity level, and an action code to determine processing flow, respectively.

When we move the methods from the base ancestor layers of each action method into the object class definition, we end up with the definition shown in Figure 22.5.

(Text continued on page 390)

Figure 22.5 Physical class definition: base custom class.

Physical Class Data

Physical Class ID:	PCD_0001	Version:	1.0
Physical Class Name:	Base custom class		
Author:	William Green	Update Date:	July 31, 1995

Object Identification Data

Functional Layer:	Base Ancestor	Ancestry:	NonVisualObject
Object Name:	cc_Base	Library:	OBJ_BASE
Object Type:	Base		

Object Class Description/Purpose

Description
Base custom class: virtualizes methods for descendants.

Methods and Attributes

Attributes

Scope		Type	Name	Default
Protected	Instance	Integer	ii_Return	Const.OK
Protected	Instance	Integer	ii_Severity	Const.Fatal
Protected	Instance	Boolean	ib_ContinueAction	True

Methods

Scope	Type	Prefix	Name	Link
(None)	Event		Constructor	
Description	Launch any object initialization routines.			
Specification	• Trigger *cue_setup* event. • Post *cue_init* event.			
Overrides	None			
Extensions	Should not be extended unless a step is required between the Setup and Init events.			
Parameters		Description		Reference
(None)				(None)

Scope	Type	Prefix	Name	Link
(None)	Event		Destructor	
Description	Launch any functionality to be executed before object shutdown.			

(Continued)

Figure 22.5 *(Continued)*

Specification	• Trigger *closequery* event/function to determine validity of closing down the object. • Determine whether object may be closed (*ContinueAction = True*). • Fire *intfc_unload* function to deactive interfaces used if closedown approved.
Overrides	None
Extensions	Should not be overridden. Can be extended to add additional setup behavior.

Parameters	Description	Reference
(None)		by Value

Scope	Type	Prefix	Name	Link
(None)	Event		CloseQuery	

Description	Event fired from the Close/Destructor event to perform application processing before shutting down the object; allows checking of data changed without being saved.
Specification	• None.
Overrides	None
Extensions	Should not be overridden. Usually extended to change default object behavior.

Parameters	Description	Reference
(None)		by Value

Scope	Type	Prefix	Name	Link
(None)	Event	cue_	Setup	

Description	Event fired from the constructor event to set up the object.
Specification	• None.
Overrides	None
Extensions	Should not be overridden. Usually extended to change default object behavior.

Parameters	Description	Reference
(None)		by Value

Scope	Type	Prefix	Name	Link
(None)	Event	cue__	Init	

Description	Event posted from constructor to perform object initialization after the object build is complete.
Specification	• None.

Overrides	None		
Extensions	Should not be overridden. Can be extended to add additional setup behavior.		

Parameters	Description	Reference
(None)		by Value

Scope	Type	Prefix	Name	Link
Protected	Function	of_p	Service_Load	

Description	Function used to instantiate declarative services.			
Specification	• Scan for declared services. • Check whether interface loaded. • If not loaded, instantiate the service. • Obtain a pointer to the service. • Increment the usage count.			
Overrides	None			
Extensions	Can be extended by developer to add additional service declarations.			

Parameters	Description	Reference
(None)		
ReturnValue	Success or Failure indicator	Constant

Scope	Type	Prefix	Name	Link
Protected	Function	of_p	Service_UnLoad	

Description	Function used to deinstantiate declarative services.			
Specification	• Decrements interface usage counter. • If usage count reaches zero, service can be unloaded completely.			
Overrides	None			
Extensions	Can be extended by developer to add additional service declarations.			

Parameters	Description	Reference
(None)		
ReturnValue	Success or Failure indicator	Constant

Scope	Type	Prefix	Name	Link
Protected	Function	of_p	Raise_Exception	

Description	Function used to process exceptions raised by the object/object class.			
Specification	• None.			
Overrides	None			
Extensions	Can be extended by developer to add to the exception-handling capabilities of the class.			

Parameters/Return Value	Description	Reference
(None)		by Value
SeverityCode	Returns Severity code	Return

The second layer contains the main set of functionality that will be used to execute the methods. Here you can see that the object's functionality begins to take form. The initialization methods are still included, but now we begin to see the class really take shape. Look at Figure 22.6 to see how the base functional layer is implemented.

Notice that we see the first implementation of a service object here, the SQLConverter service. This service is also the third level of our physical design, the base-specific class. Here we want to indicate a group of classes with very similar methods. To do this, we still define a single physical class, but indicate the differences in the methods.

When we begin to define this class, it becomes apparent that there is another line of ancestry involved. The service classes have some common processing, much like other classes. This common processing belongs in a higher-level class, too. Our services are also nonvisual objects, leading us to the conclusion that the hierarchy for services is as follows:

- *Base ancestor:* cc_Base
- *Base functional:* cc_Base_Service
- *Base-specific:* cc_SQLConverter

Based on this we can see that the base ancestor class is already defined with behaviors that are needed by the service classes. (See Figure 22.5.) Our second step is to define the base functional layer, the cc_Base_Service, which will become the immediate ancestor for all of our service classes. This physical class definition is shown in Figure 22.7.

From the base service class we can derive all of our service classes. We also realize that the SQL Access class is a service itself and should be derived from the base service class rather than the base ancestor class, cc_Base.

We also derive the specific SQL Converter service class. The converter class is a class collection; that is, there may be several implementations of the class with like methods that have different results depending on which one is executed. For example, when calling the SQL Conversion function on the ODBC class, the SQL is converted to ODBC format. When calling the same function on the Sybase class, Sybase standard SQL is returned. The class definition is very similar, however, and we define a single physical class definition for the collection of classes. The collection of classes needs a common ancestor for any common functionality, and this ancestor class and the descendant-specific classes are shown in Figures 22.8 and 22.9. Notice the multiple implementations defined in the physical class definition (PCD) shown in Figure 22.9.

Note that the SQL Converter class has a built-in function to convert the SQL to a stored procedure. This is not a feature of the application, but a feature we determined would be nice to have built into this service.

When we now approach the business functional layer, we can see that the functionality is becoming quite specific in nature. The BuildSQL function in

(Text continued on page 396)

Figure 22.6   Physical class definition: SQL Access base class (functional).

Physical Class Data

Physical Class ID:	PCD_0002		Version:	1.0
Physical Class Name:	SQL Access base class (functional)			
Author:	William Green		Update Date:	July 31, 1995

Object Identification Data

Functional Layer	Base	Functional	Ancestry:	cc_Base_Service
Object Name:	cc_Base_SQLAccess		Library:	OBJ_BASE

Object Class Description/Purpose

Description
Base SQL Access object: Defines generic functionality required by all SQL Access classes.

Methods and Attributes

Attributes

Scope		Type	Name	Default
Protected	Instance	Boolean	*ib_SQLConverter_Intfc* Determines whether SQLConverter service should be established	Const.True
Protected	Instance	cc_SQLConverter	*icc_SQLConverter* A pointer to the service object SQL converter. Instantiates the service level required for the DBMS being used	Null
Private	Shared	cc_SQlConverter	*scc_SQLConverter* Pointer to the service object instantiation	Null
Protected	Derived	Integer	*ii_Return* Return Value for calls to other methods	PCD_0001

(Continued)

Figure 22.6   *(Continued)*

Protected	Derived	Integer	*ii_Severity* Error Severity level	PCD_0001
Protected	Derived	Boolean	*ib_ContinueAction* Action code controlling logic flow	PCD_0001
Protected	Derived	Long	*il_Service_UsageCount* Usage count indicating how many instances of the service are in use	PCD_0003

Note: When default indicates a Class ID (e.g., PCD_xxxx), variable is defined in that class.

Inherited Methods

Name	Override Criteria	Defined In
Constructor	None	PCD_0001
Destructor	None	PCD_0001
CloseQuery	Extend for class	PCD_0001
Setup	Extend for class	PCD_0001
Init	Extend for default overrides	PCD_0001
Service_Load	Load SQL converter service	PCD_0001
Service_Unload	Unload SQL converter service	PCD_0001
Raise_Exception	Extend for class	PCD_0001
Increment_Usage_Count	None	PCD_0003
Decrement_Usage_Count	None	PCD_0003
Get_ServicePointer	None	PCD_0003

Methods

Scope	Type	Prefix	Name	Link
Protected	Function	ccf_p	*Build_SQL*	
Description	Build key method; accepts groups of SQL parameters to build an SQL statement.			
Specification	• Triggers SQL_Select, SQL_From, SQL_Where, SQL_Order, SQL_Group, SQL_Having methods to build various portions of the SQL statement. • Triggers Translate SQL method on SQL Converter interface.			
Overrides	New method: should not be overridden			
Extend	No	None		
Parameters		**Description**		**Reference**
(None)				(None)

Figure 22.7 Physical class definition: base interface class.

Physical Class Data

Physical Class ID:	PCD_0003	Version:	1.0
Physical Class Name:	Base service class		
Author:	William Green	Update Date:	August 1, 1995

Object Identification Data

Functional Layer	Base	Ancestor	Ancestry:	NonVisualObject
Object Name:	cc_Base_Service		Library:	Base Ancestors

Object Class Description/Purpose

Description
The base service class defines common behavior for all service classes.

Methods and Attributes

Attributes

Scope		Type	Name	Default
Inherited	Instance	Integer	*ii_Return* Return Value for calls to other methods	PCD_0001
Inherited	Instance	Integer	*ii_Severity* Error severity level	PCD_0001
Inherited	Instance	Boolean	*ib_ContinueAction* Action code controlling logic flow	PCD_0001
Protected	Instance	Long	*il_Service_UsageCount* Usage count indicating how many instances of the interface are in use	0

Note: When default indicates a Class ID (e.g., PCD_xxxx), variable is defined in that class.

Methods

Scope	Type	Prefix	Name	Link
Inherited	Event		*Constructor*	PCD_0001

(Continued)

Figure 22.7   *(Continued)*

Description	Launch any object initialization routines.		
Specification	• N/A.		
Overrides	Should not be overridden		
Extend	No	None	

Scope	Type	Prefix	Name	Link
Inherited	Event		*Destructor*	PCD_0001
Description	Launch any functionality to be executed before object shutdown.			
Specification	• N/A.			
Overrides	Should not be overridden			
Extend	No	None		

Scope	Type	Prefix	Name	Link
Inherited	Event	*cue_*	*CloseQuery*	
Description	Event fired from the Close/Destructor event to perform application processing before shutting down the object; allows checking of data changed without being saved.			
Specification	• None.			
Overrides	May be overridden			
Extend	Yes	Add CloseQuery processing for decendant service class		

Scope	Type	Prefix	Name	Link
Inherited	Event	*cue_*	*Setup*	
Description	Event fired from the constructor event to set up the object.			
Specification	• None.			
Overrides	None			
Extend	No	None		
Parameters	Description		Reference	
(None)			by Value	

Scope	Type	Prefix	Name	Link
Inherited	Event	*cue__*	*Init*	
Description	Event posted from constructor to perform object initialization after the object build is complete.			
Specification	• None.			
Overrides	None			

Extend	No	None	
Parameters		**Description**	**Reference**
Scope	**Type**	**Prefix**	**Name**	**Link**

Scope	**Type**	**Prefix**	**Name**	**Link**
Inherited	Function	*of_p*	*Service_Load*	
Description	Function used to instantiate declarative services.			
Specification	• None.			
Overrides	None			
Extend	No	None		
Parameters		**Description**		**Reference**
None				
Return Value		Method Success value		Constant

Scope	**Type**	**Prefix**	**Name**	**Link**
Inherited	Function	*of_p*	*Service_UnLoad*	
Description	Function used to deinstantiate declarative services.			
Specification	• None.			
Overrides	None			
Extend	No	None		
Parameters		**Description**		**Reference**
(None)				
ReturnValue		Success or Failure indicator		Constant

Scope	**Type**	**Prefix**	**Name**	**Link**
Inherited	Function	*of_p*	*Raise_Exception*	
Description	Function used to process exceptions raised by the object/object class.			
Specification				
Overrides	None			
Extend	Yes	Add exception-handling elements required by the SQL Access class		PCD_0001
Parameters/Return Value		**Description**		**Reference**
(None)				by Value
SeverityCode		Returns Severity code		Return

Scope	**Type**	**Prefix**	**Name**	**Link**
Inherited	Function	*of_p*	Increment_Usage_Count	
Description	Increments the Usage Count of the service			
Specification	• Increment Usage Count by 1			
Overrides	None			
Extend	No	None		

(Continued)

Figure 22.7   *(Continued)*

Extend	No	None	
Parameters		**Description**	**Reference**
Const.OK, Const.Failed		Success or Failure indicator	ReturnValue

Scope	Type	Prefix	Name	Link
Inherited	Function	*of_p*	Decrement_Usage_Count	
Description	Decrements the usage counter of the service.			
Specification	• Decrement ii_Intfc_UsageCount by 1. • If the usage count reaches zero, the service may be unloaded from memory.			
Overrides	None			
Extend	No	None		
Parameters		**Description**		**Reference**
CurrentUsageCount		Usage Count remaining after decrementing		ReturnValue

this class contains the exact definition of the SQL Select required. If this SQL statement is more variable in nature, the function would abide by the data being passed. Also notice that the business rules for potential projects are implemented in this class as services. Figure 22.10 shows the business-specific class SQL Access for potential projects.

As you can see, this single requirement has led to the establishing of several base classes and methods along the path to building the physical class. And we are not done yet! We can see that there are no application implementations, but there are some business rule implementations required. Because we want business rules to be implemented much like services, but only at the instance level and not the class level, we determine that a business rule should not be defined as a service as such, but be derived from a special new class called—you guessed it—cc_Base_BusinessRule. This class contains information to process a required rule, process any errors, and indicate whether all rules have passed or failed. The rule class is derived from our base custom class and is instantiated in the business or application levels depending on the requirement. Our base business rule class definition is shown in Figure 22.11.

Finally, we show the potential projects business rule object derived from the base business rule object. The two rules, "No duplicates allowed on potential projects" and "Cannot exist on both potential projects and active projects logs" are implemented here as methods that are either automatically executed upon update, insert, or delete, or available for on-demand execution. The rule type is defined early and may be available for both. Figure 22.12 shows the business rule class for potential projects.

Now we have completed the first of our LCDs, which, as you can see, generated seven physical classes. This will not be the case all of the time (for example, cc_Base will never have to be defined again), but you should be prepared.

(Text continued on page 400)

Figure 22.8   Physical class definition: SQL Converter base class.

Physical Class Data

Physical Class ID:	PCD_0008		Version:	1.0
Physical Class Name:	SQL Converter base class			
Author:	William Green		Update Date:	August 1, 1995

Object Identification Data

Functional Layer	Business	Functional	Ancestry:	cc_Base_Service
Object Name:	cc_SQLConverter		Library:	SQL Service Library

Object Class Description/Purpose

Description
Contains common functionality for the various SQL Converter classes.

Methods and Attributes

Attributes

Scope		Type	Name	Default
Inherited	Instance	Integer	ii_Return Return Value for calls to other methods	PCD_0001
Inherited	Instance	Integer	ii_Severity Error Severity level	PCD_0001
Inherited	Instance	Boolean	ib_ContinueAction Action code controlling logic flow	PCD_0001
Inherited	Instance	Long	il_Service_UsageCount Usage count indicating how many instances of the service are in use	PCD_0003

Note: When default indicates a Class ID (e.g., PCD_xxxx), variable is defined in that class.

(Continued)

Figure 22.8 *(Continued)*

Methods

Inherited Methods

Name	Override Criteria	Defined In
Constructor	None	PCD_0001
Destructor	None	PCD_0001
CloseQuery	Extend for class	PCD_0001
Setup	Extend for class	PCD_0001
Init	Extend for default overrides	PCD_0001
Service_Load	Extend for class	PCD_0001
Service_Unload	Extend for class	PCD_0001
Raise_Exception	Extend for class	PCD_0001
Increment_Usage_Count	None	PCD_0003
Decrement_Usage_Count	None	PCD_0003
Get_ServicePointer	None	PCD_0003

New Methods

Scope	Type	Prefix	Name	Link
Protected	Function	ccf_p	TranslateSQL	
Description	Translates SQL into DBMS-Specific SQL.			
Specification	• Parse SQL statement into separate clauses. • Translate SQL Where clause. • Concatenate translated SQL statement.			
Overrides				
Extend	No	None		
Parameters		Description		Reference
(None)				(None)

- -

Scope	Type	Prefix	Name	Link
Protected	Function	ccf_p	Generate_StoredProc*	
Description	Generates stored procedure based on SQL.			
Specification	• Build Create Proc statement. • Build procedure SQL. • Save procedure SQL to SQL file. • Generate Retrieve and Update code for stored procedure access. • Save script to script files. • Modify datawindow object to stored procedure access. • Permanently alter datawindow object.			
Overrides	None			
Extend	No	None		
Parameters		Description		Reference
DataWindow		Datawindow containing the SQL clause		By Reference
Const.OK, Const.Failed		Return Function Success or Failure		ReturnValue

*There could be a reciprocial method to convert stored procedure code and data windows back to SQL, but we found no immediate need.

Figure 22.9 Physical class definition: SQL Converter class collection.

Physical Class Data

Physical Class ID:	PCD_0004		Version:	1.0
Physical Class Name:	SQL Converter class collection			
Author:	William Green		Update Date:	August 1, 1995

Object Identification Data

Functional Layer	Base	Specific	Ancestry:	cc_Base_Service
Object Name:	cc_SQLConverter_ODBC cc_SQLConverter_Sybase cc_SQLConverter_Oracle cc_SQLConverter_DB2Net cc_SQLConverter_DB2MDI		Library:	SQL Service Library

Object Class Description/Purpose

Description
The classes can accept a standard format SQL clause and convert it to the DBMS-specific SQL statement required.

Methods and Attributes

Attributes

Scope		Type	Name	Default
Inherited	Instance	Integer	ii_Return Return Value for calls to other methods	PCD_0001
Inherited	Instance	Integer	ii_Severity Error Severity level	PCD_0001
Inherited	Instance	Boolean	ib_ContinueAction Action code controlling logic flow	PCD_0001
Inherited	Instance	Long	il_Service_UsageCount Usage count indicating how many instances of the service are in use	PCD_0003

Note: When default indicates a Class ID (e.g., PCD_xxxx), variable is defined in that class.

Inherited Methods

Name	Override Criteria	Defined In
Constructor	None	PCD_0001
Destructor	None	PCD_0001
CloseQuery	Extend for class	PCD_0001
Setup	Extend for class	PCD_0001

(Continued)

Figure 22.9 *(Continued)*

Init	Extend for default overrides	PCD_0001
Service_Load	Extend for class	PCD_0001
Service_Unload	Extend for class	PCD_0001
Raise_Exception	Extend for class	PCD_0001
Increment_Usage_Count	None	PCD_0003
Decrement_Usage_Count	None	PCD_0003
Get_ServicePointer	None	PCD_0003
TranslateSql	Extend for class	PCD_0008
BuildStoredProc	Extend for classes that support stored procedures	PCD_0008

New Methods Defined

(None)

This level of detail during the design phase takes more time than the more common "code it and we'll change it later" philosophy, but it leaves little to chance.

If we look at an illustration of our class hierarchy now, we can see that the layers are often imbedded within each other as the classes and their services are established. Figure 22.13 shows this hierarchy.

The mapping process defined. The mapping process involves looking at an object class catalog (which you should have created when you first started on the reusability path) and checking whether the class exists, the existing class contains the functionality required, and the existing attributes and the scope of both data and methods is suited for your object.

Class level. If the class already exists, we need to move on to the method interrogation to determine whether the class contains all of the functionality we require. If the class does not exist, we can immediately schedule the class for development. Again, it is important to note that we should look at the base ancestor level first, and then move down the hierarchy. This establishes a sensible schedule of events.

We can easily see from the classes we have defined that, if this were the initial project in an organization, we would need to develop all of the classes defined. If we already had a class library, we would map the classes back to the library class catalog (an example is shown in Figure 22.14), and thus determine what was available and what was not. Note that the catalog shows the potential projects PCD in the list, but also shows that it is not a preexisting class and must be developed.

Method level. If the class already exists, we can begin the next level of review: method mapping. Here we compare the methods implemented in the class with those outlined in the physical class definition. Where methods differ, or

Figure 22.10 Physical class definition: potential projects SQL Access class.

Physical Class Data

Physical Class ID:	PCD_0005		Version:	1.0
Physical Class Name:	Potential projects SQL Access class			
Author:	William Green		Update Date:	July 31, 1995

Object Identification Data

Functional Layer	Business	Functional	Ancestry:	cc_Base_SQLAccess
Object Name:	cc_SQL_PotentialProjects		Library:	SQL Library

Object Class Description/Purpose

Description
SQL Access object for potential projects.

Methods and Attributes

Attributes

Scope		Type	Name	Default
Inherited	Instance	Boolean	*ib_SQLConverter_Service* Determines whether SQLConverter Service should be established	PCD_0002
Inherited	Instance	cc_SQLConverter	*icc_SQLConverter* A pointer to the service class SQL Converter; instantiates the service level required for the DBMS being used	PCD_0002
Inherited	Instance	Integer	*ii_Return* Return Value for calls to other methods	PCD_0001
Inherited	Instance	Integer	*ii_Severity* Error Severity level	PCD_0001
Inherited	Instance	Boolean	*ib_ContinueAction* Action code controlling logic flow	PCD_0001

(Continued)

Figure 22.10 *(Continued)*

Inherited	Instance	Long	il_Service_UsageCount Usage count indicating how many instances of the service are in use	PCD_0003
Protected	Instance	String	is_Project_ID Project Identifier Mnemonic	Null
Protected	Instance	String	is_Project_Name	Null

Note: When default indicates a Class ID (e.g., PCD_xxxx), variable is defined in that class.

Inherited Methods

Name	Override Criteria	Defined In
Constructor	None	PCD_0001
Destructor	None	PCD_0001
CloseQuery	Extend for class	PCD_0001
Setup	Extend for class	PCD_0001
Init	Extend for default overrides	PCD_0001
Service_Load	Load potential projects business rule	PCD_0001
Service_Unload	Unload potential projects business rule	PCD_0001
Raise_Exception	Extend for class	PCD_0001
Increment_Usage_Count	None	PCD_0003
Decrement_Usage_Count	None	PCD_0003
Get_ServicePointer	None	PCD_0003

Scope	Type	Prefix	Name	Link
Inherited	Function	of_p	*Build_SQL*	PCD_0002
Description	Build Select from parameters.			
Specification	• Select project team ID, name, and project data. • Select from potential projects. • Select where key contains supplied project team ID or name.			
Overrides				
Extend	No	None		
Parameters		Description		Reference
Project Team ID				Reference
Project Team Name				Reference
Const.OK, Const.Failed				ReturnValue

do not exist in the existing classes, we schedule additional development work to be completed by the responsible development team. Again, it is important to note that the scheduled development should follow the same lines as before. Schedule development at the highest level first.

Figure 22.11 Base business rule class.

Physical Class Data

Physical Class ID:	PCD_0006		Version:	1.0
Physical Class Name:	Base business rule class			
Author:	William Green		Update Date:	August 2, 1995

Object Identification Data

Object Classification:	Base	Functional	Ancestry:	cc_Base
Object Name:	cc_Base_BusinessRule		Library:	Base Objects

Object Class Description/Purpose

Description
Base Business Rule class: Defines virtual methods required to implement all rules.

Methods and Attributes

Attributes

Scope		Type	Name	Default
Inherited	Instance	Integer	ii_Return Return Value for calls to other methods	PCD_0001
Inherited	Instance	Integer	ii_Severity Error Severity level	PCD_0001
Inherited	Instance	Boolean	ib_ContinueAction Action code controlling logic flow	PCD_0001

Inherited Methods

Name	Override Criteria	Defined In
Constructor	None	PCD_0001
Destructor	None	PCD_0001
CloseQuery	Extend for class	PCD_0001
Setup	Extend for class	PCD_0001
Init	Extend for default overrides	PCD_0001
Service_Load	Extend for class	PCD_0001

(Continued)

Figure 22.11 *(Continued)*

Methods

Scope	Type	Prefix	Name	Link
Protected	Function	of_p	Define Rules	
Description	Function called to define all of the rules to be used.			
Specification	• Establish the rule name. • Establish the rule type (on Insert, on Delete, on Retrieve, etc.). • Establish the rule functionality. • Establish the function call for the rule.			
Overrides	None			
Extend	No	None		
Parameters	Description			Reference
(None)				(None)

Scope	Type	Prefix	Name	Link
Protected	Function	of_p	Execute_Rule	
Description	This function executes a specified rule.			
Specification	• Retrieve rule data. • Execute given rule. • Raise errors if necessary.			
Overrides	None			
Extend	No	None		
Parameters	Description			Reference
(None)				(None)

Again we see that there should be minimal differences from our class library based on the example shown. By mapping the classes we feel the application needs and the methods required for each class, we could map the methods (per object) back to the existing classes and define whether new methods needed to be added or whether existing methods required modification.

We have spent considerable effort detailing classes and methods and boiled it down to one new class required. This is also an indication of the costs your development effort is saving if you use a comprehensive base class.

Virtualized development. Looking at this technique, it becomes obvious that the base class development team might be swamped with requests for new classes or methods. One of the means to accommodate the development teams is to virtualize development of new classes or methods. By this I mean that the class is constructed with all of the events, functions, and attributes defined, but the actual logic behind the functions and events is simply not coded until the team can schedule the development effort required. This allows the business and application class developers to go

Figure 22.12 Physical class definition: potential project rules.

Physical Class Data

Physical Class ID:	PCD_0007	Version:	1.0
Physical Class Name:	Potential projects rules		
Author:	William Green	Update Date:	August 3, 1995

Object Identification Data

Object Classification:	Business	Rule	Ancestry:	cc_Base_BusinessRule
Object Name:	cc_Rule_PotentialProjects		Library:	Rules

Object Class Description/Purpose

Description
Potential project rules.

Methods and Attributes

Attributes

Scope		Type	Name	Default
Inherited	Instance	Integer	ii_Return Return Value for calls to other methods	PCD_0001
Inherited	Instance	Integer	ii_Severity Error Severity level	PCD_0001
Inherited	Instance	Boolean	ib_ContinueAction Action code controlling logic flow	PCD_0001

Inherited Methods

Name	Override Criteria	Defined In
Constructor	None	PCD_0001
Destructor	None	PCD_0001
CloseQuery	Extend for class	PCD_0001
Setup	Extend for class	PCD_0001
Init	Extend for default overrides	PCD_0001
Service_Load	Extend for class	PCD_0001

(Continued)

Figure 22.12 *(Continued)*

Service_Unload	Extend for class	PCD_0001
Raise_Exception	Extend for class	PCD_0001
Define_Rule	None	PCD_0006
Execute_Rule_????	Individual rules defined below	PCD_0006

Methods

Scope	Type	Prefix	Name	Link
Public	Event	cue_	New_Project	
Description	Rules applied against new projects.			
Specification	• Project may not exist in Potential Projects file. • Project may not exist in Active Projects file.			
Overrides	None			
Extend	No	None		
Parameters		**Description**		**Reference**
Project_Name		Project Name		by Value
Project_ID		Project_Identification		by Value

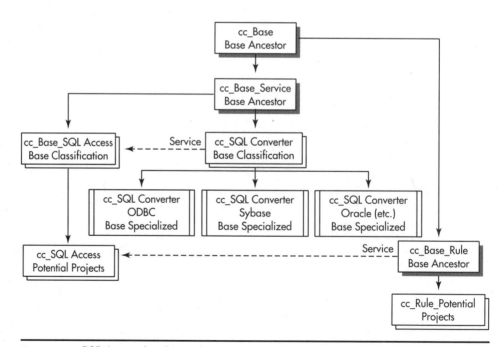

Figure 22.13 SQL Access class hierarchy.

Hierarchy	Level	Method Details	Class Exists	Xref ID
Base	Ancestor	• Base custom class.	Yes	PCD_0001
Base	Functional	• Base SQL Access class.	Yes	PCD_0002
Base	Ancestor	• Base service class.	Yes	PCD_0003
Base	Functional	• SQL Converter class collection.	Yes	PCD_0004
Business	Functional	• SQL Access class: potential projects.	Yes	PCD_0005
Base	Functional	• Base business rules class.	Yes	PCD_0006
Business	Rule	• Business rules: potential projects.	No	PCD_0007
Base	Functional	• SQL Converter base class.	Yes	PCD_0008

Figure 22.14 Class library catalog (draft).

forward with their efforts. The business class developers will also be a busy bunch. In many cases, they will be either part of the base class team or part of the application team. (I still recommend having a separate group handle the complications of developing business functionality without tailoring the effort toward an individual application, which is difficult for an application developer to do).

Basically, you are creating a skeleton that will be completed when scheduling allows, but the dependent classes can go forward with development. As the classes are built and enhanced, the completed code is passed on to the next dependent layer. Scheduling still must be a primary focus; maintain a close and careful watch on the various development schedules affected.

Object test plans

Object testing is an important aspect of the development effort. Again, without a plan, development becomes a daunting task riddled with inaccuracies. Fortunately, the CBM methodology requires method test plans that, as can easily be seen in the physical class definition, are carried forward with the object classes. Thus, developing an object test plan is a matter of gathering all of the test plans associated with the implemented methods.

Of course, you are not done yet. In Chapter 25 we go into much more detail on object testing, but the track we are going with here is that physical test cases should be designed along with the physical class definition, and actual test cases should be built along with the object. All of the tests are added to the regression test bed (at whichever level of functionality is defined) and can then be used for future automated testing. Again, testing is discussed in much more detail later on.

Navigation workflow mapping

Once we complete the physical design of our classes, we will go back to the navigation workflow that originated from the requirements analysis phase, and begin to map physical classes and objects back to the elements defined in the workflow. This will give developers a step-by-step approach to building their application. There will be no guessing involved, no mistakes in hierarchy selection, and most important of all, consistent use of the base classes in developing an application. This prepares the developer for building classes which can be reusable further down the line.

Summary

In this chapter we have discussed the process of taking a logical class design and creating a physical class definition. We have also discussed how and why services are created and implemented. Finally, we discussed object and method mapping, the process by which we determine which code is already written and which still needs to be written. We also showed how previously defined test plans are carried forward with the class definitions, automatically creating a comprehensive test plan for thorough system testing.

23

Application Development

Introduction

When building an application, especially with a language such as Power-Builder, you need to be careful and keep an open mind. Never forget that your ultimate goal is to create reusable objects. If you have a well-crafted library, your job at this point should be to build only business objects that perform business functions and application objects that hold it all together.

There are still other aspects that come into play, however, such as determining your library structure, learning what base classes and other business classes are available for your use, performing source (version) control, and developing graphical user interface (GUI) presentation.

If you do not have a solid foundation to build from, your job will be more difficult, but you should still make the effort to promote reusability by developing objects that others can use.

Chapter Objectives

The objectives of this chapter are to walk through the many elements and facets of object construction or development. The elements we will focus on are as follows:

- Constructing your libraries
- Optimizing your search path
- Encapsulation techniques
- Building from a base
- GUI considerations
- Source control
- Library maintenance

By the end of the chapter you should have a clear vision of how to construct your objects. You should also understand the many external elements that must be considered. Our goal is to save you some time and heartache.

Constructing Your Libraries

One of the first things you do when embarking on a development effort is to set up the libraries you will use for development and production. Based on our methodology, we recommend putting your application object in a separate library, with no other objects going into that library. The other library we create is the development library, which is where all objects being developed are placed. This is your work area and you will move completed objects from this library to their final destination libraries. This library also comes first in your search path during development.

After that, you would be wise to set up libraries that combine similar functionality. The reason for this is the way that PowerBuilder accesses objects.

If you have an application that contains two sets of distinct functionality, for example, chances are that the user will be working in one area at any given time. Therefore, why not have access to all of that functionality in the currently active library? For example, if you had Customers and Invoicing as two main paths in your application, it would make more sense to have all of the customer objects in a library separate from Invoice objects.

This tends to speed up the application somewhat, even though the actual time savings might seem negligible. It reduces the load created by placing objects of a like functional level in separate libraries, which is a common practice.

This holds true except for objects at base levels. Objects at base levels are accessed *less* often than other objects, but are loaded first. For example, if both a Customer and an Invoice object are derived from a common ancestor, the ancestor would always be loaded first, but would be required to load only once, regardless of whether you then choose a different option or another instance of the same option.

A common way to do this is to look at your top-level menu items. If you place all functionality relating to a top-level menu item in a library, you should gain the separation that is most effective for your application. Figure 23.1 illustrates what a typical library setup might look like if based on object types rather than functional groups.

The Search Path

The search path plays a bigger role in performance than most people think. The search path comes into play during the development phase, the compile phase and at runtime.

To explain why this occurs, we first need to dig deeper into how objects are loaded. Figure 23.1 showed the search path used in an application. Now watch

```
  ▸ Search Path
      • Application object
        (by itself)
      • Application objects
      • Base windows
      • Base user objects
      • Base functions
      • Base structures
      • Base menus
      • Business objects
      • Service objects
```

Figure 23.1 A typical library search path setup based on object types.

what happens when the application needs to access the Customer Maintenance window.

- *Search for and locate the application object (Customer).* This involves a scan of current memory, determining that the object is not currently loaded, checking an internal index to determine in which library (PBL) the object is located, open the PBD (a physical input-output operation), locate the object and load the object's definition into memory.

- *PowerBuilder now determines that the object is inherited and that the ancestor object is not loaded in memory.* A second search now takes place to locate the immediate ancestor and its definition is loaded. In this example, the Business Functional class is located in a separate PBL. Business classes are derived from Base Functional classes and another search ensues.

- *This process continues until the highest level object is located and its definition loaded into memory.* Only now can PowerBuilder build the object. Of course, once loaded, the ancestor objects will remain in memory as long as they are being used by a process. The object definitions will remain in memory for some time after the object is finally closed, but this period of time is not something we can track or rely upon.

- *If we now decide to open the invoice entry window, the process begins again.* Locate the application object, load and scan the definition. This time, however, the ancestor objects might still be loaded in memory and physical file I/O is not required. The result is a much faster load time of the second object even though it might be equal to or larger than the customer maintenance objects.

Imagine, however, that the customer maintenance window contains several objects (a datawindow or two and some command buttons). If the window, datawindow, and command buttons ancestors are located in different physical libraries, as might be the case if user object versions of the standard Power-Builder objects are being used, their definitions must be located and loaded along with their ancestors, if any.

You can now see that it makes sense for all the ancestor objects to be placed in a single library. It also makes sense for all of the objects involved in the Customer Maintenance window to be kept in the same library as the window. This also helps speed up the load time.

Figure 23.2 now shows the same application but with objects placed in a different set of libraries and a revolving search path technique used.

By carefully deciding what objects will be placed into which library, and then deciding which objects will be compiled into the executable to avoid physical I/O, you can speed up your object definition search and load times and make your application perform better.

TIP

Another reason for careful search path planning is compile time. When compiling, PowerBuilder loads the library into memory and reserves a block of memory to hold all the objects. It looks for contiguous memory for this function, and reserves several blocks of memory. When the next library is loaded, the system tries to use the blocks of memory already reserved. If they are not large enough, a new block of memory must be reserved. Not only does this take time, but it can cause your first library of objects to be swapped out of memory. When compiling, it is much more important to place your largest libraries first (with as many base objects as possible), thereby reserving blocks of memory that do not need to be changed or swapped out. This is also a reason why you need as much physical

▸ Base Object Library (Compiled with EXE)
  • Base windows
  • Base user objects
  • Base datawindows, functions, and structures in one library

▸ Revolving Object Library Setup (Compiled as PBDs)
  • Search path at load time
      Base functional
      Base specific
      Others
  • Select menu item Invoice; change search path to...
      » Business functional (Invoicing)
      » Business specific
      » Base functional
      » Base specific
      » Others

Figure 23.2 Functional library setup. Finally, based on a menu selection, you can dynamically alter the search path of the application to place the objects that will be needed first in the library list. (See the SetLibraryList() function in PowerBuilder.)

memory as possible and are better served by a permanent swap file than by a temporary swap file.

Encapsulation Techniques

I have been asked many times, "When developing an object, how do I determine what should be a function and what should be an event; of my functions, which should be private, protected, and public; and should my variables be private, protected, shared, instance, or local variables?" The following is my reply (refined over the years), which I call the eight golden rules of encapsulation. They are more guidelines than rules, but they help define these often difficult choices.

- Global variables should be avoided if at all possible.

- Shared variables should be used to restrict an attribute to a class, or to offer an area where attributes can be placed that should be shared by the class.

- Instance variables should be where most variables are kept unless the attribute is needed only within a script, in which case it becomes local.

- Shared variables are always private. Instance variables should be either private (if used only within the class) or protected if required by descendants of the class. Public variables should also be avoided if possible.

- Functions should be used instead of events wherever possible. You have no control over the scope of an event, and functions perform better.

- Functions should be private if they perform on private or shared attributes, and the functionality is wholly contained within the object.

- Functions should be protected if they are required by descendants of the class as a means of extension or as a means of accessing private or shared variables in the ancestor class.

- Functions should be public *only* if they offer access to attributes within the class to objects outside the class.

This simple collection of guidelines has served me well in developing reusable and encapsulated objects. Functions and events are the methods of your classes, and variables and object attributes make up the data these methods protect. Design them with care.

Building from a Base

The key to successful object development is a solid foundation. But even with a solid foundation, it is possible to take a long time to get little done. Using the approach of developing classes needed by your application from the ground up requires patience, an almost religious fervor for reusable objects, and the willingness to believe that the classes built according to their design will function as planned. It will not always happen that way, but it should happen more than 90 percent of the time.

The first thing you have to do is to learn about your base classes. Get a graphical map of the inheritance tree to get a quick picture of the object classes available, followed by access to an object catalog. An object catalog may take many forms. It could be a directory list from a library print, or it could be a sophisticated object repository. Regardless of the style of the catalog, the important thing is having one. A simple catalog such as the one shown in this book as our physical class cross-reference is often a good place to begin. Figure 23.3 shows a brief picture of the cross-reference class catalog.

Look at the objects available. Get to know the architecture of the class library, and the intent of the designers will become apparent very quickly. Having access to the design documentation is a key element to understanding the classes you will develop from. Only when you understand the classes, their purpose more than their content, will you truly begin to gain the benefit of this technology.

Building Objects

When you begin to construct your objects, the rules discussed for class library development[1] come back in force. Develop your objects from the lowest functional layer upward, and use the virtual development method. You will quickly put together a shell of your application where all you need to do is fill in the actual code.

Virtual development

If you have a solid foundation class library in place, you will be in position to start development of your application and business classes very quickly. If not, you must develop your classes from the ground up. The cross-reference shown in Figure 23.3 indicates that our base classes are already developed. We need to develop the classes that are not already developed, specifically the business and application classes. We define these objects according to their inheritance, place the methods required into the objects (without code), and save them, effectively building an application blueprint.

We can then go in and fill in the actual methods, starting with the base layer. Typically your development schedule is as follows:

- Base ancestor (if any)
- Base functional (if any)
- Base specific (if any)
- Business functional

---

1. See Chapter 11.

Hierarchy	Level	Method Details	Xref ID
Base	Ancestor	Virtual methods for base ancestor class.	PCD_0001
Base	Classification	SQL service methods. • Generic build capabilities to build an SQL Select statement, including dynamic parameter parsing. Generic SQL must be ANSI 92 compliant. • Call the Translate SQL method on the base-specific class to translate the SQL. • Call the Execute SQL method on the business functional class to complete the SQL statement build depending on SQL data source and to execute the SQL statement.	PCD_0002
Base	Ancestor	Virtual methods for base service class.	PCD_0003
Base	Specialized	Build SQL method encapsulating SQL dialects from various DBMSs • Convert generic SQL syntax to DBMS-specific SQL syntax.	PCD_0004
Base	Specialized	Business Rule Processor base class • Define rules. • Execute rules on Create, Retrieve, Update, and Delete. • Perform any tertiary processing indicated by rules. • Report any errors.	PCD_0006
Base	Specialized	SQL Converter methods. • Translate SQL to various SQL dialects. • Test/record/debug SQL statements. • Convert SQL to stored procedures and back.	PCD_0008
Business	Specialized	Build key method encapsulating building of potential project key data. • Build key structure for the potential projects access. • Key elements: project team name and/or project team identifier. • SQL should be a Like clause because key identifier might not be fully known at this time and project name might vary.	PCD_0005
Business	Rule	OnRetrieve. • Potential project should not exist on Active Projects log. • Potential project should not exist on Potential Projects log. OnCreate. • Potential project should not exist on Active Projects log. OnUpdate. • None. OnDelete. • Archive registration form.	PCD_0007

Figure 23.3 Class library catalog (draft).

- Business specific
- Application specific

If we look at our catalog of classes, we can determine that the first object we need to create is the business functional class Build Potential Projects SQL. This object is derived from the base functional class cc_base_SQLAccess, a service class. This indicates that this class is accessed from a datawindow. The object inherits most of its behavior from the base class, but adds some information about what a potential project is. We add the project name and project ID variables, which are used to build the access keys. When the datawindow needs to access the potential projects table, the object will automatically build the necessary SQL or stored procedure access code.

We can also see that there will be a business specific (or rule) class imbedded in this object. The rule states that on retrieve (or when the program is checking whether the project exists), the project team cannot exist on either the Potential Projects or Active Projects logs. (New potential projects should not already be active, nor should they already be registered as potential projects.)

When we build the business rule class for this object, we will include code to define the rules, code the access to rules for the various conditions, and report any errors.

Inheritance

In using a class library for development, inheritance is possibly the single most important feature of object-oriented technology you will use. The key is in knowing which class to inherit from. If you used the CBM methodology, this decision has already been made. Remember that it is often difficult and fraught with danger to attempt to change a class' inheritance hierarchy. It is much simpler to change it during the design phase.

Using your environment

Make use of the elements and the environment. In Chapter 13 we discussed using the Windows built-in About box function instead of writing your own, and using the MSInfo program instead of developing your own System Info window. By the same token, look around your desktop to see what is there that can be used. Get to know the Windows API, preferably the win32 API functions, as these are the functions you will see in Windows 95 and Windows NT workstations. (If you are planning to develop for UNIX, this obviously does not apply, but then you should get to know what is available on that platform.)

Reusing data

Another feature to consider in your application design strategy is reuse of data. We have already concluded that reusing code is an effective means of making developers more productive and efficient. Reusing data in your application makes your application more efficient and manageable. Use features such as a datastore, where commonly used data are preloaded into nonvisual datawindows and the data are referenced from these storage areas. Even updates can be made to these data and final updates made only when user involvement is not needed.

Distributing the workload

Get your system to perform as much work on your data server as possible. Or, prepare objects in such a fashion that when you make the move to distributed objects, you can take advantage of the technology without having to rewrite all of your code.

Preloading objects

Another means of reuse is to preload often-used objects or object ancestors. There are generally two methods of preloading objects. The first is to define the objects you wish to preload in an object that will be loaded at application load time, thereby forcing the load of the object definitions into memory. The second is similar in that the objects are still defined in a preloader object, but they are also physically created. In some cases, the preloaded objects can be used as base objects for your datastore objects.

GUI Considerations

A very important yet often overlooked aspect of object development is the graphical user interface (GUI) component of your application. I believe that the emphasis here should be on *user interface*. This is the portion of the system the user sees every day. If your windows are crowded with objects, users will be dissatisfied with the performance and with the eyestrain involved in locating the information they need. People are used to looking at documents. How many times have you looked at an application form or a tax form and wished it could be made a little simpler? Users have that burden on top of using your system. Do not add to their frustration.

Make your screens easily readable, place as much relevant information on the screen as is necessary to complete the function, or split the functionality between two screens. Do not stifle creativity, but do not let creativity overcome functionality. The functions should be as simple as they can be, not because users are simple, but because this is an often repetitive job. If you think doing the same thing over and over again gets boring, try adding a complicated process to something that is done over and over again. It becomes annoying, too.

Use your creativity to develop easier ways for users to get their data and create reports. I am in favor of adding graphical alternatives to viewing data, such as graphs or maps, even though the performance might not be as good as a printed report. Users need to *see* their data, and the more they can see in one pass of the screen, the happier they will be with the result. Do not worry if, like me, you are "graphically challenged." Bounce ideas off of the users. Discuss options with peers. Get opinions from people who seem to be more graphically talented than yourself. It all comes down to the users liking what they see. If the data are correct, users will take a good-looking system over an awful-looking system any time. (Some I know would prefer a good-looking system with incorrect data over an ugly one that is correct, but their experiences with bad GUI design have probably been far worse than most.)

Avoid putting too many controls on a window, or controls that scroll left, right, up, and down on the same window. Use common sense and do not be afraid to try out an idea.

Source Control

In developing applications, a key element of managing the process is source control. You need to manage the code in your project. We recommend the approach outlined in Chapter 13. Build a development "sandbox" where all new objects are created, and when they reach maturity, they "graduate" to a more permanent position in your libraries.

PowerBuilder Library Maintenance

Once your application is developed, or development is in full swing, you need to perform regular library maintenance. This involves the following elements:

- Versioning
- Archiving
- Optimizing
- Regenerating
- Compiling

Versioning

Version control is the one combination of words that strikes fear into any developer's heart. Something else controlling who does what to my objects? Not in this lifetime! But life dictates that the work we often do is critical to the company's business and we cannot take chances with what we are doing. (A year ago, that was my excuse for *not* using version control—go figure!) Now PowerBuilder and version control systems interact much better than before, allowing more confidence in the capabilities of the version control software. Of course, it was not the software that eroded our confidence, but the implementation from both sides of the fence.

My first venture into version control of PowerBuilder objects was somewhat like *Nightmare on Elm Street,* or in my case, *Frightmare on Netware.* The whole premise of archiving objects from within a proprietary structure into a text file archiving system scared me witless.

Today, however, not only has the PVCS interface to PowerBuilder improved dramatically, but there are also several newcomers on the scene, namely Mortice Kern's Source Integrity product (some may be more familiar with the term RCS, MKS's UNIX product), LBMS's Object Manager, of course Intersolv's PVCS and Legent's Endeavor Workstation. In addition, Powersoft now provides its own source control product, Object Cycle, with the Enterprise Edition of PowerBuilder 5.0.

All of these products provide a benefit. Which one is the best? As of the time of writing, I had not received the latest copy of software from each of these vendors, who had all promised significant improvements in quality and speed over their previous, non–PowerBuilder-integrated versions. I especially liked Object Manager from LBMS and Souce Integrity by MKS. Both of these vendors seemed to be making a solid move to binary object versioning.

What is perhaps more important is to decide how to version your objects. You can version individual objects, or you can version entire libraries of objects. Versioning entire libraries leaves little for the versioning software to do, but requires that you manually check each library out as soon as one person needs to work on an object in that library.

Versioning individual objects is a much more arduous task, although quite well-automated, and it gives you a deeper sense of control over individual objects.

Deciding on your version control method depends a lot on whether you choose to archive at the library or object level. Whichever way you choose to go, version control is an important element in managing your source code.

Archiving

Daily backups of your source code are recommended. I cannot count how many times I have had to go to a backup to retrieve a version of my library that does not contain any of the crud I just managed to put into it. In many organizations this is a legal requirement as well. Make sure you understand what your backup procedures are, where your backups are stored, and how to get them back.

Optimizing

Optimizing a library has the effect of copying all of your objects into a new library, deleting the old library, and renaming the new library to the old name. In effect, you are getting rid of the dead space often left when objects are moved or deleted. Optimize frequently to keep your libraries at their optimal size.

TIP

Novell users, after optimizing libraries, go into a DOS window and use the Novell FLAGS option to reset the shared attributes on the library. By default, new files created on a Novell network are not marked as shareable. Optimizing libraries is accomplished by creating a new library and copying the old source code. Resetting the shared flag prevents a common problem in a multideveloper environment: a Save Failed1.

1. Go to a DOS prompt.
2. Change to your source directory.
3. Type FLAGS *.PBL. This displays a list of your libraries and their file attributes. These are not the same attributes as DOS attributes.
4. Type FLAGS *.PBL +s. This sets the shared attribute for each library.

Regenerating

When regenerating your objects, remember to regenerate them in a hierarchical fashion; that is, regenerate base ancestor objects first, followed by the remainder of the hierarchy. PowerBuilder 5.0 offers the Object Browser window, which also allows you to regenerate objects based on the class hierarchy. By regenerating objects from their lowest levels in the Object Browser window, you are assured of regenerating objects in the correct sequence. Figure 23.4 illustrates the Object Browser window.

Keep in mind this detail: Objects, such as custom classes, that contain no functions or event scripts are not affected by regenerating because variables are not checked in the regenerate process. These objects must be physically opened and saved in order for changes to take effect in descendants. Our Constants object contains a simple function that checks the value of a constant to determine whether the object is in good condition because the object is so heavily depended upon. Adding this function ensures that the regenerate process will have an effect on the object.

Compiling

Compiling, or building your application, is one of the most exasperating experiences in using PowerBuilder. You have three options: Compile everything into one big EXE, compile some libraries into your EXE and the rest into PBDs, or compile everything into PBDs. If you choose to compile everything into a single EXE, you will end up with a rather large file that must be transported across your network regularly, you will need to physically reference dynamic objects such as windows and user objects, and you will need to recompile the entire application for every change made between compiles. This can run into several days' worth of effort!

You will also be faced with the choice of whether to compile to traditional pseudo-code or machine code. Powersoft indicates that operations that

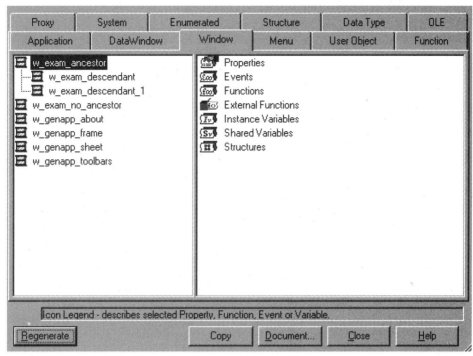

Figure 23.4 PowerBuilder 5.0's Object Browser: a leap ahead.

involve heavy calculations will benefit most from machine-code compila-
tions, and some others might actually suffer. We recommend that, on a per-
application basis, you construct both types of executables and measure
the performance of each before you decide which will be used for the final
executable.

Summary

This chapter covered the basic strategy for developing objects based on your physical design. We again discussed the virtual development theory and showed how the physical design again comes into play in detailing exactly what methods are required and where. You can quickly build your application skeleton with all methods in place, and then begin to flesh out the objects based on their position in the hierarchy. This allows developers to build objects that have dependencies in ancestor objects, without requiring that the ancestor be completely coded before you begin.

We delved into the aspects of reusability often taken for granted in that you should be trying to reuse everything, including data, objects, and methods.

We also discussed some of the external factors influencing your development effort, specifically the management and control of objects within your environment.

24

Object Integration

Introduction

When it comes to object integration, one thing leaps to the foreground: How are we going to get all of these objects to communicate with each other without knowing anything about each other? Specifically, how do we go about implementing the service objects we have designed?

We have seen how to implement a service as a shared variable that allows us to declare the service only once and the establish a pointer to the service within the object that needs access to it. But that was when there was a single service object that was known to us before the object was actually implemented. There are times that we will not know the actual service object that will be used.

One type of service that comes to mind are the business rule services. These services are known only after they are defined, and the objects that implement them will be defined and developed beforehand.

This chapter deals with these and other issues relating to object integration.

Chapter Objectives

The goals of the chapter are to discuss how to go about determining the service that will be implemented. We have defined three types of services.

- *Static services:* services that are known to us at the class library development level. The service is implemented as part of the object's initialization.

- *Declarative services:* services that are known to us at the class library development level, but are determined to be services that can be loaded or not loaded depending on the developer.

- *Dynamic services:* services that have several options available and that we will instantiate at runtime based on certain criteria. The services have a set list of options known to us at the class library development level.

We discuss each of these levels of integration and show you how to build your objects in such a way that this integration becomes automatic and effective.

Static Service

A static service is an object that is known to the developer at the class library level, usually a base-specific level object. This service is implemented within base-level objects and the instantiation code predefined. One such object is our constants object.

What are constants?

In most programming languages there is a type of variable called a constant. This variable contains a static value that the developer then refers to using the name of the variable instead of the value. In PowerBuilder, enumerated data types are a form of constant. Developers do not need to know what the value is, but instead use a familiar and documented variable name to use the value within their code. For example, when deciding whether windows should be opened as layered, cascading, or as defined in the development environment, we use the Layered!, Cascaded!, or Original! enumerated data types.

PowerBuilder does not provide this level of service to developers. We cannot declare our own enumerated data types, but we often need to.

How many times have you written code like this?

```
IF Messagebox("title", "text", Information!, OkCancel!) = 1 THEN
   /* 1 = OK */
   Do processing for OK
END IF
IF Messagebox("title", "text", Information!, OkCancel!) = 2 THEN
   /* 2 = Cancel */
   Do processing for Cancel
END IF
```

Then, a little later in your program you need another message box, but this time containing a Yes, No, and Cancel set of buttons. The code looks like this:

```
IF Messagebox("title", "text", Information!, YesNoCancel!) = 1 THEN
   /* 1 = Yes */
   Do processing for Yes
END IF
IF Messagebox("title", "text", Information!, YesNoCancel!) = 2 THEN
   /* 2 = No */
```

```
   Do processing for No
END IF
IF Messagebox("title", "text", Information!, YesNoCancel!) = 3 THEN
   /* 3 = Cancel */
   Do processing for Cancel
END IF
```

Suddenly, the value being returned for the Cancel button changes. This is a simple example, but illustrates the fact that when the value you are checking for changes, it can become difficult for the developer to remember which value you should check for. Do Message Box buttons start from 0 or from 1? What value did I assign to return from functions if the function executed OK?

These situations can be avoided if we can declare a variable called OK, and assign it the return value from the OK button every time. The same goes for Cancel and for successful function execution.

That is what constants do. They allow you to assign a fixed value to a variable name that makes the coding effort easier. Now all we have to do is find a way to implement the constants as objects that are globally available to all objects.

Where do we define this type of service?

There are three places to define constants and similar Service objects.

- As a global variable
- As an instance variable on either the application object or in the frame window
- As a shared variable within each class with a public pointer to the service

Other than the fact that we are specifically trying to avoid using global variables (and this is true of commercial class libraries even more than internally developed libraries), the global variable seems like the right place to do this.

Defining the object as an instance variable of the frame or application seems global enough, although two things stand in the way. First, we would have to know the name of the application object or the frame and second, obtain a pointer to this object in order to access the constants. This means some hard typing of object names, something else we are trying to avoid.

The third method of implementation is at the class level. We need to declare the constants as a shared service at the base ancestor level for each class. This gives us the level of encapsulation we desire, but requires that we do the same declaration in several different objects. Our base window must declare the service, as must our base datawindow object and our base custom class.

We choose to use the third method. This gives us the flexibility we desire in that services such as constants can be implemented in many object classes, but could be declared as declarative services in other objects. (You may not want constants to be declarative, but constants are only one example of static fixed services.) In some cases, the static fixed service may apply only to a certain class, such as a Window class, and not be required in other object classes.

To see how this is done, look at the code snippet shown in Figure 24.1, which shows how the constants object is implemented in the custom class base object.

Now, this class has access to all of our constants through the simple access method, objname.varname. For example, our Message Box button definitions are now as follows:

- Const.OK

- Const.Cancel

- Const.Yes

- Const.No

We no longer have to remember that yes = 1, and so does OK, and cancel = 2 except when cancel = 3. This kind of powerful value representation is not only extremely useful, but also makes code much more readable.

Declarative Service

A variation on the theme of implementing a known service is when the service is a declarative service. This is a service that is precoded, but is instantiated only when the developer declares a need for the service. An example of this type of service is the SQL Access class service. This is required only when data access is required. We know it will be required most of the time in a datawindow class, but there may be times when it is not needed. For this type of service, we need to declare a variable within the object class that indicates whether the service should be established, and then check this variable before instantiating the service.

```
/* Constants Service Load - Always required */
RC.Topic = Constants
        IF NOT IsValid (SCC_Const) THEN
IF NOT IsValid(Const) THEN
                SCC_Const = CREATE cc_ofr_constants
        END IF

        Const = 5cc_base::of_pGetPointer_Service(Constants)
        Const.of_p_IncrementUsageCount()
END IF
```

Figure 24.1 Constants object service implementation.

This also adds the flexibility of being able to instantiate this service dynamically at runtime by changing the value of the declarative and then calling the load service function. Figure 24.2 shows how the service load function first determines whether the service is required before instantiating it.

This can also be useful in declaring a service for debugging purposes that is usually not instantiated, but can be instantiated when needed. The advantage of this approach is that the service can be declared and used in one object, and not in another.

Dynamic Service

There might come a time when you know a service is required, but you do not know which one will be needed until runtime. An example of this type of class is our SQL Converter class. We have an SQL Converter class for ODBC, Sybase, Oracle, and DB2, but we do not know which one will be used by the datawindow. We know one of them will be used, though.

Because the SQL Converter classes are all derived from a single base, we can at least predeclare the service as an object of the type SQL Converter ancestor. If all of the functionality required is at least virtualized in the ancestor object, we have access to the descendant's functionality when required. To im-

```
Super::of_p_service_load()

RC.Subject = ServiceLoad
RC.ReturnValue = 1

If ib_sqlconverter_service THEN
    IF NOT IsValid(sqlcon) THEN
        IF NOT IsValid(Scc_SQLCon) THEN
            Choose Case ii_DBMS
                Case Const.ODBC
                    SCC_SQLCON = CREATE cc_ofr_SQLConverter_ODBC
                Case Const.Sybase
                    SCC_SQLCON = CREATE cc_ofr_SQLConverter_Sybase
                Case Const.Oracle
                    SCC_SQLCON = CREATE cc_ofr_SQLConverter_Oracle

            End Choose

        END IF

        SQLCon = cc_base_sqlaccess::of_p_GetPointer_Service(Const.
        SQLConverter)
        SQLCon.of_p_IncrementUsageCount()
    END IF
END IF
```

Figure 24.2 Declarative service instantiation.

plement this service we first need to determine which one is needed before instantiating. Figure 24.2 showed the service instantiation code necessary to instantiate a dynamic declarative service. Figure 24.3 shows the variable declaration for this service.

This example shows how you can predeclare the service and use a case statement to determine which service descendant is required for the object. This type of service is also specific to the object and as such is still declared as a shared variable for the class but at the SQL Access class level, not the base ancestor level. Also note that all of the various services are predeclared to make sure they are known to the object when needed.

Notice that this service is declared and instantiated in the SQL Access class, as it will not be needed if SQL Access is not used.

> *This type of service may be declared as an instance-level service if desired, based on the determination of whether the service will be needed by more than one object at any given time.*

Another form of the dynamic service is one where the class library developer knows only that a service will be instantiated, but has no idea what the name or type of the service will be. An example of this type of service is the business rule object. This object will be specific to the object class in which it is instan-

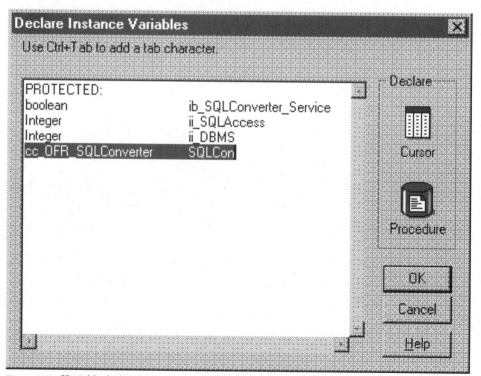

Figure 24.3 Variable declaration for the SQL Converter class.

tiated, so we as class library developers can only declare the instance variable of the type business rule ancestor. We have no idea what the name of the service will be and our job ends here.

However, we do need to provide developers with instructions on how to instantiate their own service. We do this as follows:

1. Extend the Service_Load function.
2. Call the Ancestor Service_Load function from the extended level.
3. Instantiate your service.
4. Extend the Ancestor Service_Unload function.
5. Call the Ancestor Service_Unload function from the extended level.
6. Unload your service.

The only difference between the developer's code and the class library–level code is that the developer needs to call the ancestor function first to instantiate all of the class level services, just as we showed for the SQL Converter service. In addition, the developer must code a Service_Unload and a GetPointer_Service extension.

Accessing Service Functions

When accessing services, the thing to remember is that they might not be there. Our code should therefore always be prefixed with an IsValid() statement to check whether the service is there. We can code this as shown in Figure 24.4.

This ensures that we do not call a function on an object that does not exist, and we do not pay a high price for including code for objects that might not be there. The IsValid() adds very little overhead to our object.

Object Brokers

There might come a time when two objects need to communicate with each other, but have absolutely no idea that the other even exists. An example of such a situation is a pair of objects placed on a window. If one of the objects is dynamic, you might not know anything about the object at development time, so you cannot assume that the object will be there, or even that it might be an object you know about.

To get around this we use an object called the object broker. This object behaves similarly to the way object linking and embedding (OLE) objects behave. OLE objects define their services to the calling object. The calling object knows nothing about any other functionality contained in the OLE object unless it is told about it.

Our object broker acts as the go-between for these objects. It is the known object that your other objects can communicate with. The example we will use

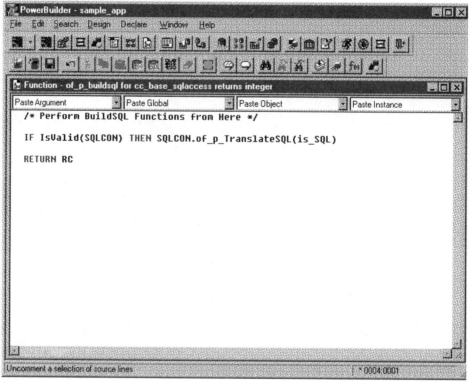

Figure 24.4 Calling service functions.

is a window I created as a Common File dialog lookalike. The window contains three dynamic objects and two static objects. Because the shape, form, and content of the three dynamic objects are entirely up to the developer, I have no idea what functionality will be available. Therefore, my object broker is built into the window and allows the objects to declare their functionality to the broker, which in turn relays requests to the other objects.

How do the objects declare functionality to another object? Well, the only way this can be done currently is through events. The object broker must contain a linked list of declared functions, event names, and objects. This is quite easily accomplished. The broker contains code to build the linked list, as shown in Figures 24.5 and 24.6.

The calling object now calls the broker (which it knows is there) and asks to route a particular function. The broker scans to see whether that function exists and, if it does, routes the function call to the recipient. If not, a return code tells the calling object there was no available recipient for their message. Note that this implementation allows the same function name to fire off multiple events in the recipient object.

Another alternative is to have the broker already know about certain functionality, such as a Load function, a Select function, a Print function. Each ob-

```
/****************Specialized Declarative Function processing***************
IS_Function is a String Instance Variable array
IF_Event is a string Instance Variable array
IPO_Object is a Powerobject Array maintaining a Pointer to the Target Object

These could also be structure, an Imbedded NVO or a DataWindow. This is the
simplest implementation.

Arguments:

as_Function = Function Name Argument - Contains a Name that will be used to
identify the function
as_Event = Event Name Argument - Describes which event will be xfired when
function is called
apo_Object = Object Pointer reference
*/

int idx, max
/*Note that MAX could be assumed value if stored as Shared*/
Max = UpperBound(is_function)
Idx = Max + 1

is_Function[idx] = as_Function
is_Event[idx] = as_Event
ipo_Object[idx] = apo_Object

/****************Specialized Declarative Function processing***************/
RC.ReturnValue = Const.OK

Return RC
```

Figure 24.5   Declare functionality to broker.

```
/*This function scans the Special Processing list to find the
        function in question and fires the associated event. if the
        function is not available, a default error message is shown
        indicating this.*/
int idx, max
max = upperbound(is_Function)
for idx = 1 to max
        /*Locate other object functions named as the passed function name
        parameter*/
        if asFunction = is_Function[idx] then
            ii_spproc_returncode = iiRC
            is_spproc_function = asFunction
            /*Launch the event on the recipient object*/
            ipo_Object[idx].TriggerEvent(is_event[idx])       /*This could be
                                                              a posted event
                                                              */

            return Const.OK
        end if

next

RC.ReturnValue = Const.Failed
RC.Reason = Const.NamedFunctionBad
```

Figure 24.6   Route functionality.

ject declares the event name to be used when calling the function on them. (They should all use the same naming conventions and try to retain consistency.) Now the calling object simply asks the broker to fire off the particular message. (This saves one scan of the linked list.)

TIP

You should consider using a datastore (a nonvisual datawindow introduced in PowerBuilder 5.0) for this process, as datawindows have special functions that allow you to store and locate data in a somewhat faster fashion than normal array processing. (DwFind is somewhat more efficient than a For . . . Next loop.) You can also use the Filter capabilities to reduce your list to a list of *all* objects that use the function and are currently active, and then route the message to each of them.

TIP

I added a SaveAs() log function to save the contents of the object broker linked lists, thus allowing me to preprogram these lists the next time the program runs. Declarations to the broker now follow the pattern of "check if you know about this function" before actually loading the function into its linked list. The object now becomes an object that actually learns a little about your system as it is used.

Summary

This chapter explained how we implement our service methodology. This is, of course, the key element in our architecture, serving to keep overhead low and processing as fast and dynamic as possible.

We showed you how to implement the four types of services we have defined, and also explained the principles behind the object broker, the flexible message router that can actually learn about your objects.

25

Application Testing

Introduction

We need to recognize when we are doing something foolish, and when we do, we should change it. Testing over the years has proven to be a very expensive portion of the development effort, accumulating as much as 40 percent of the total development time. Manual testing of applications developed in the complex client-server environment using a tool as sophisticated as PowerBuilder with its event-driven architecture and object-oriented features is what I call foolish. We cannot possibly test every nuance of every object repeatedly with any consistency without solid test planning and use of the tools available. We need to do things differently.

Much like the procedures we discussed in Chapter 14 for testing class library objects and documenting class library objects, in testing application objects you must ensure that you test each object your application will use. When putting together the application test plan, you need to define which tests to perform for each object, and combine these to form a solid test bed that tests every object class you use.

If you have followed a solid design methodology, you already have test procedures defined for each class to be developed. You should also inherit the test cases that are defined for your base classes if these are available to you.

Chapter Objectives

The goals of this chapter are to discuss the steps we follow to build test plans and test cases. The result should be a solid and thorough test plan. In all, we cover the following topics:

- Using method test plans
- Preparing test cases
- Building a regression test suite
- Using automated testing tools
- Test management

Using Method Test Plans

When we start to prepare our test plan, the first thing we need to do is to determine which objects we used, including base classes. For this we refer to our application object catalog, which is simply the cross-reference of classes we defined as necessary for this application. Figure 25.1 shows a sample of this cross-reference of classes.

This brief list shows 10 class definitions that we will use in our application. Only two of these were actually defined for the application; the remaining 8 were defined as part of our class library. Your situation might be similar, or you may have defined all 10 classes for your application. Regardless of where you started, you need to test all objects *as used by your application*. To do this we first need to gather all of the test procedures defined for these classes.

Our methodology allows us easily to collect the test procedures defined for all of the defined classes. There are two types of test procedures we have defined: logical method test procedures and physical class method test procedures. Combined, these form a comprehensive test plan for our object.

Logical method testing

Logical test plans are used to establish a requirement test plan. Physical class test procedures define an object test plan. We begin with the Register Potential Projects requirement. Figure 25.2 shows the method definitions for this requirement.

When we dig into the method definitions, we can create a list of the action methods and their associated test procedures, and end up with a list somewhat like that shown in Figure 25.3.

Each test procedure contains a definition of what is required to test both the positive and negative aspects of the method in question. Try to supply more than one negative to cover various possibilities, but do not try to cover every single combination possible. You want to test the method, but rely on the physical class test procedures to get into the lowest level.

When you pull the test procedures together for the methods, you will end up with a list of test cases like the one shown in Figure 25.4.

Each test case defined can then be built as an individual test case using your regression testing tool of choice. The test case definition defines the actual steps

Figure 25.1 Class library catalog (draft).

Hierarchy	Level	Method Details	Xref ID
Base	Ancestor	Custom Classes base class. • Setup default attributes. • Initialize object. • Load interfaces. • Unload interfaces. • Check exceptions.	PCD_0001
Base	Functional	SQL Access class. • Generic build capabilities to build an SQL select statement, including dynamic parameter parsing. Generic SQL must be ANSI 92 compliant • Call the Translate SQL method on the base-specific class to translate the SQL. • Call the Execute SQL method on the business functional class to complete the SQL statement build depending on SQL data source and to execute the SQL statement.	PCD_0002
Base	Ancestor	Base Service class. • Get an interface pointer. • Increment interface usage count. • Decrement interface usage Count.	PCD_0003
Base	Specific	SQL Converter class. • Convert generic SQL syntax to DBMS-specific SQL syntax.	PCD_0004
Business	Functional	Build Potential Projects SQL. • Build key structure for the potential projects access. • Key elements: project team name and/or project team identifier. • SQL should be a Like clause because key identifier might not be fully known at this time and project name might vary.	PCD_0005
Base	Functional	Base Business Rule Processor class. • Define rules. • Execute rules on Create, Retrieve, Update, and Delete. • Perform any tertiary processing indicated by rules. • Report any errors.	PCD_0006

➤ Check whether project team is already on file.

➤ Prepare log data.

➤ Create new log entry.

Figure 25.2 Methods for Register Potential Project.

Action Method	Attribute	Expected Result	Test_ID
Build Potential Projects SQL statement	User data/ SQL statement	Loads the expected key values in the SQL Access structure.	LIB_T001
Execute SQL call	Potential Users data/ SQL statement	Executes an SQL Select statement.	LIB_T002
Interrogate Return Value	SQL Return Value	Checks the SQL Return Value and determines whether an error occurred.	LIB_T003
[Display Error Message]	SQL Return Code/ Error Message Handler	Displays an error message if the return value indicated failure.	LIB_T004
Prepare Log data	Data Entry screen	Data structure containing potential project data is built. (May simply be data entry from a datawindow.)	LIB_T005
Build Project Team key	Log key	Build a unique key for this project team.	LIB_T006
Obtain default registration form	Registration form/ registration form storage	Retrieve our default registration form from the storage area where it is being kept.	LIB_T007
Obtain library overview document	Overview document/ document storage	Retrieve the current overview document from the document storage area.	LIB_T008
Determine proposed timetable	Timetable source	Retrieve timetable data and determine when best times would be to meet with potential projects. Pick first, second, and third best. Might initially be a manual process based on a calendar.	LIB_T009
Insert new project team	Project team data	Create a new entry on the Potential Projects log.	LIB_T010
Store registration form	Registration form	Store the prepared registration form.	LIB_T011
Send registration form and proposed overview session schedule to the project team contact	Registration form Overview session schedule	Send the prepared registration form along with the proposed overview session schedule to the requesting project team.	LIB_T012

Figure 25.3 Test procedures defined for methods for Register Potential Project.

that must be taken to satisfy the test, including setting up data, progressing through the application to the point where the test can be done, and recovering data back to the point where it was before the test took place to ensure test integrity. An example of the test case definition is shown in Figure 25.5.

As you can see, we have a system preparation step that indicates where the test begins, or the application state required for the test to begin, followed by

Test Case	Test Objective	Expected Result
LIB_C001	Test for insufficient or no data sent	Error value should indicate required key data were not received.
LIB_C002	Test for valid data sent • Existing record	Error value should be returned indicating that the project already exists.
LIB_C003	Test for valid data sent • Nonexistent record	Return value should be OK.
LIB_C004	Execute SQL successfully	SQL should execute successfully. • Expected return should be No Record Found. Record Found should indicate an error.
LIB_C005	SQL execution fails	SQL statement cannot be executed. Database returns an error.
LIB_C006	Check for return code 0	SQL execution successful.
LIB_C007	Check for return code 100	SQL execution successful, record found.
LIB_C008	Check for return code not equal to 0 or 100	SQL execution failed.
LIB_C009	Display Project Exists message	Display error message indicating that project exists.
LIB_C010	Display SQL Access error message	Display error message as determined by the database.

Figure 25.4   Test cases defined for Register Potential Project.

steps detailing what actions are required as interaction, and ending with the test case shutdown process, which describes where the system should end up when the test case is complete. The key to remember is that logical method of testing involves following typical user interaction to test the methods. Physical class testing looks deeper into the works of actual objects and may not relate to method testing at all.

Physical class test definition

When we build our object test plan, another name for the physical class test definition, we first need to establish the hierarchy of the object classes used to build the object we wish to test. For our example, we will look at the potential projects SQL Access class (as mentioned above in the logical method test definition) and see just how different these two sets of tests are. The object hierarchy for the potential projects SQL Access class indicates that eight objects are involved:

- Base custom class
- Base interface class derived from base custom class
- Base SQL Access class derived from base custom class
- Base SQL Converter class derived from base interface class
- SQL Access class derived from base SQL Access class
- Potential projects SQL Access class derived from SQL Access class
- Base business rule interface class derived from base interface class
- Potential projects business class derived from base business rule interface class.

Test Case Data

Test Case ID:	LIB_C001		
Test Case Name:	Potential projects: test for no data sent to Build Key method		
Version:	1.0	Update Date:	August 27, 1995
		Author:	William T. Green

Test Case Definition

Description
Tests the eventuality that no data is sent to the Build Key method for registering potential projects.

Test Case Steps

Step	Step Data	Expected Result
1	Test case preparation	Advance through the application login functions to the point where the selection to add a new potential project can be made.
2	Select to add potential project	Selection made, data entry object is displayed to capture potential project data.
3	Select update method without capturing required data	SQL Access functionality initiated, Build Key method returns Const.Failed, indicating that the expected data were not passed.
4	Test case shutdown	Choose to ignore the message, close the processing object and return to point of entry.

Figure 25.5   Test case definition: test for no data sent to Build Key method.

To completely test our object, the potential projects SQL Access class, we need to gather the test plans for all of the objects involved. This begins to differ from method testing because once a test is completed, there is seldom a need to test it again. This means that once we test the functions of the base custom class that are used by our various derived classes, we do not need to test again for another object that is based on the base custom class. This requires that we build a slightly different testing structure than used previously. The first object carries all the overhead, however, so we still need to begin there.

If we look at our base custom class definition, we can see the test procedure IDs linked to the class methods. Figure 25.6 shows the class definition for the base custom class. The test procedures are those that begin with LIB_T (or OFR_T if defined in our class library).

Figure 25.6 Physical class definition: base custom class.

Physical Class Data

Physical Class ID:	PCD_0001		Version:	1.0
Physical Class Name:	Base custom class			
Author:	William Green		Update Date:	August 25, 1995

Object Identification Data

Functional Layer:	Base Ancestor	Ancestry:	NonVisualObject
Object Name:	cc_Base	Library:	Base Ancestors
Object Type:	Base		

Object Class Description/Purpose

Description
Base custom class: virtualizes methods for descendants.

Attributes

Scope		Type	Name	Default
Protected	Instance	Integer	ii_Return	Const.OK
Return value used in function calls				
Protected	Instance	Integer	ii_Severity	Const.Fatal
Severity code used for exception handling				
Protected	Instance	Boolean	ib_ContinueAction	True
Action code used to control logic flow				

(Continued)

Figure 25.6 *(Continued)*

Methods

Scope	Type	Prefix	Name	Link
(None)	Event		Constructor	PCD_T001
Description	Launch any object initialization routines.			
Specification	• Trigger *setup* event. • Post *init* event.			None
Overrides	None			
Extensions	Should not be extended unless a step is required between the setup and init events.			

Parameters	Description			Reference
(None)				(None)

Scope	Type	Prefix	Name	Link
(None)	Event		Destructor	PCD_T002
Description	Launch any functionality to be executed before object shutdown.			
Specification	• Trigger *closequery* event/function to determine validity of closing down the object.			MSG_0001
	• Determine whether object may be closed (*ContinueAction = True*).			MSG_0002
	• Fire *intfc_unload* function to deactive interfaces used if closedown approved (?- Should unload be fired from CloseQuery?).			MSG_0003
	• Close down object if all unload functions function OK.			
Overrides	None			
Extensions	Should not be overridden. Can be extended to add additional setup behavior.			

Parameters	Description			Reference
(None)				by Value

Scope	Type	Prefix	Name	Link
(None)	Event		CloseQuery	None
Description	Event fired from the Close/Destructor event to perform application processing before shutting down the object. Allows checking of data changed without being saved.			
Specification	• None.			
Overrides	None			
Extensions	Should not be overridden. Usually extended to change default object behavior.			

Parameters	Description			Reference
(None)				by Value

Scope	Type	Prefix	Name		Link
(None)	Event	cue_	Setup		PCD_T003
Description	Event fired from the constructor event to set up the object.				
Specification	• Fires the Interface Load function to instantiate required interfaces.				
Overrides	None				
Extensions	Should not be overridden. Usually extended to change default object behavior.				
Parameters			Description		Reference
(None)					by Value

Scope	Type	Prefix	Name		Link
(None)	Event	cue__	Init		PCD_T004
Description	Event posted from constructor to perform object initialization after the object build is complete.				
Specification	• Set default attribute values.				
Overrides	None				
Extensions	Should not be overridden. Can be extended to add additional setup behavior.				
Parameters			Description		Reference
(None)					by Value

Scope	Type	Prefix	Name		Link
Protected	Function	of_p	Intfc_Load		PCD_T005
Description	Function used to instantiate declarative interfaces.				
Specification	• Scan for declared interfaces. • Check whether interface loaded. • If not loaded, instantiate the interface. • Obtain a pointer to the interface. • Increment the usage count.				MSG_0004
Overrides	None				
Extensions	Can be extended by developer to add additional interface declarations.				
Parameters			Description		Reference
(None)					
ReturnValue			Success or Failure indicator		Constant

Scope	Type	Prefix	Name		Link
Protected	Function	of_p	Intfc_UnLoad		PCD_T006
Description	Function used to de_instantiate declarative interfaces.				
Specification	• Decrements interface usage counter. • If usage count reaches zero, interface can be unloaded completely.				

(Continued)

Figure 25.6   *(Continued)*

Overrides	None		
Extensions	Can be extended by developer to add additional interface declarations.		
Parameters	**Description**		**Reference**
(None)			
ReturnValue	Success or Failure indicator		Constant

Scope	Type	Prefix	Name	Link
Protected	Function	of_p	CheckException	PCD_T007
Description	Function used to process exceptions raised by the object/object class.			
Specification	• Exception Code F1001: Interface Load failed. • Exception Code F1002: Interface Unload failed. • Exception Code I2001: Shutdown aborted. Data have not been complctcly processed.			MSG_0005 MSG_0006 MSG_0007
Overrides	None			
Extensions	Can be extended by developer to add to the exception handling capabilities of the class			
Parameters/Return Value	**Description**			**Reference**
(None)				by Value
SeverityCode	Returns Severity code			Return

Note that some methods are defined as virtual methods ("None" in the specification details), and as such do not have associated test procedures. So when we begin to gather the test procedures for an object, we begin at the base level for that object's class definition and gather all test procedures for the object. We gather these into an object test plan, which in reality is nothing more than a cross-reference of test procedures that apply to an object.

Figure 25.7 shows the object test plan for our Potential Projects Data Access object, beginning with the base class definition.

You can see each object definition layer in this cross-reference detailing the testing that is needed to ensure that each method on the object is completely tested. Each test procedure includes the testing that is needed to make sure the method functions correctly on the object. For example, Figure 25.8 shows the tests we feel are required for the base custom classes Destructor event.

Each of the test cases listed can be broken down into detailed testing steps if desired. (In many cases, using the debugger or a trace utility is sufficient. This can be indicated in the test case instructions, or you can detail the steps necessary as a test checklist for the object.)

Preparing Test Cases

When you build test cases for your application, there are two different processes and results based on whether you are testing the logical methods or the physical object functionality. Logical method testing is actually easier to

Test Plan ID	Test Case Description
PCD_0001	*Base Custom Class*
PCD_T001	Test Constructor
PCD_T002	Test Destructor method
PCD_T003	Setup method: declare object behavior
PCD_T004	Init event: test object initialization procedures
PCD_T005	Interface Load method: test instantiation of interfaces
PCD_T006	Interface Unload method: test unloading of instantiated interfaces
PCD_T007	Check Exception method: test exception processing
PCD_0002	*Base SQL Access Class*
PCD_T008	Test Interface Load of SQL Converter interface
PCD_T009	Test Unload of SQL Converter interface
PCD_T010	Test that the Build SQL method fires off the correct sequence of events
PCD_T011	Test the Execute SQL method
	etc.

Figure 25.7   Test plan cross-reference: base custom class.

Test Plan Data

Test Plan ID:	PCD_T002			
Test Plan Name:	Test Destructor method: base custom class			
Version:	1.0		Update Date:	July 7, 1995
			Author:	William T. Green

Test Plan Definition

Description
Test the Destructor event for the base custom class.

Test Plan Objectives and Expected Results

Test Objective	Expected Result	Test Case ID
Fire the CloseQuery method	Initiates the object's CloseQuery event.	PCD_C003
Test CloseQuery OK	Result from CloseQuery indicates OK to close: close processing should continue.	PCD_C004
Test Unload Interfaces	All instantiated interfaces should be unloaded.	PCD_C005
Test Discontinue Close	Close or unload processing indicates that object may not be closed; halt the close process.	PCD_C006
Test Continue Close	Object should close.	PCD_C007

Figure 25.8   Test procedure: Base custom class test destructor method.

remember as the testing a user could perform once the test case was developed, and in fact the user should be involved in the test case design. Physical class testing requires a developer to monitor message flow within objects and between objects. This requires one of two things: the use (and knowledge of) the PowerBuilder debugger or the use of a built-in trace/debug function.

Logical test cases

Logical test cases are much easier to prepare than physical test procedures for the simple reason that the logical test is based on the interaction between the user and the objects. There is some human involvement there. For example, consider the test procedures for the testing of Registering Potential Projects. The first method is to build the SQL required to create a new log entry. When we look at the test procedures, we see three: test with invalid data, test with valid data but existing project, and test with valid data but nonexistent project. The first two result in failure of the process and the third allows continuation.

If we now look at the actual test steps involved, you will notice something else. Our test cases always start with a Set the State of the Application step, which is a short way of saying logon, get to the menu, and select the correct option. (It also means make sure the data are prepped.) We also always end with a Reset Application State step, which is a short way of saying "Remove any added data, back out changes, and get the application back to where it was before this step started." This makes sure that each of our tests forces the QA person to make sure that the data are correct before moving on to the next test.

In between are the steps we should take. Figure 25.9 shows the steps required for the Invalid Data test.

Step	Step Data	Expected Result
1	System prep: Select option "Register New Potential Project"	Advance through the application login functions to the point where the selection to add a new potential project can be made.
2	Select to add potential project	Selection made, data entry object is displayed to capture potential project data.
3	Enter some details required for building the key, but do not complete the entry process	Data Entry function: data entered on the screen.
4	Select update method	SQL Access functionality initiated, Build Key method returns Const.Failed, indicating that the expected data were not passed.
5	Shutdown processing	Choose to ignore the message, close the processing object, and return to point of entry.

Figure 25.9 Test steps: invalid data entered.

Step	Step Data	Expected Result
1	System prep: select option "Register New Potential Project"	Advance through the application login functions to the point where the selection to add a new potential project can be made.
2	Select to add potential project	Selection made, data entry object is displayed to capture potential project data.
3	Enter project details for an existing project	Data Entry function: data entered on the screen.
4	Select update method	SQL Access functionality initiated, Build Key method returns Const.Failed, indicating that the project team already exists on either Potential Projects Log or Active Projects Log.
5	Shutdown processing	Acknowledge message; return to TestStart state.

Figure 25.10   Test steps: valid data entered, but project team exists.

Figure 25.10 shows the steps required to check for valid data entry for an existing project.

Finally, Figure 25.11 shows the valid data being entered that will ultimately be added to the database. Note the reset step at the end.

Each set of steps can easily be recorded with an automated testing tool to be used again later for regression testing (more on that later).

Step	Step Data	Expected Result
1	System prep: select option "Register New Potential Project"	Advance through the application login functions to the point where the selection to add a new potential project can be made.
2	Select to add potential project	Selection made, data entry object is displayed to capture potential project data.
3	Enter details for a new project team	Data Entry function: data entered on the screen.
4	Select update method	SQL Access function passes, project team passes remaining tests. (Project team may be added to Potential Projects log.)
5	Shutdown processing	Check whether project team was added, remove the data, and return to Test Case Start state. This includes removal of updated data.

Figure 25.11   Test steps: valid data entered, but project team does not exist.

Physical class and object testing

Testing physical classes is much more difficult. You need to be able to measure and track the effects of messages within objects, making sure that events are fired in the correct sequence. Automated testing tools still do not track individual events, but there are ways of doing this using an automated testing tool such as SQA Test Suite.

Using Automated Testing Tools

Using an automated testing tool is key to successful testing. I believe that the testing tool provides a far more accurate test of features than the human eye, unless you are lucky enough to find someone who is capable of focusing on test results for hours on end without missing any details. Automated testing tools enable you not only to accomplish accurate tests, but also to rerun the test suite multiple times with the same set of procedures.

SQA Test Suite is the tool I recommend most often to my clients. It has an easy-to-use interface that allows you to gather test cases and combine them into a test suite. Its visual object comparator can look deep into an object and allows you to preset expected results before performing any testing, which ensures much more accurate test results. Its reporting capabilities and defect tracking are also superb. The only drawback to the tool is that it is currently not multiplatform, so tests are limited to the Windows environment (Windows 3.1, Windows 95, Windows NT).

Segue's QA Partner is very competitive with SQA Test Suite in that the interface is relatively easy to use, and it provides two features not provided in SQA Test Suite. The first is the ability to establish a test state, which is where the test begins and also where the test should recover to. This feature allows more predictable unattended testing. The second feature is multiplatform availability. QA Partner runs on most of the major platforms (including MAC, UNIX, and Windows NT). The reporting capabilities and defect tracking capabilities are not as advanced as those of SQA, but are sufficient to track the defects in your system.

Microsoft Test has not gotten much press recently, but has improved greatly from the tool I saw several years ago. It does not have the capability to record and monitor the datawindow control in PowerBuilder, as it is a more vanilla testing tool, but does record accurate test scripts and provide decent reports.

Two other tools are available that I am less familiar with: Sterling Testpro and Mercury Interactive's Winrunner.

Building a regression test suite

A regression test suite is a collection of test cases used to determine whether changes made to a system (or even a single class) change the functionality of the system in such a way that it would be considered a defect. The regression test suite should be run with each build of a system to ensure that continuous quality standards are met. Using an automated testing tool allows you to build regression test suites that can be run unattended, or at least automated. Defects are tracked and you end up with a more reliable maintenance release.

Summary

This chapter dealt with the two different forms of testing we perform on objects developed. The first is the logical method test, where methods defined in the design phase are measured and general functionality is effectively measured. The second is the physical class test, where the actual methods of an object are tested to ensure that the method performs as expected and that logic flow is consistent with the object's design.

Finally, we discussed the use of automated testing tools to provide a more consistent and accurate means of capturing test cases, which can be reused to create effective regression test suites. Testing is the portion of the development effort that can quite easily expand the life-cycle if it is not performed and monitored correctly.

26

Implementation and Maintenance

Introduction

"Hit the road!" How many times have you wished this sentiment on your application? You've worked long and hard to reach this point and all you want to do now is hand the system over to someone else and move on. And then the first user call comes in.

"I really like the system, Bill, but you know that one window. . . ." And then it begins! A veritable flood of enhancement requests, hopefully very few bug reports (if we have done our job correctly), and an occasional whimper of "But the mainframe system allowed me to do this!"

You should think of application development as an iceberg. What you see above the waterline is only one-third of the total picture. What is hidden below the surface, out of view, can sink the Titanic: maintenance.

Maintenance costs typically exceed the development cost of the system over its lifetime *by more than 200 percent.* This is an important reality check. When a user agrees to pay $50,000 for a new system, how many of us tell the user that he or she will spend another $100,000 maintaining the system? Oh, by the way, you also have to pay for runtime access to production systems, upgrades to the development tool, and so on.

Application development is not cheap. System maintenance is even less forgiving.

Chapter Objectives

The goals of this chapter are to discuss the development and execution of an implementation strategy and a strategy for maintaining the system once it is in the production area.

Implementation

The big day has arrived. You have called the users to tell them that the QA group has signed off on the system, and you are ready to roll out the application to the user community and change their lives forever. A user replies "What? Already? But we don't have all of our equipment ready yet."

You had checked everything you felt was necessary for the implementation to take place smoothly and without any hassles. Now what? Your next review is less than 3 days away and this system will count 80 percent toward your getting a raise!

You can avoid this situation. We have developed the Application Deployment Checklist, a simple, expandable list of items we feel must be checked at the minimum, and scrutinized in great depth on the other end of the scale.

Chapter 33 goes into detail for each element of the checklist, so here we simply summarize the events you should go through before the users get their hands on your hard work.

Environment preparation

The first item on our agenda is preparation. Getting the environment ready for your application can sometimes feel like a root canal. You know you are not going to enjoy it, but you can apply some Novocain. Be prepared yourself before trying to prepare something as complex as a client-server environment. Our Environment Preparation Checklist helps us to prevent some elements from falling through the cracks. It has saved our bacon before, and will again. Table 26.1 shows the Deployment Checklist for environment preparation.

This table outlines the preparation steps that should be checked, double-checked, and then checked once more to make sure the gremlins of application deployment have not slipped into the process. The preparation is important. It is also important that it be done well ahead of time. The more preparatory work done before you roll out, the less chance there is of something going wrong, because it is only when time is running out that these elements choose to go wrong. Preparation also serves as documentation that you have done your job.

Installation preparation

When you are ready to install your software, you have another list of things that can go wrong. We have gathered these into the Installation Preparation Checklist. Table 26.2 shows the Implementation Checklist for the building of the application.

As you can see, the three categories cover the details we feel are necessary to track in preparing the application for installation on the users' machines. But there is yet another element we need to consider: The Users' Environment.

User environment

The users' environment can have a significant impact on how you implement. They will probably have other commercial applications. You should know about

TABLE 26.1 Application Deployment Checklist: Environment Preparation

Network preparation	Scheduled	Completed
LAN/WAN testing		
Add-user process		
Communication protocol		
Gateway requirements		
Server configuration test		
Create user groups		
Database preparation		
Database turnover request		
Database load		
Database access requests		
Environment preparation		
Documentation distribution		
Application installation routines		
Environment preparation		
User training		
Prepare user training		
Environment training		
Communications		
Set up user training		
Perform user training		
Application considerations		
Application bug reports		
Application change requests		
Application version control		
Production source control		
Other considerations		
Mainframe turnover procedures		
User equipment		
Additional hardware and software		

TABLE 26.2 Implementation Checklist: Installation Preparation

Installation build	Scheduled	Completed
Freeze source code		
Copy to secure location		
Update version information		
Optimize libraries		
Build dynamic libraries (PBDs or DLLs)		
Build application PBR		
Create project file		
Run Project Make utility		
Archive all .EXE, .PBD/.DLLs, and .PBRs		
Installation prep		
Refresh deployment kit .DLLs		
Make sure DK .DLLs are included		
Include application files		
Include routines to update INI files or registries		
If ODBC is used, include routines to update ODBC data sources		
Include setup program instructions		
Test on user machine		
Application installation		
Application directories created		
Development tool directories created		
WIN.INI updated		
ODBC data sources updated		
Program group and items created		
Run application, test key features		

these, but they have less impact than one particular element: another Power-Builder application. Typically users are set up with their applications on a server. The runtime DLLs usually also reside on the server. This means you generally have one area where the runtime DLLs are located. What happens if your application is built on a different point release than another system? You need to be aware of problems that can be caused solely by the users' environment.

We built a table that describes the users' environment, which helps us to understand what they have on the machine that could have an effect on what we are doing. The Software and Hardware Environment checklist is shown in Table 26.3.

TABLE 26.3 Implementation Checklist: Hardware and Software

Resource	Minimum	Verified
CPU		
Local hard disk available		
System memory		
Video resolution and colors		
Screen size		
CD-ROM drive		

OS Software	Minimum	Excluded	Verified
DOS	5.0	6.0	
Windows	3.1, Win95	NT, OS/2	

Software	Version	Verified

The bottom part of this checklist is where other PowerBuilder applications should be listed. Make sure you get the version numbers of the underlying software products as well.

Summary

These checklists help us to determine and track the elements that affect our implementation strategy. These checklists help us to avoid some of the pitfalls that await unwary application deployment teams, and they will help you, too.

Maintenance

Once our system is in the production environment, we need to perform maintenance. This can vary from a simple text change on a window to upgrades of the development tool, to major additions of new functionality. This can often lead to a completely new deployment of the application, where the checklists described above come back into play, but more typically means replacing a dynamic library (PBD or DLL) or executable (EXE). Keeping track of the maintenance and separating different efforts is the hard part.

Source code branching

When your first release goes live, you can be assured of two things.

- You will begin work on the next release.
- You will need to make changes to the current release.

This often means keeping two, sometimes three, sets of code for the same objects. The process is called branching by makers of source control utilities. Figure 26.1 depicts this process graphically.

The problem is in how you merge the changes made to the existing release into your new development effort. These changes become a point release. Implementing a point release can often be as painful as implementing a full-blown release. We have developed a strategy that allows us to implement maintenance changes in such a way to have less impact on both the original release and the upcoming new release of the application. The facility is called the automatic correction facility (ACF). We create an ACF PBL that is empty at implementation. The library is placed first in the search path. When an object is changed, we place the modified object into the ACF library. This allows us to roll out point releases in a single library, and it also serves to keep track of changes made to the objects in your application.

This is fine for deployment, but how do you keep the various changes you make in line with both the original release and your next major release? The answer is version control, that ugly concept most of us see as little more than an annoyance even though we all know that it is necessary. Of course, we all

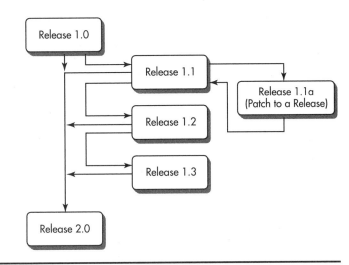

- Build first release of project (v 1.00)
- Begin development of next release (v 2.00)
- Maintenance for production release is required (v 1.1)
- Another maintenance release is required (v 1.2)
- A patch to a maintenance release is required (v 1.1a)

Release 1.0

Release 1.1

Release 1.1a (Patch to a Release)

Release 1.2

Release 1.3

Release 2.0

Figure 26.1   Source branching complicates source code control.

use the rationale that the source code maintenance programs out there do not handle PowerBuilder objects very well.

How do version control packages work? They all work differently, unfortunately; some automatically version every change, others require manual setting of versions. Regardless of the vendor's approach, we are all faced with the same dilemma: How do we control which version of the source is to be used for a particular build? PowerBuilder forces the issue. There is no means to tell the Project Painter what version of the source code to use, so the versioning must be done before the build. This means following one of two approaches: Apply versioning before changes or apply versioning only at build time.

Versioning before changes.   The method of applying versioning before changes is one that is often used. What this means is that once a build is complete (for example, v 1.0), the source code for that version is frozen and we begin a completely new build using new libraries. The version 1.0 code is copied into a new set of libraries and all modifications are made to this library.

Versioning at build time.   Versioning at build time implies that you continue to work from the same set of base code, but assign different version labels to objects as they are modified. When it becomes time to create a build of the application, you first create a separate "build" library, which you add to the top of your search path. Then, using the registration directory, you elect to Take a specified version

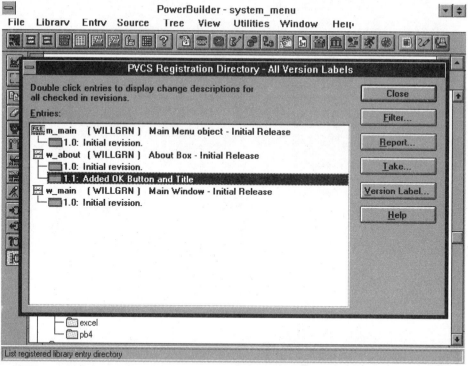

Figure 26.2   Registration Directory dialog showing multiple versions.

label. Figure 26.2 shows the Registration Directory dialog window. You can use the Filter option to filter out all objects not pertaining to the build and then select all of the objects, or you can select the objects one at a time.

The target for the Take is your build library. Figure 26.3 shows the target directory specified as build11.pbl.

When you compile the application, the modified objects are included and your build incorporates only the changes specified. If you use the Project Painter, you will be prompted and asked whether you would like to assign a new version label for the objects included in this build. Depending on your approach, you may or may not already have a version label. Figure 26.4 shows this dialog box.

Once completed, an option in the Project Painter becomes available to list all of the objects in the build and show which revision is being used. Figure 26.5 depicts this scenario. (The appearance of this dialog has been modified slightly to show as much information as possible on one screen.)

Of course, new and improved methods will come about as time goes on and we learn more about version control and how it works. One thing brought to us by PowerBuilder 5.0 is ObjectCycle. ObjectCycle is the built-in source code versioning software built by Powersoft specifically for PowerBuilder. It func-

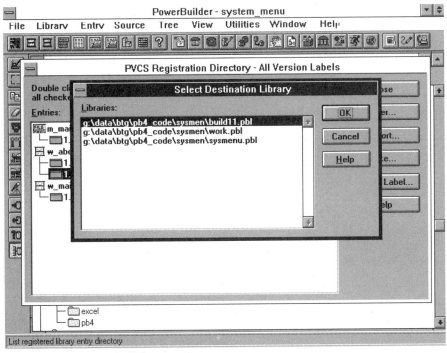

Figure 26.3 Targeting the Take operation.

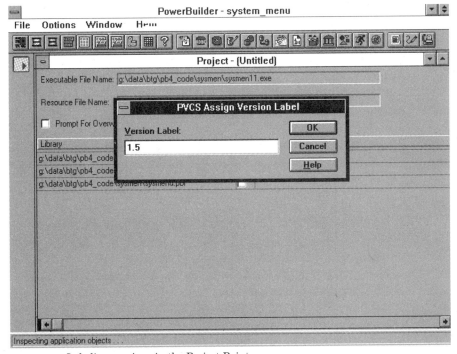

Figure 26.4 Labeling versions in the Project Painter.

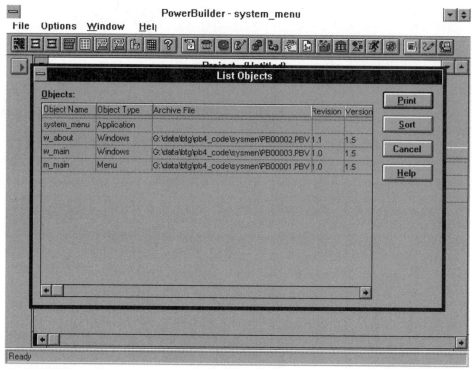

Figure 26.5 Reviewing which versions are included in a build.

tions as an Object Manager using a Relational DBMS to store version information. You can use Object Cycle to create a new release of your project.

Development tool upgrades

Generally, every 12 to 18 months, vendors release new versions of their software. While we developers gather around a CRT with feverish excitement to view the new features and gadgets that so often accompany the release, we all know the sinking feeling in our stomach: The user will want this feature, too. New development efforts with a new release of software are not affected as much as existing project maintenance teams are. We can see how the improved performance and features will benefit users, but justifying the expense to the user can leave you sweating.

Major Problem #1: You have built an extensive regression test suite to process any changes to the system. It works well. Defects are virtually unheard of in your system. (Yes, it is a dream, but I am allowed to do that.) Now you want to upgrade to the new version of software. But guess what happens when you do? Your regression test suite no longer functions as designed. You also need a new version of the testing tool to verify the results.

This usually happens 2 to 3 months after the release of the software, so you should really schedule an application upgrade to occur after the testing tool is upgraded.

What happens if you get a new version of your operating system? Now you add another step to the mix. You have to wait for the development tool to be released on that platform. Then you have to wait for the testing tools to catch up with the development tool. Suddenly it is 5 or 6 months down the road. If you are working with mission-critical data, this delay can only be considered necessary. You will have to wait—not an easy thing to do with users breathing down your neck to provide new features in the application that you know the next release of the software already has built-in.

Add one more step to the mix. If you are using a class library, you often have to wait until the library is converted and tested before you can even think about it. If we added any more, we would end up upgrading our software right around the time the *next* release of tools is becoming available. Keep this in mind when you want to jump onto the tool upgrade bandwagon. It is not easy and requires steady discipline and knowledge of the dangers involved.

Summary

You can see how the deployment and maintenance of your application depend on Murphy's Law, which says that the importance of deploying a new release of your application is directly proportional to the length of time it takes for vendors to catch up to the point that you can actually perform the upgrade.

We hope our checklists will save you some headaches in the future. They have helped for us. Hopefully, vendors will become more responsive to major upgrades in software of all kinds and help us to meet our deadlines. There are so many things that can go wrong, it is almost flabbergasting to realize how many applications we do deploy and upgrade successfully. But then again, someone once said, "This *is* rocket science."

IV

Documentation Development

Introduction

Accurate documentation enhances reusability. This part is not about the pristine glories of perfect documentation in theory. This part is about real-world documentation for real-world objects. Because time and budget constraints often squeeze the documentation efforts, it is essential to develop tools and methods that allow the accurate documentation of objects you have developed.

The primary requirement of the documentation you produce is that it be useful. It must provide meaningful information to the people who are going to use the objects and classes you have developed. A wealth of technical detail is useless if the person whom you intend to use your objects comes away from your documentation thinking, "What in the world do I do next?" How do we achieve this goal of ultimate usability? By considering the needs of the user. Try to imagine what the user wants to know about your object. The user wants to know why you would ever use this thing. The user wants to know how you use it—down to specifics—not just the fact that it exists. The user wants to know what information comes back from the function, object, attribute, or class. The user wants to know any potential side effects—any related objects that may be affected by operations on the object you are documenting.

Documentation is communication. Therefore, you must consider the tone, the target audience, and the message. You need to establish who the primary user of any given document is and aim the writing style and content so that it provides the most useful information to that person. For instance, requirements documentation is targeted toward the systems designers, the people who are going to actually design a given set of objects based on a set of requirements. The design documentation is aimed at the implementers, the people who would build a set of objects based on a design. The structure and the information content of these two kinds of documentation differ according to the targeted audiences and their needs. In the following chapters we examine the different types of documentation and their common and divergent charac-

TABLE P4.1 Document Types

Document Type	Purpose	Target Audience	Tone
Requirements	Specifies the requirements that will be met by the system or set of objects you are designing.	Logical designers	Succinct, technical, detailed, unambiguous
Method or attribute definition	Defines the attributes or methods used to satisfy the requirements.	Physical designers	Technical, aware of implementation issues
User how-to manual	Instructs the user in the typical operation of your system.	End user	Friendly, nontechnical, procedural
User reference manual	Provides a complete reference to the operation of your system.	End user	Complete, categorized, indexed

teristics. An example of some of the differing tones that your documents must adopt is shown in Table P4.1.

I would like to encourage a mental discipline in which we think in terms of a hierarchy of documentation classes. Mirroring our base object classes, each documentation object is descended from common base classes. Each descendant document class has increasingly specialized attributes and behaviors as you descend down the tree. A base documentation class contains attributes such as content, type of documentation, and target audience. Each of these objects could easily have some type of template attached to help you generate standard, easily entered, easily used documentation that fits each increasingly specific class. As we develop different types of documents, I will show how each fits into such a hierarchy. Figure P4.1 shows an example of a document class hierarchy.

You must remember that documentation always gets the short end of the stick in a project that is tight on budget, tight on resources, tight on time, or some combination of all of the above, and—guess what—all projects are! Part of the goal of these chapters is to develop documentation standards and routines and some automated tools that keep the task of documentation from being burdensome and time-consuming. The fact is that if documentation is burdensome and time-consuming, it will not get done. And if the documentation is not done, the objects will not be used.

Part Objectives
Develop a documentation roadmap

Throughout this part we deal with the specifics of documenting each phase of a development effort. We examine the types of documents and the information

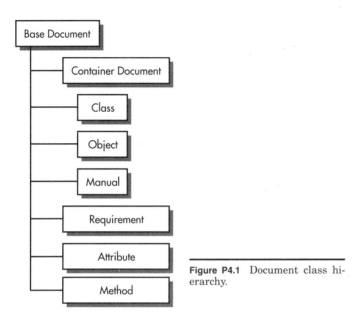

Figure P4.1 Document class hierarchy.

that makes up each one. By the end of this part, you should have a clear idea of the steps needed to produce useful and accurate documentation for design, development, and deployment of your projects.

Develop the necessary forms

We develop most of the forms you need for a complete documentation effort. You can also extend the base document to accommodate any specialized needs of your project.

Develop the documentation

You will see that each document feeds or "spawns" other documents. Just as the phases of a project lead naturally from one to the next, the information pertinent to each phase flows from each supporting document to the next. Our methodology is designed to maximize the benefit you derive from the reuse of information.

Explore automation

We believe that your documentation will be more successful if you use automation to leverage your information into thorough, accurate documents. We show you tools that can help you automate your documentation. We also give you some tips on developing your own automated documentation tools.

On-line help

On-line help is crucial to the usability of any software project. We show you some proven techniques that will enable you to provide your users with help files that really help.

Develop training

We examine the issues you must face when you are preparing training sessions and materials for your users. We cover the details of training, including the question of whether to build or buy.

Methodologies Introduced

We use the Green/Brown method of requirement analysis. In addition, we introduce the concept of document morphing as an extension of our object synthesis methodology. By document morphing we mean the creation of new types of documents from previously built ones. An example of this is the morphing of requirements documents into a features and benefits treatise.

27

Types of Documents

Chapter Objectives

This chapter has a purpose that may seem mundane, or even tedious. Do not be fooled. The organization of your documentation will make or break its usefulness. If you understand the types of documents, their purpose, and where in the project they apply, the task of documenting your project moves from tedium to something of an artistic expression. When you are finished with this chapter, you will be prepared to organize your documents for maximum clarity and content, as the information relates to each project phase.

Classifications of Documents

There are many types of documents that must accompany a programming project. Each serves a particular purpose and targets a particular audience. Some, such as the list of requirements, provide essential analysis information to the designers of the application or library. Others, such as the physical object definitions, provide guidance to the developers.

The documents that we will discuss are classified by project phase. The phases for which the project documentation will be presented are as follows:

- *Analysis:* This is the period during which the goals and requirements of the project are gathered and prioritized.

- *Logical design:* During logical design, requirements are mapped to methods and attributes that satisfy them. Logical class definitions, which group related methods and attributes, are also introduced at this stage.

- *Physical design:* Physical design relates the logical design to PowerBuilder objects, and includes a breakdown of objects into their class hierarchies. The physical design documents provide guidance to the developers as they create the objects necessary to complete the application or library.

- *Deployment:* Deployment is the point at which the application or library is released to its users. The documentation for this phase includes user manuals, technical manuals, and on-line help.

First, we give a short treatment of the essential characteristics of these project phases and the documents that accompany them. Then we cover the specific types of documents for each phase.

Analysis

The documents produced during the analysis phase gather and define the characteristics of the application or class library. Additionally, the analysis documents help to establish completion goals for the project. That is, by establishing a record of the requirements that the project must satisfy, the analysis documents provide a ready measure by which to judge a project's completion.

The benefits provided by the project are also addressed during the analysis phase. The benefits information provides a basis by which the project may be justified, and helps prioritize the requirements according to their real value.

Information gathered during the analysis phase is important in the construction of the user and technical manuals. The requirements and navigation workflow documents, the test plan, and the description of expected benefits contribute greatly to the content and organization of the final manuals that accompany project deployment.

Design

The design documents cover two distinct stages of a project: logical design and physical design. During logical design, the methods and attributes that satisfy a given requirement are grouped together to form logical class definitions. These class definitions do not relate directly to the final physical implementation of the project, but rather provide a bridge between the analysis documents and the documents that detail the specific implementation of the required functionality. Physical design documents, on the other hand, relate directly to the objects that must be developed to complete the project. The major difference between logical and physical is that logical is definition, whereas physical is design.

Logical design. Logical design documents define the logical characteristics and structure of the application or library. The logical design documents are long on architectural information and short on implementation details.

The logical design documents typically relate directly to the analysis documents:

- Requirements spawn activities.

- Activities spawn methods, methods spawn attributes. Because methods act on attributes, the definition of attributes springs from the definition of the methods that act on those attributes.

- Methods and attributes are grouped to define logical classes.

The classes defined during the logical design phase are functional groups based on requirements, as they are satisfied by methods and attributes. These classes may reflect actual implementation, but typically do not. Instead, they provide a necessary step between the requirements developed during the analysis phase and the physical implementation developed during the physical design phase.

Physical design. The physical design documents define the actual physical structure of the application or library. The class hierarchy is developed during the physical design phase, as are the definitions of the objects that must be developed. The logical design documents provide the information necessary to develop the physical design documents. In turn, the physical design documents provide the developers with implementation details at the level of objects, methods, and attributes. Object method test plans are also developed at the physical design stage.

Deployment

The documents that apply to the deployment phase are the various user and technical manuals that accompany the application or class library when it is introduced to the user community. The user documents are an important part of the user interface and must be carefully tailored to the needs of the users of your software.

In conjunction with on-line help, the user manuals guide the user's interaction with your application or library. The manuals must be accurate and up-to-date to reflect the current state of the software.

The user documents are also an important sales tool, even if the program is only for internal use. The manuals should show the benefits offered by the application or library, the purpose for its existence, and the steps the user will follow to apply the software to a business or programming challenge.

The most effective user manuals incorporate the following characteristics:

- Statement of the purpose of the software
- Statement of the benefits derived through the use of the software

- A description of the tasks that the software addresses, and the steps necessary to accomplish them

- Techniques for maximizing productivity through the use of the application or class library

These characteristics, and the ways to organize your manuals around them, are discussed in more detail in later chapters.

The content of the user documents can be derived largely from the analysis and physical design documents:

- The analysis documents provide goals, tasks, and benefits

- The physical design documents provide details of the application's or library's implementation

What follows is a short list of the suggested documents, organized under the above classifications.

Analysis Documents

The analysis documents describe and record the requirements that must be met by the application or class library. Analysis documents include the following:

- Requirements definitions
- Requirements cost-benefit analysis
- Navigation workflow
- Object map
- Test plan

Requirements definition

The requirements documents are developed based on user and developer interviews. The intent of the requirements documents is to capture, as completely as possible, statements of the desired functionality of the final product. You should associate each requirement with its purpose—what will be accomplished if the requirement is met. Closely related to the purpose, but not identical, is the expected benefit of the requirement. The purpose describes the outcome of satisfying the requirement. The benefit describes the way that the business or programming environment is enhanced if the requirement is met. Finally, you should note the identity of the submitter of each requirement. This helps if you need to find out more information about the requirement. Note also that the submitter's position in your company may affect the priority assigned to that requirement. Chapter 10 gives an example of requirements definition for a class library.

Requirements cost/benefit analysis

The requirements cost/benefit analysis helps to delineate the importance of requested features. One model we have used with great success is the $100 model described in Chapter 10. Each requirement is listed, and the users, managers, and others who have submitted requirements are asked to "spend" approximately $100, distributed among all of the requirements, with more money spent on the most important ones. This model helps to prioritize the requirements list, without resorting to lengthy theoretical studies.

Navigation workflow

The navigation workflow document is developed to help direct the development of an application. The purpose of the navigation workflow is to illustrate graphically the steps a user will take to move through the interface of an application in order to achieve a goal. The navigation workflow includes references to specific visual objects, but not their implementation.

Object map

The object map relates the graphical representations in the navigation workflow to ancestor objects and base class constructs. This helps direct the designers and developers in the correct choice of base objects, and the relationships between them. The object map also gives the benefit of documenting the application's use of the base class objects.

Test plan

The test plan is one of the most important analysis documents. The test plan developed during the analysis phase describes the indicators that will enable the designers and developers to determine whether the requirements have been met. It is a broad, general test plan, rather than a detailed, function-level plan.

Design Documents

The design documents define the way that the application or class library satisfies the list of requirements. The design portion of the project is broken into two phases: logical and physical. The logical design stage consists of associating methods and attributes with specific requirements, and then grouping those methods and attributes to form logical class definitions. The physical design stage is where the class hierarchies and the definitions of the physical PowerBuilder objects are developed. The documents that accompany each stage are similar, but each has a distinct target audience and purpose.

Logical design

The logical design documents are targeted toward the designers of the physical objects. The logical design documents bridge the gap between analysis and implementation. The analysis portion produces requirements that must be satisfied. The logical design stage defines methods and attributes, grouped into classes, such that those requirements can be satisfied.

The logical design documents are as follows:

- Method definitions
- Attribute definitions
- Class definitions

Method definitions.   Each method is linked to one or more requirements. The method definitions at the logical design phase consist of the name of the method, its purpose, and any attributes that are affected by the method. The physical design and implementation may result in many methods with the same name used in different classes. You can see an illustration of the techniques used to create method definitions in Chapters 11 and 21.

Attribute definitions.   Each attribute is linked to one or more methods and one or more requirements. An attribute should not exist in a vacuum. That is, it cannot exist if it is not manipulated in some way by some method. Likewise, each attribute is spawned as a result of a requirement.

Just as with methods, the physical design and implementation may result in many attributes with the same name used in different classes.

Class definitions.   Logical class definitions group methods and attributes together to satisfy one or more requirements. The logical classes each have a purpose and an expected benefit. Each satisfies one or more requirements. The classes defined in the logical design phase represent logical groupings, but they do not include or dictate the physical implementations of those classes.

Physical design

The physical design documents show implementation details at the object level of the application or library. During the physical design phase, the logical class definitions are used to dictate the formation of physical objects. Class hierarchies are developed at this stage. The resulting documents include definitions for each PowerBuilder library entry.

PowerBuilder object definitions.   Objects (PBL entries) are defined at this stage. Each PowerBuilder library entry should be documented at the object level, listing the object, its methods, and its attributes, with the interfaces well-defined. The details of the underlying code are not present in these documents.

At this stage, the important items to be included in each document are the name of the object, its purpose, and the attributes and methods used to interface the objects to the other objects in the application or library. The documents should also include information about the ancestry of each object. Include both ancestors and immediate descendants in each object definition. You will encounter the following PowerBuilder objects:

- Visual objects (windows and user objects)
- Nonvisual objects (custom classes)
- Applications
- Menus
- Functions
- Datawindows
- Structures
- Pipelines

Deployment Documents: User and Technical Manuals

The user and technical manuals are deployed with the application or library. They provide the user or developer with the information necessary to productively use your software. Some of the different user manuals are as follows:

- *The user's how-to manual is organized by goals and tasks.* Each objective that the user seeks to accomplish should be included, with a clear set of steps to achieve that goal.
- *The user's reference guide is typically organized by an alphabetical index.* All features of the software are included in the reference guide.
- *The developer's how-to should be organized by application constructs as reflected in objects.* The tasks that the developer faces consist of the proper application of class library and application-specific objects to the solution of programming problems.
- *The deployment checklist provides a systematic, detailed list of deployment tasks and responsibilities.* Keeping a deployment checklist and following it rigorously helps prevent essential tasks from falling through the cracks.

Some of the technical manuals that accompany an application or class library are as follows:

- *Class/object reference:* The object reference draws directly from the documents developed during the physical design phase. Every object in the application or class library should be included, with all attributes and methods listed.

- *Function / method reference:* Once again, these documents are derived from the physical design documents. Each method or function should be clearly described. List the object to which the method belongs. List the purpose, the calling syntax, the attributes that are affected, and the return type.

- *Data types / attributes reference (variables, structures, constants):* Constants and structures should be listed with their meanings and contents. Attributes can be listed separately from the objects to which they belong, or they may simply be shown as part of the documentation of the objects.

More details pertaining to the contents and construction of these manuals can be found in Chapter 28.

Deployment Documents: The Knowledge Base

The knowledge base is a living document that expands over the life of the software. As new questions are posed and answered, they should be added to the frequently asked questions (FAQ) list. Likewise, as new techniques for using the capabilities of the application or library are discovered, they should be added to the tips and techniques (TAT) section of the knowledge base. A well-maintained knowledge base can be a valuable asset, helping with support and extending the range of your technical personnel.

Deployment Documents: On-Line Help

On-line help is the first place your users will look for assistance in carrying out the day-to-day use of your software. Therefore, the on-line help must be complete, containing both how-to information and reference information for all features. Construction of on-line help is discussed in detail in Chapter 30.

Summary

This chapter presented an overview of the types of documents that accompany a development project. You saw that the documents can be classified by project phase:

- Analysis
- Logical design (definition)
- Physical design
- Deployment

We described the characteristics and purposes of each type of document for each project phase. Armed with this information, you can be assured that each aspect of your project is covered and that the results of your efforts are maintainable and usable.

Documentation Development

Introduction

The development of the documentation to accompany your application or class library is one of the most important and the most daunting steps you will face. As you read this chapter, you will learn some of the techniques we have used to strengthen the connection between the documents and the audience each document is intended to reach. You will discover how to develop each needed document based on the design documents that led to the creation of each object or application. We do not develop the complete production cycle for these manuals, but rather illustrate techniques that will improve your documentation's content and cost-effectiveness.

We cover techniques for the development of user manuals and technical manuals for an application. You will see that the user manual can be derived from the workflow diagram originally used to organize and specify the application. We show how the technical manual for an application can be based on the object map (used in the design phase to link the workflow diagram to the base class objects.) When you apply these techniques, you will speed the development of your documentation and organize the information in a way that is meaningful and helpful to the target audience.

We describe the development of technical reference manuals for class libraries based on the class hierarchy diagram. You will learn the fundamental requirements for complete, accurate, and informative documentation of each object in a class library, as well as techniques you can use to extract and present the information.

The chapter closes with a discussion on the art of turning code into documentation.

Application User Manuals Based on Navigation Workflow

Target: end user

The ideal user manual is friendly in tone and helps the user to accomplish all tasks related to the purposes of the program. The manual writer's goal is to increase the communication content or bandwidth without increasing the complexity. Each task should be listed with a clear description of purpose and with a concise set of instructions for reaching the goal. The manual should never threaten or confuse.

The Green/Brown Cooperative Business Modeling (CBM) development methodology uses the workflow diagram as the basis for the design of the application. Likewise, the workflow diagram is the best starting point for the user documentation. The tasks that the user must perform are easily visualized from the workflow. In addition, the organization of the resulting information will more closely match the users' needs and expectations when the instructions are developed from the workflow.

Develop workflow

In Chapter 21, we developed a sample workflow diagram. We use a similar but less extensive diagram to illustrate the concepts in this chapter. The sample diagram is shown in Figure 28.1. We use this diagram to illustrate the methodology used to transform a workflow diagram into user manuals.

We deliberately do not use any particular style of notation for presenting the workflow diagram. Our purpose is to show the information, not to introduce yet another notation style.

Isolate tasks from the workflow diagram

Examine the workflow diagram and isolate each task that the user needs to perform. The typical task starts at the beginning of the workflow and termi-

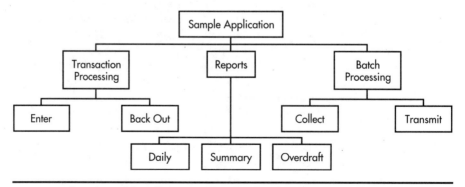

Figure 28.1   Sample workflow diagram with isolated tasks.

nates at a "leaf" or final node of the diagram. You may find many branches in the diagram. Each branch describes a different task. As you proceed, verify that the workflow diagram matches the functionality of the program. Modify the original workflow diagram if it is not an accurate representation of the way the program works.

If you find that a task is too lengthy or complicated, you should break it up into two or more smaller tasks. However, each task should be an easily described and understood entity, with a defined starting point, goal, and set of steps to achieve the goal. Never split a task at the expense of clarity and completeness. Figure 28.2 shows a task isolated from the workflow diagram.

Document each task

Document each task that you have isolated from the workflow diagram. Describe the purpose or intent of each task as it relates to the user's goals. Next, describe the steps necessary to execute that task from start to finish. Remember, illustration increases communication band width. Include screen shots and diagrams if your production techniques permit.

Explain to the user how to verify that his or her purpose has been achieved. The application provides some form of feedback, whether it is a simple "beep" or the closing of the current window. Let the user know what to expect.

The documentation of a task contains, at a minimum, the following information:

- Task title
- Task purpose
- Steps to accomplish the purpose
- Description of feedback
- Associated subtasks
- Related tasks

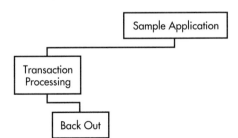

Figure 28.2 Sample workflow diagram with isolated tasks.

```
┌─────────────────────────────────────────────────────────────────────────┐
│  Task                                                                     │
│   ┌─────────────────────────┐            ┌─────────────────────────┐      │
│   │ Title                    │            │ Version                 │      │
│   ├─────────────────────────┴───┐        ├─────────────────────────┴───┐  │
│   │ Back Out Transactions       │        │ v1.0 4/15/95                │  │
│   └─────────────────────────────┘        └─────────────────────────────┘  │
│   ┌─────────────────────────┐            ┌─────────────────────────┐      │
│   │ Keywords                 │            │ Related Tasks           │      │
│   ├─────────────────────────┴───┐        ├─────────────────────────┴───┐  │
│   │ Transaction Back            │        │ Enter Transactions          │  │
│   └─────────────────────────────┘        └─────────────────────────────┘  │
│   ┌───────────────┐                                                        │
│   │ Purpose        │                                                       │
│   ├───────────────┴──────────────────────────────────────────────────┐   │
│   │ Delete improperly recorded transactions                          │   │
│   └──────────────────────────────────────────────────────────────────┘   │
│   ┌───────────────┐                                                        │
│   │ Feedback       │                                                       │
│   ├───────────────┴──────────────────────────────────────────────────┐   │
│   │ Message box stating "Transaction Backed Out"                     │   │
│   └──────────────────────────────────────────────────────────────────┘   │
│   ┌───────────────────────┐                                                │
│   │ Associated Subtasks    │                                               │
│   ├───────────────────────┴──────────────────────────────────────────┐   │
│   │ Using the calendar, choosing from dropdown lists                 │   │
│   └──────────────────────────────────────────────────────────────────┘   │
│   ┌───────────────────────┐                                                │
│   │ Steps to Accomplish    │                                               │
│   ├───────────────────────┴──────────────────────────────────────────┐   │
│   │ 1. Select "Transactions" from main menu                          │   │
│   │ 2. Select "Back Out" from submenu                                │   │
│   │ 3. Choose transaction date from calender                         │   │
│   │ 4. Choose transaction ID from dropdown list box at transaction ID field. │
│   │ 5. Choose "Edit" then "Delete" from menu                         │   │
│   │                    OR                                            │   │
│   │    Press the "Delete" toolbar button (pencil eraser)             │   │
│   └──────────────────────────────────────────────────────────────────┘   │
└─────────────────────────────────────────────────────────────────────────┘
```

Figure 28.3   Example of a task documentation form.

Figure 28.3 shows an example of a task documentation form.

Isolate subtasks

While you are documenting the major tasks each user will perform, you will notice repetitive subtasks that thread their way throughout an application. Even though you have already described these subtasks in the context of one or more tasks, you will make the user's life easier and more productive if you isolate and describe each subtask. Some examples of subtasks that might occur many times within an application are as follows:

- The choosing of a filename from a standard open-file dialog
- Cutting, copying, and pasting from within the application
- Choosing a selection from a dropdown list box
- Double-clicking on a row to "drill down" for more detail

Identify the purpose of each subtask and the ways it is used throughout the application. See Figure 28.4 for a sample subtask description.

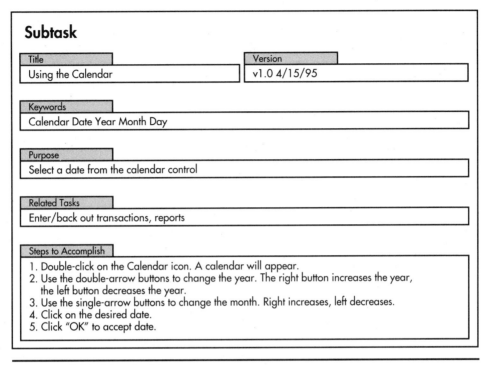

Figure 28.4 Subtask breakout form.

Identify related tasks

By definition, each subtask occurs in more than one place in the application. Document the relationships between the subtasks you have identified and the tasks in which they occur. List the related tasks following the description of each subtask to make it easier for the user to visualize the associations between the subtasks and the tasks.

You should also note the associated subtasks at the end of each task description. This allows the user to become familiar with the common elements of the application as they are encountered. You will increase the level of organization of your information and increase the bandwidth of your communication with this simple step.

Group and organize tasks and subtasks

Once you have found and described all of the applicable tasks and subtasks, you need to organize them into functional groupings. Use the workflow diagram as your guide. The tasks that grow from a common point usually have functionality and purpose in common. You will probably find that the highest-level groupings in your workflow diagram become your table of contents.

Features and benefits based on requirements

As a final touch to your user manual, you should develop a list of the features and benefits offered by the application. This is an area that is often overlooked, but is crucial to the acceptance and success of your project.

You already gathered most of the necessary information for this step when you created the requirements documents. This is an opportunity to morph the requirements documents into a form that is helpful to the user.

Each requirements document has an area in which you can specify a related benefit for the requirement. Your task during the construction of the user manual is to match the requirement with each appropriate user task and compile a list of the related benefits. This is an important step. The more a user understands about the reasons and goals that prompted the creation of the application, the more likely he or she is to make informed, inspired use of the technology.

The user benefits from this technique through greater understanding and facility with your application. You benefit through reuse of your information. The content of your manual will be more consistent with other documentation, and the cost-effectiveness of your documentation effort will be higher.

Application Technical Manual Based on Object Mapping

Target: application maintainers

Object mapping was introduced in Part II. Its function is to facilitate determining which class suits a particular object in your application. The object map can serve another purpose: documentation.

Documenting the objects that make up your application is a task often planned for, but seldom carried out. In the high-pressure, aggressive schedules imposed on development efforts today, there is seldom time to spend documenting objects for future maintenance.

What is the benefit?

Benefit: Maintenance programmers can quickly determine where in the object they need to look.

The benefit of doing technical documentation is to the maintenance programmer. It is often overlooked that system maintenance costs roughly two to three times the development effort cost over the life of the system. If you feel that the development effort was costly, even if the cost was justified, remember that this is only one-quarter of the overall cost. Making the maintenance task easier should be a primary concern. After all, this is one of the key reasons to use a class library. Providing maintenance programmers with effective documentation helps to reduce these costs. The object map and its associated object documentation are a big step in the effort to reduce maintenance efforts.

How does it all fit together?

In a traditional programming system, a programmer develops code and then creates program documentation. In a PowerBuilder environment, the concept of a "program" has disappeared. The program is replaced by a collection of integrated objects. Procedural code is replaced by methods and attributes. Figure 28.5 illustrates this difference.

In addition, the object you use may be part of a hierarchy of objects, each containing code that enhances the object you are developing. You still need to document the methods and attributes that you develop or enhance. The documentation must reflect the object state as implemented in your application. In object-oriented programming, however, you need to reflect which objects you

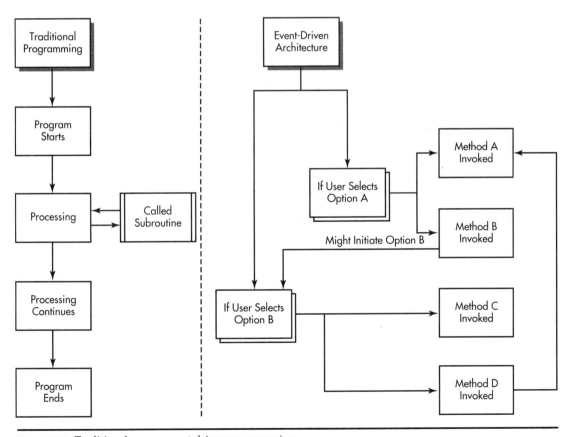

Figure 28.5 Traditional versus event-driven programming.

may have inherited from, and what methods and attributes you used, modified, extended, or added.

Figure 28.6 shows a portion of a typical object map. The window object contains two datawindows: master or parent data collection and a detail or child data collection. All three of these objects are inherited from a class library of objects. The object map shows the objects and their inheritance paths.

The object map is a graphical view of your object class hierarchy.

As we can see, all three objects are based on an ancestor class. It is also evident that the object map itself is a useful piece of documentation. All we need to do now is provide additional documentation regarding the objects created within the application. You will also notice a similarity between the object documentation used for class library technical manuals and that used for application technical manuals. The class library is based on the class hierarchy. The application extends this by adding the application objects and the object map to this documentation.

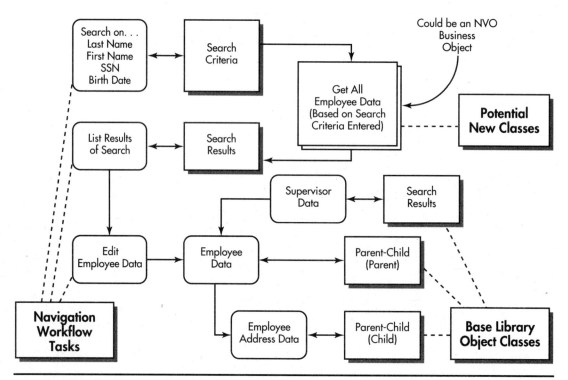

Figure 28.6 Sample object map shows how objects from the workflow are mapped back to existing reusable classes.

What do we do if we do not have an object map or ancestor classes?

If you did not create an object map, or if your application is not based on ancestor classes, you will not have to reference any ancestor attributes or methods. The formula remains the same, however. You still need to document the objects, methods, and attributes you have placed in the object. Follow the same principles used in creating class library technical documentation, but ignore the ancestor attribute references.

If you did not use an object map, but your objects are based on an existing class hierarchy, you need to create an object map or document the objects as if you had an object map. Remember that the object map *graphically* displays your object's ancestry and this can tell a maintenance programmer much more in less time than any other document.

Class Library Technical Manual Based on Class Hierarchy

Target: application developers

The technical manual for a class library may be derived from the class hierarchy and object definitions. The library documents should be organized by similarity of function and construction. The hierarchy diagram, which depicts the ancestry of your classes, is a natural place to start when producing technical documentation for your library.

Class hierarchy

A sample class hierarchy diagram is shown in Figure 28.7. The objects in this case are the physical implementations of the classes created at design time.

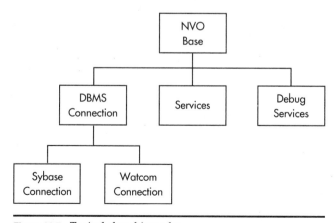

Figure 28.7   Typical class hierarchy.

The base level is shown at the top of the diagram, and each descendant level grows downward. Each descendant is associated with its ancestor by a connecting line. Each descendant inherits the characteristics of its ancestor and may extend or modify those characteristics to adapt to specialized uses.

Documentation for each object in the class library

The documentation for each object in a class library consists of three separate but related documents:

- The object overview
- The attribute reference
- The method reference

The object overview. The first step in documenting an object is to present an overview of the object. The documentation of each object should include the following:

- An explanation of the purpose for the object
- The ancestry for the object
- The immediate descendants of the object (if known)
- The attributes of the object
- The methods for the object
- A usage example, if relevant

A sample form for object documentation is shown in Figure 28.8.

The purpose of the object should be explained clearly. This allows future developers to apply the object where it is appropriate. Those charged with the maintenance of the applications that use that object will be able to ensure that it is functioning as intended.

The ancestor for each object should be part of the information you present in the technical reference. This allows users to easily reference the inherited attributes and methods. The ancestor object is easily discernible from the hierarchy diagram.

List the immediate descendants of the object. This helps prevent the needless recreation of a descendant object that already exists. Also, any time the object is changed, the potential for unexpected side effects exists. If you list the descendants, you can help future developers to ensure the integrity of the interfaces between ancestors and descendants. Of course, the likelihood of unwanted interaction and side effects is greatly diminished by good object-oriented design and techniques.

Next, break out the attributes of the object. List all newly declared (not inherited) public, private, and protected attributes. Also, show all public and pro-

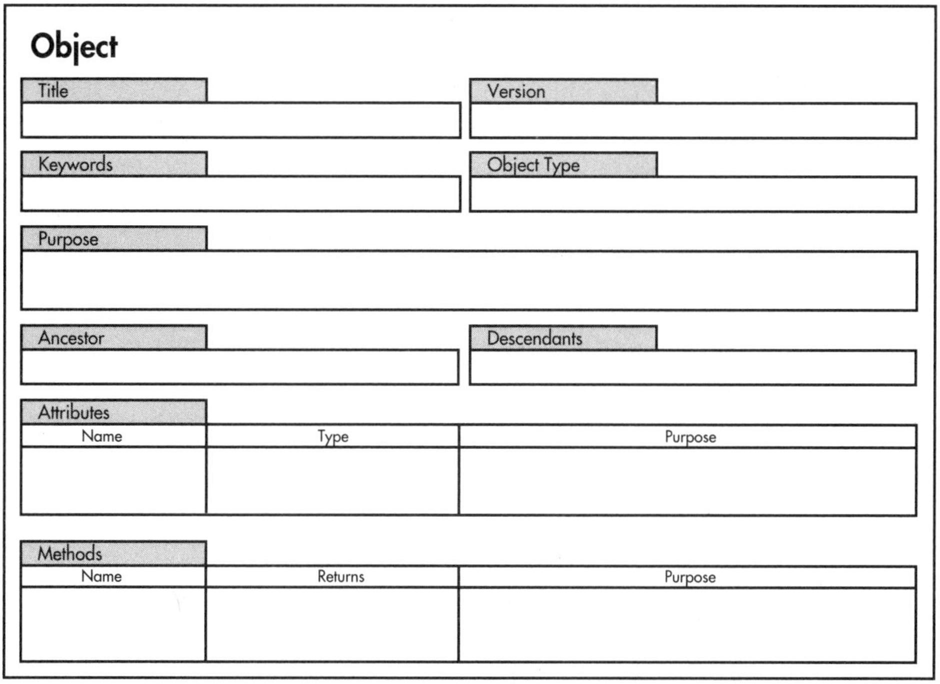
Object

Title

Version

Keywords

Object Type

Purpose

Ancestor

Descendants

Attributes

Name	Type	Purpose

Methods

Name	Returns	Purpose

Figure 28.8 Sample object documentation form.

tected attributes that have been inherited by the object. Nothing is more infuriating than chasing through a deep hierarchy in search of an inherited attribute. You should note inherited attributes with a check mark or bullet to reduce the possibility of confusion. Our own documentation uses the symbol "::," which implies a call to the ancestor. If you intend to document each attribute separately, you need not list the data type or a detailed description. In any case, you should include at least a capsule description of the function of each attribute.

Likewise, include a list of all newly declared methods (functions or events) as well as public or protected methods that have been inherited by the object. You should show the accessibility, return type, and a capsule description for each method. However, each method should be thoroughly documented separately as well.

The attribute reference. The documentation of each object should contain a list of the public, protected, and private attributes for that object. Each attribute of the object should be clearly documented. Include an example of the attribute's usage if you find it useful. The style you use to document the attributes must be fairly compact because some objects have many attributes. However, do not sacrifice completeness just to achieve brevity. The information you need to include with the attribute reference is as follows:

- The name of the attribute
- The purpose for the attribute
- The attribute type
- The range of acceptable values (if applicable)
- A usage example, if relevant

The method reference.   Each method that is newly declared or overridden in an object must be described completely in the method reference. Include as much detail as possible in the method reference. This is where developers will look to find out how to use your objects. Do not make them bounce from one area of the manual to another in search of essential information.

The method reference should contain the following:

- The object name
- The name of the method
- The type of the method (function or event)
- The purpose for the method
- The calling syntax for the method
- Each parameter (include type, purpose, and passing method)
- The return value (include type and purpose)
- When and why to override or extend the method
- Other objects referenced by the method
- Usage example

Features and benefits from requirements

Once again, you should help the users of your library understand the benefits they gain from the use of your library. Provide a description of the features and benefits provided by your library as they relate to each object. You will find that each requirement used to specify the class library has an accompanying expected benefit. If you use our forms or something equivalent, the information you need is already available from those forms. Compile the benefits into lists that correspond to the class structure of your library. Your users will be able to see what development issues are addressed by your library and where to look for solutions to their problems.

Turning Code into Documentation

An important source of documentation for your code is the code itself. The code is the reference of last resort for the actual functionality and implementation of each object. You can take a few simple steps that enhance the information contained in your code.

Develop self-documenting code

The first and most important step you can take is to ensure the development of self-documenting code. In Chapter 3 we discussed coding standards. The consistent, thorough use of coding standards contributes greatly toward the clarity and readability of your code.

When you are coding, use meaningful names for your attributes, methods, and objects. Be sure to follow the appropriate naming conventions. Use names like *ii_appInstanceCount* for an instance variable of type integer that is used to accumulate the count of application instances. Avoid jumbled or meaningless names like *iglctrx*.

Use white space creatively. Isolate functional code blocks with blank lines above and below the block. Then add a comment before the block that explains the purpose of the code.

Do not bother with comments like the following:

```
// Add 1 to counter
```

The best comments summarize rather than restate the obvious.

Add standard preamble

Each function or event should be preceded by a comment block known as the standard preamble. The standard preamble condenses all necessary information about the use and purpose of that method. The elements contained in the standard preamble include the following:

- The object name
- The method name
- The method type (function or event)
- The purpose of the method
- The parameters used in calling the method
- The return value type and purpose
- When it is appropriate to override or extend the method
- Other objects referenced by the method
- Modification history

An example of the standard preamble is shown below:

```
/*&&PREAMBLE*/
/****************************************************************
/
/ OBJECT:
/
/ METHOD:
/
/ TYPE: (Function/Event)
```

```
/
/ PURPOSE:
/
/
/ ARGUMENTS:
/ Identifier  Type    Passed By    Purpose
/
/
/ RETURNS:
/ Type       Purpose
/
/
/ OVERRIDE/EXTEND:
/ Action      Purpose
/
/
/ OBJECTS REFERENCED:
/ Object   Action Purpose
/
/
/ MODIFICATION HISTORY:
/ Date   Purpose
/
/
/*****************************************************************/
/*&&ENDPREAMBLE*/
```

Note that the use of the double ampersands before the words preamble *and* endpreamble *is deliberate. We are developing an automated documentation tool that will recognize* &&preamble *as a specific instruction. You are obviously not bound by this.*

Summary

In this chapter we examined some of the concepts that we have developed over time to help produce better, more accurate, and more informative documentation. You learned that the final documents (user and technical manuals) can be derived largely from the documents used in the design phase. We hope you take with you a conviction that, absolved of much of the tedium, you can find the documentation of your project to be a rewarding experience. Documentation is, after all, the final element in your application's presentation layer.

29

Automated Documentation

Introduction

Everyone knows that creating documentation is often a last-minute exercise. Even worse, the documentation stays in its original state even though the software continually evolves. Any efforts we can make to automate documentation will pay big dividends in reusability. In this chapter we examine what is meant by automated documentation and how you can benefit from automating parts of the documentation process.

After reading this chapter, you will have a better understanding of what aspects of documentation you can realistically delegate to machines. You will also learn the elements that can help justify the effort needed to enable your project teams to use automation. Finally, you will gain an overview of some of the tools and techniques that can help you to produce computer-aided documentation.

Automated Documentation:
Concepts and Justification

What do we mean by automated documentation?

In this chapter we do not consider every type of automation you can possibly use in the course of documenting a project. We concentrate on the areas where we have found the most gains in reusability and productivity.

Two areas of documentation lend themselves readily to an automated process. First, you can use programs to implement computer-aided documentation, which leads the documentation writer through a set of standardized steps to produce new documentation. You will find this process especially useful for architecture and preimplementation documents, but it is applicable throughout the design, development, and deployment of a system. Second, you can construct programs that scan existing application code and create documentation based on keywords and comments in the source code. Because the programs can always examine the most current source code, it is far easier to maintain up-to-date documentation with the help of a bit of automation.

Why automate?

The developers and designers among us like to produce, not document. Technical writers are often not called until the last stages of a project. The resulting documentation is often late and, thanks to the time crunch, filled with inaccuracies. Automating the more tedious and difficult areas of the documentation effort can free the developers to develop and the writers to write.

What is required for automated documentation?

The most important requirement for any documentation effort is a usable set of standards. This is true whether or not you are automating. The standards should cover the following:

- The development of design specifications
- Standard methodologies for documenting the elements of a program or class library
- Practices for embedding information and keywords into your code so that it can be automatically scanned

Many of the elements of these standards were discussed in Chapter 28.

Of course, you will need to build or buy tools that facilitate automated documentation. If you wish to automatically scan the program source, you may have to prepare the source with keywords and standardized comments. Finally, someone must make the commitment to maintain the automated documentation.

What can you expect from automated documentation?

You can expect to realize substantial gains when you make good use of automated documentation. Your projects will be delivered with usable and helpful manuals. Your project teams will spend less time and still produce meaningful documents that match the functionality of your application or library. The documents that accompany your software will be more consistent, more thorough, and more accurate. You will be able to introduce your software with timely and up-to-date documentation.

Do not expect that your teams will be relieved of the need to create clear, informative text to accompany any automatically generated information. The best we can expect from computer-generated prose is a kind of stilted consistency. Standard forms (which make up a huge percentage of the documentation surrounding computer systems) are a natural for computer production. However, the human element must be applied when explaining concepts or methods. Expect the computers to support the humans, not the other way around.

Next, we examine Powersoft's ORCA functions, a set of functions that allow programs other than PowerBuilder to access the contents of PowerBuilder libraries.

Using ORCA

In this section I discuss a powerful set of functions known as the ORCA (open repository case architecture) functions. I explain the operation and use of these functions, and the reasons a programmer would want to use them. Finally, I show how to encapsulate these functions using object-oriented techniques.

What is ORCA?

The ORCA functions make up an open interface application programming interface (API) that allows access to the contents of PowerBuilder libraries (PBLs) from languages other than PowerBuilder.

The ORCA functions are distributed as a dynamic link library (DLL) that contains all the required functions for accessing, querying, and manipulating PowerBuilder objects from code written in a programming language such as C.

Powersoft has made these functions available as part of its Client/Server Open Development Environment (CODE) initiative.

Why do we need ORCA?

ORCA fills the need to automatically examine and manipulate PowerBuilder objects using traditional programming languages. The programmer's applications for this capability can include the following:

- Batch compilation of PowerBuilder objects.

- Global find and replace operations (ORCA allows you to export object source into an in-memory buffer, change the code as you desire, and import and recompile the resulting code into a PBL in your defined search path).

- Optimizing the distribution of objects among several PBLs (ORCA can be used to identify the ancestry of objects and help you structure your PBLs to optimize their size and their order in the search path).

- Gathering statistics about PowerBuilder objects.

- Eliminating duplication of objects.
- Source code version control and archiving.
- Automated documentation.

What are the components of ORCA?

Powersoft provides the ORCA functions with PowerBuilder Enterprise as a dynamic link library (PBORC050.DLL). Powersoft includes two additional files to aid programmers:

- PBORCA.H, a header file containing the function prototypes for all of the ORCA functions and their associated callback functions
- PBORCA.LIB, an export library used for final linking

What are the ORCA functions?

The ORCA functions may be separated into four categories:

- Session management
- Library management
- Compilation
- Object query

These categories are discussed in detail below.

Session Management functions. The Session Management functions allow you to control the aspects of an ORCA session. Although no resources are allocated by a specific ORCA session, all ORCA functionality must be used within the context of a session. Table 29.1 lists the ORCA Session Management functions.

The following Library Management functions may be called without first calling PBORCA_SessionSetLibraryList:

- PBORCA_LibraryCommentModify
- PBORCA_LibraryCreate
- PBORCA_LibraryDelete
- PBORCA_LibraryDirectory
- PBORCA_LibraryEntryCopy
- PBORCA_LibraryEntryDelete
- PBORCA_LibraryEntryExport

TABLE 29.1 ORCA Session Management Functions

Function name:	PBORCA_SessionClose	
Purpose:	Closes an ORCA session.	
Returns:	Void	
Parameters:	Long pointer (hORCASession)	Session ID

Function name:	PBORCA_SessionGetError	
Purpose:	Gets the text for the current error during an ORCA session. If the most recent operation was successful, this function places a zero-length string into the error buffer.	
Returns:	Void	
Parameters:	Long pointer (hORCASession) LPSTR Integer	Session ID Error buffer Error buffer size

Function name:	PBORCA_SessionOpen	
Purpose:	Establish an ORCA session and return a pointer (Session ID) to that session.	
Returns:	Long pointer (hORCASession)	Session ID
Parameters:	Void	

Function name:	PBORCA_SessionSetCurrentAppl	
Purpose:	Sets the current application for an ORCA session. The application must be set before using any ORCA function that compiles or queries objects.	
Returns:	Integer	Return code

(Continued)

TABLE 29.1 *(Continued)*

Parameters:	Long pointer (hORCASession)	Session ID
	LPSTR	Library name
	LPSTR	Application name

Function name:	PBORCA_SessionSetLibraryList	
Purpose:	Sets the library search path for an ORCA session. The search path must be set before using any ORCA function that compiles or queries objects.	
Returns:	Integer	Return code
Parameters:	Long pointer (hORCASession)	Session ID
	Far pointer to ARRAY of pointers to LPSTR	Library names
	Integer	Number of libraries in list

- PBORCA_LibraryEntryInformation
- PBORCA_LibraryEntryMove

Library Management functions. The ORCA Library Management functions allow you to access, create, and modify PowerBuilder libraries and the entries within them. Table 29.2 details the ORCA Library Management functions.

Compilation functions. The ORCA Compilation functions allow you to import individual objects from their source code, import lists of objects, or regenerate objects within PBLs. Table 29.3 lists the ORCA Compilation functions.

Object Query functions. The ORCA Query functions return information about an object's ancestry and about the objects referenced by another object. Table 29.4 lists the ORCA Query functions.

Callback routines. Several ORCA functions require the use of callback routines. The address of these routines is passed to the ORCA function. Then ORCA calls the callback procedure as required, such as when returning a sequence of library objects. When programming in C, the MakeProcInstance Windows SDK func-

(Text continued on page 500)

TABLE 29.2 ORCA Library Management Functions

Function name:	PBORCA_LibraryCommentModify	
Purpose:	Add or modify the comment for a PowerBuilder library.	
Returns:	Integer	Return code
Parameters:	Long pointer (hORCASession)	Session ID
	LPSTR	Library name
	LPSTR	Library comments

Function name:	PBORCA_LibraryCreate	
Purpose:	Creates a PowerBuilder library (PBL).	
Returns:	Integer	Return code
Parameters:	Long pointer (hORCASession)	Session ID
	LPSTR	Library name
	LPSTR	Library comments

Function name:	PBORCA_LibraryDelete	
Purpose:	Deletes a PowerBuilder library.	
Returns:	Integer	Return code
Parameters:	Long pointer (hORCASession)	Session ID
	LPSTR	Library name

Function name:	PBORCA_LibraryDirectory	
Purpose:	Lists the objects in a PowerBuilder library. This function enumerates the objects within a library using a callback function.	
Returns:	Integer	Return code

(Continued)

TABLE 29.2 *(Continued)*

Parameters:	Long pointer (hORCASession)	Session ID
	LPSTR	Library name
	LPSTR	Library comment buffer (returned)
	Integer	Comment buffer size
	Far pointer to PASCAL procedure	List callback procedure
	Long pointer	User data to be passed to callback procedure

Function name:	PBORCA_LibraryEntryCopy	
Purpose:	Copies a PowerBuilder object from one library to another.	
Returns:	Integer	Return code
Parameters:	Long pointer (hORCASession)	Session ID
	LPSTR	Source library name
	LPSTR	Destination library name
	LPSTR	Object name
	PBORCA_TYPE (enum) Application = 0, Datawindow = 1, Function = 2, Menu = 3, Query = 4, Structure = 5,	Object type

TABLE 29.2 *(Continued)*

	UserObject = 6, Window = 7	
Function name:	PBORCA_LibraryEntryDelete	
Purpose:	Delete an object from a PowerBuilder library.	
Returns:	Integer	Return code
Parameters:	Long pointer (hORCASession)	Session ID
	LPSTR	Library name
	LPSTR	Object name
	PBORCA_TYPE (enum) Application = 0, Datawindow = 1, Function = 2, Menu = 3, Query = 4, Structure = 5, UserObject = 6, Window = 7	Object type

Function name:	PBORCA_LibraryEntryExport	
Purpose:	Exports the source for a PowerBuilder object.	
Returns:	Integer	Return code
Parameters:	Long pointer (hORCASession)	Session ID
	LPSTR	Library name

(Continued)

TABLE 29.2 *(Continued)*

	LPSTR	Object name
	PBORCA_TYPE (enum) Application = 0, Datawindow = 1, Function = 2, Menu = 3, Query = 4, Structure = 5, UserObject = 6, Window = 7	Object type
	LPSTR	Export buffer
	Long	Export buffer size

Function name:	PBORCA_LibraryEntryInformation	
Purpose:	Returns information about a PowerBuilder object.	
Returns:	Integer	Return code
Parameters:	Long pointer (hORCASession)	Session ID
	LPSTR	Library name
	LPSTR	Object name
	PBORCA_TYPE (enum) Application = 0, Datawindow = 1, Function = 2, Menu = 3, Query = 4, Structure = 5,	Object type

TABLE 29.2 *(Continued)*

	UserObject = 6, Window = 7	
	Long pointer to entry information block	Entry information block: char[256] comments Long lCreateTime Long lObjectSize Long lSourceSize

Function name:	PBORCA_LibraryEntryMove	
Purpose:	Moves a PowerBuilder object from one library to another.	
Returns:	Integer	Return code
Parameters:	Long pointer (hORCASession)	Session ID
	LPSTR	Source library name
	LPSTR	Destination library name
	LPSTR	Object name
	PBORCA_TYPE (enum) Application = 0, Datawindow = 1, Function = 2, Menu = 3, Query = 4, Structure = 5, UserObject = 6, Window = 7	Object type

TABLE 29.3 ORCA Compilation Functions

Function name:	PBORCA_CompileEntryImport	
Purpose:	Imports and compiles source for a PowerBuilder object.	
Returns:	Integer	Return code
Parameters:	Long pointer (hORCASession)	Session ID
	LPSTR	Library name
	LPSTR	Object name
	PBORCA_TYPE (enum) Application = 0, Datawindow = 1, Function = 2, Menu = 3, Query = 4, Structure = 5, UserObject = 6, Window = 7	Object type
	LPSTR	Object comments
	LPSTR	Object source code buffer
	Long	Object source code buffer size
	Pointer to far PASCAL callback procedure	Error callback procedure
	Generic pointer (LPVOID)	Pointer to user data to be passed to callback procedure
Function name:	PBORCA_CompileEntryImportList	
Purpose:	Imports and compiles the source for a list of objects. The objects and type information are passed in a set of pointers to arrays.	

TABLE 29.3 *(Continued)*

Returns:	Integer	Return code
Parameters:	Long pointer (hORCASession)	Session ID
	Far pointer to ARRAY of LPSTR	Library names
	Far pointer to ARRAY of LPSTR	Object names
	Far pointer to ARRAY of PBORCA_TYPE (enum) Application = 0, Datawindow = 1, Function = 2, Menu = 3, Query = 4, Structure = 5, UserObject = 6, Window = 7	Object types
	Far pointer to ARRAY of LPSTR	Object comments
	Far pointer to ARRAY of LPSTR	Object source buffers
	Far pointer to ARRAY of integer	Source buffer sizes
	Integer	Number of entries
	Pointer to far PASCAL callback procedure	Error callback procedure
	Generic pointer (LPVOID)	Pointer to user data to be passed to callback procedure
Function name:	PBORCA_CompileEntryRegenerate	
Purpose:	Regenerates (compiles) a PowerBuilder object.	
Returns:	Integer	Return code

(Continued)

TABLE 29.3 *(Continued)*

Parameters:	Long pointer (hORCASession)	Session ID
	LPSTR	Library name
	LPSTR	Object name
	PBORCA_TYPE (enum) Application = 0, Datawindow = 1, Function = 2, Menu = 3, Query = 4, Structure = 5, UserObject = 6, Window = 7	Object type
	Pointer to far PASCAL callback procedure	Error callback procedure
	Generic pointer (LPVOID)	Pointer to user data to be passed to callback procedure

tion must be used to create a "thunk" for the callback procedure. This provides a unique data segment for each instance, but only one code segment. This is a requirement imposed by the segmented INTEL architecture and the Windows memory model. An example C declaration and MakeProcInstance call follows:

```
typedef void (FAR PASCAL *PBORCA_ERRPROC)(PPBORCA_COMPERR,LPVOID);
PBORCA_ERRPROC ErrorCallBack(PPBORCA_COMPERR ErrorStr,LPVOID VoidPtr);
lpfncallback = MakeProcInstance(ErrorCallBack,VoidPtr);
```

If you use a language with "smart" exporting capability, such as Borland Pascal 7.0, then the callback procedures are declared much more simply:

```
procedure ErrorCallBack(ORCAErrorStruct : PErrStruct ; UserData : Pointer )
; export ;
```

The descriptions of the ORCA callback functions are shown in Table 29.5.

TABLE 29.4   ORCA Query Functions

Function name:	PBORCA_ObjectQueryHierarchy	
Purpose:	Queries a PowerBuilder object for the objects in its ancestor hierarchy.	
Returns:	Integer	Return code
Parameters:	Long pointer (hORCASession)	Session ID
	LPSTR	Library name
	LPSTR	Object name
	PBORCA_TYPE (enum) Application = 0, Datawindow = 1, Function = 2, Menu = 3, Query = 4, Structure = 5, UserObject = 6, Window = 7	Object type
	Pointer to far PASCAL callback procedure	Hierarchy callback procedure
	Generic pointer (LPVOID)	Pointer to user data to be passed to callback procedure

Function name:	PBORCA_ObjectQueryReference	
Purpose:	Queries a PowerBuilder object for references to other objects	
Returns:	Integer	Return code
Parameters:	Long pointer (hORCASession)	Session ID

(Continued)

TABLE 29.4   *(Continued)*

	LPSTR	Library name
	LPSTR	Object name
	PBORCA_TYPE (enum) Application = 0, Datawindow = 1, Function = 2, Menu = 3, Query = 4, Structure = 5, UserObject = 6, Window = 7	Object type
	Pointer to far PASCAL callback procedure	Reference callback procedure
	Generic pointer (LPVOID)	Pointer to user data to be passed to callback procedure

Encapsulating ORCA

We would like to maximize the reusability of the ORCA functions and enhance our ability to include them in the programs we write. An effective way to accomplish this is to encapsulate the functions as provided by Powersoft into classes. Then we can insert these classes into programs as needed.

Determine which ORCA classes are necessary.   The first step in encapsulating the ORCA functions is to determine what classes you need. Start by examining the actual entities involved when you are manipulating PowerBuilder libraries with the ORCA functions. The PowerBuilder entities involved are as follows:

- PowerBuilder libraries
- PowerBuilder library entries (objects)
- Object source code
- Application

TABLE 29.5 ORCA Callback Functions

Called by function:	PBORCA_CompileEntryImport	
Purpose:	Called when an error occurs during source code import.	
Returns:	Void	
Parameters:	Long pointer (PPBORCA_COMPERR)	Pointer to error structure: Integer iLevel LPSTR Message Num LPSTR Message Text UINT iColumnNumber UINT iLineNumber
	Generic pointer (LPVOID)	Pointer to user data

Called by function:	PBORCA_LibraryDirectory	
Purpose:	Called to return library entry information.	
Returns:	Void	
Parameters:	Long pointer (PPBORCA_DIRENTRY)	Pointer to directory entry structure: char[256] comments Long lCreateTime Long lEntrySize LPSTR EntryName PBORCA_TYPE objType
	Generic pointer (LPVOID)	Pointer to user data
Called by function:	PBORCA_ObjectQueryHierarchy	
Purpose:	Called to return the ancestor hierarchy for an object.	
Returns:	Void	

(Continued)

TABLE 29.5 *(Continued)*

Parameters:	Long pointer (PPBORCA_HIERARCHY) Generic pointer (LPVOID)	Pointer to hierarchy structure: LPSTR AncestorName Pointer to user data

Called by function:	PBORCA_ObjectQueryReference	
Purpose:	Called to return the objects referenced from a PowerBuilder object.	
Returns:	Void	
Parameters:	Long pointer (PPBORCA_REFERENCE)	Pointer to reference structure: LPSTR LibraryName LPSTR EntryName PBORCA_TYPE ObjType
	Generic pointer (LPVOID)	Pointer to user data

In addition, the ORCA functions add one entity, the session. We will build classes that reflect these entities.

Add attributes and functionality to the classes. In order for our classes to be useful, we must add data items (attributes) and behaviors (methods) that implement the functionality that we desire. By class, the necessary attributes can be listed. Figures 29.1 through 29.5 show the standard physical class definition forms for the ORCA classes.

The methods and attributes shown in Figures 29.1 through 29.5 support the standard ORCA functionality in easily incorporated objects. The objects may be extended and adapted to add functionality as needed. Fully commented source code for these classes can be found on the accompanying CD.

Putting ORCA objects to work

After you have completed the implementation of these ORCA classes, you can follow the steps below to incorporate the ORCA classes into your C or PASCAL programs.

(Text continued on page 515)

Figure 29.1   Physical class definition: ORCA library class.

Physical Class Data

Physical Class ID:	ORC_0001		Version:	1.0
Physical Class Name:	PowerBuilder ORCA library class			
Ancestry:	ORCA_Base			
Author:	Millard F. Brown III		Update Date:	October 2, 1995

Object Class Description/Purpose

Description
Encapsulates ORCA functions relating to PowerBuilder libraries.

Methods and Attributes

Attributes

Scope		Type	Name	Default
Protected		String	_Name_ The filename for the PBL	
Protected		Long	_Size_ The size, in bytes, of the PBL	
Protected		Date	_Date_ The PBL file date	
Protected		String	_Location_ The fully qualified path to the PBL	
Protected		String	_Comment_ The library comment	
Protected		Integer	_PBLCount_ The number of entries	
Protected		ORCA_Library_Entry[]	_EntryObject_ An array of Library Entry objects	

Note: When default indicates a Class ID (e.g., PCD_xxxx), variable is defined in that class.

Methods

Scope	Type	Prefix	Name	Link
(None)	Function		_Constructor_	
Description	Launch any object initialization routines.			
Specification	• N/A.			

(Continued)

Figure 29.1 *(Continued)*

Overrides	Should not be overridden			
Extend	No	None		

Scope	Type	Prefix	Name	Link
(None)	Function		*Destructor*	
Description	Launch any functionality to be executed before object shutdown.			
Specification	• N/A.			
Overrides	Should not be overridden			
Extend	No	None		

Scope	Type	Prefix	Name	Link
Public	Function		*Open*	
Description	Establishes attributes for the library and gathers information about its objects.			
Specification	• Initializes settings for attributes. • Creates entry object for each library entry.			
Overrides	Rarely			
Extend	Yes	Collect developer-defined attributes		

Scope	Type	Prefix	Name	Link
Public	Function		*Create*	
Description	Creates a new PowerBuilder library.			
Specification	• Creates a new library using the attributes of the library object.			
Overrides	Rarely			
Extend	Yes			

Scope	Type	Prefix	Name	Link
Public	Function		*Delete*	
Description	Deletes the PowerBuilder library.			
Specification	• Removes the PowerBuilder library from the disk.			
Overrides	Rarely			
Extend	Yes			

Scope	Type	Prefix	Name	Link
Public	Function		*GetInfo*	
Description	Returns the attributes of the library.			

Specification	• Populates the reference parameters with the library information.		
Overrides	Rarely		
Extend	Yes		
Parameters	**Description**		**Reference**
Name	The PBL name		by Ref
Size	The size of the PBL		by Ref
Date	The date of the PBL		by Ref
Comment	The PBL comment		by Ref

Scope	**Type**	**Prefix**	**Name**	**Link**
Public	Function		*ReplaceComment*	
Description	Replaces the library comment with the specified text.			
Specification	• Changes the comment attribute to match the passed parameter. • Changes the library comment on disk.			
Overrides	Rarely			
Extend	Yes			
Parameters	**Description**		**Reference**	
Comment	The PBL comment		by Value	

Scope	**Type**	**Prefix**	**Name**	**Link**
Public	Function		*AddEntry*	
Description	Adds a new entry object to the library.			
Specification	• Inserts the passed entry object into the library object's list of entry objects. • Adds the entry to the PBL on disk.			
Overrides	Rarely			
Extend	Yes			
Parameters	**Description**		**Reference**	
EntryObject	PBL entry object		by Ref	

Scope	**Type**	**Prefix**	**Name**	**Link**
Public	Function		*DeleteEntry*	
Description	Deletes the named entry object from the library.			
Specification	• Removes the entry from the PBL on disk. • Removes the entry from the library object's list of entry objects.			
Overrides	Rarely			
Extend	Yes			
Parameters	**Description**		**Reference**	
EntryName	String: the name of the PBL entry object		by Value	

(Continued)

Figure 29.1 *(Continued)*

Scope	Type	Prefix	Name	Link
Public	Function		*CopyEntry*	
Description	Copies the named entry object from the library to another library.			
Specification	• Locates the entry by name. • Copies the entry to the destination library.			
Overrides	Rarely			
Extend	Yes			
Parameters		Description		Reference
EntryName		String: the name of the PBL entry object		by Value
DestinationLibrary		PBL library object to copy to		by Ref

Scope	Type	Prefix	Name	Link
Public	Function		*MoveEntry*	
Description	Moves the named entry object from the library to another library.			
Specification	• Locates the entry by name. • Adds the entry to the destination PBL. • Removes the entry from the source PBL.			
Overrides	Rarely			
Extend	Yes			
Parameters		Description		Reference
EntryName		String: the name of the PBL entry object		by Value
DestinationLibrary		PBL library object to move to		by Ref

Scope	Type	Prefix	Name	Link
Public	Function		*ExportEntry*	
Description	Exports the entry's source code into the source code attribute of the entry object.			
Specification	• Exports the entry's source code into the source code attribute of the entry object.			
Overrides	Rarely			
Extend	Yes			
Parameters		Description		Reference
EntryName		String: the name of the PBL entry object		by Value

----

Scope	Type	Prefix	Name	Link
Public	Function		*GetEntryCount*	
Description	Returns the number of entries in the library.			
Specification	• Returns the number of entries in the library.			
Overrides	Rarely			

Extend	Yes		
Parameters		**Description**	**Reference**
Return Value		Integer: the number of entries in the PBL	

Scope	Type	Prefix	Name	Link
Public	Function		*GetEntryName*	
Description	Returns the name of the specified library entry.			
Specification	• Returns the name of the specified library entry.			
Overrides	Rarely			
Extend	Yes			
Parameters		**Description**		**Reference**
Index		Integer: the index number of the entry		by Value
Return Value		String: the name of the specified entry		

Scope	Type	Prefix	Name	Link
Public	Function		*GetEntrybyIndex*	
Description	Returns the entry object at the specified index.			
Specification	• Returns the entry object at the specified index.			
Overrides	Rarely			
Extend	Yes			
Parameters		**Description**		**Reference**
Index		Integer: the index number of the entry		by Value
Return Value		Entry object at the specified index		

Scope	Type	Prefix	Name	Link
Public	Function		*GetEntry*	
Description	Returns the entry object with the specified name.			
Specification	• Locates the specified entry object by name.			
	• Returns the entry object.			
Overrides	Rarely			
Extend	Yes			
Parameters		**Description**		**Reference**
Entry Name		String: the name of the entry		by Value
Return Value		Entry object with the specified name		

Figure 29.2 Physical class definition: ORCA library entry class.

Physical Class Data

Physical Class ID:	ORC_0001		Version:	1.0
Physical Class Name:	PowerBuilder ORCA library class			
Ancestry:	ORCA_Base			
Author:	Millard F. Brown III		Update Date:	October 2, 1995

Object Class Description/Purpose

Description
Encapsulates ORCA functions relating to PowerBuilder libraries.

Methods and Attributes

Attributes

Scope		Type	Name	Default
Protected		String	*Name* The filename for the PBL	
Protected		Long	*Size* The size, in bytes, of the PBL	
Protected		Date	*Date* The PBL file date	
Protected		String	*Location* The fully qualified path to the PBL	
Protected		String	*Comment* The library comment	
Protected		Integer	*PBLCount* The number of entries	
Protected		ORCA_Library_Entry[]	*EntryObject* An array of Library Entry objects	

Note: When default indicates a Class ID (e.g., PCD_xxxx), variable is defined in that class.

Methods

Scope	Type	Prefix	Name	Link
(None)	Function	·	*Constructor*	
Description	Launch any object initialization routines.			

Overrides	Should not be overridden		
Extend	No	None	

Scope	Type	Prefix	Name	Link
(None)	Function		*Destructor*	
Description	Launch any functionality to be executed before object shutdown.			
Specification	• N/A.			
Overrides	Should not be overridden			
Extend	No	None		

Scope	Type	Prefix	Name	Link
Public	Function		*GetInfo*	
Description	Returns the attributes of the library entry.			
Specification	• Populates the reference parameters with the entry information.			
Overrides	Rarely			
Extend	Yes			

Parameters	Description	Reference
Name	The entry name	by Ref
Size	The size of the entry	by Ref
Date	The date of the entry	by Ref
Comment	The entry comment	by Ref

Scope	Type	Prefix	Name	Link
Public	Function		*ReplaceComment*	
Description	Replaces the entry comment with the specified text.			
Specification	• Changes the comment attribute to match the passed parameter. • Changes the entry comment on disk.			
Overrides	Rarely			
Extend	Yes			

Parameters	Description	Reference
Comment	The entry comment	by Value

Scope	Type	Prefix	Name	Link
Public	Function		*Import*	
Description	Imports the entry object into the specified library.			
Specification	• Inserts the entry object into the library object's list of entry objects. • Imports the entry to the PBL on disk.			

(Continued)

Figure 29.2 *(Continued)*

Overrides	Rarely		
Extend	Yes		
Parameters		Description	Reference
LibraryName		PBL name	by Value

Scope	Type	Prefix	Name	Link
Public	Function		*SetSourceCodeObject*	
Description	Attaches a source code object to the library entry.			
Specification	• Attaches a source code object to the library entry.			
Overrides	Rarely			
Extend	Yes			
Parameters		Description		Reference
SourceCodeObject		ORCA source code object		by Ref

Figure 29.3   Physical class definition: ORCA source code class.

Physical Class Data

Physical Class ID:	ORC_0003	Version:	1.0
Physical Class Name:	PowerBuilder ORCA source code class		
Ancestry:	ORCA_Base		
Author:	Millard F. Brown III	Update Date:	October 8, 1995

Object Class Description/Purpose

Description
Encapsulates ORCA functions relating to PowerBuilder source code.

Methods and Attributes

Attributes

Scope	Type	Name	Default
Protected	String	*Name* The name for the source code	
Protected	Long	*Size* The size, in bytes, of the entry	
Protected	Date	*Date* The source code date	

| Protected | | ENTRY_TYPE | *object_type*
The type of the object (enumerated) | |
| Protected | | String | *SourceBuffer[]*
String list containing the source code | |

Note: When default indicates a Class ID (e.g., PCD_xxxx), variable is defined in that class.

Methods

Scope	Type	Prefix	Name	Link
(None)	Function		*Constructor*	
Description	Launch any object initialization routines.			
Specification	• N/A.			
Overrides	Should not be overridden			
Extend	No	None		

Scope	Type	Prefix	Name	Link
(None)	Function		*Destructor*	
Description	Launch any functionality to be executed before object shutdown.			
Specification	• N/A.			
Overrides	Should not be overridden			
Extend	No	None		

Scope	Type	Prefix	Name	Link
Public	Function		*GetInfo*	
Description	Returns the attributes of the source code object.			
Specification	• Populates the reference parameters with the source code object information.			
Overrides	Rarely			
Extend	Yes			
Parameters	**Description**			**Reference**
Name	The source code object name			by Ref
Size	The size of the source code object			by Ref
Date	The date of the source code object			by Ref

Scope	Type	Prefix	Name	Link
Public	Function		*ReplaceSourceCode*	
Description	Replaces the source code buffer with the specified text.			
Specification	• Free memory associated with current source code buffer.			

(Continued)

Figure 29.3 *(Continued)*

	• Allocate new source code buffer for specified text.
	• Copy source code text into new buffer.
Overrides	Rarely
Extend	Yes
Parameters	**Description**	**Reference**
SourceCode	The source code text	by Ref

Figure 29.4   Physical class definition: PowerBuilder ORCA application class.

Physical Class Data

Physical Class ID:	ORC_0004	**Version:**	1.0
Physical Class Name:	PowerBuilder ORCA application class		
Ancestry:	ORCA_Base		
Author:	Millard F. Brown III	**Update Date:**	October 6, 1995

Object Class Description/Purpose

Description
Encapsulates ORCA functions relating to a PowerBuilder application.

<u>Methods and Attributes</u>

Attributes

Scope		Type	Name	Default
Protected		String	*Name* The name for the application	
Protected		Long	*Size* The size, in bytes, of the application	
Protected		Date	*Date* The application date	
Protected		String	*LibrarySearchPath[]* List of search libraries	
Note: When default indicates a Class ID (e.g., PCD_xxxx), variable is defined in that class.				

Methods

Scope	Type	Prefix	Name	Link
(None)	Function		*Constructor*	
Description	Launch any object initialization routines.			
Specification	• N/A.			
Overrides	Should not be overridden			
Extend	No	None		

Scope	Type	Prefix	Name	Link
(None)	Function		*Destructor*	
Description	Launch any functionality to be executed before object shutdown.			
Specification	• N/A.			
Overrides	Should not be overridden			
Extend	No	None		

Scope	Type	Prefix	Name	Link
Public	Function		*ClearSearchPath*	
Description	Resets the search path.			
Specification	• Clear the search path. • Assign the application library as the search path.			
Overrides	Rarely			
Extend	Yes			

Scope	Type	Prefix	Name	Link
Public	Function		*AddLibraryToPath*	
Description	Adds the named library to the search path.			
Specification	• Add the named library to the application search path.			
Overrides	Rarely			
Extend	Yes			
Parameters	**Description**			**Reference**
LibraryName	String: the name of the library			by Value

Instantiate the session and application objects. Create a new instance of a session object. The constructor will establish an ORCA session and initialize the session ID and other session attributes. When you are finished using the ORCA objects you should destroy the session object.

Create an instance of the application object. This step is necessary only if you will be querying or compiling objects using ORCA. Use the AddLibrary-ToPath method to build the library path for the given application. Then use the SetApplication method of the session object to attach the application to the current session.

(Text continued on page 519)

Figure 29.5 Physical class definition: ORCA session class.

Physical Class Data

Physical Class ID:	ORC_0005		Version:	1.0
Physical Class Name:	ORCA session class			
Ancestry:	ORCA_Base			
Author:	Millard F. Brown III		Update Date:	October 6, 1995

Object Class Description/Purpose

Description
Encapsulates ORCA functions relating to an ORCA session.

Methods and Attributes

Attributes

Scope		Type	Name	Default
Protected		String	*Name* The name for the session	
Protected		Long	*Status* The current ORCA status of the session	
Protected		Long	*ErrorCode* The current ORCA error code	
Protected		String	*ErrorText* The ORCA error text	
Protected		ORCA_Application	*Application* The current application	
Protected		String	*History[]* List of ORCA operations for this session	

Note: When default indicates a Class ID (e.g., PCD_xxxx), variable is defined in that class.

Methods

Scope	Type	Prefix	Name	Link
(None)	Function		*Constructor*	
Description	Launch any object initialization routines.			
Specification	• N/A.			
Overrides	Should not be overridden			
Extend	No	None		

Scope	Type	Prefix	Name	Link
(None)	Function		*Destructor*	
Description	Launch any functionality to be executed before object shutdown.			
Specification	• N/A.			
Overrides	Should not be overridden			
Extend	No	None		

Scope	Type	Prefix	Name	Link
Public	Function		*GetSessionID*	
Description	Returns the session ID.			
Specification	• Assign the session ID to the return value.			
Overrides	Rarely			
Extend	Yes			
Parameters		**Description**		**Reference**
Return Value		The session ID		

Scope	Type	Prefix	Name	Link
Public	Function		*GetSessionStatus*	
Description	Returns the session status.			
Specification	• Assign the session status to the return value.			
Overrides	Rarely			
Extend	Yes			
Parameters		**Description**		**Reference**
Return Value		The session status		

Scope	Type	Prefix	Name	Link
Public	Function		*GetErrorCode*	
Description	Returns the error code.			
Specification	• Assign the error code to the return value.			
Overrides	Rarely			
Extend	Yes			
Parameters		**Description**		**Reference**
Return Value		Current session error code		

Scope	Type	Prefix	Name	Link
Public	Function		*GetErrorText*	
Description	Returns the error text.			
Specification	• Assign the ORCA error text to the return value.			
Overrides	Rarely			

(Continued)

Figure 29.5 *(Continued)*

Extend	Yes		
Parameters	Description		Reference
Return Value	Current session error text		

Scope	Type	Prefix	Name	Link
Public	Function		*SetApplication*	
Description	Assigns the application object for the session.			
Specification	• Assign the passed application object to the session.			
Overrides	Rarely			
Extend	Yes			
Parameters	Description			Reference
Application	The application			by Ref

Scope	Type	Prefix	Name	Link
Public	Function		*ClearHistory*	
Description	Clear the session history.			
Specification	• Remove all entries from the history list. • Free unused memory.			
Overrides	Rarely			
Extend	Yes			

Scope	Type	Prefix	Name	Link
Public	Function		*AddHistory*	
Description	Adds string to history list.			
Specification	• Add passed string to end of history list.			
Overrides	Rarely			
Extend	Yes			
Parameters	Description			Reference
HistoryString	History string			by Value

Scope	Type	Prefix	Name	Link
Public	Function		*GetHistory*	
Description	Returns history list.			
Specification	• Create copy of history list. • Return pointer to copy of history list.			
Overrides	Rarely			
Extend	Yes			
Parameters	Description			Reference
Return value	Pointer to copy of session history list			

Instantiate other objects as needed.   Once you have established a session and set up the application and search path, you can use the other classes to operate on libraries and their entries. When you instantiate a new library object, the constructor automatically gathers the information about the entries in the library. You can use the methods of the library object to manipulate the entries as you need. You will find sample code with more details on the accompanying CD.

Documenting using ORCA

The ORCA functions and the classes we have constructed can be used to help automate the documentation and control of your PowerBuilder objects. Through the use of the ORCA classes, you have complete access to the details of your PowerBuilder libraries. The uses for this capability are many and varied and can include the following:

- Automated processing of PBL entries (compilation, statistics gathering, version control, etc.)
- Automatic collection of source code documentation, including ancestry, attributes, and methods.
- Automated recording of version control information such as dates and sizes of PBL entries

Summary

This chapter has shown you some of the ways you can use automation to ease the burden of documenting your projects. You have seen the importance of standards in facilitating the automated recording of object characteristics. We have detailed for you the areas where standardization is most needed. Finally, we examined in detail the Powersoft ORCA functions. You learned how to encapsulate the ORCA functionality into reusable classes and how to apply those classes to construct your own automated documentation tools.

30

Developing On-Line Help

Introduction

No application is complete without on-line help. Users expect to find help at their fingertips, and they are more productive if help is available. Yet at its worst, on-line help can be abysmal. Clumsily linked hypertext, unclear prose, and disorganized content all contribute to the kind of help file we have all seen but never want to see again. On the other hand, artfully constructed help is a ready and able companion to the user, always handy to answer a question or provide direction and useful hints.

As you read this chapter, you will acquire a clear understanding of the role of on-line help in completing the application or class library. You will gain an appreciation for the kinds of organization that work best for hypertext help files. You will see how the structure of the application or library, the requirements, the definitions, and the descriptions of user's tasks all fit together to form a cohesive whole that is the well-tempered help system.

What Is On-Line Help?

The meaning of on-line help is known to every software developer and computer user. On-line help documents the procedures for using the software, and is accessible on the same computer as the software. *On-line* means that the help text is within easy reach of the user whenever he or she is using the application or class library.

On-line help usually provides some measure of context-sensitivity. This means that the help system is aware of the current context or state of the software, and directs the user to the most appropriate section in the help file structure.

Help topics are often linked together by keywords to allow the user to jump from one topic to any other related information. This feature, known as hypertext, is one of the most compelling capabilities of on-line help.

The best help, the sort of help we want to add to our applications, combines all of these elements through careful planning and organization of information. The result is genuine help for the user when it is needed and with access to all pertinent information.

Chapter Objectives

In this chapter we begin by discussing why on-line help is needed and how it is used. Then we introduce you to some of the tools you can use to develop help systems. You will find out how to plan, organize, and develop your help files using efficient and proven techniques. We show you the steps necessary to compile your help information into files compatible with WINHELP.EXE, the Microsoft help engine, and then distribute those files. We finish by detailing some ever-present and useful help topics that you should expect to include in your system.

Why On-Line Help is Needed

You may find yourself questioning the need for electronic on-line help. After all, your application or library addresses a well-defined need within a narrowly defined problem domain. Your interface is a model of compliance with accepted standards. Your users will be trained by the best educators available.

All true. But eventually, somebody will forget something that he or she learned. Or you will bring in new users or developers, and they will need to be productive before they have had a chance to attend a full sequence of training. Perhaps you will be blessed with developers who want to explore beyond their formal training and search for better and more efficient ways to accomplish their goals. All of these needs are best served by well-planned and well-executed on-line help.

On-line help provides ease of access

The WinHelp help engine is always just a keystroke (F1) away. Context-sensitive help is available via a key combination, usually either Ctrl + F1 or Shift + F1. In addition, users have instant access to on-line help without interrupting the flow of their work. Unlike printed and bound manuals, an application's help files are not easily misplaced.

On-line help is search-enabled

The electronic nature of an on-line help system lends itself nicely to nontraditional access methods. WinHelp provides a standard search mechanism. The user can key in a concept or keyword and get a list of topics related to that keyword. The ease and quickness of this procedure are obvious, but there is another benefit. Your users will be presented with alternative topics that they would not necessarily have even seen when searching a printed text.

On-line help offers different paths to essential information

Hypertext links in a well-designed help system allow easy reference to related items. This allows users to access the information they need, independent of the way the information is organized.

Terms that must be defined can be designated as popups. Popups allow instant access to glossary (and other explanatory) information from anywhere in the help system.

Help topics can also be arranged in a browse sequence. This allows the help developer to organize related topics in a logical order. The user simply clicks on the "<<"or ">>," button to move back and forth through a browse sequence.

The most productive help files use hypertext links, browse sequences, and popups extensively. The purpose is to present the information in a way that mimics as closely as possible the mental processes the user will use as he or she searches for answers.

On-line help is context-sensitive

Help can be keyed to the user's context within the application or class library. This is drastically different from the linear access afforded by printed material. The user can be quickly taken to the right information and be back to work before the printed-manual user has even found the index. One benefit to remember about this feature is that by making information lookup easier and faster, it encourages the user to consult the help instead of wasting time experimenting to find a solution.

Development Tools for On-Line Help

In the early days of Windows development, the construction of help files was a trying and tedious task. The help writer needed to manipulate unwieldy rich text format (RTF) files filled with mysterious codes and footnotes. Fortunately, the tools have evolved over time and we now enjoy an assortment of easy-to-use and powerful tools for the creation of help files.

RTF files

The basis of every help file is an RTF file. RTF is a file standard specified by Microsoft that contains formatting information for word processors in an independent, ASCII text–based format. The formatting information is used in specific ways to code the various parts of a help file such as keywords, context strings, titles, build tags, browse sequences, cross-references, and definitions.

The formatting codes in the RTF files are used to specify the help file elements, as shown in Table 30.1.

TABLE 30.1 RTF Formatting Codes for Help Files

Formatting Code	Help File Element
Hard page break	Separates topics.
Asterisk footnote (*)	Build tag: This element specifies topics that are conditionally built by the help compiler.
Pound sign (#)	Context string: This element signals a context string that uniquely identifies a topic.
Dollar sign footnote ($)	Title: Defines the title of a topic.
Letter "K" footnote	Keyword: This element defines a keyword used for topic searches.
Plus sign footnote (+)	Browse sequence number: Defines a sequence of topics that the user can step through in order.
Strikethrough or double-underlined text	Cross-reference: This element defines jumps to another topic in the help system.
Underlined text	Definition: Text that displays a popup containing a definition or other temporary material.
Hidden text	Cross-reference context string: Specifies the context string for the destination of a cross-reference jump.

Microsoft help compilers

Microsoft has made widely available two compilers that produce help files from RTF files: protected mode HCP.EXE and real mode HC31.EXE. The differences between these programs are primarily related to memory allocation and capacity. Because it is a protected mode DOS-extended program, HCP is capable of compiling larger help files than HC31. HCP and HC31 are adequate tools, especially given that no other help compilers exist. Unfortunately, Microsoft has never released the internal structure of the WinHelp files. This leaves us with no real choice but to use the Microsoft-provided compilers for creating help systems.

WHAT/WHPE

Microsoft has provided a tool intended to ease the task of the help author. The tool is called Windows Help Authoring Templates/Windows Help Project Editor (WHAT/WHPE). These two programs, used in conjunction with Microsoft Word for Windows, were designed to help the author construct the help topic files and the help project file.

WHAT is a set of templates that work with Word for Windows and automate the construction of topic files. Support is also provided for graphics and hotspots. The macros included in the templates ease certain facets of help file construction. For instance, the templates always save the topic files in RTF.

WHPE allows menu-driven construction of the help project file. You can add topic files to the project and edit the project-specific information. WHPE allows you to compile the finished help project, and displays the errors produced by the compiler. When you have a successful build, WHPE allows you to view the final help file.

WHAT/WHPE is available on the Microsoft Developer Network disk. Be aware, however, that the product is provided in the Unsupported Tools and Utilities section, and explicitly does not enjoy any support.

Also on the MS Developer Network disk is the excellent *Windows Help Authoring Guide*. This document contains a wealth of information regarding the design issues that face a help author.

Visual Help

Visual Help is a shareware help authoring tool. Visual Help allows easy, WYSIWYG creation of help files. Visual Help can be found on various bulletin boards and forums, and supports the shareware concept: Try before you buy.

ForeHelp

ForeHelp, a product of ForeFront Software, incorporates its own full-featured word processor, eliminating the need for MS Word or an equivalent RTF word processor. ForeHelp is a visual help development tool that supports WYSIWYG help file creation.

ForeHelp provides visual creation of standard help functionality such as topics, hypertext jumps, and popups. In addition, it supports graphic hotspots, the use of different window classes, browse sequences, macros, and embedded data.

ForeHelp's word processor allows you to define style sheets to help provide a consistent presentation. It also includes a spell-checker and thesaurus.

ForeHelp imports RTF and help project (HPJ) files from existing help projects. In addition, ForeHelp prints topics, either individually or as a group, in a format suitable for distribution as a companion manual.

Doc2Help

Doc2Help, by WexTech Software, is a template-driven help file generator. By that I mean that the product consists of a set of templates that can be used with your word processor (such as Microsoft Word for Windows) to capture your help topics and details in a manual format that can then be printed as a manual or generated into a Windows on-line help file. Doc2Help requires a help file compiler to be present in order to compile the document into a file.

Doc2Help uses a predefined set of document styles that are then used to generate the necessary help file sections. The document is first translated into an RTF file, with help file compiler codes inserted in place of the styles. Certain styles automatically become hypertext jumps. Others become referenced topics. The tool also allows you to indicate words or sentences that form index entries. The index entries are those that are shown in the Search dialog window associated with common help files.

By simply learning which styles will be converted into which help file items, you can learn how to create a user manual that can easily and quickly be converted into on-line help, including hypertext jumps, popups and automatic related topic generation.

Doc2Help allows you to create a manual consisting of multiple documents, provided you use Doc2Help templates. WexTech is a Powersoft CODE partner.

RoboHelp

RoboHelp, from Blue Sky Software, is a help authoring tool made to work in conjunction with MS Word for Windows 2.0 or 6.0.

RoboHelp supports all features of the Windows 3.1 help engine, including macros, secondary windows, and multiple hotspot graphics. RoboHelp uses a visual palette to provide an easy way to code standard help features such as topics, jumps, and popups. The tool is designed to support two-way transfer: It automatically converts existing documentation into a help system or vice versa.

RoboHelp also incorporates an Error Wizard that helps to detect and explain potential errors in your help file before compilation.

Also included with RoboHelp is a Visual Basic Custom Control (VBX) that eliminates any need to specifically code context-sensitive help into your PowerBuilder application.

Blue Sky Software is a Powersoft CODE Partner.

Planning On-Line Help

The structure of an on-line help system must be carefully planned in order to maximize the efficiency with which the user can retrieve the necessary information. The organization of the help files is the key to efficiency and information bandwidth. The steps in organizing and creating a help system are as follows:

1. Identify topics
2. Create a context map
3. Identify hypertext links
4. Identify browse sequences
5. Identify searches and keywords
6. Choose a file structure (single or multiple)
7. Decide whether to produce printed documentation directly from help document

We discuss each of these elements in greater detail below.

For our purposes, it is less cumbersome to refer to the entire collection of files in a help system as a help file, whether your final file structure is a single file or multiple files. In the discussions that follow, we do not intend to limit you to a single help file.

Identifying topics

The first step in planning the organization of your help file is to create a topic tree. A topic tree visually depicts the relationships among different topics and helps you organize the structure of the final help file more effectively. For an application, each step in the workflow document ideally relates to a help topic in an application help file. In the case of a help file for a class library, the help topics most often relate to the objects, methods, and attributes in that library.

We first examine the methods used to derive a topic tree for an application help file.

Finding topics for an application.   Examine each step or node in the application workflow document. From this examination, you should derive a tree of topics that is almost (if not exactly) identical to the workflow diagram. This represents the highest level topic organization for your help file.

As an example, you might have an item at the top level of your workflow called Transaction Processing. You should add a Transaction Processing topic to your topic tree. At this time, we are not concentrating on the *content* of the topics, just the topics themselves.

For each item on the workflow diagram that is subordinate to Transaction Processing, you should add a corresponding topic to your topic tree. For instance, you would want to include a help topic for the Enter Transactions item from the workflow.

More topics exist, however. Each on-screen object may very well be the source of a new topic. When in doubt, you should include a questionable topic in your help file plan. If you have nothing to say about it later on, you need not include it in the final help file. If you associate a help topic with each visible object, you ease the task of implementing context-sensitivity in your help system.

Add the new topics that you have identified into your existing topic tree.

Finding topics for a class library.   Take note of each object in the class library. Each object should have a help topic devoted to it. Each object that has a visual representation should also be examined for topics. As with applications, each on-screen control or object should probably be associated with a help topic.

Once again, add any newly identified topics into your existing topic tree. The result will be something like Figure 30.1.

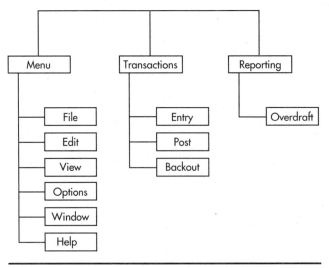

Figure 30.1   Help topic tree.

Finding topics for both applications and class libraries.   Prepare lists of frequently asked questions (FAQs). Before you deploy your application or library, these lists will of necessity be quite short. You should plan to expand and redistribute them often, however. If you keep a comprehensive list of FAQs and update them regularly, you will certainly ease the burden on your support team.

The entry points for the FAQ lists should be generic and consistent. In other words, you should begin by defining categories into which you can group the various questions. Then, the entry points into the FAQ help topics will be these categories. This allows for future expansion, adding questions and answers, without affecting the other parts of the help file. Note that the inclusion of FAQ lists is often a very good reason to select a multifile architecture for your help system. If the FAQ list is maintained in a separate file, it can be maintained and updated frequently without the necessity of distributing the entire help file each time.

Finally, identify the tasks that the user will want to perform when using your application or library. Each separate task merits instructions for accomplishing that task.

Add the FAQ lists and the task lists to your topic tree as top-level branches. Figure 30.2 shows the result.

Examples.   It is especially critical in the case of a class library, but also valid for an application, to provide numerous examples in the help file.

Start a top-level branch on your topic tree for examples. Each example should have its own topic subordinate to this branch.

This completes your search for topics. Now you need to establish the contexts and links that your help file will use to access these topics.

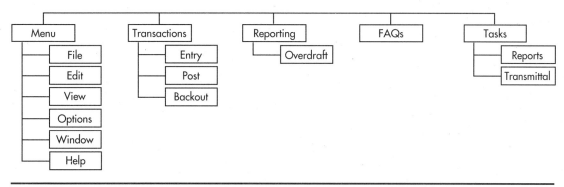

Figure 30.2 Help topic tree with FAQs and tasks.

Creating a context map

The next step in planning your help system is to create a context map based on the topic tree you have already built. A context map is a list, in outline form, of every topic you have identified. You will assign each topic two unique identifiers that will allow access to that topic. The first is a context string. The context string is simply a concatenation of each preceding topic with the current topic. The second is a context number. The context number is arbitrarily assigned but must be unique. A portion of the context map, as it stands at this point, is illustrated in Figure 30.3.

As you can see, the context numbers begin at 1 and increase by 100 for each topic. This is to allow room for later insertions. It is not necessary for the entries to be in order, but it makes it easier to find the entries.

Identifying hypertext links

Once you have completed the context map, you can begin adding information for hypertext links from one context to another. Hypertext links (or jumps) are words, highlighted in a different color from the rest of the text, that the user can click on to be transferred to another topic in the help file. Within reason, the more jumps you can embed in your help, the better the user's access to information will be. There are many useful sources of hypertext links, including the following:

- "See also" topics
- Subordinate topics
- Tasks that precede or follow this topic
- Alternative approaches to the problem

As you identify topics for hypertext links, add them to the context map, one line for each link. This is illustrated in Figure 30.4.

Context Number	Topics	Context String	Jumps	Browse Sequence
0	Contents	Contents		
1	Menu	Menu		
101	File	MenuFile		
201	Open	MenuFileOpen		
301	Save	MenuFileSave		
401	Save As	MenuFileSaveAs		
501	Print	MenuFilePrint		
601	Exit	MenuFileExit		
701	Edit	MenuEdit		
801	View	MenuView		
901	Options	MenuOptions		
1001	Window	MenuWindow		
1101	Help	MenuHelp		
1201	Transactions	Transactions		
1301	Entry	TransactionsEntry		
1401	Post	TransactionsPost		
1501	Backout	TransactionsBackout		
1601	Reporting	Reporting		
1701	OverDraft	ReportingOverdraft		
1801	FAQs	FAQs		
1901	Tasks	Tasks		
2001	Reports	TasksReports		
2101	Transmittal	TasksTransmittal		
2201	Examples	Examples		
2301	Opening a File	ExamplesOpeningAFile		
2401	Transmitting Results	ExamplesTransmittingResults		

Figure 30.3 Help context map.

Context Number	Topics	Context String	Jumps	Browse Sequence
0	Contents	Contents		
1	Menu	Menu	101, 701, 801, 1001, 1101	
101	File	MenuFile	1, 201, 301, 401, 501, 601	
201	Open	MenuFileOpen	101, 2301	
301	Save	MenuFileSave	101	
401	Save As	MenuFileSaveAs	101	
501	Print	MenuFilePrint	101	
601	Exit	MenuFileExit	101	
701	Edit	MenuEdit	1	
801	View	MenuView	1	
901	Options	MenuOptions	1	
1001	Window	MenuWindow	1	
1101	Help	MenuHelp	1	
1201	Transactions	Transactions	1301, 1401, 1501	
1301	Entry	TransactionsEntry	1201	
1401	Post	TransactionsPost	1201, 2101, 2401	
1501	Backout	TransactionsBackout	1201	
1601	Reporting	Reporting	1701	
1701	OverDraft	ReportingOverdraft	1601, 2001	
1801	FAQs	FAQs		
1901	Tasks	Tasks		
2001	Reports	TasksReports	1601, 1701	
2101	Transmittal	TasksTransmittal	1401, 2401	
2201	Examples	Examples		
2301	Opening a File	ExamplesOpeningAFile	101, 201	

Figure 30.4 Help context map with hypertext links defined.

"See also" topics.   Also often called related topics, these topics bear some relation to the topic at hand. For instance, any topic that concerns another operation that acts on the same type of data is a possible candidate for inclusion as a jump. Similarly, any topic that concerns a task that has a similar outcome might also be included. I use the words *possible* and *might* here very deliberately. This is not an exact formula, but a set of guidelines. You must use creativity and judgment when planning your hypertext links.

Subordinate topics.   Topics that appear on the topic tree as subordinate topics to the current one should be included as hypertext jumps. These usually apply to branches that the user may reach from the current context. By giving users the opportunity to jump directly to one of these topics, you increase their ability to find help according to the actual flow of their work.

Tasks that precede or follow this topic.   These topics usually answer the question "How did I get here?" They are the topics that describe stages in the workflow (or development tasks, in the case of a class library) that lead up to the current topic. Users can select one of these jumps to get a wider understanding of the context in which they are operating.

In the same way, try to include jumps to topics that answer the question "Where can I go from here?" This gives users a way to check the validity of the paths they are researching.

Alternative approaches to the problem.   Finally, if there are topics that represent other ways to address a given topic provided by your application or library, add references to these approaches as hypertext jumps. This allows the user to differentiate among alternative solutions, and pick the one that best suits the current situation.

Identifying browse sequences

The WinHelp engine provides two buttons, "<<" or ">>," that allow the user to browse through a predefined sequence of topics. This is akin to reading a book or manual in the intended order. Browse sequences provide a complete treatment of a set of related topics. Well-organized browse sequences simplify information retrieval, especially when the user is trying to learn something new.

Browse sequences should typically be based on application workflow. In the case of a class library, the attributes and methods of a class or object would form an effective browse sequence.

Each top-level item in the application workflow (or the topic tree) usually defines a browse sequence. The top-level item delineates the start of the sequence. Then, each subordinate level defines an element of the browse sequence. Number each item in a browse sequence as *sss-nnn,* where *sss* is an identifier for the particular sequence and *nnn* defines the item's place in the browse sequence. Enter the identifiers for your browse sequences into the context map, as shown in Figure 30.5.

Context Number	Topics	Context String	Jumps	Browse Sequence
0	Contents	Contents		
1	Menu	Menu	101, 701, 801, 1001, 1101	001-000
101	File	MenuFile	1, 201, 301, 401, 501, 601	001-110
201	Open	MenuFileOpen	101, 2301	001-120
301	Save	MenuFileSave	101	001-130
401	Save As	MenuFileSaveAs	101	001-140
501	Print	MenuFilePrint	101	001-150
601	Exit	MenuFileExit	101	001-160
701	Edit	MenuEdit	1	001-170
801	View	MenuView	1	001-180
901	Options	MenuOptions	1	001-190
1001	Window	MenuWindow	1	001-200
1101	Help	MenuHelp	1	001-210
1201	Transactions	Transactions	1301, 1401, 1501	010-000
1301	Entry	TransactionsEntry	1201	010-010
1401	Post	TransactionsPost	1201, 2101, 2401	010-020
1501	Backout	TransactionsBackout	1201	010-030
1601	Reporting	Reporting	1701	020-000
1701	OverDraft	ReportingOverdraft	1601, 2001	020-010
1801	FAQs	FAQs		030-000
1901	Tasks	Tasks		040-000
2001	Reports	TasksReports	1601, 1701	040-010
2101	Transmittal	TasksTransmittal	1401, 2401	040-020
2201	Examples	Examples		050-000
2301	Opening a File	ExamplesOpeningAFile	101, 201	050-010

Figure 30.5   Context map with browse sequences.

Single or multiple file structure?

Once you have obtained an idea of the range and complexity of the topics that your help file will contain, you must decide on the file structure you will use for your help system. The choice of file structure—single or multiple— is based on a number of factors.

The expected size of the final help file certainly has an influence. If your file will be small, by all means provide it as a single file. You will simplify deployment and update procedures greatly.

If you expect your file to be very large, you should plan on splitting the file into several parts. The definition of *very large* depends on how your help file is deployed. If you will deploy the help files to each workstation, the help file can be quite large, even several megabytes. However, if you plan to locate your help centrally on a file server, your maximum effective file size is probably in the 100K to 300K range. Any larger and you risk performance degradation, slow file opens, and unacceptable network traffic. If your network is fast and uncrowded, you can have larger files than if your network is slow or saturated.

The ultimate organization of the help file is also a factor you must consider. If your topic tree shows a number of primarily unrelated branches, and each branch has a high degree of complexity, a multiple file structure is ideal. Place each unique branch into its own file. This increases the responsiveness of the help system because the files are smaller, but because few links from file to file exist, performance of hypertext links does not suffer.

It is important to limit the number of jumps that cross file boundaries. These increase the number of file opens and closes and make your help system seem jumpy and unresponsive to the user. This is especially true when retrieving help files across a network connection.

Finally, if you expect any sections of your help system to be updated frequently, such as the FAQ sections discussed above, you will be better served by a multiple file structure. When the need to update the section arises, you will need to distribute only the single file relating to the updates.

Help only or help/doc?

Some help authoring tools are specifically designed to produce help files and printed manuals from the same source document. The advantage of reusability of the source document is clear, but you need to decide whether the printed documentation should be identical to the help files. In general, the answer is no.

- *Help information is best when it is presented one screen at a time.* Printed documentation often spans many pages covering a topic. The granularity of the information in a help file is far higher than the granularity of a printed document with the same content.

- *Help files rely on hypertext to increase information bandwidth.* Printed documents must convey information more serially and in a more localized fashion.

Exceptions exist, however, especially in the area of class libraries, where the topic structure corresponds primarily to objects, their methods, and their attributes. With a bit of planning, you can use the same visual presentation for your help file and your printed document, and lose nothing. You must be specific in the way you name your hypertext links. As an example, "See FooBar Object: Methods" works in either medium, whereas "See Methods" works only in the hypertext environment.

The disadvantage to using the same text for both media is that the information will be ideally suited for neither. Your printed document will seem stilted and condensed, and your help file will seem unfocused and meandering. The advantage is that your help files and your manual will contain exactly the same information. A second advantage is that the source document need only be created once, and can be used to create either the printed manual or the help file.

When you use different source texts for your help and your printed manual, you must always guard against presenting contradictory information. This means that several proofreaders should read both media thoroughly in order to spot any inconsistencies or contradictions.

Flatten the help file

A final step in the organization of your help file is to flatten any overly deep branches in the topic tree.

If your final topic tree contains branches that extend more than three levels deep, you should attempt to reduce the depth of the tree. You do your users a huge favor if you always provide a path no more than three mouse clicks away from any topic. Often you will find that a too-deep tree results from inappropriate organization of the top level topics. A simple remedy is to turn a branch point into two or more higher-level topics. Figure 30.6 illustrates the concept.

Now that the topics for your help file are identified and organized, it is time to begin creating the help file.

Development of On-Line Help

Developing a help file consists of several steps:

1. Write the topic text.
2. Identify search keywords.
3. Add jumps and popups to all topics.
4. Compile into .HLP file.
5. Test the structure of the help file.

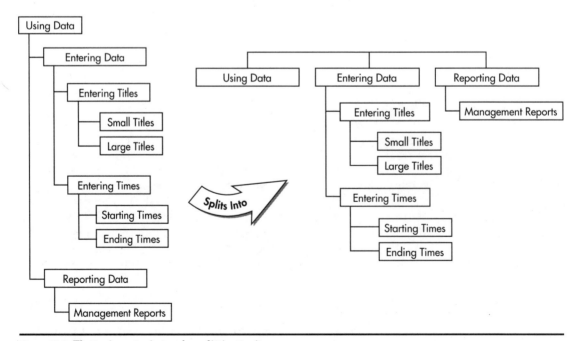

Figure 30.6 Flattening a topic tree by splitting topics.

Before you begin fleshing out your topics, take some time to identify your intended audience for this help file. Then target the information to suit their level of technical sophistication and training. Consider two areas: their general ability to navigate through a computer program and their understanding of the subject matter addressed by the application or class library.

Write the topic text

Develop each topic as an individual explanation of the task, concept, or object covered by the topic. Explain each topic as fully as you can, but try to organize your information to fit in the space of a single screen. You can use several screens to fully describe a given topic, if necessary. Just keep in mind that each individual screen should treat a complete concept, with little or no need for the user to jump back and forth.

Use styles to ensure consistent formatting

Use a consistent format and presentation when you create the help file. The easiest way to accomplish this is to use style sheets that accommodate all of the expected elements in your help file. When you set up your style sheets, avoid the "ransom note" look by using a single-family approach to fonts. That is, use a set of typefaces, sizes, styles, and weights that presents a harmonious face to the user. Because your help will be displayed on a video monitor, pay special attention to the typefaces' readability. Arial, a True Type font supplied with Windows, is very readable on a computer screen. The sizes you choose for the text should be based on the screen resolutions you expect as part of your application's environment.

Some elements for which you should define styles are as follows:

- *Banner text:* You can display a banner above your help text that does not scroll with the rest of the screen. The text should be larger than the help text and headings, but small enough to accommodate the longest topic title that you will be using.

- *Headings:* You will need several distinct levels of headings. The size and style of these headings should vary and indicate the level of detail of the following text.

- *Body text:* This is the default paragraph text. You need to strike a balance between ultimate readability and text size. The smaller you can make your text, the more information you can present in one screen. However, you should never sacrifice readability just to squeeze more words onto a screen. Be especially considerate of older users, who may have difficulty reading smaller type sizes.

- *Example code:* Use this style for code samples shown in the help file. It is best for the example code to be presented using a monospaced (nonproportional) font in order to maintain column alignment. A good choice for this is the Courier New font supplied with Windows.

It is a good practice to use fonts that you can be sure will be available to your users. The standard Windows fonts (Arial, Times New Roman, and Courier New) are almost always present.

Identify search keywords

Once you have the topics written, you can examine the text for keywords. The keywords for a particular topic appear as part of the Search dialog presented by WINHELP.EXE. This is a good place to be creative and generous. Every keyword that you can legitimately attach to a topic increases the likelihood of users finding their way to the information they need. Use the method provided by your help tool to add the keywords to the search list. The screen that ForeHelp uses to manage search keywords is shown in Figure 30.7.

Add jumps and popups to all topics

Next, use the context map to ensure that you have access points to all of the hypertext jumps you have defined. If the text contains a reference to a desired topic, connect a jump to that reference. Otherwise, you need to specifically add a See Also or Related Topics section.

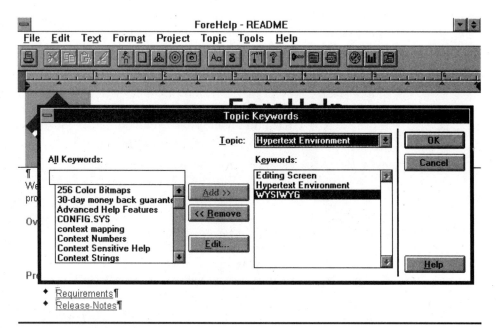

Figure 30.7 ForeHelp keyword entry.

Test the structure of the help file

Even before you attach your help file to an application, you should begin testing it for usability and accuracy. The WinHelp engine can open any help file from the menu, or you can double-click the filename from within the File Manager to open it. Note also that some help file development environments, such as ForeHelp, allow you to test the structure of a help file without even compiling it.

You should check each item in your context map to ensure that it has been included. Verify that the entry can be reached from the Table of Contents page. Next, you need to check, for each topic, that all links or popups you defined in your context map have been implemented. For each link, check first that the jump exists in the help text. Then double-click on the text marking the jump, and verify that the correct target topic is reached.

Perform the same sort of test on popups. Your goal is to make sure the box that pops up contains the text that pertains to the topic.

Select the first item in each browse sequence that you have defined. Verify that the browse sequence follows the correct order and contains all of the topics you intended.

Finally, you need to check the keywords. Bring up the Search dialog in the WinHelp engine. One by one, select each keyword and verify that the topics presented are valid for that keyword. Make spot checks to verify that you can reach the correct topic from the search dialog. Of course, an exhaustive test of all keywords and topics is preferred, but may not be practical.

Integrating Help with PowerBuilder

The final help file must be integrated with PowerBuilder in order for your users to access it. If you have developed a help file for an application, your application must have code and context information added. For a class library, you need to add the help file as part of PowerBuilder's operating environment.

Add context tags to PowerBuilder objects
for an application

Now you need to add the code and data to your application to enable the help system to respond to user requests. In the following example the user will press F1 for the Help Contents page, and Shift + F1 for context-sensitive help on any visible object.

Begin by selecting Edit/TagList from the menu in PowerBuilder's Window Painter. Figure 30.8 shows an example of the resulting dialog. Each control on the window is listed, along with a field in which you can enter the tag value for that control. You can put anything into the Tag field, but for the purposes of enabling on-line help, you should enter either context strings or context numbers. Click OK to save the Tag list, then save the window.

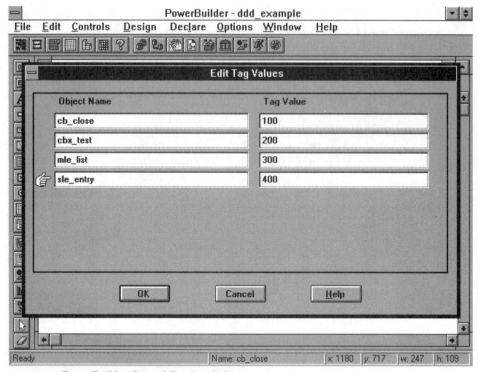

Figure 30.8 PowerBuilder Control Tag list dialog.

Using the tag value for each object is only one possible way to assign help context identifiers to objects. Some class libraries, notably Enterprise Builder from ICON Solutions, provide instance variables and access functions that allow you to maintain context identifiers for any object that is inherited from one of the library's base objects.

Add supporting code to PowerBuilder scripts

The discussion that follows takes the viewpoint that you are adding help to an application that does not gain any help functionality from a class library or application framework. The base objects (windows, controls, menus, user objects) in most class libraries have much of the functionality detailed below already in place. You will find the discussion beneficial if you are building your own class library, or if you want to understand the underlying functionality of a class library you have purchased.

It is a simple matter to add context-sensitive help to any PowerBuilder window. Begin in the menu painter. Add a menu item called Help. This item should be positioned last on the menu. Below the Help menu item, add an item called Help Index. Next, attach the F1 key as a shortcut for the Help Index menu item. Then, add a new item, Context Help, below the Help Index entry.

Assign the shortcut Shift + F1 to the Context Help item. Now you need to add code to these items to call the help system. In order to make the menus as reusable as possible, as well as to improve performance, the code in the menu simply triggers an event on the attached window.

For the Help Index menu item, enter the following in the Clicked event:

```
ParentWindow.TriggerEvent("cue_HelpIndex")
```

The code for the Context Help menu item is only slightly different:

```
ParentWindow.TriggerEvent("cue_ContextHelp")
```

Now, you need to add into the window the code that will actually call the WinHelp Engine with the appropriate file. First, in the Window Painter, create a string instance variable, is_HelpFile, to hold the file name. In your window initialization code, assign the name of the help file to the variable is_HelpFile.

Caution: Be careful how you specify the help file name. If you specify an exact path to the help file, you will complicate deployment of your application. One solution is to place the path to the help file in an application INI file, and load the INI file information when you initialize your application.

Next, add two custom user events cue_HelpIndex and cue_ContextHelp. Assign event pbm_custom01 to cue_HelpIndex and assign pbm_Custom02 to cue_ContextHelp. Figure 30.9 shows the custom Event dialog with these two additional events.

Caution: When you are assigning custom events, make sure that the descendants of your object are not already using that pbm_custom event number. You can avoid such collisions by setting sensible standards for reserved event ranges and following them assiduously.

The PowerBuilder function you will use to access the WinHelp Engine is ShowHelp. ShowHelp can be called in any of three ways. The first format will always bring up the help file at Topic 0, usually the Contents page:

```
ShowHelp(is_helpFile,index!)
```

The second format is used to go to the topic associated with a keyword (is_keyword is an instance variable containing the desired keyword):

```
ShowHelp(is_helpFile,Keyword!,is_keyword)
```

If the keyword is not found, the WinHelp Search dialog is displayed, allowing the user to choose from among the defined keywords.

The last format allows access to the help file via topic numbers (passed to ShowHelp in the instance variable ii_topic):

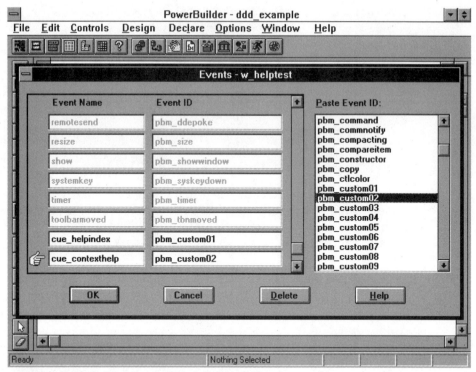

Figure 30.9 PowerBuilder Custom Event dialog.

```
ShowHelp(is_helpFile,Topic!,ii_topic)
```

Now, add the following code to the cue_HelpIndex event:

```
ShowHelp(is_helpFile,Index!)
```

The Help Index menu item is fired when the user presses the shortcut key. This in turn triggers the HelpIndex event on your window. The HelpIndex event issues a call to ShowHelp that displays the Contents page for the application's help file.

Enter the following code for the cue_ContextHelp event:

```
/*
 * eventname: ContextHelp
 */

// Obtain a pointer to the Current Object
ig_currentObject = GetFocus()

// Get the tag Value from the Current Object
is_TagValue = ig_currentObject.Tag

IF isNumber(is_TagValue) THEN
// Use the Context Number if the Tag is numeric
```

```
 ii_TagValue = Integer(is_TagValue)
 ShowHelp(is_helpfile,topic!,ii_TagValue)
ELSE
// Use the Tag as a Keyword
 ShowHelp(is_HelpFile,keyword!,is_TagValue)
END IF
```

As you can see, the code first obtains a pointer to the current object. Then the tag value for that object is assigned to is_TagValue. The tag value is then checked to see whether it is numeric. This feature allows you to set the tag values to either keyword strings or context numbers depending on your needs. If the tag value is a number, ShowHelp is called with a numerical topic. Otherwise, ShowHelp is called with a keyword.

Testing in context with your application

Once you have verified the help file itself, you need to ensure that the application works properly together with the help file.

The first test is that the Help Index menu item brings up the Contents page of your help file. Press the F1 key or select Help/Help Index from the menu. The help file should appear with the Contents page visible.

Next, you need to make sure that the context-sensitive help is functioning as intended. Follow the application workflow for this testing sequence.

Follow the application workflow, opening the appropriate windows or sheets for each task. Set the focus (using the Tab key) to each control on each window. Press Shift + F1 (or select Help/Context Help from the menu). Verify that the proper help topic is displayed for each object on each window.

Adding a help file to PowerBuilder for a class library

You can integrate the help file for your class library into the PowerBuilder help environment. PowerBuilder displays an additional button labeled User in its help window. By default, PowerBuilder sets the WinHelp engine to open a file called PBUSR050.HLP when the User button is pressed.

You can attach your own help file to the User button by using the following steps:

1. Set the context ID string for the CONTENTS topic to index_user_help.

2. Rename the original PBUSR050.HLP file to another name.

3. Copy your help file into the PowerBuilder directory, using the name PBUSR050.HLP.

Now, when you press the User button, your own help file will appear at the Contents page instead of the User Help file installed with PowerBuilder.

You can use the same file to provide context-sensitive help for your functions. PowerBuilder opens the User help file if the user presses Shift + F1 while the cursor is placed on a function beginning with uf_.

TIP

You can use the PB.INI variables UserHelpFile and UserHelpPrefix to alter the default User help filename and function prefix. The PBUSR050.HLP file that is shipped with PowerBuilder has more details on the use of these variables.

Compilation and Distribution

Distribution of help files is usually managed through the same mechanisms used to distribute an application. However, you may decide that the help files can be deployed on each workstation while the application resides on the server, or vice versa. The decision on where to place the help files should be based on considerations such as impact on network traffic and user needs.

Useful On-Line Help Topics and Files

Some topics that you should always include (and, in fact, you can usually create as reusable modules) are as follows:

- *Standard Windows menu items:* The items on the File, Edit, and Windows menus should be included, and their descriptions are almost always the same. Consider developing a standard menu help file for these and other common items.
- *Class Library:* For a class library, it can sometimes be useful to document the Windows API and how it can (or need not) be used by users of the library.

In addition, you can implement the Help on Help topic by including a jump that transfers to the Contents (0) topic of WINHELP.HLP, found in the Windows directory.

Summary

In this chapter we have shown you how to create functional, efficient, and *helpful* help files. We discussed the need for on-line help and the characteristics of well-implemented help systems. We examined several of the tools available to aid in the creation of help files.

We presented a step-by-step method for identifying and organizing help topics, jumps, and keywords. We gave you some guidelines to help you present your help data in a consistent, informative style.

Finally, we showed you how to add the hooks into a PowerBuilder application to allow the user to access context-sensitive help.

31

Training

Introduction

Whether you are developing training to train people in PowerBuilder itself, in a class library you purchased, or in the use of your application, developing training is the hardest task of all. The reason for this is that you are putting yourself on the line. Your knowledge, your communication skills, and your very beliefs are portrayed in the training materials you develop and the training delivery itself.

This is no ordinary skill. Look at all the great teachers in history and you will see one thing in common: They could put their hearts out on their sleeves and draw the audience into themselves, creating a willingness to learn.

Many of us are developers, some qualify as great developers, but few of us have the gift of teaching. Some of the people whose technical skills I respect the most are not great teachers. Technologists, especially good ones, have an ego that they prefer to keep hidden except in technical conversation.

A few of my esteemed colleagues are born teachers, a skill I envy. I, like many of you, have to work too hard and too long to be able to deliver a decent class. If you are one of those with the gift, you need not go any further in this chapter. You already know more than I ever will. For the rest of us, this chapter highlights many of the tricks, tips, and techniques I have learned, along with many I have solicited from those I respect and admire (and wish they did not make the rest of us look so bad).

Chapter Objectives

The goals of this chapter are to introduce the technologies of the day, ranging from a typical classroom environment to the latest methods of computer-based training and computer-based video training.

To help you develop training for any reason, this chapter outlines the necessities that must be covered, such as choosing between developing your own training and buying a professionally produced training course, planning the course materials, developing the course outline, developing the course materials, developing workshop exercises, delivering the training effectively, and following up on your students after the course is completed.

These tips and techniques will help you to bridge the gap between an average training course and a good training course. I cannot teach you to be a great teacher, but I can pass on to you what I have learned to be the other elements necessary for good training materials and effective delivery.

Technologies

There are many forms of training materials today. The technology of the era is beginning to find the student. Of course, there is still the traditional classroom, but even there, the technology being used is getting more sophisticated.

Video-based training

Besides traditional training classes, the industry is experiencing the growth of several new media designed to allow students to teach themselves at their own pace. Of course, video-based training has been around for quite some time. The problem with traditional video-based training has always been the lack of interaction between the instructor and the student. You might be able to stop, pause, or fast-forward a videotape, but when a task needs explanation, the student is often left wondering about the answer. The quality of videotaped training has suffered because of this lack of appeal to students and teachers.

Computer-based training

Computer-based training is a hot new medium. An interactive computer program that works at the student's pace, directly on the computer, using the software that is being taught, is very close to a hands-on workshop. The student still does not have the interaction with a teacher when questions arise that are not included in the program, but the step-by-step "I'll show you how it's done, then you do it," with constant feedback from the training program, helps students to accelerate self-study courses. The sophistication of today's technology affords software vendors a great opportunity to build these types of training materials. You can, too. Companies such as CBT have interactive training material-building programs, which are expensive; however, the cost can be justified when compared to the average cost of $1000 per student for on-site training. In larger organizations, where student counts are expected to be high, it becomes obvious that such a training materials development tool can be justified.

Computer-based training with video

The latest technology to hit the streets is the inclusion of computer video with computer-based training materials. Now, instead of textual instructions on how to use the piece of software, an instructor's advice can be captured on video, as well as "screen-cams," computer video taken of actual usage of the product that shows how it should be used. Used without the computer-based software, it provides a more inexpensive hands-on training method to be used by smaller vendors and development teams that cannot afford the interactive media. If the video is coupled with written media, the student can not only read about how it should be done, but use the screen-cams to see how it is done on the machine. Screen-cam developers can also record their voices on the video track, allowing them to talk to their students.

All of the new media can help alleviate the training requirements of an organization, but nothing can quite replace the interpersonal communication between a teacher and students. Perhaps in time, technology will advance the interactive media further than it has today, but for my money, personal instruction with a good teacher is worth the investment.

Develop or Buy?

Of course, the question arises even with the classroom training: Should you develop the materials yourself, buy the materials (if available), bring in an instructor, or teach the class yourself? There are various pros and cons for each, and the decision is affected by the subject matter, but you should explore the alternatives and find the balance between cost and benefit to the students. Remember that it is their education you are concerned about, and that should remain your primary consideration.

Developing your own materials is time-consuming, but delivers a known product.

Developing your own materials and delivering them to your students is a time-consuming effort, full of rewards and criticism, and generally a difficult task to accomplish. By default, it therefore provides you with the greatest reward upon successful completion and delivery of the training. Much of the remainder of this chapter is dedicated to the preparation and delivery of your own training. If you plan to become an instructor, the topics will help you to develop and deliver training for other materials down the road.

Buying prepared training is cost-effective, but usually not customized. Customized costs more.

One of your alternatives is to purchase training services from a vendor qualified to supply the training materials you need. This works out pretty well with commercialized software products, as most vendors provide training (or training programs through partners) that will satisfy your needs. Of course, if you are developing the product, you become the vendor. This is true whether it is a class library, business objects, or an application. Someone will become the user of the product and will require training. You are the vendor who must provide that training.

Hiring a company to develop training provides highly customized, and usually expensive, solutions.

You can also buy "unprepared" training from a training development company. This means that you hire a company qualified to develop instructional materials to come in and develop training materials based on your product. Again, the product is of little concern. All products need some form of training available for the users of the product, be they end-users or developers. This is often a good approach because an outside professional vendor can develop a good training course in a relatively short period of time, based on a lot of prior experience. The downside is that there is no way an outsider can know your product as well as you do. You will need to build in time and effort to review and modify the training materials they deliver.

Certified training provides guaranteed quality of materials and relatively guaranteed quality of instruction.

For some products, certified training materials and instructors are available. I advise you to use this form of training for products you purchase, making sure that the vendor has some form of training material certification. If not, inquire as to when certified material would be available, and perhaps you can even strike a deal with them to assist in the development process in exchange for reduced costs on training at your organization.

Noncertified instruction is usually less expensive, but not guaranteed.

One path often chosen by companies is to use what is commonly called bootleg instruction. This is instruction developed and usually delivered by companies that either develop their own training materials instead of using the prescribed training offered by the vendor or its partners, or promise to develop and deliver "customized" training for your organization. Although there are definitely some companies or individuals out there who will develop and deliver high-quality training, for the most part, you should be very careful. Often, you get what you pay for. Make sure you check around the community to determine whether the vendor offering the training has a reputation (good or bad).

Planning

Okay. You have made the big decision. You are going to develop your own training course. What now? Where do we begin? What tools and techniques do we use to make the most of what we have to do a good job? The place to start is with planning. As in anything else, without good planning, you are setting yourself up to fail. Of course, some people succeed no matter what the odds are. I, on the other hand, need to plan what I want to accomplish. Planning serves two purposes: It forces me to think of what I want to accomplish and it provides a checklist of what I have accomplished.

The importance of planning is often underrated.

The first item on my plan is, of course, to develop the plan. Now that this element is out of the way, we can get down to the real stuff. The following items are tasks I usually put onto my plan. The list is high-level, but covers all of the areas that I feel are important and should be covered.

- *Get to know your audience:* Whenever you are preparing training materials, it is important to know who your audience will be. The number of people, existing skill level, and current political climate all affect the way your audience will receive your materials. Adjust and modify your materials to suit your class.

- *Develop an outline:* Prepare an outline of the training materials you are going to deliver. Like a book, training material must flow from one topic to the next. Topics should be arranged sequentially. Introduce new functionality and methodologies before going into depth. A good method for this was introduced to me by my colleague and coauthor, Millard Brown. Break your major topics out into short but descriptive topic sentences. Each topic sentence tells you what needs to be fleshed out and assigned a presentation medium.

- *Choose the media:* Select the medium you will use for each topic in your outline. In fact, you should choose the medium for each of your topic sentences. Overhead slides, computer program demos, exercise example code, and screen-cam recordings are just a few possibilities.

- *Develop the materials:* Develop the materials according to the outline and topic sentence breakouts you have made. Stick to the subject and do not try to amuse or entertain. If you are experienced as an instructor, you can build in a few amusing anecdotes to keep your audience entertained, but you should always remember that your students have usually paid money to be taught, and you have wasted their money if they leave your class entertained but untaught.

- *Develop multimedia and exercise materials:* Develop the additional materials you need for the training session, be it a multimedia presentation or exercise materials.

- *Rehearse and practice delivery:* Rehearse and practice the delivery of your training classes. If you can rehearse with others, it works out better.

These are the major tasks I outline and adhere to for every training session I prepare, regardless of the size of the training class or the size of the training materials. Skip any of these steps and your are exposing yourself to possible failure.

Get to Know Your Audience

Finding out who you are training is really more important than most people think. Knowing whether they are experienced or beginners at the skill you are teaching can mean the difference between effective training and having people bored or confused. Try to find out the makeup of your class. Having one experienced person in your class among several beginners can be devastating. The experienced developer might feel slighted by being included in the class, or feel that the pace is far too slow to be beneficial, and begin distracting the rest of the class. Even worse, the experienced developer may try to show off his or her knowledge to the rest of the class, usually at your expense. Always remember that you are a teacher. Your job is to teach the students in the class.

The same thing could occur if a beginner ends up in an advanced class with some experienced developers. The pace might be slowed, or the one person learns little because he or she does not understand enough to keep up with the class.

Simply being aware of the skill levels of the people who are in the class will help you with training development and delivery.

Find out what you can about the organization. A friend of mine once taught an introductory course for PowerBuilder to a group of mainframe users. Nothing unusual about that, right? In this case, they were taking the training because they had been laid off and the company was offering alternative training modules to help the employees extend their skills. Needless to say, the classroom climate was unusual. Finding this out, the instructor was still successful in what he had to do. By adjusting his normal strategy to empathize with the students, he was able to effectively deliver the training, leaving the students feeling that they learned something worthwhile. This could have turned out a lot worse.

The more information you have on hand going in, the more likely you are to develop an effective training course and deliver the course effectively. Learn what you can about your class as soon as you possibly can.

The other thing to remember when you are developing training materials is that you are targeting a specific group of employees. If the class is introductory, make sure you include elements explaining why the class is occurring at all. If the class is more advanced, keep it at an advanced level, but be prepared to explain a concept or technique that might be foreign to a student, even in an advanced class.

Outline Development

Break out self-contained units.

When developing an outline for training material, you could think of each high-level item in the outline as a unit. A unit of training material covers a topic completely, and leaves the trainee knowing the materials. The equivalent in a book is a chapter. The unit should be as self-contained as possible, and should have a definite start and end. It should begin with an introduction describing the unit and the objectives of the unit. The unit should close with a summary and an evaluation of the objectives of the unit.

Break out encapsulated major topics.

When writing a book, an author breaks a chapter down into major topics. Each major topic is then broken down into topic sentences. A training unit should follow the same method: Break the unit down into major subject areas, then break down the subject areas into small, encapsulated topics. This makes it much easier to develop training material that maintains a consistent flow of connected information and avoids subject-jumping.

Maintain flow of data; keep students interested.

Maintaining the flow of information is vital to keeping your students attentive and interested. Try not to refer to future topics as much as possible, and highlight elements that reinforce or detail prior topics. Flow of information is vital to the success of the training materials, as an audience that gets confused will be concentrating on figuring out which topic you are describing rather than concentrating on the material you are presenting. If a future topic must be referred to, it should be because the current topic relates to the material in such a way that an explanation regarding when that particular topic will be covered is necessary.

Developing an outline, therefore, ensures that your subject matter continues to build on the students' knowledge in a linear fashion that is easily comprehended and absorbed. It also ensures that you cover the material desired and present a tangible starting and ending point, after which the students feel they have absorbed the topic. Pause between topics for questions, and have a few pointed questions of your own to ask the students to ensure that they have grasped the material you are presenting. Nothing is more frustrating than delivering a well-planned course to a group of students and finding out afterward that they were lost on the second topic and absorbed none of what was covered from then on. Exercises are a good way to test the level of comprehension.

Materials Development

Now that the outline is complete, you can begin to flesh out the topics you want to present. Begin the process by going through the subject areas and topics and highlighting the areas that will include alternative media such as a hands-on exercise, video clips, or computer-based interactive media. You can follow this by fleshing out the explanation for the media involved (be it code samples or whatever) and, finally, flesh out the remaining topics. This method allows you to develop the materials as they will be presented, and gives you an accurate gauge of what you will teach. Try to be as thorough as possible. You can go back later and remove subject matter that is not relevant to the unit; you can also customize your class to match the students' skill levels, which you should determine before delivering the class.

Choose the right media.

When choosing the media to use in the training materials, be aware that sometimes the media hardware and software may not be available, or may not function when you are delivering the materials. Have a backup plan for the media portions that does not rely on the media. For example, a video clip can be replaced by a slide that explains the point you want to get across. A slide can be replaced by an overhead or printed material. Hands-on exercises should not be replaced, if at all possible, but if necessary, present the class with the challenge of writing the pseudo-code for the materials on paper. If you are well-prepared, the impact of your presentation need not be diminished by glitches in your multimedia equipment.

Use graphical materials when possible.

The training materials themselves should be as clear and concise as possible. If points need to be made, remember that more than three or four points in a list cannot easily be absorbed. Make the point as much as you can with the written materials, and use graphical or visual material to emphasize and re-iterate the point. Why? Because students take the course materials home with them. They can reread the hard copy, but not the video clips and handsome slides. Include all graphical portions of the training materials with the hard copy, and if you can, have the graphical materials printed in color to match the training materials. If you are developing computer-based training where an instructor may not be physically present, make sure the written materials cover the topic in even more detail to ensure that the students can use it to confirm their level of comprehension.

Hands-on material should accomplish an objective.

The use of hands-on materials is critical. If code is to be developed, or shown, make sure that your code is clean, follows a conventional standard of format and naming conventions, and develops a feeling of accomplishment when completed. Even when developing a complex set of code, ensure that the code is broken up into easily absorbed chunks that develop the whole rather than a slice at a time. This technique is called knowledge transfer through expanded objectives.

Alternative media must be informative, not spectacular or flashy.

If you plan to develop video or other media to use as part of your training material or as your entire course, the material should be adequately covered in the written materials associated with the media. Like any other graphical materials, graphical and interactive media should be informative, but not spectacular. Do not include flash to prove you are an artist.

Workshops

If your training plan includes a workshop, the same guidelines discussed above apply. The materials should conform to an accepted standard, be self-documenting, and be tested. I attended a high-level strategy workshop once where one of the presenters, delivering an example of the strategic product in the form of a demo, showed code that contained clearly visible, obvious errors. The people attending were all high-level technologists and I sensed their loss of respect and confidence. The subject matter, although actually informative, was considered irrelevant by the attendees. This is unacceptable practice, unless errors are introduced specifically to make a point. You will lose the audience's confidence in your abilities, and if students do not perceive you as more knowledgeable then they are, you cannot hope to have them believe what you are teaching.

Delivery of material should lead toward the final goal.

Planning the delivery of the subject material is also crucial. The materials presented in a workshop format should relate to the subject matter being presented and should lead the student through a series of steps that are guaranteed to satisfy the desired result.

Develop materials that illustrate the point being made.

Developing materials is crucial to the success of your workshops. The material must accurately illustrate the point being made. Make the exercises long enough to teach the lesson, but not so long as to distract from the remainder of the materials. Make sure every aspect of the materials is tested thoroughly. Errors in your workshop materials can kill the class. Losing your students' confidence in the materials is distracting and destructive. Test each exercise from different angles. Finally, make sure that example code is well-documented and follows an accepted naming convention.

---

*Plan the timing of delivery so that you maintain the students'
attention.*

When your materials are ready, begin rehearsal. Rehearse each element of
each unit, allowing time for questions or repeated explanation. Also, allow
enough time at the end of each unit for a summary, extra questions, and a brief
break to allow the lesson to sink in. Time the breaks so that they are regular,
but short.

Delivering Training

Delivering training is crucial. After all the time spent on preparation (if you
developed it yourself, you know what you went through), you want to deliver
the training material not only for your students' enlightenment, but for your
own satisfaction as well. Take a few steps to help ensure correct delivery. You
will become more effective with practice, so do not be afraid to be a little ner-
vous. By the way, someone once said that to put yourself at ease when speaking publicly, imagine your audience in their underwear. This might work for
some people, but if you have a sense of humor like mine, it might do more
harm than good. Just remember that your students are as anxious as you are
to get started and settle down. Take the time to get to know them and you will
soon find that the common ground, the subject matter, will ease everyone's
anxiety and you will soon become confident.

One of the key elements to delivering your class successfully is to know your
audience. If you can prepare beforehand, do it. You will be able to empathize
with your class much more quickly. If not, spend a little time at the beginning
of the class to get to know them, their expectations, and their current skill levels. As the class progresses, each student's personality will become known to
you. Learn to recognize when a student is struggling, or when you are not
making your point. Treat each student as an individual and you will leave
them feeling that they received your personal attention throughout.

One of the critical factors in training is time. Your time is limited, and the
students have taken time out from their daily tasks to attend the training.
Make the most of their time and yours. Start your sessions on time, break at
the scheduled times, and restart promptly after breaks. Show that you respect
the value of their time; your students will appreciate it.

Rehearse your materials and your delivery, but be careful to not over-
rehearse. This can cause your delivery to become stale. Make sure you get to
the classroom early on the first day and check the machines your students are
going to use.

When you are delivering the training, remember to go as fast as your slowest student without losing the interest of others. Your goal is to teach all of the
students. Keep the pace brisk and the materials interesting. As much as possible, reference the students' organizational standards and guidelines so that
they can continue to relate to what they may already know.

Follow Up

Once the training is completed, the students will return to their development areas to put what they have learned into practice. They will often not hear from the teacher again. Making a habit of following up with your students shows them that you are genuinely interested in their progress and in their opinions of you as a trainer. Your job is to continually improve your training materials and delivery.

Follow up with your students. Their success relates to your success. If they become more successful due to your training, you have accomplished your goal. Remember also that these people might hire you later on to do additional training for them or for others in their group, so follow-up is also a marketing tool.

Find out where students feel there is room for improvement. This allows you to continue to build your class to become more and more effective in delivering the knowledge you aimed to deliver.

And, of course, if you are a training vendor who relies on students attending your classes in the future, identify additional training requirements as soon as possible.

Summary

This chapter outlined the requirements for developing and delivering good training classes. We discussed the alternatives available to you for training acquisition (standard training solutions, customized training solutions, or developing your own) and outlined the tasks you must handle when developing your own training.

We also discussed the technologies being used today and how each of these can be used either in a classroom or for self-study classes. The result should be training materials that teach students what they need to know effectively and efficiently. Training is the one element of any development program that is not technology-dependent. When new technologies surface, training needs will be right behind them. Training is the one need that will never go away.

Implementation and Beyond

Introduction

The planning is over. The design is complete. The development effort is under way. What are you going to do with this thing once you finish it? The only fulfilling answer is to deploy your project to its users. This step, notwithstanding the preceding question, is accepted as a given, and is sometimes paid only scant attention in the overall plan. However, the deployment (or implementation) phase is one of the most critical for your project's acceptance and success. Your project may be a class library, aimed at developers, or an application whose target is users. In either case, their opinion of and willingness to work with your software is heavily influenced by their first impression. Careful attention to planning and a watchful eye for detail assure you of winning users' acceptance. This part guides you through the planning and details that will make a success of your deployment and, by extension, of your project.

What We Cover

This part covers the implementation phase of your project. The first chapter presents you with a detailed guide to help you in the deployment of a class library. The chapter after that gives a similar treatment to the deployment of an application.

There are three sure things in life: death, taxes, and new versions of your development tools. You need to make sure that the tools you and your developers use are kept up-to-date. You need a system to ensure that the updates you apply are certified, synchronized, and distributed in a timely manner. We discuss version maintenance of your development tools in the final chapter of this part.

The Implementation Chapters

Two of the chapters in this part bear a startling resemblance to each other. These chapters discuss the implementation of class libraries and applications. Many of the principles are the same, but some are different. Each chapter is presented as a coherent whole, so that you can direct your interest to the topic that meets your current needs. Where the information is shared between the two chapters, we repeat it, changing the wording and context to accommodate the differences between class library deployment and application deployment. You can read one of these chapters or both, according to your needs.

The implementation chapters each include a specific, point-by-point checklist that guides you through the maze of details you need to address during the implementation of a project. These checklists represent the synthesis of the experience gained through library and application development in the client-server environment since the early days of PowerBuilder. Remember, though, that these lists are only a starting point. You should add to these lists, drawing from your own experiences in the world of client-server development.

Development Tool Maintenance

You cannot stop the evolution of your development tools. Users will clamor for features that can easily be implemented using newer versions of Power-Builder, but would be nearly impossible with older versions. However, you can control the impact that new versions of your tools have on the developers and users in your domain.

The methods at your disposal to control the impact of new releases include the following:

- Regression testing
- Certification procedures
- Controlled distribution
- Rollback procedures

These methods are covered in detail in Chapter 34 as we discuss the maintenance of development tools.

Summary

Once you have designed and built your class library or application, you need to deliver it to the users. This part will help you deliver everything necessary, everywhere it needs to be, and in the right order. Remember, a perfectly executed project is a success only if the deployment of that project is a success. You will succeed by maintaining the attention to planning and detail that has brought you this far. Read on, and good luck!

32

Library Implementation

Introduction

We have all been part of application development teams. In many ways, we have encountered the various challenges that must be overcome when deploying an application into the corporate environment. This chapter, on the other hand, is about the issues pertaining to the deployment of a class library. There are many similarities between the rollout of a class library and the rollout of an application. The similarities as well as the differences are worthy of our attention. In each case you must deliver a product that satisfies the end user's requirements. Both require attention to details that are seemingly beyond the scope of the application or library. However, in the case of a library, your attention is most often directed to issues of access, documentation, and functionality.

In this chapter, we examine the elements that add up to a successful rollout of a class library. You will see the fundamental differences between application rollout and library rollout. We introduce you to the kinds of preparation and the various details that you must manage during the rollout of your library. Finally, we present a detailed checklist that will allow you to monitor the progress of your library deployment.

This chapter is directed toward the deployment of a class library throughout a corporate development environment. If you are planning to distribute your library as a shrink-wrapped product, you will find that some of the guidelines presented here do not apply. Of course, you will not be able to exercise control over the network structures and development environments that receive your library. However, many of the principles still apply. For shrink-wrapped distribution, follow the guidelines that pertain to library and documentation preparation, as well as preparation of the support infrastructure.

The rollout: what is different about a class library?

The target audience for a class library is developers, not end users. A developer must be sold on the benefits of a package before investing the time and effort required to include that package in his or her application-building toolkit. What this means is that you need to spend considerable effort identifying and explaining the benefits that the developer will derive using your library. Furthermore, you will find that the imagination and creativity of a really good developer often stretches your class library to (and sometimes beyond) its limits. The robustness of your design, the flexibility of your architecture, and the quality of your documentation all come into play when your library must be revised to keep up with developer demands.

The focus is on functionality, not workflow. An application is defined largely by the work it accomplishes and the flow of that work through the application. A library has one identifiable task: to enable the developer to create better applications faster. By better, we mean more consistent, more feature-rich, and more reliable.

The interface for a class library must remain stable. That is, even if the underlying superstructure changes drastically, the outward appearance must remain identical throughout the life of the library. Functionality can be added at any time, but elements of the library that have already been incorporated into applications must remain as unchanged as possible.

Prepare the production environment

The production environment for a class library consists of the following:

- The PBLs and PBD/DLLs that compose the library
- The directory structure that supports the library
- The network configuration for distributing the library
- The technical support infrastructure for the library

You must ensure that all of these elements are in place when you introduce your class library to the development community. The guidelines and checklist that follow are designed to help you toward that goal.

Implementation Guidelines:
The Implementation Checklist

The implementation checklist that follows will help you focus on and manage the details during the rollout of your class library.

The format for the checklist is a simple form containing a few identification elements and a four-column table allowing check-off of completed tasks. You will see this format again in Chapter 33, where we examine application rollout. Some tasks may not require more than a simple check-off, and serve simply as reminders to make sure that everything is checked.

A complete, printable checklist is included on the attached CD in the file ch32_ck.DOC. This is a Word for Windows 2.0 file. A Windows Write file equivalent is attached as ch32_ck.TXT. The checklist is also available as a Microsoft Project 4.0 project plan (ch32_ck.mpp).

Network preparation

You need to identify the servers on which the library will be deployed. The key element in this decision is accessibility of the library to the developers who will be using it.

Table 32.1 highlights the network preparation steps.

Identify development locations. Throughout your company you should identify the development areas that will be using your library. In many cases, the library is adopted as a company standard, and the list of PowerBuilder development teams is the list of library users. Once you have identified your users' locations, you need to determine their access to the company's file servers.

Identify servers. Each development area or team may have access to different file servers. You need to identify the servers that are available to each team. Then select the servers for library deployment such that each team has access to one copy of the library.

Create library directories. On each server where the library will be implemented, create the supporting directory structure. The directories you probably need are as follows:

- A binaries directory to hold PBD/DLLs
- A doc directory to hold documentation
- A resource directory to hold bitmaps and other resources
- A source directory to hold the PBLs
- Other supporting directories for items such as library utilities

Establish user group rights. Once you have created the directories for your library, you should establish access rights and user groups for those directories.

TABLE 32.1   Network Preparation Checklist

Task	Scheduled	Completed
Identify development locations		
Identify servers		
Create library directories		
Establish user group rights		

The rights should be set up so that each developer has access to the directories in your library structure, but cannot write, erase, or modify the contents.

In some cases, we have found that read-only access to PBLs or PBD/DLLs in your PowerBuilder search path causes the white screen of death. This is an error message screen from PowerBuilder with a title bar saying Compiler Errors and no accompanying information in the box.

Installation preparation

Take steps to prepare for the installation of your library. Before the library is deployed, you should ensure that the documentation is distributed to all sites where the library will be used. Next, if you want the installation to be automated, you need to create a setup routine that will distribute the various elements of your library into their respective directories.

Table 32.2 illustrates the steps necessary to prepare for library installation.

Documentation distribution.   The documentation should be distributed as part of the standard directory structure used for library deployment. There should be a clear overview of the functionality of the library, as well as detailed documentation for each class, method, and attribute. In addition, you should provide a roadmap that suggests the best ways for users of various levels of expertise to approach the documentation.

By including the documentation as part of the basic library directory structure, you ensure that any replication technique you use to distribute the library also includes the documentation in its most up-to-date form.

Library installation routine.   Prepare and document the installation routines for the class library whether the process be manual or automated. Test the routines on a production or production look-alike server, not the development area. Strive to simulate the production environment as best you can.

The library installation should be constructed to enforce, as much as possible, consistency across installed sites. This simplifies support issues and increases the likelihood that application developers will be able to access the library objects throughout the organization.

Replication plan.   If you are planning to use a replication method to distribute your library, you need to develop a plan that ensures that your class library is

TABLE 32.2   Installation Preparation Checklist

Task	Scheduled	Completed
Documentation distribution		
Library installation routine		
Replication plan		

properly deployed to each development server that requires access to the objects. Include a mechanism that allows for distribution of regular maintenance releases, as well as emergency bug fixes (yes, you will have bugs). You also need to make allowances for adding new development servers to the list of distribution targets.

Additional software

In some cases you need to deploy software created by other parties along with your library. Some examples are custom control DLLs and VBXs. You need to attend to issues of licensing, distribution, training, and documentation related to these third-party products. Keep in mind that the licensing requirements are often different when you are distributing a developer's tool, such as a class library, that makes use of a third-party control or function library. The publishers expect to receive payment for each developer using their product, not just the developers of the class library. An elegant but expensive solution to this problem is to obtain a site license for the product. A different, possibly less expensive solution is a per-seat license for a limited number of developers who will use the final class library. This approach is harder to administer, but may pay off in reduced costs.

Table 32.3 shows an example of the checklist you can use to verify the inclusion and licensing of additional software.

User training

You must ensure that the developers are trained in the use of your class library. Properly trained developers are one of your best marketing tools. Training should be arranged and in place before the library is deployed to the developers. However, the training should not precede the deployment by more than about a week. Without the ability to apply what they have learned, the developers will lose some of their facility with the features and functionality of the library. Table 32.4 lists the steps you need to follow in establishing and carrying out user training.

Prepare user training. You should ensure that the development of the training courses and the associated materials is nearing completion 4 to 6 weeks before

TABLE 32.3 Sample Additional Software Checklist

Software	Verified
CPALETTE.DLL	
VIBX.DLL	
THREED.VBX	
CTL3DV2.DLL	

TABLE 32.4   User Training Checklist

Task	Scheduled	Completed
Prepare user training		
Communications		
Set up user training		
Perform user training		

the library is due to be deployed. The training you present to the developers should be weighted toward two specific goals:

- Explaining the benefits in time, features, and functionality that the developers will enjoy through the use of your library.

- Ensuring that the developers have the skills necessary to apply the elements of your library efficiently and correctly.

In constructing the training curriculum, it is important to include as much hands-on training as possible. Use thorough exercises to illustrate the use of your library's features. And make sure that the students have the opportunity to actually enter the code that accompanies the examples. Remember, if they do not type it, they will not remember it.

Communications.   Make sure developers know what type of equipment and protocols they are using so they can communicate this easily to a technical support person if the developer's site is remote. Also, let the developers know how to get in touch with the various support people, and which support organizations (such as hardware configuration, software configuration, or training) are likely to handle a given issue best.

Consider setting up a hotline to allow the developers a single entry point into the support infrastructure.

Set up user training.   Schedule training sessions to familiarize developers with the class library 1 to 2 weeks before implementation. Remember that morning sessions are often more productive than afternoon sessions. After lunch you may find that people are drowsy or preoccupied, and you will not get their full attention.

You need to verify that the training rooms you will use are up to the job. Are there enough seats for the expected class sizes? Is there enough writing space? Does the available audiovisual equipment meet the needs of the course material? Is the lighting adequate? Will the room still be comfortable (not too hot, not too cold) when it is full of people? If you need a computer (and perhaps a large screen), how do you obtain it? Verify in advance that hookups exist in the training room to allow you to connect to the required network resources.

Once you are satisfied with the training rooms, verify the schedule and confirm that the rooms are reserved for your use. Then publish the schedule and stick by it.

There are several ways to provide training to developers. Try to provide training that affords as much actual interaction with the computer system as possible. Hands-on training gets the developers familiar with the features and functionality of the library and helps them to learn more quickly. Some new methods of training are also available if hands-on classes cannot be prepared or given.

Video-based and computer-based training are becoming increasingly popular. These methods allow the users to learn at their own pace, with interactive media guiding them through different facets of the class library.

Perform user training.   Perform the training as soon as possible and then allow the developers to begin working with the class library. At first, keep the classes small and focused so that you can efficiently revise the course material to reflect the developer's needs.

Please remember: Respect others' time. They have work to do. Do not start late to accommodate the stragglers, and never allow a session to extend beyond its scheduled end unless the class unanimously agrees.

Library considerations

Table 32.5 lists some other considerations that apply when you deploy a class library throughout an organization.

Library bug reports.   Establish technical support procedures for the user. Make sure the use of these procedures is covered in the training sessions. Support procedures should include the following:

- Whom to contact and how to contact them
- How to submit a support request
- What information to include in a support request (such as error messages and library version information)

TABLE 32.5   Library Considerations Checklist

Task	Scheduled	Completed
Library bug reports		
Library change requests		
Library version control		
Production source control		

- When to expect acknowledgment of a support request

- How to escalate a support request

Library change requests.   Every day, each user of your class library will learn something new about the library's capabilities. As they learn, their creativity and development needs spawn new requirements for the library.

Change requests are an inevitable part of your library's support needs. Be prepared for them, and put procedures in place to allow the developers to request changes.

A companion procedure should exist for notifying the developers of receipt, status, and expected disposition of library change requests.

Library version control.   Establish a procedure to maintain versions of the library binaries. Inform developers of new versions and predicted impact on user productive time.

Production source control.   Establish a procedure for maintaining production source code that matches the current binary versions of the libraries. Also establish procedures to allow changes to be made to the production environment that may be separate from a new development phase. Mismatches between production source code and the binaries will cause many major problems during and after deployment of the library. A more detailed explanation of source control is covered in Chapter 23.

Installation build and test

You need to complete the final build of your class library. Typically, you will have a dummy (or demo) application that you will use to complete the regeneration and build of your library files. Table 32.6 details the steps required for your library build.

TABLE 32.6   Library Build Checklist

Task	Scheduled	Completed
Freeze source code		
Update version information		
Copy to secure locations		
Regenerate libraries		
Optimize libraries		
Build library PBR files		
Build dynamic libraries		

Freeze source code. When you prepare to do your final build of your class library, you come to a point where the code for the distributed version must be frozen. Resist the temptation to unfreeze it for last-minute changes. Save the changes for a minor release at a later date.

Update version information. Ensure that any version information contained in and distributed with your library is up to date with the current version and release numbers. Often this information is stored in a Data-Retained-on-Save datawindow that lists the names and version numbers for each PBL or PBD/DLL.

Copy to a secure location. Keep a copy of the library source for each distributed version in a secure location. If your organization has access to off-site storage, you should consider using it to house your library source. Neither library developers nor library users should have access to the only existing copy of the frozen source code that accompanies a library release.

Optimize libraries

TIP

Novell users, after optimizing libraries, go into a DOS window and use the Novell FLAGS option to reset the shared attributes on the library. By default, new files created on a Novell network are not marked as shareable. Optimizing libraries is accomplished by creating a new library and copying the old source code. Resetting the shared flag prevents a common problem in a multideveloper environment: a "Save Failed—Probable File I-O Error" message when you attempt to save an object.

Steps:

1. Go to a DOS prompt.
2. Change to your source directory.
3. Type FLAGS *.PBL. This displays a list of your libraries and their file attributes. These are not the same attributes as DOS attributes.
4. Type FLAGS *.PBL +s. This sets the shared attribute for each library.

Build library PowerBuilder resource files. In order to distribute bitmaps, icons, cursors, and, in some cases, datawindow objects with a library, the developer

TABLE 32.7   Sample PBR File Entries

Picture Object Resource Path	PBR File Entry
c:\libs\pb\rc\mybitmap.bmp	c:\libs\pb\rc\mybitmap.bmp
..\rc\mybitmap.bmp	..\rc\mybitmap.bmp
..\rc\mybitmap.bmp	c:\libs\pb\rc\mybitmap.bmp ← This is incorrect even though the ultimate paths may point to the same place.

has two choices: Either all of the external files must be included and distributed with the library (with the exception of datawindow objects) or the resources can be built into a resource (PBR) file. Adding a PBR file to the library build has the effect of binding the resources directly into the binaries. Binding the resources at build time helps to make the loading of the resources faster at runtime. It also ensures that all resources the developer's application requires are included with the PBD/DLLs of your class library.

Table 32.7 shows some sample PBR entries, as well as some incorrect ones.

Resource files are a recommended method of distributing the resources required by the library. The inclusion of a resource file ensures that the necessary objects are included with each application using the library, regardless of the application's working path.

PowerBuilder 4 only: regenerate all libraries.   Once all of the object libraries have been optimized, the libraries must be regenerated to ensure that all interobject communication pointers, especially when inheritance is used, are relinked and accurate. Although a common practice is to select all of the objects in a library and then regenerate, one has to be careful to regenerate in the sequence of inheritance. A common solution to regeneration problems is to always regenerate all objects a number of times corresponding to the number of inheritance layers

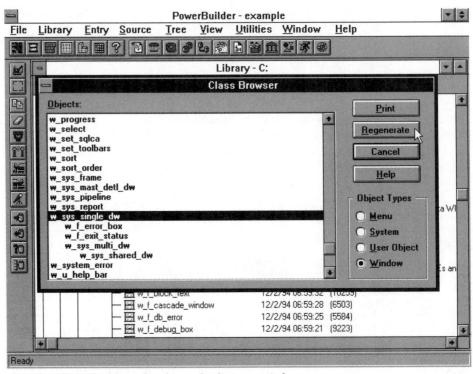

Figure 32.1   PowerBuilder 4 class hierarchy diagram: windows.

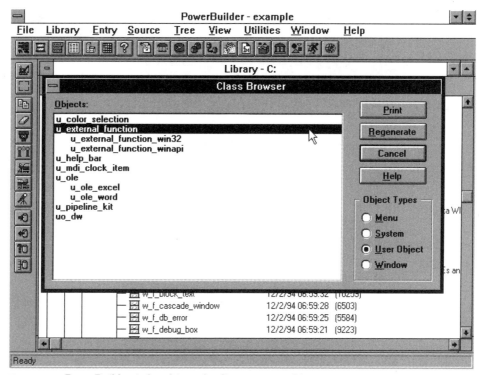

Figure 32.2   PowerBuilder 4 class hierarchy diagram: user objects.

you might have. This allows the object pointers to establish their binding paths and synchronizes the object's internal pointers. Another, safer method is to use the Library Painter's class hierarchy and regenerate the objects from the class hierarchy. This reduces the chance of an object pointer being incorrectly bound.

Figures 32.1 and 32.2 show the Class Browser hierarchy dialog for windows and user objects (PowerBuilder 4.0 browser).

As the diagrams show, the leftmost (parent) indentation contains the lowest level of any class hierarchy. Selecting this object and then choosing Regenerate will regenerate the object and all of its descendants in hierarchical sequence and ensures the correct regeneration of the object class.

PowerBuilder 4 only: build dynamic libraries.   The dynamic libraries (PBD/DLLs) should be created now. Building dynamic libraries in PowerBuilder is easy. Select the Library Painter Utilities menu option, then select the Build Dynamic Library menu item. A dialog is presented to select the library to be built. Choosing the library and selecting OK builds a PBD/DLL file for the application. Figure 32.3 shows the Build Dynamic Library menu option. Once the PBD/DLLs are built, copy or move them to the binaries directory in your library structure.

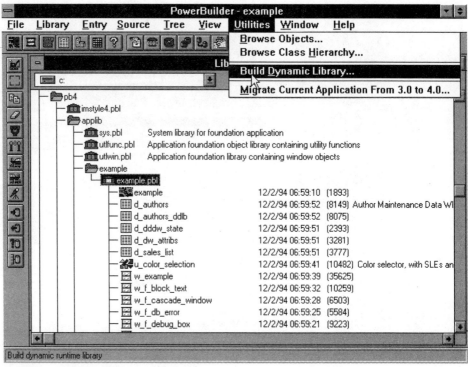

Figure 32.3 Building PBDs in PowerBuilder 4.

In PowerBuilder 5.0, there is a new feature for maintaining your objects: Incremental Rebuild. This option works as follows. When you change an object and save it, you are, in fact, compiling the object. What you are not compiling are the objects referenced by or within the object. These referenced objects are flagged as needing to be recompiled. When you choose the Incremental Rebuild feature (shown in Figure 32.4), the compiler builds a hierarchy of required compilation based on these reference maps. These objects are recompiled, reducing the amount of time needed to regenerate all your objects and ensuring that regenerating is done in the correct sequence. Of course, you still have the option of full compile, which recompiles all objects in the correct sequence automatically. Recompiling may take longer on an individual pass, but overall (because we are used to regenerating multiple times, with prayer), you will find it to be much more productive.

Library Distribution

In order for your library to reach its intended audience, you need to develop and implement a plan for software distribution. Take into account the hierarchy of your organization, the number of workstations and servers that will be affected, and the usual methods used by your company.

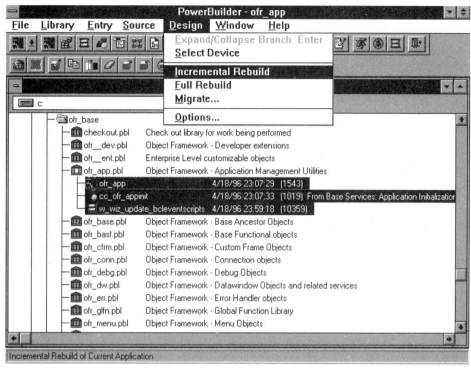

Figure 32.4 Regenerating in PowerBuilder 5.

Single-server access. The simplest distribution method is that of a single-server installation. All of your library software is installed on a single server, and all developers attach to that server to access the library. The advantages of this configuration include ease of maintenance and upgrade as well as simplicity of version control. The disadvantages include limited capacity and vulnerability to server outages.

Multiple-server installation. If your organization has several LANs at different sites that are not interconnected, you need to distribute your library using separate installation packages. This type of distribution is the most difficult to control and maintain. The administrator of each LAN must be instructed on the method of installation and must be counted on actually to perform the installation on schedule and accurately. Additionally, the different LANs may exhibit a tendency to drift away from each other in matters of configuration and capacity.

Multiple-server replication. When you deploy your library across several interconnected servers, it is best to use a replication technique. You or your staff installs and maintains a central copy of your library software. The network services personnel then distribute the library to the target servers whenever an installation or update is required. If your organization is set up to perform this task smoothly and accurately, this is the least troublesome and highest-capacity scheme for software distribution.

Automated software distribution.   There are some products available today that allow for the automated distribution of software. Although these systems are well-established in the mainframe and UNIX worlds, the software available today has yet to catch up to the frantic changes occurring in the client-server world. The environment is stabilizing, however, so your organization may want to look into the use of an automated software distribution system to alleviate many of the distribution problems we face today. If you are looking at such products, use the checklist defined in this chapter to ask tough questions of the vendor.

Performance Metrics

You developed a set of library performance metrics when we discussed library testing in Chapter 18. Now that you have completed implementation, but before you turn the developers loose, measure library performance once again against your performance metrics. Often this step is ignored, and performance is measured on a "Hey, looks pretty good" basis.

Summary

The deployment checklist can be used for initial installation and maintenance release installation. Some of the items are not applicable for maintenance release rollouts. Even though these are typically not changed, make sure that each item is at least discussed and checked off again. Botched maintenance releases can destroy the user's confidence in the product even more quickly than the initial installation.

The key to success in deployment was, is, and will always be planning and preparation!

33

Application Implementation

Introduction

The rollout: avoiding the pitfalls

The implementation and rollout of a production client-server application requires several specific elements to be considered and checked. All too often, one or more of these steps are omitted or overlooked, and the result is a chaotic scramble to get the application implemented on the client workstation.

Your application needs a properly prepared (and soft) landing field. The details of implementation, if you attend to them with care, will allow your project to be appreciated and admired instead of feared and reviled. Your goal is to make sure your users believe that the new application will make them more productive and more valuable. For a new application, the first impression does count.

A smooth rollout is what you desire. However, you will find plenty of traps along the path to that glorious result:

- Workstations do not meet your applications requirements.

- The network does not work.

- The network works, but nobody added the users.

- The users have inadequate or excessive network rights.

- The database does not exist.

- Everything runs, but the documentation is unavailable.

- Nobody was trained to use the application.

- Something is wrong, but nobody tells you.

The typical environment for a client-server application, as shown in Figure 33.1, is a distributed one. Although this makes the application's efficiency lev-

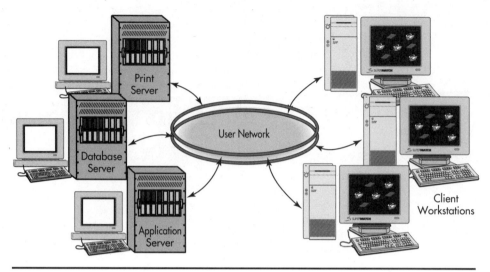

Figure 33.1 A typical distributed network.

els rise, it introduces a level of complexity in deployment that exists in no other environment. Multiple computers are usually involved, not counting the user's workstations, and the environment becomes a critical part of your deployment planning and execution.

This list can grow rather long. Simply remember to take the time and effort to prepare adequately for your rollout, and you reduce the probability of ugly surprises.

Prepare the production environment

You should ensure that the production environment for your application has been designed and put in place by the time you are ready to roll out the application. Be especially sensitive to items that you might have taken for granted in the development environment. You will need to develop a heightened awareness of the real requirements of your application if your rollout is to succeed.

Prepare for the workload

Be aware that the demands placed on the application team will be greater and more insistent as you prepare to deploy your application. Users will require support and training. The geographical extents of your job will expand as you configure the sites that will use your application. You will need to contact many new people, fill in forms, and follow up to ensure that required tasks have been completed. All the while, last-minute polishing of the application will be taking place.

This is the time to consider additional staffing. Take the time to prepare realistic workload estimates. You increase your chance of success if you prepare detailed documentation of your additional staffing needs. You will probably have to fight for the resources you need, and the more justification you can provide, the more likely you are to obtain the workforce you need.

Prepare for testing

By the time you are 4 to 6 weeks away from implementation, you should have testing scripts available to verify that each step in the preparation has succeeded. Where it is relevant, such as in performance metrics, include expected results. The more test cases you include, the less chance you have of being surprised when the application finally rolls out.

Implementation Guidelines

Now let's examine the implementation process, which is shown in Figure 33.2. We review each step in the process, is present just as a pilot reviews a pre-takeoff checklist.

The implementation checklist

What follows is an exhaustive checklist that will aid you in a smooth, successful rollout of your application. You may find that time, funding, or staffing limits your ability to realistically address every issue listed below. However, you should strive to tackle as many of these items as you can manage. Each of these items will happen. Your goal should be to cause as many of them to happen in advance and by design as possible.

By using the checklist, the developer and implementation staff can keep these elements from slipping through the cracks. The checklist is similar to the library implementation checklist, but there are several areas where the two are different enough to warrant a separate discussion.

The format for the checklist, again, is a simple form containing a few identification elements and a four-column table allowing check-off of completed

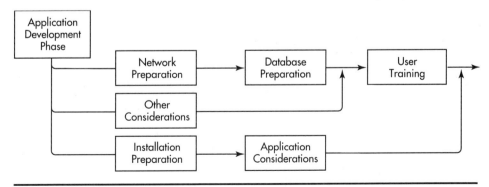

Figure 33.2 The implementation process.

tasks. Some tasks may not require any more than a simple check-off, and serve simply as reminders to make sure that everything is checked. The world of client-server is young, aggressive, and ever-changing, and the checklist should be used with every application or application upgrade.

A complete, printable checklist is included on the attached CD in the file ch33_ck.DOC. This is a Word for Windows 6.0 file. A Windows Write file equivalent is attached as ch33_ck.TXT. The checklist is also available as a Microsoft Project 4.0 project plan (ch33_ck.mpp).

Network preparation

We need to make sure that the network is established, set up, and tested before moving anything to the network. This step should be done in preparation regardless of whether an established network is in place. Impact on existing systems should be considered and measured, if possible. It is important to test the type of network and database being used as early as possible in the implementation cycle.

If your application uses multiple databases, be sure that at some point before deployment you have tested your application with all the applicable architectures. Table 33.1 highlights the network preparation steps.

LAN/WAN testing.   The network where the users are to be located should be set up and tested 4 to 6 weeks before implementation. You should check the physical connectivity as well as the logical connectivity. This ensures that a solid foundation is in place before you attempt to roll out the application.

Process for adding and removing users.   Ensure that a procedure is in place to add or remove users of the application to or from the network. Before you add the real users, use the identical procedures to add and test some sample users. This step ensures that the procedures for adding users to the network are functioning correctly.

Communication protocols.   Ensure that all communication protocols are established. If a vehicle such as transmission control protocol/Internet protocol (TCP/IP) is being used, make sure all users have IP addresses created. If additional hardware is being used, ensure that hardware is tested at the user site and is able to connect to the expected production environment.

Gateway requirements.   If gateways are required, make sure that the gateway is established and tested. Make sure users and user groups have access through the gateway and that password changes have minimal impact on the user.

Server configuration test.   Test the server in its production configuration. If the application is ready for testing, use an automated tool to stress-test the envi-

TABLE 33.1 Network Preparation Checklist

Task	Scheduled	Completed
LAN/WAN testing		
Add-user process		
Communication protocol		
Gateway requirements		
Server configuration test		
Create user groups		

ronment. Use the database size estimates produced earlier to verify that enough space exists to accommodate the expected load on the server.

Create user groups. Create the user groups that will allow the users to access the network, the application, and all other necessary DLLs.

Database preparation

Preparation of the production database is another vital step in implementation. The database, if not already a production database, must be prepared, loaded, and tested well ahead of the intended schedule. If it already is a production database, some of the tasks become more simple check-offs. (See Table 33.2.) Client-server applications that access production databases require significant effort in setting up the database, database connections, and security levels even before you load the actual data (if necessary). Make sure that the database is prepared, loaded, and tested at least 2 weeks before implementation.

Prepare for reloads of the database before they become necessary. Be sure to account for any views, triggers, or stored procedures that may be affected by a reload.

Database turnover request. Create and submit a production database turnover request to have the database established in the production environment at least 3 weeks before implementation.

TABLE 33.2 Database Preparation Checklist

Task	Scheduled	Completed
Database turnover request		
Database load		
Database access requests		

Database load.   Load all expected production data to the database 2 to 3 weeks before implementation. Verify that all tables, views, triggers, and stored procedures have been migrated to the production database. Compare the actual load times with the benchmarks you have developed during development and testing. If you find that the load times differ significantly from the observed benchmarks, you may discover that a problem has occurred during the loading of the database. This is a case where a bit of preparation and cross-checking can save you a large headache later.

Database access requests.   Submit the necessary forms to establish the expected user base on the database. Make sure all security levels are established and correct. If your location includes any kind of table-based security, you must verify that the administrator creates the tables, and that the tables are populated in advance with the information necessary to allow the users access to the database.

Installation preparation

Preparing the environment and the user for the upcoming implementation is important. The sooner the users become familiar with their environment and procedures, the easier it will be for them to make the transition to the application when it is implemented. (See Table 33.3.)

Documentation distribution.   Distribute user guides and technical references as soon as possible, preferably before training begins. If on-line help files and context-sensitive help are being supplied, make sure that all help files are also distributed. This allows the user to become familiar with the style and look and feel of the help formats. Provide a feedback form that the user can use to comment on the content and accuracy of the documentation.

Application installation routines.   Prepare and document the installation routines for the application, whether the process is manual or automated. Test the routines on a production or production look-alike server, not the development area. Strive to simulate the user environment as best you can.

Environment preparation.   Make sure the user environment is set up the way the application is expecting. Make sure that the application does not refer to any file via a hard path.

TABLE 33.3   Installation Preparation Checklist

Task	Scheduled	Completed
Documentation distribution		
Application installation routines		
Environment preparation		

TABLE 33.4   Hardware Resource Checklist

Resource	Minimum	Verified
CPU	486 66 MHz	
Local hard disk available	95 MB	
System memory	16 MB	
Video resolution and colors	$800 \times 600 \times 16$	
Screen size	17″	
CD-ROM drive	Yes	

Consider the workstation environment for your application. Are there any special requirements? During the development of the application you will have reached a conclusion about the minimum hardware requirements for acceptable performance. Spell these out. Then do everything in your power to make sure every target workstation is up to your declared minimum standards. (See Table 33.4.) An application struggling with insufficient resources can frustrate users and leave you with a failed rollout.

The software operating environment is equally important. You should be able to list the software that your application requires to run smoothly and without failure. Be sure to consider the impact of different DOS and GUI versions or implementations. Will your application work equally well under Windows 3.1, Windows for Workgroups, Windows95, OS/2, and NT? Are there any DOS versions that can cause your application to perform poorly? Be prepared to answer such questions, and check each workstation against your list. (See Table 33.5.)

Next, compile a list of other software required to run your application. (See Table 33.6.) Make no assumptions about what is available on each workstation. Include utilities on which your program relies. For example, if your program launches NOTEPAD.EXE, add that to the list of required software. List the OLE and DDE clients and servers that your program expects to find. Specify the runtime and utility DLLs that your application requires.

If you know of any software that interacts poorly with your application, add that software to a list of software that should be specifically excluded.

Finally, configure each workstation to receive your application. Add the directory tree where your application and supporting files will reside. Make any necessary changes to the system configuration files (such as DOS path and CONFIG.SYS changes). Verify that all other required software and libraries

TABLE 33.5   Sample Software Configuration Checklist

Software	Minimum	Excluded	Verified
DOS	5.0	6.0	
Windows	3.1, Win95	NT, OS/2	

TABLE 33.6   Sample Additional Software Checklist

Software	Verified
VISIO.EXE	
NOTEPAD.EXE	
EXCEL.EXE	
CPALETTE.DLL	
CTL3DV2.DLL	

are present, and that (to the extent of your power over the situation) no troublesome software remains.

User training

The preparation and execution of user training are critical. Users always need training on the application, and in many cases, require training in the environment they will be working in, technical support procedures to obtain assistance, and other procedures used to report bugs, request enhancements, and contact the developers to ask questions or make comments. (See Table 33.7.)

Prepare user training.   Ensure that the development of user training is nearing completion 4 to 6 weeks before implementation. Add resources to this task as necessary to keep it absolutely on schedule. If your users do not know how to use your application, they will not like it. If the users do not like your application, they will find ways to break it. Your life will be miserable. Trust me on this.

Environment training.   Make sure training includes some instruction on the platform and some of its quirks when it comes to memory management and resource management. Obtain a tool such as SysMon to visually monitor resources or include a resource check utility in the application and show the user how to check it. Make sure the users know the acceptable range of memory and resource usage, and what to do if they are running out of either.

TABLE 33.7   User Training Checklist

Task	Scheduled	Completed
Prepare user training		
Environment training		
Communications		
Set up user training		
Perform user training		

Communications. Make sure users know what type of equipment and protocols they are using so this can be communicated easily to a technical support person if the user site is remote. Also, let the users know how to get in touch with the various support people and which support organizations (such as hardware configuration, software configuration, and training) are likely to handle a given issue best.

Consider setting up a hotline to allow the users a single entry point into the support infrastructure.

Set up user training. Schedule user training sessions to familiarize the user with the product 4 to 6 weeks before implementation. Remember that morning sessions are often more productive than afternoon sessions. After lunch you may find that people are drowsy or preoccupied, and you will not get their full attention.

You need to verify that the training rooms you will use are up to the job. Are there enough seats for the expected class sizes? Is there enough writing space? Does the available audiovisual equipment meet the needs of the course material? Is the lighting adequate? Will the room still be comfortable (not too hot, not too cold) when it is full of people? If you need a computer (and perhaps a large screen), how do you obtain it? Verify in advance that hookups exist in the training room to allow you to connect to the required network resources.

Once you are satisfied with the training rooms, verify the schedule and confirm that the rooms are reserved for your use. Then publish the schedule and stick by it.

There are several ways to provide training to the users. Try to provide training that affords as much actual interaction with the computer system as possible. Hands-on training gets the users familiar with the feel of the system and helps them to learn more quickly. Some new methods of training are also available if hands-on classes cannot be prepared or given.

Video-based and computer-based training are becoming increasingly popular. These methods allow the users to learn at their own pace, with interactive media guiding them through different facets of the application.

Perform user training. Perform the user training as soon as possible and then allow the users to work with the proposed system before implementation to accomplish user testing, user familiarization, and an indication of performance expectations.

Please remember to respect others' time. They have work to do. Do not start late to accommodate the stragglers, and *never* allow a session to extend beyond its scheduled end unless the class *unanimously* agrees.

User training should never be completed too far in advance of the actual implementation of the application. The training materials should still be familiar to the users by the time they begin using the application.

TABLE 33.8   Application Considerations Checklist

Task	Scheduled	Completed
Application bug reports		
Application change requests		
Application version control		
Production source control		

Application considerations

Before you implement the application, several items should be prepared and followed to ensure that the application remains in a controlled environment. (See Table 33.8.) The following procedures enable you to maintain a high level of application stability and user feedback responsiveness. These tasks must be completed at least 1 week before implementation.

Application bug reports.   Establish technical support procedures for the user. Make sure the use of these procedures is covered in user training. Support procedures should include the following:

- Whom to contact and how to contact them
- How to submit a support request
- What information to include in a support request (such as application messages, other applications in use, and application version information)
- When to expect acknowledgment of a support request
- How to escalate a support request

Application change requests.   Someone once said that an application, once developed, is obsolete. In the days of multiyear development efforts, this was more often true than not. In the client-server world, things are a little different. Users are more involved in the product, development cycles are much shorter than before, and the user gets the finished product relatively quickly after development begins. Users get a product that more closely matches their requirements because the product is delivered in a shorter time frame. However, this does not mean that the user will accept the application and never want anything changed. In my experience, users need changes made for three major reasons:

- The application does not meet business requirements.
- The users have changed their mind from what they first wanted.
- Users are becoming more familiar with their environment and are learning they can expect more from the application.

So change requests will come, even if the application meets the business requirements. Be prepared for this, and put procedures in place for users to use when submitting application change request data.

A companion procedure should exist for notifying the user of receipt, status, and expected disposition of application change requests.

Application version control.   Establish a procedure to maintain versions of the application executable. Inform users of new versions and predicted impact on user productive time.

Production source control.   Establish a procedure for maintaining production source code that matches the executable. Also establish procedures to allow changes to be made to the production environment that may be separate from a new development phase. Mismatches between production source code and the executable will cause many major problems during and after application deployment.

Other considerations

Table 33.9 lists some additional considerations that should be checked if they apply.

Mainframe turnover procedures.   Make sure all processes and loads on the mainframe are tested in a production mode. Turning the mainframe procedures live before implementation allows additional time to test the data and processes before the implementation date.

User equipment.   Make sure the user has the proper equipment in place and tested at least 1 week before implementation. Make sure equipment is configured to handle the application load.

Additional hardware and software.   Make sure that the user has access to all additional hardware and software required to run the application. Ensure also that the user has any necessary runtime licenses to the hardware or software required.

TABLE 33.9   **Other Considerations Checklist**

Task	Scheduled	Completed
Mainframe turnover procedures		
User equipment		
Additional hardware and software		

Installation build and test

Preparing the executable for distribution to the user is one of the most critical tasks encountered along the way to successful application implementation. An application must be carefully prepared, and there are sufficient pitfalls along the way to make this a daunting task.

TIP

PowerBuilder 5 contains an object called the Project object. This object records details regarding your application build and helps to alleviate many of the problems commonly associated with application builds in prior versions. Unlike previous versions, PowerBuilder 5 does not allow you to build an application from the Application Painter; you must use the Project Painter.

The steps in Table 33.10 outline the tasks you need to address in order to ensure a safe application build. If all steps are followed, chances of error are greatly reduced.

Freeze source code.   It is vital that source code changes be prevented after the final system test. It is too easy to make a quick fix here or there in the Power-Builder environment, especially with the use of PowerBuilder dynamic libraries (PBDs). Quick fixes to problems, or last-minute modifications of code that are not included in final system testing, allow the possibility of introducing bugs into the application. Users expect a bug-free application. They are usually paying a lot of money for the application development effort. It is the developer's job to deliver a high-quality product.

Copy to a secure location.   Making a backup of the production release source code is important. It provides a means to restore source code to a known baseline.

TABLE 33.10   Application Build Checklist

Task	Scheduled	Completed
Freeze source code		
Copy to secure location		
Update version information		
Optimize libraries		
Build dynamic libraries		
Build application PBR		
Create project file		
Run Project Make utility		
Archive all EXEs, PBDs, and PBRs		

Update version information. If version information is imbedded in the application (a recommended practice), make sure that this information is updated to help identify the version level of the application the user is using. Trying to trace a problem reported with a version of an application that does not match the user environment is a very difficult task.

Optimize libraries. Optimize all of the PowerBuilder source code libraries before application build. This removes unneeded object references that are left behind from code moves and deletes, reducing the size of the library to its optimum.

TIP

Novell users, after optimizing libraries, go into a DOS window and use the Novell FLAGS option to reset the shared attributes on the library. By default, new files created on a Novell network are not marked as shareable. Optimizing libraries is accomplished by creating a new library and copying the old source code. Resetting the shared flag prevents a common problem in a multideveloper environment: a "Save Failed—Probable File I-O Error" message when you attempt to save an object.

Steps:
1. Go to a DOS prompt.
2. Change to your source directory.
3. Type FLAGS *.PBL. This displays a list of your libraries and their file attributes. These are not the same attributes as DOS attributes.
4. Type FLAGS *.PBL + s. This sets the shared attribute for each library.

Build application PowerBuilder resource files. In order to distribute bitmaps, icons, cursors, and, in some cases, datawindow objects with an application, the developer has two choices: Either all of the external files must be included with the application (with the exception of datawindow objects) or the resources can be built into a resource (PBR) file. Adding a PBR file to the application build has the effect of binding the resources directly into the executable. Binding the resources at executable build time helps to make the loading of the resources faster at runtime. It also ensures that all resources your application requires are included with the application. (See Table 33.11.)

TABLE 33.11   Sample PBR File Entries

Picture object resource path	PBR file entry
c:\pb5i32\rc\mybitmap.bmp	c:\pb5i32\rc\mybitmap.bmp
..\rc\mybitmap.bmp	..\rc\mybitmap.bmp
..\rc\mybitmap.bmp	c:\pb5i32\rc\mybitmap.bmp ← This is incorrect even though the ultimate paths may point to the same place.

TIP

When building application PBRs, developers should note that the entries in the PBR file must contain paths to resources that match the path specified on the object exactly.

Resource files are a recommended method of distributing the resources required by the application. The inclusion of a resource file ensures that the necessary objects are included with the application regardless of the application's working path.

PowerBuilder 3 and 4 only: regenerate all libraries.   Once all of the object libraries have been optimized, the libraries must be regenerated to ensure that all interobject communication pointers, especially when inheritance is used, are relinked and accurate. Although a common practice is to select all of the objects in a library and then regenerate, one has to be careful to regenerate in the sequence of inheritance. A solution to regeneration problems is to always regenerate all objects twice. This allows the object pointers to establish their binding paths and synchronizes the object's internal pointers. Another, safer method is to use the Library Painter's class hierarchy and regenerate the objects from the class hierarchy. This reduces the chance of an object pointer not being correctly bound. Figures 33.3 and 33.4 show the PowerBuilder 4.0 Class Browser hierarchy dialog for windows and user objects.

As the diagrams show, the leftmost (parent) indentation contains the lowest level of any class hierarchy. Selecting this object and then choosing Regenerate will regenerate the object and all of its descendants in hierarchical sequence and ensures the correct regeneration of the object class.

PowerBuilder 3 and 4 only: build dynamic libraries.   If your application is going to use dynamic libraries (PBD), the libraries should be created now. Building dynamic libraries in PowerBuilder is easy. Select the Library Painter Utilities menu option, then select the Build Dynamic Library menu item. A dialog is presented to select the library to be built. Choosing the library and selecting OK builds a PBD file for the application. Figure 33.5 shows the PowerBuilder 4.0 dialog for building a dynamic library (PBD).

TIP

Remember that PowerBuilder stores only the library name in the executable, and not the full path, as you have to specify in the Application Painter search path. This means that if another library with the same name is found earlier in your search path (current directory, Windows directory, DOS path map), this library will be loaded instead of the one you might be expecting. Make sure that your application's search path does not encounter another library of the same name.

PowerBuilder 3 and 4 only: create executable.   Creating your application executable with PowerBuilder 3.0 or 4.0 is the final step in the application build

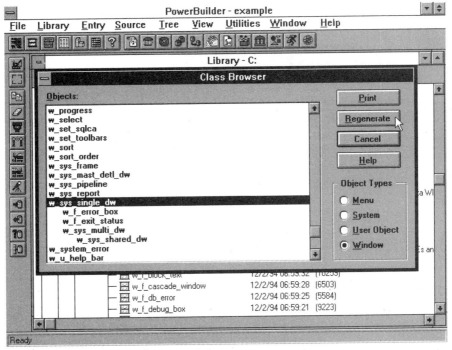

Figure 33.3 Class hierarchy diagram: windows.

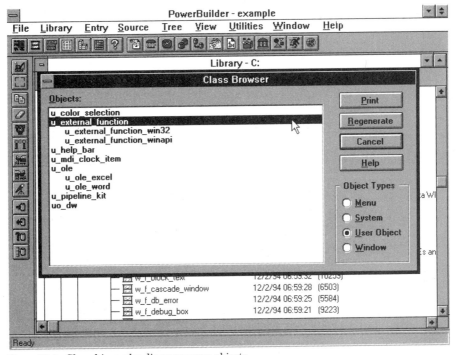

Figure 33.4 Class hierarchy diagram: user objects.

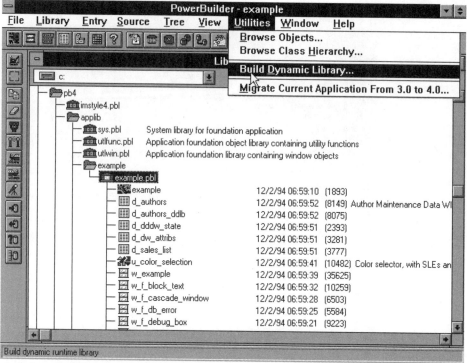

Figure 33.5   Build Dynamic Library menu option.

process. A decision needs to be made as to how the application executable will be built. The options are to create a standalone executable with no dynamic libraries, to create an executable with some dynamic libraries, or to create a simple executable with all libraries specified as dynamic libraries. There are advantages and disadvantages for each method, and a few development techniques will help decide the path.

Standalone executables.   Standalone executables are the easiest builds to accomplish. All resource files and objects are contained in the executable and are loaded into memory when the application starts up. This means that the application will take longer to load initially, but file I/O is reduced significantly thereafter. One choice of development technique affects this. If multiple window instances are supported and the Open Format 2 is used, the window being opened is referenced through a string variable, and therefore is not bound within the executable. These windows, and any dynamic datawindows used, must be included in a PBD and this alternative is then excluded.

Large projects may also find that the executable size is prohibitive. Not only for distribution, but in loading to memory, part of the application may be swapped out to disk.

Executable containing some dynamic libraries. If an executable is created with some of the objects contained in dynamic libraries, the developer can use some knowledge about how the system will be used to place less frequently used objects in the dynamic libraries. This gives the developer some control over which objects to place in the executable (loaded directly to memory) and which objects to place in external dynamic libraries, to be loaded when needed. This can improve the efficiency of the system.

___
TIP

If this approach is used, it will prove beneficial to build dynamic libraries for objects that are considered reusable. That way, multiple projects could use the library, especially if the library contains a group of well-defined, functionally similar objects.

Some care must be taken with this approach because objects that are part of a class hierarchy follow slightly different rules. If an object is a descendant of another object and the object is placed in a dynamic library, then its ancestor must also be placed in a dynamic library. It need not be the same library, but for efficiency, the ancestor object should be placed higher in the library search path than the descendant. Likewise, all descendants of the object must also be placed in dynamic libraries.

The approach also introduces the need to keep track of which libraries are built as dynamic libraries and which are not.

All libraries contained in dynamic libraries. If all object libraries are built as dynamic libraries, the developer does not need to keep track of which libraries are built as dynamic libraries. The developer is also relieved of the need to track down dynamic objects, as they are all contained in PBDs. Object class hierarchies are also eliminated from the issue list.

The executable built in this fashion is small and does not have to be rebuilt when code changes are made to existing objects. It must be rebuilt if the library search path changes in any way. This allows for maximum flexibility during maintenance, but if the PBDs are located on a network, the file I/O across the network increases as each object is loaded.

Another benefit is that only the object required is loaded from the library. The entire library is not loaded, as is the case with a DLL or EXE.

The biggest disadvantage is that the libraries are dynamic and replaceable. This exposes the application to the danger of accidental overlay or deletion.

PowerBuilder 4 and 5 only: create project file. In PowerBuilder 4.0, a new object was introduced: the Project object. This object allows the developer to set up a makefile that automatically regenerates the objects, rebuilds all dynamic libraries, and builds the executable with associated PBR files. This utility object reduces the possibility of error and can be saved and reused, making the developer more productive. The Project object's responsibility has been expanded in PowerBuilder 5.0 because the Project Painter is the only place from which you can create an executable. Figure 33.6 shows the PowerBuilder 5.0 project object.

As you can see, the Project object allows you to specify PBR files for each library in the search path. The developer can also choose which libraries to automatically build as dynamic libraries. With a little experimentation, you can determine which of the application build methods you should use to make your application more efficient and maintainable. The Project object ensures that the correct sequence of events takes place.

PowerBuilder 4 and 5 only: run Project Make utility.   Running the Project object builds the application executable according to the parameters set by the executable builder.

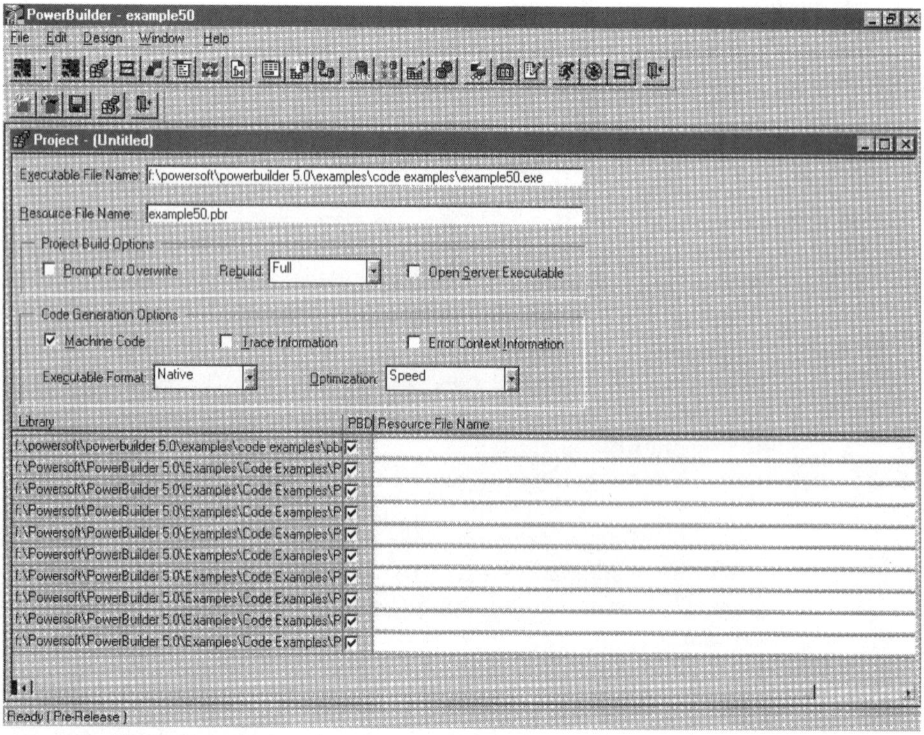

Figure 33.6   The Project object.

TIP

PowerBuilder 5.0 gives you the opportunity to create machine code executables. Powersoft advises that some applications will benefit greatly if they are compiled as machine code, but others may actually perform worse. We recommend that you build each application both ways (as traditional p-code and as machine code), then test performance thoroughly before you decide which mode you want to use.

Archive all EXE, PBD, and PBR files.   Make a backup copy of all EXE, PBD, and PBR files.

Test the executable.   Even though the application has been built and tested before, during systems testing, retest the application before distributing it to the users.

Application installation preparation

Preparing an application for installation is another task fraught with danger. A single missing resource file can bring an otherwise successful application install to its knees. Take care and make sure that you test your installation thoroughly. (See Table 33.12.)

Refresh deployment kit DLLs.   When distributing your application with Power-Builder DLLs, make sure that the deployment kit files you are using always match up with the set of DLLs you built the application with. Nothing is worse than building and testing an application thoroughly and building and testing the executable, only to find that on the user's machine, problems suddenly begin to appear and cannot be reproduced. Often, one hears of the comment, "It works everywhere, except on this machine." One of the causes for this is an incorrect version of a DLL on the client's application workstation or server.

TABLE 33.12   Application Installation Checklist

Task	Scheduled	Completed
Refresh deployment kit DLLs		
Make sure DK DLLs are included		
Include application files		
Include routines to update users' WIN.INI or registry		
If ODBC is used, include routines to update ODBC data sources		
Include setup program instructions		
Test on user machine		

Be aware that the user's machines and their application server may already have a PowerBuilder application running, and that application may not have been built with the same set of DLLs. Even placing the DLLs in a separate directory is not enough to ensure that the correct DLLs are being used. A DLL, once loaded into memory, will not reload, even if the versions are different. This problem is discussed in detail in Chapter 34.

Make sure deployment kit DLLs are included on installation. If you are building install disks, make sure that the deployment kit files are included on the disks. Figure 33.7 shows the files contained in the deployment kits for PowerBuilder 5.

Files for Windows 3.1 and Windows 3.11	Files for Windows 95 and Windows NT
PBBGR050.DLL	PBBGR050.DLL
PBCMP050.DLL	PBDBT050.DLL
PBDPB050.DLL	PBDPB050.DLL
PBDSE050.DLL	PBDSE050.DLL
PBDWE050.DLL	PBDWE050.DLL
PBHLP050.DLL	PBNPC050.DLL
PBIDBF50.DLL	PBNPS050.DLL
PBITXT50.DLL	PBODB050.DLL
PBLAB050.INI	PBOSC050.DLL
PBODB050.DLL	PBOSS050.DLL
PBODB050.INI	PBROI050.DLL
PBOSC050.DLL	PBRTC050.DLL
PBOUI050.DLL	PBRTE050.DLL
PBROI050.DLL	PBRTF050.DLL
PBRTC050.DLL	PBSHR050.DLL
PBRTE050.DLL	PBSMI050.DLL
PBRTF050.DLL	PBSYB050.DLL
PBSHR050.DLL	PBSYC050.DLL
PBSMI050.DLL	PBTYP050.DLL
PBTYP050.DLL	PBWSC050.DLL
PBVBX050.DLL	PBWSS050.DLL
PBWSC050.DLL	

Figure 33.7 PowerBuilder deployment kit files.

Make sure all application files are included. When building the installation routines, make sure that the following application files are included:

- Application executable
- Application dynamic link libraries
- Class library dynamic link libraries
- Resource files (if PBRs are not used)
- Application initialization file (INI)

It might seem redundant to mention this, but I have witnessed more than one failed installation because files were missing, especially resource files.

Include routines or procedures to update user's system settings files. Typically, an application refers to a Windows initialization file (INI) for initial application settings. The most common usage I have seen is to create a section in the user's WIN.INI file labeled to match the application. A setting in this section then directs an application to the location of the application INI file. Other settings may be incorporated. If you are using this method (which I recommend), make sure your installation routines make this update.

Include routines or procedures to update ODBC.INI file if ODBC data source is used. If ODBC (open data base connectivity) data sources are used (Sybase SQLAnywhere databases, for example), make sure your installation routines update the ODBC.INI and ODBCINST.INI files (or their registry counterparts) with the information relevant to the connection.

Build setup program. PowerBuilder 5.0 (Enterprise edition) comes with its own setup program, called Install Builder, which allows you to set the options and files needed for your application. A setup program is built with this information and reduces the amount of time developers need to spend creating this.

Include setup program instructions. Always make sure that a complete set of instructions on how to use the setup program is included on your installation disks.

Test install on a user machine or equivalent. Always test the install program on a user workstation if at all possible. The user workstation will almost definitely be configured differently from your development workstation and will be the place where something goes wrong. If this is not possible, have a similar workstation set up in the development area where this testing can take place. The workstation should be set up to simulate the following:

- A brand new machine with no software loaded
- A user machine with other applications loaded

This tests your installation both on a new machine and on a machine that has previously gone through an install process. The first situation tests that the necessary DLLs are included and installed correctly; the second tests the impact of installing your application on a machine that already has other applications installed. You should test the software to see that it runs in both cases, but you should also test the other applications in the second case to ensure that your application install does not affect the other applications. Finally, run both your application and a second PowerBuilder application simultaneously to make sure there are no DLL dependencies.

Client workstation installation

The final step is to install the application on the user workstation. This entails loading all the files required, making sure that initialization files are updated or created, and testing the installed software before the users begin to look at their brand new system. (See Table 33.13.) This final step ensures a polished installation that gives the user an initial impression of professionalism, which leaves the user with a comfortable feeling that the developers have done a thorough job of preparation before installation. To users, impressions are important.

Create application directories. Create the application directories required for your application. This may be a feature of your install program, but make sure this gets done. Scanning hard disks to determine where files were loaded is not only time-consuming, but embarrassing.

Create development tool directories. If the PowerBuilder DLLs are going to be loaded locally, make sure that the location of the DLLs is set up correctly. If you are installing these DLLs to a network drive, make sure that the network connection has been made before attempting the install.

Update WIN.INI, system registry, or other system initialization files. Unless your installation program is automatically updating the WIN.INI file, make sure

TABLE 33.13   Client Workstation Installation Checklist

Task	Scheduled	Completed
Application directories created		
Development tool directories created		
WIN.INI/registry updated		
ODBC data sources updated		
Program group and items created		
Run application, test key features		

TABLE 33.14   ODBC.INI: SQL AnyWhere Database: Powersoft Demo DB V5 (ODBC Data Sources)

Powersoft Demo DB V5=Sybase SQL Anywhere 5.0
[Powersoft Demo DB V5]
DatabaseFile=f:\Powersoft\PowerBuilder 5.0\Examples\Code Examples\PSDEMODB.DB
DatabaseName=PSDEMODB
UID=dba
PWD=sql
Driver=f:\SQLANY50\win32\WOD50T.DLL
Start=f:\SQLANY50\win32\dbeng50.exe -d -c512
Driver32=f:\sqlany50\win32\WOD50T.DLL

that this file is updated with the correct information. If your target is Windows NT or Windows 95, update the system registry instead. Carry a diskette with you containing a text file with the correct settings or REG file, and check the WIN.INI file or system registry after installation.

Update ODBC.INI for ODBC data sources.   If ODBC data sources are being used, make sure that the ODBC and ODBCINST.INI files are updated as required. Tables 33.14 and 33.15 show typical additions to these files.

Create program groups and items.   If your install program created a program group and items, check that they were created successfully. Most auto-setup programs use DDE (dynamic data exchange) to communicate with the Program Manager to create these groups, and DDE conversations can be interrupted quite easily by other Windows applications. If you are creating the group and items manually, do so now.

TIP

Be creative when designing an application icon; the application title should be clearly defined on the program item. Remember that this is the user's first view of your application!

Run application, test key features.   Once the install is completed, run and test the application. Test a few key features of the application as well as one or two

TABLE 33.15   ODBCINST.INI: SQL Anywhere Databases

[Sybase SQL Anywhere 5.0]
Driver=f:\SQLANY50\win32\WOD50T.DLL
Setup=f:\SQLANY50\win32\WOD50T.DLL

items that require external file access, such as dynamic data objects or resource files, to make sure these load correctly. Do not turn the application over to the user until this process is completed. If your application requires the user to sign on when he or she normally uses the application, have the user sign on to the network and the application for you. This will leave the impression that your application is secure and that you do not have the access to do what the user is able to do. Again, the "warm, fuzzy feeling" is important to the user.

Software Distribution

In order for your application to reach its intended audience, you need to develop and implement a plan for software distribution. Take into account the hierarchy of your organization, the number of workstations and servers that will be affected, and the usual methods used by your company.

Single-server access

The simplest distribution method is a single-server installation. All of your application software is installed on a single server, and all users attach to that server to run. The advantages of this configuration include ease of maintenance and upgrade as well as simplicity of version control. The disadvantages include limited capacity and vulnerability to server outages.

Multiple-server installation

If your organization has several LANs at different sites that are not interconnected, you need to distribute your software via separate installation packages. This type of distribution is the most difficult to control and maintain. The administrator of each LAN must be instructed on the method of installation and must be counted on to actually perform the installation on schedule and accurately. Additionally, the different LANs may drift away from each other in matters of configuration and capacity.

Multiple-server replication

When you deploy your application across several interconnected servers, it is best to use a replication technique. You or your staff installs and maintains a central copy of your software. The network services personnel then distribute the software to the target servers whenever an installation or update is required. If your organization is set up to perform this task smoothly and accurately, this is the least troublesome and highest-capacity scheme for software distribution.

Automated software distribution

There are some products available today that allow for the automated distribution of software. Although these systems are well-established in the mainframe and UNIX worlds, the software available today has yet to catch up to the frantic changes occurring in the client-server world. The environment is stabilizing, however, so your organization may want to look into the use of an automated software distribution system to alleviate many of the distribution problems we face today. If you are looking at such products, use the checklist defined in this chapter to ask tough questions of the vendor.

Test a single instance

Start by testing a single instance of your application. This shows you the best-case performance you can expect from your application in the production environment. If you have performance problems at this stage, correct them before moving to the next step.

Test average expected workload

Run your application simultaneously on enough workstations to simulate your expected average workload. Be sure to record quantifiable results and check them against your expected outcomes. Because this situation represents your expected average case, you should take extra care to verify that your application will perform adequately.

Stress-test

If you have automated testing tools (or an army of dedicated testers), run your application at full throughput on all available workstations. Do not expect record-shattering speed during this test. Look for unexpected situations that can result from this intentional overloading of the system. Remember, if you can head off a disaster before production begins, you will safeguard data, everyone's nerves, and your reputation.

Deployment FAQs

How can you manage your resources with PowerBuilder?

Managing resources with PowerBuilder is still a darkly kept secret. It is no secret that PowerBuilder requires significant resources to run well. It is also no secret that most of the tools available today require significant amounts of resources to run comparably, some less than others. The real secret lies in discovering how to make your application run well with the resources available.

Using the PowerBuilder PBD. A PowerBuilder dynamic library (or PBD) is the binary representation of your source code in libraries that match your source code. Objects (including functions) are loaded from the PBD into memory on an as-needed basis. This means that your executable size will be smaller (by far) and execution will be more efficient—not necessarily faster, but more efficient. Because only the required objects are loaded at any time, memory swapping is far less likely (which would make your application faster). Although this concept seems like the best way to implement a PowerBuilder application, it has some pitfalls. You are now required to perform version control on the runtime version of each PBD. Each PBD can be swapped out by another version of the PBD without recompiling the application; this can make things simpler and, at the same time, much more difficult. If objects are inherited, the objects' descendants must also be regenerated and the libraries they reside in rebuilt. PBDs are more efficient, however, as long as the basic rules are followed.

There are some factors that force the use of PBDs. Use of the Open (Format 2) functions using a string variable to identify the object (creating multiple instances of objects) forces the developer to use PBDs or the object requested will not be included in the runtime. When using PBDs, follow these steps to ensure success:

- Always regenerate and recreate PBDs based on your class hierarchy.
- Make sure you regenerate all descendants of an object.
- Make sure you replace all of the PBDs that have been rebuilt.
- Provide a means of runtime versioning for your applications that can check each PBD as necessary.

There are two immediate drawbacks to this technique. The first is the danger of replacing a PBD at any time. If linked objects (inherited or descendant) are in different PBDs, the developer must ensure that all of the required PBDs are replaced. The second drawback is in software distribution. Instead of distributing your EXE file whenever changes are made and tested, you now have to distribute multiple files, increasing the risk of error. Some automated software distribution programs can alleviate the problem, but the danger remains.

The unknown drawbacks lie in the sometimes incorrect techniques used in generating the executable. Techniques range from attempting to place the PBDs in specific sequences to facilitate quicker location of source code, to dynamically modifying the search sequence with special code. These techniques may be successful in some cases, but they are not reliable and expose the application to dangers not covered in the user guide.

Why is this better than compiling everything into a standalone EXE?   There are two reasons for doing this. The first is that you will not end up with a huge executable file that needs to load itself, generally across a network, whenever your application is run; second, when memory resources are low, a large executable will not load at all or will swap in and out of virtual memory more often. It is therefore a recommended practice to use PBDs, and the key to success is organization.

Does changing the search path of the libraries used in an application make the application run faster?   It is true that the correct sequencing of PBDs improves performance. If ancestor objects are located faster, objects load faster. However, the difference in speed is noticeable only to the CPU unless your load sequence is in reverse (your most-often-used or highest-level ancestors are in the last of more than four PBLs). The average user will not notice the nanoseconds ticking by while the object ancestry is located. It is far more important to place objects in a sequence that makes sense to the object scanner that searches for your objects, and to preload objects that provide the basis of your object hierarchy.

Although it may make more sense to place objects of common ancestry or style in the same PBL (or PBD), from the interpreter's point of view it makes more sense to be able to locate objects in an ordered fashion. If you have used inheritance in PowerBuilder, you know that the deeper you go down a hierarchy, the slower your objects seem to perform. This occurs because when a descendant object is required, the interpreter has to first locate the object's ancestor and load this object. Remember that inheritance never tells the interpreter about more than its immediate ancestor. This ancestor may be a descendant itself, and the circle repeats itself until the highest level of ancestor is located and loaded. Only then can the object begin to perform its processing. It therefore makes sense to have the highest level of ancestry be highest in the search path, then the second level, followed by its descendants. It seems that the highest level of ancestors in a single PBL should be located first in your search path. Although this is true, it is not always practical. Search paths are used much more in the development environment than in the production environment. The gains are minimal and the effort could be substantial.

TIP

If you choose to adopt this method, save your search path in a TXT file that can be imported and copied into each developer's library search path so that everyone uses the same path. There is nothing worse than building an application and paying attention to your search path only to find that another developer, with a different search path, has regenerated and rebuilt your application with a very different search path sequence.

Why do my system resources not always return to normal after I run my application?

Of great concern to developers and users alike is the memory leak. A memory leak occurs when an object is loaded, memory is allocated, and the memory is not freed up when the object is closed. Although we are not responsible for monitoring memory leaks created by the development tools we use, we are responsible for the memory leaks we create with our code.

The biggest culprit for memory leaks is the Create of an object without a corresponding Destroy. Any time you create an object using the Create function, you are responsible for destroying the memory allocated to that object once completed. For example, I create my own transaction object thus:

```
Transaction MyTransaction
MyTransaction = CREATE Transaction
```

When I have finished using this object, I should destroy the object.

```
DESTROY MyTransaction
```

SQLCA is created by your application automatically and is also closed automatically.

One of the objects that exposes you to this danger more readily than others is the nonvisual user object (called the nonvisual custom or standard class in PowerBuilder 5.0). This object can be instantiated only by a Create and the developer is therefore more likely to omit the corresponding Destroy. Another logical candidate is the dynamic user object. This object is created using OpenUserObject and OpenUserObjectWithParm. These objects should have a corresponding CloseUserObject when you have finished using them. Why does PowerBuilder not destroy these objects automatically as it does regular objects placed on a window? Because PowerBuilder can destroy only objects that are in its control list. Only objects that are present on the object's surface are listed in the control list. (This includes invisible objects.) Dynamic user objects and nonvisual objects as well as instances of PowerBuilder global objects (such as transactions, message, and error) are added to the object after its control list is created. Closing the parent object does not automatically mean that the parent object knows to destroy the dynamically added objects. These remain in memory until you can recover memory through a utility or by closing Windows itself. Using a memory resource monitor such as that provided by the Windows 3.1 Resource Kit allows you to monitor resources during test cycles to ensure that they are freed as expected.

How can I get more speed from my application?

Getting more real speed from your application can be accomplished with Power-Builder, although you should pay more attention to good coding techniques rather than global techniques, as listed below. Techniques such as not using a function to determine Loop or Do While limits improve code execution speed; for example, for 1 to upperbound(arrayname) or do while Rownumber < RowCount() forces reexecution of the upperbound or RowCount() functions for each iteration of the loop. Simply setting a variable for your loop limit before executing the loop can have a significant impact on code execution speed. This and many other tips are available in the PBTIPS.HLP file distributed with Power-Builder. The global techniques I have used successfully are described below.

Compiling resources into the application. Another technique that should be practiced is compiling application resources (such as bitmaps, icons, cursors, and dynamic datawindows) into resource files. PowerBuilder supports the use of a resource file known as a PBR. This is simply a line indicating a path that identifies a resource file. Remember that this path name must match exactly the path name you originally supplied on the object. The purpose of this is that a copy of the bitmap, icon, or cursor is attached to the executable and loaded into memory when called upon. This is much faster than searching paths for objects that may not be there and, if they are, opening them and loading the resource into the object. When the object's memory is freed, so is the memory of the location of the resource file. Next time, the circle repeats.

Should I run my application on the client machine or the server machine? Excellent question. Tests we have run have indicated a performance improvement of 50 percent in some cases by running the software on the client machine. This may entail additional software distribution problems, but if your application is performance-dependent, you may be well-served to run your application locally.

Why do I get Out of Memory messages no matter how I compile and, usually, no matter what is running on the user's machine? The Out of Memory message in Windows is a misleading one and usually is accompanied by irritable grunts of disbelief and yells of, "I have 32 MB of RAM on this machine. How can I run out of memory with only two applications running?" Annoyed users experienced in Windows programs immediately begin shutting down other applications until they find one that frees up enough room for their PowerBuilder application to run. Almost without fail, the developer blames PowerBuilder, and the user blames the developer. In most cases, neither one is to blame: Windows 3.1 is.

Keep in mind that Windows is not a standalone operating system. It is a DOS program. It still requires fixed program address space. This space is located below the 1 MB memory line in upper memory. If you use the DOS MEM program with the /C option, you will see something like the display in Table 33.16.

MS-DOS is resident in the high memory area. Notice that although there is 360 K (approximately 384,000 bytes) of memory available between the 640 K DOS limit and the 1 MB upper memory block, the display shows a total of almost 500 K available between upper memory and reserved memory. Most of this is reserved. This is memory not available to the developer. This reserved space is usually for network software and other drivers. The memory available is the remaining 42 K shown in the win386 line. This is the memory used by applications that require fixed address space. Some programs use more of this memory, in small pieces, than others. When Windows creates a new task, the Windows loader module creates a task database (TDB) for it. The task database must be loaded below the 1 MB line and is a minimum of 200 bytes in length. The reason is that the second portion of the task database entry is a program segment prefix (PSP), an artifact from Windows 1.0, 2.0, and 3.0 real mode. The only reason this is still used is to make things easier for the built-in MS-DOS extender, as it is not actually required for protected mode windows. Why is this still implemented in Windows 3.1 protected mode? Only Microsoft engineers have the answer.

Regardless of the reason, your program still has to compete for this available space, and there is no way to extend it further. Even systems with

TABLE 33.16   Available Memory Display

Modules using memory below 1 MB			
Name	**Total**	**= Conventional**	**+ Upper memory**
MSDOS	17,533 (17 K)	17,533 (17 K)	0 (0 K)
HIMEM	1,120 (1 K)	1,120 (1 K)	0 (0 K)
EMM386	4,144 (4 K)	4,144 (4 K)	0 (0 K)
POWER	80 (0 K)	80 (0 K)	0 (0 K)
COMMAND	3,888 (4 K)	3,888 (4 K)	0 (0 K)
win386	44,816 (44 K)	2,384 (2 K)	42,432 (33 K)
NAVTSR	7,984 (8 K)	7,984 (8 K)	0 (0 K)
MOUSE	25,328 (25 K)	272 (0 K)	25,056 (24 K)
SHARE	26,368 (26 K)	26,368 (26 K)	0 (0 K)
DOSKEY	4,144 (4 K)	4,144 (4 K)	0 (0 K)
WIN	1,760 (2 K)	1,760 (2 K)	0 (0 K)
COMMAND	4,048 (4 K)	4,048 (4 K)	0 (0 K)
POWER	4,672 (5 K)	4,672 (5 K)	0 (0 K)
SMARTDRV	29,024 (28 K)	29,024 (28 K)	0 (0 K)
Free	581,312 (568 K)	581,312 (568 K)	0 (0 K)

Memory summary			
Type of memory	**Total**	**= Used**	**+ Free**
Conventional	655,360	74,048	581,312
Upper	101,184	101,184	0
Reserved	393,216	393,216	0
Extended (XMS)	19,821,760	18,773,184	1,048,576
Total memory	20,971,520	19,333,632	1,629,888
Total under 1 MB	756,544	175,232	581,312
Largest executable program size	581,296 (568 K)		
Largest free upper memory block	0 (0 K)		

32 MB RAM are bound by this restriction. (This and the 64 K GDI and
USER heaps are among the most restrictive pieces of code in Windows
today.) Windows programs all require some of this "below the line" memory
in order to function, and all allocate some fixed memory. Sometimes, programs allocate storage in this area although the memory required is not
fixed. These "misbehaved" programs chew up this space quickly. Fortunately,

PowerBuilder prevents us from being able to grab all of this scarce resource for ourselves. Unfortunately, this also means we have no control over what does or does not. C programmers will be familiar with the GMEM_FIXED memory allocation and possibly GlobalDosAlloc. Both of these functions try to allocate memory below the 1 MB line. A program such as HEAPWALK.EXE (with the Windows SDK or C++ compilers) allows you to view the allocated memory blocks below the 1 MB line to determine more accurately which applications are chewing up your most valuable resource. Also, experiment with the LoadHigh features of MS-DOS. Loading high frees up conventional memory, but reduces the amount of upper memory available at the same time. Balance is the key.

What are the other Windows resources?   There are two other resources used in Windows that often cause applications some grief. These are the USER and GDI resources. These resources, like the task database area described above, are limited by Windows, not your machine's capabilities. These resources have a 64 K limit. This means that the amount of memory you have on your machine usually does *not* play a part in out-of-memory situations.

GDI resources are probably more well-known than USER resources. GDI resources are handles to resources and device contexts used in your application. Every bitmap, icon, cursor, datawindow, user object, and window uses up these resources. Large custom toolbars are the biggest culprits of GDI mania, but are by far the least of your problems. Every window, datawindow, and button uses up GDI resources, and these are usually the first resources that dwindle down below 20 percent free. At this point, you are at the mercy of the system and may not be able to open your next object.

USER resources are also used with each object. If a user object comprises a collection of objects, each of these objects uses USER resources (such as handles and task management), so the call for dynamically opened and closed objects might prove beneficial. The use of a datawindow as a collection of objects is also a good way to use less of these resources, as it is truly a single object.

It becomes quite clear now that you have far less memory available for applications than you might first think. Windows 95 alleviates this problem to a great extent for 32-bit applications, but 16-bit applications still encounter GDI and USER resource limitations even on Windows 95.

Should I compile my application into a machine code executable?   Many of us hoped that PowerBuilder 5.0's ability to compile our applications into native machine code would provide an instant, easy speed boost. This is not quite the case. Some applications, particularly those that require heavy computation, benefit greatly from native code. But the truth is that PowerBuilder p-code has become quite optimized over the years, and other applications benefit little, if at all, from native machine code. We recommend that you build your application both ways (native code and p-code) and choose the version that provides the best combination of speed and size.

Summary

The deployment checklist can be used for initial installation and maintenance release installation. Some of the items are not applicable for maintenance release rollouts. Even though these are typically not changed, make sure each item is at least discussed and checked off. Botched maintenance releases can destroy the user's confidence in the product even more quickly than the initial installation.

The key to success in deployment was, is, and will always be planning and preparation!

Good luck!

34

Maintaining Your Environment: DLLs and Other Three-Letter Words

Introduction

Despite efforts to control releases of software, I would hazard a guess that there is no group in any corporation that has ever applied an upgrade, where multiple versions of the same product are resident in their network, without feeling like they are living a nightmare. Even on a single machine this becomes frightening.

We work with dozens of software products every day to accomplish our tasks. Seldom do we have to ask ourselves, "Which version of software are we running today?" When we use a tool such as PowerBuilder, the problem becomes much more obvious much more rapidly. Keeping track of which version of software our applications are built with and which versions are running on our users' machines is a daunting task, especially in today's world of maintenance upgrades. Maintenance upgrades do not give us a new suite of DLLs; rather, they are updates to existing DLLs, and are much harder to monitor and control. This chapter looks into these issues, which we face once every 3 months or so.

Chapter Objectives

The goals of this chapter are to provide you with some information and tools to help alleviate the problem of applying upgrades and patches to your environment. There are steps to take to avoid some of the common problems associated with the environment we virtually live in:

- Certifying new releases and upgrades
- Distributing new DLLs
- Controlling versions within your application
- Monitoring the ever-changing environment

We discuss these issues and outline the methods we use to circumvent the typical problems we face.

What Is There to Maintain?

In the PowerBuilder environment, unlike most commercial applications, we use an array of DLLs: everything from the myriad of PowerBuilder DLLs, to ODBC driver DLLs and OLE control DLLs that require significantly more synchronization, all the way to the operating system's executable files themselves.

How many times have you installed a commercial application (such as MSWord or MSExcel) and found that you had a different set of ODBC drivers or a different CTL3D.DLL than you had before? Most applications perform some version checking of their own to determine whether the DLL being replaced is more current than the one you already have. Some do not. And I would guess that many of us do not concern ourselves with what particular version of PowerBuilder we are going to place on users' machines or the network.

When looking at what needs to be monitored, maintained, and continually checked, we find a staggering list of items we need to be aware of going in:

- System files such as CTL3D.DLL
- Database driver files such as ODBC.DLL
- Third-party tools
- PowerBuilder DLLs
- Class library PBLs and PBDs
- Application PBLs, PBDs, and EXEs

How do we keep this under control? Certification.

What Is Certification and How Does It Help?

Certification implies that any new DLL or other form of executable is thoroughly tested with *all* possible tool and product combinations to ensure compatibility. I remember the surprise I felt one day when logging into the system at a client's workstation to find that PowerBuilder, MSAccess, and every other product I used to access our databases failed. It took almost 4 hours to determine that our DBLIB access module to Sybase had been upgraded to accommodate a problem that had been occurring with a batch-reporting tool. The DLL solved the tool user's problems, and simply killed other products because the DLL was not compatible with another system DLL, WLIBSOCK. Another patch was hastily applied to upgrade WLIBSOCK, which was great except that the two-file combination caused a particularly nasty problem to occur in conjunction with our PowerBuilder Sybase DLL combination. After a frustrating and unproductive day, we eventually figured out that we needed a later version of the PBSYBM??.DLL file that would work with the latest releases of the other DLLs.

Another example of this type of behavior occurred when I installed a small commercial program. The program used a Visual Basic control GRID.VBX, a special Visual Basic DLL extension I received with my program, the latest and greatest GRID.VBX, which promptly prevented my use of Lotus Notes!

We learned a simple lesson from this. No upgrade should ever be thought of as a single-environment update. Unless you make changes on a nonnetworked PC (and even this environment can be affected), any change made can affect your entire development and user communities and can result in significant losses in revenue.

We learned quickly, although with a great deal of pain, that any change to any DLL can result in chaos and should be handled like nitroglycerin—very carefully.

We discovered that we needed to develop a procedure that could handle all upgrades. We called this the certification procedure; as its name implies, its purpose is to certify which DLLs are being used, which applications and products are using them, and the impact of applying changes. We developed groups of people whose task it became to receive and test any modified DLL.

The installation

We set up a special environment where all known cross-usage files were marked as read-only to highlight possible version problems. After determining which files were affected, we could then formulate a plan to have the modified DLLs tested before applying these against our network. Many commercial products use other commercial products either as their development tools or as add-ons. These can often become "targets": two different tools using the same DLL as part of their development efforts that suddenly come into conflict with each other when placed in the same environment. If you are developing a commercial product, be aware that any shared file such as a DLL may already be used by other vendors. On one such occasion, I was fortunate to find I had two DLLs with the same name from two different products. The problem was that the two DLLs actually did two very different things!

The testing process

We developed a set of test cases for each DLL and for each tool that used that DLL. This test suite continues to grow as more and more tools are introduced and used. We used the same formula and forms for test case management as we use for our development efforts, keeping consistency. One of the key elements to success is to incorporate all *known* failures into your test suite. Once a problem is discovered with a DLL (and you may be sure of only one thing: You will never find every problem with every DLL), you should *immediately* prepare a test case that validates the problem. Once the test is included, you can at least be sure that it will never return. This implies that there is a need to communicate outside your organization. Use electronic communication media to gather information about releases of software to learn how others are performing this task and what problems others have encountered, and to share your knowledge with others.

Another important problem-discovery tool is the release notes put out by the vendor. The release notes highlight what problems are being resolved and what new enhancements are being added in. Try to develop test cases for each of the known problems that are "fixed" before applying the fixes. (You will generally find you were not aware of 20 or more other problems that the test cases reveal). This also ensures that these problems do not suddenly begin to occur in your environment.

Certification

Only when all of your tests are concluded satisfactorily can you begin to relax—briefly. You can now state that the new and improved DLLs are certified, and you can begin to publish the upgrade requirements.

Upgrading issues

Unfortunately, all of your hard work is not yet done. Now that you have a version of DLLs that you have thoroughly tested and certified, you begin to learn about your environment. How many of us have developers or users on more than one different file server? My experience is that less than 1 percent of client-server development efforts reside on a single file server. This means that you take your odds of applying a solid set of DLLs, and apply a factor of (number of possible DLL conflicts times the number of file servers) against it to realize what you are up against.

Since PowerBuilder 3.0 was released, and up to and including the release of PowerBuilder 5.0, I have gone through five "official" releases of PowerBuilder 3 and five "official" releases of PowerBuilder 4. Fortunately, the DLLs used by PowerBuilder 3 and 4 are different. Unfortunately, they all use ODBC.DLL (or ODBC32.DLL, depending on your environment and platform). This adds up to a staggering number of maintenance releases that could possibly be applied to a DLL in a 3-year period. That does not include the ODBC.DLL supplied by other tool vendors! I learned pretty quickly that almost every tool I use that has a database behind it includes an ODBC.DLL (testing tools, word processors, spreadsheets, reporting tools, you name it).

I also learned another lesson. Once you upgrade to a "named" release such as PowerBuilder 3.0b from PowerBuilder 3.0a, or PowerBuilder 4.0.03 from PowerBuilder 4.0.02, the road back is an arduous one. Point release changes such as these are seldom backward compatible. By this I do not mean that an application compiled under PowerBuilder 4.0.02 will not run with 4.0.03 DLLs, but rather that once you update your application to 4.0.03, the migratory path back to 4.0.02 is not due south. It is more like going from New York to Los Angeles by boat: There is a known path, but it takes longer. This is another reason for establishing an isolated and secure testing facility: a separate machine where versions of application and software can be maintained totally separate from each other.

The problems do not stop there. Once you have certified the DLLs, the next step is to verify your class libraries, which are the foundation of your application's development, and your current production or near-to-production applications. As you can imagine, the entire process is time-consuming and often painful. It is the price we pay for power and flexibility. You need to be aware of the possible pain and the prescription for cure.

Anatomy of an Upgrade

System files

System files such as CTL3D.DLL and network files such as WLIBSOCK.DLL and W3DBLIB.DLL (for Sybase users) rank high on the list of DLLs we need to monitor when installing a new product or applying an upgrade to an existing product. This does not apply only when you upgrade PowerBuilder; if you are using other tools or products, these must certainly be a concern. Files such as these should always be maintained in a central location and upgrades should be applied automatically. Using network update scripts that update everyone's machine when they first log in and using a central location for access to these DLLs are definitely good ideas. Remember that many tools and products work with newer versions of a DLL, but few work with an older version. Monitor the system files your application uses and make sure you are running with a version compatible with your application.

Network files

One of the most difficult tasks I faced was in determining a version of network DLLs that worked together with the tool I was using. If your environment is like mine, it is not a pure environment where you use one toolset with unconflicting DLLs. Most of my clients use not only PowerBuilder, but other development tools as well, not to mention different databases such as Sybase and Watcom. Generally, organizations standardize on a database a lot faster than they do on development tools. This makes this task a little easier, but by no means alleviates the problem.

The team responsible for maintaining the DLLs must be aware that more than one toolset uses the DLLs to access elements on the network. The certification process must be aware of all systems and applications that use the DLLs and the testing should take this into consideration. An update to a Lotus Notes DLL, for example, affects not only Lotus Notes but all products that have struggled to build a decent VIM interface to Lotus Notes.

Third-party tools

We often make use of the power of add-on tools. These tools can often cause the same type of problems that an upgrade to your PowerBuilder DLLs causes because your code is based on a set level of execution code. Any change to this means that a complete retest is necessary.

Third-party tools generally are used by more than your PowerBuilder developers, especially when DLLs are involved. I remember one instance when a particular set of DLLs offered by a vendor was being used by my client. An upgrade to a totally different tool overwrote this set of DLLs because the third-party tool was being used by that vendor as well. This caused some severe problems that were particularly difficult to track down, as the second tool passed certification easily. The possible effect was unknown because the two tools were completely unrelated except for their common usage in both products. Again, the need to establish an environment where *every overlaid file is reported* becomes critical. After all, we are talking about mission-critical applications.

Another problem is that you might be using a tool for development and implement your application based on a predefined set of runtime DLLs, including third-party DLLs. The user might use a product that is not part of your environment that also uses a particular DLL. Your application, or their product, could have a nasty and unexpected effect on both your application and their commercial product. Be aware of this and, as stated in Chapter 33, get to know your users' environments as well as your own.

PowerBuilder DLLs

Powersoft releases a maintenance release every 3 months or so. In order to ensure that we stay current with the latest code base, we need to use these fixes. To perform a thorough certification, however, we need a thorough test bed. All known problems should have a test case defined that exploits a particular weakness and can be retested. Powersoft's own internal testing has improved greatly since PowerBuilder 3.0. I have found very few cases of old problems reappearing in a maintenance release. Powersoft uses an automated testing tool to test releases.

However, you should not put all your trust in vendor testing. A vendor can never test for every condition or explore every method of use. This goes for all vendor products, not just PowerBuilder. Today's environments are becoming increasingly complex and your environment might highlight a particular problem area that other testing might not reveal. If problems are found, they should be reported to the vendor immediately, along with the test case that allows reproduction of the error condition.

Another common occurrence with maintenance releases is the problem of multiple version use. Once you recompile your objects using a new maintenance release, it is often difficult to use the older version with the same objects. Again, separation of code and DLLs is a necessity. Your best bet is to have a specific environment set up for this kind of testing, where a set of objects can be converted, tested, and manipulated without fear of affecting a current development effort.

Your testing environment should also be established in such a way that only one version of DLLs can ever be loaded. DLLs are not renamed with a maintenance release, so it becomes almost impossible to tell which version of the DLL is currently in memory when your program calls for it. Writing a small module in C or C++ whose sole purpose is to load or unload a set of DLLs from memory before your application can be started in this environment is a good idea. The code is simple enough. This code snippet shown in Figure 34.1 unloads all of the specified PowerBuilder DLLs from memory. The PowerBuilder application then loads the version of the DLLs it finds in its search path.

Caution: Remember to use this code only in your testing environment. Running it in your production environment will prove to be an experience you might never forget.

The next problem we run into with maintenance releases is that when a development effort ends and a system goes into production, the DLLs used to develop the application must be installed in the users' production environment. This could mean that when System A goes into production using, for example, PowerBuilder 5.0, the user must then have the PowerBuilder 5.0 DLLs installed as runtime DLLs. A few months later, when System B goes into production, it may have been built using PowerBuilder 5.0.01. These are different DLLs from System A. The certification process must ensure that once approved, all development and production efforts are moved to the current certi-

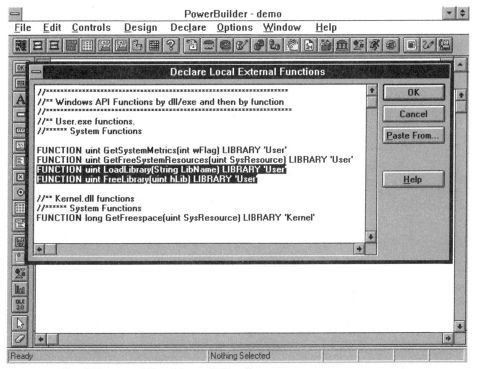

Figure 34.1 LoadLibrary and FreeLibrary DLL calls.

fied level of DLLs, or you will encounter the strangest problems with applications that are fully tested.

Class library code

Class libraries add an additional layer of complexity to this process. Now you have a version of PowerBuilder DLLs that is certified, but before an application begins using these, its library code must be upgraded to that level of DLL or the mix of library code based on earlier DLLs will cause unnecessary headaches for the application developer. It therefore makes sense to have a member of the library development team as part of the certification team. This ensures that the developers and users are always using the latest release of products that form their development work base.

Application code

Application code is the least affected by maintenance releases, or at least it should be the least affected. The problem is that when you compile the list of DLLs (or other files) that your application depends on, it becomes frighteningly obvious that there is a great deal that could go wrong quickly. Your only chance of survival in this cruel environment is to be aware of what is out there and build certification processes to accommodate the eventualities.

What Is Coming Next?

This is the really scary part. We are only at the beginning of client-server architecture. Coming up in the near future are various new architectures that will add to the already muddied pool of DLL disaster planning. Three-tier architectures, OLE, and new operating systems all add to this mix. If you establish a well-rounded and carefully-thought-out certification process, however, you can avoid many of the problems.

One particular concern to me is the frighteningly powerful OCX. An OCX is a special type of DLL object used for OLE 2.0–compatible applications. These are tools that will make your development effort more flexible and your applications more powerful, but will inevitably make your certification process much more difficult. OCXs will be coming out of the woodwork pretty soon, and they add a totally new layer of version control problems.

Tips and Techniques to Avoid
the Impending Disaster

We see more and more problems, but are there any solutions? The answer is yes. There are some techniques and precautions you can take that will help to alleviate the common problems. Following are three techniques we have found to be very useful in averting major disasters.

Automated software distribution

One of the easiest means of controlling the environments is the use of an automated software distribution product. Some vendors, such as Legent, offer such tools, but you can develop your own methods relatively easily. The best time to initiate these products is when the user or developer logs on to the network. A utility program can quickly scan the developer's specified runtime directories for DLLs or EXEs and compare the version information against that in a small central database. The database can contain not only the version information, but also a pointer to the latest certified version of the software.

Another method is to create a single runtime environment where *all* executable code, such as EXEs and DLLs, is placed. This ensures, at the minimum, that a single version is used. However, it does not guarantee that the version is the correct version. It also places a much higher load on network traffic.

The runtime version control interface

We developed a small module that allows our applications to check version information for themselves. Again, the problem is that the module checks only the version of DLL that would be loaded if one is not already loaded. It does not check whether the module is already resident in memory. The module also depends on accurate information being maintained.

Our version check module contains a Data-Retained datawindow that holds information about runtime DLLs that will be used by the application. A second Data-Retained datawindow allows developers to capture information pertaining to the versions of EXEs and PBDs their application will produce. The version check module then calls a small C routine that retrieves the date, time, and size information about the registered file and compares this with the information stored in the datawindows. If the data do not match, error processing is initiated. The C routine is needed because Windows does not provide adequate directory- and file-processing capabilities. You could write this function quite easily in C or Pascal, or use an existing DLL such as Funcky.[1]

Setting up DLLs as read-only

Another effective means of controlling the environment, as much as we can control it, is to write a small module that searches for DLLs and executables and changes their file attributes to read-only. This prevents the specified DLL from being overwritten either accidentally or by a completely different tool. Adding a pre-setup program to the installation that checks which files are (and should be) affected by an upgrade, and makes these files overlayable again, is an effective method of controlling exactly what is affected by any tool.

---

1. Funcky is a third-party library of prebuilt C routines available from Powersoft.

If the module is run periodically, it will track down all DLLs and other executables, report on them if necessary, warn of duplicates, and set them up to avoid being overwritten. You can even prevent users from affecting an important file through installation of a totally separate commercial product installation.

Summary

This chapter dealt with some of the many issues we face every time you apply an upgrade to any product in your environment. We covered the following topics:

- Product certification (why and how we should certify releases of software)
- Distribution of DLLs and other executable code
- Controlling versions within your application
- Monitoring the ever-changing environment

We also provided you with some techniques that will make your environment a safer place for your application.

35

The Future of Client-Server and PowerBuilder

Introduction

The future looks brighter than ever for PowerBuilder developers. With the new features of PowerBuilder 5.0, we are, I believe, only a few technological years away from reaching the level I have been looking for since 1989. An environment is fast approaching in which a single development tool will provide the means to develop all of the code and objects needed to satisfy all of your requirements, with the capability to run any or all of these objects in any environment configuration you set up. Of course, with this level of power comes complexity and more hidden dangers.

PowerBuilder is an incredibly powerful tool that we have found to be even more advanced (sometimes by accident) than we thought. Capabilities exist today that we would not have dreamed of 7 years ago, so I can only imagine what the next 7 years will bring.

More and more competitive products are being born, and with the raised level of competition, I believe we all benefit. This is a tremendous product with a bright future. The client-server vision is beginning to be realized. We are not there yet, but we are no longer drifting in deep space.

Chapter Objectives

The goals of this chapter are to outline (without a hierarchy control) what we believe the future holds. Some of this is based in fact, the remainder in wishes. We will have to wait and see. We cover the PowerBuilder 5.0 release and how to exploit the new features, multi-tiered architecture, OLE 2.0 and OCXs, the future of Windows, Windows NT, and Windows 95 as development and user platforms, and also the Macintosh and UNIX releases.

PowerBuilder 5.0

PowerBuilder 5.0 promises to answer many of the questions we ask. Some of the new features are as follows:

- Compiled code
- Full OLE 2.0 compatibility
- New development environment
- Distributed objects
- Nonvisual datawindows (datastores)
- Inheritable application objects
- Constants
- New controls
- Standardized user interface

Compiled code

PowerBuilder 5.0 compiles Powerscript as C code executables and DLLs. What does this mean? How does this really help us?

The first thing to understand is that your code in the development environment is unchanged. Only when you compile is your code converted to C code and then compiled into an executable (EXE or DLL). You do not have access to the underlying C code, and one misconception must be clarified right away: This is not C code that we can use, handle, or manipulate. The code generation is completely behind the scenes using Watcom C compiler technology. Existing PowerBuilder runtime DLLs are still required as part of the runtime, but the native code runs significantly faster.

The true benefit, I believe, is not in processing speed, but in added flexibility. The ability to compile a single PBL into a DLL means that you can develop truly reusable layers that can then be more easily used by other applications. A common error handler, for example, can be imbedded into a DLL and used by all applications. Business rule processing will also benefit greatly from the new feature.

PowerBuilder 5's DLLs are not true Windows DLLs as we know them. They are OLE 2.0 server DLLs. What this means is that the DLLs can easily be used in your PowerBuilder application, but external applications (such as Excel or other tools) must support the OLE 2.0 paradigm in order to use the built-in functionality of the DLL. You must connect to these DLLs as objects rather than by declaring function prototypes, as we would do with SDK calls. For this to happen, Powersoft has introduced the best OLE 2.0 browser I have seen. The browser works with the OLE 2 objects' own internal methods to display attributes, methods, and help available. This allows you to hook up to an OLE 2 object quickly and, generally, painlessly. As the OCX (and OLE 2) technology improves and grows, this will become more and more apparent.

Full OLE 2.0 compatibility

With PowerBuilder 5.0, Powersoft is taking OLE 2.0 compatibility to the next level: full OLE 2.0 compatibility. This means that PowerBuilder applications are able to be OLE clients *and* servers.

PowerBuilder 5.0 OLE support extends not only to the development environment as an OLE 2.0 container object with extensive browser support, but also as a datawindow control, allowing the developer to integrate data with OLE 2.0 controls that support uniform data transfer, such as MS Word documents.

New integrated development environment

Powersoft has created a new integrated development environment (IDE) for PowerBuilder 5.0 including automatic keyword highlighting and coloring and automatic indentation. This makes PowerBuilder a better product for developers to use, comparing favorably with other editing tools.

The new IDE also conforms with the Windows 95 interface design and effort was made to ensure consistency of GUI application throughout. This makes the product more polished and commercially acceptable.

Distributed objects

Distributed objects is a current buzzword. The ability to develop an object on one client and run it on another client workstation using automated remote procedure calls will help push PowerBuilder to the front of the distributed objects queue. This type of flexibility allows the developer to reduce the load on a client workstation and place it on a server or even another client workstation.

Nonvisual datawindows

Nonvisual datawindows, known as datastores, allow developers to add datawindow capabilities to their nonvisual functions and objects. Datastores containing often-reused data can be imbedded within and passed between objects, further reducing the workload that must be performed during the life of an application session. Nonvisual objects can also run on a server machine using the distributed objects technology, giving the developer more control of workstation and server load distribution. Nonvisual datawindows also add several other capabilities, such as the ability to be used in place of arrays! The possibilities are limited only by the imagination.

Multi-Tiered Architecture

Multi-tiered architecture is another buzzword of the day. Along with this technology come such elements as application partitioning and multi-threaded distributed objects. But what does this all mean to us? And how is it better?

First, let's look at how PowerBuilder supports multi-tiered architecture. PowerBuilder is the only tool available that supports multi-tiered architecture in both a native mode and through the use of technology such as distributed computing environment (DCE). Some of the more popular technologies being used today include Transarc's Encina, AT&T's Tuxedo, and Open Environment's Entera. PowerBuilder's own distributed objects are themselves a multi-tiered architecture, allowing the development of an object on a Windows client, but coding the object to run on a UNIX or NT server as a standalone object that you "connect" to, much as you would connect to a database. This provides the additional level of abstraction (and adds much more to the complexity of your design), as the object can now run on either the client or the server machine.

Three-tiered architecture is the separation of the client-side application logic from the server-based data. Today, we have to wire our client application to our data directly, using a tool such as the sophisticated datawindow. Now you can add a level of separation to this. Your client application (presentation layer) can now be coded to talk to distributed objects (PowerBuilder distributed objects or other DCE components), otherwise known as the logic layer, which is coded to access the data from your data sources, the data layer. We have already seen that reusing code is good. It saves time and money that far outweigh the added complexity it can bring. This is simply an extension to the reuse paradigm, allowing further reuse of complex business objects, which can run on a distributed server, often a long way away from the client. Figure 35.1 shows the typical two-tiered architecture.

Figure 35.2 shows a typical three-tiered architecture. The three-tiered architecture is clearly much more adaptable to future change with the least amount of impact on the presentation or data layers or partitions. Because the technology is still pretty new, and with the wave of Internet technology in the not-too-distant future, there appears to be no rush to move from the two-tiered client-server technology to the multi-tiered distributed technology.

How is this actually better for us? This is still an unproved science, but if we understand the concept of saving through reuse, then the same applies

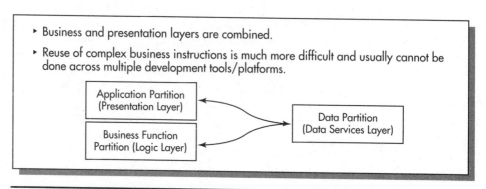

Figure 35.1 Two-tiered architecture.

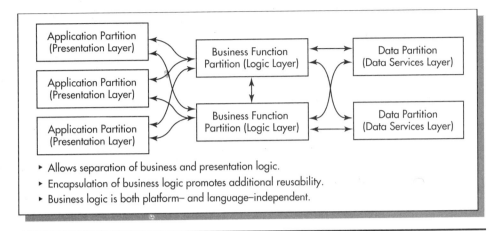

> ▸ Allows separation of business and presentation logic.
> ▸ Encapsulation of business logic promotes additional reusability.
> ▸ Business logic is both platform– and language–independent.

Figure 35.2 Three-tiered architecture.

here. If a developer were to develop an object that accesses some data and returns this to the user, then, if we reuse this object, we save development and maintenance costs. This sometimes works, but more often than not, the code being reused today is application framework architecture. Class libraries cannot provide business objects because the developers usually do not know the business.

What makes this even more difficult is the distributed nature of data today. We may require some data from a mainframe, some from a file server, and still more from an updated combination of both. This makes developing truly reusable business objects very complex. Once you tie a datawindow to a particular database and table, you are pretty much locked in. If you require stored procedures to access the data, you are locked in even more securely. Although this might add to security, it restricts flexibility and increases redundancy. Data must be replicated and replication must be monitored and maintained. All of this is a very expensive process.

Three-tiered architecture proposes to provide a common access point for data access. We have spoken about common access points to methods and attributes of our own objects. Multi-tiered architecture provides the common access points to the methods and attributes of your business. Applications are coded to connect to the distributed objects and the client application no longer cares where the data come from. The middle layer (tools used to develop on this middle layer are called middleware) is used to isolate the client from the data. Objects in the middle layer are coded to return data to the client in a specific way, and are also coded to retrieve the data from its source. If the source changes, the middleware object must change, but the multitude of applications accessing the data need not change or be recompiled.

Of course, this adds complexity to design and development, requiring expensive software and other resources to set this up and maintain it (not to mention the training and development of resources to code the middleware layer), but, just as a foundation class object can provide tangible benefits in the development and maintenance of PowerBuilder systems, three-tiered architecture adds a level of reusability to your applications, but on a much larger scale. (Middleware layers can provide data to other products, not just PowerBuilder.) It's like adding Powersoft datawindows to all of your databases, where your application simply has to choose which datawindow to use.

OLE 2

What is OLE 2? OLE stands for object linking and embedding, the technology designed initially by Microsoft to make objects able to talk to each other through a common medium. OLE 1.0 allowed you to select objects created by other applications and place these objects in your own application and communicate with them. The technology was, at best, crude but effective.

OLE 2 is the next evolution of the object linking and embedding paradigm. OLE 2 objects are much more capable than their predecessors, having the ability to communicate bidirectionally. An OLE 2 object "publishes its interface"; it tells the calling object what methods and attributes are available to it.

To get a real feel for OLE technology, I highly recommend Kraig Brockschmidt's book—*Inside OLE 2.0: the fast track to building powerful object-oriented applications.*[1]

If anyone wants to know which technology is the most important to get to know, I would point to OLE 2.0. PowerBuilder's distributed objects are, in fact, OLE 2.0 server objects, and the PowerBuilder compiled DLLs are OLE 2.0 servers. Powersoft has recognized this technology and Microsoft is banking its future on it. If you want to stay on the forefront of technology and be able to use objects written by others, learn this stuff!

Windows 95/Windows NT

The great debate over Windows 95, Windows NT, and OS/2 rages on. Everyone recognizes that the Windows 3.1 technology is dead, but the wake is taking an awful long time. There is no question that the new 32-bit technologies will eventually replace the millions of copies of 16-bit technology, but we can probably count on Windows 3.1 development and maintenance going forward well into the next century. This is my prediction.

The newer debate, however, centers around Windows 95 and Windows NT. Which is better as a development platform and a user platform? There were no questions before. You developed on Windows 3.1 client and ran on some other server system, usually UNIX. The architecture was pretty closed in.

---

1. Brockschmidt, Kraig. *Inside OLE 2: the fast track to building powerful object-oriented applications.* Microsoft Press, 1994. ISBN: 155 615 6189

Now it is opening up. Windows 95 and Windows NT can both connect very easily to a number of back-ends, including the latest rage, the Internet.

My preference is to use Windows NT as the development platform simply because of its more robust resource and operating system protection offered. Windows NT is closer, in my opinion, to the processing power of UNIX with the ease of use of Windows. I might have users with Windows 95 (and/or Windows 3.1), and PowerBuilder 5.0 on NT allows me to compile both 16- and 32-bit objects on one platform.

Multiplatform Compatibility

Powersoft has entered the multiplatform arena with a thump. The long-awaited UNIX and Macintosh products are now available, marking Powersoft's entry to this arena and confirming its commitment to keeping an open architecture. Powersoft was more-or-less forced into this arena with its vision of distributed objects. Objects running on a server, be it UNIX or NT, must be compiled as standalone with 32-bit architecture. PowerBuilder 4.0 was the first step, moving up to the 32-bit architecture internally. This allowed Powersoft to create the variations of PowerBuilder that run on UNIX, NT, and Macintosh.

The importance of supporting multiple platforms cannot be overstated. Most of the Fortune 1000 companies will not select a product, especially a development product, that does not support their environments. Most of them are widely distributed in their internal architecture, and require support for at least Windows 3.1 and UNIX. Many also require NT and Macintosh support. Whether they will ever develop a single object on those platforms using Power-Builder depends greatly on their reaction to PowerBuilder 5.0's compiled code initiative. Whether they will accept PowerBuilder as a development tool depends on the product's *ability* to support multiple platforms. You can look forward to PowerBuilder 5.0 code on UNIX and Mac within a relatively short time after the PowerBuilder 5.0 release.

Summary

In conclusion, this chapter might well be obsolete by the time you read it. Technology is advancing in ever-quicker cycles, and it is impossible to keep up with it without using the tools made available. We all need to embrace change, sometimes try to influence its direction, but in all cases, remember that change is like a hurricane. It has the ability to wipe you off the face of the earth, but if you stay in the center, the sun shines on your face. You have to keep moving to stay in the same place.

36

Summary, Conclusions, and Appendix Z

Introduction

There comes a time when we all have to make choices. We made our choice some time ago, believing that the upstart company Powersoft actually had something to offer a few years back. The feelings have proven justified. I do not think any tool I have ever used has had the same impact on my life. From the most frustrating yells of "Another GPF? I didn't even do anything," to "Wow! This is unbelievable," I have enjoyed a love-hate relationship with Power-Builder.

Everybody remarks on the product's potential power. Every time you use a new feature, the possibilities ring up inside your head like the express lane at a supermarket. Many remark on the product's stability as a problem. I believe that when you develop new technology such as this, you are living on the edge. And when you live on the edge, sometimes you get cut. The real question is whether the company is willing to spend some of its enormous profits doing something about it. I believe PowerBuilder 5.0 will answer that with a re-sounding "yes." Several of our TeamPowersoft colleagues had an opportunity to spend some time on the tech support lines at Powersoft, and they all re-marked that they had to revamp a test case here and another there to bolster the regression test suites being developed in Concord. My experience with the new product so far (and it is very new) is that it is a remarkable improvement over PowerBuilder 4.0, which I thought was a good improvement of Power-Builder 3.0.

This book not only was an opportunity for us to share the knowledge we have accumulated, but it also taught us a great deal. (For one, I learned an awful lot about Microsoft Word.) We discovered we had a methodology that we followed from day to day. And where our development efforts did not go exactly as planned, we discovered we had omitted a step in the methodology.

Summary and Conclusions

We took you through several processes in this book. We began with discussing what management needs to understand about the technology and commitment to this crazy little thing called reuse. We introduced you to CBM, the Cooperative Business Modeling approach we have adopted and found to work very well, using the process of object synthesis to take a requirement and develop methods and attributes that would satisfy the requirement. Collecting the methods and attributes into logical classes formed the next phase, logical class definition. Logical classes then become physical classes, reducing the development effort to one of building the objects you actually designed.

We showed this process for both class library development and applications development, and introduced the concepts of navigation workflow and object mapping. We even illustrated the art of producing (ugh) documentation and demonstrated how the built-in ORCA functionality can be used to help automate this delightful process.

We covered the details of implementation and deployment. These elements are often glossed over or taken for granted, leaving your users with a bad impression of a good system.

There is a lot of subject matter contained between these covers. The client-server environment is a complex one, requiring significant effort to develop integrated distributed systems.

We hope that this book has turned out to be a valuable investment for you. It certainly was a valuable learning experience for us.

Appendix Z, or What the Publisher Did Not Want You to See

Over the course of the past year, we happened across several things that we found to be amusing. Of course, our warped sense of humor picked up on the littlest things, from the smallest spelling error that changed a word's meaning, to some of the things that happened while we were writing and testing. We chose to keep a record of the "outtakes" and share some of these with you. We hope you enjoy them as much as we did.

The Winnie the Pooh coding technique

Ever needed an event to execute quickly? Just use the new keyword "TiggerEvent" and your code will really bounce. Just avoid the nuisance of the "PestEvent."

Emphasize, emphasize, emphasize

In describing how something works you need to emphasize; for example, "The function contains functionality that functions as a global function or object function." Oh well, as long as it is functional!

"Politically correct" naming conventions

When coming up with an acronym for the dynamically preinherited classes (customization classes), we first chose Integrated Dynamically Inherited Object Template, or IDIOT classes. (We settled for DIO.)

Pronunciation

It is important to pronounce things correctly when talking, especially acronyms. One of the more amusing pronunciations we happened across was PBORCA (Puh-Borka).

It is all in the translation

Sometimes you happen across something that just sounds good, even if the actual meaning is irrelevant. One such item was a message we saw from someone in Germany who was describing Edit-Insert: Bearbeiteneinfügen.

Edit-Insert never sounded this good in English!

Fin.

Index